The Colonel and Hug

The Colonel and Hug

THE PARTNERSHIP
THAT TRANSFORMED THE
NEW YORK YANKEES

Steve Steinberg and Lyle Spatz

Foreword by Marty Appel

University of Nebraska Press | Lincoln and London

Library of Congress Cataloging-in-Publication Data

Steinberg, Steve.
The Colonel and Hug: the partnership that transformed the
New York Yankees / Steve Steinberg and Lyle Spatz;
foreword by Marty Appel.
pages   cm

Includes bibliographical references and index.
ISBN 978-0-8032-4865-6 (cloth: alk. paper)
ISBN 978-0-8032-8413-5 (epub)
ISBN 978-0-8032-8414-2 (mobi)
ISBN 978-0-8032-8415-9 (pdf)
1. New York Yankees (Baseball team)—History—20th century.
2. Huggins, Miller, 1879–1929. 3. Ruppert, Jacob, 1867–1939.
I. Spatz, Lyle, 1937–II. Title.

GV875.N4 S2015
796.357097471—dc23
2014041596

Set in Fournier MT Pro by Lindsey Auten.

To Colleen, whose understanding
and flexibility have enabled me to travel to the
early twentieth century on a regular basis.

———————

SS

To Marilyn, who has good-naturedly
tolerated my "first love" for fifty-five years.

———————

LS

CONTENTS

PHOTOGRAPHS

FOREWORD

Marty Appel

Shortly after George Steinbrenner's death in 2010 questions arose about his worthiness for inclusion in the Baseball Hall of Fame. As one who worked for him for many years, I found myself on the receiving end of that question many times. And I would answer, "Mr. Steinbrenner often said that owning the New York Yankees was like owning the *Mona Lisa*. If that was true, then Jacob Ruppert was Leonardo da Vinci—the man who painted it. So before we debate Mr. Steinbrenner, let's take care of the unfinished business of getting Jake Ruppert elected first."

Ruppert did at last find enshrinement in 2013, and George Steinbrenner's name was back on the ballot for 2014. All was in order, although he fell well short of election.

You could not work for the Yankees without thinking about the history of the franchise on a daily basis. Babe Ruth was everywhere. Young fans today don't care as much about baseball history as previous generations did, but there is no escaping Ruth. And ninety years ago, there was no escaping Ruth if you were Jacob Ruppert or Miller Huggins. Ruth was oversized in every way—the easiest to pick out of a team photo, and the one most likely to be in the newsreels at your movie theater. But the dynamics of Ruth and Ruppert, Ruth and Huggins, Huggins and Ruppert (over matters concerning Babe) require a book like this to sort it all out.

Poor Hug. When he died in 1929, largely because penicillin hadn't yet been invented, Ruth mourned him as "my friend; a great guy." This would have likely made Huggins laugh. Babe seemed to exist to make Miller's life miserable. His propensity for circumventing the rules was forever a bane to Huggins, who tried so hard to impose discipline on the Yankees. It was what managers did! But it just could not be accomplished with Babe laughing at the rules and getting into mischief like your worst junior high school detention-ridden malcontent. There would be few enforceable rules that applied to everyone until Babe left the Yankees after 1934. And by then, poor Hug was long gone.

And then there was the conflict between Babe and Ruppert. At least Babe knew who signed his paychecks and who he had to at least show the same respect he had shown to his elders at St. Mary's. But, yes, he wanted to manage the Yankees. And in a time when player-managers were common (usually to save a salary), he was feeling ready by the time Huggins died. Ruppert decided then that Babe was not managerial material. So he shot him down in 1930, and then after Bob Shawkey was fired after one year, he shot him down again in 1931 when Joe McCarthy got the job. And when McCarthy didn't win in '31, Babe was probably campaigning again. And he did not get it, not in '31, and not between 1933 and 1935 when the Yankees failed to win the pennant. "C'mon, Colonel," he probably said. "Sorry, Root," was the almost annual response.

The request to manage probably coincided with Christmas season. You could cast Scrooge and Cratchit in the parts of Ruppert and Ruth.

I'm not sure what kept Ruppert out of the Hall of Fame for so long, other than a long stretch in which owners simply weren't considered. Most of them simply "owned" and didn't run things, as Ed Barrow did during the Ruppert years. I do know that I always felt that a Ruppert plaque would have been an easy one—Bought Babe Ruth, Built Yankee Stadium, Created Yankee Dynasty. But of course, as we see in this book, there was a lot more to the man than sitting back and watching those first-inning leads grow.

He knew how to live the life of a man of wealth. His homes and estates, his hobbies, his refined tastes, were all pure twentieth century, inherited from European opulence, which his parents would have seen and Americanized in the nation's most vibrant city. It was not smooth sailing for Jake, of course. The money and the homes and the servants and the horses and the show dogs and the rest were all fine. But he did also have to live his very public life in the wake of anti-German feelings following World War I (The Great War), owning a brewery during Prohibition (put THAT in your business plan), and then his mighty Yankees had to be reined in during the Great Depression, which essentially crippled the growth of the baseball industry. So it wasn't just sitting back and watching the runs score. It was staying afloat while maintaining a smile.

I wish I knew the "mystery lady," Helen "Winnie" Weyant, the Colonel's regular companion, to whom he left a third of the Yankees. I could have known her—she lived not far from me in Westchester County, New York, and she lived into the 1980s. But she receded from whatever small spotlight she occupied and apparently chose a life of reclusiveness. There were no obituaries for her when she passed. What an interesting Old Timers Day guest she might have been.

I did know Dan Daniel near the end of his life, but I did not know that he had done some work with Colonel Ruppert on a memoir. What a gift to baseball that would have been! What a missing link to know the whole story behind everything from the purchase of the team to the hiring of Huggins to the acquisition of Carl Mays to the Ruth deal to the Stadium construction and onward.

We could certainly have used a Huggins memoir, too. Or one from his sister, revealing what he *really* thought of Babe Ruth when he unburdened himself in the evenings.

But now, in this volume, a lot of those moments are carefully reviewed through the eyes of baseball historians and put into perspective. We didn't get the firsthand accounts of Jake or of Hug, but this book fills the gap quite well. Ruppert and Huggins were the principal figures in the transition of the Yankees from an afterthought on the New York baseball scene to the nation's greatest sports dynasty of the twentieth century. And they are well served here.

PREFACE

A visit to Yankee Stadium's Monument Park, just beyond the center field wall, is a journey to baseball's past and a reminder of the rich history of the National Pastime. For even the casual fan, the experience conjures up a strong sense of the game's continuity and the exceptionalism of its stars.

Five Yankees greats—only five over more than a century of play—have been honored with red granite monuments in Monument Park. Four are among the best who have ever played the game. Their names and faces are instantly recognized by millions: Babe Ruth, Lou Gehrig, Joe DiMaggio, and Mickey Mantle—American icons all.

Yet there is a fifth monument, and this last one was actually the first—and the only tribute in stone at the Stadium for almost a decade. It is dedicated to Miller Huggins, not nearly as well known as the others. One of the smallest men ever to have played the game, as a second baseman for the Cincinnati Reds and the St. Louis Cardinals, he emerged as a baseball giant. He is memorialized here as the manager of the New York Yankees from 1918 to 1929, when they won six pennants and three world championships, the first titles for the club. He brought together an unruly collection of stars in the early 1920s and rebuilt the team with youngsters later in the decade. Both groups were among baseball's best.

Nearby is a substantial plaque for Yankees owner Jacob Ruppert. Under his watch (1915–39), the Yankees won ten pennants and seven World Series, and they won the eleventh and eighth the year that he died. When Yankees historian Marty Appel was asked if anything surprised him or jumped out as he worked on his definitive history of the club, *Pinstripe Empire*, he replied that the importance of Jacob Ruppert—the man who bought Babe Ruth and built Yankee Stadium—has been largely overlooked.

There is a third member of the Yankees' management who played a vital role in the team's rise to the top, business manager Ed Barrow, who joined the club late in 1920. Barrow already has a biography, and a fine one, Dan Levitt's *Ed Barrow: The Bulldog Who Built the Yankees' First*

Dynasty. Our focus in this book is on the two men whose stories have not yet been told, Ruppert and Huggins.

In a 1931 article in the *Saturday Evening Post*, Ruppert said, "Getting him was the first and most important step we took toward making the Yankees champions." "Him" was not Babe Ruth but Miller Huggins.

Ruppert and Huggins were intensely private men. In the case of Ruppert, that reserve generated an air of regal mystery. In the case of Huggins, it generated misunderstanding and criticism. But Ruppert understood. Sportswriter Frank O'Neill wrote in the *New York Sun* in 1924 that Ruppert saw in Huggins "a man worthy of confidence, a man hung on the cross of propaganda which was as cruel as it was false, and as unfounded as it was detrimental to the cause of the Yankees."

Ruppert and Huggins both have been hiding—in plain view. They weave in and out of countless Yankees histories and biographies. Before they came onto the scene, the Yankees were a sorry, losing franchise. Both men had an almost fanatical commitment to winning, to making the New York Yankees the best in the world, and to keeping them there. They brought enormous strengths to the club, but it was also the synergy and mutual respect of their partnership that started the Yankees on their winning ways and laid the foundation for the club's future greatness.

When Ruppert's plaque was dedicated in April 1940, the *Sporting News* noted that it was going up next to the monument of Huggins, markers for two men who had brought so much success to the Yankees. They would not be forgotten by fans of the current era, the weekly predicted. We hope that with the publication of this book, they will long be remembered by future generations, too.

STEVE STEINBERG

LYLE SPATZ

ACKNOWLEDGMENTS

Rob Taylor, our editor at the University of Nebraska Press, for his
faith and trust in our judgment.

Marty Appel, who wrote our foreword and provided valuable
insights into the Yankees' history.

A special thank-you to Jennifer McCord, who provided editorial
advice and support from the start.

Our readers: Mark Armour, Tom Bourke, Rick Huhn, Dan Levitt,
and Eric Sallee, and our fact-checker, Gabriel Schechter, for their
insight and expertise.

The following people were most generous with their advice and
answers to our inquiries: Oliver Allen, Bill Ayrovainen, Cliff
Blau, Lynn Drigant, Jonathan Eig, Bill Francis, Irv Gold-
farb, Michael Haupert, Chuck Hildebrand, Lawrence Hogan,
Mike Lackey, Robert Lifson, Doug Lowry, Mike Lynch, Nor-
man Macht, Trent McCotter, Tony Morante, Maureen Ogle, Pete
Palmer, Brian Richards, K. Jacob Ruppert, Ron Selter, Robin
Shulman, Dave Smith, Barry Sparks, Glenn Stout, Joan Thomas,
Stew Thornley, David Vincent, and Craig Wright.

Members of SABR, the Society for American Baseball Research,
beyond those listed above.

National Baseball Hall of Fame Library and Archives, New York
Public Library's Microforms Reading Room, SABR Lending
Library, Stephan Saks of the New York Public Library, and Seattle Public Library's Interlibrary Loan and Magazines and Newspapers Departments.

Our Statistical Sources: Baseball-Reference.com and Retrosheet.

Our Photo Sources: Matthew Schneider and Melissa Ramhold, Bett-
mann/CORBIS; Jane Winton, Aaron Schmidt and the Trustees
of the Boston Public Library; Chicago Daily News Collection,
Chicago History Museum; Margaret Baughman and the Cleve-

land Public Library Photograph Collection; Bill Barrow and the Cleveland Press Collection, Cleveland State University; Pat Kelly and the National Baseball Hall of Fame Library, Cooperstown, New York; Library of Congress, Prints and Photographs Division; New York Daily News/Getty Images; Rosemary Morrow and the New York Times/Redux; Linda Briscoe Myers and the Harry Ransom Center, University of Texas at Austin; Mark Rucker and the Rucker Archive; Mary Wallace and the Walter P. Reuther Library, Wayne State University; Matt Fulling; Mark Fimoff; and the private collections of Tom Carwile, Chris Gamble, Dennis Goldstein, Michael Mumby, and Steve Steinberg.

The Colonel and Hug

Prologue

A Collaboration Is Born

It was mid-August 1917, and Miller Huggins's St. Louis Cardinals were making their final visit of the season to New York. Meanwhile, the Yankees had just suffered through a seven-game losing streak, and co-owner Jacob Ruppert was beginning to realize that his easygoing manager, Bill Donovan, was not the kind of leader the team needed.

Just a few months earlier, Huggins, the diminutive thirty-nine-year-old manager of the Cardinals, had expected to become the owner of the St. Louis team, and now he was contemplating leaving the ball club altogether. This meeting with Ruppert could lead Huggins away from St. Louis and toward baseball's biggest stage, New York City.

Huggins had managed the Cardinals since 1913; he was the player-manager until 1916, although 1914 was his last season as an everyday player. Team owner Helene Britton decided to sell the club and the dilapidated Robison Field after that 1916 season, and she promised Huggins the right of first refusal.[1] After lining up his financing, he discovered Britton had sold the club to a local group. Shortly thereafter, the new owners hired an executive of the American League's St. Louis Browns, Branch Rickey, as president.

A disconsolate Huggins could see that his influence in St. Louis would be greatly diminished in the revamped organization. Not only had he lost the opportunity to become the Cardinals' owner but he would be limited to managing the team on the field and no longer responsible for putting it together. Even as manager, he would have Rickey looking over his shoulder.

In spite of the team's severe financial constraints—something he faced all five years as the Cardinals' manager—Huggins surprisingly had them in third place this August, where they would finish the season.[2] The July 12, 1917, issue of the *Sporting News* featured Huggins's photo with the headline "Little Miracle Worker of the West." Huggins probably welcomed the attention, as he recognized it was time to move on. Detroit sportswriter Joe S. Jackson later noted, "Huggins was out [as the Cardinals' manager], to all intents and purposes, long before the season ended."[3]

American League president Ban Johnson took notice of what Huggins was accomplishing in St. Louis. Johnson was almost as disappointed as Huggins over the move of Rickey to the Cardinals, though for a very different reason. Johnson viewed Rickey as a rising star in the baseball world and was stung by his move to the rival National League.

Ruppert also may have noticed. The Yankees had thrilled New Yorkers in 1916 when they occupied first place for almost the entire month of July before being devastated by injuries and fading to fourth place. "Two or three broken bones were all that stood between [Yankees manager Bill] Donovan and greatness in 1916," wrote sportswriter George Daley.[4] Much had been expected of the 1917 Yankees, but they were floundering. Ruppert and his partner, Capt. Tillinghast "Til" L'Hommedieu Huston, had little to show for their investment and efforts of the past three years.

Johnson, who also wanted a winner in New York, was also coming to the conclusion that the Yankees needed a new manager. That summer he played a key role in connecting the Yankees' owners and the Cardinals' manager. He informed Ruppert of the likely availability of the highly regarded Huggins and told Taylor Spink, the publisher of the *Sporting News* (headquartered in St. Louis), to let Huggins know that an opportunity might arise in the nation's largest city.

Ruppert and Huggins had connected briefly earlier. "I had met Huggins only once," said Ruppert later. "It was in a hotel lobby. He didn't impress me at all. Just a little fellow slouching around with a cap and a pipe." Ruppert added that his first reaction was, "Who, that little grouch!" He later admitted, self-mockingly, "In view of the fact that getting Huggins was, beyond all question, the most important move toward building the Yankees from almost nothing into a consistent winner, you can see how much my first impression of him amounted to."[5]

In August, Huggins went to the Jacob Ruppert Brewery on East 90th Street in Yorkville to meet the Colonel. When he entered the office, Ruppert looked at the slightly built man with his cap pulled over his face and was taken aback. This was not his image of a leader. Spink recounted the meeting: "Coupled with his gnome-like appearance, the cap accentuated his midget stature and made Huggins look like an unemployed jockey. And Colonel Ruppert, an immaculate dresser, instinctively shied away from a cap-wearing job applicant."[6]

Yet Ruppert described a different impression of Huggins this time. "I saw in a very few minutes that my former estimate of him was way off the mark."[7] Sportswriter Bill Slocum quoted him as saying, "I like the business-like way he walked in on me, and the business-like way he talked to me."[8] Damon Runyon recalled that Ruppert went further, saying, "I picked him the moment I saw him walk into the room. I liked the way he came in."[9] Huggins also recalled a positive encounter. He said that Ruppert told him, "I have been interested in you for a long time."[10]

Ruppert was impressed by the depth of baseball knowledge and grasp of the intricacies of the game the little fellow sitting across from him possessed. Both men were direct and even blunt in their conversation. "I realized," said Ruppert of the meeting, "that Huggins's baseball ideas were all of a constructive nature, that he had great organizing ability, and that with the financial resources necessary to put his plans into operation, he could build a championship team."[11]

Huggins, in turn, was struck favorably by Ruppert's commitment to building a winner, his having the financial resources to do so, and his willingness to let his manager run the club without interference. In St. Louis Huggins had always lacked the first two, and the arrival of Branch Rickey now precluded the third. With Huggins still under contract in St. Louis and Donovan still managing the Yankees, he and Ruppert agreed to reconnect after the season.

Damon Runyon later provided insight into Ruppert's thought process. A few weeks after the meeting, Runyon and Slocum traveled with Ruppert to Plattsburgh, New York, for a Yankees exhibition game. Runyon explained: "All the way to Plattsburgh he talked of Miller Huggins, not to me exactly, but more as if he were talking to himself—as if he were arguing himself into favorable consideration of Huggins. It was a strange procedure. 'I liked him,' the Colonel kept saying, to which I could offer no comment because I did not know Huggins." By the time they reached their destination, said Runyon, Ruppert had made up his mind. "I'm going to make Miller Huggins manager of the Yankees. I like the fellow." Runyon noted that the selection was "in a measure snap-judgment, but the Colonel never wavered from that judgment."[12]

The Yankees played the exhibition game in Plattsburgh (for army troops in training) on September 23—before the end of the 1917 season— and the coverage of the game noted Ruppert's presence.[13] The following day, sportswriter Dan Daniel wrote that Huggins admitted he had been offered Donovan's position.[14] "Hug Almost Sure to Lead Club in American League" was the headline in the *St. Louis Star* on September 24.

Previous stories that Huggins was taking over the Yankees had surfaced in August.[15] In mid-September Ban Johnson told a St. Louis newspaper, "I do not know that Huggins is to manage the Yankees. I hope, however, that he is to do so. I regard him as a great manager."[16] Donovan was still the team's manager, yet Johnson was already anticipating getting back at the National League by capturing one of its bright young baseball minds. One story circulated that Johnson was so angered by the loss of Rickey that he had secretly signed Huggins to an American League contract during the 1917 season, without knowing at the time just what team Huggins would manage.[17]

At the end of the season, Johnson invited Huggins to New York as his guest for the World Series between the Chicago White Sox and the Giants and another clandestine meeting with Ruppert.[18] On the train to New York, Huggins had an awkward encounter with Rickey. The frugal Rickey was surprised that the equally thrifty Huggins was spending his own money to travel "to see the World Series."[19] Did Rickey suspect Huggins had an added reason to make the trip?

Now the Yankees did need a manager. They had finished the season in fifth place, and Ruppert had informed Donovan that he would not be rehired. "I like you, Donovan," Ruppert told him, "but we have to make some changes around here." The good-natured Donovan did not put up any resistance and replied, "I know it, Colonel."[20] Still the brewery executive found the firing excruciating. "If I live fifty years more," moaned the Yankees' fifty-year-old owner, "I hope I never have to face such a painful task."[21]

Managing in New York was a career ambition for the Cardinals' skipper.[22] Huggins realized it would not be easy, though he probably underestimated just how tough it would be. Years later he explained: "Going into New York from some other city is not like, we'll say, going from St. Louis to Cincinnati. New York is like no other city. . . . The psychology of New York is entirely different. . . . You've got to make good!"[23] Huggins mentioned two prerequisites for him to take the position: to have the authority to acquire and trade players, and to bring along his confidant and chief scout, Bob Connery, who had found many players for the Cardinals, including Rogers Hornsby. Ruppert agreed.

Til Huston was in Europe overseeing engineering projects for the Allied war effort. On October 18, his good friend Boston Red Sox manager Ed Barrow wrote him a letter. "Well, your old ball club didn't finish very well. There are all sorts of stories about a new manager for the Yanks. The scribes here are tipping Miller Huggins strongly, but the Colonel has not made any announcement so far. There is no doubt but that Huggins would be a fine man for you. He is a great hustler and builder."[24]

But Huston favored someone else. He was a close friend of Wilbert Robinson, the popular manager of the Brooklyn Dodgers.[25] Robinson had surprised many observers when he led Brooklyn to the 1916 National League pennant. Huston wanted "Uncle Robbie," as he was affectionately known, to become the Yankees' next manager.

Ruppert felt that, at age fifty-three, Robinson might not bring enough energy to the challenge of turning the team around. Perhaps Ruppert's business instincts told him that hiring the friend of a partner would create problems in the future, should the day come when the manager would have to be let go. Sportswriter Frank Graham said that Ruppert was brusque when he met Robbie, shaking his head and dismissing the Brooklyn manager with the words, "No, you will not do. For one thing, you are too old."[26]

Huston was at a distinct disadvantage in the hiring process: he was in France, 3,500 miles away. He could merely flail away in telegrams touting Robinson to Ruppert, which his partner conveniently ignored. Huston's main opposition to Huggins was that he was not Wilbert Robinson. But

Huston also did not care for Ban Johnson, and Huggins was considered "Ban's man" because Johnson had pushed hard for the St. Louis manager.

While the prevailing account is that Ruppert never seriously considered Robinson, he said otherwise more than a decade later. "We wanted Wilbert Robinson: in fact, we had wanted him from the start." But Brooklyn owner Charles Ebbets still controlled Robinson and demanded to know if the Yankees were trying to take his manager. Ruppert backed down.[27]

Considering the strong evidence that Ruppert did not want Robinson, this 1931 statement is hard to reconcile, unless it was Ruppert's attempt to show respect for a beloved icon of the game, one he had rejected out of hand years earlier. Or was it his penchant for recalling events from his past differently at different times?

On October 25, 1917, Jacob Ruppert announced he had signed Miller Huggins to a two-year contract to manage the Yankees.[28] The *Sporting News* saluted Ruppert for the hire: "Huggins' record with the Cardinals, considering his material, was not less than brilliant. . . . From the collar upward, little Miller Huggins was one of the biggest men in the game."[29] St. Louis sportswriter John Sheridan noted that the departure of Huggins conveniently cleared the way for Rickey to put his stamp on the Cardinals. What had been Huggins's team would now be Rickey's.[30]

John McGraw, the manager of the New York Giants, complimented Colonel Ruppert for the hire. "I believe that Huggins will build up the Yankees. . . . He knows baseball from every angle and is a fine fellow personally. It will help baseball in this city if the Yankees can win. . . . I feel sure that in due time the Yankees will be a worthy foe."[31] Yet McGraw, a brilliant tactician with an exceedingly high opinion of himself, did not feel threatened. When someone suggested that he and Huggins would now share the limelight in New York, he replied, "No man will go 50-50 with me there."[32]

In 1917, after the Giants won the National League pennant for a sixth time since 1903, few observers would have argued with McGraw. The New York Yankees were a team with virtually no winning tradition. There was often talk of "the Yankee jinx." Players who came to the Yankees seemed to get injured or suffer a decline in performance. Even respected managers, such as Frank Chance, winner of four pennants and two World Series with the Chicago Cubs, failed miserably in New York.

So perhaps few people took great note of Jacob Ruppert's statement to the press after he hired Huggins: "I think we made a ten strike in selecting Miller Huggins to lead the Yankees. He will have full power to do what he thinks best. . . . I have informed him to go the limit to give the American League rooters in New York a winner. I will spare no expense to give the Yanks a place in the sun."[33]

Part 1

THE EARLY YEARS

1

Everything He Touched Won First Prize

That Miller Huggins was on time for his first formal meeting with Jacob Ruppert did not go unnoticed by his future employer. "He is amazingly punctual in everything he does," said sportswriter Damon Runyon in a 1924 column about Ruppert. "He expects everybody else to be equally exact." Runyon described Ruppert as a "solidly built man of medium height, with iron-gray hair, which he wears slicked back in the Broadway mode, and a short iron-gray moustache. He commonly carries a serious expression. He wears clothes of the latest cut, is very particular about his apparel, but never deviates from snowy white linen shirts and collars. He never displays any jewelry, not even gold cuff links."[1]

With the exception of the color of his hair and moustache being iron-gray, this 1924 description of Ruppert could have been made at any time in his adult life. His passport application, dated March 15, 1892, when he was twenty-four years old, listed him as five feet eight, with brown eyes, a broad forehead, dark hair, and a dark complexion. Yankees historian Leo Trachtenberg called him "a dignified, portly man with a pleasant smile, an astute mind, and a ready bankroll."[2]

In a June 1918 interview held at Ruppert's brewery, the reporter portrayed him as sitting in his office at a desk littered with papers in "a spacious room decorated very simply with massive bronze statuary." He described Ruppert as "in every sense a man of big business, quick of speech, decisive in his statements, yet courteous and discriminating in his treatment of the men who approach him in a continual stream on a thousand varied errands."[3]

Waite Hoyt, who pitched for Ruppert's Yankees from 1921 to 1930, also talked about Ruppert's fourth-floor office at the brewery. "Of course, when you went into the place you entered a long hall, a long marble hallway. . . . All the woodwork was rosewood and paneled, and the brewery was immaculate. You could eat off the floor. You could not imagine it was a brewery." Hoyt called Ruppert one of the best-dressed men of his time. "His Rolls Royce always looked brand new when it was 10 years old. He was that way about everything."[4]

At the time of the Huggins signing, fifty-year-old Jacob Ruppert had been a success in everything he had ever put his hand to—except baseball. His Ruppert Brewery was among the most productive and profitable in the nation, his kennels of St. Bernards were consistent prizewinners, and his stable of racehorses was highly successful. It was only the Yankees, the American League club he co-owned with Captain Til Huston, that had been a consistent failure. Bringing Huggins to New York would be the first step in rectifying that failure, and by the time Ruppert died in January 1939, it could be accurately stated that his beer won gold medals, his dogs won blue ribbons, and his baseball team won world championships. "Everything he touched won first prize," was a quote New York Daily News sports editor Jimmy Powers used to sum up Ruppert's life.[5]

Born into a wealthy family that owned a successful brewery, Ruppert had amassed a personal fortune by steadily increasing output and making the Jacob Ruppert Brewery one of the largest and best-equipped breweries in the world. The Ruppert family had been brewers since before the American Civil War. Jacob's grandfather, Franz Maximillian Ruppert, was born in Bavaria in 1811. Like many of his fellow citizens, Franz eventually immigrated to America, in his case to New York City, where he opened a grocery in 1837. The business prospered, allowing him to buy a malt house in 1845, becoming the first German malt dealer in New York. He added to his holdings in 1850 when he bought the Aitken Braueri. The braueri (or brewery) was at 322 East 45th Street, just off First Avenue in a section of New York City then known as Turtle Bay. Franz Ruppert renamed his new brewery the Turtle Bay Brewery.[6]

Franz and his wife, the former Wilhelmina Zindel, born in 1813, also in Germany, had one son, Jacob (our subject's father), born in New York City on March 4, 1842. Wilhelmina died in 1865, whereupon Franz, who by now had anglicized his name to Francis, married New York City native Sophia Gick. They had four children: John, Frederick, Charles, and Annie.

Jacob started working in the brewery at age ten. By 1863, when he was just twenty-one, he was the manager. In 1867, he bought eleven lots of forested land on Third Avenue between 91st and 92nd Streets in Manhattan's Yorkville section and started his own brewery. Doing much of the physical labor required on his own, he cleared the land and built the Jacob Ruppert Brewery. A *New York Journal-American* article, written in 1957, described the Yorkville area as mostly farmland in 1867. "The population of New York was about 1,300,000 and the more populated parts of the city ended at 42nd Street. Only about 30,000 people lived in the Yorkville area. It was the old 12th Ward, bounded by 86th Street to the south and the Harlem River to the north, and stretched from the Hudson River to the East River. The whole area was filled with "squatters, goat farms, and wooden shanties perched on the rocks in the woods and marshes."[7]

On February 4, 1868, the first beer was brewed at the Jacob Ruppert Brewery, with Jacob serving as brewmaster, salesman, and distributor.[8] Francis Ruppert retired from brewing in 1869, but Jacob's brewery grew and prospered. In 1874, he bought a larger piece of land one block north on Third Avenue and 92nd Street. The brewery continued to flourish, and in 1883 Jacob bought a country home near Rhinebeck-on-the-Hudson in Dutchess County, New York.[9] He used the profits from his real estate investments to buy a silk factory, a lumberyard, a livestock farm, and an ice plant.[10]

The elder Jacob Ruppert had started with a handful of employees and sold 5,000 barrels of beer in his first year. When he died in 1915 after a lengthy illness, the brewery, now run by Jacob Jr., had 1,500 employees and production had grown to 1,200,000 barrels a year. Jacob Sr. had invested most of his profits in real estate, operated by the Jacob Ruppert Realty Corporation, which increased greatly in value during his lifetime. His principal hobby had been the breeding of trotting horses at his farm in Poughkeepsie, New York, the site of his Hudson River Driving Park, a scenic trotting track that later became the site of the Poughkeepsie Speedway.

The Ruppert lived amid all the trappings of great wealth. Their mansion and country estate were elegantly furnished. They threw lavish weddings for their children, which the society pages of the New York newspapers covered in detail. Their Manhattan neighbors included steel tycoon Andrew Carnegie and famed banker Felix Warburg. Neverthe-less, the Rupperts never were considered "blue-blooded" members of the New York City social elite. Their overall net worth, great as it was, did not compare to that of the Carnegies, Vanderbilts, and Astors. As a nouveau riche family who had made their fortune brewing beer and were Catholic rather than Protestant, they were never part of "the Four Hun-dred."[11] Yet they did attend many of the same social events, such as the 1902 christening of Kaiser Wilhelm II's yacht.

Ruppert Sr. was also fond of music and owned the Central Opera House in New York City.[12] A Mason and a longtime member of Tammany Hall, New York City's Democratic Party machine, he had served as an elector from the state of New York for Grover Cleveland's second election as president in 1892.[13] He was a forceful, single-purposed man with a great capacity for work. His charities were numerous but not ostentatious, a tradition Jacob Jr. would continue.

Because of British influence dating back to the thirteen American colo-nies, most beers brewed in the United States had been ales. In the colonial period, brewers such as Murray, Beekman, Van Cortlandt, and Rutgers were among the most distinguished New York families. Vassar College's founder, Matthew Vassar, directed his family's brewery in Poughkeepsie, which in 1836 was one of the nation's largest.[14] Ales are made with yeast that ferments on the top of a vessel; the process uses warm water, and the brew is often served warm. But the arrival of German immigrants, beginning in the mid-1830s, mostly from Bavaria, transformed the brew-ing craft, weaning Americans away from ale and onto lager beers, which were bottom-fermented and stored cold.[15] On the website Smart Planet, technology expert David Worthington wrote: "A major difference between brewing ale and brewing lager beer is the amount of refrigeration that's involved; lagers ferment at relatively cooler temperatures. German immi-grants began to arrive in earnest during the mid-1800s and needed a way to cool their drafts."[16] In New York, brewers used the ice that floated down the Hudson River to aid in the production of their lagers.[17]

By 1880, Yorkville, the Lower East Side of Manhattan, and the Williams-burg and Bushwick sections of Brooklyn, which had all become home to large populations of German immigrants, were also home to more than a hundred breweries. In 1866, George Ehret opened Hell Gate Brewery in

Yorkville, stretching from 91st to 94th Streets between Second and Third Avenues. Three years later Jacob Ruppert Sr. opened his brewery almost next door. As one of the earliest brewers to use the new technology of refrigeration, which allowed for year-round brewing, Ruppert expanded his brewery to become one of the leading beer producers in the United States, though almost all of his sales were in the New York City area.[18]

In 1865 Ruppert married Anna Gillig, the twenty-three-year-old daughter of New York brewer George Gillig, another native Bavarian and one of the country's first brewers of lager. The couple had six children: Cornelia, Jacob Jr., Frank, Anna, George, and Amanda.[19]

Jacob Jr. was born on August 5, 1867, at his family's mansion on Fifth Avenue and 93rd Street and reared under a stern Germanic influence. Although he, like his father, was native-born, both spoke with a German accent throughout their lives.[20] Trachtenberg, however, wrote that Ruppert Jr. would lapse into a German accent only when he was excited or agitated.[21]

An 1897 article in the *New York World*, when Jacob Jr. was the Tammany candidate for president of the Municipal Council, described his childhood as a period of firm discipline. There were no private tutors or coddling. He attended school just as if his father's income were in the hundreds of dollars instead of the thousands.[22]

Jacob was an average student at New York's Columbia Grammar School, where his formal education began and ended. He was a member of the school's baseball team, though there are no records of any prizes or awards to his credit. He did apply to the School of Mines at Columbia College and passed the entrance examination, but his parents had different ideas for their son. Ruppert's mother in this staunchly Bavarian Catholic family wanted him to enter the priesthood, while his father wanted him to enter his business, in much the same way he had entered his own father's business.

His father won out, although another version of how Jake got into the family business appeared in the *Sporting News* after his death. He had received an appointment to West Point, he told sportswriter Dan Daniel, but never got to go. "My mother called me into her room one day and said: 'Jake, father is 72. He can no longer attend to business. You must sacrifice college and become a practical brewer, so you can run this business. You must make the sacrifice for the family.' So I forgot about college and about West Point and proceeded to become a brewer."[23] While it is true that Jacob had an interest in West Point, his recollection of the timing of this story does not ring true. The year "father was 72" was 1914, the younger Jacob was 47 and well established in his career, not a recent graduate of the Columbia Grammar School.

Ruppert, like many successful men who lived full and eventful lives, often gave varying accounts of even his most important decisions. In a poignant 1937 interview with Taylor Spink, he gave yet another version of his entry into the family business. "It seems to me I never have got around to doing the things I wanted to do most. For example, when I was a youngster, I wanted to be a ball player. My ambition was to be a member of the team at West Point. I wanted to be a soldier. I belonged to the Knickerbocker Greys, an organization of military-minded lads. I played second base with their team. I really could play ball too. I envied the Giants. There were no Yankees then. My mother was very sympathetic. But my dad, who was a brewer, said, 'This West Point stuff, this ball playing business, is all nonsense. You go into the brewery.'"[24]

When he did go to work in the brewery as an eighteen-year-old common laborer, his father told the foreman, "Do no favors for this new worker. If he does good work, give him a better job. If he shirks, fire him." The foreman put Jake to work washing kegs and carrying hundred-pound sacks for $10 a week.[25] The most pleasant of Ruppert's memories of working in the brewery as a young man were those of driving brewery-wagon horses. "Brewery teams were as pretty to see operate as a nicely stepping ball-team."[26]

"There are many departments in Ruppert's mammoth establishment," noted the *World*, and in each of these, the young man served an apprenticeship. It was not until he was twenty years of age that young Ruppert was graduated from the real drudgery of brewing and entered the business department."[27] In 1891 Ruppert Sr. named his twenty-three-year-old son the general manager of the company. Under his leadership, the brewery became one of the biggest in the country, and by 1911 he had become president and chairman of the board of trustees for the United States Brewers Association.[28]

When he took over the brewery from his father, it was producing

350,000 barrels a year. "Son, when I founded this business my big ambition was to sell 5,000 barrels of beer a year—and I did it," his father said on yielding control. "Dad, my ambition is to sell 5,000 barrels a day," Jake replied.[29] Eventually he would realize and surpass that lofty goal. In 1919, the last year before Prohibition, that number had grown to 1.3 million barrels a year.[30] When Repeal came in 1933, he hired hundreds of new workers, built a new plant, and was soon producing 2.5 million barrels of beer a year.[31]

Yet when asked years later if there was anything in the world he had not been able to do, he answered, "I was never able to be a major league catcher. That was my boyhood ambition." Ruppert said as a youngster he had been the captain, manager, and catcher on his neighborhood baseball team, the Millrocks of Hellgate. But after a new boy moved in and won the catching job, Ruppert moved to second base and later to center field. "I always could hit, and could catch flies or handle grounders. But I always wanted to catch." Ruppert said his mother always considered catching too dangerous and preferred it when he played the outfield. "Catching is not easy," he admitted.[32]

That Ruppert would want to play the most difficult and demanding position is not surprising. Catching had acquired a "special mystique" by the 1880s, wrote historian Peter Morris. Young men who came of age in post–Civil War America "saw the man behind the plate as an iconic hero who embodied unbounded courage, extraordinary skill, and unmatched value." "The 1880s saw a new emphasis on the catcher as the embodiment of such attributes as teamwork, leadership, and resourcefulness," Morris wrote.[33] Ruppert would later employ all these attributes in building his brewery, baseball, and real estate empires.

2

The Colonel Makes a Name for Himself

The teenage Jacob Ruppert's ambition to attend West Point had ended when his autocratic father and his own sense of familial obligation led him to join the family brewery instead. As in all his endeavors, he approached it with determination to succeed. "Young Jake was willing," wrote Gerald Holland in *The American Mercury*. "He had his father's romantic passion for brewing. He loved it with a tender devotion."[1]

Ruppert also recognized that for a family-owned business to succeed in New York City, a political connection was mandatory. His family was a regular contributor to Tammany Hall, the Democratic machine that dominated New York City politics. Jacob, who had joined Tammany as a twenty-one-year-old in 1888, began to cultivate the Tammany representatives in his district. In addition, wrote Holland, "He assembled celebrities for dinners still famed," while acquiring "the reputation of a gay and witty young beau."

In 1886 Ruppert had joined the New York National Guard as a member of the Seventh Regiment, what he called the "silk stocking troop."[2] Three years later, Governor David B. Hill appointed him as aide-de-camp and gave him the rank of colonel. Ruppert would be "Colonel Ruppert" or "the Colonel" for the rest of his life.[3] Colonel Ruppert served on Governor Hill's staff from 1889 through 1891 and then as a senior aide to Hill's successor, Roswell P. Flower, from 1892 to 1894.[4] Citing Ruppert's "grace and aptitude" as a public speaker, Flower chose him as his representative at Chicago's Columbian Exposition of 1892–93. And it was Ruppert, on behalf of the governor, who delivered the acceptance speech at the unveiling of the Christopher Columbus monument in New York City in 1892.[5] When Republican Levi P. Morton, the nation's former vice president, became governor of New York in

1895, Ruppert, a Democrat, was temporarily out of the political arena, but not for long.[6]

While he had become influential in Democratic Party affairs, serving for a time on the powerful Finance Committee, Ruppert was fully aware that the Democratic machine was swindling the citizens of New York. In 1892 he called them "polluted harpies that, under the pretense of governing this city, are feeding day and night on its quivering vitals."[7] Nevertheless, Tammany leader Richard "Boss" Croker selected him to run for the city council presidency in 1897. One of the methods Tammany used to retain power was to reward each of the city's ethnic groups for their support. Croker believed the nomination of Ruppert would satisfy Tammany's German American constituency.[8]

However, the city's German Americans were not satisfied with having one of their compatriots serve as city council president; they wanted a mayor.[9] On October 8 Ruppert removed himself from the race, citing "business reasons" for his withdrawal. He claimed the time necessary to devote to the job would greatly interfere with his tasks at the brewery. The more likely reason for his withdrawal was his refusal to contribute $50,000 to Tammany in return for the nomination.[10]

An undeterred Croker selected him to run for the U.S. House of Representatives in 1898 instead. Ruppert was the Democratic candidate from New York's Fifteenth Congressional District, which included parts of Manhattan and the Bronx, but was situated primarily in upper Manhattan's heavily German Yorkville section. Croker believed Ruppert, as the son of a prominent and well-known German American Democrat, had a strong chance to defeat Philip B. Low, the two-term Republican incumbent.

Although the Fifteenth District was thought to "lean Republican," Low's predecessor had been a Democrat: Isidor Straus, a native of Germany and co-owner, with his brother Nathan, of Macy's department stores.[11] In the election that fall, Ruppert overcame opposition from organized labor to defeat Low easily, garnering almost 31,000 votes to Low's 20,000.[12]

He was reelected in 1900, despite continued hostility from organized labor, which was opposed to Ruppert and his fellow brewers for employing non-union workers. Moreover, he defied his own party with his support for the Republican-backed bill supporting the Gold Standard, a position opposed by Free Silver Democratic presidential candidate William Jennings Bryan and most congressional Democrats. "I represent a sound money constituency, and I propose to act in accordance with their wishes and with the best interests of this great commercial city," Ruppert said.[13]

Ruppert defeated Republican Elias Goodman, but his margin of victory was much smaller than it had been in 1898. In all, Ruppert served four uneventful terms in Congress, with perhaps the most memorable moment coming in 1902. Returning from a day of watching the horses at Washington's Benning Race Track, he and fellow New York City congressman Oliver Belmont were arrested when Belmont's auto sped by a police officer on a bicycle at about 20 miles per hour. The two congressmen were eventually able to convince the officer to let them go free.[14] Ruppert was no stranger to speeding vehicles. Ten years later, the Colonel was racing his motorcycle against a car driven by John Gernon, a wealthy Rhinebeck garage owner. The race ended when Gernon crashed his vehicle into a tree and died.[15]

During his tenure in Congress, Ruppert served on the Committee on Militia and the Committee on Immigration and Naturalization. He declined nomination to a fifth term in 1906. That year the *Washington Post* identified him as one of fourteen millionaires serving in the House. Ruppert, one of three Democrats on the list, was judged the ninth wealthiest, with an estimated net worth of $4 million. (Belmont was also on the list.) The *Post* called him an "extremely modest man" who "has served four terms in Congress and never made a speech, although he is rarely ever absent from his duties."[16] Another of the *Post*'s lists, this one in 1902, included him among the twenty-three bachelors in the 356-member House.[17] "Colonel, clubman, Congressman, sportsman and bon vivant, young Jake Ruppert was now the Prince of Wales of beer."[18]

Ruppert had entered Congress at a time before an income tax was levied on persons and businesses, which led to his and many other families amassing great wealth.[19] His four terms had been undistinguished legislatively, but as a moneyed young bachelor he thrived socially. He was a regular attendee at White House receptions, thrown by fellow New Yorker Theodore Roosevelt and First Lady Edith, and at the numerous diplomatic and charitable events that made up the capital's social calendar.

The *New York World* described the thirty-year-old freshman congressman as a good-looking man, a trifle below medium height, broad-shouldered, and stoutly built. His round, plump face showed the Teutonic blood the newspaper believed had made him Tammany's choice in the Fifteenth District. "His friends will tell you he is a prince of good fellows, one of the best-groomed men in the city and a glorious entertainer," claimed the *World*. Ruppert, with the assistance of his valet, was always impeccably dressed. There were few "dressier" men than the Colonel, according to the *World*. "But his intimates go further. They testify to a very long head on Col. Ruppert's shoulders, to his industry and judgment in business and to the careful avoidance of the social pitfalls into which other sons of wealthy men have stumbled now and again."

Calling him more modest than some other rich men's sons, the *World* noted that he did "make merry occasionally," recalling the 1896 Arion Ball when he was said to have shocked several of his father's old friends with his merry-making. And while Ruppert had generally avoided notoriety, it had been rumored a few years earlier that he was about to marry a music hall favorite known as "Trola," a rumor he denied. "Not that he runs to brilliant waistcoats or rainbow shirts, for he doesn't. It is in cut, in finish, and in the nicety of detail that the Colonel excels. He patronizes an American tailor—a Fifth Avenue artist, to be sure, and he pays him, by the year, enough to sustain a large family in the most substantial kind of comfort."[20]

Ruppert's immense wealth afforded the young man-about-town an opportunity to enjoy life to the utmost, and he took full advantage. Living in his parents' mansion on the southeast corner of Fifth Avenue and 93rd Street, he awoke each weekday at eight and was at the brewery at 9:30. He worked until noon and then had lunch with his father in their private dining room at the brewery, where a special chef prepared their meals. After lunch, the two men usually spent a half hour or so in the brewery's private billiard room. His day's work completed, Ruppert returned home and spent the rest of the day enjoying such pleasures as riding his bicycle through Central Park.[21] After his bath, dinner was at Delmonico's or one of the other eateries that catered to people of wealth. Dinner was followed by a lively evening, most often at the theater.

Like most men of his social class, Ruppert was a member of many clubs.

During his lifetime he was associated with the Lambs Club, the Manhattan Club, the New York Athletic Club, the Catholic Club, and two German societies, Arion and Liederkranz. In August 1895 Ruppert purchased the 113-foot steamer yacht, *Judge*, and renamed it *Albatross*. The next year he and his brother George took a course in navigation at the New York Nautical College. They then passed an examination that licensed them to command and pilot the boat.[22] An avid sailor, Ruppert belonged to the Atlantic, the New York, and the Larchmont yacht clubs, and he spent many hours aboard the *Albatross*, sailing on Long Island Sound.

Jacob Sr.'s lifelong passion had been the standardbred trotting horses he bred at his farm at Rhinebeck-on-the-Hudson, twenty miles north of Poughkeepsie.[23] He retired from breeding these horses in 1899, yet when horsemen from around the country formed the Association of Trotting Horse Breeders in 1906, they named Senator J. W. Bailey of Texas president and Ruppert second vice president.[24]

Jacob Jr. followed a similar path, but his interest was primarily in thoroughbreds rather than standardbreds. He was one of fifty wealthy horsemen who established New York's prestigious Jockey Club in 1894. From 1890 to 1898 his racing stable was among the nation's finest. Among his best-known horses were Ajax, Counter Tenor, Gotham, and Concord.[25] Perhaps his favorite horse was St. Domingo. "I always considered that St. Domingo was worth every cent of the $30,000 I paid for him," Ruppert said of the horse he felt was the country's best three-year-old in 1893, "but he had bad luck."[26] St. Domingo broke down during the running of the 1893 Belmont Stakes and finished last.

The Jockey Club arose as a response to the corruption and mismanagement of the Board of Control that had run horse racing in New York since 1891. The *New York Tribune* argued in 1894 that "racing had to change its ways . . . to flourish and gain public acceptance.[27] But by that time a change in the old order had already begun. The new ruling body modeled itself after the English Jockey Club, whose members would ensure the integrity of the sport. Ruppert, a senior aide to Governor Flower, but already at age twenty-six a prominent horseman, was chosen to attend that first meeting on February 10, 1894. In addition to Ruppert, the membership included many of New York's bluebloods and WASP elite: August Belmont, J. J. Astor IV, J. P. Morgan, and Cornelius Vanderbilt.[28]

Horse racing was extremely popular among New York's sports fans. Most of those fans knew little and cared less about who controlled racing. Unlike the breeders, they were for the most part working-class city people and first- and second-generation Americans. Along with the pleasure of attending sporting events and following them in the newspapers, many liked to wager on the events' outcomes. This fondness for betting led to New York horse racing's greatest crisis.

Gambling had long been a cancer on the body of sports, leading to fixed ball games, fixed fights, and fixed horse races. For those who cared about the integrity of sports, there was no doubt that reform was needed. Perhaps because thoroughbred racetracks were centered in and around New York City, legislators from the rural parts of the state, who found any kind of gambling immoral, took special aim at the betting taking place at those tracks.[29] Even Ruppert's mother objected to his involvement in horse racing because of its close association with gambling. "While I was ill with diphtheria," Ruppert told sportswriter Dan Daniel in 1938, "my mother saw a box in a New York newspaper which insinuated that a horse of mine, favorite in a race, had not done his best because jockey or trainer had not wanted it to win. Mother said 'Jake, no Ruppert can afford to be mixed up with anything like that.'"[30]

In 1908 Charles Evans Hughes, New York's Republican governor, set out to eliminate gambling at racetracks.[31] Hughes signed the Hart-Agnew bill into law in June 1908. The bill, which essentially prohibited on-track betting, crippled the horseracing industry in New York City.[32] Police were instructed to arrest men at racetracks who congregated in groups of more than three and to arrest anyone who was seen writing anything that might be construed as betting on a newspaper, racing program, or even a piece of plain paper.

In 1910 the New York legislature passed even more restrictive legislation that made it possible for racetrack owners and members of its board of directors to be fined and imprisoned if anyone was found betting, even privately, anywhere on their premises. A 1911 amendment to the law that would have limited the liability of owners and directors was defeated, after which every racetrack in New York State shut down.[33]

Ruppert's entry in the 1958 edition of the *Dictionary of American Biography* says that he sold his racing stable in 1910, after Hughes closed the racetracks, and that he later lost interest in breeding horses after his disagreement with a judge's decision at a national horse show.[34] However, an 1896 article in the *New York Times* indicates that Ruppert's major involvement in horseracing had ended much earlier, even before he entered Congress. "The racing stable of Col. Jacob Ruppert was sold at auction at the Sheepshead Bay racetrack yesterday. The Colonel will retire from racing, much to the regret of his many friends." For reasons unknown, those prize thoroughbreds were sold very cheaply. Gotham, a four-year-old ($6,100) and Concord, a two-year-old ($4,000), were the highest priced of the thirteen sold. Ajax, now six years old, went for a mere $675.[35] Nine months before that, the *New York Herald* noted that Ruppert had sold his brood mares and intended to retire from breeding but would retain his racing stable.[36]

An 1897 *Times* article gave another possible reason for Ruppert's abandoning horse racing. "Col. Jacob Ruppert, with all his business cares, finds time to take more than a passing interest in sport, and is a patron of the racetracks, the athletic field, yacht races, and bench and horse shows. For several years he owned a powerful stable of racehorses, but last season, although very successful on the turf, he decided that he could not properly attend to his business and his stable, and so decided to sell his horses. He has now two race horses, which occasionally carry his colors."[37]

Ruppert also kept a hand in his father's trotting horses. In a lively auction held at Madison Square Garden in 1902, he paid $15,700 for Oakland Baron, rated the country's best trotter. The new acquisition was immediately sent to the Ruppert stock farm at Rhinebeck-on-the-Hudson, where he would be used as both a racer and a stud.[38]

Ruppert was now focusing most of his sporting attention on his dogs, which he would continue to show and breed long after he got out of horse racing and even after he bought the Yankees. He had developed the world's finest kennel of St. Bernards, spending thousands of dollars buying and breeding them. A note in the November 1, 1911, *Boston Daily Globe* reported that Ruppert had purchased three St. Bernards for a total of $6,000. One of the dogs, Champion Young Stormer, winner of five championships and twelve blue ribbons, sold for $2,500.[39] In return for his investment, Ruppert's St. Bernards were regular winners at dog shows. His prize St. Bernard was Oh Boy, who won Best of Breed in four classes at the Westminster Kennel Club Dog Show in Madison Square Garden in February 1919.

In addition to St. Bernards, Ruppert was also breeding Boston terriers. "His exhibits of this breed have been the admiration of half-a-dozen dog shows, and the Boston breed has been made popular through his lavish efforts," stated the *World* in 1897. It mentioned the dozen dogs, St. Bernards and Terriers, each a blue-blooded aristocrat with a prodigiously long pedigree that resided at the Ruppert family's palatial country home in Rhinebeck-on-the-Hudson. The *World* described Ruppert's passion for choice first-edition books, which he had started collecting even before he entered Congress. "Beautiful artistic bindings are all important for the purposes of this collection. He has accumulated 1,300 volumes at a modest expense of $30,000 to date, and still the work goes on."[40] Later on, Ruppert would also collect jade, Chinese porcelain, and Indian relics and keep a private zoo at Eagle's Rest, his 135-acre country estate in Garrison, New York.

When Jacob Ruppert Sr. died in 1915, he left his estate, valued at $20 million (a sum worth well over $400 million today) to his widow and his four remaining children.[41] He specified that Jacob Jr. should continue running the brewery and replace him as president. "In this connection I wish to emphasize the fact that my son, Jacob Ruppert, has had practical management of the said brewing business for some years and the progress and success of said business have been due largely to his ability and attention. It is my wish that upon my death he shall be elected president of such corporation and continue as such as long as he shall be willing."[42]

Sons of very successful men are often driven to establish their own identities. This is especially true when the son, whether by choice or not, enters the same industry or profession as his father. In Jacob Ruppert's case he was not only up to the task but he far surpassed his father in the brewing industry. By 1911 he had moved up from first vice president to president and chairman of the board of trustees for the United States Brewers Association, a post he would hold for sixteen years.[43]

Early in his presidency he was forced to deal again with those who felt it their duty to dictate morality. The same kinds of groups that had found gambling immoral were now campaigning for a nationwide ban on the sale of alcoholic beverages. The opposing forces were mainly the same.

On one side, advocating the ban, were native-born Americans, mostly Protestant, rural and small town. On the other side, opposing the ban, were recent immigrants, mostly Catholic and Jewish, along with city dwellers in general.

Millions of new immigrants, mostly Italians and Jews from Eastern Europe, had come to the country in the past thirty years. They had settled in the nation's cities, bringing their strange languages, strange customs, and, in many cases, foreign ideologies with them. Nativist groups, such as the Immigration Restriction League founded in 1894, opposed the influx of what they called "undesirable immigrants" from southern and eastern Europe, who brought with them poverty and organized crime. "To temperance advocates, beer was code for immigration filth and sloth," wrote author Robin Shulman. "The brewers were foreign interlopers who came to America to fatten themselves on sales of their vile lager, leaving a trail of drunk and debauched citizens in their wake."[44] Noting that more than two-thirds of New York City residents were foreign-born or the children of immigrants, one Prohibition publication called the nation's biggest city "the least American part of the United States."[45]

Among the most vocal critics of the immigrants was Billy Sunday, the former Major League ballplayer turned evangelist. "America has become the backyard in which Europe is dumping its paupers and criminals," Sunday said in 1914. "They settle here and become a carbuncle on the neck of the body politic."[46]

Ruppert addressed the issue of banning the sale of alcohol at the 1912 Brewers convention. He reported that the tide was turning against those who favored Prohibition. "It has been clearly shown," he stated, "that beer is the national beverage, and its use is increasing far faster than the population. The light beer made by American brewers appeals to the popular taste and is peculiarly adapted to a nation of moderate drinkers." He exhorted his fellow brewers to make their product's desirability better known. "We must, however, reiterate its good points again and again, after the manner of a successful advertiser, so that everyone may at last understand that beer is from the very nature of its composition and manufacture hygienically clean and pure, besides possessing undoubted food value; a light, bright, sparkling, germ-proof and health-giving beverage, which contains only about 3 to 4% of alcohol, is deliciously palatable, and without a rival in popular flavor." He ended his speech by quoting *Louisville Courier-Journal* editor Henry Watterson, who wrote, "The introduction of beer in America has done more for temperance than all the temperance societies and all the prohibition laws combined."[47]

In urging his fellow brewers to advertise their product, Ruppert was preaching what he himself practiced. This 1912 ad in the *Brooklyn Daily Eagle*, welcoming in the New Year, was one of many he ran in the New York newspapers.

> Nineteen hundred and eleven recorded the most remarkable epoch in the history of the Jacob Ruppert Brewery. The largest beer stockhouse in the world was completed and equipped with the best and most modern machinery ever installed in a brewery. When the present plans and buildings now under construction are completed, which will be this year, the Jacob Ruppert Brewery will be one of the three largest breweries in the world. We desire to thank the millions who appreciate our efforts in producing the pure, unadulterated beverages that go out under our name and seal, and wish to drink a health to all for the New Year.[48]

The ban on on-track betting at the racetrack had been a financial blow to Ruppert's involvement in the commercial end of horse racing. But breeding and racing horses was as much a hobby for him as it was a business. His main business was brewing beer, which had been and continued to be the foundation of the Ruppert family fortune. So he well understood just how catastrophic a law prohibiting the manufacture, sale, and transport of alcohol might be.[49]

With both perceived vices—gambling and alcohol—Ruppert sided against the moral reformers and "do-gooders." We cannot know his feelings on the morality of each of these battles, although it is most likely he did not see betting on horses and drinking alcohol as moral failings. There was, however, one case where Ruppert sided with the reformers, but again not doing so would have harmed his business interests.

In 1908 a reform group called the Committee of Fourteen was trying to clean up prostitution in New York, especially in the midtown Times Square area. The committee estimated that between 80 and 90 percent of the city's 11,000 saloons tolerated, and even encouraged, commercial sex. The committee earned the cooperation of the New York Brewers Association, which was joined by the Brewers Board of Trade, led by Ruppert, its president, in severing ties with saloons that allowed illegal activity.[50] "We are opposed to the dives as much as we are to drunkenness," Ruppert said. "They are the worst foe of the brewers, and they can and will be done away with by concerted action."[51]

It is difficult to determine how many saloons allowed "illegal activity," yet despite Ruppert's condemnation of them, business relations between saloons and brewers, including him, were an important part of the business. "The Committee of Fourteen," reported the *New York Times*, "has entered into negotiations with brewing concerns and surety companies with a view of establishing an 'unofficial discretion' that would have the effect of preventing the opening of saloons or hotels of a disorderly character in the future."[52]

In 1914 the Ruppert brewing empire expanded with the purchase of the Haffen Brewery, the largest brewery in the Bronx. Formerly operated by the J. & M. Haffen Brewing Company, the plant occupied the entire frontage between 151st and 152d Streets on the west side of Melrose Avenue.[53] Ruppert had organized the brewery into an efficient vertical production, wrote Robin Shulman, "investing in an ice factory (for cooling), horse stables (for transportation), forestry concerns (for making wooden barrels), real estate (for saloons), banks (for credit), and the German-language paper the *New Yorker Staats-Zeitung* (for favorable press)."[54]

Jacob Ruppert's brewery products, including his signature Knickerbocker brand, ranked at the top of the industry. As Elisabeth Bradley has written in *Knickerbocker: The Myth behind New York*, that name and image for decades had conveyed "a shorthand for all things New York. . . . His name and image had become synonymous with a real New Yorker."[55] His horses, when he had raced his own stable, were the finest money could buy. As a dog fancier, he bothered with nothing but blue-ribbon winners. His collection of first editions, etchings, china, and other objets d'art again reflected his discriminating taste.[56] Not yet fifty years old, Ruppert seemingly had no worlds left to conquer. However, a chance encounter with two fellow brewers years earlier, when he was in Congress, had set in motion a venture that would forever change his life.

3

Nothing at All but Ambition
and Pluck and Brains

Miller Huggins began his love affair with baseball while growing up in Cincinnati. He idolized Bid McPhee, the Reds' great second baseman of the late nineteenth century.[1] Huggins excelled as the captain of his baseball team at Walnut Hills High School. He also played on the area's semipro teams as a teenager "on about as many teams as there were sandlots in 'Cincy,'" he later recalled.[2] Huggins often played under the assumed name of Proctor, accomplishing two things by doing so.[3] He kept his eligibility for high school and university baseball, and he hid his ball playing—especially on Sundays—from his religious father.

James T. Huggins, an accomplished cricket player, was born in England, as was his wife, Sarah.[4] When he settled in Cincinnati in his twenties, he went to work in the grocery business, where he remained for the rest of his career. His son, Miller, was born in Cincinnati on March 27, 1878, the youngest of three sons and the third of four children.[5] James was a strong disciplinarian, and his serious nature was probably something his son inherited. Damon Runyon reported, humorously yet with a kernel of truth, that Miller Huggins had laughed—once.[6]

"The head of our family," recalled Miller's sister Myrtle, "was a strict Methodist who abhorred frivolity and listed baseball as such, especially baseball played on Sunday."[7] Miller later recalled reaching an understanding with his father. "We argued the matter at length. I was stubborn and argumentative, and in a way I won. I got a compromise by which I could play ball at times and study law at others."[8]

After playing semipro ball in and around Cincinnati for a few years, Huggins began his professional career with the Mansfield (Ohio) Haymakers of the Interstate League in 1899, still under the name of Proctor. He juggled law school and his baseball career, pursuing baseball in the summers when school was out.

In the summer of 1900, Huggins played for Fleischmann's Mountain Tourists, a team the *Cincinnati Enquirer* called "the strongest independent team in America." Julius Fleischmann was Cincinnati's mayor from 1900 to 1905; his brother Max was more "a man of leisure." He captained the baseball team that played in the upstate New York town that later became known as Fleischmanns.[9] The brothers, whose family made its fortune in the yeast business, were also part owners of the National League's Cincinnati Reds. In the 1880s their father, Charles Fleischmann, had transformed the town into a summer resort for wealthy Hungarian Jewish families, at a time when Jews were barred from many mountain resorts.[10] Max Fleischmann took over a Cincinnati semipro club and relocated the team to upstate New York. Formally known as the Mountain Athletic Club, it was made up of many top Cincinnati area players. The team traveled in a special railroad car and drew big crowds for its games. Late in his life, Huggins looked back fondly on that 1900 season. "I probably had the most fun in my baseball career when I captained the Fleischmann Mountaineers. . . . That was a joy ride that year—1900—we won about 60 out of 66 games."[11]

At the University of Cincinnati Law School, where he earned a varsity letter, Huggins captained the baseball team, an early reflection of his leadership skills. Among his professors were the law school's dean, future president and chief justice of the U.S. Supreme Court William Howard Taft and former U.S. attorney general and future Ohio governor Judson Harmon. At one point Huggins had to appear before the school's executive committee to explain why he should not be dropped from the school.[12] He pleaded his case successfully and graduated in 1902; he clerked that winter in St. Paul, Minnesota, under District Judge Grier Orr.

Huggins was at a crossroads, and Taft sensed it. "You can become a pleader or a player—not both," he told him. "Try baseball; you seem to like it better." Taft added words of encouragement, telling his student not to look back once he made his career choice.[13] For Huggins, it was an easy choice. Years later, he explained that he fell in love with baseball at an early age. "No suitor ever laid out as careful a plan to obtain his love as I. . . . I loved baseball, I went to it. I had to, for in it I was happy."[14]

It was around this time that Huggins almost joined forces with John McGraw, the famous third baseman of the National League's great Baltimore Orioles of the 1890s. McGraw became the player-manager of that team in 1899. In one version of the story, Huggins said when he was playing for Mansfield, McGraw wanted him to come east and try out for the Orioles. But McGraw did not provide the train fare, and Huggins declined the invitation.[15] McGraw told a somewhat different story. When he was managing the 1901 Orioles, at that time an American League team, he was looking over prospects on Cincinnati's Shamrocks, a semipro club. He passed on Huggins. "'That shrimp,' I said to myself. 'He's too little to be of any use as a big leaguer.'"[16] Two decades later, McGraw and Huggins would cross paths again as opposing World Series managers.

Huggins was indeed a "shrimp," much more so than is reflected in baseball databases, which list him as five feet six and 140 pounds. In 1924 Huggins said that he weighed just 120 pounds and that his weight never varied much from that.[17] When he debuted with the Reds in 1904, Cincinnati sportswriter Ed Grillo wrote that there was no smaller man in the Major Leagues, maybe in all of baseball.[18]

Perhaps to compensate for his size, or perhaps simply because of who he was, Huggins always had a fierce determination to succeed and improve. As a youngster, he loved to play marbles. He and his brother Clarence amassed 21,408 marbles and confessed to "our unique method" of acquiring them, one that led to a number of scraps. They would put chewing gum on the soles of their shoes, and marbles just followed them home.[19] Huggins was a serious youngster, and he also was crafty, creative, and competitive.

In 1901 Julius Fleischmann helped Huggins land a spot on the Western League's St. Paul Saints, a team at the highest level of the Minor Leagues. When Saints owner George Lennon first met Huggins, he was said to exclaim, "Why damn you, I have a boy at home bigger than you!"[20] A year later the Saints were part of the inaugural season of the American Association, and in 1903 they won the pennant. Huggins hit better than .300 in both 1902 and 1903. He also grew close to player-manager Mike Kelley, with whom he would develop a lifelong friendship.

Huggins was offered a contract with his hometown Reds in the fall of 1902. Yet he turned the offer down. Huggins's brother Clarence, who was a decent sandlot player himself (the two had been teammates a few years earlier), was managing a semipro team in Cincinnati. Lennon agreed to hire Clarence as the Saints' treasurer if Miller would stay with the team for another season. Lennon also gave Miller the food and scorecard advertising concessions at the Saints' ballpark.[21] Additionally, Miller felt he still needed to work on improving his game.

While at St. Paul, Huggins undertook a change to his playing style, one that revealed a fierce determination to gain a winning edge. He had essentially no power at the plate.[22] Unlike boxing, where there are different weight classes, he noted, "In baseball they meet in different packages, the large and the small." He wanted to beat out more ground balls for infield hits. So the right-handed hitting Huggins undertook a systematic program over three winters to learn to hit left-handed, which would allow him to gain a couple of extra steps to first base. He had to train new muscles and untrain old ones.[23] "He was grievously handicapped by his lack of size," wrote John Sheridan in the *Sporting News*. "Huggins worked at this job night and day for three years. He did road work and gymnasium work in winter, threw the ball, chopped wood, drove spikes, used the knife and fork, ate, drank, walked, and talked left-handed. At the end of three years, he 'went up.'" Huggins also worked at maximizing the advantages he did have. His size presented pitchers with a small strike zone, made even smaller by his crouching in the batter's box. "He never looked at a ball that was a hair's breadth off the plate. He always took two strikes before hitting," wrote Sheridan.[24]

Huggins persuaded Saints owner Lennon to let him sell his services to a Major League team after the 1903 season. When the Cincinnati Reds agreed to pay $3,500 for the prospect, Lennon gave Huggins $1,000 of the purchase price. Lennon sent a telegram to Reds owner Garry Herrmann in which he said that Huggins was the best ballplayer in the country. Lennon then told reporters, "He is a finer man than he is a ballplayer."[25]

Huggins saved the money and a couple of years later used it to open a cigar store on Fountain Square and the city's largest roller-skating rink in Walnut Hills, both in his hometown. He later invested in other Cincinnati skating rinks and converted one into a dance hall during the dance hall craze of the 1910s.[26] One of Huggins's "hobbies" was to visit rinks in different cities during his baseball travels, something he continued to do even after he retired as a player. One of his dreams was to own a chain of such rinks.[27] He also invested in real estate and a company that built homes in Cincinnati.[28] Huggins was simply an "all business" kind of person, usually focusing on business ventures in the off-season—when he was not training for baseball.

Miller Huggins became the Reds' starting second baseman and lead-off hitter beginning with his big league debut in the second game of the 1904 season. That season—perhaps even his career—almost ended the day it began. Running to second base late in the game, Huggins was hit in the neck and knocked unconscious by the Chicago Cubs' second baseman, Johnny Evers, who made a wild leap for an errant throw he had no chance of catching. He came down on Huggins; one paper said that Huggins could have suffered a broken neck by the reckless play of the young infielder who was playing "unclean ball."[29] After the game, Huggins brushed off the incident and didn't blame Evers.

A player can succeed in the big leagues, Huggins said, if he has the confidence to play the same kind of ball that he played in the high Minors.[30] He captured the city of Cincinnati by storm, earning comparisons to his boyhood idol, Bid McPhee. "The Rabbit is a little firecracker," wrote the *Cincinnati Enquirer*. "He is all over the infield like a flea skating around on a greasy skillet."[31] Reds teammate Larry McLean later gave him the fitting nickname of "Little Everywhere." A quiet and soft-spoken man off the field, Huggins was chirpy and even confrontational on it. He goaded and mocked opponents for their weaknesses, which earned him comparisons to John McGraw—scrappy and always with something to say.

Huggins still had no power at the plate; he actually sacrificed what little he had when he hit left-handed. He modeled himself after the scientific-hitting Willie Keeler, yet he wished he were a better batsman and wistfully commented on the Reds' number-two hitter. "I'd give anything if I could hit the ball like Mike Donlin. . . . Donlin has the greatest swing at a ball of any player I have ever seen."[32]

Huggins continued to play the waiting game with great regularity. He led the National League in walks four times. He also stole twenty-seven or more bases in those four years. But his Reds struggled, finishing as high as fourth place only twice. The manager position was unsettled, too. Joe Kelley was player-manager in 1904 and 1905 and was followed by Ned Hanlon for the next two seasons.

Hanlon had won five National League pennants from 1894 to 1900, but he had losing records in his two seasons with Cincinnati. He had limited playing talent and trouble motivating some of his players, who bristled at his harsh style. There is no indication that Huggins was among the rebellious players, and Hanlon admired his approach to the game. For men like Huggins, said Hanlon, "The game is everything to them. Victories make them feel as though they owned the earth; defeat makes them angry." Yet there was something else that set Huggins apart from most players: a cerebral approach to the game. Hanlon acknowledged his young infielder's baseball IQ. "That boy Huggins is in the game up to his ears from the time the first ball is pitched until the last man is out."[33]

He smoked his silver-studded pipe from his first days with the Reds, which only underlined that he was a different kind of baseball man.[34] He also liked an occasional cigar. A St. Louis newspaper later wrote that his hobby was "to sit and smoke and think."[35]

After the 1908 season, Huggins traveled to Cuba with his Reds' team for games against the Almendares and Havana clubs.[36] In one game Huggins broke up a no-hitter with two outs in the ninth inning against emerging star pitcher José Méndez. The exhibition series had far-reaching effects. First, with twenty-five shutout innings against Cincinnati, Méndez emerged as a national hero who would become a legend in his homeland. Beating an American team during the Second Occupation of Cuba enhanced his iconic status. "The conqueror's mantle of superiority in economic and military power could not be denied," wrote Robert Echevarria in his history of Cuban baseball, "but it was removed in the mock battlefield of sports."[37]

Second, this was the first of many exhibition games that Major League teams would play on the island in coming years. The growing popularity of baseball outside the United States led Huggins to predict in 1909 that the world championship would someday be played between the United States, Mexico, and Japan.[38] Third, two of Méndez's Almendares teammates would join the Reds in 1911, and one, Armando Marsans, would play for Huggins's Yankees in 1918.

The Cuba excursion had another consequence. On the trip south, the Reds stopped in St. Petersburg, Florida, and played against a semipro team. Huggins took a liking to the city and would eventually call it home—for himself in the off-season and his Yankees during spring training.

Clark Griffith, the former manager of the New York Americans, took over as skipper of the Reds for 1909. Early that season he benched Huggins for rookie Dick Egan. Griffith was complimentary of Huggins but felt that Egan was better.[39] Huggins appeared in only fifty-seven games that year, often as a pinch-hitter, and hit only .214. Less than a year later, in February 1910, Griffith traded Huggins to the St. Louis Cardinals in a five-player deal. Observers in his new city cheered the trade as a "steal," and the headline in one St. Louis paper declared, "Fans Are Wild with Glee."[40] Griffith may have considered Huggins a rival, someone who might replace him as the Reds' manager. Huggins had been rumored to be taking over the club as early as 1908. In making the trade, Griffith made a strange comment. "No matter who I get for Miller Huggins, I'd be cheated. . . . Hug is one of the best players of the game."[41] Yet still he made the deal in order to acquire the man he called the league's best pitcher, Fred Beebe.

As with Dick Egan, Griffith's evaluation skills proved faulty. Beebe went on to win only twenty more games in the Majors. Years later Reds owner Garry Herrmann said his one big mistake was trading Huggins instead of making him the team's manager.[42]

For the little second baseman, the trade sparked a resurgence in his playing career. He stayed healthy and led the league with 688 plate appearances in 1910, a career high. His batting average rose more than 50 points to .265, and he led the league in walks (116). Years later, as a manager, Huggins explained his philosophy on why trades often help players by looking back at his own. "It is the freshening of the player's mind, the possibility of a new field to conquer, that accounts for his spurt."[43]

After the Reds finished in fifth place in 1910 and were floundering again in 1911, *Sporting Life* wrote that Huggins had been railroaded out of Cincinnati and would have become the team's manager, had he still been there.[44] A *Sporting News* headline during that season shouted that the trade might result in the firing of Griffith.[45] At the end of 1911, Griffith was fired.

Huggins was approaching the age of thirty-two when he was traded, though his "baseball age" was only twenty-nine. His life still revolved around baseball, followed by his business interests. He had simple tastes, enjoyed reading and playing billiards and pinochle, and he did not seem to have an active social life. He never married, though he dated the future wife of Reds pitcher Bob Ewing around 1898.[46]

When Huggins joined the Cardinals, their manager was Roger Bresnahan, the fiery former star catcher of John McGraw's New York Giants. A year later, Helene Britton inherited ownership of the club. Lady Bee, as the press called her, was an accidental owner who came into the team when her uncle, Stanley Robison, had died early in 1911 with no children of his own.[47]

The Cardinals had their most profitable year in 1911, driven by a spirited run toward the top of the standings. Yet it was a season marred by the team's near-brush with death. In the early hours of July 11, their *Federal Express* train was involved in a horrific wreck near Bridgeport, Connecticut, one of the worst in U.S. history.[48] Fourteen people died, and dozens were seriously hurt. The Cardinals were the first responders to the rescue efforts, and Huggins used his small size to crawl into a tight space and rescue a victim. The team's members were not injured, saved by a fortuitous switch of their car to the back of the train shortly before the accident. Had that move not been made, July 11, 1911, would be etched in major league baseball history as the day of its worst tragedy ever.[49]

The Cardinals finished fifth in 1911, and Huggins finished sixth in the voting for the league's initial Chalmers Award.[50] They performed poorly the following season, accompanied by a dramatic drop in attendance. During that 1912 season, Bresnahan may have sensed that his second baseman was becoming a threat to his position. He tried to trade Huggins, but Lady Bee vetoed the deal.[51]

When the 1912 season came to a close, after repeated clashes with her brusque and overbearing manager, Britton fired Bresnahan. She replaced him with Huggins, who became the team's player-manager. His shortcomings had been offset by his intensity and intelligence. John Sheridan would later write in the *Sporting News*, "Smart little chap. Started in baseball with nothing but a clever head. No arm. No legs. No hands. No strong back. Nothing at all but ambition and pluck and brains."[52]

4

No Smarter Man in Baseball

Miller Huggins became the Cardinals' manager under trying circumstances. Roger Bresnahan's departure had created both a void at catcher and a fissure on the club, split between pro-Bresnahan and pro-Huggins factions. It fell to Huggins to negotiate contracts with his players, many of whom were holding out for higher salaries. He inherited a team of limited talent that had won barely 40 percent of its games in 1912.

Star first baseman Ed Konetchy led the Bresnahan clique. Less than three years earlier, "Koney" had called Huggins the smartest player in the history of the game.[1] Now he was saying that Huggins was no manager and never would be one.[2]

The 1913 Cardinals played at a .500 pace for a few weeks and then fell off badly, finishing in last place.[3] Even Huggins's size was held against him. Sid Keener, the young sports editor of the *St. Louis Times*, wrote what many fans believed: "Huggins cannot manage players. Nature is against him. The big huskies have refused to listen to his commands. And why? It's the baseball team. A little fellow can't manage the big fellows."[4]

During the course of the season, a number of Huggins's players had begun ignoring him and even talking back to him. Some claimed he nagged and overmanaged. St. Louis reporter Marion Parker noted that Huggins was "too nervous and high strung" to handle his men.[5] The *Sporting News* said that if Huggins continued as manager he would have to get rid of many of his best players, who had turned against him.[6] Huggins's friends reported that summer that he was "daft with worry" and on the verge of a nervous breakdown. He would soon resign, they predicted.[7]

Despite his managerial problems, Huggins's 1913 season was one of his best as a player. He hit .285 with a league-leading .432 on-base percentage.

Meanwhile, Helene Britton selected her husband, Schuyler, as the club's president, and they backed their manager as firmly as owner Jacob Ruppert of the Yankees would years later. "Why, I have not even considered changing leaders," Schuyler Britton told the *Post-Dispatch* in August.[8]

Huggins did not resign, although a month into the 1914 season he may have wished he had. The Federal League, a rival with Major League aspirations, began competing with Organized Baseball that year and placed a team in St. Louis. The city now had three teams, and the upstart league lured away two of Huggins's starting outfielders.[9] The Cardinals started poorly with a 10-15 record in mid-May. The clamor for Huggins's head intensified, yet Schuyler Britton did not waver. He would "go the route" with his manager, he declared.[10]

Following the 1913 season, Huggins, with the Brittons' approval, sent his unhappy star first baseman, Konetchy, to Pittsburgh in what became known as the "five-for-three" trade.[11] Most observers felt the Pirates got the better deal, a view that seemed warranted when they won fifteen of their first seventeen games in 1914, while the Cardinals started so slowly.[12]

Suddenly both teams' fortunes changed. While the Pirates tumbled to seventh place by the season's end, the Cardinals began winning. The trade was a big reason for both those reversals of fortune.[13] The improvement in team morale, Huggins wrote a decade later, was both dramatic and immediate.[14]

The Cardinals had lost their biggest star, but Huggins was not perturbed. In a prescient statement that would ring true during difficult times with the Yankees in the early 1920s, he said, "A team of stars will never succeed if all the players do not harmonize. Give me a bunch of youngsters who are hustling and trying to win all the time, and sore when they don't, in preference to those players who are looking out for themselves, and I'll fare better." Jack "Dots" Miller, an underrated, versatile player who also set the tone in the clubhouse, exemplified that team's spirit. "I wouldn't trade Jack Miller for any player in baseball today," said Huggins that summer.[15]

Huggins now had a team built around speed and pitching. The club stole almost 20 percent more bases than it had in 1913, and thirty-six-year-old Huggins stole thirty-two. The Cardinals' 2.38 earned run average was the league's best. Veteran pitcher Slim Sallee (2.10) worked with two youngsters, Bill Doak (1.72, lowest in the league) and Pol Perritt (2.36), to anchor the staff.[16]

On Wednesday, August 26, 1914, the Cardinals hosted the New York Giants for a doubleheader before 27,500 fans at Robison Field.[17] They were just one game out of first place behind the Giants and the onrushing Boston Braves. When St. Louis won the first game, 1–0, and the Braves lost by the same score, the three teams were tied for the lead.[18] But after Giants manager John McGraw read the "riot act" to his men, Christy Mathewson shut out the Cardinals on two hits in the second game.

St. Louis then faded from contention, as did New York. The Braves kept winning, going 34-9 after that day, to win the pennant by 10½ games. The Cardinals' solid third-place finish, just behind the Giants, surprised almost every preseason prognosticator and brought acclaim to their second-year manager.[19] One reporter who had predicted Huggins's firing in May now called him "probably the best manager in the old league. . . . He has made a team out of practically nothing."[20]

No less a critic than McGraw commented on what Huggins had accomplished in 1914. "He is a wonderful developer of a young pitcher. If I were a youngster breaking into the game, and especially a pitcher, I would ask nothing better than to have Huggins for my manager."[21]

With a limited budget, exacerbated by the competition from the Federal League, Huggins had no choice but to develop his own talent. It was a skill he would use in New York, for very different reasons, after the Yankees' collapse of 1925. He took enormous pride in the development of Doak and Perritt. Huggins said of Perritt, "He considered himself the greatest pitcher in the league. And I agreed with him."[22]

Late in the season, Huggins was spiked. The infected wound led to blood poisoning and caused him to miss some games. It would not be the last time he faced such an infection, which was a serious health concern before the advent of antibiotics. That winter Huggins developed pneumonia, which his doctor attributed to the season's stress.[23] Injuries and illness seemed to bedevil him, and illness would continue to do so after his playing career.

The Federal League may not have been a financial success in its first season, but it continued to raid the Cardinals in 1915. They lost yet another starting outfielder from their 1913 team, Lee Magee.[24] Most painful for Huggins was the loss of his protégé, Perritt, whose jump to the "Feds" shocked Huggins. McGraw then lured the pitcher back to the National League, to his Giants. It was "legal tampering," since Perritt would otherwise have been lost to Organized Baseball.[25] Once again, the neon lights of New York, higher salaries, and the "seductive voice" of McGraw had drawn a ballplayer to the Giants.[26]

Some observers felt that Huggins could have retained most, if not all, of the players he lost to the Federal League, had the Brittons shown some flexibility and willingness to increase salaries.[27] A decade later, Huggins said that his greatest challenge as Cardinals manager was getting the team's female owner to understand the issues and nuances of baseball.[28]

McGraw still had to compensate St. Louis for the loss of Perritt, but Huggins had little leverage. He settled for another speedy base runner, Bob Bescher.[29] Huggins believed he would have won the 1915 pennant, had he not lost so much talent to the Federal League, and he became an ardent foe of that upstart group. But that did not stop him from using the Federal League war to sign his own long-term contract with the Cardinals at a sizable salary increase.[30] When the rival league was negotiating with Organized Baseball at the end of 1915, Huggins persuaded Helene Britton not to sell out to the owner of the Terriers, Phil Ball, and urged her to let the rival league die under its own weight.[31]

The year 1915 would be Huggins's last season as a regular player. Late in 1914, he had told scout Bob Connery that the Cardinals could not afford prospects from the high Minors. "How about looking over some of the smaller leagues?" Huggins suggested. "You might find a kid who might help us."[32] In the spring of 1915, Connery found one. While managing the Cardinals' "B" squad playing in small Texas towns, Connery took a liking to a kid in Denison named Rogers Hornsby. Connery signed the nineteen-year-old that summer for $600. Connery, who played briefly in the Minor Leagues, had excelled at sandlot ball in St. Louis when Huggins was doing the same in Cincinnati. He then managed Hartford of the Connecticut State League for five seasons before joining the Cardinals as head scout when Huggins became manager.[33] For the rest of his life, Huggins would count Connery as one of his closest friends, along with Mike Kelley, his former St. Paul manager.[34]

The Cardinals almost missed signing Hornsby. When the Brittons hesitated over the outlay of $600, Huggins offered to loan the club the money, so confident was he in his scout's evaluation. Huggins said he would quit and take Hornsby with him if the Brittons were not satisfied with the Texan at the end of the year.[35] The Brittons eventually did sign Hornsby, who hit .313 in his first full season, 1916. Huggins then had to fight off cash offers for the emerging star, which the Brittons wanted to consider.[36] Huggins liked him from the start. "Hornsby is going to be one of the real stars of the game. . . . I've looked over the entire field this spring, and I haven't seen one who comes close to the Texas youngster."[37] Hornsby also had enormous confidence from the start, a cockiness that Huggins loved.

During Organized Baseball's battle with the Federal League, when all three St. Louis clubs were losing money, Huggins paid some salaries and expenses out of his own pocket.[38] When he left St. Louis for the Yankees, the *Sporting News* wrote in an editorial, "He was all there was to the club practically, under petticoat management even to the extent of being its financial savior."[39]

On August 7, 1915, Huggins pulled off a trick on an unsuspecting opposing player, a story that has been immortalized in books of baseball anecdotes and lore. In a tie game against Brooklyn, St. Louis had the bases loaded and Huggins was coaching at third base. Brooklyn rookie reliever Ed Appleton was on the mound when Huggins shouted to him that the ball had a rip on the cover and asked to look at the ball. When Appleton tossed it his way, Huggins moved aside, the ball rolled to the grandstand, and the Cardinals scored what proved to be the winning run.[40]

Baseball historian Bill Deane has tracked incidents of the hidden ball trick, when an infielder pretends to throw the ball back to the pitcher and instead holds onto it and then tags an unsuspecting base runner when he steps off the bag. In his work-in-progress, Deane has identified eight instances of Huggins executing this play, the most of any player in National League history.[41] No surprise that when Huggins was named manager of the Cardinals. Harold Lanigan of the *Sporting News* wrote, "He is a deep little cuss, a thorough student of the national game, and knows as many tricks as the next."[42]

The Cardinals struggled in both 1915 and 1916, even though the Federal League ceased operation after 1915. When players of that league became available to sign with American and National League teams, the Brittons refused to purchase any of them, including their former outfielders, Steve Evans, Rebel Oakes, and Lee Magee.[43]

In 1916, John McGraw picked off another top Cardinals' pitcher, Slim Sallee, and he did it without the help of the Federal League. Now in his ninth season with St. Louis, Sallee suddenly announced that he was "through with baseball" and quit the team.[44] It was not the first time he had taken leave of the team; his bouts of drinking had earned him suspensions going back to Bresnahan's days as manager. Yet this time was different: Sallee said he was upset with his food and accommodations on the road. Huggins was concerned that Sallee had caught "New York Fever" from John McGraw. He felt uneasy because whenever his Cardinals played New York, his players seemed to be "auditioning" for McGraw.[45] After both Huggins and Schuyler Britton had said they would never trade or sell Sallee, the Brittons did just that—selling him to McGraw's Giants for $10,000 on July 23. For the tenth time since 1903, the Cardinals would lose ninety or more games. The following season, the Giants would win the pennant, with Perritt and Sallee winning thirty-five games between them.

By competing against Huggins over the years, McGraw had come to recognize his potential as a manager. "Miller Huggins is my ideal of a real leader, and some day, if they will leave him alone long enough, he will win a championship for them out there," McGraw had said a year earlier. "There is no smarter man in baseball today than Miller Huggins."[46] The admiration was mutual: Huggins often spoke highly of McGraw, asked him for advice, and called him the "ideal manager."[47]

Huggins began his fifth season as manager of the Cardinals just days after the United States entered the Great War. The war would have little impact on the 1917 baseball season, as the country mobilized slowly. Huggins again rebuilt his team, and the Cardinals pulled off another surprising third-place finish. It was a startling accomplishment, considering the limited talent and budget he had to work with. Huggins credited teamwork—along with some good pitchers—with which, he said, he would beat "a so-called star aggregation any time."[48]

One can only imagine how much higher the Cardinals would have finished in 1917 had Perritt and Sallee been pitching and had Evans, Oakes, and Magee been patrolling the outfield for them. A St. Louis sportswriter recognized what the team's manager had accomplished. "Huggins' record with the Cardinals, considering his material, was nothing less than brilliant. . . . From the collar upward, little Miller Huggins was one of the biggest men in the game."[49]

Through it all, Huggins revealed different personalities on and off the field. "When battling for victory, he is sharp, aggressive, belligerent, fiery and perhaps a trifle overbearing," wrote a Philadelphia sportswriter. "Off the field he is a mild-mannered, quiet-spoken gentleman."[50] Huggins may have overcompensated with an outsized feistiness, yet a few years into his managerial career, he recognized that he had to be a diplomat as well as a fighter. Leading would not come easy to him.

Huggins's aggressive nature during games was reflected in his aversion to umpires, which he attributed to an early run-in he had with umpire Hank O'Day. "In spite of the fact that he is a great umpire, I always felt that he was a stone wall in my way." Huggins recalled that after he lost his temper with O'Day, the umpire replied, "Young feller, if you want me to pay any attention to you, you had better come in out of that tall grass so that I can see you."[51]

After the Cardinals' last-place finish in 1916, Helene Britton finally decided to sell the team. With a world war on the horizon, Organized Baseball facing an antitrust lawsuit, her marriage crumbling, and the team drawing an average of only around 3,000 fans per game, she had good reasons to do so. She promised her manager the first chance to buy the club.

This was not the first time Huggins had considered owning a ball club. As early as 1909 he tried to buy into the Birmingham Barons of the Southern League. Late in 1914 he negotiated to buy the Buffalo Bisons of the International League and, when that deal fell through, the St. Paul Saints.[52] Years later, in 1928, Huggins would tell sportswriter Dan Daniel that he had not fulfilled his "fondest ambition," owning a baseball club.[53]

After the 1916 season, when Huggins lined up his financing with the Fleischmann brothers to purchase the Cardinals, Britton instead accepted an offer from a local group with thousands of citizen-owners.[54] They came up with the novel idea that each share of stock in the club would provide a pass for a youngster to attend weekday games at no charge.[55] When the team hired Branch Rickey, an underutilized executive with the St. Louis Browns, as president, Miller Huggins knew it was time to move on.[56]

Huggins and Rickey had been teammates briefly in 1904 and had a publicized "debate" over training methods back in 1913, when Rickey was managing the cross-town St. Louis Browns.[57] Rickey had been discussing his training ideas, including batting cages and sliding pits, with reporters. "I believe manager Rickey has a lot of good ideas, but I'm not strong for this theory stuff," Huggins commented at the time.[58]

Despite his disappointment, Huggins approached the 1917 season, the final one of his three-year contract, the only way he knew: determined to do his best to lead and win. That spring he told Sid Keener, "I'm going to hustle and I'm going to show them who's the big man on this ball club."[59] Bob Connery, who would move on to New York with Huggins, looked back on their St. Louis years, as challenging as they were, with nostalgia. "They were really five happy eventful years; we had our worries, yes, but funny things were happening to the club and in the front office all the time. We were younger then, could take it, and the laughs eased a lot of tough situations. Hug could stand his grief better then than in his later years in New York. We were together in both places, and those five years with the Cardinals were happier than any five years in New York, even when Huggins was winning pennants."[60]

Part 2

RUPPERT BUYS THE YANKEES

5

How about the Yankees?

Owners of Major League baseball teams have two main responsibilities. They must (or at least should) attempt to make their team better than the teams of the other owners. But they are also partners, in effect, with all those other owners and must work in tandem with them. Throughout its history, baseball has had its share of "difficult" owners, those who violated one or both of those responsibilities. For many historians, the title of "most loathsome team owner in baseball history" belongs to Andrew Freedman.[1] Freedman biographer William Lamb called him "chronically impatient with his team's standings" and labeled the eight years of his ownership (1895–1902) "the darkest in New York Giants history." Lamb wrote, "Freedman inflicted 13 managerial changes on the Giants during his tenure as club owner. Worse yet, Freedman's peevish battles—with players, umpires, fellow owners, league officials, the sporting press—and his ferocious vindictive streak drained vitality from the National League's flagship enterprise and hurt the game itself in the process."[2]

In 1899 the Giants finished tenth in the twelve-team league, much to Freedman's delight. "Base ball affairs in New York have been going just as I wished and expected them to go," he said. "I have given the club little attention and I would not give five cents for the best base ball player in the world to strengthen it."[3] The other owners, aware that a forlorn team and an antagonistic owner in New York were harmful to their joint interests, began looking for someone to buy the Giants. One day in 1900, Harry Von der Horst, owner of the Baltimore Orioles, and Frank De Haas Robison, co-owner with his brother Stanley of the St. Louis Cardinals, ran into Congressman Jacob Ruppert on a train leaving Washington.

"Colonel Ruppert, you are just the man I am looking for," said Von der Horst, a fellow brewer. "How would you like to get into baseball?"[4]

When Ruppert signaled his willingness, Von der Horst suggested that he make an offer to buy the Giants from Freedman. "If you do," Robison chimed in, "we will see that you get four players as a gift. We will give you John J. McGraw, Wilbert Robinson, and two others."[5] McGraw and Robinson were members of Robison's St. Louis club, but had made no secret of their desire to move back east. The two budding entrepreneurs wanted to be near their jointly owned Diamond Cafe in Baltimore, a billiards parlor that included a bar, dining room, and bowling alley.

Ruppert, who knew Freedman from their service together under Richard "Boss" Croker on Tammany's Finance Committee, asked him if he had any interest in selling the Giants. "Well, I don't know whether I do or not," Freedman responded, "but if I decide to sell I will let you know."[6] He had promised Ruppert the first call, but did not fulfill that promise. Moreover, after he sold the club to John T. Brush in 1902, he never even bothered to call his old Tammany associate. Ruppert had offered $150,000 for the Giants. So when he learned that Brush had bought the club for that exact amount, it soured him on baseball for many years.[7]

A Giants fan since boyhood, Ruppert never forgot his failure to purchase what once had been his favorite club. In August 1938, five months before his death, he was asked how he became involved in baseball. "I have always enjoyed watching baseball and had been interested in purchasing a baseball team since the turn of the century but with truly no success," he said. "I had wanted to buy the Giants for more than a decade, but I was never successful."[8]

Ruppert did have another chance at ownership in 1913. Charles Murphy was selling his controlling interest in the Chicago Cubs, but Ruppert had no desire to be associated with a non–New York team. After briefly considering it, he declined, saying he was not interested "in anything so far from Broadway."[9]

In that 1938 interview, Ruppert claimed he again became interested in buying the Giants in 1912, after Brush died. "The Giants had an unmatched clientele that on almost any afternoon might include the cream of New York's sporting and social life. So you can understand why I would be interested in buying such a team."[10] However, Brush's son-in-law, Harry Hempstead, had taken control of the club, and Ruppert was informed there was no chance for him to acquire the Giants.

The Giants may have been unattainable, but ownership of a Major League team was not. Ruppert's story, as it appeared in a 1938 reminiscence in the *New York World-Telegram*, was that one day a man suggested to him that he purchase the Yankees. That man was likely New York Giants manager John McGraw, who knew that Yankees owners Bill Devery and Frank Farrell were having serious financial problems and were anxious to sell the team.

"I discussed the idea with Billy Fleischmann, an intimate friend, who was very much interested in baseball," Ruppert remembered. Fleischmann thought it was a worthwhile investment, but suggested he not undertake it alone. "I have a partner in mind," said Fleischmann. A week later he introduced Ruppert to Til Huston at a dinner in the Claridge Hotel. "We agreed to become fifty-fifty partners in the purchase of the Yankees," Ruppert said.[11] Frank Graham, in his history of the Yankees, told a slightly different story. He wrote that when McGraw learned that Ruppert and Huston were both interested in buying a team, he arranged for the two men to meet. McGraw then posed the question that would forever change Ruppert's life (and McGraw's too). "How about the Yankees?" he asked.[12]

The forty-seven-year-old Ruppert, a prototypical New Yorker, and the forty-five-year-old Cincinnati-born Huston were as mismatched in appearance as they would prove to be in temperament. Huston's suits and derby hats always looked crumpled, as opposed to Ruppert, whom author Robert Creamer described as "urbane, sophisticated, [and] impeccably dressed."[13]

Ruppert "was not one to pal around with the boys," Rud Rennie wrote in the *New York Herald-Tribune*. "For the most part, he was aloof and brusque.... He never used profanity. 'By gad' was his only expletive."[14] Creamer called him "the quintessential owner, a quiet, mannered rich man with an aristocratic reserve."[15] Huston, whom sportswriters generally called "Cap" because of his wartime service, was a "man's man"— informal, familiar, rumpled, self-made.[16] Yankees historian Marty Appel contrasted the two men in a way that made their dissimilarity easily understood. "While Ruppert looked like the sort of fellow who expected to be handed a towel each time he washed his hands, Huston looked more like a fellow who would give a quick glance toward the sink and decide he could skip it."[17]

Til Huston, an engineer, had remained in Cuba after the Spanish-American War, where he secured lucrative contracts improving the sanitation, harbors, and rivers throughout the country. Huston had struck up a friendship with John McGraw back in 1911, when the Giants were touring Cuba. McGraw occasionally visited Huston when he vacationed in Havana in the off-season, while Huston occasionally visited McGraw's Giants at their spring training home in Marlin, Texas. Huston was also McGraw's guest at several World Series games between the Giants and Athletics in 1911, and then joined the New Yorkers when they played a series of exhibition games in Cuba later that fall.[18]

Before teaming up with Ruppert, Huston had come close to partnering with McGraw in purchasing the Chicago Cubs. While considering offers for the Cubs in 1914, Charles Taft, then their majority owner, granted an option to Huston and McGraw.[19] The plan was for McGraw to get his release from the Giants and manage the Cubs, as well as become the club's co-owner. When he failed to get free of his New York contract, he and Huston let the option lapse. At the time of the negotiations, Taft did not release the names of the prospective buyers, and there was much speculation about who they were. Only after Huston and Ruppert bought the Yankees did New York sportswriter Joe Vila reveal their identities.[20]

McGraw suggested that Ruppert and Huston, both Giants season ticketholders, speak to American League president Ban Johnson about buying the New York club. That McGraw would do something to help Johnson, his bitter enemy, yet his "curious ally" here, is an indication of how secure he was in presuming his Giants would always be New York's most popular team. And while McGraw had fought the American League in its early days, he had come to accept it as part of Organized Baseball. Because he did not have that same attitude toward the Federal League, he thought it crucial to bring Ruppert and Huston's financial resources into the American League.[21]

"It had never really occurred to me to acquire the Yankees, because they were such a, well, mediocre team at the time," Ruppert remembered. "Like all Giants fans, and like most businessmen, Col. Huston and myself weren't too interested. To us, the Giants were still the only team in town. . . . But McGraw convinced us . . . and we eventually decided to purchase the team for a sum of $450,000. Many said that we were buying a 'pig in a poke' and that it was unwise to make such an investment with the Great War bearing down upon our country." Ruppert acknowledged that he was buying a bad team but that he and Huston believed that if they could get the right manager and some good ball players, they could build the Yankees into a winning club. They recognized the difficulty of drawing fans away from the Giants, yet hoped to "offer New York an answer to the otherwise unanswerable Giants."[22]

Years later, Ruppert reflected on his and Huston's purchase of the Yankees. "For $450,000 we got an orphan ball club, without a home of its own, without players of outstanding ability, without prestige."[23] When the sale was finally completed, Ruppert's assessment of his new team was indeed accurate.

The Yankees had come into existence in 1903, although Ban Johnson had wanted to put a team in New York since declaring his American League a Major League two years earlier. He failed because Giants owner Freedman, opposed to having competition in New York, used his Tammany Hall connection to Croker to prevent Johnson from finding a suitable site to build a ballpark.[24] Meanwhile, the new league had conducted a successful two-year raid on the established National League for players. The raids ended on January 10, 1903, when the two leagues reached a peace agreement at Cincinnati's St. Nicholas Hotel. As part of the agreement, Johnson finally gained entry into New York by getting the National League to allow him to relocate the disbanded Baltimore franchise there. *New York Evening Sun* sports editor Joe Vila, an enthusiastic supporter of the American League, helped Johnson find an owner for the new club. Vila introduced Johnson to Frank Farrell, owner of a racing stable and a major figure in the New York gambling scene. Farrell, in turn, chose William "Big Bill" Devery, a retired New York City police chief, to be his partner. Devery was a former bartender with his own connection to Tammany's Croker. He used that connection to get himself appointed to the police force. Eventually Mayor Robert A. Van Wyck named Devery chief of police, where his record for honesty was dubious and his attempt to root out corruption was nonexistent. His personal motto was "Hear, see, and say nothin'; eat, drink, and pay nothin'," wrote Luc Sante in his social history of old New York.[25]

Perhaps to appease Johnson, who would have preferred a less unsavory pair, Joseph Gordon, a respectable businessman and former state assemblyman, was chosen to be the club's president, with Farrell serving as treasurer. Farrell and Devery purchased the club for $18,000, and the Greater New York Club of the American League (the press dubbed them the Highlanders) was incorporated on March 18, 1903.[26] The owners used their relationship with Tammany's "Big Tim" Sullivan to lease land in upper Manhattan from the New York Institute for the Blind. Hilltop Park, a wooden structure that seated 16,000, was built in Washington Heights, west of Broadway between West 165th and 168th Streets. The site was accessible by trolley car and later by an IRT subway stop at 168th Street and Broadway that began service on March 16, 1906.

By convincing Chicago White Sox owner Charles Comiskey that a thriving franchise in New York was vital to the financial success of the league, Johnson succeeded in getting Comiskey to allow his manager and star pitcher, Clark Griffith, to move to New York. Griffith's team would include five holdovers from the 1902 Baltimore Orioles and three National League stars: pitchers Jack Chesbro and Jesse Tannehill from the pennant-winning Pittsburgh Pirates, and outfielder Willie Keeler from the Brooklyn Superbas.[27]

After finishing fourth that first year, the New Yorkers stayed in the 1904 pennant race until the final day of the season.[28] Led by Chesbro's forty-one wins and Keeler's .343 batting average, Griffith's team entered needing to win both games of a doubleheader against defending champion Boston to win the pennant. The teams were tied at 2–2 in the ninth inning of Game One when a Chesbro wild pitch allowed Boston to score the run that won the game and the pennant.

The Yankees finished second again in 1906 and 1910, but were mostly also-rans, with eight second-division finishes in their first twelve years of existence. In June 1908, with the team in sixth place, Griffith was fired. Under his replacement, shortstop Kid Elberfeld, the Yankees won only twenty-seven of their remaining ninety-eight games and finished last with a record of 51-103.[29]

George Stallings replaced Elberfeld in 1909, and the team finished fifth and drew a record 501,000 fans to Hilltop Park. But Stallings grew tired of front-office meddling (as had Griffith) and quit, or was forced to quit, late in the 1910 season. He had also grown tired of Hal Chase, his star first baseman, whom he suspected of throwing games. To replace Stallings, an undaunted Farrell chose Chase, who had been a demoralizing force in 1908 when he was bypassed in favor of Elberfeld.

Harry Wolverton succeeded Chase in 1912, but after the club's 102-loss performance, he was gone after the one season. Ban Johnson, worried that a noncontending team in New York was causing financial problems for his league, brokered a deal that brought in Frank Chance, "The Peerless Leader," to manage the Yankees. As a player-manager, Chance had won four National League pennants and two world championships with the Chicago Cubs, but the Cubs had released him late in 1912. On January 8, 1913, the Yankees signed him to a lucrative three-year contract.

Despite the high hopes engendered by Chance's arrival, the 1913 Yankees finished in seventh place. One positive development was the jettisoning of Hal Chase, "addition by subtraction," as Branch Rickey would later call such a move. Early in the season, Chance, like Stallings before him, began to suspect Chase was "throwing" games and traded him to the Chicago White Sox.[30]

Chance had been brought to New York to lift the club from the second division, but he said he was unable to do so because he was furnished with third-rate material and told to build a first-class team.[31] "I know there are boneheads in baseball," he said, "but I didn't believe so many could get on one club. Mine."[32]

The team moved up one place in the standings in 1914, but Chance, unhappy with the way ownership was running the team, resigned with twenty games left on the schedule. Twenty-three-year-old shortstop Roger Peckinpaugh finished out the season as manager. Peckinpaugh remains the youngest man ever to lead a Major League team. Such was the status of the ball club Ruppert and Huston were attempting to buy.

6

The Rocky Road to Ownership

After Jacob Ruppert and Til Huston agreed to pursue the purchase of the Yankees, they met with Ban Johnson and other American League owners. "I told them," Ruppert said, "that it seemed to Capt. Huston and myself that there wasn't much of a club to purchase, merely a few individual players of merit and a rather disorganized team." Nevertheless, Ruppert said that he and Huston would be interested in buying the team, provided the other owners helped in the construction of a winning club. "I emphasized the fact that we asked no charity, that we were able and willing to pay a liberal cash price." He also stressed that a winning club in New York meant greater crowds not only in New York but in all the other cities in the league.

Ruppert reminded them how much a strong Giants team benefited all the National League owners and seemed baffled that they could not see how a strong Yankees team would do the same for them. "This is, in my mind, a failure to appreciate facts at their face value, which has cost the American League a lot of prestige it might have had, and has cost every club owner in the circuit the loss of valuable revenue."[1]

Sportswriter James R. Crowell agreed with Ruppert. "As it is now, and has been for years," he wrote, "New York is largely a one league city. The Nationals hold complete sway here and will continue to stand far ahead of the Americans as long as the Giants are able to keep among the pacemakers and the Yankees are unable to do better than they have done. Baseball fever runs high while the Giants are at home and sags to almost nothing when the Yankees are providing the entertainment."[2]

While the other American League owners professed their agreement, their actions never matched their words. Ruppert said that once he and Huston took control of the Yankees, other owners offered them "can't-miss" prospects at inflated prices. All were turned down, and all turned out to be much less than advertised. "The generous magnates were willing to palm off their shoddy goods on the new 'suckers,'" wrote Sid Mercer.[3] "In fact," said Ruppert, "the only concrete evidence that the American League would give us unqualified support finally simmered down to players Pipp and High, for both of which men we paid the full market price."[4] Twenty-two-year-old Wally Pipp had batted .314 for the Rochester Hustlers in 1914, while hitting an International League–leading fifteen home runs, but had only 12 games of Major League experience. Hugh High was already twenty-seven and had played in 171 games for the Tigers in 1913–14, with a combined .247 batting average.

The official transfer of the franchise from Devery and Farrell to Ruppert and Huston would have to survive many rumors, false starts, and intense negotiations before it was made final. The rumors started in early December 1914 when the *New York Herald* reported that Rudolph Hynicka was a partner with Ruppert and Huston and that he had already purchased Devery's stock in the Yankees.[5] Hynicka, a Cincinnatian with offices in New York, was a friend of Cincinnati Reds president Garry Herrmann. An amusement promoter and president of a company controlling a chain of theaters, Hynicka had been trying to buy a big-league team for the past several seasons. Ruppert was vacationing in French Lick, Indiana, and refused to comment on any aspect of the supposed deal with Hynicka.[6]

The *New York World* also cited a report affirming Hynicka's purchase of Devery's stock and another that claimed Connie Mack, manager of the Philadelphia Athletics, had bought out Devery's stock. The *World* added that the Athletics would trade Eddie Collins, their star second baseman, to the Yankees, where he would become the team's new manager. The same day this appeared in the *World*, Philadelphia sold Collins to the Chicago White Sox. Nevertheless, most of the talk focused on Ruppert and Huston as the sole buyers, but even that was denied by Huston. "There is no truth to the report that Colonel Ruppert and I have bought the New York club," he said. "I don't know how the story started that we had bought the club. We have not even made an offer to Mr. Farrell or Mr. Devery." However, Huston did confirm his and Ruppert's interest in the club. "A short while ago, a friend of Colonel Ruppert told him that the New York club could be bought at a reasonable price," he said. "The Colonel asked me about it. I told him that I had heard the same story. However, neither the Colonel nor I made any proposition to Mr. Farrell for the sale of the club."[7]

Ban Johnson, closely monitoring every aspect of the possible sale, said that Herrmann and Julius Fleischmann, also a part-owner of the Cincinnati Reds, had been lobbying on behalf of Ruppert getting the Yankees. But, he added, others also were interested, namely, William Smith and James McGill, owners of the American Association's Indianapolis club. Johnson did indicate that he thought Ruppert would be the eventual owner. "I have every reason to believe that Col. Ruppert would prove an excellent addition to the American League and to organized baseball. Mr. Farrell has set his price on the club. He is only awaiting a favorable reply before closing."[8] Farrell and Devery wanted $500,000 for the Yankees, reported the *Baltimore Sun*, while Ruppert was said to have offered $400,000 and agreed to build a stadium for the team.[9]

In addition to top-drawer players, it was apparent to Ruppert and Huston that to succeed in New York they needed a top-drawer manager. They would have liked their friend John McGraw to fill that role, but McGraw was already the toast of the town in New York and was not going to leave the lordly Giants for the lowly Yankees. One soon-discredited rumor that Philadelphia's Connie Mack had bought out Devery's share was replaced by another that had him leaving the A's to manage the Yankees.

Mack was said to be unhappy with the fan support his team had gotten in 1914, despite winning the pennant.[10] However, he quickly ended those rumors. "Say for me that I will not leave Philadelphia," said Mack, whose managerial reputation was equal to McGraw's.[11] "I am well satisfied here and am already making my preparations for the 1915 season."[12]

Yet the December rumors kept coming, with the New York newspapers seemingly printing them all, no matter how far-fetched. One had Hughie Jennings coming from Detroit to manage the Yankees, while another had the Yankees trading pitcher Ray Caldwell to the Giants for Christy Mathewson, who would then become the manager.

Through it all, the negotiations dragged on. Ruppert was again at the French Lick resort he often visited, but Johnson remained in contact with Huston and with Fleischmann, who was representing Ruppert. "Colonel

Ruppert has kept in close touch with the negotiations," Fleischmann said. "I have reason to believe the proposition is now viewed more favorably than at any time. But Mr. Ruppert is a shrewd business man and will wish to take a personal hand before closing a transaction of such magnitude. Therefore, there seems little likelihood of completing the final details of purchase until Mr. Ruppert returns."[13] Speaking from French Lick, Ruppert said, "I have made up my mind what I will do. I want the New Yorks and hope to purchase the club, but not until the American League agrees to sell or trade me five players and a manager. I shall not go out with a bad ball team and try to make a pennant winner out of it."[14]

While in French Lick, Ruppert was visited by Federal League president James Gilmore and Charlie Weeghman, who owned the league's Chicago team. Both men tried to persuade Ruppert to back a Federal League team in New York. "They wanted me to buy the Indianapolis team of their league and transfer it to New York. This was the club which [millionaire oilman and Federal League investor] Harry Sinclair took over and brought to Newark [in 1915]," he remembered. "While Weeghman and Gilmore were talking me into the Federal League, Ban Johnson got wind of the effort and dashed into the scene. I owe to Ban Johnson my escape from what would have been an expensive and unhappy experience."[15]

After the Colonel's death, sportswriter Sid Mercer told a tale that highlighted the different approaches to money taken by millionaires Ruppert and Sinclair. One winter night during the time the Federal League was threatening to invade New York, the American League was holding its annual meeting at the Wolcott Hotel on West 31st Street, just west of Fifth Avenue. A few blocks up Fifth Avenue, between West 33rd and West 34th Streets, Sinclair was holding forth in the bar at the Waldorf-Astoria Hotel. "If you think they've got more money to spend than we have," Sinclair boasted, "just tell Col. Ruppert that I'll stand up with him and pitch dollar for dollar into the ocean." When Ruppert heard what Sinclair had said, his reaction was indicative of the man. "That's ridiculous," he responded. "Why should I pitch dollars into the ocean? Won't do anybody any good. I've got better use for my dollars."[16]

At a special meeting of the American League owners, held in Chicago on December 20, 1914, Johnson announced that Ruppert and Huston had officially purchased the New York Yankees from Farrell and Devery.

Johnson was a bit premature in calling it "official." The stock had not yet been transferred, and some sources said that Farrell was still claiming the club was for sale to the first man or group willing to pay $500,000, a price Huston and Ruppert were not willing to pay. There were also whispers that Huston was having second thoughts about getting into baseball and that Ruppert might become the sole owner.[17]

The day before the American League owners met in Chicago, Ruppert and Huston arrived in Indianapolis. There they met with Harry Hempstead, the president of the New York Giants, to make sure the Yankees could continue to play as tenants in the Polo Grounds, as they had since 1913. A week earlier a story in the *Baltimore Evening Sun* had questioned whether the lease the Yankees had would continue after the team changed owners. It has been stated on "good authority," the paper claimed, that the Giants would not allow Ruppert and Huston, the Yankees' prospective new owners, to use the Polo Grounds beyond 1915 and that the Yankees were looking to build a new home in the Bronx. The *Sun* article pointed out that Ruppert owned a lot of real estate in the Bronx and that he would choose a site accessible by the new subway system being constructed in that borough.[18]

It was now just a few days before Christmas, and Ruppert and Huston had not yet completed the purchase; still the partners said they expected the deal would be made soon. They were convinced that Ban Johnson and the American League owners would do what was necessary to make it happen. "We think that the American League magnates will see the matter in the same light," Ruppert said, and "they will give us the players we need to put New York on the American League map. We are asking merely that we get options on the players we need and at prices that we can afford to pay before we take over the Farrell and Devery interests in New York." Both men again dismissed the possibility of acquiring a team in the Federal League and moving it to New York.[19]

While Ruppert had no interest in the Federal League, some of the players on the 1914 Yankees did. Not knowing which players might leave had an obvious influence on the sale price and further contributed to delaying the transfer of the franchise. Ruppert and Huston wanted to be assured that the team's top two players, shortstop Roger Peckinpaugh and third baseman Fritz Maisel, would return to the Yankees in 1915.

Joe Tinker, manager of the Federal League's Chicago Whales, had spoken to Peckinpaugh about making the jump, but found the twenty-four-year-old shortstop's initial demands "outrageous and preposterous."[20] Nevertheless, there was a strong sense that Peckinpaugh was leaning to the Feds. And because Tinker was still a viable shortstop, he was perhaps acting on behalf of the league and, if signed, Peckinpaugh would be moved to another team.

With the New Year only a week away, Farrell was still insisting the deal was not final, though Ban Johnson proceeded as if it were. "Everybody is satisfied," he said. "The league has agreed to aid Colonel Ruppert and Captain Huston bolster up the club, which I can safely say will be the strongest that has represented New York in the American League in many years. The team we propose to establish there should be a pennant contender from the start."[21]

On December 31, 1914, at the Wolcott Hotel in New York, the parties reached a tentative agreement.[22] Ban Johnson, Huston, and Farrell were present. Devery was not, nor was Ruppert, although he stayed in constant telephone contact with Huston. The transfer of the New York Yankees from Farrell and Devery to Ruppert and Huston was greeted with near unanimous acclaim from the baseball world. *Sporting Life* praised the new Yankees ownership editorially. They now have owners of "character, ability and wealth." They will make the Yankees "impregnable" and secure in the ongoing baseball war.[23] "There is now a possibility of raising the New York American club to local parity with the New York Giants," wrote the *Reach Official American League Guide*. "Messrs. Ruppert and Huston, who, in point of character, wealth, and popularity, measure up to the most exacting standards of the game."[24]

Loose ends, including the haphazard financial paperwork of the previous owners, resulted in the sale not being finalized until January 11, 1915.

Ruppert had been somewhat of a mystery man during the whole process. He had kept a low profile throughout, and many members of the press covering the sale would not have recognized him had they passed him on the street. Yet as one of the city's wealthiest "men-about-town," a former congressman, and an extremely successful brewer, his name was not unfamiliar to New Yorkers. The sporting public remembered him from his days as an owner of race horses. But aside from being a regular at Giants games, there was no indication as to what kind of baseball owner he would be.

The local papers rushed to print articles and interviews designed to introduce the Yankees' new co-owner to the team's fans. This one, featuring a set of Ruppert responses that appeared in the magazine section of the March 28, 1915, *New York World*, was typical: "Like most boys I played baseball on my high school team. It has been one of my favorite sports since then, but I doubt if it ever occurred to me to own a baseball club until recently. I have been a regular box-holder at the Polo Grounds for years and shall continue to be. My interest in other years always has been to the Giants, and I do not intend to abandon them, even if they're my rivals. The truth is I always saw several Giant games every week they were playing at home. I have seen comparatively few games in my own league."

Finally Ruppert let New York's sporting public know how important winning was to him. "To be quite honest, I have no expectation of winning a pennant this year, but I do expect to build up, as quickly as possible, a winner. We will get all the players that money can buy as we will work to the one end of winning." For long-suffering Yankees fans, those were exactly the words they had been waiting to hear since the birth of the franchise.

Ruppert then switched from talking as a fan to talking about the business aspect of owning the Yankees. "I want them to be primarily a sporting proposition, but that doesn't mean they will not be run as a business proposition. I think one can do both."[25]

7

The New Owners Get to Work

In January 1915 the United States was still maintaining a position of neutrality in the Great War in Europe that had begun six months earlier. Most Americans, including President Woodrow Wilson, preferred that the country remain uninvolved, though a majority probably sided with Great Britain and its allies. Yet in a nation where approximately one-third of the people were either foreign-born or the children of immigrants, more than ten million Americans had their origins in Germany or the nations of the Central Powers. Furthermore, millions of Americans of Irish descent sided with the Central Powers because of their hatred for the English.

The National German-American Alliance was an association of German groups—representing millions of people—whose mission was to promote and preserve German culture in America. Its lobbying efforts focused primarily on fighting the rising forces of Prohibition, not foreign policy, and it drew much of its financial support from German American brewers. But by early 1915, when the Alliance felt the American government was continuing to favor Great Britain, it acted. At their January 30 meeting in Washington, the Alliance demanded that America maintain a true munitions embargo.[1]

The *Brooklyn Eagle* took a position that was not unusual in the American press when it called this conference "a close resemblance to treason."[2] But New York's numerous German-language newspapers did not back down. In February a series of editorials appeared in several German papers berating President Wilson, Secretary of State William Jennings Bryan, and the Congress for what they considered their anti-German stance in the war. They called America's so-called neutrality a farce and criticized the administration's harsh communications with Germany, as opposed to what they called the gentle requests sent to England. An editorial in the German-language *New Yorker Herold* warned of "grave complications if the United States should persist in the course indicated by the most recent note to Berlin."[3]

Germany had begun submarine warfare shortly after the Alliance's January 30 conference. On May 7 a German submarine sank the British luxury-liner RMS *Lusitania* off the coast of Ireland.[4] Nearly 1,200 people died, including more than 100 Americans.[5] While the United States would not enter the war for almost two more years, the Alliance, like other German American groups, was greatly marginalized by the disaster. It would cease operation in the spring of 1918.

The possibility of war between America and Germany must have caused Jacob Ruppert much anguish. As a native-born American and former member of Congress, his loyalty was unquestioned. Still, so much about him was culturally German, even his accent. K. Jacob Ruppert, the great-grandson of Jacob Ruppert Sr., claimed that while Jacob Jr. spoke German fluently, he really did not have a German accent. "He just used the accent when it was favorable to do so."[6] Others, like pitcher Waite Hoyt, claimed he always spoke with a German accent, which got more pronounced when he was excited. (For example, he called Babe Ruth "Root.") In either case, Ruppert almost certainly was a member of the Alliance, or at least involved with the affairs of the Alliance, and like many German Americans, he was in an awkward situation.

German associations now felt compelled to proclaim their loyalty to America. Typical was the statement of the prominent weekly *New Yorker Staats-Zeitung* shortly after the *Lusitania*'s sinking. "There has never been but one flag under which the German American has fought. There can never be but one under which he can ever fight, and the flag is the Stars and Stripes."[7]

The loyalty of "hyphenated-Americans" became an issue in 1915 and gathered momentum as the country entered into the presidential election year of 1916. Yet for most Americans, including Ruppert, the war had not yet begun to affect them, and life went on as before. The official transfer of ownership of the New York American League club was made on January 11, 1915, at the law offices of Elkus, Gleason, and Proskauer at 170 Broadway. Til Huston sent a telegram that day to Ban Johnson.

"Deal closed. We are signed, sealed, and delivered."[8] Because the Yankees had $300,000 of debt at the time, which the new owners assumed, baseball business analysts Michael Haupert and Kenneth Winter estimate that Ruppert and Huston probably paid no more than $160,000 in cash and then settled the debt at considerably less than 100 cents on the dollar.[9]

Nevertheless, the $450,000 sale price remains in the literature. Almost a quarter-century later, John Kieran of the *New York Times* wrote that Ruppert, a solid conservative businessman, came to the closing with a lawyer and a certified check for $225,000, his half-share. Huston, who admitted he liked to "raise a ruckus," paid his half by casually plunking down 225 $1,000 bills on the table.[10] While Kieran's story may be apocryphal, it is symbolic of just how different the partners were from each other. Moreover, the story just might be true, except for a difference in the dollar amount.

Ruppert assumed the presidency, and Huston became both the secretary and treasurer. In his book *Baseball as I Have Known It*, Fred Lieb wrote that one of the major motivations for Ruppert to buy the Yankees was his belief that he could rename them the "Knickerbockers," the name of his best-selling beer. Lieb said the managing editors of New York's thirteen daily newspapers did not like the idea of the long name, and Ruppert backed off.[11]

The new owners praised John McGraw for the advice he had given them in their quest to buy the club. McGraw expected to be compensated for his services. In early 1918 the matter still had not been resolved, and Huston wrote to Ruppert while he was still stationed in France: "McGraw felt all along that he was to be entitled to some compensation," which seemed reasonable. He had agreed to pay McGraw $5,000 that coming summer and wanted the club to reimburse him. Huston noted that McGraw wanted the deal to be kept strictly confidential, "absolutely graveyard and to go no further than you and I."[12] There is no record of Ruppert's reply and no entry in the Yankees' financial records of a payment to McGraw.

Ban Johnson, who was there to oversee the sale, gave it his blessing. "I am satisfied," said Johnson, "that we have in Messrs. Ruppert and Huston two staunch supporters who will stand with our league till the crack of doom. They have impressed me most favorably. Never once throughout the long drawn negotiations have they wavered a quarter-inch from their original stand. The fact that they were most deliberate and conservative throughout their calculations proves to me that they are men who may be depended upon."[13]

Both Ruppert and Huston were strong-willed men, used to giving orders and getting their way. Neither man like divided authority, and neither was capable of playing second fiddle to the other. Those who knew the domineering character of the two men predicted the partnership would not last.

Following the December 31, 1914, meeting at the Wolcott Hotel, at which he and Ruppert took control of the Yankees, Huston, who would be the face of the franchise for the next few years, spoke to the press. "Colonel Ruppert and I have finally bought the New York Club. We have engaged Bill Donovan to manage the team. We probably will play at the Polo Grounds next season, but it is the intention of Colonel Ruppert and myself to erect an immense baseball park for the team; one that will be the equal of any that is now controlled by the other owners in organized baseball."[14]

The site of the park Huston mentioned was rumored to be at 145th Street and Lenox Avenue, which was supposed to have been the site where the new Highlanders were to play in 1903. That deal had fallen through, and the Highlanders ended up at 168th Street and Broadway.

Huston had on several occasions stated publicly his opinion that Yankees and the Giants could not continue to share the Polo Grounds. The Yankees' owners believed "separate grounds are absolutely necessary to give their club the distinct individuality that they desire," wrote Bozeman Bulger of the *New York Evening World*, after the 1916 season. "Without separate grounds they also feel that there will never be any healthy local rivalry between the Yanks and the Giants."[15]

In a July 16, 1915, letter to Ban Johnson, Huston mentioned the feasibility of a park on 42nd Street, along with a statement laying out the financial aspects of the project. "It seems from the amount of carrying charges we would have to combine with some exhibition scheme to bring the matter within our reach," he wrote.[16] While both owners agreed the Yankees needed their own ballpark, Huston was more aggressive in pursuing it. He continued his push for a new park during the 1915–16 off-season. In February 1916, he said: "I am just as much in favor of building now as I ever was, and if the question is left to me, we will certainly build. . . .

While Colonel Ruppert does not object to building, I must say he is a little more conservative on the subject than I am."[17]

Joseph Lannin, the owner of the Red Sox, had allowed Bill Donovan, the manager of the Providence Grays, a team Lannin controlled, to go to New York to manage the Yankees. Donovan, a thirty-eight-year-old former star pitcher for the Brooklyn Superbas and Detroit Tigers, had managed the Grays to the International League pennant in 1914.[18] Ban Johnson, who also spoke after the December 31 meeting, intimated that the Yankees had wanted Tigers manager Hughie Jennings, but were refused by Detroit owner Frank Navin. Jennings then suggested they hire Donovan.

"All that remains to be done is to make a first division team out of the Yankees," Huston said after the completion of the stock transfer that made him and Ruppert the new owners. "It is now up to Donovan entirely. He is the boss from now on." Huston added that the club would soon announce the signing of a business manager. However, he continued, it would be Donovan who would decide where the club would train in the spring and who would make the decisions on players. "Donovan is free now to make any trades, purchases, or any other deals he may see fit."[19]

Donovan was given full liberty in running the club without any interference from the front office. That was the policy set down by the new owners, and a look at the recent standings suggested it was a wise policy. The 1914 pennant-winning managers, Boston's George Stallings and Philadelphia's Connie Mack, had similar control, as did most of the managers of first-division teams.[20] "When I take hold of the New York club," Donovan said after agreeing to manage the 1915 Yankees, "I shall endeavor to follow a few simple rules that I think have earned me some friends in my time. I shall treat my players with every courtesy and friendship, for I feel that I shall always be one of the boys. I shall try to encourage every man of the squad and give all a square deal. I have not the least apprehension," he said with naiveté, "that any player will try to take advantage of me."[21]

Along with refurbishing the club's offices at 30 East 42nd Street, Ruppert and Huston made their first personnel move. Ruppert appointed Billy Fleischmann, who had been of great help in engineering the purchase, as his assistant.[22] Then, at McGraw's suggestion, they hired Harry Sparrow to be the team's business manager. The thirty-nine-year-old Sparrow was a Broadway friend of McGraw's who had managed the business arrangements for the Giants when they and the Chicago White Sox made their 1914 world tour.

John McGraw had a well-deserved reputation for having a win-at-all-costs mentality, yet recommending a valuable man like Harry Sparrow to the Yankees was consistent with another of his traits. Throughout his career he would always help his current players and other employees advance their careers. He was also always there to lend a hand to former players and employees who had fallen on hard times. Of course, at the time McGraw had a personal interest in the Yankees' success that went beyond Sparrow. He wanted them to do well because Huston and Ruppert had purchased the Yankees "largely on my advice," he said in July 1916, when the Yankees were briefly in first place. "Therefore, I want to see the club make good for him," referring to Huston, the partner to whom he was closer.[23] It was yet another indication of how much McGraw believed that he and his Giants would always rule New York baseball.

Business manager Sparrow chose Mark Roth and Charlie McManus to assist him. Roth was a former *New York Globe* sportswriter, and McManus had worked for Ruppert at the brewery's business office since 1907. Heeding another McGraw suggestion, Sparrow hired Joe Kelley to be the Yankees' chief scout. Kelley, a longtime National League star and McGraw's teammate with the 1890s Baltimore Orioles, replaced Arthur Irwin, who had signed to manage the Lewiston (Maine) Cupids of the New England League.[24]

Donovan was cautiously optimistic in the manner of all new managers taking over bad clubs. "From what I read in the papers some folks have an idea I am taking over a terrible proposition, but I don't figure it that way," he said. "If we can strengthen ourselves at one or two positions, we will have a fine ball team."[25] He chose Duke Farrell, who had been his catcher in Brooklyn for several seasons, to serve as a coach and a pitching instructor. Farrell had been with the Yankees in 1910 and 1911, when George Stallings was the manager, and he had tutored pitchers Ray Caldwell, Ray Fisher, Russ Ford, Jack Quinn, and Jim Vaughn. The club released Farrell after a run-in with management and replaced him with Lou Criger and then with Tom Daley, both of whom proved ineffective. Now Farrell was back.

Caldwell had been the club's top pitcher in 1914, with an 18-9 record and a 1.94 earned run average, but during the off-season it appeared unlikely he would return in 1915. He had announced in the fall that he was leaving the Yankees for the Buffalo club of the Federal League. Determined to retain his best pitcher, Donovan and a lawyer went to Caldwell's hometown of Salamanca, New York, to attempt to persuade him to stay with the Yankees. Whatever they told him worked. Sportswriter James Isaminger wrote, at least partly in jest, that the heavy-drinking Caldwell returned when he learned that a brewer had bought the Yankees.[26] Caldwell, who was working in the off-season as a telegraph operator for the Pennsylvania Railroad, signed a three-year contract at an annual salary of $8,000. However, the Yankees agreed to repay the $5,000 the Buffalo team had advanced to him.[27] The agreement called for Ruppert to deduct the $5,000 over the next three seasons.[28]

The Frank Farrell–Bill Devery duo had mismanaged the Yankees franchise for years. The club had been $96,000 in the red in 1914.[29] They had a twelve-year record of 861-937 and an average attendance of 345,000 per season, or less than 5,000 fans per game. Those that came to see them were mostly there to see opposing players, such as Nap Lajoie, Eddie Collins, Ty Cobb, and Walter Johnson. Clearly Ruppert and Huston were faced with a challenge. The new owners inherited the rights to twenty-eight players, but by 1920, just five years later, only Roger Peckinpaugh remained from that original group.[30]

The Yankees' first game under the new regime was in Washington, where Walter Johnson shut them out, 7–0, on two hits.[31] First baseman Wally Pipp, batting cleanup, singled in his first Yankees' at bat, one of New York's two hits against Johnson. Left fielder Hugh High, the other acquisition from Detroit, was also in the opening-day lineup.

Neither Pipp nor High had been happy about leaving the Tigers, whom they expected to be pennant contenders, for what they considered an "experimental" team in New York.[32] Pipp demanded a two-year contract, while both men asked for more money to help alleviate their potential financial sacrifice. They even suggested that the Yankees compensate them with a World Series share should the Tigers win that honor in 1915. Pipp later claimed that owner Navin told him he had made a mistake in letting him go to New York and asked him to refuse to report."[33]

After winning four of their first seven games at Washington and Philadelphia, the Yankees made their first home appearance on the wintry afternoon of April 22. Mayor John Purroy Mitchel threw out the first ball, and Ruppert and Huston watched as their team lost to the Senators, 5–1. The Yankees finished in fifth place in 1915, but for the first time ever they led the American League in home runs, a promising sign of things to come.[34]

8

Fritz Maisel Follies

On February 15, 1916, the Yankees purchased Frank "Home Run" Baker from the Philadelphia Athletics. Adding Baker was the club's most significant acquisition since they landed pitcher Jack Chesbro and outfielder Willie Keeler following the 1903 origin of the franchise. Ban Johnson had helped make the Baker deal possible by persuading Connie Mack to sell his star third baseman to the Yankees rather than to Baker's other suitor, Charles Comiskey's Chicago White Sox.

This was not the first time the Yankees had gone after Baker. They had made a serious effort to get him in the spring of 1915, after manager Bill Donovan told Ruppert and Huston to meet any reasonable terms. Heeding Donovan's plea, the rookie owners offered $25,000, but Mack wanted $50,000. Huston then went to see the A's manager in person and told him he would add Fritz Maisel to the offer. At the time Maisel was considered by many to be the American League's second best third baseman, behind only Baker.[1]

Mack still refused, but Philadelphia had been unable to sign Baker. The taciturn farmer was displeased with the way Mack was purging the A's of their best players and with the contract offered to him. He chose to sit out the 1915 season, which he spent at his farm in Trappe, Maryland, while also playing some semipro baseball in the Peninsula League.

Baker remained the property of the Athletics, and when the Yankees offered Mack $37,500 for him in early 1916, he accepted. The thirty-year-old Baker was still the game's greatest slugger. He had won or tied for the league's home run crown in each of the four seasons prior to 1915. Some Philadelphia sportswriters had begun calling him "Home Run" Baker during spring training of his first full season, 1909. Baker had earned the sobriquet after winning three consecutive exhibition games with home

69

runs.[2] The name became forever identified with him when the national press started using it after he hit home runs in consecutive games against the Giants' Rube Marquard and Christy Mathewson in the 1911 World Series. In addition to his hitting, Baker was an excellent base stealer, and contemporary pundits ranked him among the steadiest defensive third basemen in the game.[3]

A month before acquiring Baker, Huston had negotiated a deal with Federal League representative Harry Sinclair to purchase the contract of Lee Magee from the Brooklyn Tip-Tops for $25,000. Magee's sale to the Yankees made him the first player from the failed Federal League to return to Organized Baseball.[4] In 1915, his one season in the Federal League, Magee batted .323 as the manager and second baseman for the Tip-Tops.[5] Before jumping to the Feds, he had been a full-time outfielder for three seasons with the St. Louis Cardinals. Donovan said he would likely return him to the outfield in 1916, which he did.[6] Magee, however, was a disappointment, batting just .257, and in July 1917 the Yankees traded him to the St. Louis Browns. In return, they received Armando Marsans, a speedy outfielder. But Marsans suffered a broken leg shortly after the trade and also was a disappointment in his two seasons with the Yankees.[7]

Baker was not the only member of Connie Mack's "$100,000 infield" whom the new owners had wanted to bring to New York. In late 1914 Ruppert confirmed the accuracy of reports that second baseman Eddie Collins had been offered to the Yankees for $45,000.[8] "It is true that Collins was offered to us, but at that time we had no assurance that we were going to get the club. There was no sense in buying a player for a lot of money and then finding that you have no franchise" was Ruppert's rationalization for not pursuing the sale. "When the deal was finally closed we were informed that Collins was sold to the White Sox. I can add that Collins is wildly anxious to play with the Yankees. He likes New York."[9]

Ruppert's explanation for why the Yankees missed out on the American League's best second baseman is understandable. Nevertheless, in the early Ruppert-Huston years, before they hired Miller Huggins and Ed Barrow, the Yankees did not have a baseball man with the knowledge to make advantageous deals.[10] Had Huggins or Barrow been on board in 1915–16, one, or possibly two, of the league's best outfielders might have come to the Yankees in trades.

After the White Sox failed to get Frank Baker, Comiskey and man-ager Clarence "Pants" Rowland traveled to the American League meet-ings in New York with plans to make a trade for Yankees third baseman Fritz Maisel. With Baker available to play third base, they reasoned, the Yankees would be willing to trade Maisel. In return, the White Sox were offering outfielder Joe Jackson, one of baseball's most feared hitters.[11]

Astonishingly, in hindsight, the Yankees turned down the offer.[12] Per-haps they were influenced by a combination of Maisel's league-leading seventy-four stolen bases in 1914, followed by fifty-one in 1915, and Jack-son's 1915 late-season slump. Jackson had batted just .272 in forty-five games for Chicago following his August trade from Cleveland. Or perhaps they were influenced by the press. Newspapers in Chicago had repeat-edly pointed out Jackson's shortcomings during his 1915 fall-off. At the same time, the New York press, no less an influential force then than it is today, questioned whether the wily old Comiskey was trying to put one over on the relatively inexperienced Yankees' owners. They wondered if the twenty-eight-year-old Jackson had seen his best days, while Maisel, more than two years younger and very popular with the New York fans, had his best days in front of him.[13] A *New York Tribune* writer counseled that this would have been a terrific deal for the Yankees two years ear-lier, but it would not be so now. "For all the power of Jackson's bat," he cautioned, "there are reasons for believing he is not so valuable a ball-player as Maisel."[14]

Sam Crane was equally hesitant about a possible Jackson-for-Maisel trade. "Jackson is a great batter—a cleanup man, who is very valuable in his way," he wrote, "but the question arises: is not the fiery little Bal-timorean [Maisel] of more value to the Yankees on account of his run-making abilities than Slugger Joe?" Crane cited Maisel's popularity as an additional reason not to make the trade. "Maisel has proven his worth with such steady consistency and is, moreover, so extremely popular with the Yankees' supporters that Captain Huston and Manager Dono-van have done the proper thing in turning the deal down. Joe Jackson is a big card, but Fritz Maisel is a bigger one right here in New York, and is the kind of player who will retain his popularity. There is nothing that enthuses the average fan more than base stealing, and Maisel is par excel-lent in that important department of the sport." Crane wrote that he was present for Jackson's long home run over the right-field grandstand in the Polo Grounds and other long drives of his. "But still I pin my faith on Maisel in preference to Jackson." He added that "figures" can show that Jackson's worth exceeds that of Maisel, "but there are other things besides statistics to be considered as between the two players."[15]

In his Sport Views column, Walter St. Denis of the *New York Globe* echoed Crane. "Rumor has it" the Yankees will trade Maisel for Jackson. "Let's hope that no such deal is put through. The majority of fans agree that in view of the acquisition of Frank Baker the team can get along very well without even such a fine batter as Shoeless Joe. It is the general belief that the little Yankee [Maisel] is far more valuable a man to a ball club than is Jackson. There is no question that the New Yorker is a more versatile player."[16]

Then, on April 7, 1916, the *New York Evening Journal* revealed that at those same American League meetings in February, Ruppert and Huston had discussed a deal for center fielder Tris Speaker with Red Sox president Joseph Lannin. Speaker, twenty-eight years old and in the prime of his career, was having salary problems with Boston. With the demise of competition from the Federal League, Lannin and the other owners were intent on rolling back salaries. The Yankees offered to buy Speaker, but Lannin also wanted a player in return—Fritz Maisel. Although the Yankees were willing to pay a substantial amount of money for Speaker, they again refused to give up Maisel. "We would like to have Speaker," Huston said, "but we won't let Maisel go. Why should we trade a young fellow who has ten good years ahead of him for a veteran who may not last only three or four years more at the most?"[17] As in the Jackson case, the age factor's influence on the trade is particularly difficult to comprehend. Speaker was only twenty months older than Maisel.

In January 1918, the Yanks traded Maisel, the man who might have brought Joe Jackson or Tris Speaker to New York, to the St. Louis Browns, along with four other players, for second baseman Del Pratt. Maisel played one season for the Browns and then was gone from the big leagues. "I'd like to play in New York," Speaker had said when he heard of the possible trade, "although I prefer to stay in Boston. It's simply a case of where I can get the salary I want."[18] A few days after the *Evening Journal* story surfaced, Boston sent Speaker to the Cleveland Indians for pitcher Sam

Jones, second baseman Fred Thomas, and $55,000. Speaker, of course, lasted a lot longer than "three or four years" in Cleveland. He won the batting championship in his first year with the Indians and accumulated 2,187 more hits before he retired in 1928.[19]

While the Yankees might be ridiculed for turning down the opportunity to get Speaker, that opportunity may have existed for only a brief time or not at all. It was around this time that Indians ownership was in the process of being transferred from Charles Somers to a group headed by Jim Dunn. Ban Johnson, still in complete control of the American League in 1916, had recruited Dunn, no doubt with promises to help build up the club. If Johnson wanted Speaker to play in Cleveland, he would have shut down any other trade option, no matter what the Yankees might have offered.

In his article in the *New York Press* of April 9, 1916, Fred Lieb quoted Huston as saying that a player like Speaker would rehabilitate the game in Cleveland and increase the strength of the league. Lieb went on to say that Johnson was "behind" the deal, that he had to "take control of the club [Cleveland] himself" when it was hard to find a purchaser. It appears that Lannin may have "pulled a bone" that would cost him the pennant by letting Speaker go. "The Red Sox were no longer a great team, just a good team," he said.[20]

P. T. Knox, of the *New York Evening Telegram*, believed that Johnson had the last word on which teams landed star players. As an example, he offered Johnson's holding back other teams from bidding against the Yankees for Frank Baker. The policy, wrote Knox, is based on the principle that "it is more effective financially to have baseball strength distributed in as many teams in the league as possible." Knox also noted that Cleveland fans "had virtually decided to boycott the club" when Jackson was sold, and "it was imperative" that they get another star.[21] Moreover, Huston's dismissively calling Speaker "a veteran who may not last only three or four years more at the most" was an opinion shared by at least one astute member of the New York press corps. Sid Mercer called the $50,000 the Indians paid for him "an excessive amount to have paid for a man "who has seen his best years."[22]

Nevertheless, there remain innumerable thought-provoking scenarios suggested by a Joe Jackson or a Tris Speaker joining the Yankees in 1916. Had the deal been made, would the White Sox (minus Jackson) have won pennants in 1917 and 1919? The Yankees did not win their first pennant until 1921, after getting Babe Ruth from Boston. However, with Jackson or Speaker on the team, might they not have won before then? How imposing would the Yankees' teams of the early 1920s have been with Ruth and Jackson or Ruth and Speaker?

Then again, had one of those two led the Yankees to pennants in the late teens, Ruppert and Huston might not have gone after Ruth in 1920. Just imagine how different the next fifteen years would have been if Ruth had remained in Boston or had gone to another team. It is difficult to envision the Babe Ruth legend developing in quite the same way if the Babe had never played in New York. And we have to wonder whether Ruppert would have built such a magnificent Yankee Stadium without Ruth.

One of the more intriguing questions to ponder concerns the relative positions of Ruth and Jackson in baseball's hagiology and how they would have changed. Might not Joe Jackson have been among that first group of men voted into the Hall of Fame in 1936? Writing in the wake of the Black Sox revelations, Dan Daniel reminded his readers how close the Yankees came to having the services of two of the other banished players. Happy Felsch had asked Charles Comiskey to trade him to the Yankees in the fall of 1918 and again following the 1919 season. Buck Weaver asked to be traded to New York in the spring of 1920, during his holdout. Had both men been Yankees in 1920, the club likely would have won the pennant, but would now have had two players under indictment on their roster.[23]

Not only were the Yankees passing on superior players in the first years of the Ruppert-Huston ownership but they were spending a lot of money on inferior ones. On May 22, 1916, the *New York Press* reported the Yankees had spent $150,000 on new players in their first few years. The June 7, 1920, *New York Evening Mail* placed the total at $200,000.

Among those who produced less than expected was pitcher Dan Tipple, purchased for $7,000 from the Indianapolis Indians of the American Association, whose Yankees career consisted of three games in 1915. Huston had highly recommended the purchase of Tipple, something Ruppert would use against him whenever he wanted to emphasize his claim of superior knowledge regarding personnel. Another notable flop was pitcher Cliff Markle, who started well in both 1915 and 1916, but appeared in a combined fourteen games in the two seasons.

The Yankees finally gave up on Markle, releasing him after the 1919 season. Fred Lieb believed Markle's early success went to his head, which caused him to get into arguments with many of his teammates, "and overnight his pitching skill vanished." On the day they released Markle, the Yankees also released future Hall of Fame pitcher Dazzy Vance, who like Markle had joined the club late in the 1915 season.[24]

There was, however, the occasional success. On June 28, 1915, after several days of negotiations with the Athletics, manager Donovan announced the purchase of pitcher Bob Shawkey. Newspaper estimates placed the price Mack received for the twenty-four-year-old right-hander as low as $18,000 and as high as $80,000. The actual price was $3,000.[25]

Getting Shawkey that cheaply was a rare personnel triumph in the early years of the new ownership. Conversely, it was one of the worst deals ever made by the usually shrewd Mack. Donovan also announced he had purchased another pitcher that day, George Mogridge, a twenty-six-year-old left-hander who was with Des Moines of the Western League.

The Yankees of the mid-teens had missed out on getting superstars Eddie Collins, Joe Jackson, and Tris Speaker. That would all change in January 1920, when they landed the biggest superstar of all. Shortly after they purchased Babe Ruth, Sam Murphy of the *Evening Mail* reflected on those early years: "It takes nerve and the patience of an army of Jobs as well as a bankroll—large, loose, and easily reached—before one can get a winner at the gate or on the grounds," wrote Murphy. "For five long and lean years the Yankee owners have been stripping their bank accounts to put a winning ball club in New York. . . . When Ruppert and Huston started out, they bought freely and paid high."[26]

9

Anti-German Hysteria and
Two Disappointing Seasons

Despite the Yankees' poor showing in 1915, Jacob Ruppert was clearly delighted about owning a baseball team. Seated in the stands at training camp in Macon, Georgia, in 1916, the onetime sandlot player decided to take a few cuts. When the pitchers were taking batting practice, he asked to step in to see what he could do with the bat. The rookie pitcher on the mound threw three soft ones right down the middle, but Ruppert whiffed on all three. "I guess this is not as easy as it looks," he said as he threw down his bat and took a seat back in the grandstand.[1]

Ruppert's beer business continued to flourish. His brewery was now selling a million barrels of beer a year, the first brewery without national distribution to reach that milestone.[2] Yet he was still waiting for a winner on the baseball field. The addition of Frank "Home Run" Baker had excited New Yorkers, who began predicting the slugging third baseman would lead the club to its first pennant.

But the 1916 season would be a difficult one for Ruppert, both off the field and on. In December he was criticized by Dave Fultz for what Fultz called abuses against the disability clause in some players' contracts the past two seasons. Fultz was a former Major Leaguer and the center fielder for the Yankees in their first-ever game in 1903.[3] He later became a lawyer, and in 1912 he created an organization called the Baseball Players Fraternity, whose goal was to unionize Major League players.

Fultz cited the case of Yankees pitcher Ray Keating to show that the clause harmed the players. Ruppert, on vacation in French Lick, responded that his club had always given its players fair treatment and that the criticism lodged against the Yankees by Fultz was not based on fact. He argued that the disability clause in Keating's contract had not prevented him from collecting his full 1915 salary from the Yankees. "Keating won three games and lost six," Ruppert added, "making his winning games cost us for his services $1,666.66 a game."[4]

He further pointed out that the disability clause did not keep the club from paying King Cole his salary of $3,800 and a physician's bill of $365 in 1915, although Cole had been unable to pitch all season.[5] Ruppert went on to list all the injured players in 1916. Those injuries "undoubtedly cost us the pennant," he contended. "The medical treatment which the club assumed for the players I have mentioned amounted to $3,000, while the actual salary loss on these players for the time of their disability was $17,000. Yet neither Captain Huston nor myself ever dreamed of dodging behind any technical interpretation of the disability clause to ease the strain on the club's bank balance."[6]

The injuries Ruppert alluded to had indeed played a major role in preventing the Yankees from winning their first pennant. On July 29, 1916, they were in first place, where they had been for a month. They led the Boston Red Sox by a half-game, but after five losses in three days to the St. Louis Browns, they dropped to third place, three games out. They never recovered, in large part due to their string of injuries.[7] The press, which could be savage in its criticism, fully acknowledged the role injuries had played. "No major league club in the history of the sport ever experienced such a run of ill luck," wrote Joe Vila of the *Evening Sun*. "Maisel, Gilhooley, Baker, Magee, High, Cullop, Mogridge, Nunamaker, and Peckinpaugh sustained injuries at various times that put the team out of the running."[8]

The 1916 Yankees went 80–74 to finish in fourth place. It was the first time they had finished in the first division since George Stallings's second-place club of 1910. Wally Pipp became the first Yankee to lead the American League in home runs, with twelve. Baker was second, with ten. The team's total of thirty-five again topped the league. Bob Shawkey led the pitchers with twenty-four wins (second in the league to Walter Johnson's twenty-five), followed by Nick Cullop's thirteen. Based on the Yankees' 1916 showing, both the press and the fans had high expectations for 1917.

Before spring training had even started, Damon Runyon wrote, "Many followers of the game firmly believe that only bad luck cheated Donovan of a pennant last season, and that he has a great chance to win this year."[9]

The war in Europe had mostly been ignored by Americans until just prior to the start of the 1917 season, on April 6, when the United States entered the conflict against Germany on the side of the Allies.[10] "My only regret is that I myself am not ten years younger and physically fit to bear arms in the titanic struggle abroad," Ruppert said.[11] He added that he received greater pleasure from seeing players from his club answer the call of duty than he would from winning a World Series. By early June, Huston had left the Yankees to rendezvous with his regiment of engineers en route to the European Front. With Huston gone, Ruppert took over running the club, which was stumbling along in third place, and for the first time he became personally involved in its day-to-day affairs.

Following a 6–1 home loss to Cleveland, a distraught Ruppert went into the clubhouse and voiced his displeasure at the way the team was playing. He castigated the players, letting them know he would not stand for listless playing. He was particularly upset at the lack of production from outfielders Hugh High and Lee Magee.[12]

On August 26 Ruppert was in Chicago, where he saw the Yankees lose to the White Sox, 8–3. The game confirmed his suspicion that certain players were not "loyal" to Donovan, while others were just incompetent or slow-thinking, and a shakeup was necessary. He focused particularly on catcher Les Nunamaker, who had hit into three double plays and missed a sign.[13] Ruppert was already making plans for newcomers Muddy Ruel and Truck Hannah to solve his catching problems. "The time to rip the Yankees apart and sew them up again is at hand," wrote Sid Mercer. "The house cleaning is at hand—in fact, it has already started," Mercer said, adding that Ruppert does not hold Donovan responsible.[14]

For one reason or another, Donovan had never gotten to manage a Yankees team that included an Eddie Collins, a Joe Jackson, or a Tris Speaker. One more name can be added to that list of "almost-Yankees," although how likely he would have been traded to New York is uncertain. The August 27, 1917, *New York American* reported a deal was in the works that would bring Walter Johnson, the league's best pitcher, to Donovan's club. The Yankees would also get outfielder Clyde Milan and catcher Eddie Ainsmith. Washington would receive $100,000 in what would be the biggest cash deal in baseball history. Both Ruppert and Ban Johnson were anxious to see a winning team in New York. Meanwhile, Washington had not drawn well and continued to lose money, and while Johnson denied it, plans were being made, it was rumored, to move the franchise to Baltimore.[15]

Preseason optimism that 1917 would bring the Yankees that elusive first pennant went unrealized. Even worse, the team fell from fourth place to sixth. Pipp, the Yankees' six foot one, 180-pound left-handed cleanup batter, retained his home run title, though he hit just nine, six at the Polo Grounds. The onetime architectural student at the Catholic University of America in Washington DC also saw his runs batted in total decline, from ninety-three to seventy, and his batting average was a full-season career low .244. Shawkey won only thirteen games, which tied him for the club lead with Ray Caldwell.

Perhaps the highlight of the season came in an April 24 game at Boston, when George Mogridge outdueled Dutch Leonard, 2–1, in pitching the Yankees' first-ever no-hitter. Overall, however, it was a disappointing season, which did not prevent sportswriter W. S. Farnsworth from predicting that "Donovan undoubtedly will be retained as manager of the Yanks next season." While conceding that Ban Johnson preferred someone else, Farnsworth believed Ruppert would now be running the club as he saw fit.[16]

After the season, Ruppert and Huston made the decision to fire Donovan. Among the replacements they considered was Brooklyn's Wilbert Robinson, a longtime friend of Huston's. "Are you trying to take Robinson away from me?" Dodgers president Charles Ebbets had asked. Ruppert disingenuously explained the interest in Robinson, which, in effect, was tampering. "I didn't know at first in baseball you weren't supposed to make offers to men employed by other clubs," he said.[17]

With Robinson out of the picture and Huston serving in France, the choice of a new manager fell to Ruppert. Ban Johnson had been pushing for Miller Huggins. Ruppert resisted initially, but after conferring with Huggins, he was so impressed with the former Cardinals manager that he hired him. Huggins's managerial skills and ability to control his players would be a constant source of conflict between Ruppert and Huston and a major impetus to ending their partnership.

Early in his new manager's first season, Ruppert explained the obstacles Bill Donovan had faced and why he had chosen to replace him. "He had been handicapped by the worst of luck as I well realized," Ruppert said of Donovan, "but after three years we didn't seem to be advancing very fast, and I felt that it was to the best interests of the club to make a change." Ruppert added that he would "take personal credit for Miller Huggins's appointment if he succeeds as I believe he will, and I also shall take full blame for his failure if he fails."[18]

Ruppert had at least one ally in the press. "I have great faith in Miller Huggins being successful as leader of the Yankees," wrote Sam Crane of the *Evening Journal* weeks after Huggins was hired. But as New Year's Day 1918 approached, Crane was lamenting Huggins's lack of success in making an off-season trade, a failure he blamed on the rest of the American League clubs. All of Huggins's deal-making experience was in the National League, Crane pointed out, and the way things worked in the American League was quite different. Primarily he pointed to the fact that any American League sale or trade, particularly if it involved a star player, had to have the approval of Ban Johnson. Despite the new owners of the Yankees being promised "everything in sight" when they took over, any deal that did not have Johnson's approval did not get made. Captain Huston, serving in France, had often voiced his opinion that the Yankees were being discriminated against by "men higher up" in the American League.[19]

Discrimination of a more serious kind was also intruding on Ruppert's life. This was a difficult time for a man proud of both his German heritage and his American nationality, as it was for so many German Americans. While Ruppert did not hesitate to make clear his loyalty to America and the Allied war effort, there was one battle in which he was on the losing side—the battle against the movement to mandate Prohibition.

In his classic study of late nineteenth- and early twentieth-century immigration, John Higham noted, "The fury that broke upon the German Americans in 1915 represented the most spectacular reversal of judgment in the history of American nativism."[20] The anti-German fervor played into the hands of Prohibitionists, and they took full advantage. They questioned the loyalty of the German-American Alliance because they defined American brewers (most of them of German origin) and their beer as threats to American productivity and the war effort.

Newspaper editor Arthur Brisbane purchased the *Washington Times* in 1917, with the help of a secret $375,000 loan from German American brewers. The government's alien property custodian, A. Mitchell Palmer, had uncovered the money donated by the brewers, which had prompted a congressional investigation. While the brewers had hoped for a sympathetic voice in their battle against Prohibition, which Brisbane was, the sale raised suspicion of German government subversion and war propaganda.[21] Ruppert, the head of the United States Brewers Association and its finance chairman, had contributed $50,000. America's entry into the war had an adverse effect on every brewer in the country. "The United States Brewers Association came to be looked on as a flank of the Hindenburg Line," wrote Gerald Holland.[22]

One victim of this hysteria was German American brewer George Ehret, owner of the Hell Gate Brewery in New York. Ehret, a friend and competitor of Ruppert's, had been in Germany in 1914 when the war broke out. Although the eighty-year-old Ehret was an American citizen, his son George Ehret Jr. agreed to turn over the family's $40 million business to the government. Palmer said the action was triggered by Ehret's temporary residence in Germany.[23] Ehret returned home in 1918, and the brewery was returned to the family after the war. Prohibition crippled the business, and the brewery, located near Ruppert's, at Third Avenue and 92nd Street, ceased operating in 1929.[24] Ruppert bought the property in 1935 and began to brew ale there.

Secure in his choice of Huggins, Ruppert looked forward with great anticipation to the 1918 season. "Huggins had vision," Ruppert wrote in the *Saturday Evening Post* in 1931. "Getting him was the first and the most important step we took toward making the Yankees champions. Huggins had constructive ideas. Far-seeing judgment. He planned on a big scale."[25]

Part 3

HUGGINS ARRIVES

10

An Impatient City with
an Unforgiving Press

As Miller Huggins prepared for the 1918 season, his first as manager of the Yankees, he had substantial financial resources at his disposal for the first time. He had signed a two-year contract for $12,000 annually, and he had an open-ended budget for players.[1] Yet while the outlook seemed bright, outside forces were impacting baseball at the national level.

America had entered the Great War in April 1917. However, only now, in the spring of 1918, was full mobilization resulting in large numbers of both players and fans joining the war effort. In January there were barely 100,000 American soldiers in Europe. By the summer, more than 200,000 were arriving in France every month.[2] Eventually the 1918 season was shortened, and with no end in sight to the fighting in Europe, even the 1919 season seemed in jeopardy.

Just before Christmas 1917, Congress had proposed the Eighteenth Amendment to the Constitution and sent it to the states for ratification.[3] The "manufacture, sale, or transportation of intoxicating liquors," including beer, could soon be prohibited. While Jacob Ruppert had given Huggins his commitment to spend whatever it took to build a winner, Prohibition now loomed as a threat to his primary source of income.

The Anti-Saloon League (ASL) had led the battle against the alcoholic beverage industry by mastering single-issue politics and leveraging legislators' ultimate fear: losing their seats in the next election. The nonpartisan group became national in scope in the early twentieth century. Congress's overwhelming support for the amendment was testimony to the group's influence. Aided by the rise of Progressivism and the women's suffrage movement, both of which had also targeted the saloon culture as an enemy of the public good, the ASL then turned its focus to the state legislatures.[4] The League also deftly created a link between the Allies' major enemy in the war, Germany, and America's brewers, most of whom had their roots in Germany.

Drawing its strongest support from Baptist and Methodist churches in the South and the rural Midwest, the philosophy of the ASL was rooted in rural and nativist values. Eliot Asinof wrote in *1919: America's Loss of Innocence* that the ASL framed the issue as a fight against "the corruption of the cities, those sprawling, violent, chaotic centers of polyglot populations dominated by political bosses who bought power through bribes and deals and favors, where nothing was on the square."[5]

In his study of the early twentieth century, Mark Sullivan noted, "Much of the social history of the United States, and not a little of its political history, consisted of resistance by the country, especially the rural portions of it, to influences emanating from New York."[6] Small wonder that the *New York Times* found humor in saying its home was in "Satan's last stronghold."[7] Prohibition was also a threat to Tammany Hall's political machine, which was closely tied to the saloon and to the lifestyle of millions of New Yorkers, especially immigrants. Everything in New York City was done on a large scale. "New York sits upon the surplus wealth of America; it is Cinderella, the Fairy Godmother, the handsome prince, and the wicked sisters all in one," wrote the *New York Globe*. "If New York is on the whole a vulgar city, it is because the soul of America is tainted with vulgarity."[8]

Midwesterner Miller Huggins was about to learn how different the nation's largest city was from Cincinnati and St. Louis, his previous places of employment. He also would soon learn that New York City had an unforgiving press and a demanding fan base. John McGraw and his New York Giants "owned" the city's sports scene. The defending National League champions had won six pennants in fourteen years, starting in 1904. The Yankees, on the other hand, had been so bad for so long that Fred Lieb wrote of a "strange fatality" of injuries and accidents that had followed the team for years.[9] In the summer of 1916, one writer suggested that the team's history should be written by Edgar Allan Poe, an author preoccupied with loss and misfortune.[10]

Huggins worried about whether the metropolis would give him enough time to succeed. Before he managed his first game, he told his sister, Myrtle, "New York is thumbs down on a losing club. They're too impatient, and they may not give me a chance to build a winner all the way up from the cellar."[11] A few years later, he looked back and explained, "The psychology in New York is entirely different. . . . You've got to make good!"[12]

This realistic evaluation led Huggins to abandon what had been one of his core concepts as a manager in St. Louis, developing young players and building a team from the ground up. New York, said Huggins, "is not the place to do it, as a general thing." Young teams rarely win pennants, and with the heightened competition between two New York clubs, a manager must "scheme and plot for one year only, leaving the future to take care of itself."[13]

Not only did New York teams need established players. Huggins understood that the Yankees also needed stars—and colorful ones at that. "A ball team with no 'color' is an awful thing," he said. "You can bet there will be plenty of 'color' in this bunch this year."[14] This shift in approach would generate frustration for Huggins. Stars were often temperamental (colorful stars even more so), and they often felt they did not need "managing."

The former star second baseman also understood that the Yankees needed to be strong defensively "up the middle." So just three months after signing with New York, he made a major trade with the St. Louis Browns. The Yankees acquired second baseman Del Pratt in exchange for five players, including pitcher Urban Shocker.[15] Pratt was arguably the second best second baseman in the American League (after Chicago's Eddie Collins), both in the field and at the plate. "Pratt was the man who put our ball club on its feet," Huggins later explained. "The improvement was immediate."[16]

Ruppert continued his active involvement in running the ball club and encouraged Huggins to make the Pratt deal. He told *Baseball Magazine* that he had had his eye on Pratt for a number of years. "I paid fifteen thousand dollars in cash and gave away a number of good players for him. But what can you do? I needed this player and everyone knew I needed him."[17] Pratt did have a reputation for stubbornness and litigious behavior. He had sued the owner of the Browns, which prompted St. Louis's willingness to give him up.[18] Staying in character, before Pratt reported to the Yankees, he held out for more money.

The trade was not an unqualified success for the Yankees. Shocker blossomed into one of the game's great pitchers. He averaged almost twenty-three wins a year from 1920 to 1923, despite missing about a month each season. While Huggins later suggested that he knew Shocker would develop into a fine hurler, the reality is Huggins traded him based on bad advice. He was told that Shocker was a troublemaker and should be dealt away to break up a problematic clique on the team. "I had not been correctly advised," Huggins later said.[19]

Just who gave him this advice and what was the "clique" can only be surmised. Scouts Joe Kelley and Bobby Gilks are likely "suspects." They had been with the Yankees before Huggins was hired and stayed on afterward. Shocker was friendly with hard-drinking pitcher Ray Caldwell; the two men had been fined after a "night on the town" in 1917. Caldwell had gone AWOL and had been suspended by New York's previous two managers.[20]

Huggins brought in a new pitching coach, Paddy O'Connor, to replace Duke Farrell. O'Connor had coached for Huggins in St. Louis in 1914, when the Cardinals had the best pitching staff in the National League.[21] He had a long career as a catcher, mainly in the minors, and was a member of the 1909 champion Pittsburgh Pirates.

Huggins then focused on upgrading his outfield. In February he entered into discussions with the Detroit Tigers to acquire Ty Cobb. The Tigers needed pitching, and many of Cobb's teammates did not get along with him; some detested him.[22] When those talks did not progress, Huggins sat down with Charles Comiskey, the owner of the Chicago White Sox, to again discuss acquiring Joe Jackson. Those discussions also went nowhere.[23]

In March Huggins did acquire an outfielder, slugger Ping Bodie, the first of many San Francisco area Italian Americans who would find their way to the Yankees.[24] The rotund, earthy outfielder, while lacking in speed, was one of the league's top home run hitters and had once hit an incredible thirty home runs in the Pacific Coast League.[25] The New York press heralded Bodie's arrival. "In New York Ping will be a character, an institution, one of the sights," wrote a sportswriter of the *Globe*.[26]

Bodie was known for his gargantuan appetite as well as his aphorisms.[27] He once observed that home plate and the dinner plate were similar for a ballplayer. "A guy can't get hits if he pulls away from either of them."[28]

He could also be rowdy. When he struck out in a spring training game and cursed loudly, a bemused Jacob Ruppert was in the stands. "My, my, we have a man who swears," he chuckled. "What are the Yankees coming to?"[29]

But the rest of the Yankees, in both 1918 and 1919, were lacking in the "color" Huggins had hoped to present to the fans. The veteran infielders were solid players, yet quiet and even aloof. Sam Crane described the biggest star of the group, third baseman Frank Baker, as "a mechanical player" who "hasn't enough ginger to keep him warm."[30] George Daley of the *World* put it well when he wrote that the Yankees were "too earnest," lacking a "firebrand" such as Ty Cobb, Hal Chase, or Johnny Evers.[31]

Miller Huggins showed a surprising flexibility in his approach to the game after taking over the Yankees. Many people assumed he would run his offense as he had in St. Louis, scratching out a run or two with walks and speed, and then making them hold up with pitching. Instead, he told New York reporters he would tailor the tactics of the Yankees to the talent at hand.[32] With the addition of Pratt and Bodie to an already powerful lineup, he had one of the top slugging teams in baseball.

On opening day, Sid Mercer wrote of Huggins's relying on his "Murderers' Row" to score runs. When the Yankees battered Washington in the opener, Mercer's headline the next day read, "'Murderers' Row' Too Brutal for Walter Johnson."[33]

Huggins had modeled his own place-hitting style after Willie Keeler's, and he was the first player of the modern era to accumulate 1,000 walks. But now he was sensing a change in the style of play, one that had not fully emerged yet—one in which there would be more of an emphasis on power-hitting. His thinking was also driven by his understanding of New York fans, their expectation of entertaining as well as winning baseball.

At the start of the 1918 season, Crane wrote that he was "strong for Hug" because the Yankees' manager understood that his team "must hit to become popular favorites." Fans, wrote Crane, remember "the slugger, the swatter, the walloper, of course."[34] Five years later, Huggins looked back and told Fred Lieb that his Yankees—including the pre-Ruth teams of 1918 and 1919—"had a lot to do with revolutionizing the style of play."[35]

There was a lot of discussion in the New York newspapers about the managerial style of the Yankees' new leader, with conflicting opinions emerging. Was Huggins a "driver" (like John McGraw and George Stall-ings) or a "salve" manager (like Connie Mack and Wilbert Robinson)? Crane noted that he could be both: a disciplinarian when needed and a "diplomat" at other times.[36] A year later Huggins would expand on his style and his philosophy: "One system will not rule. It is impossible, because you will find temperamental players, you will find players who do not need any rules, and you will find players who insist that they know more than the manager."[37]

Sportswriter Hugh Fullerton, who said he had known Huggins since he was a "kid," predicted success for the Yankees, but worried that perhaps too much was expected of the new manager.[38] Damon Runyon, who had a knack for sizing up people both vividly and accurately, captured Hug-gins at the start of the 1918 season:

> We would say he is a manager of the Huggins type. He impressed his style and personality upon the National League strongly enough to create his own type. . . . He has stage presence and atmosphere. People know he is around. Off the field he is quite self-effacing, and rather given to solitude. He is no mixer with the world at large. His exterior manner suggests the crustacean known as the crab. . . . The casual observer is apt to gather the idea that Mr. Huggins is some-what brusque. . . . Mr. Huggins has a way about him in the baseball arbor which inspires the feeling that he knows his business.[39]

There was virtually no discussion in the New York newspapers about Huggins's personal life or his hobbies and interests. Perhaps baseball fans did not realize it at the time, but that was because Huggins did not have a particularly interesting personal life. As Runyon had noted, the new Yankees' manager was not especially outgoing or engaging. New York reporters would soon understand that baseball was his life.

The *Reach Guide* called 1918 "a disastrous baseball season," with increased competition from the auto and cinema, plus "the culminating blow" of the Great War.[40] When Germany went on a dramatic and initially suc-cessful offensive that spring, the Allies' need for fresh troops from Amer-ica became overwhelming.[41] By summer, the war's impact—on baseball and the nation as a whole—had become enormous. The National Pastime was not considered an "essential industry"; baseball players were not exempt from the draft. They had to report for military service or to a war-related industry, such as steel factories and shipbuilding, before the end of the summer.

After a series of shifting positions by American League president Ban Johnson, the National Commission, baseball's governing body, announced that the regular season would end in early September, followed by the World Series.[42] Baseball attendance in 1918 fell by more than 40 percent from 1917, which had seen a drop of 20 percent from 1916.[43]

When Jacob Ruppert joined the American League, he was said to be for Johnson "first, last, and all the time."[44] Yet Johnson stumbled badly on the war issue when he announced late in 1917 that he would ask Secretary of War Newton Baker for draft exemptions for 288 ballplayers (18 per team) from the draft. Many owners were outraged, none more so than Jacob Ruppert. "Germany must be whipped, and whipped thoroughly," declared one of the nation's most prominent German Americans. Ruppert continued by noting sarcastically that Johnson's proposal was "a fine suggestion," while Til Huston and many others were risking their lives in France.[45] Ruppert told Damon Runyon in May 1918 that his position was simple: "The war first, baseball last."[46]

Huston had volunteered for the army back in 1917. He caused an uproar in early 1918 when he wrote an open letter from "Somewhere in France." He castigated baseball's executives for not contributing more to the Allied war effort, from 1917 World Series proceeds to volunteering their own service. "The lack of patriotism shown in baseball circles is a disgrace," he wrote.[47] There was speculation that Huston's position led to the secretary of war's ruling a few months later that baseball was not an "essential industry."[48]

Miller Huggins, though beyond draft age, volunteered for the war effort during the off-season and served as the assistant athletic director for the Pelham Bay Naval Station in the Bronx. He organized the base's sports program for about four thousand enlisted men.[49]

That summer Johnson was both indecisive and inconsistent. He then veered wildly in the other direction, suggesting that the baseball season be shut down far earlier than was necessary. Most of baseball's owners opposed his position. For almost two decades, Johnson had ruled over the American League (and all of baseball, to some extent) in an imperious style. He rarely consulted with the owners—ultimately, the people for whom he worked—before he made pronouncements and took action. Now for the first time there were serious doubts about his judgment and leadership. Red Sox owner Harry Frazee had been in open conflict with Johnson ever since he bought the Boston club after the 1916 World Series. Now Frazee had potential allies in the owners of the Yankees to lead the battle against Johnson.[50]

Frazee had not been personally vetted and approved by Johnson, who usually took an active role in the selection of new owners. Late in 1917 Frazee said that Johnson was conducting "a war of extermination against me." It was "ridiculous" that Johnson would be able to drive him out of baseball. Frazee also took the novel (but accurate) position that the league's president worked for the owners. "I am one of the eight employers of Ban Johnson," he declared.[51]

For the Yankees, 1918 was an up-and-down season, one the 1919 *Spalding Guide* called "heterogeneous."[52] The team won about half its games the first few weeks of the season. Then, starting in late May and continuing for about a month, they won two of every three games and even moved into first place for a day. But once July rolled around, the Yankees could not sustain that pace. After reaching a 36-25 record, they lost 61 percent of their remaining games and finished in fourth place.

It did not help that pitching ace Bob Shawkey enlisted in the navy and missed almost the entire season.[53] He could have avoided going to Europe by joining a shipyard, but he genuinely wanted to serve and also did not want to be booed after the war for shirking service. "Ruppert begged me not to go," Shawkey said to historian Eugene Murdock more than a half century later. "In fact, I think he was a little mad that I did."[54] Shawkey's comment suggests that Ruppert's private position on baseball and the war may have been different than his public one.

With Shawkey lost, the Yankees tried to sign veteran pitcher Chief Bender in late May. Winner of more than two hundred games, Bender was beyond draft age at thirty-four and was working as a foreman at the Hog Island Shipyard in Philadelphia. When the shipyard said it would not hold his job for him if he joined the Yankees, he declined their offer.[55]

Earlier in May, the Yankees swept a three-game series from the even-tual world champion Red Sox. But in losing, Boston had showcased a dangerous hitter of its own, Babe Ruth, whom they were in the process of converting from a pitcher to an everyday player. On May 6, playing first base against the Yankees, Ruth hit his second home run in two games. Harry Frazee was in the Polo Grounds with Jacob Ruppert that day. Rup-pert reportedly offered Frazee $150,000 for the nascent slugger during the game. Both men laughed. It may have been a joke, but as Leigh Montville says in his Ruth biography, "it was a joke to be remembered."[56]

Sam Crane, a player himself in the late nineteenth century, had seen a lot of baseball. After witnessing Ruth's blast, he wrote, "I do not think any player ever lived who could hit the ball any harder."[57] Ruth already had displayed a flair for the dramatic and a special one for doing so in New York. This was his eleventh career home run, and he had hit six of them against the Yankees—five at the Polo Grounds.[58] The previous September, pitching before a large crowd at the Polo Grounds in a game honoring soldiers, he blasted a home run and won his twenty-second game of the year.

In early June the Yankees visited St. Louis for the first time in 1918, and Del Pratt returned to face his former team. He quieted the jeers of Browns fans with a dramatic double that knocked in the game's only run. It held up to beat Urban Shocker, who had shut New York down twice in four days in May.[59] Shocker would cause the Yankees much misery in his first four years in St. Louis.

By now Huggins was tiring of Ray Caldwell's antics. The pitcher had announced that he would win thirty games in 1918; he won only nine. He pitched the Yankees into first place on July 1, but he had long stretches of ineffectiveness. Huggins assigned two detectives to Caldwell, but he would elude them and find his way into bars. Huggins later said, "Caldwell was one of the best pitchers that ever lived, but he was one of those char-acters that keep a manager in a constant worry." If he had had "a sense of responsibility and balance," lamented Huggins, Caldwell would have achieved greatness.[60]

The last month of the season was chaotic—and not just for the Yan-kees. With players leaving the game for positions in essential industries (where they often played baseball on company teams and, more important, avoided going off to war), marginal players made the rosters. "Line-ups These Days Seem Like a Joke" was the headline of a *Sporting News* article in mid-August.[61]

Just one week after he pitched the Chicago White Sox to a win over the Yankees in August, spitball pitcher Jack Quinn was awarded to the Yankees (starting with the following season, 1919), resolving a difficult and unfortunate dispute between the two teams.[62] Both clubs thought they had acquired Quinn after his Minor League team disbanded because of the war, and Ban Johnson ruled in favor of the Yankees. Quinn had seemed washed up when the Yankees sent him to the Minors back in 1912. Now, at age thirty-six, he was returning to the Majors, where he would continue to pitch for fifteen more seasons, setting age and longevity records along the way.

The most immediate impact of the ruling would be the forty-one games Quinn would win for the Yankees over the next three years. The greater long-range impact may have been its causing the final rupture in the friendship of two powerful American League men, White Sox owner Charles Comiskey and league president Ban Johnson—who ruled against his old hunting buddy. The opposition of Ruppert and Huston, Frazee, and now Comiskey to Johnson would contribute to the latter's downfall, the end of the National Commission, and the rise of the commissioner system, as personified by Judge Kenesaw Mountain Landis.

The Boston Red Sox won the pennant and went on to beat the Chicago Cubs in the World Series, with Babe Ruth winning two games and Carl Mays winning the other two, including the Red Sox's last twentieth-century World Series clincher.

In retrospect, the press had overreacted to the Yankees' late spring surge. A front-page feature in the *Sporting News* in early June, accompanied by Huggins's photo, had called him "the man of the hour in Gotham." Joe Vila went so far as to write that Huggins had replaced John McGraw as the new idol of New York fans.[63]

A few weeks later, reporters were growing critical of Huggins. Vila, in a distinct minority of columnists who would defend Huggins in his early New York years, was upset. "The real trouble with baseball in this city is the Fourth Estate. In no other major league town is such merciless hammering permitted in the daily newspapers."[64] Vila went so far as to call these reports "insane or vicious writings of alleged critics."[65]

Too much had been expected of the 1918 Yankees. Grantland Rice felt this New York team was similar to the club Huggins had taken over in St. Louis: both had little "pep" and few "hustlers." Rice suggested that Huggins would have to turn over practically the entire club before he could turn it around.[66] And that is exactly what Huggins was doing. He would go into his second season in New York with only nine of the men he had inherited a year earlier. His work of building a winner was just beginning.

The war ended in November, following a stunning and successful August counterattack by the Allies. Ruppert credited American forces in general and American sports—including baseball—in particular as having been crucial to the Allied victory. He once again made clear that his allegiance had not been divided: "There is no question that the physical and mental condition of the American troops was the deciding factor in the war, and that our boys were able to throw into the balance the fighting power which broke the deadlock, sent the Huns reeling back, and ultimately brought about their complete defeat," Ruppert said. "And the reason that the Americans, many of them but hastily trained troops, were able to make such a splendid showing was because of their athletic bringing up—their physical fitness, their ability to think quickly and to act individually in emergencies. And these qualities they acquired on the ball lots, the gridiron, and other fields upon which brain, muscle, and brawn were put to the test."[67]

Ruppert and Huggins could now focus on baseball in 1919 without major disruptions. The Colonel would return to the job at hand and make "baseball first." Just a few weeks after the conclusion of the Great War, he told a reporter that he was prepared to spend a million dollars to secure a championship.[68]

11

The Nation in Upheaval

Baseball never operates in a vacuum, and the months following the 1918 season were a whirlwind of change. The celebration of the war's ending was tempered by a worldwide influenza pandemic that seemed to have been fueled, at least in part, by the concentration and movement of troops in Europe.[1] The epidemic spread across the country in the fall of 1918, intensified by the extreme overcrowding in the military camps and the ships heading to the European front.

More American soldiers died from the flu than in the Vietnam War, most in the ten weeks starting in mid-September 1918. Almost all government officials and agencies were inexcusably silent in the early stages of the epidemic, when they should have been recommending precautionary measures. Most publicity was aimed at protecting morale and keeping the focus on the war, as it was entering a critical phase. "Don't Get Scared" and "Don't Let Flu Frighten You to Death" were typical slogans the authorities placed in newspapers across the country. But as the disease continued to spread and intensify, so did people's fears.[2]

Typical was the spread of the flu in Philadelphia in the early fall. The shortened baseball season mercifully prevented, in a small way, the spread of the disease. Had the baseball season maintained its regular 154-game schedule, both the Phillies and the Athletics would have been playing at home in September. As it was, a Liberty Loan rally to sell war bonds and raise millions of dollars was scheduled for September 28 in the heart of the city. Despite doctors' pleadings, the mayor and director of public health refused to cancel the event, saying there was no danger. The rally was held, and hundreds of thousands of people stretched over the two-mile parade route. Within forty-eight hours, the city was reeling. In just one day in early October, 759 Philadelphians died from the flu. (By comparison, before the outbreak of the disease, an average of 485 people died of all causes each week in the city.) Several hundred thousand were sick. "The city began to implode in chaos and fear."[3]

Historian John Barry captured the terror. "In Philadelphia meanwhile fear came and stayed. Death could come from anyone, anytime. People moved away from others on the sidewalk, averting conversation; if they did speak, they turned their faces away to avoid the other person's breathing. People became isolated, increasing the fear."[4]

As officials pleaded for volunteers for everything from amateur nurses to picking up the sick and the dead, few responded. Doctors and nurses were dying in large numbers too. Two of the unsung heroes in the city were former Athletics catcher Ira Thomas and his wife, Katherine. "They had no children. Day after day he carried the sick in his car to hospitals and she worked in an emergency hospital. Of course there were others. But they were few."[5]

By the start of the 1919 season, the virus had run its course. While an accurate death toll from the pandemic is hard to determine, estimates range from twenty to fifty million worldwide, more than half a million in the United States.[6] Among the fatalities were umpire Silk O'Loughlin and former Major League outfielder Larry Chappell.[7]

Recognizing the dislocation and social and labor upheaval the war had generated, baseball's owners believed a return to a full 154-game schedule would be both impractical and unprofitable. So they decided on another shortened season for 1919, only 140 games. But they badly misjudged America's return to what President Harding would call "normalcy." Attendance more than doubled from 1918.[8]

The nation was ready for a break. In *The Big Change*, Frederick Lewis Allen recalled a friend, who was a small boy in 1918, asking his father after the Armistice was signed on November 11, "Now that the war's over, what will they find to put in the newspapers?"[9] Allen noted that many dailies, especially the tabloids, began to present life in America as one of sports, crime, and sex.

Sports coverage increased dramatically in most papers. Bylines topped many articles, which often had appeared unadorned with names beforehand. In the highly competitive battles for circulation among urban papers, wrote Tom Clark, a Damon Runyon biographer, "A top bylined sports column could pull in readers like nothing else. . . . The slight edge a 'name' sportswriter could provide was worth plenty to editors and publishers, as indicated by the high salaries men like [Grantland] Rice and Runyon eventually commanded."[10] With so many dailies in New York City, all expanding their sports coverage, New York would provide a powerful platform for a big star. For the Yankees, that man was still a year away.

Prohibition was drawing closer. On January 16, 1919, Nebraska became the thirty-sixth state legislature to approve the Eighteenth Amendment. The momentum created by the Drys had been overpowering. Fueled in part by the war, though that conflict was now over, Prohibition would go into effect in one year.[11] The amendment's enabling law, the National Prohibition Act, known as the Volstead Act, defined intoxicating liquor as a beverage of more than 0.5 percent alcohol, a crippling blow to the breweries. They had hoped for a designation of 2.75 percent, which would have allowed for low-alcohol brews. Instead they were left with "near beer," which was hardly beer at all.

The Volstead Act became law in late October 1919, overriding President Woodrow Wilson's veto. It was then that Jacob Ruppert decided on a final stand against the impending law, using the courts to challenge the legality of the Volstead Act. The case went all the way to the United States Supreme Court, which ruled in a 5–4 decision that the act was legal.[12] With this ruling, Ruppert ended the fight. "I shall naturally, as a law-abiding citizen, carry out both the spirit and letter of the law," he declared.[13] From all indications, he fully complied with Prohibition for its entire duration.

There was another "culture war" going on in the United States, one that was being fought on a state-by-state basis: the battle over Sunday baseball. Conservative religious groups, known as Sabbatarians, had kept Sunday baseball illegal in New York State, primarily with the support of upstate Republicans.[14] Evangelist Billy Sunday had been one of the leaders of the opposition to Sunday ball for years. "The first day of the week is holy and such blatant sport as baseball pollutes its sanctity. Baseball is a great game and too much cannot be said in its favor, but . . . when it usurps the day of the Lord it has overstepped itself and must be curbed. One day a week is not too much to give up to higher things."[15]

A 1921 editorial in *Baseball Magazine* framed the issue in different terms.

"Do not mistake the issue, supporters of Blue Law legislation. That issue is not one of Sunday observance. It is one of freedom of belief. . . . Trampling on athletic sports may be a small issue. But trampling on human rights is a very broad issue."[16]

As with Prohibition, the country's urban and rural communities lined up on opposite sides. Yet while the Great War helped make Prohibition possible, it made the battle against Sunday baseball increasingly indefensible.[17] Ballgames were often presented as patriotic events, preceded by military marches and concerts. It was noted that soldiers and workers in war industries had to fight and toil on Sundays, and when they had time off, they deserved the opportunity to attend Sunday games. With the growth of the motion picture industry, baseball had an invaluable ally, and the forces of secularization were gaining momentum.[18]

Jacob Ruppert himself explored the possibilities the cinema presented. *Variety*, the entertainment weekly, reported that he had invested in the Film Clearing House, a distributor of independent films, in 1918. "The advent of the wealthy brewer as a film man possesses a greater significance," wrote the magazine. There was talk of a merger of film distributing companies, but it did not occur.[19]

Ruppert had been pushing for Sunday baseball since 1917. Along with Brooklyn Dodgers owner Charles Ebbets, he lobbied politicians and community leaders for legalization. Ruppert pointed out that the 1787 "blue law" banning public sports on Sundays "was enacted in response to the sentiment of a primitive community, differing vastly from that of the present age."[20] As historian Charles DeMotte pointed out, New York's German American community wanted a more "unrestricted Sunday," both because of the group's culture and because many of them resented the efforts of Protestant churches on behalf of both Prohibition and Sunday observance. "Since beer and baseball had always enjoyed a close, uneasy relationship, the issues of temperance and Sunday baseball were singular matters to New York's German community."[21]

On June 17, 1917, Ruppert had served as the master of ceremonies at the first regular-season Sunday game played at the Polo Grounds, with 25,000 fans attending. It was a festive and patriotic event with colorful flags, music, a marching band, and soldiers present. The Browns beat the Yankees in the game, whose proceeds went to the Reserve Engineers

Regiment, which was about to head overseas.[22] Yet because of political maneuvering in the state capital, regularly scheduled Sunday baseball in the city was still almost two years away.

In early 1919, state senator Jimmy Walker introduced a bill into the New York legislature to legalize Sunday baseball, similar to one that almost became law two years earlier. It passed on April 19 and was signed into law by Governor Al Smith, who was in favor of Sunday ball almost as much as he was opposed to Prohibition. Walker's sponsorship of bills to legalize boxing and Sunday baseball "permanently allied Jimmy Walker's name with ideas of sweetness and light in the minds of New York's sporting crowd."[23] He would parlay those efforts into the city's mayor's office in 1926.

On May 4, 1919, the New York Giants drew 35,000 fans for their first Sunday game since the law went into effect.[24] Another 25,000 attended a Robins game at Ebbets Field. Working-class fans who toiled six days a week—what one newspaper reporter called "holiday fans" and another described as "the bone and sinew of the country"—could now attend games regularly.[25]

The *New York Tribune's* reporter described the makeup of the Sunday crowd. "Up to yesterday, baseball in greater New York was for the semi-idle. . . . Yesterday those bleachers teemed with life. The men from the docks and the factories came and they brought their wives and children. Those dark green benches held thousands of fans who never in their lives had seen a big league game."[26]

Sunday baseball would have a profound impact on the economics of baseball in New York; overnight, the potential live gate had grown dramatically. When the Yankees did a feasibility study on building their own stadium a couple of years later, Sunday baseball played an enormous role in the analysis. With an annual attendance of 950,000—"exceeding conservative, perhaps absurdly so"—the Yankees would make a profit of $460,000 a year, the report estimated. The increased revenue "has taken baseball from the speculative category and placed it in the safe business class."[27]

The Yankees had their first Sunday game a week later. It was preceded by two days of rain, and more was forecast on Sunday. Only three thousand fans turned out, and they were rewarded with a classic pitchers' duel that had an unusual ending. Washington's Walter Johnson and New

York's Jack Quinn twirled scoreless ball for twelve innings. After a dozen years and almost four thousand innings pitched in the Major Leagues, some observers were questioning whether Johnson was still the dominant pitcher he had been. Grantland Rice put such concerns to rest. "Johnson seems to have slowed up in the same way that John D. [Rockefeller] has gone broke—both have lost something, but they still have enough."[28]

At one point in the contest, Johnson retired twenty-eight men in a row.[29] While there was still plenty of daylight remaining, umpire Bill Dinneen halted play on the advice of Ruppert. The Yankees owner mistakenly thought no game could continue past 6:00 on Sunday; in reality, the law simply required that no Sunday game could start before 2:00.

The next day, the teams played another tie game; this one went fifteen innings. The Yankees' lead-off hitter, George Halas, struck out three times. "It was taken for granted that his name is pronounced to rhyme with *alas*," wrote the *New York Times*.[30] This was one of Halas's first games in the Major Leagues. It was also one of his last, as the Yankees released him and his .091 batting average in July. Halas always appreciated the decency Huggins had shown him, including the fact that he had delivered the difficult message himself.[31] "I am grateful for the manner in which Miller Huggins told me my big league career was over," he wrote in his autobiography. "Through the years, whenever I have had to cut a player, I have tried to emulate his grace and consideration."[32] Halas would go on to a Hall of Fame football career as the owner and coach of the Chicago Bears.

12

A Season of Transition

In the spring of 1919, Boston's Babe Ruth hit a home run against the New York Giants at the Tampa Fair Grounds that was reported to have traveled five hundred feet in the air. New York reporters were already raving about the slugger's power, and this blast made such an impression on them that Fred Lieb and Frank Graham put a tape measure to the shot.[1] W. O. McGeehan wrote in the *Tribune*, "The ball sailed so high, when it came down it was coated with ice."[2] Red Sox manager Ed Barrow later told Miller Huggins about the blast. Huggins, who had had his eye on Ruth for some time, "listened intently," in the words of sportswriter Dan Daniel.[3]

A week later, the Red Sox were in Baltimore, where the Babe was born. He had a couple of remarkable games against the International League's Orioles, the team Ruth had played for in 1914. On April 19 he had six plate appearances, hitting four home runs and walking twice. The following day, he hit home runs in his first two at bats. Six home runs in six official at bats.[4] The 1919 regular season had not even started, and word about Ruth was getting around. When the former heavyweight champion James Corbett asked him how he did it, the slugger replied, "I just step in and bust the ball. That's all there is to it."[5]

The 1919 Yankees' winning percentage improved by nearly 100 points (.488 to .576) in Miller Huggins's second season. But it translated to just one place in the standings, up to third. Bob Shawkey returned to the top of the rotation and won twenty games, including ten in a row. Jack Quinn made a fine comeback, with a 2.61 earned run average and eighteen complete games. On July 9, Cleveland's Stan Coveleski ended Shawkey's streak with a shutout that knocked the Yankees out of first place. Shawkey allowed seven home runs on the season, three of which were to Babe Ruth, including a dramatic late September blast that tied the game in the ninth inning. It was the longest ever hit at the Polo Grounds. Although Ruth started fifteen games as a pitcher in 1919 (he won nine of them), he was rapidly making the transition to an everyday player, with 432 at bats in 130 of the Red Sox's 137 games.

It also was Ruth's twenty-eighth home run of the season, which broke Ned Williamson's 1884 single-season mark.[6] The game had additional long-term significance for the Yankees. Boston's young pitcher, former Brooklyn high school star Waite Hoyt, went the distance in the thirteen-inning contest. At one point, he retired twenty-seven Yankees in a row, pitching a "perfect game within a game," before giving up the losing run in the thirteenth. Hoyt probably made quite an impression on the cerebral Yankees manager, although the press mostly ignored his performance while heaping their accolades on Ruth.[7]

Frank Baker had announced his retirement after the 1918 season. He was coming off a solid season, but he had fulfilled his three-year contract and wanted to get back to his family and farm. After meeting with Huggins, however, Baker changed his mind and decided to return to the Yankees. The 1918 season had been so disrupted by the draft and the war that he wanted to give the Colonels another year. "It is because of my sense of duty and devotion to the game that I feel it almost obligatory to return," said Baker.[8] He would have another strong season in 1919. For the second time in his four years with the Yankees, he would rank second in the league in home runs, with ten.

Led by Baker, the Yankees topped the Major Leagues with forty-five home runs.[9] Their infield was one of the best in baseball, combining for twenty-eight home runs and a .291 batting average. Shortstop Roger Peckinpaugh had always been a respected glove man; now he was also hitting with authority. Peckinpaugh's .305 average was the first time in eight seasons he had batted above .270. The team's regular catcher, Muddy Ruel, a former St. Louis sandlot star with the Wabadas, was acquired from the Browns in 1917.[10] They had given up on the young backstop because of his small size.

The Yankees' pennant chances were diminished by an outfield that was slow and nondescript.[11] Ping Bodie led them with a .278 batting average and led the Murderers' Row with a modest .406 slugging percentage.

In late July, the ponderous Ping did make a dramatic ninth-inning steal of home against the league-leading White Sox, to send the game into extra innings.[12]

Except for Bodie, the Yankees were not a colorful team, and neither was their manager. Huggins had no more personality, wrote one New York reporter, "than a stark old oak tree against a gray winter sky."[13] He did not play to the "gallery"—the press or the fans; he did not believe it was in his character or his job description to make friends or build alliances.

That he was not outgoing did not mean he was not demonstrative. He had his share of run-ins with umpires and—occasionally—even fans. On May 12, in the fifteen-inning tie game with the Senators, Huggins was so upset with a steal of home call that allowed the Senators to tie the score that he pounded his fists on the chest protector of umpire Brick Owens, earning himself an ejection.[14] A couple of years earlier, with the Cardinals, Huggins had verbally attacked a fan who had been "riding" him and "almost pulled a Ty Cobb" before the umpire restrained him from going into the stands.[15]

On August 2, an enormous Polo Grounds crowd of 33,000 turned out to see the irrepressible Cobb, considered along with Pittsburgh's Honus Wagner the greatest player the game had yet seen and certainly one of the most colorful. Cobb slashed four hits and also slashed the leg of Frank Baker when he slid into third base.[16] When Cobb passed away in 1961, sportswriter Shirley Povich, who had written about him for four decades, described Cobb's brand of baseball. "To Ruth, a single was a single. For Cobb, it merely was the start of a progressive tour around the bases, with excitement at each point."[17]

Cobb played the game as well as it had ever been played. He was on his way to his twelfth batting title in 1919.[18] Only now, Babe Ruth was playing the game in a new, very different way. Why bother with a single, when one swing could generate a tour around all four bases? Added to his ability was the flair and color that he brought to the game. Damon Runyon explained that the Babe had "a knack of presenting his talent to the public in the most appealing manner. That is, he knows how to 'sell himself.' It amounts to an art."[19]

At some point, perhaps in 1919 when Ruth was still with the Red Sox, Cobb must have begun to realize that he was being challenged—if not as the game's greatest player, then surely as the game's greatest attraction. Ruth was "turning ballparks into theatres of tumult" with his long drives.[20] Looking back on the 1919 season in early 1920, the *New York Times* reported, "Ruth was such a sensation last year that he supplanted the great Ty Cobb as baseball's greatest attraction."[21]

While Cobb never would consider Ruth his equal or superior on the diamond, fans were beginning to do so, even in Cobb's hometown. In late August Boston played three games in Detroit, and Babe Ruth hit four home runs—and made headlines. Detroit papers marveled at his slugging. The *Detroit Free Press* wrote, "The equal of Ruth's homer [a bases-loaded blast over Cobb's head and the center field bleachers into the street beyond] has never been witnessed in the history of Navin field, and it is doubtful whether it ever will be." The *Detroit News* noted how opposing teams' fans went wild when he struck out and even wilder when he hit a home run. The *Detroit Journal* praised "this goliath of base ball. One hears murmurs of wonderment every time Ruth steps to the plate."[22]

The Yankees' 1919 season had an eerie similarity to 1918. The team started slowly, caught fire, and moved near the top of the standings (41-24 on July 10), and then went into a summer swoon. By July 21 they had fallen from one game out of first place to seven and a half out, and they finished third with an 80-59 record. Once again, their early summer flirtation with first place proved to be a tease.

In December 1918, the Yankees had made their first deal with Harry Frazee and the Red Sox, and it was a big one. Miller Huggins sent Ray Caldwell to Boston in a seven-man trade that brought three Boston stars to New York: pitchers Ernie Shore and Dutch Leonard and outfielder Duffy Lewis.[23] The trade had all the makings of a one-sided transaction in the Yankees' favor. The *New York Herald* called it a "master stroke" for the Yankees.[24] The *Sporting News* saluted Huggins for "electrifying the baseball world . . . in snaring three of the Red Sox most brilliant stars."[25] Shore, Leonard, and Lewis all were key contributors to the Red Sox's championship seasons of 1915 and 1916.

To the surprise of most observers, and certainly to Huggins, the trade did not benefit the Yankees. Leonard had a salary dispute and never played a game for New York.[26] Shore seemed to have lost his pitching ability during his year in the navy. Just twenty-eight years old, he won only five games in 1919 and would win only two more the rest of his career. Lewis did have a decent 1919 season, but the Yankees traded him to Washington after his injury-plagued 1920 season. His last year in the Major Leagues would be 1921.[27]

The trade had an unusual postscript. Ray Caldwell did not turn his game around in Boston, and the Red Sox released him in early August. His career seemed to have come to an end. As Fred Lieb put it, "Baseball writers wrote the swan song of a man who might have been a Mathewson, but for the temptation of the ages—wine, women, and song."[28] Just two weeks later, Tris Speaker, the player-manager of the Cleveland Indians, signed the pitcher. He used reverse psychology with Caldwell, inserting a clause in his contract that Caldwell "must get drunk" the day after he pitches.[29] On September 10, he pitched a 3–0 no-hitter against the Yankees in the Polo Grounds. Lieb called it all the more remarkable because he was thought to be finished in baseball. Sam Crane wrote that never had a ball player—even a New Yorker—received such a sustained and loud ovation as that accorded the former Yankee after the game.[30] Caldwell finished with a 5-1 record with the Indians and would win twenty games for them in 1920.

Even as the elusive first pennant slipped away from the Yankees, Huggins stuck with his veterans rather than giving playing time to his youngsters. In the *Sporting News*, John Sheridan wrote that this "Ancestor Worship" would cost Huggins the pennant. "The 'Little Old Man of the Sea,'" he wrote, "has become a confounded Confucian. He adores old-timers."[31]

The Chicago White Sox returned to the World Series for the second time in three years. Only this time, their performance—when the Black Sox scandal would surface a year later—would be immortalized. After the World Series, the Yankees again tried to acquire Joe Jackson from the Chicago White Sox, not knowing that he had been one of the Black Sox players who "threw" the Series at the behest of gamblers.[32]

The press began to question Huggins's ability as the Yankees faded that summer. A reporter from the *New York American* made the attack both personal and insulting: "We have come to the conclusion that if Huggins is a big league manager, then we are a Brisbane [Arthur Brisbane, a prominent New York newspaper editor] in the newspaper field."[33] The

Washington Post declared unequivocally that Huggins had failed, noting that his team was one of the strongest clubs ever assembled.[34]

By early September, with the Yankees more than ten games out of first place and Huggins's contract coming to an end, the name of Brooklyn's Wilbert Robinson again began surfacing in the press—as the Yankees' next manager. On September 25, the *Sporting News* ran a photo of Robinson with the words, "Picked to Lead Yankees" above it. Huggins demanded clarification of his status, and Colonel Ruppert gave him a one-year contract for the 1920 season. For the rest of his Yankees career, Huggins would have only one-year deals.[35]

Whether Huggins was retained because Robinson chose to stay in Brooklyn (where he would win his second National League pennant in five years in 1920) or because Colonel Ruppert did not want to replace him is not clear. The October 2 *Sporting News* had conflicting stories. In one, Robinson explained that he did not want to be a future source of conflict between the Yankees' owners and therefore decided to remain with the Dodgers.[36] Yet an editorial in the same issue said that Ruppert simply did not want to fire Huggins.[37] Most likely, Robinson sensed Ruppert's reluctance and the potential problems his candidacy would present. So he bowed out and remained with Brooklyn.

Some veteran sportswriters were not nearly so critical of Huggins. Hugh Fullerton said that the Yankees were simply not a great ball club, and Dan Daniel spoke out against the "propagandista," some of it outspoken and some of it "insidious," all aimed at undermining Huggins. More important, Huggins was not getting the most out of his men because "they will not get the most out of themselves. . . . Give the man a chance."[38]

Huggins's predecessor, Bill Donovan, is a mostly forgotten figure now, yet his popularity as a factor in Huggins's difficulties cannot be ignored. Damon Runyon once wrote, "No other baseball man, not even excepting Christy Mathewson, had greater personal popularity here than Bill."[39] Huggins, by contrast, projected a personality that was "almost repellant to would-be acquaintances," in Daniel's words.[40] Some observers wondered why he acted that way. "Despite the fact that he is one of the smartest men that ever trod on a ball field, and is a lawyer in the bargain," wrote a *New York Sun* columnist, "he does not seem to realize what assets popularity and publicity can be to a successful manager."[41]

Daniel wrote that Huggins had suffered from some kind of abdominal problem toward the end of the 1919 season. (Huggins told him it was probably appendicitis, but that he was not going to have it checked out until the season ended.) Daniel added that Huggins would sit in hotel lobbies for hours, in apparent pain, with his feet "doubled up."[42]

Years later, Huggins's sister recalled how fans had booed him in his early years with the Yankees and how Colonel Huston stirred up "the newspaper men" against him. "It upset my brother greatly," she said, even when the Yankees won and even though the team was improving. "'I'm not going on with this thing,'" he told her one night at the close of the season. "'The players are aware of differences of opinion between the owners. That's bad for discipline. They criticize me for what I don't do and what I can't do. It's too much and I won't stand it.'" "My advice was 'Stick it out,'" she continued. "'Make them fire you; don't quit under fire.' It was the best advice I ever gave my brother."[43]

Or was it? "This thing" began to take a toll on the Yankees' manager, who was not a strong man to begin with. And for someone whose life revolved around baseball to get so little positive reinforcement from it had to weigh on him. "Huggins was all wrinkles and bones. He was overanxious and underfed, a victim of chronic insomnia," wrote Lou Gehrig biographer Jonathan Eig. "His false teeth fit him poorly. He looked like hell and felt worse most of the time."[44]

Organized Baseball was now sharing a portion of the World Series proceeds with second- and third-place teams. An ugly dispute broke out over the distribution of their third-place money. Yankees management had decided to give some of the proceeds to players they had traded away midseason, as well as to nonplaying members of the team.[45] Del Pratt led a group that demanded the current Yankees players be given all the money. A decade later, sportswriter John Kieran called Pratt "the greatest clubhouse lawyer baseball ever knew."[46] In the end, Ruppert and Huston made up the difference with current players out of their own pockets.

John Sheridan was outraged over what he called "pitiful penuriousness . . . the most contemptible thing I have ever known in baseball." In writing about the controversy, he revealed some of the challenges Huggins faced as he tried to build a winning team. "Men with such petty spirits can't win anything. The all-star system weighed heavily against the chances of the Yankees anyhow. I have never known an all-star team to do any good. Who is to blame? Huggins? I do not think so. I cannot believe that Huggins countenanced some of the deals made by the two Colonels, who seem to be thoroughly imbued with the New York idea that money can buy anything."[47]

Miller Huggins was trying to put a winning team together quickly. Jacob Ruppert agreed, saying that the Yankees would win "on the foundation of 'made' players."[48] When Sheridan suggested Huggins may not have wanted to acquire so many stars, he may have been implying something more. Ruppert may not have been agreeing with Huggins on how to win, but rather, perhaps Huggins may have been agreeing with Ruppert. (And Ruppert's partner, Cap Huston, had shown an equal impatience and willingness to spend money for a winner.) Ruppert had operated that way in horse racing and dog shows, with "made" thoroughbreds and St. Bernards. The little Yankees manager not only had a demanding and impatient press and fan base; he also had a demanding and impatient owner.

Late in the 1919 season, the Yankees would acquire one of the game's most temperamental stars. And before the start of the 1920 season, they would purchase the biggest star in the history of the game. If the Yankees were going to win, they would do so with an all-star team. When Miller Huggins came to New York, he explained just what that would entail. "Stars help to maintain public interest in baseball just as they do on the stage. . . . But when stars interfere with the machinery of a ball club I'd rather sacrifice the star. However I expect no such difficulties here in New York."[49]

13

A Battle Leads to a War

On July 29, 1919, the Yankees sent pitchers Bob McGraw and Allen Russell, along with $40,000, to the Boston Red Sox for pitcher Carl Mays.[1] One of the best hurlers in baseball, Mays also had one of the most difficult personalities the game has ever known. From 1916 to 1918, only Walter Johnson won more games in the American League. But Mays was having a tough time in 1919, as was his team, mired in sixth place. He was getting little run support, as reflected in his 5-11 record, despite having an earned run average well below the league average.[2]

He quit the team during a game on July 13, saying he would never pitch for Boston again. The Red Sox saw an opportunity to rid themselves of a player whom manager Ed Barrow called "a chronic malcontent" and to generate both cash and young arms for owner Harry Frazee.[3] Little did anyone know that this trade, the second between Frazee and the Yankees, would set off a firestorm that would change the face of baseball's power structure.

Mays had lost all his belongings in a mysterious house fire that spring. He suspected arson but could not prove it, and the insurance had been woefully inadequate to cover his losses. Teammate Harry Hooper found Mays crying in the clubhouse the day he walked out on his team, "in a condition of great nervous tension, and indeed of practical nervous collapse."[4] Yet Mays probably evoked little sympathy, even from his teammates.

Historians Harold Seymour and Dorothy Seymour wrote that Mays had been described as "a person with a permanent toothache."[5] *Baseball Magazine*'s F. C. Lane declared, "It has been Mays' misfortune to arouse a deeper feeling of enmity in his associates on the diamond than any other player who ever lived."[6] He also had a reputation as a pitcher who threw at the heads of batters. In his rookie season, he threw at Ty Cobb, provoking a near-riot in Fenway Park.[7]

Mays made no secret of throwing at the heads of hitters who crowded the plate and tried to take away what he called his "bread and butter." He knocked his former teammate, Tris Speaker, unconscious in 1918. When Speaker came to, he rejected Mays's apology. "I worked on the same team with you long enough to know different."[8] In the mid-teens, the Red Sox pitching staff—not just Mays—had a reputation of throwing the "beanball."

Mays was outspoken about his aggressive approach. "The backbone of pitching is guts," he told Lane near the end of his career.[9] More than forty years after he joined the Yankees, Mays gave a revealing interview to Cleveland sportswriter Hal Lebovitz. "I was a fighter all my life. Everything I ever got I had to fight for. I loved to fight," he said. "Do you understand that I'd skip a meal and walk two miles for a fight?"[10]

This was the man the Yankees were adding to their clubhouse. Decades later, Waite Hoyt, who would rejoin Mays as a teammate on the Yankees before the 1921 season, told historian Eugene Murdock, "Oh, sure he threw at hitters. . . . He was a trouble-maker. . . . But he was a great pitcher, there's no doubt about it."[11] The man who won sixty-one games for Boston in the past three years would win sixty-two games in just over two seasons, after his arrival in New York.

However, despite the announcement of the trade, Mays was not yet a Yankee. Ban Johnson was in St. Louis having breakfast at the home of Taylor Spink, the publisher of the *Sporting News*, when he read of the trade in the morning paper. "Johnson was furious; I thought he would hit the ceiling," Spink later wrote. "I never saw him so riled."[12] Johnson overruled the trade and ordered Mays suspended. He explained that since Frazee did not suspend his recalcitrant pitcher for leaving his team, it was now Johnson's duty as league president to do so. A contract-breaker simply could not be rewarded by forcing a trade—in this case, to a pennant contender.

Frazee, Johnson's foe, was benefitting by getting rid of a troublesome player and receiving both cash and players in return, which made Johnson's action more understandable. Until Frazee had bought the Red Sox late in 1916, Johnson never had an American League owner challenge his authority. From the start, Johnson saw Frazee as independent and therefore unpredictable, not beholden to him in any way. Colonel Huston claimed that Johnson once told him, "I am going to drive that little rat out of baseball."[13] Perhaps by stopping this trade he could force Frazee to sell.[14] Only now he was also crossing Til Huston and Jacob Ruppert, both determined and deep-pocketed.

Johnson's biographer, Eugene Murdock, captured his subject's personality. "It was his nature to demand subservience. He was unused to the art of compromise, so essential to the proper functioning of his own office. Disagreements over policy matters frequently escalated into personal jealousies, which would quickly pass the point of recall."[15] It is not surprising that Ruppert found this man so difficult to work with.

Huston and Ban Johnson, both from Cincinnati, had a mutual hostility that went back many years, though its source remains unclear. (Huston and Frazee, by contrast, were close friends.) Upon hearing of Mays's suspension, Huston promised Johnson "one of the most interesting baseball fights this game ever has seen."[16] Initially, Colonel Ruppert thought that his partner was being overly negative and that Johnson would be open to reason. As John Kieran wrote upon Huston's death, "The old soldier went roaring into that battle, dragging Colonel Ruppert with him."[17] After all, thought Ruppert, other teams had been negotiating for Mays's services for two weeks, and Johnson had taken no action.

Ruppert sent a telegram to Johnson requesting that he allow the trade. While Ruppert's telegram was "in the friendliest spirit," he did not preclude any options, noting that the Yankees were not waiving their legal rights.[18] Almost twenty years later, Ruppert said that he and Colonel Huston "were in the wrong" in dealing for Mays, since "a player under suspension cannot be traded." Actually, Mays was not suspended until after the Yankees acquired him.[19] However, a few days before the trade, Johnson had warned teams not to negotiate for Mays.

Johnson agreed to meet the Colonels, but their August 3 session in New York City became heated and resolved nothing. The Yankees' owners believed that Johnson had a financial interest in the Cleveland Indians, one of the teams that had been negotiating for Mays. They felt his conflict of interest had facilitated the Indians landing Tris Speaker a few years earlier.[20] Now that Cleveland had not acquired Mays, the Colonels felt that Johnson's duplicitous motives were behind the Mays suspension.

In fairness to Johnson, he had never made secret that he was a silent investor in the Indians, not to enrich himself but rather to save the franchise. "He was there simply to keep baseball alive in Cleveland," wrote Murdock.[21]

After the meeting, Huston called Johnson a "carbuncle" that needed to be removed from the league.[22] He said that Ruppert "thought diplomacy would prevail, but after Ban practically insulted him with those short answers, Jake was three times as tough as me." Ruppert was blunt in his reaction to Johnson's high-handedness. "I'll spend a million dollars if I have to but I'll beat him."[23]

Baseball observers sensed that a significant shift in the power structure of the American League was taking place. As the *New York World* wrote, Johnson thought "he was fielding an ordinary pop fly from Col. Ruppert, and discovered it to be a live, sputtering whizz-bang that knocked the ground from under him and left him dazed."[24]

The Yankees' owners went to the New York State Supreme Court and secured a temporary injunction from Justice Robert F. Wagner, allowing Mays to play for the Yankees.[25] Baseball had prided itself in staying out of the courts and keeping the courts out of baseball, but Johnson had encouraged a dangerous break with that precedent a year earlier. He had encouraged Athletics owner Connie Mack to dispute in court a National Commission ruling that had awarded a contested player to another team.[26]

The following day, August 7, the umpires at the Polo Grounds were presented with a copy of the injunction, and Carl Mays pitched a six-hitter for the Yankees to beat the Browns. He would fashion a 9-3 record with New York over the last two months of the 1919 season.[27] He was a key factor in the Yankees edging the Tigers for third place by a half-game. He had demonstrated he was still one of the game's best pitchers.

Articles and editorials in the *Sporting News* supported Johnson's position in the dispute.[28] Typical was an October 2 column disparaging the Yankees' owners. "The efforts of this little group of short-visioned, strong-lunged magnates who are threatening to 'drive' President Ban Johnson out of baseball are certain to prove as futile as they are foolish."[29] Sportswriters

Joe Vila and John Sheridan were particularly passionate in their support of Johnson and all the good he had done for the game. They were equally critical of the Yankees' owners for dragging baseball into the courts and "trying to smear Johnson with a technical, legal decision."[30]

On October 25, Justice Wagner granted the Yankees a permanent injunction in the Mays case, delivering a stunning blow to Johnson. The suspension, Wagner ruled, threatened contract and property rights of the team owners, was arbitrary, and was driven by animosity toward Harry Frazee. He also noted that the real "sufferer" was the New York club, which was guilty of no offense.[31]

Colonel Huston had testified in Wagner's courtroom about Johnson's behavior. "It was against such autocratic and Kaiser-like acts as those that our American Army went to France to fight." He also noted that the Yankees had acquired Frank Baker—who refused to play for his team (the Athletics) in 1915 and was then sold to the Yankees—with no action taken by the league president.[32]

Colonel Ruppert made it clear that the battle was about much more than Carl Mays. He told Sid Mercer, "The league isn't big enough for us both. For the good of the game Johnson must go. He's making a joke of the American League by carrying his animosities into such petty channels. Johnson is a positive menace to baseball, and if the American League is to survive, he must be curbed. So far I have only tried to protect the interests of the New York club, but now I'll go the limit. This man, I believe, would wreck the league to serve his own ends."[33]

When the National Commission decided to withhold third-place money from the Yankees (claiming their finish had been tainted by the Mays victories), the battle was renewed. Eugene Murdock wrote that "what unfolded [on December 10 in New York City] was the bitterest league meeting in history."[34] Ruppert could be heard screaming from behind closed doors, "You can't drive us out of baseball!"

Johnson had the support of five of the league's eight owners and outvoted the three "Insurrectos," Ruppert-Huston, Frazee, and Charles Comiskey of the White Sox, on every issue in contention. Connie Mack, one of the "Loyal Five," told reporters, "The Yankees' owners are making a lot of trouble for a team which has no ball park. The American League would be better off without them."[35]

Huston could not resist a retort. Noting that Mack had broken up his great club after winning the pennant in 1914 and had had terrible teams since then, he compared the A's owner to the little boy who took a watch apart and could not put it back together. "He [Mack] says we have a ball club but no ball park. He has a ball park but no ball club."[36]

Huston declared, "They rode over us with a steam roller, and we are going to send the steam roller right back at them."[37] That the Yankees' owners soon did. They served Johnson with three lawsuits for damages they suffered from the Mays conflict. A few weeks later, they consolidated the suits into one $500,000 lawsuit for damages from Johnson's efforts to drive them out of baseball and to cancel the Yankees' Polo Grounds lease.[38]

The *Sporting News*, the voice of Organized Baseball, continued to defend Johnson, one of the leaders of the game for almost two decades. A January 1920 article in the weekly, for example, said the Yankees' owners "have lost sight of the Mays case altogether, and that their sole object is the persecution and harassment of President Johnson."[39]

While the Yankees' battles with Johnson played out in the courts and the press, there was much more to the conflict beneath the surface. On November 5, 1919, Huston wrote Comiskey that Johnson had leaked the location of a possible ballpark for the Yankees and was killing any deal they could make in order to force them to sell. "This fellow assuredly has become both a knave and crazy and must be eliminated at all costs or all our property will become worthless." Huston also testified before Justice Wagner that earlier in the 1919 season, he had asked Frazee whether he would consider selling or trading Babe Ruth. (Frazee had replied that Ruth was not available.) Huston then had asked Johnson his opinion of the Babe. Within two days, Frazee said, the Indians—the team Johnson had an interest in—contacted him about Ruth's availability.[40]

While the battle for control of the American League was raging, another governance conflict was unfolding: the unraveling of the National Commission. Baseball's governing body consisted of the presidents of the two Major Leagues and the Commission's president, Garry Herrmann, the owner of the National League's Cincinnati Reds. This structure seemed to favor that league, which had two of the three seats on the body. Yet Herrmann had been a friend of Johnson's and often deferred to him. As the *New York Sun* wrote in early 1919, "For years it has been common talk in baseball that Herrmann is a mere figurehead on the commission and is completely swayed by the domineering personality of Johnson."[41]

Ever since Herrmann had cast the deciding vote to award George Sisler to the American League's St. Louis Browns in January 1915, Pittsburgh's owner Barney Dreyfuss had campaigned to replace Herrmann.[42] Johnson had helped save Herrmann's job with a dramatic plea in January 1919. Now, a year later, with so many problems swirling around Johnson, he was unable to protect Herrmann. At the owners' meetings of February 1920 in Chicago, Herrmann's resignation became official.[43]

While an owners' committee had been assigned the task of finding a new chairman a year earlier, it had made little progress because of Johnson's lack of cooperation. Now, with Herrmann's departure, the dysfunctional Commission became nonexistent for 1920. On January 15, 1920, the *Sporting News* featured Chicago federal judge Kenesaw Mountain Landis on the front page, writing, "He is declared to be just the man to bring peace and order in Organized Baseball—a man who will have the respect of magnates, players and public in all leagues."[44] Landis would be selected as baseball's commissioner, but not for another ten months.

At those same meetings, the American League owners had a contentious all-night gathering on February 10. Reports said that Ruppert almost came to blows with Phil Ball, the owner of the St. Louis Browns and Johnson's biggest supporter.[45] But in the face of the determined fight of the Colonels (who had named the Loyal Five as parties in the $500,000 lawsuit), those owners' support of Johnson melted away, and as morning approached, a settlement was reached. In exchange for the Yankees dropping their lawsuits, Mays was officially reinstated, and the Yankees were awarded third place (and third-place money) for the 1919 season. As a final insult to Johnson, Ruppert would be one of two owners on a "Board of Review" that would examine all fines of $100 or more and all suspensions of ten days or more.

But that was not all. The Board of Review had the authority to look into "any act that any member feels affects his constitutional rights as a member of the association."[46] The only consolation for Johnson was that he still had his job, but "Ban Johnson, sans power, is rather a sad spectacle," wrote Damon Runyon. "It is like ham and eggs, without the ham."[47] Johnson quietly left the meeting, almost unnoticed. "Nobody gave him a thought," Monitor of the *World* wrote. "The world quickly forgets a loser."[48]

The *Sporting News* maintained the fiction that the outcome was not a defeat for Johnson. Joe Vila wrote, "Johnson's authority hasn't been curtailed to a degree that he now is merely a figure-head." An editorial went further. "Of course everybody knows it was a substantial victory for Johnson."[49] Murdock was more blunt—and accurate—in his Johnson biography more than sixty years later. "There is little question that it was a crushing blow for the former czar."[50]

This had to be an immensely satisfying day for Jacob Ruppert. Not only was he victorious in the Chicago showdown, but he was also winning competitions of a different sort back home in New York City. At the Westminster Kennel Club Dog Show on February 11, his St. Bernards Oh Boy and Bulgari captured awards.

Throughout the Mays controversy, Miller Huggins was silent. He was in an awkward position, a classic "man in the middle." He probably had mixed feelings at best about acquiring Mays, a talented pitcher but a potentially disruptive team member. When John Sheridan wrote in the *Sporting News* that he did not think Huggins agreed with some of the deals the two Colonels made, the Mays trade was likely one of them.[51]

Further complicating matters for Huggins was that, in some ways, he was "Johnson's man." The league president was the driving force behind Huggins's move to New York. Huston never embraced Miller Huggins as Yankees manager when his friend Wilbert Robinson did not get the job. But the Huston-Johnson hostility was another reason for Huston's fierce opposition to Huggins. Frank Graham explained that Huston had "nothing personally against Hug, but merely was striking through him at Johnson, whom he hated."[52] Westbrook Pegler noted that Huston viewed Huggins as "a human zero mark" because Huggins did not "detest" Johnson.[53] The Yankees' manager may have been collateral damage in the bitter feud.

After Huggins's death, Joe Vila wrote, "Huggins never forgot Ban Johnson. He sought the advice of the former head of the American League on numerous occasions, and when Johnson virtually was forced into retirement, the Yankees' little manager expressed deep regret."[54]

14

A Home Is No Longer a Home

The Yankees played their home games at the Polo Grounds, the ballpark of the New York Giants, beginning in 1913. Their departure to a stadium of their own is a complex story that remains shrouded in mystery.

During a December 1919 court hearing for the Carl Mays case, the Yankees' owners presented excerpts from a "personal and confidential" letter Ban Johnson had written to the Loyal Five on August 6, 1919. (The Yankees had somehow "obtained" it from Johnson's files.) "It is my judgment," wrote Johnson, "that they [Ruppert and Huston] should be retired from our organization. . . . I am sure that other people can be interested in the proposition and that a satisfactory arrangement [to play at the Polo Grounds] can be made with the present owners of the New York National League club."[1] The Colonels used the letter to buttress their argument that Johnson was conspiring to push them out of baseball.

Yet not only had the letter been secured illicitly but the portions released were taken out of context. Johnson emphatically denied the charge and provided the context.[2] A few weeks later, Phil Ball, St. Louis Browns owner and Johnson's biggest supporter, released the full letter. It cast the previously released excerpt in a very different light.[3] Johnson's interest in "retiring" the Yankees' owners was in response to their desire to get out of baseball, Johnson said. Back in the summer of 1918, a year before the Carl Mays case, the Yankees received a "peremptory notice" from the Giants to leave the Polo Grounds (after the 1920 season, apparently). Giants owner Charles Stoneham was supposedly furious with Til Huston's letters from France, criticizing baseball executives for not supporting the war.

Faced with the prospect of having no ballpark and a war that had no end in sight, the Yankees' owners felt they were "doomed to suffer almost unbearable losses." Under those circumstances, they were unwilling to spend money on a new ballpark. "They insisted it was quite desirable the franchise be taken off their hands," Johnson elaborated. "They declared the stock of the New York club was for sale and I could have it on five minutes' notice for $600,000."[4] In the August 6 letter, Johnson went on, "The following day they 'buckled up' on the offer they made to me, and said they were going to remain in baseball." It was in this context that Johnson wrote that the Colonels should be "retired." Johnson concluded, "We all appreciate how impossible they are."[5] Johnson may not have fully realized just how "impossible" they would become. On the day he wrote the letter, Ruppert and Huston went to court to get the temporary Carl Mays injunction from Justice Wagner. They secured it the following day. They never publicly denied Johnson's account.

There are some puzzling aspects to Johnson's story. He talks about the Yankees' owners wanting "out" in the summer of 1918, yet he wrote the letter in August 1919. Moreover, since Stoneham did not buy the Giants until January 1919, the eviction notice would have been written by the previous Giants' owners. If indeed Stoneham had served the eviction notice, as Johnson said, would he have done so and sacrificed $65,000 annual rent because of Huston's war accusations from the previous year, before he bought the Giants?

Johnson's role in the threatened loss of the Polo Grounds for the Yankees remains murky. One thing is clear: this matter arose before the Yankees acquired Babe Ruth, though it would emerge again in 1920. Evidence suggests that Johnson had persuaded the Giants to cancel the Yankees' lease and let him control it in the league's name.[6] "If you haven't got any park you can't play in the league. You forfeit the franchise," he told the Yankees' owners.[7] In response to this move, Ruppert threatened to build a ballpark that would seat only 1,500 fans on property he owned in Manhattan between Madison and Fifth Avenues, between 102nd and 103rd streets. He told Johnson, "If you press us to the wall we will play Yankee games where every hit will be a home run. Your league will become the laughing stock of the country."[8]

At times Ruppert and Huston had expressed interest in building their own ballpark. At other times, they did not want to make the enormous cash outlay for a new stadium. Stoneham surely found the rent he received from the Yankees very attractive, yet he probably wanted the Giants alone to play in the Polo Grounds. While the Yankees' owners were frustrated with the year-to-year leverage their landlord maintained over them, Stoneham in turn was irritated by the Colonels' ongoing flirtation with exiting the Polo Grounds.

The controversy over the Polo Grounds made headlines on May 15, 1920, when newspapers reported that the Giants had notified the Yankees they would no longer share the ballpark with the American Leaguers after 1920.[9] Ruppert responded by claiming such a move was in violation of a verbal agreement the Yankees had with the previous owners of the Giants, which, he said, was part of the January 1916 Federal League settlement.

Ruppert's assertion raises a number of questions. First, what did such a Giants-Yankees agreement have to do with the Federal League war? Second, why would Ruppert not have gotten such an agreement in writing? Third, in early 1916, Til Huston stated that the Yankees had only a year-to-year lease at the Polo Grounds.[10] And Harry Hempstead, the owner of the Giants at the time, said a long-term agreement was never finalized because the two clubs could not agree on terms.[11] However, the former head of the National Commission, Garry Herrmann, who played a key role in the Federal League settlement, confirmed Ruppert's contention. He noted that Ban Johnson refused to sign the settlement until the Yankees received that Polo Grounds promise.[12]

Some sportswriters claimed this eviction notice was given because of jealousy over Babe Ruth, who joined the Yankees that season, and the crowds he was drawing. Ruth pulled a muscle in his ribcage early in the season, missed a few April games, and was hitting only .226 at the end of the month. The Babe did not hit his first Polo Grounds home run until May 1, yet he hit five there in the first two weeks of May.

Other observers, such as Fred Lieb, felt the Giants' move may have been based on a desire for more lucrative Sunday games at the Polo Grounds, dates they were forced to share with the Yankees. Only that could explain the Giants giving up $65,000 a year in rent, he wrote. With Sunday baseball now legal in New York, so the thinking went, if the Yankees had their own ballpark, the Giants would have many more Sunday dates. Even when the Giants were on the road in Boston or Philadelphia, which still banned

Sunday baseball, they could return to the Polo Grounds for Sunday games with the Braves or the Phillies, if the Yankees were not playing there.[13]

But that was not and would not be the case. Sid Mercer explained that Organized Baseball avoided scheduling conflicting dates in the same city, especially if one team did not want them.[14] That would be the case in New York City, as it was in Boston, Chicago, Philadelphia, and St. Louis. A review of the Sunday dates of the Giants and Yankees from 1921 to 1924—two years before and after the opening of Yankee Stadium— shows that the Giants did not gain Sunday dates after the Yankees had left the Polo Grounds.[15]

For some reason, the Brooklyn Dodgers were more fortunate. Schedulers considered Brooklyn, a borough of New York City since 1898, as a separate city, and the Dodgers had many home games when the Yankees were playing at home in the early 1920s.[16] Since the Giants likely knew they would not gain additional Sunday home games, their decision was probably not financial. The reason for the Yankees' eventual departure from the Polo Grounds may have been more fundamental. As Mercer explained, "The men who operate the National League team want the place to themselves. The Giants have long been an institution in New York and would be in danger of losing their identity as the 'home team' if they should encounter a bad season while the Yankees were winning."[17]

Lieb made the same point. With the rising popularity of the Yankees, the Giants' owners "may have feared that the Polo Grounds might become known as the home of the Yankees rather than that of the Giants."[18] Those Giants would have included their manager and part-owner, John McGraw, who had enjoyed being the city's dominant baseball figure for a decade and a half.

During the 1919 season, when Ruth hit a record-breaking twenty-nine home runs, he and his Red Sox drew huge crowds at the Polo Grounds, and the New York press was in awe of the slugger's performances. Boston drew almost 100,000 fans to the Polo Grounds over four days in June.[19] The *Times* saluted "the mighty Ruth," who "has struck terror in the heart of many a pitcher."[20] In September, the paper described him as "the batting sensation of all time."[21]

Surely the proud and arrogant McGraw had taken notice. Now that

Ruth was a Yankee, playing his home games in the Polo Grounds, his surging popularity grated on McGraw even more. As if to underline the Giants' concern, the Yankees drew more than 60,000 fans for two games at the Polo Grounds in mid-May, just after the Giants notified them that they had to leave.[22]

Stoneham said that in the summer of 1919, the Yankees had requested a long-term lease for the Polo Grounds, or else they would build their own ballpark. The Giants turned them down. "We believed it would be a good thing for baseball if they built their own grounds." Stoneham said the Yankees must have had a change of heart because in May 1920, they again raised the issue of a long-term lease. Stoneham then met with McGraw to review the Giants' position—as the Babe was hitting three home runs in two days—and the Giants reiterated their position. "New York is a big city," said Stoneham, "and there is ample room for another plant of this kind."[23]

When Ruppert looked back on his career in a 1938 radio interview, he confirmed that he had approached Stoneham about a long-term agreement to share the Polo Grounds because "I felt that New York did not need two ball parks." Stoneham had replied, "Colonel, I like you. I'd be willing to do anything to keep you at our park. But McGraw and Judge [New York City magistrate and Giants treasurer Francis X.] McQuade object." Ruppert then proposed going in with Stoneham as an equal partner in a new stadium for 100,000 fans on the Polo Grounds site. When he did not get agreement to that, Ruppert said that he and Huston closed the deal on the future site of Yankee Stadium.[24] "We felt like outsiders and we had very little security," said Ruppert in the 1938 radio interview. "We never knew when the arrangements might be terminated, and if they were, our team would be homeless."[25] Ruppert was ready to move on. "If the Giants do not want us any longer on the Polo Grounds there is no use trying to stay around where one is not wanted," he had said in 1920.[26] Colonel Huston was in complete agreement. Yet while the Yankees maintained a brave front, noting they had options on a few locations, it would have been nearly impossible for them to have their own stadium built in time for the 1921 season.

On May 21, 1920, a week after they had announced the eviction of the Yankees for 1921, the Giants agreed to extend the Yankees' lease for two more seasons, at a significant increase in rent, from $65,000 to $100,000. Garry Herrmann, who had played key roles in settling both the American League–National League and Federal League wars, helped facilitate the compromise.[27] Apparently so did Ban Johnson, who must have had a change of heart.[28]

Part 4

RUTH AND BARROW ARRIVE

15

Buying the Babe

Jacob Ruppert had two businesses, both of which he loved: his brewery and his baseball team. Both brought him great joy throughout his life, and occasionally, though far less often, they brought him disappointment. On January 5, 1920, he experienced both those emotions full force: a low for his brewery and a high for his baseball team. That day, the Supreme Court, in a 5–4 ruling, upheld as constitutional the wartime prohibition sections of the Volstead Act.[1] Ruppert had led the nation's brewers in challenging the legislation.[2] It was also the day Ruppert announced that he and Colonel Huston had purchased Babe Ruth from the Boston Red Sox. The move would not only radically transform the Yankees but also accelerate the change in the way baseball would be played. The headline in that day's *New York Times*, trumpeting the purchase, was typical. "Ruth Bought by New York Americans for $125,000, Highest Price in Baseball's Annals," it blared.[3]

Ruppert appeared confident that by landing the game's greatest young star, he had assured his team's success for years to come.

> It is not only our intention, but a strong life purpose, moreover, to give the loyal American League fans of greater New York an opportunity to root for our team in a world's series. We are going to give them a pennant winner, no matter what the cost. I think the addition of Ruth to our forces should [be] held greatly along those general lines. Yet the fans can rest assured we by no means intend to stop there. Eventually we are going to have the best team that has ever been seen anywhere.[4]

A reporter asked Ruppert if he had notified Ban Johnson, who had been the two Colonels' and Frazee's antagonist in the Carl Mays contretemps of the previous summer. "No, we haven't advised Ban Johnson of the deal as yet. We shall let him know about it tomorrow," Ruppert responded. "However, what Ban Johnson thinks of the deal doesn't particularly interest us. Baseball fans already know he is one bogey man we are no longer afraid of. Whether Mr. Johnson approves or disapproves of our deal, Ruth will be in our opening day lineup. I can promise that much to our fans."[5]

The *Times* applauded Ruth's coming to New York and also predicted a bright future for the Yankees. "If the club, strengthened by Ruth and other players the owners have in mind, does not carry off the flag, it will not be the fault of the owners," it wrote."[6] Other newspapers expressed similar sentiments. While not saying explicitly whose "fault" failure would be, clearly fingers would be pointed at manager Miller Huggins if the Yankees did not win the 1920 pennant.

However, not everyone looked on the biggest transaction in baseball history with approval. One *Times* writer warned that "the concentration of baseball talent in the largest cities, which can afford to pay the highest prices for it, was a bad thing for the game. It is still worse," he added, "to give a valuable player stranded with a weak club the idea that if he holds out for an imposing salary he can get somebody in New York or Chicago to buy his services."[7] Ruppert would hear such criticism, whether overt or covert, for the rest of his life. His answer was always a variation of one he gave to the *Sporting News* in 1932. "I found out a long time ago that there is no charity in baseball and that every club owner must make his own fight for existence."[8]

Ruth's sale from the Red Sox to the Yankees had its genesis two years earlier, when Boston manager Ed Barrow made the bold decision to move Ruth from the mound to the outfield. By the end of the 1919 season, Ruth had completed the transition from one of baseball's best left-handed pitchers to its greatest-ever power hitter. The twenty-four-year-old slugger had set Major League records in home runs (29) and slugging percentage (.657), while also leading the American League in runs batted in (114) and runs scored (103). Moreover, he was drawing people to the ballpark, something he had begun to do even as a pitcher.

In his six seasons with Boston, Ruth had twice won twenty games and had an 89-46 record with a 2.19 earned run average. In 1916, he defeated

Walter Johnson four times, including a 1–0 decision that went thirteen innings. "When he pitched against Walter Johnson, the Red Sox would take out ads in the paper: 'Babe Ruth vs. Walter Johnson, today at Fenway,'" said Richard Johnson, curator of the Sports Museum of New England. "The Red Sox started to promote him, and there was a real spike in attendance."[9]

Ruth's leading the Major Leagues in home runs in 1918 and 1919 had been accompanied by an enormous rise in his fame and popularity.[10] He had now surpassed Ty Cobb as the game's greatest attraction. And he knew it. "A lot of people think that Ruth was up in Boston, and then he came to the Yankees and became famous," said Ruth biographer Robert Creamer. "But he was really famous when he was still with Boston. He was so outsized; I mean baseball changed completely when he started hitting the home runs. It took a few years for a lot of the sluggers to get in the general area with him, but he was so far ahead."[11]

By swinging for the fences from the end of the bat, the Babe was replacing the hitting style of the Deadball Era, when almost everyone choked up on the bat. Ruth was showing the way and setting an example, and other batters would begin to emulate him. Moreover, managers had begun to adjust their tactics, playing for the big inning rather than trying to scratch out a run with a bunt and a stolen base.

The fans were turning out not only in Boston, but in the league's seven other cities, and the Babe wanted Red Sox owner Harry Frazee to pay him accordingly. Ruth had just completed the first year of a three-year deal calling for a salary of $10,000 per year. But after completing his record-breaking season, and aware of his extraordinary effect on attendance, he wanted the Red Sox to double his yearly salary to $20,000 for 1920 and 1921, the contract's two remaining seasons.[12] When Frazee refused to renegotiate, and Ruth made a half-hearted threat to quit the game, Frazee began to look for a buyer. He now felt Ruth's attempt to renegotiate his contract had made his continued employment with the Red Sox untenable. "When Ruth announced that he was not going to play for the figures on his contract, I lost all respect for him as a player and a man," Frazee said.[13]

Though he kept a home in Boston, Frazee's main residence was in Manhattan, where he lived with his wife, Elsie, and their son at 565 Park Avenue, between East 62nd and East 63rd Streets. His office was also in

Manhattan, within walking distance of the Broadway theaters where his shows were performed. It was also within walking distance of the Yankees' offices. "The best thing about Boston is the train ride back to New York," he sometimes joked.[14]

The Yankees had long coveted Ruth. Ruppert had been impressed when he saw him in spring training or as a visiting player, and Huggins told the Yankees' owners that if Ruth were to become available, they should try to acquire him, whatever the cost. Huggins later told Ruppert that Frazee would consider $100,000 a fair price for Ruth. "Huggins, you are crazy," exclaimed Ruppert, "and this man Frazee is even crazier. Who ever heard of a ball player being worth $100,000 in cash?" Huggins was quick with his reply. "Colonel, take my advice. Buy Ruth. Frazee is crazy, yes. He's crazy to let you have the Babe for so little."[15]

So when the opportunity to acquire Ruth arose, the Colonels acted. The sale was agreed to and formally signed on December 26, 1919, though not officially announced until ten days later.

Ruth was in Los Angeles when Johnny Igoe, his business manager, telegraphed him with the news of his sale to New York. He sent a telegram back to Igoe. "Will not play anywhere but Boston. Will leave for the East Monday." Later, perhaps after learning that Ruppert was glad to meet his salary request, Ruth changed his mind about playing in New York. Huggins met with him in California and confirmed that the Babe, despite his supposed initial reluctance, was glad to be joining the Yankees. "I'm not surprised," Ruth said of his sale to New York. "When I made my demand on the Red Sox for $20,000 a year I had an idea they would choose to sell me . . . and I knew the Yankees were the most probable purchasers in that event."[16]

"Ruth knew his value," historian Richard Johnson said. "This was a guy who certainly understood there was money to be made and glory to be gained in New York."[17] Recounting the deal more than ten years later, Ruppert praised Huggins's early recognition of just how great a force Ruth would be. "I doubt if anybody except Huggins had any foreknowledge of just how predominant Ruth would become in the baseball world." Huggins was a product of the Deadball Era, Ruppert pointed out. Yet he "foresaw that the game of baseball was entering an era when batting would be the predominant feature."[18]

Ruth, however, was not impressed with his new manager's predictive powers, focusing instead on his unimpressive physical stature. He later said of meeting Huggins, "I wondered how such a little guy could ever have been a good ballplayer. He didn't seem strong enough to swing a bat, or live through a spiking job."[19] Meanwhile, Huggins was receiving "condolences" from people in Boston and elsewhere, warning of how difficult Ruth would be to manage. Noting that Barrow could not get along with him in Boston, sportswriter Ed Fitz Gerald wrote, "Poor Miller Huggins is apt to be bald-headed before the season closes."[20]

Ruppert said Frazee had asked $450,000 for Ruth. "The bank held a lot of his notes and could put him in a tight place if they chose to call," Ruppert said. "Only about $125,000 of the $450,000 he wanted was outright purchase money. About $325,000 was to be applied as a mortgage on Fenway Park. . . . It would be a sort of loan, but it would take care of Frazee's notes."[21] Huston agreed to the purchase price, but balked at the mortgage-loan deal, so Ruppert personally covered the mortgage part of the transaction. "In effect," wrote Yankees historian Marty Appel, "the Colonels would be the mortgage holders on Fenway. The loan is what put the deal over the top."[22]

Frazee was fully aware of how great a ballplayer Ruth was and the likely possibility he would become even greater. But the Red Sox had won pennants in 1916 and 1918 after trading the great Tris Speaker. He assumed they would win again, this time with players he could buy with money acquired from the sale of Ruth.[23] Additionally Frazee claimed that having Ruth on his team presented problems: "It would have been impossible to start next season with Ruth and have a smooth working machine."[24] According to Frazee, "Ruth had become simply impossible and the Boston club would no longer put up with his eccentricities. . . . Twice during the past two seasons, Babe has jumped the club and revolted. He refused to obey orders of the manager."[25]

Perhaps he had, but when Frazee informed manager Ed Barrow he was going to sell Ruth to the Yankees, Barrow had replied: "I thought as much. I could feel it in my bones. But you ought to know that you're making a mistake."[26]

In a 1943 article, Fred Lieb described the conversation between the owner and his manager. "I'm sorry, Ed, but I had to do it—it was the only way I had of saving the club," explained Frazee. "We'll get a few players from the Yankees."

"The hell with the kind of players they'll give us," said Barrow. "They made me look ridiculous when I had to take pitchers Bob McGraw and Allen Russell in the Mays deal last year. I don't want to look silly again by taking some bushers for a player like Ruth." [27]

Despite his justifications for the sale, Frazee was faced with a public relations debacle as he attempted to pacify infuriated Bostonians. To this day, Harry Frazee has few defenders in Boston. "History has maligned my great-grandfather," said Max Frazee in July 2003, during a panel discussion at Manhattan's Museum of American Folk Art. According to Max, Harry sold Ruth mostly because of the Babe's misbehavior and salary demands. Harry could afford to pay Ruth what he wanted, said Max, but he could not stand him.[28]

Yet a 2008 article by Daniel Levitt, Mark Armour, and Matthew Levitt makes a very strong case for the sale being motivated strictly because of Frazee's shaky financial status. All parties to the transaction—including Frazee himself—consistently maintained that Frazee needed money. Ruppert and Huston each stated that Frazee sold Ruth because he needed the funds. Both, particularly Huston, were close friends of Frazee and were well acquainted with his financial situation. "With his financial squeeze mounting," the authors wrote, "on January 5, 1920, Frazee announced the notorious sale of Babe Ruth to the New York Yankees. In return, Frazee received the record sum of $100,000: $25,000 up front and three promissory notes of $25,000 each at a 6 percent interest rate, due in November 1920, 1921, and 1922. In addition, Ruppert gave Frazee a three-month commitment that he would lend him $300,000 to be secured by a first mortgage on Fenway Park."[29]

Whatever Frazee's reason for doing it, Boston's sale of Babe Ruth to the Yankees remains the most significant player transaction in American sports history. Legends have grown up around it, and it would affect the fortunes of both teams for decades to come. Ruth attained near-mythical status in New York, while also leading the Yankees to seven pennants and four World Series titles before they unceremoniously released him following the 1934 season.

The Red Sox, meanwhile, did not bounce back after selling Ruth, as they had after trading Speaker. Frazee did not use the money he got from Ruppert and Huston to bring new and better players to Boston. The club that Ruth helped lead to a world championship in 1918 would not finish in the first division again until 1934, would not win another pennant until 1946, and would not win another World Series until 2004.

In 1929, Babe Ruth looked back at the fortuitous timing of his career evolution. "I've been a pretty lucky fellow. . . . In the old days when defense was the big thing I was a pitcher. . . . And when things switched over and hitting became the rage Ed Barrow, then managing the Red Sox, turned me into an outfielder and gave me a chance to 'take my cut' with the rest of the sluggers. So I got a break going and coming. You can't beat that!"[30]

Ruth also could not have timed his arrival in New York any better had he orchestrated it himself. Hitting and scoring began rising, and so did attendance. As W. R. Hoefer wrote in *Baseball Magazine*, "There is very positive evidence in the jammed ballyards that the multitude finds the cruder, more robust, freer walloping game of the present more attractive. And in baseball, more perhaps than in any other sphere, the majority rules."[31]

Ruth was having a profound impact on the game. During the 1919 season, he had generated enormous excitement and large crowds. For example, after his home run beat the Browns early in the 1920 season, one St. Louis paper wrote, "Bedlam in its wildest hours had nothing on that crowd which had seen a ball hit as only Ruth can hit it."[32] In addition, he was aided by a major rules change approved by the owners at the February 1920 winter meetings. Pitchers were no longer allowed to "doctor" the baseball; they could not roughen it or apply a "foreign substance" to it.[33] The penalty—even if the umpire was not sure who had tampered with the ball—was the ejection of the pitcher and an automatic ten-day suspension. Umpires were also instructed to remove discolored or damaged balls from play.[34] Batters would now have a bright, white ball coming at them throughout the game.[35]

One New York newspaper quickly recognized that these changes were the most radical since the foul-strike rule.[36] Occurring just as Ruth was joining the Yankees, they had an enormous impact in ushering in the Lively Ball Era. Manufacturers of baseballs were adamant in claiming they had not changed the ball's construction.[37] Independent tests confirmed this.[38] However, after the war, they began using a higher-grade yarn made of Australian wool. Coupled with improvements in sewing machines, which allowed for tighter and countersunk stitches, the ball was more firmly wound and thus more elastic.

In short, the increase in offense in the 1920s probably came more from "lively bats" (led by Babe Ruth's batting style) than lively balls. If the ball played a role in the spike in offense, it was what could no longer be done with the ball (trick pitches) and what umpires were now doing with it (removing discolored balls from play), and not just the ball itself.

In his biography of Ruth, Kal Wagenheim wrote, "Ruth's joining the Yankees in the spring of 1920 was a perfect marriage of personality and circumstance. Here was the champion slugger of all time, in all his uncouth splendor, walking onstage precisely at the outset of America's most flamboyant decade. America was ripe for a hero like the Babe. The country had recently ended its involvement in a grim world war. People wanted fun, and fun they got. . . . New York was the ideal—perhaps only—place for the creation of a modern demigod."[39]

16

The Risks of Ruth

The Yankees' purchase of Babe Ruth was a seminal event in the history of baseball's dominant franchise and a key element in the club's ascendancy. Conversely, their acquisition of the Babe has been called "the Rape of the Red Sox" and the origin of "the Curse of the Bambino." Yet when Red Sox owner Harry Frazee sold Ruth, he noted that the Yankees were taking a risk in acquiring the high-priced slugger. He spoke of how difficult and disruptive the slugger had been and how risky his behavior and lifestyle were. A close look at Ruth's illnesses, rebellions, accidents, and dangerous conduct during his career confirms the accuracy of Frazee's warning. How close the Yankees came to losing the game's greatest slugger. How close Ruth came to not even becoming the game's greatest slugger.

Frazee defended the deal as a smart baseball move with reasoning that seemed logical. He said the Babe had become arrogant and unmanageable. Frazee then stated his philosophy with words that could have been spoken by Miller Huggins, Ruth's new manager. "A team of players working harmoniously together is always to be preferred to that possessing one star who hugs the limelight to himself."[1] Frazee said he would reinvest the money he gained from the sale on other productive, more manageable players. However, considering his financial problems at the time, it is doubtful Frazee planned on doing so.[2]

Frazee said the Yankees were taking a gamble—investing so much money on one player in general and this one in particular—and indeed they were. First, Ruth was not immune to the infections and illnesses that could strike anyone in an age before antibiotics. Most famous was his 1925 sickness during spring training, which sent him to the hospital for several weeks. At one point during that illness he fainted on a train and struck his head against a bathroom sink. He was fortunate not to have fractured his skull.

What sportswriter W. O. McGeehan called "the tummy ache heard 'round the world" was actually venereal disease, Ed Barrow told "one of the most respected of sportswriters."[3] Yet Ruth—whose appetite for food was as voracious and uninhibited as it was for women—did have an operation and the abdominal incision to support it. Robert Creamer pointed out that surgery is not the treatment for a sexual infection and suggested the slugger may have had an intestinal abscess.[4]

During Ruth's first summer with the Yankees, on the set of the movie *Heading Home*, his arm became severely inflamed from the bite of a wood tick.[5] During the 1921 World Series, his arm was so badly infected (he had scraped it while sliding) there was genuine fear it might require amputation.[6] In the spring of 1924, the Babe returned from a baseball tour of Cuba very much overweight and became seriously ill with a fever and either influenza, pneumonia, or both.[7]

While fans of the Babe—as well as the Yankees' organization—were probably afraid such maladies would end his career or even his life, Ruth never showed concern. As a young sports reporter and future television host, Ed Sullivan, wrote about Ruth, "There never has been a great champion who didn't think like a champion. . . . Great champions are often insolently self-confident."[8]

Ruth was fearless, a trait he exhibited behind the wheel of his automobiles, a number of which he crashed. "Ruth was inclined to take unnecessary risks, most of all when driving an automobile," wrote Marshall Smelser in his Ruth biography. "Perhaps ballplayers come from a group of men who take death less seriously than most of us."[9] He already had been in at least one accident in Boston, in July 1918, when his car was hit by two trolleys.[10] During the summer of 1920, Ruth had a widely publicized car crash near Wawa, Pennsylvania. He and his passengers were thrown from the car; there were even reports he had been killed.

The Babe loved to drive fast, and Yankees management feared not only for his safety but also for the safety of pedestrians and other drivers. He once crashed his new Packard near Boston, left the car at the scene, hitched a ride, and went to the nearest Packard showroom, where he bought another one and drove off in it.[11] In another accident, he ran his Packard head on into a truck near Middletown, Connecticut.[12]

The Babe's Yankees career almost ended before it began. During a 1920 spring training game in Jacksonville, Florida, he went into the stands after a heckler, who then pulled a knife. Colonel Huston managed to restrain his player from going after the abusive fan. Two weeks later, after a night of partying and drinking in the Florida Keys, a hungover Ruth and the Yankees played an exhibition game in Palm Beach. While chasing after a fly ball, the Babe ran full speed into a palm tree in the primitive outfield, knocking himself unconscious. Recalling the incident years later, the Babe commented humorously, "I guess my reflexes were a bit off that day."[13]

There was also the Babe's insolence and rebellious nature, which Frazee had noted and about which some New York sportswriters expressed concern. When the Yankees acquired Ruth, Sid Mercer wondered if he would be "tractable."[14] At different times between 1920 and 1925, there was the real possibility he would simply quit—and play exhibition baseball games and take up movie acting, vaudeville, or even boxing. Christy Walsh, his agent beginning in 1921, probably impressed upon him that his fame—what was landing him lucrative cinema and stage contracts—emanated from his success in Organized Baseball.

Yet Ruth went on a fall 1921 barnstorming baseball tour, despite a baseball rule forbidding it and in spite of express warnings from Commissioner Landis not to go. The resultant fine and suspension that Landis levied were significant.[15] They also led Ruth to consider walking away from the game, something he had already done more than once as a member of the Red Sox, though only temporarily.

When he returned to the Yankees in late May 1922, after his suspension, Ruth was suspended several more times after run-ins with umpires.[16] League president Ban Johnson said of Ruth that year, "He has the mind of a fifteen-year-old."[17] This was a particularly difficult year for the Babe, who was going through marital difficulties.

Then there were the Babe's "dangerous liaisons." A married man since 1914, when he was only nineteen, Ruth's sexual escapades have become legendary. His teammate, Waite Hoyt, provided some context when he explained, "He was like a kid who has never been allowed candy and is suddenly presented with a truckload. Baseball was the instrument which pried off the lid to his treasure chest."[18]

The Babe faced not simply the danger of venereal disease from the prostitutes he frequented; he also risked physical threats from jilted lovers and jealous husbands. These reports never appeared in the newspapers. This was the age in which sports stars were built up and protected as larger-than-life heroes. That aura was preserved in memories, oral histories, and books that appeared after the Babe's death, with only rare glimpses behind closed doors.

It is impossible to know how many such incidents occurred. But those that did surface hint at the risks Ruth took. On a train to New Orleans, during spring training of 1921, a woman with a knife chased a naked Ruth through the parlor car past the sportswriters. As the train pulled into a station, the Babe escaped by jumping off, with the woman following; he then jumped back on as the train was pulling out of the station.[19] More unusual, even amusing (had the situation not been so rife with danger), wrote Robert Creamer, was that the reporters did not intervene and pretended to ignore what was going on. Two more events reportedly occurred in 1921. In one, an irate husband chased an almost-naked Ruth out of a Detroit hotel. Perhaps most frightening was when some of the Yankees, including the Babe, were relaxing at a roadside café near Shreveport, when he suddenly ran out and drove off in his car, with another in pursuit. Teammate Harry Harper decided to follow. He soon came upon a man in the middle of the road, pointing a gun at Ruth. Harper broke up the showdown by driving his car directly at the gunman, who jumped away, and Ruth climbed into Harper's car.[20]

Besides the danger of such incidents themselves, there was a lingering threat. Ruth was a public figure, and security for public figures was almost nonexistent at the time. People from whom he got away could have easily reached him again, as could any fan or person in the street.

Ruth's public persona did not fully reveal such a wild side. He was idolized by millions of children and presented as a role model. In the foreword to one of Dan Daniel's Ruth books, the Babe had his "Ten Commandments" for youngsters. They included "Get at least eight hours of sleep" each night and "Do everything in moderation."[21]

It is remarkable that the sheer amount of liquor Ruth consumed and the number of women with whom he had liaisons did not seem to have a negative impact on his baseball performance. Waite Hoyt noted the wonder of it all. "Among baseball players Ruth's hardiness in face of late hours and over-indulgence was more talked about than his home runs."[22] His teammate in both Boston and New York, Ernie Shore, explained, "You have to remember, he had grown up in that Catholic reformatory. When they let him out it was like turning a wild animal out of a cage. He wanted to go everyplace, and see everything and do everything."[23]

When the Yankees signed him to a three-year contract before the 1922 season, Colonel Huston spoke to the Babe about moderating his "nighttime activities." He replied, "Colonel, I'll promise to go easier on drinking and get to bed earlier. But, not for you, not for fifty thousand dollars, or two hundred fifty thousand dollars will I give up women. They're too much fun." Huston would tell that story with a grin and add, "What can you do with a fellow like that?"[24]

The following year, the Yankees' owners hired an undercover detective to probe Ruth's after-hours activities. In May 1923 "Investigator X-77" reported on Ruth's drinking and lascivious behavior, based on conversations with Broadway chorus girls. They spoke of a recent party at which the Babe served as bartender and master of ceremonies, where he "baptized himself more than anyone else."[25] Just how the Yankees planned to use such "evidence" is not known, but Huggins did not discipline him. Ruth did not curtail his nighttime pursuits and had a spectacular 1923 baseball season.

Babe Ruth was unique, and his foibles made him even more popular. In 1927 sportswriter Joe Williams wrote of him, "The truth is he cannot afford to change too much, if at all. The customers, sadly, aren't wild about perfect people. Mr. Ruth has always been looked on as something of a 'character.' This has added to his appeal at the box office."[26] Small wonder that the Yankees insured their most valuable asset for $300,000.[27]

17

Ruth Roars into the Twenties

Babe Ruth would spend fifteen years as an employee of Jacob Ruppert. During that time the two men, so different in upbringing, lifestyle, and public persona, engaged in the most heavily reported salary negotiations of the era. They had their first official meeting at the Yankees' 42nd Street office in late February 1920. Ruth had come down from Boston, where he had tried, without success, to obtain a portion of the money Red Sox owner Harry Frazee had received for selling his contract to New York.

From a financial standpoint, Ruth had benefited greatly from the sale. He remained under contract for the next two seasons, but the Yankees doubled his salary to $20,000 for both 1920 and 1921. They also paid him a $5,000 bonus for each of his first two seasons.[1] "We will pay Ruth any salary in reason," Ruppert had said shortly after the purchase. "We want him to come here satisfied."[2]

However, Ruppert had another purpose in mind for this first meeting, as did Colonel Huston and Miller Huggins, who also were present. Fully aware of Ruth's off-the-field escapades and occasional disregard for Boston manager Ed Barrow's leadership, they were reminding their new acquisition what they expected of him. He was to behave and fully obey Huggins's directions, warned Huston. Smoking a cigar, the twenty-five-year-old "man-child" responded to Huston in typical Ruthian manner.[3] "Look at ya! Too fat and too old to have any fun! That goes for him too," he added, indicating Ruppert. Turning to Huggins, he said, "As for that little shrimp. He's half dead right now."[4] If they had not suspected so before, Jacob Ruppert and Miller Huggins were now on notice that dealing with Babe Ruth would be very difficult at times, principally for Huggins. Ruth's criticism and mini-rebellions against him would come close to costing Huggins his job and would adversely affect his health.

Health, more specifically Ruth's health, had been on the minds of the Colonels since his acquisition from Boston. They had been talking to various insurance companies and expected to sign a policy that would insure the Babe for $150,000. The owners had a policy that insured the team as a whole, but only the Cleveland Indians had insured an individual player—their manager and star center fielder, Tris Speaker. "It will be a life and accident policy," Huston said. "Baseball is a business as well as a sport with both Colonel Ruppert and myself, so why shouldn't we insure one big asset as much as in other businesses in which we are interested?"[5]

A "big asset" does not begin to describe what Ruth immediately became to Ruppert. He was to his baseball team what his prized St. Bernard, Oh Boy, already was to his dog breeding ventures. Oh Boy, like Ruth, had above-normal physical attributes—he weighed 230 pounds—and had dominated the awards at the Westminster Kennel Club Dog Show at Madison Square Garden in each of the previous two years.[6]

Prohibition was now law, but the Ruth-led Yankees paid no attention to the Volstead Act. They enjoyed a riotous spring training in Jacksonville, Florida, on trips to Miami, and in the small southern towns as they played their way north. Wherever they appeared, people came out in record numbers, primarily to see Ruth hit home runs. They usually got what they came to see.

Ruppert had spent two weeks in Jacksonville during spring training in 1919. Columnist Sid Mercer recalled a conversation in which the Colonel suggested that Mercer had a "better time" than he did. "I don't seem to have fun anymore," Ruppert said. "Take it from me, Sid, money is only a burden after you have enough for a comfortable living. It becomes a responsibility. I go to bed at night and maybe I can't go to sleep for a couple of hours. Why? Because my mind will be working on some business deal and I can't let go of it. Maybe it involves only a few thousand dollars. Here I am trying to snatch a few days with my ball team and I'll bet you I'll have to cut my vacation short."[7] Ruppert proved to be prophetic, as just two days later, he received a wire from Chicago Cubs president William Veeck to come to Nashville to inspect some coal property.

On Opening Day in Philadelphia, more than 15,000 fans were at an unseasonably cold Shibe Park to see Ruth's Yankees' debut. Most fans were paying higher ticket prices this season. At a joint meeting in February, the baseball establishment had decreed a new and higher price structure for all parks: bleacher seats would now cost 50 cents, pavilion seats 75 cents, and grandstand seats one dollar.

Ticket scalping would not be a problem in Philadelphia this season, but it would continue to be one in New York, the entertainment capital of the nation. Ruppert and others, working with assistant district attorney Edwin Patrick Kilroe, hoped to put the business of scalping on a legitimate basis by not allowing the agencies to charge any more than an additional 25 cents above the face value of a ticket. Ruppert, reports said, had plans to compete with these agencies by starting one of his own and charging just an additional 10 cents a ticket.[8]

Three months after the sale of Ruth to the Yankees, it remained the biggest news story in baseball, and many Philadelphians had come out expressly to see him. The Babe, playing center field, had a pair of singles, but his eighth-inning drop of Joe Dugan's fly ball allowed two runs to score and led to the Yankees' 3–1 loss. Although Ruth was in center field for the opener, he would play mostly right field in 1920, with Ping Bodie, the team's regular center fielder in 1919, reclaiming the position. Huggins had benched Bodie for the opener, the result of a heated spring training incident between the two.[9]

With Aaron Ward sidelined by an injured knee, rookie Bob Meusel was playing third base. Yankees scout Bob Connery had signed Meusel by outbidding several Major League teams who had been after the six foot three Californian. Meusel was coming off a sensational year with Vernon of the Pacific Coast League, in which he had batted .337 and had 330 total bases. "If Meusel is half as good as they say he is," said Huggins, "then the Yankees have corralled a great player who can play first, third, or the outfield. Right now, it's my intention to play him in the outfield."[10]

In 1921 Huggins would move Meusel to the outfield full time, where he and Ruth would play together through the 1929 season. Ward would be the Yankees' regular third baseman in 1920 as the replacement for Frank Baker. Baker's wife, Ottalee, had died in February, and he had chosen to leave baseball to look after his two young daughters.[11] When he decided to return in 1921, Huggins moved Ward to second base.

On the day the Yankees opened the new season, a portion of Ruppert's library, consisting of several thousand volumes of finely bound sets of the

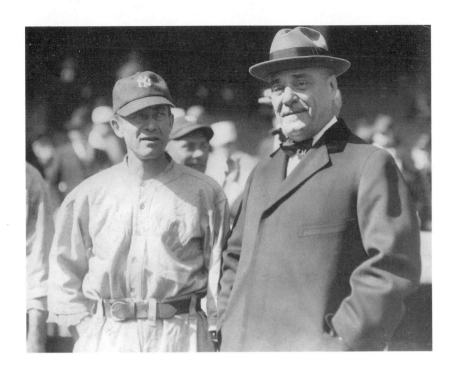

1. At their first meeting, the impeccably groomed Jacob Ruppert was unimpressed with Miller Huggins's gnome-like appearance. A few weeks later, he decided to make Huggins his manager. Ruppert called the hiring "the first and most important step we took toward making the Yankees champions." Courtesy Trustees of the Boston Public Library.

2. (*above*) Jacob Ruppert, in the center, with younger brothers George (*left*) and Frank. George took over the brewery when the Colonel died. Frank died at age thirty of typhoid fever. Tom Carwile Collection.

3. (*left*) Jacob Ruppert, a Democrat, was elected to the House of Representatives in 1898 with the support of Tammany Hall. He served four uneventful terms and was more active on Washington's social circuit than in the halls of Congress. Tom Carwile Collection.

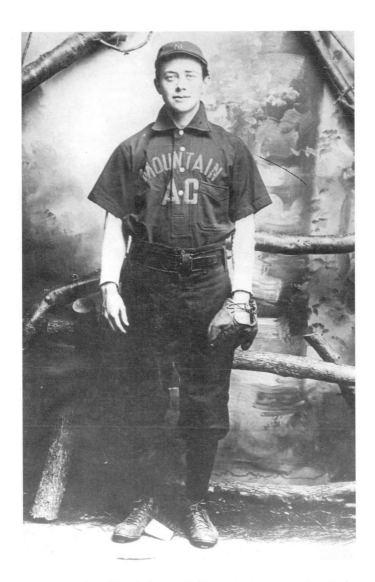

4. Huggins played baseball in an idyllic setting in upstate New York in 1900. Cincinnati's wealthy Fleischmanns had a powerful semipro team, the Mountain Tourists, in the town named after their family. Steve Steinberg Collection.

5. (*above*) "The 'Rabbit' is a little firecracker," noted the *Cincinnati Enquirer* of the hometown boy who made good from the start. In 1905, only his second season, he scored 117 runs and led the National League in walks and the league's second basemen in assists. *Chicago Daily News* Collection, Chicago History Museum; negative SDN-002985.

6. (*opposite*) The tiny Huggins's style of play exemplified baseball in the Deadball Era. During his playing career, he was known as "the Waiter" for taking pitches and as "Little Everywhere" for the ground he covered playing second base. Courtesy Trustees of the Boston Public Library.

7. (*opposite top*) Yankees owner Frank Farrell looks on as Frank Chance signs a lucrative three-year contract in 1913 to manage the team. A frustrated Chance quit after less than two years, claiming he was furnished with third-rate material and told to build a first-class team. *Chicago Daily News* Collection, Chicago History Museum; negative SDN-058117.

8. (*opposite bottom*) Co-owner Til Huston (*right*) and manager Bill Donovan. Huston and Jacob Ruppert's first manager was unsuccessful in making the Yankees a serious pennant contender. Steve Steinberg Collection.

9. (*above*) Mayor John Purroy Mitchel (*left*) and Jacob Ruppert at the Polo Grounds on April 22, 1915. Mayor Mitchel threw out the first ball at the Yankees' home debut under the team's new ownership. Library of Congress, Prints and Photographs Division, LC-DIG-ggbain-18929.

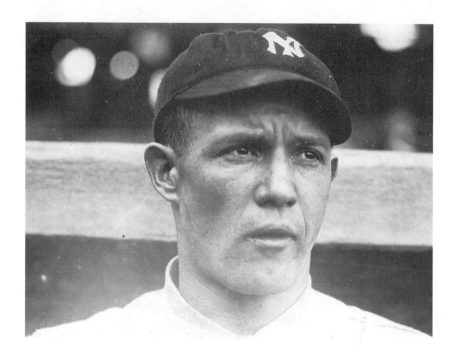

10. (*above*) Before Miller Huggins and Ed Barrow joined the Yankees, the team had little front-office expertise. They made a colossal blunder after the 1915 season, when they chose to keep Fritz Maisel rather than trade him for Joe Jackson or Tris Speaker. Steve Steinberg Collection.

11. (*opposite top*) In May 1915, German submarines sank the British ocean liner RMS *Lusitania*. Of the 1,195 people who died, 128 were Americans, causing a dramatic rise in anti-German sentiment in this country. Library of Congress, Prints and Photographs Division, LC-USZ62-55384.

12. (*opposite bottom*) Huggins joined the Yankees with a reputation as a resourceful and cerebral manager with the St. Louis Cardinals. Early in his Yankees years, Hugh Fullerton wrote, "He is a crabby little man who knows about as much baseball as there is to be known." Steve Steinberg Collection.

13. (*above*) Colonels Ruppert and Huston with future New York governor Al Smith and his son, Al Jr. Like Ruppert, Smith had strong ties to Tammany Hall and firmly opposed Prohibition. The oft-mentioned contrast in appearance between the dapper Ruppert and the disheveled Huston is evident. Steve Steinberg Collection.

14. (*left*) The Yankees' 1919 acquisition of Carl Mays triggered a conflict that almost tore apart the American League. Mays won sixty-two games in his first two-plus years with the Yankees, but later fell out of favor with his manager. Steve Steinberg Collection.

15. American League president Ban Johnson played a key role in Huggins's move to the Yankees. Huggins felt a debt of gratitude to his fellow Cincinnatian and surely was anguished when the Yankees' owners took on Johnson and eventually brought him down. Steve Steinberg Collection.

16. (*above*) John McGraw's New York Giants had dominated baseball in New York when Miller Huggins joined the Yankees. The proud and arrogant McGraw thought that by evicting the Yankees from the Polo Grounds, he would make them outcasts. How wrong he was. National Baseball Hall of Fame Library, Cooperstown NY.

17. (*opposite top*) Miller Huggins, Colonel Ruppert, and Babe Ruth relaxing at spring training. Something in the sky, likely an airplane, has caught the attention of Huggins, an avid fan of aviation. © Bettmann/CORBIS.

18. (*opposite bottom*) The actions of the larger-than-life Babe Ruth dominated the sports pages. On the field, his power changed the game. Off the field, the press discreetly ignored his sexual exploits. Women of the 1920s found him irresistible. National Baseball Hall of Fame Library, Cooperstown NY.

19. (*opposite top*) Miller Huggins is smiling as he and Jacob Ruppert welcome their prize acquisition, Babe Ruth, to New York. Dealing with the Babe would entail a series of challenges for both men. National Baseball Hall of Fame Library, Cooperstown NY.

20. (*opposite bottom*) Ban Johnson had led the American League with an iron fist since its founding. But Jacob Ruppert led a group of owners that stripped him of much of his power in 1920 and made way for Commissioner Landis. Steve Steinberg Collection.

21. (*above*) Managers Wilbert Robinson and Miller Huggins pose before an April 1921 exhibition game. Rumors during the off-season had the two men switching places; nevertheless, they remained close friends over the years. © Underwood & Underwood/CORBIS.

22. (*above*) The 1921 Yankees appear loose before playing in their first World Series. Carl Mays (*far left*) and Waite Hoyt (*center middle*) pitched shutouts to win the first two games, but the Yankees eventually lost to John McGraw's Giants. Steve Steinberg Collection.

23. (*left*) Miller Huggins examines Babe Ruth's injured elbow after Game Five of the 1921 World Series. The Babe scored the winning run, but the severity of the injury restricted him to very limited duty for the rest of the Series. *Chicago Daily News* Collection, Chicago History Museum; print ICHi-65706.

complete writings of various American, British, and French authors, was sold at the American Art galleries. The works included an autographed edition of the writings of Bret Harte, the complete writings of Nathaniel Hawthorne, and the works of William M. Thackeray. The auction netted Ruppert $54,445.[12]

After the Yankees lost four of their first five, Ruth played his first home game, against the A's on April 22. The New Yorkers won, 8–6, but the large crowd, anxious to see the Babe, went home disappointed. During batting practice, they had been clamoring for their latest hero to put the ball in the seats. Trying to impress his new fans, Ruth took a vicious swing at a Rip Collins pitch. He immediately dropped his bat, grabbed his right side, and dropped down to one knee. Several teammates helped him to the bench, where trainer Doc Woods administered to his injured side. Ruth tried again, but quit after one swing.

Nevertheless, he was in the starting lineup and was greeted with a tremendous roar from the fans when he came to bat in the first inning. But after two foul balls and a swinging third strike, Huggins replaced him with Frank Gleich when the Yankees took the field in the second inning. It was a foolish injury— the kind Harry Frazee had in mind when he said the Yankees were taking a gamble on Ruth—and it caused him to miss several games.

When Ruth returned, he had trouble getting untracked. He did not hit his first home run as a Yankee until May 1, against Boston's Herb Pennock. The long-awaited blast, the fiftieth of his career, cleared the right-field grandstand and landed in adjoining Manhattan Field. But by May 9, after going hitless in three consecutive games, his batting average was a lowly .210, and he had only two home runs. Ruth matched that total with two against the Chicago White Sox in New York's next game, and then was nearly unstoppable for the rest of the season.

"I use a heavier bat than any man in baseball, and I swing with all my might," Ruth said in 1920 in describing his long-ball slugging. "I happen to be able to handle that bat as freely as a smaller man handles a smaller bat. If I time my swing perfectly, and if I get the full force of my arms and shoulders and back behind the swing, I get a homer."[13]

Early May had been a difficult time for Ruppert. His star player was not performing as expected, nor was his team, which had a losing record and was in sixth place. Of greater consequence was the May 6 death of business manager Harry Sparrow. Sparrow was one of the first men hired by Ruppert and Huston in 1915. They had done so on the advice of John McGraw, Sparrow's employer with the Giants, at a time when the relationship between McGraw and the Colonels was still cordial.

The forty-five-year-old Sparrow had suffered from heart trouble for the past three years and was further weakened by influenza and pneumonia. Sparrow had been more than a business manager in his years with the Yankees. During the war, with Huston serving in France and Ruppert devoting much of his time to his brewery, Sparrow had performed some of the administrative duties usually reserved to the owners.

Less than a month later, Ruppert suffered an even more severe setback, this time to his brewery. On June 6, the Supreme Court dealt the final blow to all those, like Ruppert, who believed the Volstead Act was unconstitutional. The court heard challenges to the Eighteenth Amendment from seven jurisdictions and rejected them all unanimously. The opinion, rendered by Justice Willis Van Devanter, "held that the amendment not only came within the amending power conferred by the Federal Constitution but was lawfully proposed and now was the law of the land."[14] The lead paragraph in the *New York Times*'s coverage of the court's decisions described the defeat of the "wets" in unmistakable language. "Every contention raised against the constitutionality of the Volstead Prohibition Enforcement Act and the validity of the national prohibition amendment to the Federal Constitution was swept aside today by the United States Supreme Court in a decision which held constitutional and regular all phases of the existing law and amendment."[15] Speaking from the Republican National Convention in Chicago, Wayne B. Wheeler, counsel for the Anti-Saloon League, claimed the decision "kills the liquor traffic as dead as slavery."[16]

Ruppert and other representatives of the brewery and liquor interests, along with saloon owners, had hoped for a favorable decision. All expressed their disappointment and in many cases disgust. They warned of the dangers of passing a law that could not be enforced, a lesson the nation was about to learn.

New York Congressman (and future mayor) Fiorello LaGuardia said enforcement of the law "would require a police force of 250,000 men, and a force of 250,000 men to police the police."[17] Several years later, Assistant United States Attorney General Mabel Willebrandt attested to the futility of the so-called noble experiment. "It cannot be truthfully said that prohibition enforcement has failed in New York," said Willebrandt. "It has not yet been attempted."[18] The inability to enforce Prohibition, wrote Michael Lerner, "had completely undermined the viability of the noble experiment, diminished public respect for the law, and made a mockery of the dry mission."[19]

The problem the "drys" faced, Eliot Asinof wrote, was that Americans thought it was their right to drink.

> As it turned out, the problem [enforcement] did not disappear. Liquor did not disappear. Only the law disappeared. In time, the massiveness of this onslaught bewildered, then overwhelmed, the nation. There was no movement behind it, no conspiracy, no organization: quite simply, the American people wanted to drink, just as they had always wanted to drink. It was their natural right to drink. In this great free country, how could anyone deny such a God-given right? There was no talk of the law. No one cared about the law. The law was what anyone chose to make of it.[20]

H. L. Mencken, the Baltimore newspaperman and social critic, summed up the battle in his typically acerbic way. "What lies under it [Prohibition] and under all the other crazy enactments of its category is . . . the yokel's congenital and incurable hatred of the city man—his simian rage against everyone who, as he sees it, is having a better time than he is."[21]

The 1920 Yankees' team was the best they had ever had, and the pressure was on Huggins to produce a pennant. "It is up to Huggins to drive his club home first or forever hold his peace" was a sentiment representative of the New York press. "Few managers have ever had such material as he. Colonels Ruppert and Huston have spent with a lavish hand to produce a championship club. Now Huggins and his men must do their part."[22]

Yet one month into the season, Huggins acknowledged that the Yankees were not playing his style of baseball. "It's not that the players don't do what they are told," he said, but "I like a fast team, and one that can fly around the bases. They compose a team of the slugging type." Still,

Huggins, more than most, had recognized that Ruth was changing the game from one of speed to one of power, and he was ready to adapt to the new style. "That system is to keep pounding away at the pitcher until he breaks, and they will break a lot of them. . . . And the team has such offensive strength that it can't help but bring results despite its deficiency in speed."[23]

As Ruth began to hit—he had twelve home runs in May—the Yankees began to win. Beginning on May 25, they won eighteen of twenty, and Ruppert's hopes rose. According to Damon Runyon, at one point in late May the Colonel attended three consecutive games, something he had never done previously.[24]

Ruth hit his thirty-third home run on July 23, in a win against the Indians. After two months of chasing Cleveland, the Yankees were now in first place. The next day the Babe smashed another home run, but the Yankees lost, to drop percentage points behind the Indians. At this point, his batting average was .393, fourth best in the league.[25] "I could have a lifetime average of .600 if I hit singles, but they don't pay off on singles," Ruth was quoted as saying. "They pay me all that dough for them four-base knocks and I keep swinging for the fences."[26]

For more than a decade, Ty Cobb had reigned supreme as baseball's greatest player. But during the 1920 season, as Ruth drew ever-greater attention from the press and the public, Cobb became "increasingly contemptuous" of him. Cobb biographer Charles Alexander describes a "special rivalry of two men who represented radically contrasting approaches to the game. . . . Cobb grasped early and completely the threat Ruth posed to his whole set of values. . . . Cobb's harassment of Ruth was steady, systematic, and often vicious."[27]

In the second week of August, the Yankees swept a four-game series in Cleveland, which moved them within a half-game of the first-place Indians. During the series, the Yankees suggested some of the league's other teams were favoring Cleveland over New York in the pennant race. Neither team had yet won an American League flag.

The Yankees pointed to what they considered questionable plays in a recent series between the Indians and the Red Sox. They claimed Boston made "an unusually large number of errors" in the late innings. Moreover, they said, the St. Louis Browns and Detroit Tigers had used their best pitchers, Urban Shocker and Howard Ehmke, twice in a series against the Yankees and had done nothing similar when they played the Indians.[28]

The charge gained a degree of credibility when Ruppert also weighed in on it. "We shall watch the next series St. Louis and Detroit play against Cleveland," said the Colonel. "We are anxious to see whether Shocker and Ehmke will each work twice against the Indians as they did against New York."[29] The complaints generated little sympathy in the New York press; the general reaction was that Ruppert and the Yankees should stop squawking and trying to dictate the way other managers used their pitchers.[30]

Oddly, no mention was made of the Chicago White Sox, who along with New York and Cleveland were waging a dramatic three-way race for the American League pennant. A week later, when the Indians came to the Polo Grounds for a three-game series, they were tied with the White Sox for first place. The Yankees, who had used nine-game and ten-game winning streaks to stay in the race, trailed by half a game.

The Indians won two out of three, but the series is remembered most for the tragedy of its opening game, on August 16. A fifth-inning pitch by the Yankees' Carl Mays hit Cleveland's star shortstop Ray Chapman in the temple, fracturing Chapman's skull and leading to his death the next day. "It hit him so solid that we weren't sure that it hadn't hit the bat," said Roger Peckinpaugh, the Yankees shortstop that afternoon.[31] Mays did think it had hit the bat. He fielded the ball and threw it to first baseman Wally Pipp.[32]

Mays, who threw with a submarine delivery, had a well-deserved reputation as a "head-hunter." As *Baseball Magazine* described it, "Carl slings the pill from his toes, has a weird looking wind-up and in action looks like a cross between an octopus and a bowler. He shoots the ball in at the batter at such unexpected angles that his delivery is hard to find, generally, until along about 5 o'clock, when the hitters get accustomed to it— and when the game is about over."[33]

Meanwhile Chapman had a batting stance that tended to crowd the plate. "Once a player digs in with his front foot [as Chapman did] it is almost impossible for him to dodge clear of that sort of ball," said Miller Huggins in an attempt to exonerate his pitcher.[34] Given Mays's style of delivery, Chapman's crowding of the plate, and a cloudy, drizzly day, with poor visibility and perhaps a slippery ball, it was an accident waiting to happen.

Because of Mays's reputation, he received criticism from some umpires and numerous opposing players.[35] Some teams went so far as to threaten to boycott any games against New York in which Mays was the pitcher. Still, most agreed that Mays had not deliberately attempted to hit Chapman. Among them was Indians manager Tris Speaker. "Mays was absolutely blameless," said Speaker, at least for public consumption.[36] "Many players are hurt in baseball," Speaker noted, "and I don't see how they can hold Mays responsible for yesterday's accident. There is not the slightest ground for any such [boycott] action as is reported to be planned by the Detroit and Boston players."[37]

Colonel Huston, speaking personally and not on behalf of the club, said: "I am terribly sorry that Chapman was killed. I'm sorry such an accident had to happen in our park or that any of our team had any connection with it."[38] In response to Ban Johnson's claim that Mays was now a "broken reed," the Colonels issued a statement refuting Johnson. "He will take his regular turn in the pitchers box and we expect him to win games as usual."[39] It was Johnson, however, who played a key role in quashing the threat of boycotts. "The talk about boycotting Mays was preposterous. I'm glad Mr. Johnson has put a stop to it," said Ruppert.[40]

Mays responded as the Colonels expected, going 8-2 over the final six weeks of the season. "I fooled them. I went out and pitched the rest of the year," Mays told Jack Murphy of the *San Diego Union*, more than fifty years later. "Why should I let it ruin the rest of my life? I had a wife and two children and they had to eat. I had to make a living. I had to provide for them."[41]

On August 26, the Yankees began a three-game series at home against Chicago, as they attempted to catch the White Sox, who had surged into first place and led them by three games. Chicago started Dickie Kerr (15-5) in the opener, while Huggins chose George Mogridge, who had won only five games all season (5-8). The Sox jumped on Mogridge for seven runs in three-plus innings on their way to a 16–4 win.

In the clubhouse immediately following the defeat, a group of Yankees players criticized Huggins's decision to start Mogridge in such an important game. Most vocal was Ruth, whose forty-fourth home run of the season was the game's one redeeming feature for the fans. Why start Mogridge, they wondered, when superior veterans like Mays and Jack

Quinn were available? The dispute was eventually settled; however, Huggins did not use Mogridge for two weeks, and he pitched him only three more times the rest of the season, all in relief. Ruth, meanwhile, missed a week of action, not for insubordination, but rather from an insect bite on his right wrist that had become infected.

Huggins's pitching selections again came under fire three weeks later in another game against the White Sox. This time the press was not only reporting players questioning his decision but voicing criticism of their own. The September 16 game was the opener of a three-game series at Comiskey Park. New York was in first place, a game ahead of Cleveland and two and a half games ahead of Chicago. Dickie Kerr, now 17-9, was again on the mound for Chicago, and Jack Quinn, with an identical record, was Huggins's choice to oppose him.

But as sportswriter Harry Schumacher argued, "Quinn has pitched only one or two good games in the last six weeks." In his article, accusingly titled "Huggins's Judgment Suicidal to Yankees," Schumacher claimed that Mays, Hank Thormahlen, and Rip Collins all were available, and all would have been better choices.[42] Quinn did not make it out of the second inning. New York's 8–3 loss ended their five-game winning streak and started them on a four-game losing streak that dropped them behind both Cleveland and Chicago.

Schumacher continued his assault on Huggins's judgment after the White Sox swept the series. He called the starting of Quinn in game one "a tactical blunder" that revitalized the White Sox and devastated the Yankees. "The panic in Manager Huggins's heart spread throughout the club and the infield defense went to pieces," he wrote, concluding that the Yankees were now "hopelessly out of the pennant race."[43]

Huggins was now in his third year as manager of the Yankees, yet he had never had the full support of all his players. Their questioning of his judgment and decisions had continued throughout the season. It had begun in spring training when he benched veteran second baseman Del Pratt in favor of young Chick Fewster.[44] The season was only two days old when another Huggins move allegedly drew criticism from several players. During the seventh inning of a 4–1 win at Philadelphia, Huggins sent Sammy Vick up to pinch hit for Quinn. Several Yankees on the bench objected, saying Lefty O'Doul would have been the better choice.

Sportswriter James P. Sinnott had taken Huggins to task when he felt it was called for, but he objected strongly to the benchwarmers' actions. "The question is not one of whether O'Doul or Vick is the better batter," he wrote. "It is whether Huggins is going to run the Yankees or the players are."[45]

Detroit Tigers manager Hughie Jennings had hinted at these potential problems back in February. While predicting the Yankees were in an excellent position to win the pennant, he said a great deal depended on how Ruth acted, adding that the Yankees had several temperamental players. "If things do not start off right, there will be disputes that will tend to form the club into cliques."[46]

For the first time since 1904, their second season in New York, the Yankees stayed in the race almost until the very end. They were not eliminated on the last day, as they had been in 1904, but they did lead the league as late as September 14. They eventually finished in third place, a game behind the Chicago White Sox, and three behind the Cleveland Indians, who overcame the Chapman death to win the pennant and then the World Series.[47]

Merely staying in the race was far from being sufficient to satisfy New York's pennant-hungry populace. Yet again, many in the press and among the fans were calling for Huggins to be fired. One observer, identified only as "an old time student of the American national sport," spoke for many with this assessment of Huggins: "Huggins is a smart baseball man, but he is not a leader of men where great pennant fights are raging," he said. "He is too fearful. . . . That is the root of his trouble. . . . In the heat of a battle for a pennant under certain conditions [he] lacks confidence and for that reason—especially in handling pitchers—is guilty of fatal indecision and sometimes panic."[48]

Ruth finished the season with fifty-four home runs, shattering his own single-season record of 29, set a year earlier with the Red Sox. He had more home runs than any other team in the American League, and his total accounted for an astonishing 15 percent of all home runs hit in the league.[49]

In addition, Ruth batted .376 and led the league in runs scored (158) and runs-batted-in (137). He established new Major League highs in walks (148) and in slugging percentage (.847), the latter of which is still the all-time American League high.[50] With a team total of 115 home runs, the Yankees became the first Major League team to exceed 100.[51] "How shall I describe Babe Ruth's batting," said Miller Huggins. "You can't describe him; you can't compare him with anybody else. He's Babe Ruth."[52]

Meanwhile, Ruth's addition to the club was paying off, not only on the field but also at the box office, where the Yankees had more than doubled their 1919 attendance. They outdrew the Giants for the first time—by more than 350,000—setting a Major League attendance record as they attracted 1,289,422 fans to the Polo Grounds. While disappointed at falling short in the pennant race, the Colonels were beginning to see a significant return on the investment they had made five years earlier. Home gate receipts totaled $864,830, and the club showed an operating profit of $374,079. Any questions that the Yankees purchase of Ruth had been a sound investment "is being answered daily at the Polo Grounds in a manner entirely satisfactory to Jacob Ruppert," Sid Mercer had written back in May. "And the Yankee colonels say he's cheap at the price," he added. That was an understatement. The return on their investment in Ruth was unprecedented. After losing a combined total of about $30,000 in their first five years of ownership, the Yankees recouped three times what they had paid for Ruth in the Babe's first year in New York.[53]

Mercer quoted one fan as saying: "I'm going up every day the Yankees are here because Ruth is going to break that distance record at the Polo Grounds some afternoon and I want to say I was there to see it."[54] As historians Harold and Dorothy Seymour wrote, "He [Ruth] attracted people who might be untutored in the subtleties and refinements of inside baseball but who could understand and respond to the clear, uncomplicated drama and beauty of one of his towering drives."[55]

Additionally, when the Yankees played on the road they drew some of the home team's biggest crowds ever. The locals came to see Ruth hit home runs but also to cheer when the home team pitcher fanned him. Typical was the Sunday, August 1, game at Comiskey Park. More than 15,000 fans had to be turned away, and special grounds rules had to be established after fans lined up twenty deep along the foul lines and in the outfield.[56] "Ruth will go down in history as probably the greatest drawing card," wrote Sam Murphy in an early-season article. "What he can draw cannot be seated in the largest modern ballpark. They'll have to build them bigger."[57]

18

Squabbling Owners and Scandal
Lead to Landis Coronation

Ban Johnson had not considered his crushing defeat in February 1920 as final. For the next eight months, he fought a rearguard action against both a reconstituted National Commission and the selection of a powerful new commissioner. Jacob Ruppert and Til Huston had to battle their league president once again. Only after the Black Sox scandal broke into public view in September 1920 was enough momentum generated to again thwart Johnson and bring about a new governing structure.

During the spring and summer, Johnson and National League president John Heydler could not agree on a candidate to head the National Commission. When two stars of the 1919 White Sox confessed to "throwing" the World Series at the behest of gamblers, the press turned its wrath on the nonfunctioning Commission and Johnson's delaying tactics.[1] Grantland Rice noted that "crooks" had taken advantage of the absence of a governing body for baseball. "Ban Johnson's gross inefficiency has proven that he is utterly incapable of protecting the interests of the game," he wrote.[2]

The National League and the American League's three "Insurrectos," the Yankees, Red Sox, and White Sox, supported a plan developed by Albert Lasker, a Chicago advertising executive and minority owner of the Chicago Cubs. Lasker had proposed that baseball be ruled by a three-man board of non-baseball men, with one of the three as commissioner. Ideally, the commissioner would be "a man of commanding mental stature, a man of national prominence, with force and vision and sufficient courage to remain independent."[3] In other words, they wanted a man not handpicked or controlled by Johnson. All agreed with Sid Mercer's observation that Johnson's judgment had become "warped through long association with men who danced when he played the piper. He opposes anything that will remove him as a dictator. . . . Apparently he is still blind to the handwriting on the wall."[4]

Ruppert laid the blame for the failure to bring about the adoption of the Lasker plan on Johnson's unwillingness to abide by the vote of the majority of the sixteen clubs. Unhappy with all the infighting and airing of dirty linen in public, Ruppert issued a warning to his fellow owners. "When I was interested in baseball years ago, I got so disgusted reading about politics in baseball I would not go to a baseball game any longer. The time will come when it will be too late to remedy conditions and again a great many will stay away from baseball and it will take considerable time to get them to come back again."[5]

Ruppert had emerged as the informal leader of the eleven clubs opposing Johnson. "Mr. Johnson and his supporters seem to think that we are bluffing," he said. "They are grievously mistaken if they do. . . . We intend to have a new form of government."[6] Many baseball observers believed that had Johnson not blocked the selection of a strong executive, the Black Sox scandal would have been avoided. At the least, baseball would have caught the culprits and cleaned the scandal up sooner and without a criminal investigation.[7]

Unlike Huston, who fiercely opposed Johnson, Ruppert was still willing to let him remain as league president, though with limited power. Huston's dislike of Johnson was so strong that at one meeting, Ruppert and Harry Frazee had to spend an hour persuading him to allow Johnson to remain in place.[8]

A week after the 1920 World Series ended, Ruppert made a surprising declaration, one that was in harmony with the rival New York Giants, at least in the matter of hiring a strong non-baseball commissioner. If Johnson and his five owners would not agree to reorganize as the majority of teams wanted, he said, the Yankees would not invest in a new ballpark. They would instead remain at the Polo Grounds indefinitely.[9]

Ruppert's group had coalesced around Chicago federal judge Kenesaw Mountain Landis as their choice for commissioner. Landis was a passionate baseball fan who had done Organized Baseball a big favor when he delayed ruling on an antitrust lawsuit to the benefit of the Major Leagues.[10] As a judge, Landis was mercurial and pretentious; many of his rulings were overturned on appeal.

> For all his vituperative Americanism, Landis' formal judicial career was an abysmal failure. His decisions in the Rockefeller and Berger cases, as in so many other cases which initially appeared in his court, were later overturned. President Calvin Coolidge, to Landis' endless dismay, later commuted the sentences of the I. W. W. members. Landis' was the failure of a past which could only fume at the present, a Populism lost and irrational in an alien world. Unsuccessful in imposing his will upon society at large, Landis would find himself the island of baseball fertile ground for his authority.[11]

The three disenchanted American League teams threatened that if Johnson's group did not accept Landis, they would join the National League, creating something called the New National League. Such a move would leave Johnson with a five-team league—and no clubs in Boston, Chicago, or New York. "They could no more have a grandstand built in New York before a year than they could stand on their heads," Ruppert said.[12]

Johnson was blunt in accepting the challenge. "There will be war to the bitter end," he responded.[13] Damon Runyon wrote, "Ban will either wind up ruler of his own particular universe, or his name will be mud. And in either event there will be left a great deal of wonder at the uselessness of it all."[14]

Ruppert then played a key role in defusing the conflict. First, he met with Connie Mack, the usually taciturn owner-manager of the Athletics who had been an outspoken supporter of Johnson. Then he organized an informal meeting of all the owners, to which Johnson was not invited. On November 11, 1920, two years after the Armistice ended hostilities in the Great War, Organized Baseball signed an armistice of its own. The sixteen teams then unanimously offered the position of commissioner to Landis.[15]

With the Black Sox scandal swirling around them, the owners welcomed a new leader with near-dictatorial authority. They gave Landis broad powers to investigate and levy fines; they also waived the right to contest any of his rulings in civil court. Landis would operate as "a one-person court of both first instance and last resort."[16]

In hiring Landis, in the words of G. Edward White, "they could have appointed no more visible personification of militant old-fashioned morality."[17] John Dos Passos described him more critically, recalling the harsh jail sentences the judge had handed down two years earlier in the celebrated trial of labor union activists. "The judge could hand out twenty-five-year sentences as lightheartedly as he'd fine some Joe five bucks for speeding. . . . Underneath he was a butcher."[18]

Landis's approach to the Black Sox scandal was to minimize baseball's exposure to charges of corruption by painting the scandal as a unique anomaly. "Landis surely did not want to tear down the very game he loved and now oversaw. . . . Landis continually focused on the Black Sox players . . . and thus diverted attention from a broader story and wider investigation. . . . By focusing on the players, Landis deflected attention from the owners and their repeated failures to confront gambling in baseball."[19]

In keeping with what Professor David Voigt called "the myth of baseball's single sin," Landis "threw the book" at the eight Chicago players involved in the scandal.[20] At their trial in August 1921, a jury found them not guilty despite a preponderance of evidence to the contrary. The next day, an undeterred Landis banned them from baseball for life. While that draconian action surprised many, it should not have. Shortly after he was hired as commissioner in November 1920, Landis gave a long interview. "Whether or not they [the indicted Black Sox] are convicted of a crime— and there seems to be a great deal of doubt that they can be," Landis said, "they have been cast out of baseball forever. . . . To permit them to return to baseball would be impossible and unthinkable."[21]

The reality was that gambling by players and fixed games were far more widespread than Landis would admit. In *Baseball: The Golden Age*, Harold and Dorothy Seymour devote an entire chapter to such incidents, entitled "Warning Shadows." "Wagering on athletic contests is as old as the contests themselves, and certainly baseball was no exception to the practice. . . . Wherever gambling flourished, its insidious offspring, 'the fix,' lurked nearby."[22]

Sportswriter Hugh Fullerton had tried to expose the Black Sox fix right after it occurred and was ignored, if not vilified, for trying to do so. Now, almost a year later, he wrote about it in *The New Republic*, with more than a tinge of bitterness. "The officials in charge of baseball adhered to their policy of curing an evil by declaring it did not exist and by using their influence over consciously or unconsciously subsidized sportswriters to suppress the accusations and punish those who demanded an investigation."[23]

Damon Runyon wrote a revealing article in the 1940s on why he had stopped covering sports a couple of decades earlier. He eloquently addressed the challenge that sportswriters faced. "I had softened up too much long before I quit it. . . . To be a great sports writer a man must hold himself pretty much aloof from the characters of the game with which he deals before his sympathy for them commences to distort his own viewpoint. There is nothing more engaging than an engaging rogue and there are many engaging rogues in professional sports. I fear I knew most of them, and that is not good for a sports writer."[24] Runyon also said that gambling influences on baseball continued well after Landis's arrival. In the mid-1920s notorious criminal attorney William Fallon told Runyon that dozens of players were "up to their necks" in gambling.[25]

When the scandal broke, Chicago White Sox owner Charles Comiskey suspended his eight players suspected of involvement in the fix. At the time, the White Sox were only a half game out of first place, but the personnel losses devastated their pennant prospects. That very day, the Yankees' owners made a remarkable offer to Comiskey (who had supported them in their Carl Mays battles). "Your actions in suspending players under suspicion . . . not only challenges our admiration but excites our sympathy and demands our practical assistance. . . . Our entire club is at your disposal," announced Ruppert and Huston.[26] The White Sox's secretary responded, "Of course, it is impossible [to transfer players so late in the season], but the offer will bring tears to the old man's eyes."[27]

Many observers now felt, in retrospect, that when Organized Baseball did not punish the corrupt Hal Chase in 1919 for "throwing" games, other dishonest players saw little risk in doing so. John Sheridan of the *Sporting News* went even further and blamed the Black Sox scandal in part on the owners. "The whitewashing of Chase and the encouragement of Mays in his notorious indiscipline and disregard of all fair dealing have done more to bring about the present condition in baseball than all other things."[28]

Jacob Ruppert certainly did not make such a connection when he spoke at length about the scandal a few days after the story broke. First, he naively reinforced the fiction that this was a unique and isolated incident. "I do not think that there has been much gambling [in baseball] before last year," he said. He then addressed the future of the suspected players—weeks before Landis did so. "Of course they are forever out of organized baseball. They will never have a chance to return." Ruppert explained why Organized Baseball was so opposed to gambling on the game. "Baseball club owners are sensible business men. . . . If they permitted gambling to get a hold they would destroy the game and with it their property; their business would go to ruin." He then promised "for my life and yours, baseball will be kept clean."[29]

19

Huggins Stays

On October 12, 1920, Jacob Ruppert spent the evening at West Side Park, home of the International League's Jersey City Skeeters.[1] Along with many celebrities and politicians, he witnessed the light-heavyweight championship fight between Frenchman Georges Carpentier and Battling Levinsky. Carpentier, a French war hero who was being promoted as a worthy challenger to heavyweight champion Jack Dempsey, won in a fourth-round knockout. However, the general agreement among the press and the fans was that Carpentier would be no match for Dempsey. When they did meet, on July 2, 1921 at Boyle's Thirty Acres, also in Jersey City, that assessment proved correct. In a fight that drew more than 90,000 spectators and generated boxing's first million-dollar gate, Dempsey scored a fourth-round knockout.

Dempsey's rise to the championship in 1919, along with Ruth's arrival in New York in 1920, had launched a golden age in sports.[2] On October 13, 1920, three major sports stories were featured on the front page of the *New York Times*: Cleveland's World Series triumph over Brooklyn; Carpentier's knockout of Levinsky; and Man O'War's match race victory over 1919 Triple Crown winner Sir Barton in Windsor, Ontario.

Thoroughbred racing's Man O'War would join Ruth, Dempsey, football's Red Grange, tennis's Bill Tilden, and golf's Bobby Jones as their respective sports' most memorable figures of the 1920s. But baseball was the most popular sport and the one most ingrained in people's everyday lives. And among baseball players, Babe Ruth was by far the best known and liked. "Ruth replaced Christ as the center of attention on Sunday," claimed one historian—an overstatement, no doubt, but one that rang true among some segments of baseball-loving America.[3]

Sport "had become an American obsession," noted historian Frederick

Lewis Allen just after the decade ended. He wrote that newspapers (and soon, radio) found profit "in exploiting the public's mania for sporting shows and its willingness to be persuaded that the great athletes of the day were supermen."[4]

Modern historians have sounded a similar theme. Michael Parrish explained how heroes helped maintain the myth of individualism. "The selling of individual personalities became as important to the maintenance of social order as the selling of durable goods," he wrote. "And the American appetite for vicariously participating in their lives proved nearly inexhaustible."[5]

Ruth's "superman" status had become such that his addition had raised expectations for a Yankees' pennant in 1920, and when they fell short, the critics grew fierce. The target of that criticism was Miller Huggins. If Huggins had been on the hot seat at the end of the 1919 season, it was even hotter a year later. "He undoubtedly lost last season's championship by mistakes in selection of pitchers during the final western trip," wrote Hugh Fullerton.[6] Stories revolving around Huggins's weaknesses as a manager and his impending departure from the Yankees dominated the press. For the first and only time in his Yankees career, his biggest supporter, owner Jacob Ruppert, wavered in his support. "Huggins, I hear, is a marked man. Already the little fellow is receiving the full blame for the Yankees' failure to walk off with the pennant. . . . The gossips say that a certain clique in the Yankee team is out to get Hug's scalp."[7] Those were the words of *New York Evening Sun* columnist Joe Vila, written late in the 1920 season. Vila, who always gave Huggins the benefit of the doubt, felt he had made the best of a difficult situation.

Sid Mercer spoke for many when he wondered about the lack of discipline in the clubhouse and wrote of Huggins, "He is a student of the game, but not a commanding figure among men. . . . Do the Yankees need a professor of baseball or a disciplinarian?"[8] Damon Runyon explained away Huggins's alleged failure as a disciplinarian, the chief complaint against him. "It must be remembered," Runyon wrote, "that he is handling a club made up largely of men who got their baseball elsewhere, and such a club is more difficult for a manager than one he makes to suit himself."[9]

Some observers agreed with Vila; they were not surprised that the Yankees did not win the pennant. At the start of the season, John Sheridan wrote in the *Sporting News*, "If he finishes in the first division with that oddly assorted and expensive crew, I shall be greatly surprised. Manhood, the love of the game, the spirit to win, these things make for success— and his team has them not."[10] One New York sports editor hinted at the carousing and nighttime activities of some of the Yankees. Had they been as concerned about "their mode of life as they are of getting the last dollar for their services," wrote Sam Murphy, they would now be preparing for the World Series.[11]

After the 1920 season, Hughie Jennings resigned as manager of the Detroit Tigers. Jennings had led them to pennants in each of his first three seasons (1907–9), but had never won again and called it quits following Detroit's seventh-place finish. He immediately joined the ever-growing list of those rumored as replacements for Huggins. In addition to Jennings, the list now included Yankees outfielder Duffy Lewis; Pants Rowland, former manager of the White Sox; Bill Carrigan, former manager of the Red Sox; George Stallings, current manager of the Boston Braves; and most prominently, Wilbert Robinson, who had just led Brooklyn to its second pennant in five years.[12]

On October 13, the day after Cleveland defeated Brooklyn in the World Series, the *New York American* went so far as to report that Robinson would definitely be managing the Yankees in 1921, with Huggins switching to Brooklyn. The managerial swap was seen as a victory for Til Huston, who had preferred Robinson when Ruppert chose Huggins back in 1917. Brooklyn sportswriter Tom Rice noted that Robinson had an engaging personality (something that Huggins lacked), with "the knack, or gift, of winning the public and doing it unconsciously . . . he radiates personality without knowing how or why."[13]

Years later, Jacob Ruppert admitted that this one time, in October 1920, he vacillated in backing Huggins. "The argument finally broke me down and I told Huston that if Robbie wanted to come to the Yankees it was okeh with me."[14] Ruppert met with Robinson and offered him the position of Yankees' manager. Just after the Robins had lost the World Series to the Cleveland Indians, Brooklyn owner Charles Ebbets said, "I wouldn't stand in Robinson's way if he wanted to manage the Yanks, but I hope he will never lay such a proposition before me."[15]

The October 12 *Evening Telegram* reported that Robinson had signed with the Yankees and quoted Huggins as expressing surprise that the Yankees' owners had not notified him beforehand. He admitted they had been noncommittal to him, but he said he had no plans for resigning. "My contract with the Yankees expires this year," he said, "but in view of my work with the club I have not worried much about losing my job."[16]

The next morning, the *American* reported that Huggins had met with Ebbets about managing Brooklyn. Robinson had accepted the Yankees' offer, the paper stated, and "Huggins permitted it to be known that he will not manage the Yankees next season. . . . Colonel Ruppert was finally convinced that Robinson, who accomplished remarkable results in Brooklyn, was the ideal man to manage the Yankees." However, the paper also reported a denial from Robinson, who said he had not decided to leave Brooklyn. "The owners of the Yankees aren't negotiating with me and I'm not negotiating with them," he said. "Reports that I am going to change teams are foolish and untrue."[17]

A couple of weeks went by. Wilbert Robinson had second thoughts. He talked the matter over with his wife, Mary, and perhaps felt the responsibility and pressure of leading the Yankees would be too great. Perhaps he could not bear leaving Brooklyn, where he had become a treasured part of the community, practically a Brooklyn institution. Maybe he feared becoming the source of a Ruppert-Huston conflict, should the Yankees falter sometime in the future. Robinson signed a three-year contract with Brooklyn, practically on his own terms, at a substantial pay raise.[18]

Following the Colonel's death, George Perry, a friend and advisor to Ruppert, talked about the alleged pursuit of Robinson.[19] Perry believed that by offering the job to Robinson, he was calling Huston's bluff, knowing that Robinson preferred to remain in Brooklyn, where he was comfortable and beloved. "I have always thought that Jake knew what was coming when he 'gave in' to Til."[20]

Ruppert had publicly denied he was contemplating a managerial change, and he ended all speculation that Huggins would not return when the Yankees re-signed him on October 28. Huggins came to New York from his off-season residence in Cincinnati to sign his 1921 contract. He then returned home to vote for his fellow Ohioan, Senator Warren G. Harding, in the November 2 presidential election.[21] Colonel Ruppert commented on the signing. "Huggins may have his faults, but in justice to the man, it must be admitted that under his management the New York Americans have played their most interesting ball in the history of the club."[22]

Ruppert had prevailed over Huston, who wanted Huggins gone, but did not have another candidate besides Robinson to replace him. Nevertheless, Sam Murphy of the *New York Evening Mail* thought Ruppert was making a mistake in keeping his manager. He praised Huggins's ability as a judge of players and recommended he be kept on as an advisor. It was his failure to control men on the playing field that Murphy believed adversely affected him as a manager. "Whether the players are right or wrong, the mere fact that they are ever ready to condemn the decisions of Huggins would convince any student of the value of men as leaders that the Yankees need a man who is more stern than Huggins."[23]

Vila wrote that Huggins must be given the authority to "rule with an iron hand" in 1921. The problem on the team was "the inflation of several craniums," players who thought they knew more than Huggins and even some who wanted his job. Next year, warned Vila, "If there are swelled heads on the team, he must flatten them."[24]

Shortly after the Yankees acquired Babe Ruth, the *Sporting News* wrote that it took a special leader to handle a group of stars, each requiring special handling. If Huggins could succeed with these Yankees, "they ought to erect a monument to him up there along Riverside Drive. But if reverses come they may as well begin to figure upon his tomb."[25]

On the same day that the Yankees re-signed Miller Huggins, they made another important personnel move, one that would prove crucial for the team's long-term success. They hired fifty-two-year-old Ed Barrow, the manager of the Boston Red Sox, as their business manager. "They were building," Barrow explained in his autobiography. "They had Ruth. . . . And it was New York."[26]

Barrow brought a rich resume of baseball positions, most of them away from the dugout, including being president of two Minor Leagues and the owner of Minor League teams. His temperament and skill set lent themselves more to an executive position than that of a field manager.

After business manager Harry Sparrow's sudden death on May 7, at age forty-four, Colonel Huston attempted to handle his responsibilities, but he did not have the patience to do so on a long-term basis. In his history of the Yankees, Frank Graham noted, "Huston was more concerned with

rooting for the team than he was with the books, its scouting system. . . .
Ruppert was the first to realize where they were drifting."[27] Harry Frazee
was willing to let Barrow go, in part because he was looking to reduce
overhead and in part because he wanted to solidify his relationship with
the Yankees' owners.

When Barrow joined the club, Huggins did not know what to make
of the newest Yankee. There were stories that Barrow might take over as
manager should Huggins not succeed in 1921. There were other reports
that Barrow would help Huggins enforce discipline with the unruly members of the club. Early on, Barrow set Huggins's mind at ease. He told
him, "You're the manager, and you're going to get no interference or
second-guessing from me. Your job is to win, and part of my job is to see
that you have the players to win with. You tell me what you need, and I'll
make the deal—and I'll take full responsibility for every deal I make."[28]
Not only did Barrow support his manager; he also provided a buffer to
protect him against interference from Huston. Barrow was acutely aware
of such meddling from the problems he had with owner Frank Navin as
manager of the Detroit Tigers back in 1904.

Barrow began to expand his role into that of a modern-day general
manager, handling executive functions from salary negotiations to player
acquisitions, though he worked in tandem with Ruppert on the former
and Huggins on the latter. Barrow also brought his coach, Paul Krichell,
with him from Boston. Krichell would work with Barrow and Bob Connery as a scout, concentrating in his first years on college prospects, a talent pool the Yankees had previously left untapped.[29]

The arrival of Barrow in many ways provided the Yankees with an
essential link in building a professional organization. Ruppert quickly
grew comfortable in delegating to Barrow, as he already was to Huggins.
"It was Barrow who started the Yankee organization on its way, who laid
the foundation that enabled the club to carry on," wrote Tom Meany in
his history of the Yankees.[30]

Part 5

THE YANKEES

RISE TO THE TOP

20

One of the Fiercest Pennant Battles Ever

Led by Babe Ruth, who hit fifty-four home runs, the 1920 Yankees had shattered individual and team home run records. In late May Miller Huggins claimed, "The team has such offensive strength that it can't help but bring results despite its deficiency in speed."[1] That deficiency was evident by the Yankees' 64 stolen bases (in 145 attempts), second to last in the league, and almost 100 fewer than Washington.[2] Although committed to the power game, Huggins, very much a product of the Deadball Era, was intent on adding speed to his lineup.

"I realize that lack of speed is one big handicap of the Yankees as the club is constituted today, and my main task is to add speed to the team," Huggins explained on signing his 1921 contract in October.[3] He said he would probably make changes in his outfield and pitching staff while standing pat with his infielders and that he was mostly satisfied with his catchers.

Yet despite the manager's statement that he was satisfied with his infielders and his catchers, newly hired business manager Ed Barrow's first deal involved a major shakeup to both positions. On December 15, 1920, Barrow, with Huggins's full approval, engineered a trade with the Boston Red Sox, the team he had managed for the past three seasons. Second baseman Del Pratt, catcher Muddy Ruel, outfielder Sammy Vick, and pitcher Hank Thormahlen went to Boston, along with $50,000, in exchange for pitchers Waite Hoyt and Harry Harper, catcher Wally Schang, and infielder Mike McNally.

Personnel evaluation was one of Huggins's strengths, and he was the driving force behind the trade. Barrow confirmed its logic once he joined the team. The two key players in the deal were Pratt for Boston and Schang for New York. Pratt had batted a combined .295 in three seasons with the Yankees, including a .314 mark in 1920, but his trade was expected. He was a leader of the team's anti-Huggins clique and had campaigned for Huggins's job late in the 1920 season. Huggins did not want to lose twenty-four-year-old Muddy Ruel, but the pressure was on him to win in 1921 or likely be fired. To do so, he felt he needed a more experienced catcher, like Schang, the starting backstop for two World Series winners: the 1913 Athletics and the 1918 Red Sox. Schang, reasoned Huggins, could better handle veteran pitchers Bob Shawkey, Carl Mays, and Jack Quinn.

While it seemed a fairly even deal at the time, it would prove to be among the Yankees' best trades ever. Schang was arguably the best all-around catcher in the league and would continue to be so with New York. Hoyt had made a big impression on Huggins in that thirteen-inning 2–1 loss in September, when he retired twenty-seven men in a row. "Young Hoyt is a pitcher of infinite promise," Huggins said. "I cannot tell you how pleased I was to be able to secure him from the Boston Red Sox. I expect great things of him and do not think he will disappoint me."[4] The hotheaded and sometimes impetuous youngster would achieve immediate stardom with the Yankees, while McNally would be a valuable utility man on three pennant winners.[5]

Two weeks later, the Yankees acquired Bobby "Braggo" Roth from Washington in exchange for outfielder Duffy Lewis and pitcher George Mogridge. Huggins hoped that Roth, who had stolen twenty or more bases in each of the past six seasons, would be the answer to the team's need for speed. The Yankees would be the sixth team in eight seasons for Roth, a talented and temperamental player with a reputation for frequent run-ins with his managers.[6]

After the two big off-season trades, only pitcher Bob Shawkey and infielders Roger Peckinpaugh, Wally Pipp, and Frank Baker remained from the 1917 Yankees' team Huggins had inherited. In his ongoing attempt to assemble the best team he could, both on the field and in the clubhouse, he had even parted with ten players from the 1920 squad that had come so close to a pennant.

The Yankees had made some significant additions, but Colonel Ruppert was not satisfied. "We intend to go right ahead and build up a strong ball club for next season. Colonel Huston and I have but one objective in mind. That is to win the world's championship. We shall not be content to finish second or third. We want that title," he said.[7] "If we don't win this year, I cannot see how we could ever win," said Huston."[8]

During the winter, Ruppert had been forced to confront yet another legislative scheme hatched or supported by New York's rural upstate Republicans. For more than a quarter-century, the urbane New York City Democrat had been the unwitting victim of several of their proposals. They had, to some degree, driven him from the business of racing thoroughbreds and were intent, through Prohibition, on dismantling his primary source of income. Now, following the election of Judge Landis as baseball's commissioner in early 1921, they were considering a new plan, one that would limit Ruppert's control over his ball club. Their proposal, which had the support of numerous upstate politicians and in certain high circles of the state government, was for a commission to administer the affairs of baseball, boxing, racing, and other major sports in New York State.[9]

National League president John Heydler reacted immediately, saying such an arrangement would be a terrible mistake. "Never in the history of baseball has there been so little need for outside interference. Such a commission as the one proposed would be a colossal blunder," he said. "It would absolutely disrupt the sport at the very moment its legislative department is in the very best possible condition. It would destroy the good that baseball has accomplished through the last few months. Never, in fact, has professional baseball been better able to regulate itself and to regulate the players and the club owners as a whole than at the present."

Heydler had a strong ally in Ruppert, who since his purchase of the Yankees in 1915 had fought vigorously to put the government of the game on a businesslike basis. "We have been fighting for dignified and sagacious handling of baseball's affairs for a long time, and now we are getting it from Judge Landis, who is so splendidly equipped both as to personality and mental fiber to undertake such an important assignment," said Ruppert. "Why not let baseball and other sports alone? I fail to see any definite reason why there should be any tampering with any of them. But baseball, beyond any other branch of sport, is able at last to govern itself as well as the best regulated business establishment in the country. Let the game alone." The views of Ruppert and Heydler prevailed, and no such commission was ever launched.[10]

After two years in Jacksonville, Florida, the Yankees moved their spring training to Shreveport, Louisiana, in 1921. Huggins had pushed for the move in an attempt to cut down on his players' partying, drinking, and general hell-raising in Florida. Prohibition was having a serious effect on Ruppert's income, as his brewery was now limited to making only "near beer." But Prohibition was having no effect on his players. The same wild behavior of the past two training camps continued unabated in Shreveport. The old accusations that Huggins was unable to control his players picked up just where they had left off at the end of 1920.

Late in spring training, as the Yankees were preparing to leave Shreveport, Huggins was bedridden with what one paper termed a "catarrhal attack of the appendix." Yet, unknown to most, he was dealing with far more serious health issues. A nervous man by nature, he had found the strain of the 1920 pennant race too much to handle, though his "nervous collapse" was reported only after the 1921 season and by only one newspaper. Veteran reporter Bill Slocum divulged after Huggins's death that the little manager had almost ended his relationship with the Yankees that winter of 1920–21 when his health was so bad.[11]

Huggins had turned forty-three in March, yet he looked years older. "His wrinkled forehead and the creases around his eyes suggested a life of struggles, or health problems, or both. He was not a natural leader, and managing a big-league ball club had not come easy for him. Doing so these past three years in New York, a city with an unforgiving press and demanding fans, only added to the stress."[12]

Back in January, the *Sporting News* front-page headline had announced, "Mite Manager Has Strengthened Himself on Field and at Same Time Has Rid Himself of Some Unruly Spirits."[13] Yet while Pratt, one of his leading critics among the players, was gone, Huggins still had "troublemakers" on his roster, led by Babe Ruth. More threatening to his job security was co-owner Huston, who would continue to undercut his authority. Fred Lieb was one of many who thought the Yankees were the best team in the American League, calling them "the greatest combination of clouters in history."[14] Many others expected Cleveland, led by player-manager Tris Speaker, to repeat. "Cleveland wins largely because of Speaker. . . . If the Yankees win, it will not be because of Miller Huggins, but in spite of him," wrote Ralph Davis of the *Pittsburgh Press*.[15]

Huggins expected his fiercest competition would come from the defending champion Indians, while acknowledging the Yankees were "wonderfully well equipped this year to make a hard and determined fight of it."[16] William B. Hanna thought the Yankees' "pennant chances depend chiefly on how they fight and hustle and their steadfastness in keeping it up."[17]

The pennant quest got off to an uneven start. On April 27, the Yankees lost their fourth straight game to Washington—all come-from-behind wins by the Senators. Making the loss even worse for Huggins were the contributions made by two players he and Barrow had recently traded away. George Mogridge got the win in relief, and Duffy Lewis hit the ninth-inning, game-winning double. Huggins knew both men were still viable players, but he had personal reasons for trading them. He suspected Lewis of wanting his job and therefore considered him "persona non grata."[18] Mogridge had fallen out of favor when he refused to leave the mound one afternoon after Huggins had called for another pitcher.[19]

The loss was the Yankees' fifth straight overall and dropped their record to 5-6. Of immediate concern to Huggins was the state of his pitchers. "The celebrated right-handed pitching staff is as shot full of holes as a Swiss cheese," declared Sid Mercer.[20] For Huggins, frail and often ill, this was just the beginning of a 1921 season that would become a considerable ordeal.

In early May, Huggins made some lineup changes that included moving third baseman Aaron Ward to second base, which allowed Frank Baker, who had sat out the 1920 season, to return to third. The team started to win, but some of the Yankees' players continued to defy Huggins and question his managerial strategy. In one game Carl Mays's refusal to issue an intentional walk ordered by Huggins cost the Yankees a game.[21] In another, Ruth hit a home run after ignoring an order to sacrifice. The fans cheered the Babe, unaware that he had defied his manager's orders. Huggins let Ruth know of his displeasure and fined him, a move that *Evening Mail* sports editor Hugh Fullerton applauded: "No player is a good player who disobeys orders or who plays for personal glory at the expense of team work."[22] Reports that Ruth was "not staying in condition" and was "violating training rules" drew criticism of the Babe in the press, even from his supporters.

The Yankees were two games behind the first-place Indians when they arrived in Cleveland on May 14. New York took three of four, including a win by Carl Mays. It was his first appearance in Cleveland since one of his pitches had killed Ray Chapman in the Polo Grounds the previous August. Any doubt that Mays would pitch in the series was quickly squelched by Huggins. "Mays is going to pitch just as sure as my name is Miller Huggins," he declared.[23]

In first place after the Cleveland series, the Yankees then split a four-game series with the scandal-depleted Chicago White Sox to fall out of the lead and to again set the Huggins critics howling. The team was suffering from "the lack of inspiring leadership," wrote George Daley, trying to explain why the Yanks lost to weak teams. "[Huggins] is without the personal magnetism so necessary in holding his men on a level they are quite capable of reaching."[24]

The Indians and Yankees continued their seasonlong battle for first place, and by July 20, when the Yankees next visited Cleveland, the New Yorkers were one game behind. They had won sixteen of their past nineteen, including eight straight with Huggins on the sidelines after an attack of blood poisoning forced him to take a leave of absence. While he was gone, Roger Peckinpaugh, the Yankees' shortstop and former manager, and Huggins's trusted coach, Charley O'Leary, ran the team. Huggins had returned for the Cleveland series, but, not unexpectedly, there were those who thought the team would fare better had he not. W. J. Macbeth wrote, "Writers with the club say that under Peckinpaugh it was one of the most formidable machines ever seen. . . . It is up to Huggins to make good in like fashion or gracefully retire."[25]

Some players, no doubt, preferred to play for the easygoing Peckinpaugh. In a thinly veiled swipe at his manager, Babe Ruth said in his syndicated column, "Unlimited credit belongs to Roger Peckinpaugh for the way he handled the club during the absence of Miller Huggins."[26] And while noting that Huggins deserved a fair chance to succeed, Hugh Fullerton reported there was a good chance the Yankees would replace him with Peckinpaugh. He explained that unnamed "experts" felt Huggins was "a 'wet blanket' sort of manager whose manner and actions tend to discourage the players, while Peckinpaugh is an inspiring leader."[27]

Several players, unhappy with Huggins, were said to be planning a meeting with Colonel Huston to persuade the team's owners to fire him.

"When Hug admonished the players for some of their pranks off the field, they simply laughed at him. . . . They had reason to believe that any shackles placed on them by Huggins would be struck off by Cap [Huston]," wrote Frank Graham.[28]

Joe Vila, who continued to be one of Huggins's few friends in the New York press, was outraged. He accused those involved of sabotaging their skipper. He also chastised the fans, "grandstand managers" he called them, for wanting "to hurl him [Huggins] into outer darkness" whenever the Yankees lost a game.[29] Colonel Ruppert, as he had in the past, defended his manager, informing the press that Huggins would remain.

Even as Huggins was steering the Yankees toward their first-ever pennant, he remained continually subject to criticism from the press and derision from the fans. In late September a caption in the *Sporting News* declared, "The Mite Manager fights his way through, sans diplomacy, sans personality, and makes it harder for himself; that's not his fault: he was born that way."[30]

The Yankees clinched the pennant on October 1, at the Polo Grounds, after what Damon Runyon called one of the fiercest pennant battles in baseball history. As the fans celebrated, Runyon described Huggins as he "tramped across the yard in the wake of his men, his head bowed in a characteristic attitude. In happiness or sorrow Huggins is ever something of a picture of dejection. The crowd cheered him as his familiar Charley [*sic*] Chaplin feet lugged his small body along, and Huggins had to keep doffing his cap."[31] It was now time, said Runyon, to give Miller Huggins his due. "He is entitled to all the credit and the glory that goes with the leadership of a pennant winning ball club. He is entitled to an apology from those who have belittled his efforts."[32]

The New York Giants, seemingly out of the National League race in August, had staged a dramatic late-season comeback to snatch the pennant from the Pittsburgh Pirates. The World Series would be a match not only for the championship of baseball but for supremacy in the nation's largest city.[33] "It is more than possible that the victor in this combat will plunge ahead as the chosen team of the city, and if the American Leaguers bring home the bacon it will mean much, very much to them. . . . McGraw has never lost his hold on the popular imagination of New York, and the legend that he is the greatest still exists and is still potent."[34]

The Series would prove to be a watershed moment in baseball, particularly in New York. In one corner stood John McGraw and the old, established Giants, a fixture in the city since the "Rosie O'Grady" days of the Gay Nineties. In the other stood Babe Ruth and the brash Yankees, the perfect sports symbol for what would come to be called America's "Jazz Age." McGraw was one of baseball's two most outsized characters featured in the Series; the other, of course, was Ruth, the game's greatest slugger. The Babe had just put together the most productive batting season ever. In addition to his .378 batting average, he hit fifty-nine home runs, which broke the single-season record he had set in 1920, scored a league-leading 177 runs, and set a new runs batted in record, with 171. His on-base and slugging percentages were an astounding .512 and .846.[35]

Still, McGraw felt his pitchers could cope with Ruth. "Why shouldn't we pitch to Ruth?" he responded when asked before the Series if the Giants would pitch to the home run king. "I've said it before, and I'll say it again, we pitch to better hitters than Ruth in the National League."[36]

Adding to the drama surrounding this first all–New York World Series was McGraw's jealousy of the Yankees, who were threatening to replace the Giants as the city's favorite team. He also resented Ruth, due in part to the Babe's role in moving the game away from the "inside baseball" McGraw had helped foster. The Yankees' exciting power game had moved them much closer to being the Giants' equals in the estimation of New York's fans, as reflected by the Yankees' home attendance exceeding that of their Polo Grounds landlords. However, they were not yet on a par with the Giants in the eyes of the Wall Street and Broadway crowds or with most older New Yorkers. "This is a National League town," declared Sid Mercer. "John J. McGraw put his label on it years ago, and the Giants are firmly established. Up to a couple of years ago, the Yanks were just the 'other New York team.' But the immense personal popularity of Babe Ruth and the dynamite in the rest of that Yankee batting order have made the Yanks popular with the element that loves the spectacular."[37]

The confrontation between McGraw and Ruth captured the headlines, but it was the confrontation between McGraw and Huggins that drew the focus of the experts. The decisive edge, they decided, belonged to McGraw. Sam Crane spoke for many in the press when he said the Giants' manager was more creative and more of a risk-taker, while Huggins was more deliberate and predictable.[38] William Hanna, a reporter familiar with both managers, disagreed. He thought Huggins was not getting his due. "Tactically Huggins plays second fiddle to nobody, nor is he behind anybody in quick grasp of openings," Hanna declared.[39] McGraw himself had thought highly of Huggins's abilities ever since he led the Cardinals to a surprise third-place finish in 1914. "Miller Huggins is my ideal of a real leader. . . . He can take a player who has shown only a mediocre supply of ability on some team and transform him into a star with his club. . . . He will make a high mark as a manager in baseball one of these days."[40]

The Yankees got off to a great start in the Best-of-Nine World Series, winning the first two games, as Mays and Hoyt pitched back-to-back 3–0 shutouts. "I don't see why people should be so awfully surprised by our showing in the first two games of this series," Huggins said after Game Two.[41] Perhaps the surprise, if there was any, came not from the Yankees winning those two games but rather in the manner in which they won. Aware of how good the Giants' pitching was likely to be, and knowing runs would be scarce, Huggins had abandoned the slugging game for more of a small-ball type attack. "The team supposed to be composed of heavy-footed sluggers depending exclusively on the big blast for victory," wrote Grantland Rice, "has suddenly turned and played a series of inside rings against one of the smartest teams in the game."[42]

Led by the pitching of Art Nehf, Phil Douglas, Fred Toney, and Jesse Barnes, the Giants bounced back to take the Series, five games to three. In contrast to McGraw's pitching depth, Huggins could depend only on Hoyt and Mays. With his limited pitching options, noted Sid Mercer, Huggins "remains just one jump ahead of dire necessity."[43] Also, the Yankees missed Ruth, who batted .313, with one home run, but sat out the final three games with a badly injured left arm. McGraw's pitchers walked him five times but struck him out eight times. Hoyt, who pitched three complete games without allowing an earned run, lost the final game, 1–0. The Giants scored in the first inning on a slowly hit, routine ground ball that shortstop Peckinpaugh allowed to go through his legs. When Peckinpaugh failed to go into short left field to retrieve it, Dave Bancroft, who had been the runner at second base, came around to score. Nehf made the one run stand up.

Losing the World Series was a great disappointment for Huggins, but if there had been a nadir to his 1921 season, it came in a game at the Polo Grounds on September 19. The Yankees, behind Carl Mays, held a comfortable 4–0 lead over Detroit, but Mays collapsed in the eighth inning as the Tigers scored eight runs on their way to a 10–6 victory.[44] The crushing defeat pushed the Yankees out of first place and, combined with the insults from the fans, the hostility of the press, and the rebellion from his own players, severely affected the troubled and sickly Huggins. After the game, he wrote a letter of resignation and sent it to Ruppert, who refused to accept it.[45] Ruppert recognized the difficult situation in which Huggins operated; nevertheless, he had confidence in his manager's leadership qualities. "It was Ruppert's words of encouragement in the darkest hours that kept Huggins from losing his nerve," wrote Joe Vila.[46]

Peckinpaugh, who was seen as a likely replacement should Ruppert ever sour on Huggins, was gone before the end of the year.[47] Barrow, again with Huggins's endorsement, traded him to the Red Sox in a multiplayer deal that brought pitchers Joe Bush and Sam Jones to New York, along with Everett Scott, who would replace Peckinpaugh at shortstop.[48] Bush and Jones were both twenty-nine years old, while two of the pitchers going to the Red Sox, Bill Piercy and Rip Collins, were both twenty-six. The *Sporting News* concluded that the Yankees were again looking to "win now," by giving up prospects for proven veterans.[49] "The insistence of the [Yankees] club owners and their patrons on an immediate winner has worked against the retention and development of these prospects."[50] However, Jones and Bush helped New York win two pennants and were the top two winners on the club's first world championship team.

The trade of Peckinpaugh came as a big surprise to the fans and an absolute shock to the Yankees' team captain. "I am too stunned to make any statement," he said. "The deal is entirely news to me, but it seems that no matter how good a player one is or how loyal service he gives the New York team, his position is never safe."[51]

A few months later, in April 1922, Hugh Fullerton questioned just how much control Huggins had over the team in 1921 and particularly in the World Series. He wrote that late in the 1921 season, the players "practically assumed charge of the team ten days prior to the World Series last fall. The series was run by a committee rather than by the manager, with Ruth and Peck cutting in or dictating. The results were not entirely happy."[52]

Ruppert, meanwhile, continued to back his manager in every aspect of the game. "I consider Huggins one of the ablest, smartest and best managers in baseball. . . . But for a combination of circumstances, over which Huggins had no control, the Yanks would have won the big series with the Giants in five or six games."[53]

21

The Struggles and Troubles of Huggins

The strain of the 1921 season took a terrible toll on Miller Huggins. Shortly after the World Series loss to the Giants, he suffered a nervous collapse.[1] Recovering at the home of his brother Arthur in upstate New York, he was reported to be playing over the events of the recent Series in his delirium.[2] In 1924 reporter Will Wedge wrote of the Yankees' manager, "He admits he has never felt quite the same since his nervous breakdown several years ago."[3] Huggins had no idea that the 1922 season would be far more trying for him than 1921. It was the stress of managing that gave the gaunt manager the appearance, as one writer put it, of "a jockey grown old."[4]

There were a number of reports that Huggins would soon retire, but when 1922 rolled around, he was preparing for another season with the club.[5] He had few interests outside of baseball; on off days during the season, he would often go to the Yankees' offices downtown.[6] The truth was he had nothing better to do.

Huggins took an interest in the burgeoning field of aviation, where it seemed that virtually every week in the early years, a pioneer of the skies was killed in flight.[7] He also enjoyed reading about finance and real estate in the *Wall Street Journal*.[8] Joe Williams captured Huggins's colorless personality with a vivid portrayal. "Mr. Huggins smokes a pipe, reads the market quotations, talks little, has a sad smile, makes friends reluctantly, has his own ideas about baseball and baseball players, votes a straight Republican ticket, and thinks Tiger Flowers [a black boxer] is a florist. . . . He seldom says anything beyond a guarded, indecisive comment on the character of the prevailing weather, if any."[9]

The Yankees moved their spring training from Shreveport, Louisiana, to New Orleans, where they could draw bigger crowds. But New Orleans nightlife proved too tempting for many of the players and certainly was not conducive to serious training. One New York sportswriter filed a report with the headline, "Yanks Training on Scotch."[10]

While the Volstead Act was "the Law of the Land," it was routinely ignored, and alcohol was readily available, especially in urban areas—and not only for celebrities, athletes, and the wealthy. Essayist and satirist H. L. Mencken noted, "I believe there is more bad whiskey consumed today than there was good whiskey before Prohibition."[11] While most government officials publicly supported Prohibition, many—including President Harding and Judge Landis—continued to drink.[12] More women drank after the ban than before, finding speakeasies far more attractive than saloons.

During an exhibition game in Little Rock, Arkansas, Carl Mays threw a tantrum and heaved the ball into the stands when Huggins pulled him from a game. Hugh Fullerton saw Mays's "petty display of temper" as symptomatic of deeper problems. He noted that the team was still riddled with anti-Huggins players, even after Roger Peckinpaugh (a rallying point as a possible managerial alternative to Huggins) had been traded away. Joe Vila wrote about "know-nothing second guessers" and Huggins's "cowardly enemies."[13] Should Huggins again not have the real authority to enforce discipline, wrote Fullerton, "the team may collapse utterly."[14]

Perhaps in response to such columns, Til Huston backed up his manager (an unusual show of support) when Huggins fined Mays $200 for his ball-throwing tantrum.[15] A *Sporting News* editorial suggested that Huston, who had had "frequent outbreaks of vocal rash" in the past, should now take a back seat to Ruppert in presiding over the club and supporting Huggins. Maybe Colonel Ruppert had found something for Huston to do, the paper opined, such as "excavating at the site of the new ball park."[16] The paper had never forgiven Huston for leading the battle against Ban Johnson, a good friend of the Spink family.

That new ballpark, the future home of the Yankees, was finally moving forward. It had taken almost a year from the 1921 purchase of the land for the city to close the streets that ran through the property. Work began in early May 1922. Huston did spend much of his time at the site during construction.

Huggins was facing a much bigger problem than dealing with the temperamental Mays. The Yankees would have to play the first six weeks of the season without Babe Ruth and Bob Meusel, who were paying the price for violating the baseball stricture against barnstorming by World Series participants. Ruppert and Huston did not fight the player suspensions; they did not have much choice.[17] They thought the rule was unjust, but "as long as it exists, it should be obeyed," they said in a joint statement.[18] When Commissioner Landis attended a Yankees' spring training game, he saluted "two of the gamest owners in organized baseball . . . who have not complained or sought surcease from one of the hardest jolts it has been my lot to deliver."[19]

Primarily on the strength of their pitching, the Yankees were in first place, two games ahead of the St. Louis Browns, when Ruth and Meusel returned to play on May 20. Thirty-eight thousand fans turned out at the Polo Grounds to see "Ruth and Company" host the powerful Browns. The huge crowd saw an exciting game, an apparent 2–1 New York victory. But the Browns appealed the final out, saying the ball was juggled at first base as the Browns' Jack Tobin crossed the bag. Umpire Ollie Chill eventually agreed and reversed his call. The Yankees were called back from the clubhouse, and the field was cleared of fans. Play finally resumed, and before the Yankees were able to get the third out, the Browns exploded for seven runs and a stunning 8–2 win, to climb to within one game of the Yankees. After the game, a stunned and speechless Huggins just stared at his locker.[20] It would be that kind of a topsy-turvy season.

The Babe did not get the ball out of the infield against Browns ace Urban Shocker and reliever Billy Bayne. It would be that kind of season for him, though he did have some explosive stretches.[21] In the first month after his return, Ruth was twice ejected by umpires and suspended by Ban Johnson for a few days.[22] Joe Vila continued to be critical of the struggling slugger, "the eminent Swatless Sultan of Swat, who has been laboring under the delusion that he owned the national game, lost his temper and made a fool of himself."[23] A few weeks later, Vila was even harsher. "Ruth as a home run king is through. . . . Ruth's downfall was inevitable. He was always overrated, as the Giants realized."[24]

Ruth was hitting below .200 as June rolled around and was batting only .267 with eight home runs at the end of the month. For the first time as a Yankee, he was hearing persistent booing from the crowd; for a man who loved the adoration of the fans, the heckling rankled him. Hugh Fullerton explained a seeming paradox in an age of entertainment stars. "If there is one thing that pleases an American public more than cheering a hero as he is elevated, it is jeering him when he falls."[25]

The suspensions took Ruth away from the game he cherished. When he returned from his second enforced absence to hit five home runs in four games in early July, Miller Huggins and millions of fans hoped he was settling back into form. As one New York sportswriter wrote, "The Babe does love baseball. That may prove his redemption. No matter how far he may stray from the straight and one-way paths, the deep-seated yearning for the crack of the bat against the ball is the biggest thing in Ruth's life."[26] It was this longing for the game and the roar of the crowd that Vila and other critics did not account for. It was this craving that would pull him back from the edge more than once in his career.

Huggins continued to face challenges to his authority from a number of his players. Early in the season, twenty-two-year-old Waite Hoyt took a swing at his manager in the dugout after a fourteen-inning loss to Boston.[27] Fullerton noted that since the World Series of the previous fall, "Hoyt has shown aggravated symptoms of inflation" and had joined "the unruly ones" in the clubhouse.[28] Huggins minimized the incident as a temporary outburst by a hot-headed youngster in the heat of the moment. "I always remember that I, too, once was a ball player. I know he [Hoyt] has his heart and soul in that game," he said.[29] Fullerton felt that the Yankees' manager handled the scrap with class and had gained respect by doing so.

Another member of the group that enjoyed carousing and who gave Huggins a hard time was outfielder Bob Meusel, an immensely talented ballplayer who often appeared lackadaisical on the diamond. Huggins said of him, "Meusel could be one of the greatest centre fielders the game has ever produced. . . . He has been content thus far to sort of drift along, playing brilliant ball one day and lapsing into mediocrity the next, simply for lack of sustained effort. He is one of those players who can be just as good as they want to be, and up to now he hasn't seemed to care a whoop whether he developed into a star or remained just an ordinary outfielder."[30]

All season long, the Yankees and the Browns staged a fierce see-saw race for first place. What was going on in the Yankees' clubhouse was not fully reported, but as in previous seasons, it seemed that some players were undermining their manager. Joe Vila charged that some of the Yankees were indifferent to winning games, if not losing them on purpose, and should be treated by the commissioner just like the banned Black Sox. Huggins was dealing with "swollen craniums, jealousy, indifference and downright inefficiency," he wrote.[31]

The Yankees were also fighting among themselves. Babe Ruth and Wally Pipp got into a scrap on June 10 in St. Louis. They both hit home runs that day, a 14–5 shellacking of Urban Shocker, who had dominated the Yankees since they traded him.[32] Afterward, Browns coach Jimmy Austin muttered, "You birds ought to fight every day." When two other Yankees fought the next day, Huggins threatened fines and suspensions if such behavior continued. "I'm running a ball club, not a fight club," he said.[33]

There were reports that the Yankees would sell or trade the trouble-makers. Hoyt, Meusel, Mays, and Aaron Ward were regularly mentioned as the culprits.[34] When the team lost eight straight games in mid-June, rumors swirled that Huggins would be fired. He demanded that Ruppert confirm his status. "Colonel Ruppert, I am the manager of your team or I'm not. Make the announcement, or you can have my job."[35] Ruppert quickly clarified matters. "We wish to deny emphatically that we are considering a successor to Huggins. He is not to blame for the slump of the team. The players themselves are, in the main, responsible for the losing streak."[36] Business Manager Ed Barrow shored up his manager's position even more. Early that season he asked the Yankees' owners not to enter the clubhouse unless invited by Huggins.[37]

In late June Commissioner Landis made a special trip from his office in Chicago to Boston, where the Yankees were playing. The club, on Huston's suggestion, had hired a detective who posed as a newspaperman and traveled with the team.[38] He reported to the Colonels about the Yankees' drinking and other nighttime activities. He even produced a photograph of a number of the Yankees (including Ruth and Meusel) at an Illinois brewery, an obviously illicit endeavor during Prohibition. In a rare display of Huggins's sense of humor, he later hung the picture in his office.[39]

The Yankees' owners in turn passed the investigator's report on to Landis, perhaps because they were searching for help in establishing discipline among their unruly group. Landis met the team in the visitors' clubhouse and focused on accounts that a number of the Yankees were betting heavily on horse races. He read the team the "riot act," warning that when he got hard evidence of such activities, "No matter how big you are, no matter how great a star you may be, punishment will be swift and sure."[40] Landis's remarks were delivered to all the players, even though they were intended for some more than others. One Ruth biographer wrote that Landis told Ruth, "If I ever hear of you bettin' another hoss, I'm gonna put you out of baseball."[41]

Huston later said that a number of the Yankees had been fined for betting on horse races. He was asked how the team had the right to control what the men did off the field. "Off the field is just it. They bring it onto the field. We found them running out between innings to get horse-race returns."[42]

One bright spot for the Yankees was the play of their recently acquired shortstop, Everett Scott. Vila felt he was the best player in the game at his position, a definite improvement over the man for whom he had been traded, Roger Peckinpaugh.[43] In late June, Scott played in his 900th consecutive game. James O'Leary of the *Boston Globe* wrote, "No other player has come anywhere near this mark, and it is doubtful if ever one does."[44]

A week before the August 1 trade deadline, New York made another big trade with the Red Sox, acquiring one of the game's best third basemen, Joe Dugan. Since mid-June, the Yankees had been stalled in second place behind the Browns, and third baseman Frank Baker had been hobbled by a rib injury that kept him out of action for a month. Huggins and Barrow sent Boston three players who had never developed as the Yankees expected, infielders Chick Fewster and Johnny Mitchell and outfielder-pitcher Lefty O'Doul, as well as veteran outfielder Elmer Miller and $50,000.[45]

In a "quantity for quality" deal, the Yankees got the twenty-five-year-old Dugan in return. Cleveland's player-manager Tris Speaker called the trade "a crime."[46] When *Baseball Magazine* chose Dugan as the game's best third baseman of 1922, F. C. Lane wrote that his "all-round class is superior to that of any of his competitors."[47] Huggins later called the Dugan deal the best trade he ever made.

The St. Louis Chamber of Commerce (representing the interests of their city's Browns) sent a letter of protest to Commissioner Landis, who said he would push for making the trade deadline earlier in the season. A week later, the other New York team, the Giants, acquired pitcher Hugh McQuillan from the other Boston team, the Braves, for $100,000 and three players. In the winter meetings late that year, that deadline was moved up to June 15, starting in 1923.[48]

St. Louis sportswriter John Sheridan lamented the fact that the New York teams, because of all their money, had their choice of the game's best players.[49] Another *Sporting News* columnist declared that there were only two big-league clubs left, the New York ones. All the others were either "pawns or farms [farm clubs] or foils."[50]

There was a real "community of interest" between the owners of the Yankees and the owner of the Red Sox. Ruppert and Huston wanted to spend money to build a champion, and Harry Frazee needed money for his theater interests and other pressing financial concerns. Yet knowing that did not make things any easier for Red Sox fans, who were pained, embittered, or both.

A neutral observer, Chicago's Irving Vaughn, looked at all the New York–Boston trades of recent years and wrote, "Frazee's dealings have done more than to make the Yankees champions. He handed over players who, had they been retained, would have kept Boston in the title or near-title class, instead of the doormat class."[51] The influx of Red Sox talent to the Yankees was invaluable. However, many contemporary accounts thought the Yankees–Red Sox trades of these years (1918–23) were fairly equitable (and that some even favored Boston), even though they turned out to be anything but.[52]

Right after Dugan joined the Yankees, they went on a western road trip and won eleven of fifteen games. Their key contributor was the team's quiet and solid first baseman, Wally Pipp. He went thirty for fifty-five (a .545 batting average) with fifteen runs batted in on the trip. When the team came home, Babe Ruth had a hot streak. From August 16 to August 20, he too batted .545. He also hit five home runs in four games, as the Yankees moved into first place.

Huggins realized he had to hold the Babe answerable to some rules. Sid Mercer noted that most of the manager's woes came from having two sets of rules—one for Ruth (hardly any rules at all) and one for everyone else. Huggins was in a difficult and awkward position, Mercer explained.

If he fined the Babe, his star might quit in anger. If he suspended the Babe, the team's owners would suffer a large revenue loss from the drop in attendance.[53]

Ruth had repeatedly stayed out late at night and arrived late for pregame warm-ups, despite having a clause written into his contract forbidding late-night excursions.[54] On August 20, Huggins told traveling secretary Mark Roth, "This has gone far enough"; he was going to say something to Ruth after the day's game. The Babe hit two home runs, including a three-run game-winning blast in the ninth inning. Fans carried him off the field in celebration. Afterward, Huggins did say something to his slugger: "Hiya, Babe!" He explained to Roth, "Say something to him? What the hell can you say to a guy like that?"[55]

Intuitively Huggins knew that to succeed as a leader, he could not treat all his men the same way. Early in his Yankees career, he said, "One system will not rule. It is impossible, because you will find temperamental players, you will find players who do not need any rules, and you will find players who insist that they know more than the manager."[56]

Yet as long as Huggins was unwilling or unable to confront the Babe and hold him accountable on basic matters such as curfew and limits on carousing, he could not lead effectively. Huggins's defenders may have blamed the lack of discipline on the easygoing Huston, who enjoyed his nights on the town drinking with Ruth and undercut the lines of authority. Yet in private correspondence with Ruppert, Huston was adamant that he had pushed for discipline and regularly reported Ruth's transgressions to both Ruppert and Huggins, to no avail.[57] Ruppert would admit at the end of the season that he too had muddied the water by suggesting leniency for his players.[58]

Huggins must shoulder at least some of the blame. As long as one member of the Yankees had no rules, discipline for the rest of the club had a hollow ring. One wonders how John McGraw, a fierce disciplinarian, would have handled Ruth and whether he too would have had interference from the owners' suite. The fact remains the Babe was one of the world's biggest celebrities and would have been a challenge for any boss.

Hoyt reminisced about the party atmosphere of those days in a 1965 interview: "It was the birth of something new, and everybody from the Astors [a prominent wealthy New York family] to gangsters wanted to meet baseball players. It was fashionable to say, 'I met so and so last night at such and such night club.' Another thing that is forgotten: Then we played strictly day baseball and we had ample time at night to go here and there."[59]

In 1929 Damon Runyon looked back at Huggins's early years and saw a lonely soul. "Huggins always struck me as rather a pathetic figure in many ways early in his managerial career. He was inconspicuous in size and personality. He seemed to be a solitary chap, with few intimates. He wasn't much of a mixer. And for a long time there was no doubt that some of the high-priced giants that surrounded him viewed him with some contempt. But the little man 'had something,' no doubt of that."[60]

Ruth and Meusel were not the only Yankees who were suspended in 1922. In early May Huggins was suspended for a few days after new umpire (and former pitching great) Ed Walsh tossed him from a game for questioning his calls—and his eyesight. In August Huggins was fined (based on the umpires' report) for stalling during a rain squall, to prevent a game the Yankees were losing from becoming official.[61] Another ejection has become a part of baseball lore. Huggins and center fielder Whitey Witt, whom the club had acquired early that year to shore up their depleted outfield, were ejected from a game that summer by umpire Bill Guthrie. Guthrie supposedly told Witt, pointing at Huggins, "Take the bat boy with you."[62]

The Yankees came back to win the pennant, edging the Browns by only one game, on the strength of taking two of three games in what was called "the Little World Series" in St. Louis in mid-September. New York won the deciding game by rallying against Urban Shocker, who had come in to nail down the victory in the ninth inning. Shocker won twenty-four games in 1922, but the Yankees beat him seven times, three by the score of 2–1.[63] When the Yankees clinched the pennant in Boston a couple of weeks later, "they were hooted and jeered as no other pennant winning outfit" by the disgruntled Red Sox fans.[64]

The Yankees were favored in their World Series rematch with the Giants on the strength of their pitching. They had added Joe Bush, who posted a 26-7 record, while the Giants had lost Phil Douglas, one of the stars of the 1921 Series.[65] The Yankees also had a healthy Babe Ruth. While the Yankees were 7–5 betting favorites, Hugh Fullerton analyzed the teams and felt the Yankees should be overwhelming favorites.[66] Jacob Ruppert was also confident, saying, "Those boys will win. They smell the money."[67]

In a stunning outcome, John McGraw's Giants swept the Yankees and held Ruth to a meager .118 batting average. (After three years of Best-of-Nine games, the Series had returned to a Best-of-Seven games, which has remained to this day.) The Yankees did not win a game, though they played a ten-inning tie in Game Two, called on account of the approaching darkness.[68] When the commissioner decided that the entire proceeds of the game would be donated to charity, the Colonels could not agree on the charities, which added to their already strained relationship.[69]

The Series ended when the Giants came from behind with three eighth-inning runs and a 5–3 win. When Huggins signaled for Joe Bush to walk the dangerous Ross Youngs intentionally, Bush loudly cursed at his manager seated in the dugout and shouted, "What for, you stupid oaf?" This outburst was heard by hundreds, if not thousands, of fans.[70] Bush did walk Youngs, but then threw a pitch down the middle of the plate that George Kelly hit for a two-run single, the lead, the game, and the Series. After the game, Huggins and Bush were heard yelling at each other in the clubhouse.[71] F. C. Lane described Huggins when he met the stunned manager afterward. "The Yankee leader sat hunched in a chair, his slouch hat pulled down over his eyes, a battered pipe in his mouth. His attitude was that of a man who had experienced all that misfortune could bring and was rather indifferent as to what would happen next."[72]

That night Frank Graham wrote, "Ruppert was fuming and Huston was bellowing."[73] More than forty years later, Fred Lieb wrote that a possibly inebriated Huston shouted in the bar of the press headquarters hotel, "Miller Huggins has managed his last Yankee ball game. He's through! Through!"[74]

In the wild aftermath of the World Series that night of October 8, Ruppert got word of his partner's rant at the bar of the Commodore Hotel. Fred Lieb described his reaction. "Ruppert then slammed his fist on a table and said, 'If anybody wants to know who the next manager of the Yankees is, I'll tell him. His name is Miller Huggins.'"[75]

While the Yankees did not win a single game, each contest was close, and the Giants had to come from behind in three of their wins. John McGraw called it the best World Series ever played.[76] Babe Ruth came in for the brunt of the criticism for the loss. Joe Vila continued his anti-Ruth crusade, calling him "an exploded phenomenon" who had built his reputation on American League pitchers "who lacked either skill or brains."[77] Even Grantland Rice wrote that Ruth was "one of the most demolished idols who ever fell over the precipice."[78]

Ruppert said that Bush should be fined for his public outburst at his manager. He also admitted that the "baby tactics" the Yankees had been using with their star players had been a mistake. "Miller Huggins has been hampered too much by the owners of the Yankees. That includes myself. We catered to the whims of ball players, always believing that Huggins was wrong in his desire to execute discipline. . . . From now on Miller Huggins is going to manage those players. He is going to sign them, trade them, fine them and suspend them—and Babe Ruth is included. That goes. That is my reward to Huggins. There isn't a man on the club who is going to be bigger than Huggins."[79]

Ruppert noted that John McGraw had lost three straight World Series (1911 to 1913), yet neither the New York press nor the fans had called for his firing. "Huggins has won two pennants for us," said Ruppert. "That accomplishment speaks for itself. He has made good."[80] A couple of days later, Huggins signed to manage the Yankees again in 1923. Perhaps this was when Ruppert decided he had to consolidate control of the team. His relationship with Huston—as exemplified by their dispute over Huggins—had become terribly dysfunctional. The two Colonels simply could not remain partners.

The *Sporting News* editorialized, "Perhaps never in the history of the game has any manager been so flouted, reviled, and ridiculed." For the past three seasons, rebellious Yankees had probably overplayed their hand as they plotted to get their manager fired. Huggins gave sportswriter Arthur Mann his thinking on the matter. "You will find that ball players who get too ambitious are always dumb. They are easy to outsmart, but they usually outsmart themselves."[81] An acquaintance told Huggins, the editorial added, that if he had "a spark of manhood, he should chuck the job."[82] But Huggins was not a quitter, especially when he had the staunch support of Jacob Ruppert, and he did not want to leave his owner in the lurch either. If the team needed to be blown up," wrote Frank O'Neill, "Huggins himself will ignite the fuse."[83]

During his Yankees years, Huggins's friends would also tell him to quit for health's sake. He probably heard such advice both before and after the trying 1922 season. Huggins's reply was always the same. "Baseball is my life. I'd be lost without it. Maybe, as you say, it will get me some day—but as long as I die in harness, I'll be happy."[84]

22

Huggins Is My Manager

Shortly before Christmas 1922, the Yankees announced that Jacob Ruppert was buying out Til Huston and would become the team's sole owner. Huston explained his decision to sell as a desire to slow down and provide for the financial future of his family.[1] The price was reported as $1,250,000, an enormous return on his initial investment of $225,000.[2] Huston and Ruppert were complimentary of each other and said they got along "splendidly," though there were many veiled comments in the press suggesting this was not the case.

The fifty-fifty ownership arrangement had been uncomfortable for two men accustomed to getting their own way. Ed Barrow was more direct in his autobiography, written almost three decades later, describing "two self-willed personalities, who by background, manner, and outlook were worlds apart." Barrow had even played a role in precipitating the buyout. Tiring of the infighting between the two owners, he threatened to quit unless one bought the other out.[3] Barrow's preference was for Huston to sell: Ruppert's professional approach to running the organization corresponded to his own, and like Ruppert, Barrow believed in Miller Huggins as a manager.

Huston was frustrated that Huggins was still managing the club, over the dispute with Ruppert about where to donate the money from the tie game in the recent World Series, and with having so much of his net worth tied up in the new stadium. Huston was even more candid in his correspondence with Ruppert; it was clear their working relationship was irreparably broken.[4] "Huston wanted out as badly as Ruppert wanted him out," wrote Daniel R. Levitt in his Barrow biography.[5]

The Colonels had previously received and turned down offers from circus impresario John Ringling and boxing promoter Tex Rickard. More recently, oil millionaire and horseman Edward F. Simms had offered $3 million for the Yankees.[6] In 1938 Ruppert recollected that he and Huston had agreed to a buyout of $2.5 million from Simms, but the negotiations had fallen through.[7] Perhaps Ruppert had considered selling in 1922, before Huston had agreed to sell, because neither Colonel could tolerate partnering with the other any longer.

The 1922 World Series was the final blow in the owners' battles over Huggins. Huston felt the sweep by the Giants necessitated his firing. Ruppert felt his partner's intemperate anti-Huggins tirade was beyond the pale. When Ruppert got word of Huston's post-Series outburst, he said, "If Miller wants to manage the Yanks next year, the position will be there waiting for him. . . . We are with Huggins, first, last, and all the time."[8] Just three days after the World Series, after "a verbal battle" in which Ruppert "asserted himself so vigorously," the Yankees signed Huggins for 1923.[9] Ruppert was able to get his way but he realized—as did Huston—that they could no longer continue as partners. Sixty days later, Ruppert's buyout of Huston was announced. Ruppert said, "Running a ball club has its worries, and I think the 'Cap' [Huston] wanted to be relieved of the strain." Ruppert wanted to remain in the game and said he would rather continue alone than have another partner. "I realize it is quite a responsibility I am taking over. . . . However, I am willing to tackle the additional care and think I can get away with it."[10]

The convivial Huston was beloved by many sportswriters, who were saddened to see him go. "Magnates of his type are too valuable to be lost," wrote Bill Phelon in *Baseball Magazine*. "Col. Huston was the gamest kind of sportsman, a royal good fellow, and the soul of integrity."[11]

Yet there were dissenting voices in the national press. The *Sporting News* attributed the Yankees' clubhouse problems—as well as those of baseball as a whole—to Huston's meddling. The weekly blamed his battles with Johnson over Carl Mays as contributing to a general breakdown of authority and discipline throughout the game.[12] The paper's long-held animosity toward the departing Colonel distorted its view; it gave his actions more influence than they really had and blamed many of the game's ills on him.

Despite how often he had called for Huggins's firing, Huston maintained that no manager ever had more backing from his owners than

Huggins had received from Ruppert and him.[13] He insisted that his only objection to Huggins was that he was too lax with his team. Three years earlier, in his column in the *Sporting News*, John Sheridan had captured the shortcomings of the emotional Huston. "He has so often let his heart run away with his head, and passions run away with his prudence that one almost despairs of him."[14] Sid Mercer noted somewhat amusingly that Huston was "a good hater, but he hates openly and not surreptitiously."[15]

Because Huston had been in the public eye much more than Ruppert, newspapers saw the buyout as an opportunity to reintroduce Ruppert to the public. Joe Vila recalled that back in 1918 Ruppert had told him he was not in the game to make money. "It's pure sportsmanship."[16] Sid Mercer wrote of Ruppert's integrity. "When he tells you something, you can rely on it. In a game where deceit and skullduggery are rife it is refreshing to find such a man." That is why "the Yankees will always stand for big things."[17]

Just after New Year's Day 1923, as the Yankees were preparing for their first season in their new stadium, Huston met with the press to announce that he and Ruppert were objecting to the scheduling of conflicting Sunday home games with the Giants. Newspapermen wondered why the former Yankees owner was involved with a problem relating to the upcoming season. After a flurry of questions, Huston admitted that the buyout had fallen through and that he would remain as the team's co-owner.

While he insisted he was back to stay, the press sought to determine why the deal had collapsed. One theory suggested Ban Johnson and his supporters were gloating about Huston's leaving, and the proud owner refused to quit "under fire." But the real reason, according to many accounts, was that the final papers had a non-compete clause: Huston could not become a baseball owner in New York for ten years, and he had refused to accept that restriction.[18]

The obstacle may have developed at baseball's winter meetings a few days after the sale was originally announced. Johnson had recommended the clause to Ruppert so he would not have to deal with Huston as a potential competitor in his own city.[19] There had been reports that Huston would buy (or buy into) the Dodgers, managed by his friend Wilbert Robinson, or even the Giants. Charles Stoneham, the Giants' owner, was facing criminal indictment, and stories circulated that he would soon sell his team.[20] Ruppert had endured enough battles with Huston in the boardroom; he did not want to resume them in a crosstown rivalry. Ruppert wanted to be done with him for good.

Ruppert tried to put a good face on the news, saying he was pleased his partner was remaining. One paper reported that Huston had offered to buy Ruppert out, but the latter made it clear he was not leaving. "My share of the Yankees is not for sale. . . . I am heart and soul with the team."[21]

Concurrent with the return of Huston were reports that the Yankees were again trying to acquire Eddie Collins from the White Sox. Collins had broken into the Major Leagues in 1906 and appeared to be nearing the end of his playing career. The thirty-five-year-old also had made no secret of his desire to manage a Major League club. The Yankees had come close to acquiring the star second baseman from Philadelphia in 1915 but passed because new owners Ruppert and Huston were not sure they would acquire the franchise.

W. J. Macbeth reported that the Yankees would send Bob Meusel, Aaron Ward, and Waite Hoyt to the White Sox in exchange for Collins in a blockbuster deal. Macbeth also wrote that the Yankees were close to acquiring pitcher Herb Pennock, which would mean they could afford to trade Hoyt.[22]

Did Huston's return and the club's renewed interest in Collins mean that Miller Huggins was once again on the firing line? With Collins on the way in, was Huggins on the way out? The Yankees' roster of moody, egotistical stars had made his job impossible, wrote sportswriter Warren Brown. He noted that if Huggins ever gave up managing a baseball team, he could "make big money by entering a cage of hungry lions to lecture therein on baseball deportment and temperament."[23] But Huggins was thinking beyond his managerial career—even beyond baseball—to a more sedate profession than either baseball or lion-taming.

George Daley of the *New York World* had a revealing story the week after Huston was back "in" with the Yankees. He wrote that the driving force behind the push to secure Collins as a replacement for Huggins was none other than Huggins himself. The Yankees' manager recognized how fragile his health was. "I have higher ambitions than to manage a ball club all my life. . . . I love it but the strain is too much year in and year out, for the money there is in it. If I stay in baseball, it will be as an owner, and I'll let someone else do the worrying." Huggins was thinking of retiring after the 1923 or 1924 season, wrote Daley. He enjoyed dabbling in real estate and was considering managing properties. While some people thought Huggins would consider the capable and intelligent Collins a threat to his position, the Yankees' manager said the truth was just the opposite; he wanted Collins because of those very strengths. "I want to see Col. Ruppert fortified when I retire, for I certainly am not going to work for someone else [in baseball]."[24]

F. C. Lane seconded Daley's account in *Baseball Magazine*: "Huggins, with the strong support of Colonel Ruppert, is doubtless assured of his position indefinitely. But it doesn't necessarily follow that he wants the job indefinitely. Huggins' task of managing the Yankees has been the toughest managerial assignment in either league. He is not a robust man and his labors have made tremendous demands upon his nervous energy."[25]

How can Huggins's comments about his unwillingness to leave baseball and love of the game be reconciled with those in which he discussed retiring? The answer lies in human nature. He was not the first person—nor would he be the last—to have mixed feelings about his lifestyle and career choices. He recognized his health problems and vulnerability to stress, but he also did not see alternatives that offered him as much satisfaction as his current job did.

Huggins also felt Collins still could play at a high level. In January 1923, he said of the White Sox second baseman, "He ought to be a great player for several years more. . . . At thirty-six he looked better to me than any second baseman in either league."[26] Huggins was right. Collins would play as a regular for four more seasons (1923 to 1926) and hit over .340 in each, with an on-base percentage of more than .440 each year. But he put up those numbers for Chicago.

While Macbeth was right about the Pennock trade, the Collins deal never happened. As with many proposed trades, sometimes the ones not made turn out to be the best. Hoyt's 3.02 earned run average was the league's second best in 1923, while Meusel's ninety-one runs batted in and Ward's eighty-two contributed greatly to the Yankees' offense. Moreover, Hoyt and Meusel would be two of the league's best at their positions for the next six seasons.

A month after the opening of Yankee Stadium on May 21, the buyout was back on again, this time for good. The non-compete clause that had derailed the original sale was removed. The price and terms had changed only slightly.[27] More important for Huston, he got out from under the massive debt related to the building of the stadium. "It's all over now," Ruppert said. "The papers have been signed, sealed, and delivered. They go into effect on June 1. By law and every other way I am now the sole owner of the Yankees, or at least I will be within another ten days."[28]

Actually, Ruppert allowed Barrow to buy a 10 percent ownership stake in the team.[29] The Colonel recognized that Barrow attended to the myriad details that he did not want to get bogged down with and also freed up Huggins to focus on the game between the lines. With Barrow handling the back-office functions and Huggins dealing with the players on the field (and to his dismay, their nighttime activities), Ruppert understood he had a management team that worked well together and would drive the Yankees to excellence—and keep them there.

He recognized Barrow's operational skills and, in the words of Tom Meany, that Barrow had a "singleness of purpose . . . absolutely ruthless in his fight for dominance."[30] The Colonel wanted to lock his talented business manager, a man with a varied baseball career, to the Yankees, long term.[31]

While Ruppert declared his association with Huston had "been a delight and truly remarkable for its few differences of opinion as to the policy to be pursued," the truth was much the opposite.[32] In a letter to Ruppert shortly before the buyout, Huston revealed just how strained the relations between the two men had become.

I am especially bitterly dissatisfied over the way in which our business is being conducted at present. We went into this business as a partnership basis, but now you have arrogated to yourself so much authority and doing continually so many things without consulting me that it is becoming a one man show and only a question of time when you will drive me into an open rebellion. . . . The other day in talking over the phone regarding the fence advertising you said brusquely you would give me an 'answer' on such and such a day. Please be informed that you can give me an 'answer' on no question of this club's affairs. You can give me your 'opinion' only. . . . The fact that you seldom visit our office is a serious handicap to our business. . . . It is absurd we see one another so infrequently . . . As it is now, our office is a mere annex to your Brewery, which is intolerable.

Huston was not through.

As to Ed Barrow I think you have insidiously bribed him like [President Woodrow] Wilson did labor during the war. In my opinion he thinks you are alone responsible for his large raise in salary. You vaingloriously made Mrs. Barrow a present of $1,000 of our money over the phone not saying a word to me about it. . . . Your policy as a whole, it seems to me, has been to belittle me. [Ban] Johnson and his five club owners blame me for the Carl Mays fight.[33]

In another letter, this one to Barrow, Huston reminded him that it was he, not Ruppert, who had the idea to hire him as the team's business manager. He then criticized Barrow for a number of actions that he found underhanded. Huston closed by writing in part: "From the preceding it is apparent that the camaraderie and friendship which has existed personally between us cannot continue."[34]

The *Sporting News* was again pleased with Huston's exit and portrayed Ruppert as an unwilling partner in the battles against Ban Johnson. The weekly said that Ruppert had "grown in grace" and now regretted challenging the league president over Carl Mays.[35]

There is no question that Ruppert had been a very willing partner in the battle against Johnson in the Carl Mays dispute; a review of his statements at the time makes that abundantly clear. However, almost four years later, Miller Huggins had turned against Mays, and Ruppert's views on discipline had evolved. He may very well have regretted picking the fight over Mays, though it is doubtful he ever admitted so in public.

Frank Graham wrote that Ruppert was "supremely happy" when he completed the buyout. "Nothing he ever had done before had pleased him so much."[36] His press release looked back at how far his Yankees had come since 1915. "The team which was bought had only one good player on it. Today it is the best. . . . The club when acquired was a waif. It had not playing grounds, but was a tenant at the mercy of a rival league and subject to the tender caprice of an opposition club. It has now a home of its own in the most magnificent baseball stadium in the world in the heart of the greatest city of America."[37] Yet there was still work to be done; there was one thing that would please him more: winning a World Series.

Even though the Giants had beaten the Yankees in the last two World Series, the attendance numbers for each team told a different story, one in which the Yankees were the clear winners. One *Sporting News* columnist noted that the club had achieved "the seeming impossible task of displacing the Giants as favorites in New York." They did so by "imitating and then surpassing the Giants' ancient star-buying policy."[38]

With Huston gone, Ruppert told reporters, "I'll have to give it [baseball] more attention." He added, "Huggins can stay as manager as long as he wants. He's doing pretty well, isn't he?"[39] When the buyout was announced, the Yankees were in Chicago, where they had just swept the White Sox to push their league-leading record to 23-8. Ruppert sent a simple yet emphatic telegram to his team, which he instructed to be read in their clubhouse. "I am now the sole owner of the Yankees. Miller Huggins is my manager."[40]

When Miller Huggins looked back on his years working for Huston, he said, "I owe a lot to Colonel Huston. . . . The Colonel thought I was so rotten and said so in so many columns of spaces so many times that nobody expected anything from me. Even the little things I happened to do right stood out like mountains."[41]

Yet the reality was quite different for the team's skipper; it was a brutal time for him. Huggins told Fred Lieb in late 1924, "I will be frank with you. I would not go through those years again (1920–22) for a million dollars. Money is a nice thing to have, and we all like honors. But money and honors are nothing compared with peace of mind and health. I was a sick man during a good part of the time, perhaps sicker than my friends knew, but I held on and stuck it out."[42]

23

This Is the Happiest Day of My Life

"An institution is the lengthened shadow of one man," wrote Ralph Waldo Emerson. So it was no surprise that when Jacob Ruppert, who had always sought to be the best in any endeavor he undertook, decided to build a new ballpark for his Yankees, he built the biggest, most modern baseball stadium in the country. In February 1921 he and co-owner Til Huston had paid the estate of William Waldorf Astor $600,000 for a ten-acre parcel of land in the Bronx—just across the Harlem River from the Polo Grounds.

Once scoffed at as being too remote a site for a baseball team, the Bronx was undergoing a population boom. Between 1900 and 1930, the number of Bronx residents would increase more than sixfold, from 201,000 to 1,265,000.[1] Moreover, the new stadium would be reachable by New York's ever-expanding network of subways and elevated lines. The 161st Street station of the Jerome Avenue line, opened in 1917, would be just a short walk from the new stadium.[2]

John McGraw, who had quipped that no one would go to see the Yankees play in the Bronx, had not considered the changing demographics of New York City. "As a demographer, McGraw was stuck at the turn of the century," wrote Neil Sullivan in his history of Yankee Stadium. The new subway, noted Sullivan, had helped the Bronx change from "the Northwest Territory of Manhattan" to a functioning part of the city.[3] "Yankee Stadium is a mistake. Not mine, the Giants," Ruppert would often say with a sense of satisfaction."[4]

In May 1922 White Construction Company began work on Yankee Stadium, under the directions of architects from Osborne Engineering Company of Cleveland. Colonel Huston, a trained engineer, was on site almost every day, overseeing the sinking of the foundation, the pouring of the concrete, and the erection of the steel girders.[5] When finished, Yankee Stadium had three concrete decks that extended from home plate to the left- and right-field corners, with a single deck in left-center and wooden bleachers around the rest of the outfield.[6] "In short," wrote the *New York Times*, "the Yankees' Stadium is just about the last word in baseball plants."[7]

Ruppert chose to name his creation Yankee Stadium, because he wanted the name to depict a grand venue "that would be made impenetrable to all eyes, save those of aviators."[8] He had made it clear that he was building the park primarily for his baseball team. He opposed the idea of boxing at ballparks because he did not believe baseball and boxing were a good mix. "Boxing is legal in this State and not in others," he said. "Then there are times in New York when it is legal and other times when it is illegal." His protestations aside, Ruppert did not completely rule out boxing at the Stadium. "I would not object if our new park was used for an occasional big fight, and I would not want too many of those. But I am unalterably opposed to a ball club staging regular weekly boxing shows."[9]

Nevertheless, the first "occasional big fight" came less than a month after the Stadium opened. A benefit for the Milk Fund on May 12 featured two heavyweight bouts designed to determine a challenger for champion Jack Dempsey's crown. The two winners were rising Argentinian star Luis Angel Firpo and former champion Jess Willard.[10]

The construction of Yankee Stadium was completed in eleven months at a cost of $2,500,000, including the price of the land. The American League lent the Yankees $400,000 toward the cost of building the stadium.[11] Opening Day was April 18 against the Red Sox, and head groundskeeper Phil Schenck and his crew did an excellent job of getting the field ready.[12]

The Stadium had 60,000 seats, which was not nearly enough for the opener; more than 20,000 disappointed fans were turned away. Ed Barrow estimated the attendance at approximately 74,000. That was probably on the high side; still, it was by far the largest crowd ever for a baseball game.[13] Surprisingly, the police reported only two arrests for ticket-scalping outside the Stadium; one man tried to sell his $1.10 grandstand ticket for $1.25, and another man tried to sell a similar-priced ticket for $1.50.

The huge turnout delighted Ruppert, Huston, Barrow, and everyone associated with the business end of the Yankees' operation. It was also a lucrative day for concessionaires Harry M. Stevens and his son and key lieutenant, Frank, as they watched the fans spend their money not only on food but on first-game mementoes. The enterprising father-son duo had expanded the information contained in the scorecards, which normally sold for a nickel, renamed them "souvenir programs," and were selling them for 15 cents.[14]

Guest conductor John Philip Sousa and the Seventh Regiment Band led the teams in a parade to the flagpole in center field. Miller Huggins and Frank Chance, the new Red Sox manager, raised the American flag and the Yankees' 1922 American League championship flag.

Governor Al Smith of New York and baseball commissioner Kenesaw Landis led the parade back to the front of the Yankees' dugout, where Huggins was presented with a large horseshoe of roses. Colonel Ruppert removed one rose and wore it in his lapel throughout the game. Red Sox owner Harry Frazee sat in the owners' box as a guest of the Yankees. Also at the game was New York Giants owner Charles Stoneham, though two who had planned to be there were notable absentees: Mayor John F. Hylan, too ill to attend, and American League president Ban Johnson, suffering from a "sudden attack of influenza."

Huggins gave the honor of pitching the Yankee Stadium opener to Bob Shawkey, who had been with the Yankees since July 8, 1915, and was second only to first baseman Wally Pipp in length of service with the club.[15] Boston first baseman George Burns got the first hit in the new stadium, one of only three hits that Shawkey allowed in a 4–1 win.

The distinction of hitting the first home run in the new park went, as if willed by the baseball gods, to Babe Ruth.[16] It came against Howard Ehmke in the fourth inning, with Whitey Witt and Joe Dugan aboard. "Grinning as he followed Witt and Dugan around the bases, he waved his cap at the fans, who responded with the loudest roar of the day. Given the size of the crowd, the ovation Ruth received following his home run may have been the biggest ever heard at a ballgame."[17]

A month later, on May 21, the on-again, off-again sale of Huston's share of the club to Ruppert was finalized. "It was too good to refuse," Huston said about the deal. "I simply couldn't pass it by. In justice to myself and my family I had to accept." But, he added, "My interest in baseball will never wane. I expect to see every game played in New York unless I am out of town."[18]

Despite the bitter behind-the-scene infighting related to the sale, things on the field were going splendidly. The Yankees won their first four games, took over first place in early May, and had a record of 21-8 at the time of the Huston buyout. They were never seriously challenged and won the pennant by sixteen games over Detroit. As early as May, after a successful 12-1 western swing, Joe Vila was predicting a romp for the Yankees: "In my opinion the Yankees are sure to get into another World Series."[19]

With both the Yankees and the Giants seemingly headed for their third consecutive pennants, voices of anti–New York sentiment continued to be heard in the hinterlands. "The prominence of New York in Major League baseball has become a disturbing element," wrote F. C. Lane. "The task of keeping New York strong, but not too strong, still remains one of the great problems in the politics of the National game." Lane noted that because visiting teams shared in gate receipts, "New York is a gold mine of both Major League circuits." Lane acknowledged that baseball faced a problem not easily solved. "The combination of brains and money," he wrote of the two New York clubs, "is a hard pair to beat. . . . The attempt to divorce wealth and intelligence from all advantage has never succeeded anywhere."[20]

By mid-July the Yankees had a twelve-game lead over Cleveland, but Ruppert wanted more. "He doesn't relish excitement," Vila wrote of the Colonel. "He'd rather see his team score 14 runs in the first inning and shut the other fellows out the rest of the way, than pull for a 1–0 victory."[21]

Clearly, the days when baseball in New York "belonged" solely to the Giants were long gone. Attendance figures over the past four seasons had shown the Yankees were now the dominant attraction in the city. As much as that pleased Ruppert, he wanted to be more than the dominant attraction—he wanted to be the dominant team.[22]

Vila believed Ruppert had an additional incentive, that he was driven by a desire to gain revenge on John McGraw and the Giants for the Series defeats of the previous two years. "The Colonel's thirst for the Giants' gore," he wrote, "is the result of the intense rivalry between the two clubs."[23] The battle between the Yankees and the Giants for baseball supremacy in New York had been waged since the arrival of Babe Ruth in 1920. A World Series win by the Yankees would leave no doubt that they were now supreme.

Ruth followed his "off" year of 1922 by batting .393 and leading the league in home runs (41), runs batted in (131), runs scored (151), and slugging percentage (.764).[24] His league-leading 170 walks helped contribute to his career-high .545 on-base percentage.[25] The Babe was chosen unanimously as the league's most valuable player.[26] Powered by Ruth, the Yankees led the league in home runs and slugging percentage.[27]

It had now become apparent even to Huggins's biggest detractors that much of the credit for the Yankees' success belonged to their manager. "He more than ever this year," wrote the *New York Times*, "asserted his remarkable managerial talents in piloting the Yankees to the top with a team no stronger than last year, but one that played the game all the time and simply won through the punch of Ruth, excellent pitching, and the added asset of Huggins's brilliant strategy."[28]

Huggins had seen the need to add a left-handed pitcher to his 1922 all right-handed rotation of Shawkey, Joe Bush, Sam Jones, Waite Hoyt, and Carl Mays.[29] He had gotten his man in January, when the Yankees acquired Herb Pennock from the Red Sox. Pennock joined fellow hurlers Bush, Jones, Hoyt, Mays, catcher Wally Schang, shortstop Everett Scott, third baseman Joe Dugan, and, of course, Babe Ruth, on the list of Yankees' front-liners who had come from the Red Sox.

Designed originally as a one-for-one swap of Pennock for outfielder Norm McMillan, Frazee had persuaded the Yankees to include pitcher George Murray and outfielder Camp Skinner, leading one team official to call it the worst trade the Yankees ever made. "Murray is a first-rate pitcher," Huggins said in defense of the deal, "but he would only sit on the bench next year. I have enough right-handers now—all I need. The staff needed a left-hander of experience."[30] Huggins claimed Pennock was that man and that he should win fifteen games for the Yankees in 1923. Known more for his steadiness than for possessing any great ability, Pennock, 10-17 for the last-place Red Sox in 1922, exceeded Huggins's hopes by winning nineteen games (19-6) in 1923.

As he usually did, Ruppert had backed his manager. "John McGraw once was accused of being an 'opportunist,'" he said. "We are opportunists in this case. We are taking Pennock to make reasonably sure of the present. We are willing to take a chance on the future. Other Murrays and McMillans will come along."[31]

Sam Jones led the pitchers with twenty-one wins, followed by Pennock and Bush with nineteen each, Hoyt with seventeen, and Shawkey with sixteen. Those five started 143 of the team's 152 games, with rookie George Pipgras making two starts and Carl Mays seven. Pennock had, in effect, replaced Mays, whom Huggins disliked intensely, as did many of Mays's teammates.

Putting aside whatever negative feelings he had toward Mays, Huggins had given him thirty starts in 1922, including one in the World Series. He also appeared to have Mays very much in his plans for 1923. The day before the opener, Huggins had said: "If I can give Mays enough work, I believe he is good enough to win twenty-five games."[32] Yet while Mays was perfectly healthy in 1923, Huggins used him in only twenty-three games, mostly in relief.

Huggins's evolving feelings about Mays revealed themselves in a July 17 game at Cleveland, where George Uhle shut out the Yankees, 13–0. Huggins humiliated Mays by forcing him to pitch the entire game despite his being shelled for twenty hits. In Huggins's defense, the Yankees' pitching staff had been hit with numerous injuries, and Huggins did not want to waste another arm in a lost cause. The situation was such that Ruth even offered to start a game in Detroit. Huggins considered it seriously, but did not take him up on the offer.[33]

When Jones defeated the White Sox, 10–4, on September 15, the Yankees clinched their third consecutive pennant. Next was another World Series against John McGraw's Giants. McGraw still had most of the players who had won the Series in each of the previous two years, including the National League leaders in runs batted in (Irish Meusel), runs scored (Ross Youngs), and hits (Frankie Frisch).

The 1922 sweep by the Giants (there was one tie) had been seized upon by Huggins's critics, who claimed that he did not have control of his men and that an ironhanded manager was needed. To silence the detractors, Ruppert had signed Huggins to a one-year contract a few days after the Series ended. This year Ruppert, recognizing the three consecutive pennants Huggins had won, signed him to a contract for 1924 following the final game of the 1923 season.

"Miller Huggins will manage the Yankees next season," Ruppert announced to the press on October 7. "He signed a one-year contract Saturday, and when that contract expires he can have another one and another one as long as he cares to keep the job."[34] The terms of the contract were not disclosed, but Ruppert acknowledged that he had given his manager a substantial increase in salary.

Baseball men interpreted the re-signing of Huggins prior to the beginning of the World Series as a strategic move by Ruppert. It would, he hoped, prevent the repetition of last year's stories that Huggins did not have the support of the Yankees' management, which resulted in several players ignoring his instructions.

"As a strategist he [Huggins] rates with the best," a well-known baseball man told the *New York Times*. "I know that he retains the respect of every one of his men, for they all have reason to know that he is thoroughly versed in baseball and all the fine points. He is real modern and quickly adapted himself to the change in the style of play brought about by the lively ball." "As for discipline," added the *Times's* source, "you can bet that Huggins will enforce it this year. Every player on the Yankee team knows that Huggins is the boss and that his orders in the coming series will be carried out. There will be no back talk and no laying down on him. Watch Huggins in the coming series."[35]

Still, Huggins expected he would be overshadowed by McGraw, just as he had been in 1921 and 1922. Both men were "keen students of the game," noted sportswriter Ford Frick, but of a different order. "McGraw has the smashing, dashing brilliance of a Napoleon. Huggins has the tenacious, bulldog capacity of a Grant. McGraw is as absolute in his government as a czar. Huggins plays to his men's personality with all the suavity of a Gladstone or a Disraeli."[36]

Huggins was well aware of the public appeal edge McGraw had over him. "I know you can't sell my stuff like McGraw's," he told Christy Walsh, who was Babe Ruth's agent and also represented McGraw and Huggins. Walsh agreed the public was more interested in reading about the colorful Giants manager than about the taciturn Yankees skipper. "But what Miller Huggins lacked in color, showmanship and crowd appeal, he made up in intellect and education," Walsh said. He then told of one incident where Huggins was assertive. Walsh would always gather a few of the key figures in the World Series for a pre-Series photograph. In 1921 and 1922 the picture was taken in front of the Giants' dugout, with Huggins crossing the field at Walsh's request. In 1923 Huggins asked Walsh, "How about getting McGraw to come over here for a change?" Which McGraw did.[37]

While New Yorkers relished another battle between Huggins's Yankees and McGraw's Giants, many others decried the New York monopoly on the Series. "Gad, will I never get out of New York to see a World Series?" asked Judge Landis, who was attending his third as commissioner, all of which had been in the city.[38] The *Philadelphia Inquirer* complained that "the color and atmosphere of the usual World Series has entirely been lost. The fans have come to look upon the battles of October as merely a family quarrel among Pegleg Peter Stuyvesant's scions, and have given but a tithe of the old attention and interest to the outcome. The monopoly of Gotham has had the effect of suffocating the interest and of killing the series as a great finale to the baseball season."[39]

There was one change, however, significant to New Yorkers, but hardly an appeasement to fans in other cities. Unlike the previous two seasons, when all the games were played at the Polo Grounds, the first game of the 1923 Series, on October 10, was at Yankee Stadium.[40] The Giants won, 5–4, on Casey Stengel's ninth-inning, inside-the-park home run off Joe Bush.

Back at their former home, the Polo Grounds, the next day, the Yankees evened the Series, 4-2, behind Herb Pennock.[41] Ruth smashed two home runs, one clearing the right field roof, and Aaron Ward had one. The win broke the Yankees' string of eight consecutive Series losses to the Giants.[42]

Stengel was the hero again in Game Three, with a seventh-inning home run off Sam Jones that was the game's only run. As he rounded the bases, the clownish Stengel blatantly thumbed his nose at the Yankees' bench. The gesture upset Ruppert, who demanded that Commissioner Landis fine Stengel. Whether because of Ruppert's demand or because of his own sense that the dignity of the World Series had been tarnished, Landis fined Stengel $50. Yet, the commissioner noted, "A fellow who wins two games has a right to be a little playful, especially if he's a Stengel," wrote Casey's biographer, Robert Creamer.[43]

The Yankees evened the Series behind Bob Shawkey in Game Four and won the next two games to claim their first world championship. Joe Bush tossed a three-hitter to win Game Five, and Herb Pennock, with relief from Jones, won the 6–4 clincher at the Polo Grounds. Trailing 4–1, the Yankees scored five runs in the eighth inning; Bob Meusel's bases-loaded single off Rosy Ryan was the key blow.

The Yankees' only run in the game to that point had been Ruth's first-inning home run, his third of the Series. He finished with a .368 batting average, a .556 on-base percentage, and a 1.000 slugging percentage. It was sweet retribution for the Babe following his abysmal showing in the 1922 Series. And despite McGraw's oft-repeated claim that he was not afraid of Ruth because the Giants had faced better hitters in the National League, his instructions to pitch the Babe extremely carefully resulted in eight walks. Pennock, winning twice and saving Game Four, was the pitching star.

Ruppert called the Yankees' first world championship in 1923 and the wild ride back from St. Louis after the 1928 World Series his biggest thrills in baseball. "I was a happy man the day Bob Meusel bounced that single over Rosy Ryan's head in 1923 and gave us our first world's championship."[44]

Never known as a gracious loser, McGraw impressed Huggins by his appearance in the Yankees' clubhouse during the winners' post-game celebration. "Instead of the perfunctory congratulations on the field, the Giant manager had made a point of coming right into the clubhouse in the face of the jubilant celebration," wrote Huggins. "A thing like that is rarely done in baseball. His visit was sincere and we felt it."[45]

Ruth took a break from the celebrating to present Huggins with a diamond ring on behalf of the players. "Boys, we've won the world championship and we owe a lot of the accomplishment to the guiding hand of Mr. Huggins," the Babe said. Huggins thanked the players and told them how much happiness the championship had given him. "We have had our little arguments during the season, but they were not real hard feelings; they only appeared so at the time. . . . This token of your friendship is one that I shall always treasure and I want to thank you all for the loyal spirit in which it is given."[46]

Damon Runyon wrote that he never before had seen a man who so visibly betrayed his feelings as Colonel Ruppert had while marching from the ball field after the Yankees' final victory. "The possession of great wealth is an old story to him. There was no novelty for him, no thrill, in the buying excesses of great wealth. It was the thing that money couldn't buy that brought him his big, bright hour."

Runyon went on to praise Ruppert for his sense of decency and fair play in competition. He called him "a fine man, a gentleman, a real American sportsman," the type of American sportsman who would disregard all other considerations when a question of sportsmanship was involved. Runyon then compared Ruppert to other great sportsmen, like thoroughbred racing's Harry Payne Whitney and English yachtsman Sir Thomas Lipton.[47]

"This is the happiest day of my life," an overjoyed Ruppert told Commissioner Landis in the clubhouse. "This is a wonderful occasion," he announced that night at a victory party at the Commodore Hotel. "I now have baseball's greatest park, baseball's greatest player, and baseball's greatest team. . . . But let's give credit where credit is due and give most credit to little Hug."[48]

One celebrator began singing "It's a Long, Long Trail A-winding into the Land of My Dreams," the war song American soldiers sang in France. Others joined in, and when they had finished, Ruppert walked over to their table and asked them to sing it again. After they did, there was a moment of absolute silence. Then Ruppert said, "I like that song; it's apropos of the Yanks."[49]

The owner's faith in his manager, in the face of seemingly never-ending criticism, had finally been rewarded. With a new contract and a World Series championship in hand, Miller Huggins had finally gained the respect of many of the naysayers in the New York press. Following the Series win, Harry Cross of the *New York Evening Post* placed Huggins's six-year tenure in perspective.

There probably never has been as patient a manager in the national game as Huggins. Ever since he took the helm at the head of the American League club here, everyone in the world has tried to tell him how to run his ball club. Someone or other was always telling Hug that he was all wrong. He just listened patiently and then did as he thought best. No manager had been the recipient of so much criticism as Huggins. They said he was too easy with his players, and what he needed was discipline. They said that he didn't know when to take his pitchers out when they were getting hit hard. They also said that he wasn't smart and had no inspiration or imagination. Hug took it all and never said a word. Col. Ruppert stood by him and his judgment. They were both right.[50]

Part 6

THE YANKEES AND
THE BABE STUMBLE

24

It's Tougher to Manage
a Pennant Winner

After the 1923 Yankees romped to their third consecutive American League pennant, they were strong favorites to win again in 1924. Miller Huggins worried that the Yankees' primary threat would come from overconfidence. "Winning, to the Yankees, is already something of an old story. They are a little too inclined to take things for granted, to be too sure of themselves," he explained.[1] He decided to tighten discipline for the coming season, threatening fines for players who did not follow training rules. "We must win that fourth pennant this year, and if any of you have talked it into yourselves that you can walk in and be in any kind of condition you are sadly mistaken," he warned his men during spring training.[2]

Huggins, a chronic worrier, was unable to enjoy his success fully. After winning the 1923 World Series, he had garnered national recognition, including a banquet held in his honor in Cincinnati, but he felt as much—if not more—pressure. "Winning a pennant is much like climbing a mountain. You brave all kinds of obstacles to get to the top, but when you have reached the top, all you can do is stay there for a while and then come down again."[3]

Huggins realized that New Orleans, where the club had trained since 1922, was not conducive to serious training. As Dan Daniel wrote, "New Orleans is no place to train a ball club. The city is too big and its distractions after dark are too numerous."[4] A few months later, the Yankees announced a six-year deal to train in St. Petersburg, Florida, starting in 1925.[5]

While Huggins was planning to start the season with the same lineup of 1923, he recognized that shortstop Everett Scott and first baseman Wally

Pipp were slowing down. Scott's consecutive-game streak had become "a real obsession," causing him "nerve-straining anxiety" and loss of sleep, in the words of the *Sporting News*.[6] Since June 20, 1916, Scott had not missed a game. He had broken Fred Luderus's twentieth-century mark of 533 back in 1920 and had played more than 1,100 straight games by the end of the 1923 season.[7]

Meanwhile, Huggins continued to groom the young Columbia University slugger Lou Gehrig, focusing his efforts on the first baseman's lumbering play in the field. To his credit, Pipp went out of his way to help Gehrig—his probable eventual replacement—with his fielding that spring.[8]

There was little question about Gehrig's potential at the plate. The *New York Times* was already calling him the "second Babe Ruth," for his long-ball hitting the past fall and this spring.[9] Another New York paper gave a vivid description of the youngster. "Gehrig is a leviathan of the baseball world; he is built on ponderous lines; his shoulders are as broad as a boulevard in Paris and he has barrel-like arms with powerful wrists."[10]

Huggins sent Gehrig back to Hartford of the Eastern League, where he would see action every day under the watchful eye of manager and former Yankees coach Paddy O'Connor. Huggins explained his approach to developing young players. "Ball players and ball clubs are like any business people or business places. They do not just spring up and become something. They grow into it."[11]

Pipp had a solid season with New York, hitting .295, with 114 runs batted in and a league-leading nineteen triples. Meanwhile, Gehrig hit .369 with thirty-seven home runs in Hartford before the Yankees called him back for the final month of the season.

With the Yankees' January 1923 acquisition of pitcher Herb Pennock, there was little playing talent remaining on the Red Sox; the Yankees had acquired almost all their best players. Harry Frazee had sold the Red Sox in July 1923, a transaction that Jacob Ruppert had encouraged. Ironically, the Yankees' owner now supported Ban Johnson's efforts to get rid of his erstwhile trading partner. Ruppert realized it was time for the Boston club to have new ownership and restore the league's prestige in that key market.[12]

Every team was hesitant to trade with the Yankees, lest a deal make the New York club even stronger. There was widespread grumbling throughout Organized Baseball that the dominance of the New York teams was hurting the game. Faced with the challenge of finding a new source of players, the Yankees had to look to the Minor Leagues.

In early January, Ruppert announced that the club had purchased Louisville's star outfielder Earle Combs for $50,000. Combs had hit a combined .365 for manager Joe McCarthy the past two seasons. "The chief idea I had in mind in getting this sensational youngster," declared the Yankees' owner, "was to build for the future. The present Yankees won't last forever."[13]

As was often the case with championship teams, many of the Yankees wanted raises and returned their 1924 contracts unsigned. Ruppert noted the men had been offered "liberal" terms that had been supplemented the past three seasons by World Series checks. One of the holdouts was the rookie Combs, and Ruppert himself handled the Yankees' end of the negotiations. At one point he wrote to the Kentuckian, "As it is almost a certainty that the Yankees will again win the American League pennant, you will not fare so badly your first season as a major league player."[14]

A *Washington Post* reporter was sure the Yankees' owner would do what it took to keep his team intact. Ruppert "has learned the lesson that it takes money to get a championship team together, and he is not going to let it disintegrate for the lack of the same commodity."[15] Eventually Ruppert did get all of his players signed. As the season approached, he was confident, more so than his manager. "The boys are just as sure and enthusiastic about repeating as I am. . . . Unless there is an unforeseen collapse in some department, I see a fourth Yankee pennant on the pole. Personally, I think this team is great, the best ever."[16]

Ruppert revealed his management philosophy, probably the same one that had served him well in growing his brewery. His marching orders to Huggins were simple. "Do with it [the Yankees] what you think best, and I hold you responsible for the results. There will be no interference with you in your methods."[17] Just before the start of the 1924 season, the Colonel conveyed his opinion of his manager. "Huggins is the boss. He is having his own way in everything. It is a pleasure to have such a man on the job. Also it is gratifying to remember that I stuck to Huggins when a lot of people wanted him removed."[18]

Ruppert's aide, Billy Fleischmann, had predicted late in 1922 that once the Colonel won a World Series, he would lose interest and sell the Yankees. "He'll build this team up, just as he has built up other things, until he gets to the top. As soon as the Yankees win a world's championship, he'll probably tire of baseball for there will be no more worlds to conquer."[19]

Fleischmann was wrong. Ruppert had reached the top of the mountain and wanted to stay there as long as he could. As he said just before the end of 1923, "Here I am deeper than ever in baseball and more in love with the game than ever."[20] His love of baseball had grown to the point that Ruppert was now a sportsman first and a businessman second. Damon Runyon wrote a year later, "I believe Colonel Ruppert would sacrifice his entire baseball investment rather than knowingly be a party to an unsportsmanlike action."[21] Like Huggins, Ruppert was aloof. When Ruppert bought the Yankees, he was "rather standoffish," Runyon wrote, "accustomed to the formal deferential atmosphere of the business world." His fellow owners called him "Colonel" at first. Over the years, he had become somewhat more accessible, and now they called him "Jake."

The two men were similar in another way. The Colonel was a perfectionist. "Winning was a mania with him," wrote Sid Mercer after Ruppert's death.[22] In Huggins he had found a kindred spirit. "'Miller always was scheming, always was trying to better his team,' Ruppert once said."[23]

Just before spring training, outfielder Bob Meusel narrowly escaped death in a California car accident that killed Boston Braves outfielder Tony Boeckel. The automobile was becoming more affordable and transforming American society, but it was doing so at a price. Virtually every day, newspapers had reports of car accidents in which people were seriously injured and killed.[24]

Also transforming American society was the cult of celebrity and hero worship, helped along by the tabloid newspapers, typified by the *New York Daily News*. Founded in 1919, laden with photos and sensationalist stories, it grew dramatically in circulation, in no small part because of its in-depth coverage of Babe Ruth.[25] The growing popularity of radio and motion-picture newsreels also helped publicize and popularize the National Pastime.

These mass media "helped convince a nation divided by race, class, and ethnicity that it had a common identity," wrote historian Nathan Miller. Yet the reality was that the country was deeply divided, and the early 1920s saw the backlash against immigrants from Southern and Eastern Europe reach a crescendo. At the start of the Great War, 80 percent of the nation's immigrants were coming from those regions.[26] After the war, Congress began restricting immigration to a small number each year, culminating in the Immigration Act of 1924, which dramatically limited Southern and Eastern Europe immigration, which was heavily composed of Jews and Italians.[27]

Annual immigration fell from about 650,000 before the war to about 150,000 in the late 1920s. Moreover, most of those people now came from Northern Europe.[28] The idea of America as a melting pot, evolving and never finished, was rejected, and "old-stock" Americans could take comfort in winning at least one front of the culture war.

Baseball reflected American society, both its myths and reality. Fred Lieb wrote in 1923 that the National Pastime provided a wonderful "melting pot" for Americans of different origins. Yet the game would remain dominated by players originating from Northern Europe for years to come, though Italians and Eastern Europeans were beginning to make their mark.[29]

One of the talented yet mercurial players Huggins no longer had to worry about was Carl Mays. The pitcher had been marginalized in 1923, when he started only seven games, and the Yankees had excelled without him. Huggins once made a shocking statement to Fred Lieb, so out-of-character for the soft-spoken manager. "Any ballplayers that played for me . . . I would give him a helping hand. I make only two exceptions, Carl Mays and Joe Bush. If they were in the gutter, I'd kick them." Lieb then wondered, "How can such a kindly gentleman carry such a deep hatred?"[30]

In Mays's biography, he ridiculed Huggins and said that Babe Ruth had publicly mocked his manager. Mays accused Huggins of many things, including publicly humiliating Waite Hoyt by calling him "gutless."[31] Hoyt later said that Mays's accusations were simply not true.[32]

After the 1923 season, the Yankees sold Mays to the Cincinnati Reds. Huggins felt he could spare him, with the Yankees' deep and talented pitching staff. Lieb rather cryptically noted that Huggins and Mays "did not pull together, and that being so, they were both better off apart."[33] *Baseball Magazine* was more blunt. A February 1924 editorial noted,

"Mays' hostility to his own manager, Miller Huggins, was notorious and profound. He took no pains to conceal this hostility." Huggins knew Mays could still pitch, which is probably why he wanted him out of the American League. "I would not stick my old friend [Reds owner] Garry Herrmann. I sold him a mighty fine pitcher."[34] *Baseball Magazine* agreed. "Mays is far from through. . . . He is a man of far more than usual player-intelligence. He is ambitious and he deeply resents being shoved thus unceremoniously into the discard. If Mays does not pitch good ball next season, we shall miss our guess."[35]

Carl Mays did indeed have plenty of pitching left in his arm; he won twenty games for the Reds in 1924 and nineteen in 1926. The Yankees could have used some of those wins, but Huggins knew what he was giving up when he dealt Mays.

The Yankees were challenged for the 1924 pennant by the most unlikely of competitors, the Washington Senators. Washington had never won a pennant and finished twenty-three and a half games behind New York in 1923. They now had their fifth manager in five years, twenty-seven-year-old second baseman Bucky Harris. Earlier in the year, the Senators had offered the manager's job to Yankees business manager Ed Barrow, who turned them down.[36] The Senators had four former Yankees: pitchers Allen Russell and George Mogridge, shortstop Roger Peckinpaugh, and catcher Muddy Ruel. All were major contributors to the 1924 team.

Huggins conceded he had misjudged Ruel when he traded him away following the 1920 season. "Muddy fooled me completely. . . . I thought he was too small."[37] Huggins said he had learned from that mistake. "Now, every time I'm tempted to pass snap judgment on a youngster, I think of Muddy—and I wait a while!"[38]

Washington also had an aging pitching great, thirty-six-year-old Walter Johnson.[39] Early that season, Johnson lamented that he no longer had the speed and strength he had ten years earlier. "If only I could be for one short month the pitcher I used to be!"[40] Johnson emerged as the season's biggest surprise: a 23-7 record with the league's top marks in wins, winning percentage, earned run average, strikeouts, and shutouts.

In late June, the Senators came to Yankee Stadium, swept a four-game series from the Yankees, and moved into first place. Huggins said, "After that series Washington was a changed club."[41] Earlier that month, Earle Combs had fractured his ankle sliding into home plate; he was hitting over .400 at the time. It was a big loss for the Yankees, though Whitey Witt filled in admirably the rest of the year. Combs would have only one more at bat that season, when he returned in September.

In late August, the Senators returned to New York and won three of four. Following their win in the second game, the *New York Times* portrayed the intensity of the Senators. "Although not outhit, the Yanks were outscored, outplayed, outfought, and outlucked by the Senators. The Senators were irresistible. They had exuberant spirits, a dash and a fire that the Yankees could not match."[42]

After the Senators prevailed in the final game in extra innings, Huggins told the Senators' great relief pitcher, Firpo Marberry, "If my hurlers had the guts that you have, young fellow, we'd have beaten you today."[43] The Senators were ahead of the times with their heavy use of relievers, and Marberry was the best.[44]

"Pitchers. It rather frets me," said Huggins early that summer.[45] Three years earlier, the Yankees' manager noted, "Handling pitchers is, perhaps, the most difficult part of a manager's job. . . . The manager who spends his time in coddling glass arms won't do much else."[46] Sore arms plagued his staff all season. Huggins was so desperate for pitching that he signed Cliff Markle, the Yankees' 1916 bust.[47] Only Herb Pennock came close to his 1923 numbers, and he improved upon them.[48] Huggins once said of the slender and elegant lefty, "If you were to cut that bird's head open, the weakness of every batter in the league would fall out."[49]

As the season wound down, Damon Runyon wrote that it would be "great" for baseball if Washington won the pennant. "This is treasonable from a New Yorker, but true. New York has become satiated, blasé, with baseball championships. It no longer appreciates the thrill of the World Series."[50] Even Jacob Ruppert wondered aloud that it might be good if both New York teams would be beaten out for the pennant because that would generate renewed baseball interest in the city in 1925.[51]

The Yankees reeled off fourteen wins in eighteen games to start September and were tied with the Senators for first place when they went to Detroit on September 19. New York dropped three agonizing one-run games to the Tigers. Detroit's player-manager, Ty Cobb, was as brilliant and irascible as ever. He went 6-for-13 and reached two hundred hits for the ninth time.[52] He also managed to taunt and provoke the mild-mannered Lou Gehrig, who had recently rejoined the Yankees, resulting in Gehrig's first career ejection. After the season, Cobb expressed satisfaction at "kicking the Yankees out of the race."[53] *New York Daily News* sportswriter Paul Gallico wrote of Cobb's personality, "There was a burning rage in Ty Cobb never far from the surface. . . . His compulsion to excel was far beyond anything which had been seen perhaps in any sport."[54]

There already was bad blood between the teams. Back on June 13, Tigers pitcher Bert Cole hit Bob Meusel in the back, and Meusel rushed the mound, triggering a fracas and subsequent riot. Cobb had a reputation for ordering his pitchers to throw at opposing batters, even at their heads, and Babe Ruth claimed he saw Cobb signal Cole to hit Meusel. Thousands of Detroit fans stormed the field, and the game was forfeited to the Yankees.[55]

New York may have conceded one win to Detroit that summer. In order to catch a train to the Midwest, they had agreed with the Tigers that their July 24 Yankee Stadium game would end after eight innings. The Yankees gave up a chance to rally in the ninth inning and lost the game, 5–4. More surprising was that they were catching a train to Indianapolis, where they had scheduled an exhibition game on their way to Chicago. The *Sporting News* declared it was "rather appalling" that the schedule was made "a football for exhibition games."[56]

New York finished just two games back of Washington, while John McGraw's Giants won their fourth straight National League pennant. The Senators then edged them in a dramatic seven-game World Series.[57] Yet the transfer of baseball power from Manhattan to the Bronx was continuing. The Yankees outdrew the Giants by more than 200,000, bolstering their status as New York's number one team.[58] The club generated so much profit that Ruppert paid off Til Huston that summer, earlier than their agreement had called for.[59]

Despite the disappointment of finishing in second place, Jacob Ruppert reaffirmed his support for Huggins. "He won pennants and world championships for me, and the club has been a splendid financial success. Could anyone ask more of a manager?"[60]

There was one man the Yankees could not blame for failing to repeat in 1924, at least not for his on-field performance: Babe Ruth. He again led the league in many offensive categories, including home runs (46), batting average (.378), and slugging percentage (.739). In his biography of the Babe, Marshall Smelser's 1924 chapter is entitled "It Wasn't the Babe's Fault."

Ruth's popularity was at an all-time high, and he was proving to be a perfect fit for both New York City and the 1920s, a decade of excess and celebrities. Huggins, who always let Ruth operate under his own set of rules, probably understood what sportswriter Ford Frick wrote about the Babe. "Into each of us there is born a secret hatred of conventions. But most of us lack the nerve to defy the conventions which we secretly detest. When we find a man who has such nerve, then we put him on a pedestal of notoriety. While we question his judgment at times, we admire his daring and his originality. That's Babe Ruth."[61]

Huggins had put up with a lot from Ruth over the years. He understood Ruth's personality when he said, "To be at his best, he must be a happy, carefree boy."[62] Huggins exaggerated the harmony of their relationship. "As a manager I have found Ruth very easy to handle. He is intensely ambitious and always wants to do what is best for the club," Huggins said before the season. Coming off a World Series win, it was easier for him to overlook problems. Even then, he noted of Ruth, "He has his own notions about how he ought to do it [what is best for the club]."[63]

Lieb wrote after the season that Huggins had stayed with his veterans as long as he could and would now tear the team apart and rebuild it. He said that Huggins would consider trading most members of his club to improve it. That winter Huggins explained the importance of trades. "It is a good thing to keep shifting the personnel of even a seasoned and successful team. It keeps the players alert, and new faces usually please the fans and keep them interested."[64] Yet while Huggins understood the theory behind necessary change, he admitted to a human weakness. "I kept my team intact as long as I could. I have always been loath to break up a combination of players, and I have a certain sentiment toward the men who have stood by me through four hot and heavy pennant races."[65]

The tragedy of the Yankees of the early 1920s was that they "could have won, should have won" five pennants in a row (1920 to 1924), instead of just three, Huggins later told sportswriter Arthur Mann. Huggins also spoke of one of his favorites, a talented young player who was "one of the most foolish," whose career was cut short "all on account of liquor."[66]

Huggins was already looking ahead to 1925. He still toyed with the "bug" of owning a Minor League team, especially when the stress of managing impacted his health. But he hoped to continue as the Yankees' manager for several years. "Ruppert is a wonderful man to work with. After seven years of close association I guess two men get to understand each other pretty well," he said. "If I really want a man, he will go the limit to get him. And he never tires of winners." Huggins noted that his health had improved since 1923. Even during the difficult 1924 pennant race, he had not lost the positive "nervous vitality" that had deserted him in earlier years. Nevertheless, he explained, "there is no business or game I know where nerves can be worn more raw than in one of those 154-game grinds in which pennant hopes hinge almost on every ball pitched."[67]

Huggins planned to rest and recover in his favorite way down in Florida. "I'll be in a small boat away out in the bay, a fishing pole in my hands and a floppy, wide-brimmed straw hat on my head. I'll be smoking my pipe and catching fish."[68]

Almost a half century later, Dan Daniel provided a revealing vignette of the man often referred to as "the Mite manager" and derogatorily, in other cities, as "the mouse" [for his size]: "I learned more about the mechanics and the winning system of baseball from Miller Huggins than from anybody else. Huggins was not in very good health. He wasn't a very strong man. On the road, after a game, he'd go up to his room and get into his long drawers and lie there exhausted. Then, he'd begin to discuss the game, inning by inning, move by move. Why he did this, why he did that, and it registered with me because I heard so many of his lectures and dispositions and analyses. He knew an awful lot about baseball."[69]

25

New Homes for Single Men
and Their Team

On New Year's Day 1925 Bob Connery, the Yankees' chief scout, resigned from the club and announced he had purchased the St. Paul Saints of the American Association. He had tired of the peripatetic lifestyle of a scout and saw the Saints as a good business investment. The *St. Paul Press* noted that the Yankees and the Saints would make an "unbeatable combination" because of the former's money to spend on players and willingness to send them to Connery for development.[1] Nevertheless, noting there was no formal relationship between the two clubs, Connery declared the Saints would not become a "feeder" to any specific big league team. "If the Yankees, at any time, want to purchase a St. Paul player, they will have to give our club what we want just the same as any other club."[2]

Yet the Yankees would work closely with Connery, purchasing a number of Saints players and sending prospects there for seasoning. "A regular shuttle of players between the Yankees and the Saints would become a cornerstone of the New York team's player acquisition and development program."[3] The Yankees would spend around $300,000 on St. Paul ballplayers in the next few years, with little to show in return.[4]

What was not widely known at the time—it emerged only after Miller Huggins's death—is that the Yankees' manager was a silent partner, a one-third owner, in Connery's purchase of the Saints, the team he had played for more than two decades earlier.[5] When Jacob Ruppert bought a Saints player recommended by Connery and Huggins, he knew Connery would benefit financially. Did he also know that Huggins would profit from the deal? While Huggins kept his investment from the general public, he probably shared it with his boss, the Colonel.[6] Their mutual trust would have had it no other way. Perhaps Huggins kept his investment from public view because he feared Commissioner Landis might have disallowed it.

Before the end of 1925, Ed Barrow would add two scouts to his staff, Bill Essick, the former manager of the Vernon, California, club of the Pacific Coast League, and Eddie Herr, who had scouted for Huggins's Cardinals back in the teens.[7] Together with Paul Krichell, whom Barrow brought over from the Red Sox, they would provide the Yankees with a powerful weapon in identifying and securing Minor League talent for decades to come.

While Branch Rickey and the St. Louis Cardinals were acquiring Minor League clubs, the Yankees were buying individual players from independent Minor League teams, often at high prices. In one of his bitter letters to Ruppert in early 1923, Colonel Huston stated that Huggins had swayed Ruppert against the idea of owning farm clubs, which Huston favored.[8]

The scouts worked under Barrow's direction, and he in turn worked closely with Huggins on the club's needs—current players and possible acquisitions. In evaluating the former, Huggins had the clearest view and deciding opinion. When it came to the latter, Barrow had his scouts and was "the senior partner."[9] He said of working with Huggins, "Ours was an ideal partnership. We respected each other's abilities and ideas."[10]

The Yankees moved their spring training to St. Petersburg, Florida, in 1925. Al Lang, known as "the Sunshine Salesman," was the city's former mayor and current chamber of commerce president. He had moved from Pittsburgh when he was diagnosed with a life-threatening respiratory illness more than a decade earlier.[11] Given just a few months to live at the time, the tireless promoter of the city lived until 1960. Lang, who looked like a cross between Connie Mack and Commissioner Landis with his tall, angular body and white hair, had convinced Jacob Ruppert that "the minds of the players would be more on baseball and less on wine and wild women" in St. Petersburg than in New Orleans.[12]

Historian Charles Fountain explained that "while not exactly bereft of temptation—and Ruth could find an opportunity for sin in a church—Lang's St. Petersburg was more in keeping with the sort of image Ruppert was trying to cultivate for the Yankees."[13] Sportswriter Joe Williams noted that the town, a haven for northern retirees, was known for three activities: sitting on park benches, throwing horseshoes, and playing checkers.[14]

It also helped Lang's efforts that Miller Huggins called St. Petersburg home. He and his younger sister, Myrtle, shared an apartment in New York City during the baseball season; they lived just a short subway ride from both the Polo Grounds and Yankee Stadium.[15] She was a schoolteacher who had studied "domestic science." They returned to Cincinnati during the off-season until the early 1920s, when they moved to Florida.[16]

The Yankees' manager enjoyed following the stock and real estate markets, and now he could put his interest and skill to use in his booming hometown, making real estate investments. W. O. McGeehan noted that Huggins had been bitten by the Florida real estate boom "virus," with "more options on Ivory Belt realty than the average south-bound suitcase holds pints of Scotch."[17] More important, he seemed to get revitalized after the baseball season in the leisurely pace of the subtropical city on Tampa Bay. And he liked nothing more than having his favorite activity, fishing for hours on end, so close to home.

Huggins had first visited the city back in the fall of 1908, when his Reds were on their way to a baseball exhibition series in Cuba. He and Myrtle built a new home there late in 1924, just a few minutes' walk to Crescent Lake Park, where the Yankees practiced.[18] His mother's sister, Matilda Reed, lived with them. Huggins found few pleasures in life and even fewer ways to relax; living in St. Pete provided both.

He had few friends, and two of his intimates, Connery and his former St. Paul manager Mike Kelley, were now both living in Minnesota.[19] One of those he was closest to, his agent Christy Walsh, hinted at how difficult it was to get to this intensely private man. "You know him intimately, and you don't know him at all."[20]

Like his sister, Miller never married, and Myrtle was his closest confidante. He rarely spoke about loneliness. He did, however, lament not having a son. "My chief regret is that I haven't a boy of my own to take an interest in," he told sportswriter Bill Corum in 1924. "I could give him so many things that I didn't have. A first-class college education would be one of them. Money doesn't mean much, unless you have somebody to spend it on."[21]

Huggins did comment on marriage. He told Dan Daniel, "That's my one big regret. Married life gives a man varied interests. What interests have I? To make a stronger ball club, to win more pennants, to set records and make money? Why, it's got so I get the biggest kick just out of making money. I think I cannot let go."[22] If ever there was a baseball manager married to his job, Miller Huggins was that man.

He grew close (fatherly, perhaps) to a young sportswriter, Arthur Mann, who was just starting a family in the 1920s. "Take care of it all," Huggins told him with a twinge of envy. "You don't realize what you have," referring to the reporter's family.[23]

Huggins was not the only Yankee who moved into a new residence in 1925. After Jacob Ruppert's mother died of heart disease in 1924, he no longer wanted to live in the family's Fifth Avenue mansion. He moved into a twelve-room apartment across the street, at Fifth Avenue and 93rd Street.[24] His apartment office was described as "extremely masculine," with dark-wood paneling.[25] He lived "alone," with his butler, maid, valet, cook, and laundress.

Around the same time, Ruppert bought and developed Eagle's Rest, an estate with a spectacular mansion, in the village of Garrison, New York. The property sat on the Hudson River, across from West Point, less than sixty miles from New York City.[26] Ruppert kept Eagle's Rest virtually baseball-free.[27] He transported and reconstructed much of his New York City mansion in the upstate retreat. He maintained a shrine to his mother in one room, "arranging furnishings there as she had left them."[28]

Damon Runyon wrote that Ruppert would never retire to a life of leisure in Garrison. "You can take the Colonel out of the city, but it's a sure thing you can't take the city out of the Colonel."[29] Ruppert would spend many weekends in Garrison but never lived there for any period of time.

Like his manager, Ruppert never married. Unlike Huggins, he was not known to have addressed the absence of children in his life, but he made comments on marriage and wives, perhaps with a bit of humor. He told Fred Lieb that back when he was younger, he did not want to marry because "it was too much fun being single."[30] In a free-wheeling 1928 interview with a female reporter, Ruppert said, "There are too many attractive girls in New York to ever allow a man to be lonesome."[31] As he grew older, he told Lieb, he feared marrying. "I was afraid that I would kill her. I would be certain that she had married me for my money and that sooner or later she would take on a younger lover. And then I would have no alternative but to kill her."[32] In a somewhat more serious vein, the Yankees' owner said men marry only when they are lonely or in need of a housekeeper—and neither circumstance applied to him.[33]

In May 1937 Ruppert was featured in the short-lived men's fashion magazine *Bachelor*, along with actor Tyrone Power, author and literary critic Alexander Woollcott, playwright Noël Coward, and fashion photographer and costume designer Cecil Beaton. "The shrewd, fastidious bachelor," wrote the monthly about the Colonel, "is a gifted, good-humored gentleman with an extremely vital and interesting personality."[34]

In the first issue's lead article, Dr. Louis Bisch wrote, "Gossip about the whys and wherefores of bachelorhood usually tends to be vicious. . . . From what I can gather from the bachelors of my acquaintance, it is not 'woman' that bothers them but marriage as an institution."[35] The lead article in the May issue noted, "Marriage will destroy his [a man's] egoistical glory; will precipitate his glamorous individuality to mediocrity. . . . The wedded man cannot dream in terms of self-glory. His fancy is not free. . . . So we have the bachelor. We have had some rather famous ones. He is such because he must have his freedom."[36]

Ruppert himself predicted marriage would disappear in one hundred years. "The only way marriage can be a success is for the husband and wife to live separately and see each other only a few times a week."[37] He did admit that married women were charming—"if you are not married to them."[38] He explained, "After marriage every wife gains in assurance and fascination. They're the most successful companions in the world for the bachelors." Ruppert concluded that 1928 interview by saying, "But no matter how old and lonesome I get, I'll never get married. If it becomes necessary for me to find companionship I'll go to an Old Man's Home."[39] The Colonel had many acquaintances, especially in brewery and real estate circles, but not many friends. Most of his closest relationships were with male companions, notably club secretary George Perry, personal secretary and club treasurer Al Brennan, and realtor Fred Wattenberg.

The Colonel often appeared at social events with an attractive, younger woman at his side. A single woman he drew close to, starting around 1925, was Helen Weyant, the daughter of a friend and more than thirty years his junior. She had a brief career as a Broadway actress and chorus girl, appearing under the name of Winthrop Wayne.[40] Their relationship was hidden from the press and retains an air of mystery to this day. They did not appear in public together in the city, though she often spent weekends with him in Garrison, where she served as the informal hostess of Eagle's Rest.

26

Huggins Waited One Year Too Long

Despite predictions that the Yankees would undergo a major overhaul after finishing second in 1924, Miller Huggins chose mostly to stay with his veterans for another season. He told Fred Lieb that while he did fear what he called "mental disintegration," he expected one more pennant from this core group, comparing his club to the 1910 Chicago Cubs.[1] "Every championship team goes only so far before it begins to break up," he said. "That has been true through baseball history; there have been no exceptions."[2] He saw it coming to his Yankees. He just did not see it coming in 1925.

Huggins had convinced himself he still had a great team. At one point in the spring of 1925 he said this was the best squad he had ever managed.[3] When the Cubs faded after the 1910 season, their player-manager, Frank Chance, was asked just when he knew they could no longer win. "I never knew they couldn't," he replied. "I simply found they didn't."[4]

Huggins constantly fretted that things could (and would) go wrong, which played havoc with his stomach as well as his ability to sleep. While Ruppert may have been a more resolute decision-maker than his manager, they were kindred spirits in agonizing over whether their Yankees would play championship ball. W. O. McGeehan wrote of the Yankees' owner that spring, "The Colonel has an infinite capacity for mental anguish and likes to do his worrying early. There is nothing to worry about [so McGeehan thought at the time], but trifles like that cannot deter the Colonel from worrying."[5]

The Yankees made only one major trade in the off-season. They reacquired pitcher Urban Shocker, sending Joe Bush and two young pitchers to the St. Louis Browns.[6] Huggins had long admired the feisty Shocker, whom he regretted trading away seven years earlier. He felt Shocker, who had won more games the past five seasons than any other pitcher in baseball, would add a key ingredient to the Yankees, one that was missing from the 1924 club. "Shocker may not win many more games than Joe Bush, but Bush is a world's series veteran," declared Huggins. "Shocker, on the other hand, is as eager to get into his first world's series as was Walter Johnson last season. He will give our pitching staff a mental stimulus."[7]

Huggins was so anxious to land Shocker that he was willing to include his promising first baseman, Lou Gehrig, in the deal, though he later denied it. Shortly after Gehrig's death, Dan Daniel reported that Huggins once told Gehrig, "I hate to think of the terrible mistake I would have made had I sent you to the Browns for Urban Shocker. If they had insisted, you would have gone."[8]

Gehrig, meanwhile, credited Huggins with talking him out of quitting that spring, when the twenty-two-year-old first baseman was not seeing much action.[9] Gehrig also noted Huggins's patience. "When I broke in, I was green and awkward, and half afraid. I made boot after boot and bad play after bad play. . . . He stuck with me and encouraged me and helped me. . . . He is the best teacher I ever had the privilege of being with."[10]

Huggins worked countless hours with Gehrig on his fielding; Bozeman Bulger noted that the Yankees' manager "had the patience of a Chinese philosopher."[11] He knew how to get the most from his men, by tailoring his approach to the individual. "Some players must be coaxed, and some must be driven," he told Frank Graham.[12]

The Yankees suffered a major blow when Babe Ruth collapsed in early April at the end of spring training. Tagged as "the bellyache heard 'round the world" by McGeehan, it was attributed to acute indigestion from eating too many hot dogs and drinking too much soda pop. It was also ascribed to influenza; Ruth had suffered bouts of the flu the past few springs while shedding weight and getting into shape.

There were even whispers that the Babe was suffering from a sexually transmitted disease. But the hospital said he had an abscess, which required abdominal surgery. Robert Creamer noted that "abdominal surgery is not standard procedure for correction of venereal disease, and there is no question that Ruth bore a long vivid scar on the left side of his abdomen."[13] Ruth remained hospitalized for a few weeks and did not return to the lineup until June 1. By that time, the floundering Yankees were mired in seventh place with a 15-25 record.

Center fielder Earle Combs was a rare bright spot for the club, as he bounced back from the ankle injury that sidelined him much of his rookie season. Miller Huggins often spoke about the importance of seeing a prospect in actual games, not just practice and spring training. "You never know what a player is until you get him into strict competition. . . . How do I know that he has brains and guts? Can't be figured out until he gets into a regular game."[14]

Combs moved into the starting lineup on opening day and quickly proved he had both brains and guts. He was a consummate professional who quietly excelled, day in and day out. Huggins once told Ed Barrow, "If you had nine Combses on your ball club, you could go to bed every night and sleep like a baby."[15] On June 1, when a still-weakened Ruth returned to the lineup, Combs was hitting .366.

The Yankees lost six of eight April games to the Senators, yet Huggins reaffirmed his faith in his core players. "A few more beatings, and they are likely to snap out of it," he said hopefully.[16] A week later, Huggins mustered what little humor he could find and declared, "When I retire from baseball, my first work will be a little brochure on 'Slumps and How to Cure Them.' . . . I say you must let nature run its course."[17]

On May 6, after fielding complaints from his pitchers that Everett Scott was no longer covering much ground at shortstop, Huggins benched him and said, "I'm sorry. I've got to do it, Everett. But the record's got to go."[18] Scott's consecutive-game streak ended at a seemingly insurmountable 1,307. He was furious and demanded his release. The following week Huggins and Ed Barrow went to St. Paul, looking at Bob Connery's prospects. On May 29 the Yankees acquired twenty-year-old Saints shortstop Mark Koenig for $50,000.[19]

McGeehan noted that Huggins's ability to blend young players into the lineup would now be put to the test. "Colonel Ruppert no longer can buy ready-made players. There are no ready-made players for sale. The scouts will have to find them and Mr. Huggins will have to develop them."[20] What McGeehan and others overlooked was that a decade earlier, as the manager of the Cardinals, Huggins had great success nurturing young ballplayers.

With his team crumbling around him, Huggins finally decided to change his lineup. On June 1, the day the Babe returned to action, Huggins used Gehrig as a pinch-hitter for weak-hitting shortstop Pee Wee Wanninger. The next day Huggins told Gehrig, "You're my first baseman," and he replaced Wally Pipp as the starter.[21] On the same day, Huggins benched second baseman Aaron Ward and catcher Wally Schang, both of whom had played regularly most of the season.

It has often been said that Pipp lost his job to Gehrig because he had a headache on June 2.[22] He may have had a headache that day, but Huggins simply decided to shake things up and bench Pipp and his .244 batting average. Pipp did suffer a concussion, but not until July 2, a month after Gehrig had replaced him. By the time Pipp returned on August 7, Gehrig was firmly ensconced on first base. "A pair of oxen couldn't drag him away from first base," wrote the *New York Times*.[23]

Stories of dissension and dissatisfaction with Huggins's leadership, similar to those of 1922, swirled around the Yankees. In mid-June the Yankees' manager fought back, telling Joe Vila, "I'm going to stick, and for a long time too. I love baseball and wouldn't know what to do with myself if I got out of the game. . . . Some radical changes in the team will be made before next year."[24]

That season, when Huggins overheard a couple of his players discussing how lucky their manager was that Ruppert was so loyal to him, he exploded in anger. "Don't kid yourself about Colonel Ruppert carrying me. Ruppert is not carrying me or anyone through sentiment. If Ruppert has stuck by me it is because he knows that I know this game," Huggins told the men. "He has confidence in my judgment. . . . I have no apologies to make to anyone for being here. I am here because I am delivering."[25]

Baseball writer John Foster wrote in June that four players had rebelled against Huggins. One had been dealt away the past winter, he wrote, though he mentioned no names. This was almost certainly Joe Bush, who had openly disobeyed Huggins at the end of the 1922 World Series and thus earned his manager's enmity. Another was a young pitcher "whose egotism has nearly ruined his physical ability. His conceit is terrific."[26] This was probably Waite Hoyt, whose name repeatedly surfaced as a trade candidate until 1926. Typical of the articles that did suggest more names was that of Davis Walsh, the sports editor of the *International News Ser-*

vice. He listed the club's "trade material": Hoyt, Ward, Sam Jones, and Bob Meusel.[27]

Vila wrote that "scandal mongers" were again reporting that Huggins had lost control of his club and that Ruppert had lost faith in him. Ruppert was furious about reports that he would replace Huggins with Ed Barrow or Rochester manager George Stallings.[28] "It's a lie, pure and simple. . . . It would be shabby treatment to remove him now or at any other time. . . . Huggins can remain in control of my team as long as he feels like it," Ruppert declared.[29]

The Yankees' owner was bitterly disappointed with his team's performance. The man who did not like finishing second in any competition had a baseball team that was stuck in seventh place most of the year. "You can bet when the present campaign is over, he will begin to act," wrote Vila. "He will have another winner, no matter what may happen."[30]

Huggins was obviously disappointed as well. "Colonel Ruppert and I thought sure last winter that the Yankees would not only last one more season, but that they would be strong enough to win the pennant," he said in early August.[31] He rarely gave reporters headline-grabbing quotes, and this season was no different. When asked how the Yankees would do in the second half of the season, he replied, "We shall see what we shall see."[32]

While Vila defended Huggins in the press, McGeehan was an outspoken critic. "The little Florida realtor has all the parts of a first-class automobile. . . . But it stalls and wheezes like a flivver and apparently goes nowhere in particular." McGeehan noted a lack of discipline in the clubhouse. "Not a whip has been cracked. The detonation resembling the crack of a whip was caused only by the Yanks cracking a little further."[33]

A famous story revolves around Babe Ruth and Bob Meusel almost throwing their little manager off a moving train. Did it happen, or is it another one of baseball's legends? If it did occur, it might have happened during the 1922 season, but more likely it was during the terrible 1925 campaign. Both were seasons in which the Babe struggled mightily. Ruth biographers Robert Creamer and Leigh Montville say it never happened. Other chroniclers of Ruth's life, Marshall Smelser, Kal Wagenheim, and Bob Considine, maintain it did indeed occur, during the summer of 1925.

Huggins was lecturing his players about their excessive carousing when

"Ruth picked him up like a doll" and held him over the tracks, Smelser wrote.[34] Ruth did the lifting, and Meusel was at his side. Both Bob Shawkey and reporter Frank Graham said that Ruth told them in advance that he was going to "throw Hug off the train."[35] Sportswriters Joe Williams, Arthur Mann, and Ford Frick also wrote about the incident.[36] Mann did not name the culprit, described as "one outraged Yankee, fueled by an alcoholic temper." He wrote that a desperate struggle to prevent a tragedy ensued, and Huggins was rescued.

Williams said that "an unnamed Negro porter" intervened and saved the manager's life. "To Huggins this incident was just a laugh. Ruth was Ruth and Meusel was Meusel. . . . It was fortunate for all that it ended in a mere prank."[37] A final word on the matter comes from the Babe's second wife, Claire. She said the Babe "denied to his deathbed" dangling Huggins off a speeding train during the 1922 season. However, she said, a player did do so in 1925. "And this time the player was my husband."[38] The evidence suggests that the incident did indeed occur.

Journalist Gene Fowler wrote in his memoir, "Mr. Ruth always made his own rules. Rather, he had but one rule: never to go halfway in anything, on or off the baseball diamond."[39] For once, fortunately, Ruth did something only halfway.

Early in the summer, Huggins had fined Ruth $1,000, probably for his late-night activities, yet when the Babe homered the next day, the fine was rescinded.[40] However, on August 29 in St. Louis, Huggins fined Ruth $5,000 and suspended him.[41] The Yankees were still in seventh place (with a 49-71 record), and the Babe was hitting only .266. The fine and suspension were the culmination of years of misbehaving on the part of the slugger, whose drinking and womanizing were all the more disappointing, coming so soon after his serious illness.[42]

Since 1922, Ruth's contract prohibited him from drinking or staying out past 1 AM.[43] But fining one of the nation's biggest celebrities was not easy for anyone to do, much less the soft-spoken Huggins. Now, however, with his team and "former" star slugger struggling in the "dog days of summer," Huggins had picked his spot. The season—for both the Yankees and for Ruth—was already gone.

After unloading a string of profanities at his manager, the Babe declared him incompetent and that he would quit if Huggins remained the club's manager. Huggins told reporters, "Patience has ceased to be a virtue. I have tried to overlook Ruth's behavior for a while, but I have decided to take summary action to bring the big fellow to his senses."[44]

"What happened in the case of the Yankees is obvious," wrote Damon Runyon. "Miller Huggins waited one year too long before dismantling his club and starting to build anew."[45] For years, reporters—in New York and across the country—had favored the Babe over Huggins. There was a powerful economic logic to their bias toward Ruth and ignoring his faults: he sold newspapers and made money for them, a lot of papers and a lot of money.

Many people probably agreed with columnist Heywood Broun, who wrote after Ruth's suspension, "You can't make a Spartan out of an ancient Goth."[46] Broun felt that Ruth would never accept any supervision that repressed him. Even Huggins himself had written the previous year, "If the harness were strapped too tight on Ruth I believe it would cramp his style."[47]

The press held its collective breath as Ruth went to Jacob Ruppert's brewery to meet with the Yankees' owner, whom he felt would back him. But the Babe was sadly mistaken. After the meeting, the two men emerged, and Ruppert announced that Ruth would have to work out his differences with Huggins, who would remain as manager. "Anything Miller Huggins says, goes with me. I will support him to the limit," Ruppert declared. "Huggins is running the club, not Ruth. Ruth can do as he pleases. He can quit if he wants to."[48]

The press, reversing course, moved quickly to support Huggins and criticize the Babe. *Baseball Magazine*'s F. C. Lane stated the reality that had been avoided for years. "The fact is that Babe Ruth has bedeviled baseball for years. . . . He has been egotistical, unmanageable, a questionable influence on his club and on the game. . . . Miller Huggins is an earnest, intelligent working baseball man. He knows his business, is always on the job, and is eminently fair. The player who has trouble with Miller Huggins deserves trouble."[49]

Ruth also understood the shift in the public's reaction and was contrite. He told *Collier's*, "I have been the sappiest of saps. . . . I have been a Babe and a boob."[50] He apologized to Huggins, but his manager was not ready to have him back. "I may reinstate him, but not until I believe that he has let this lesson seep into him. . . . Ruth will have to realize that the club is bigger than he is."[51]

Damon Runyon observed that when Ruth was "busting those home runs all over the landscape," he did not have to apologize to anyone.[52] (The Babe had hit only fifteen so far in 1925.) Richard Lipsky has noted a paradoxical relationship that fans have with their heroes, and not only those in sports. "We live vicariously in the ability of the hero to transcend all the pointless routines of everyday life. . . . Yet we secretly rejoice when he is forced to atone for overstepping the bounds of that transcendence. In both instances the social order is reinforced."[53]

The suspension, which kept him away from the playing field, was very difficult for the Babe. When he did return, on September 7, he went on a batting hot streak. In the season's final twenty-nine games, he had twelve multi-hit games and hit ten home runs with thirty-one runs batted in, as he raised his batting average to .290.

Yet questions remained as to whether Ruth could return to his old form in 1926. He would be thirty-one years old, and with his hard-living lifestyle, an "old" thirty-one. As St. Louis Post-Dispatch sports editor Ed Wray wrote, "There is another and much more serious battle pending [beside the one with Huggins] for the Bambino. That fight is with himself. His ultimate career is the prize of victory."[54] A determined Ruth told Collier's that he would make good again. "I am going to start all over, and I hope they'll all be watching my smoke in 1926."[55]

In his autobiography, Ed Barrow tells the story of Huggins concluding in the summer of 1925 that his team as constituted was "through." He told Ruppert and Barrow he could no longer get any reaction from his men, not even anger, no matter what he said to them. A 1926 article by Frank Graham confirms the story, including its timing.[56] Graham wrote that Huggins told Ruppert late in the 1925 season, "It's gone. There isn't anything you can do with a team that has become listless." When Ruppert asked him what was wrong with the team, Huggins told him, "It's gone. Just gone. I have tried everything—threats, cajolery, everything— but I can't get a rise out of it."[57] Barrow's reaction to Huggins's remarks was as forceful as it was terse. "Get rid of them. We'll get a new team."[58]

Sports teams—and companies in general—usually fire the manager rather than "get a new team." This was "a moment of truth" for the Yankees, which handled it in a professional way that sent a clear message—to the team and all the baseball world.

The Yankees did not have to get an entirely new team, though they did get rid of a number of players. Smelser noted that some veterans—he mentions Witt, Pipp, Schang, Scott, and Ruth—were united in opposition to Huggins in 1925. Ruth was disciplined, and by the start of the 1926 season, the other four men were no longer Yankees.

John Kieran of the *New York Times* noted one aspect of Huggins's understated style. "He appeared to be so quiet and harmless that he deceived even the players on his club for a while. They took advantage of him. They even poked fun at him. But not for long. When the boys began kicking up their heels, Huggins began making gifts. . . . Railroad tickets . . . some of them giving the holder the right to one first-class ride to Boston, others offering similar privileges to men headed for Atlanta or St. Paul. The Yankees remaining on the club noticed these gifts and the resultant departures."[59] Those remaining included three who had presented Huggins with challenges over the years, Ruth, Hoyt, and Meusel.

Ed Barrow noted more than a quarter of a century later that Huggins's action against Ruth had a profound impact on the club. "You can call it the turning point in the history of the New York Yankees. Thereafter the so-called bad boys realized that we meant business."[60]

Part 7

THE YANKEES RISE AGAIN

27

Florida's Boom to Bust and
the Yankees' Bust to Boom

Miller Huggins's life revolved around baseball. It was a source of both satisfaction and frustration. In 1926 he said, "Baseball is a funny game. You can cuss it and drive it out of your mind tonight and tomorrow morning you're wrapped up in it again and eager to get to the ball park."[1] As he prepared for the 1926 season, he realized the extent of the challenge that lay ahead. Yet he also saw an enormous opportunity. Huggins wanted to rebuild a team that would be, in the words of Fred Lieb, "his own handiwork, a team of dashing, young players which will lift the Yankees back to their former proud position."[2]

Huggins had invested heavily in Florida real estate, as had Colonel Ruppert, John McGraw, and a number of Major Leaguers. The new credit system made the boom possible; the slogan of the country was "Enjoy while you pay." Improved autos, tires, and roads, as well as Henry Flagler's Florida East Coast Railway and the Orange Belt (West Coast) Railroad, made the state more accessible to people from other parts of the country. The summer and fall of 1925 saw that frenzied market reach a peak. A summer 1925 edition of the *Miami Daily News* carried so many real estate ads that it had 504 pages—said to be the largest newspaper ever published to that time.[3]

Huggins had already seen his share of financial investments go bad. Frank Graham mentioned a financial setback suffered in Cincinnati and a Florida freeze that had destroyed a large orange grove, shortly after he had turned down an offer of $100,000 for the property.[4] After the Yankees' difficult 1922 season, Huggins's doctor—concerned about his health—had made him sell his stock portfolio.[5]

Jacob Ruppert had recently asked Huggins half-jokingly, "What are you, Miller—a real estate man or a baseball manager?"[6] Critical sportswriters, including Westbrook Pegler and W. O. McGeehan, not-so-jokingly referred to him as the Yankees' "little realtor."

Economist John Kenneth Galbraith had called the booming markets of the 1920s "mass escape into make-believe."[7] Now, early in 1926, with cracks already showing in the Florida land craze, Huggins decided to liquidate his real estate holdings. He sold them to J. B. Creamer, a Brooklyn investor, for $150,000.[8] He may have sensed the market was wildly inflated and got out when it was near, if not at, its high. But most of all, Huggins wanted to "clear the decks" for baseball. "Baseball and real estate don't mix," he said, "and I like the game the better of the two."[9]

With his time freed up from orange groves, Huggins did find a diversion outside of baseball, in addition to fishing. He took up golf. He fell in love with the game and found it relaxing because it did not weigh him down with responsibility. He never took a lesson, shot in the 90s, and dreamt of shooting 80. "Mention golf and everything changed," wrote sportswriter Bill Slocum. "Those eyes lighted up, the smile broadened and Huggins was a happy youngster again."[10]

Yet Huggins still had a real estate connection. He was the vice president of the Ruppert Beach Development Corp. In the fall of 1925 Ruppert had acquired extensive waterfront holdings at Pass-a-Grille Key, on the southern tip of St. Petersburg Beach. "There is a wonderful opportunity, in my judgment, for developing another Miami Beach on the Gulf of Mexico in St. Petersburg," the Colonel declared. "I am backing my opinion in this respect by making a substantial investment."[11]

Six months later, in a glorified ad couched as an interview, Colonel Ruppert touted Ruppert Beach. "I do not go into things hurriedly," said Ruppert, "but when I do I stick until it is finished. I want to repeat that I regard my investments in Florida as substantial as any I have made."[12]

Before the end of the year, triggered by the devastating September 1926 Miami hurricane, the Florida land boom collapsed. The extent of Ruppert's losses is unknown. Galbraith noted that the boom reflected the mood of the 1920s that believed "God intended for the middle class to be rich." More remarkably, he noted, this mood survived the Florida collapse and moved into the stock market.[13] Baseball historian Robert Smith wrote of the speculation of the 1920s, "It was like playing a lottery that had nothing but winners, or betting on a race where every horse came in first place at long odds."[14]

It seemed destined that 1926 would be a rebuilding year for the Yankees, a time to reinvest for the future, particularly in the infield, where Huggins had decided to go with a rookie double-play combination of shortstop Mark Koenig and second baseman Tony Lazzeri.[15] Huggins explained that spring that operating a ball club was "the quality of being able to look ahead and size up the future by the signs of the present. . . . In a way this business instinct is nothing but a keen gambling sense. It is knowing when to throw a lot of new capital into the organization." That very instinct led the Yankees to buy Ruth. "We looked ahead and saw the value Ruth would be to the Yanks."[16]

Ford Frick noted the risks involved in using two rookies at such vital positions and said the Yankees would be lucky to finish in the first division. "No team in baseball history has ever won a pennant with a kid infield," he pointed out.[17] The backbone of the team's defense ("up the middle") also included Earle Combs, who was starting only his second full season with the Yankees, as was first baseman Lou Gehrig.

Many observers were harsher than Frick. The Yankees' chances were "hopeless," wrote Ed Wray, the sports editor of the *St. Louis Post-Dispatch*. The club had lost its "super-hitting strength and enjoys only middle-aged pitching. Its infield is still a question mark and its main attraction is the once great Bambino, whose luster is dimming." The outlook for Huggins? "His head may come off," concluded Wray.[18]

The *New York Times* went so far as to call the Yankees' manager "almost a baseball Bolshevik" for entrusting key positions to youngsters: Koenig was just twenty-one years old; Lazzeri and Gehrig were just twenty-two. "Miller Huggins is no faint-hearted gambler; he is betting the roll on flaming youth," wrote the paper's columnist.[19]

Huggins knew exactly what he was doing; the Yankees had sold Wally Pipp to Cincinnati after eleven years with the team. "If those kids fail me, we'll wind up in sixth place. If they come through, we'll win the pennant," he declared.[20]

The Yankees had bought Lazzeri for $50,000 from Salt Lake City of the

Pacific Coast League, where he had a sensational 1925 season. He hit .355 with sixty home runs and 252 hits in 197 games.[21] Lazzeri was an epileptic, and when that information surfaced, other teams backed away from him. But the Yankees did not. Before finalizing the deal, Barrow asked Bob Connery to take a look at Lazzeri in Salt Lake. "Buy him. He's the greatest thing I've ever seen" was Connery's terse evaluation.[22] In his entire career, Lazzeri would never have a seizure on the field.[23]

Both Koenig and Lazzeri had played mostly shortstop in the Minors. Huggins, a former second baseman, felt Lazzeri would be the more likely to succeed at second base. While working with Gehrig on his fielding that spring, Huggins spent countless hours with Lazzeri, teaching him the finer points of his new position.[24] The Yankees' manager was doing what he had done so well a decade earlier in St. Louis: developing young players.

Lazzeri repaid Huggins's faith in him. He played in every game in 1926, batting .275 with eighteen home runs and 117 runs batted in; the latter was second-best in the league, behind the Babe. Huggins later called Lazzeri "a tower of strength to Gehrig and Koenig when they were unsure of themselves. . . . Ball players like Lazzeri come around once in a generation."[25] An appreciative Lazzeri later said of Huggins, "He made me; that's all. And I don't think anybody could bring along a kid player the way Huggins could."[26]

Years later Frank Graham wrote that of all the Yankees who played under him, Huggins probably liked Lazzeri best. Tony was "a ball player's ball player and a manager's ball player. He did everything right and was a dead game guy and a terrific competitor."[27] While Huggins never specifically said so, he probably took enormous satisfaction in seeing young players succeed. "You could tell the man he was by watching him bring along a kid player hopeless for anybody but Huggins," said Lazzeri.[28]

Koenig had far less self-confidence than his double-play partner. While he too delivered at the plate in 1926, batting .271, he was shaky in the field. His fifty-two errors led the league's shortstops in 1926, and some of them cost his team ballgames. A worrier like his manager, Koenig sometimes questioned his own ability. When newspapers were critical of his play, Huggins always reminded him there was only one person's opinion that mattered—and he believed in his young shortstop. "He made you feel like a giant" was how Koenig spoke of Huggins.[29] "Keep Your Eye on

Koenig, Says Huggins" was the headline of one New York paper as the season began.[30]

Huggins, perhaps thinking of Koenig, later spoke of players who conquered fear. "Too often a case of nerves is mistaken for a lack of nerve. . . . Give me the bird who knows what fear is but conquers his fear. That's the game guy."[31] He believed his three young infielders had the mettle—as well as the talent—to succeed.

Huggins took a fatherly, paternalistic approach to some of his players. He once walked up to Gehrig and punched him. When the puzzled (but unhurt) first baseman asked what that was for, Huggins explained he was upset when he heard Gehrig had spent $5,000 on a new car. When Gehrig explained he had spent only $700 on a used Peerless auto, Huggins told him, "Well, let that punch be a lesson to you; that's what will happen to you if I ever hear you are throwing your money away."[32]

Pitcher Waite Hoyt was another Yankee Huggins doted on. "Huggins was sort of a fatherly guy," Hoyt explained. "He was sort of a baseball father and sort of a psychiatrist. He had a couch in his office, and I was on that couch more than I was on the field. I was always being lectured, because he always said to me, 'You should lead the league every year with your stuff, but you don't because you don't concentrate.' And it would go on for hours."[33]

There were many uncertainties about the Yankees' upcoming season, but the biggest was not a youngster. It was thirty-one-year-old Babe Ruth. Hugh Fullerton questioned whether Ruth could stay healthy all season.[34] Ford Frick wrote that the Babe would never again match his earlier home run performances.[35] But he did acknowledge that Ruth was in his best shape in years. The Babe was determined to come back and had worked all winter at Artie McGovern's gym across from Grand Central Station; he had even hired a "digestion specialist." On the eve of spring training, the *New York American* described Ruth's "Apollo-like proportions." He had lost about forty pounds.[36]

The Yankees started spring training by losing their first few games, including an 18–2 thrashing at the hands of the lowly Boston Braves. The next two days they were shut out by the Yannigans, the term given to a team's back-up players. On March 14 Huggins was subjected to a withering attack by one of the nation's leading syndicated sportswriters, Chicago's Westbrook Pegler. "If Miller Huggins knew how to manage a ball team he might manage a pretty good club this year if he had a ball team to manage. . . . Huggins neither leads nor drives and the middle course between these two is nagging. . . . There is no evidence that he matters enough to deserve hostility. . . . The playing strength of the Yankees matters little. . . . They aren't a ball team; they're just a lot of ball players who think their manager is a sap."[37] Pegler had already ripped into the Yankees a week earlier. "The gossips in the smart tea places have been saying that the Yankees are a terrible flock of muggs who will be lucky to finish ahead of Peoria."[38]

Huggins used the attacks as a rallying point for the team and ultimately for his career. He ventured out of his comfort zone and went on the attack. In the next few days he was twice ejected from games for arguing on behalf of his players. He also defended his team. "I have never had a bunch of fellows who worked harder for me. . . . Why should a team be panned for taking a few socks in early practice games? That doesn't mean anything. I feel I have a good team and I like their spirit."[39]

The critics took notice. W. O. McGeehan quickly sensed that something was happening with the Yankees—a team spirit was coalescing. "There remains hope. The Yanks showed the first signs of real truculence. . . . Miller Huggins, the demi-tasse manager of the Yanks, was the first to declare war. He declared war against the critical correspondents and against the world in general. . . . The Yankees may do much better than any expert will predict at the current writing. If they do, their success will have to be attributed to the turning of the demi-tasse manager into a man of violent words."[40]

Then it all came together on the field. One day, then the next, and then the day after that. The Yankees won their final sixteen games of the exhibition season, including twelve games against the Brooklyn Dodgers. Brooklyn manager Wilbert Robinson was not simply impressed; he was stunned by the firepower he was seeing. "They're just a bunch of hitting fools. Anybody on that club is likely to bust up a game any time. . . . Mark my word, that club will win a lot of games in any league."[41] Jacob Ruppert, who had agonized through the early losses, was pleased. "We have a good ball club, much better than New York fans have been led to believe," he said. "The Yankees will be in the pennant race this season. . . . The Babe looks very good to me, and I expect him to make a great comeback."[42]

Miller Huggins, never mistaken for an optimist, liked his team that came together in Florida. As the club headed back home for the start of the season, he said, "I am taking North the most interesting team I have ever brought to New York."[43]

28

Huggins Silences His Critics, for Good

The city the Yankees called home had a flamboyant new mayor in 1926, Tammany favorite Jimmy Walker. His sponsorship of the laws legalizing Sunday baseball and boxing in New York (1919 and 1920, respectively), while in the state senate, made him immensely popular with New York's sporting crowd. His first term (1926–29) would be "one long champagne party" plagued by corruption and mismanagement.[1] Yet most New Yorkers loved their mayor because of "his immense wit, his warm personality, and because his days of wine and roses coincided with a postwar time which cast off the moral restraint our elders had decreed," wrote journalist Gene Fowler.[2]

Jacob Ruppert had lent his public relations man, George Perry, to the Walker mayoral campaign for four months. The Colonel also hosted the mayor-elect's victory party at his new Fifth Avenue apartment. This reflected the Colonel's genuine friendship with Walker, as well as his ongoing efforts to maintain his Tammany connections.[3]

Walker was a reflection of the city and of the times. "Wasn't Jimmy the quintessence of New York?" wrote Lloyd Morris in *Incredible New York* in 1951. "Didn't he represent its holiday mood, its vivacity and splendor, its pre-eminence among American cities as the pleasure capital of the hemisphere?"[4] In his history of the 1920s, Mark Sullivan wrote, "The part of America lying outside New York City felt itself frequently infected by noxious seeds carried by the winds from the metropolis. Much of the social history of the United States, and some of its political history, consisted of resistance by the country, especially the rural portions of it, to influences emanating from New York."[5]

Despite the spring training win streak, few sportswriters picked the Yankees to be in the 1926 pennant race, much less to win it. *Baseball Magazine* predicted they would finish fourth.[6] Fred Lieb was in the distinct minority when he wrote, "The Yankees should be the big sensation of baseball this year," led by what he called their "remarkable offensive strength."[7] Umpire-columnist Billy Evans, who had seen them firsthand in Florida, wrote, "Despite the fact that most of the experts have been roasting the New York Yankees to a dark brown, I still think it is a mighty good ball team."[8]

The Yankees started the season strongly; after beating Washington on May 1, their record stood at 13-3. In late April they beat the Red Sox in a game the *New York Times* called "as pretty a pitching duel as has been seen in these parts since they introduced the rabbit ball."[9] The winning pitcher was Herb Pennock, the supposedly washed-up lefthander the Yankees had acquired from the Red Sox three years earlier. The losing pitcher was Red Ruffing, a twenty-year-old pitcher who—like Pennock—would have little success in Boston.[10] Huggins kept a close eye on Ruffing over the next few years and tried to acquire him as early as 1927.[11]

On May 10 the Yankees began a sixteen-game winning streak, replicating what they had done in spring training. They averaged almost seven runs a game during that stretch. Early in the streak, Huggins confidently remarked, "All the Yankees need is good pitching. . . . All other worries have been eliminated."[12] That pitching did come through. Pennock, Hoyt, and Shocker all won at least ten games by the end of June. By mid-June New York had built up a ten-game lead over their nearest rivals.

Ruppert attended every home game this season, something he could not bear to do in 1925.[13] W. O. McGeehan wrote that when a Yankees opponent started a rally, "the Colonel would dive down beneath the stands and remain there, pacing nervously to and fro." He would "come up for air again" only if the Yankees retook the lead. If they did not, he often left the ballpark altogether.[14] There are many such stories about Ruppert's nervousness watching his Yankees play. While generally true, they should not be taken literally, especially those embellished by writers with a dramatic and even exaggerated style such as McGeehan. Ruppert almost certainly did not leave the Stadium every time the Yankees lost a lead or were losing a game.

In late June, Vila called the Yankees' owner one of the happiest men in baseball.[15] On the occasion of his seventieth birthday more than a decade later, Ruppert told *News-Week* that baseball made him feel twenty years younger. Unfortunately, he added, Prohibition and the fortune he lost in Florida's land boom had aged him twenty years. "So he's all even," the weekly concluded.[16]

Early in his career, outfielder Bob Meusel had been a source of frustration for Huggins. But he had emerged as one of the game's most dangerous hitters, and in May the Yankees' manager called him the best player in the American League. "I wouldn't trade Meusel for another outfielder in the league as he is playing now. He is finally showing the form that we all knew he could show if he put his mind to it."[17] By late May, Meusel was leading the league in hitting with a .400 batting average. Unfortunately, he broke a bone in his foot in late June and missed more than six weeks of the season.

Another of Huggins's problem players, Waite Hoyt, continued to test his manager's patience. The pitcher's ego and temper limited his effectiveness. When Huggins lifted him from an August game in the third inning, Hoyt "addressed harsh and insubordinate words toward Mr. Huggins" and was reported to have made a "gesture of derision" to his manager. The following day Huggins levied a $200 fine on his temperamental pitcher.[18]

Despite the enormous satisfaction Huggins must have drawn from his first-place team—Vila noted that the "knockers" had been "stricken dumb"—Huggins could not relax. When the Yankees' lead shrank to six games in July, he bemoaned the pressure of being at the head of the pack. "In piloting a pace setter there is more mental strain. . . . It takes a constant effort to keep a team that has a good lead from slumping. . . . I'll probably get just as many new gray hairs this year with a likely winner as I got last year when we finished seventh."[19]

This was a man who found it very difficult to enjoy his achievements, even when others were taking note of them. In a midseason editorial, the *Sporting News* stated, "Of the managers of major league baseball, there are few, almost none, who have achieved, in the face of great handicaps, what Miller Huggins has achieved."[20] The Yankees stumbled in early July but quickly reversed course in late July; their "remarkable offensive strength" reemerged, and they ran off eleven wins in a row, averaging seven runs a game.

Perhaps the season's biggest surprise was the stunning comeback of the Babe. He was batting .400 in late May and .390 in early July. Fred Lieb called his play "an inspiration" to the club.[21] A writer for a year-old magazine, the *New Yorker*, noted that "baseball's bad boy is now a good boy," but observed that "he is a boy, alternately good and bad—and will, I dare say, never grow up."[22] Ruth finished with a .372 batting average and led the league in home runs (47) and many other offensive categories. Fans embraced his return to form; the growth of newsreels at the cinema spread his fame to an ever-growing audience.

Author Jerome Charyn once noted that Ruth did not invent the home run—"he simply turned it into a lethal weapon."[23] Huggins had said something similar decades earlier. "Ruth was the most destructive force in baseball. I don't mean the force of Ruth's homers alone. The mere presence of the Babe created a disastrous psychological problem for the other team."[24]

Many baseball purists had been critical of the surfeit of home runs and high-scoring games since the early 1920s. Vila called the high-octane offense "farcical and disgusting."[25] Pitchers certainly agreed. The Giants' hurler Hugh McQuillan made a memorable statement when he said, "The lively ball is making stars of infielders and outfielders, and bums out of pitchers."[26] Huggins disagreed. He had foreseen the slugging era baseball was entering when the Yankees acquired the Babe. "We've got to play the game the way the fans want it played. They build the stadiums and they pay the Ruths and Gehrigs. And they like the home runs."[27]

In August Ruppert celebrated a sporting accomplishment of a very different kind, when New Yorker Gertrude Ederle became the first woman to swim the English Channel. Her primary opponents were the elements. She came home to a hero's welcome and a tickertape parade. Ruppert praised her for "a great American triumph."[28] There was one New York City group that especially wanted to claim her as their own: the German American community. Her parents were both German immigrants.

While Ruppert was probably wise to frame her swim as an American accomplishment, he did add "felicitations to her splendid mother and father." The United German Societies, which represented 2,500 German American groups, publicized her ancestral roots. These groups had been on the defensive—if not invisible—since the war and saw the perfect opportunity to resurface.

But the nation was in the midst of a fierce nativist, anti-immigrant mood, as reflected in the restrictive immigration laws that Congress had been passing in the 1920s. A few days after the Ederle swim, the *New York Times* attacked "the pompous German American gentlemen" who wanted to claim her as "Gertrude of Arc" and "cover again with honor the German name in the United States."[29]

When the Yankees went into an August tailspin, Huggins bolstered the team by acquiring veteran southpaw Dutch Ruether, who had compiled a 30-13 record in the past two seasons with Washington.[30] Ruether had a reputation as a hard drinker and a difficult player to manage; all the other American League teams had passed on him. A couple of months earlier, Chicago Cubs manager Joe McCarthy had released former pitching great Grover Cleveland Alexander for similar bad habits. The St. Louis Cardinals claimed him off waivers, and his nine wins proved crucial in their pennant drive in the National League.

The Yankees pulled into Cleveland in mid-September for a six-game series, holding a five-and-a-half game lead over the Indians. After winning the first game, the Yankees lost four in a row, and the lead shrank to two and a half games. After their third consecutive loss, the *New York Times* wrote, "Outfought, outthought, outplayed and outclassed, the Yankees gave a very poor imitation of a championship team."[31] Tension was so high that Huggins and Cleveland player-manager Tris Speaker almost came to blows in the fifth game.[32]

With the season on the line, Huggins sent Ruether back out—he had pitched well earlier in the series—to start the final game.[33] He beat the Indians 8–3, helped along by three doubles and a home run by Lou Gehrig. This was just the kind of game for which Huggins had secured Ruether, known as a "money pitcher."

The Yankees staggered to the pennant, losing eleven of their last sixteen games, including the Cleveland series, but held on, eventually edging the Indians by three games.[34] The *Sporting News* saluted them in an editorial entitled "Hail New York." In the spring, they had been given a "scurrilous greeting by incompetent ignorance" as never before.[35] When the season ended, they had climbed from near the bottom to the top of the league—in just one year. "That just about ended the debate over the ability of Miller Huggins. The scoffers ceased to scoff and the skeptics were convinced," wrote John Kieran in the *New York Times*.[36]

Westbrook Pegler admitted that the Yankees had seriously embarrassed him. He wrote that he had "innocently jabbed their manager with a fork and so aroused him" to abandon real estate and win a pennant, though surely Huggins would not have credited Pegler with either occurrence. The writer said he had merely repeated what a Yankees' player told him a majority of his teammates believed—that Huggins knew no more about running a club or leading men than a jeweler knew about locomotives.[37]

Marshall Smelser, one of Ruth's biographers, also felt that Huggins lacked the ability to manage other men. "His [Huggins's] judgment of people was faulty. He did not know how to lead his star-spangled team. He tried to master them after the fashion of a lion tamer. Overrigid discipline has been a problem in baseball since the beginning. Managers try despotism, but if despotism fails then anarchy threatens." Smelser saw similarities between Huggins and another small man who led larger men, Napoleon. Both were "shrewd, cold, selfish, and sometimes cruel." In 1925, Smelser noted, "Huggins's job became steadily harder. His men were ill-tempered and so was he. His attempt to rule with a firm hand met resentment among bored players."[38]

He is the only baseball historian of the past seventy-five years who has been critical of Huggins's dealings with his players, and Smelser is harshly critical. Even Pegler revised his opinion after the comeback of 1926. Smelser, who had the perspective of time and the manager's entire body of work, seems to have missed the skills Huggins brought into play.

In the summer of 1926 Huggins discussed leadership, providing a look at his philosophy and depth of thinking. "Leadership means keeping the morale and spirit of the team at the right level. Sometimes overconfidence has to be toned down. That has been the case this year, at times. Again the team must be lifted from a mental slump. You've got to be patient when plans go wrong, when a young player gets into a slump. . . . When fans and the newspapers are riding you hard—that's when patience becomes the most necessary of managerial virtues."[39]

Huggins went on to say there was an even more important element to leadership: common sense. That meant not treating all players alike. Some needed a "firm hand"—Huggins said as he glanced at Waite Hoyt, whom he recently had fined. Others needed a "loose rein"—and Huggins looked out toward right field, where Ruth was playing. Even after their late 1925 showdown, Huggins recognized that he could not smother Ruth. He also recognized that was not necessary. Once the Yankees had set the boundaries and Ruth had acknowledged them and accepted his manager's authority, Huggins and the Babe had a good—and even affectionate—working relationship for the rest of their years together.

The Yankees met Huggins's former team, the St. Louis Cardinals, in the World Series.[40] They were an exciting team led by player-manager Rogers Hornsby. The thrilling Series featured Herb Pennock's two complete-game wins and Babe Ruth's three home runs in one game. But in the end, the thirty-nine-year-old Alexander was the difference. He too won two games and saved Game Seven, a 3–2 win, with his legendary strikeout of Tony Lazzeri with the bases loaded in the seventh inning.

Waite Hoyt pitched well enough to win that final game, and the Babe's fourth Series home run would have been the game-winning blow. But the Yankees' defense melted down in a three-run fourth inning; all the runs were unearned. Koenig, perhaps rattled by the Cardinals, who had been "riding" him the entire Series, muffed an easy ground ball. He and Meusel then let a catchable fly ball drop between them, and Meusel followed that "hit" by dropping a routine fly. The Series ended with the Babe thrown out trying to steal second base, with Bob Meusel at the plate and Lou Gehrig on deck. While Ruth was criticized for the attempted steal—Ed Barrow called it the only dumb play the Babe ever made—Huggins defended Ruth's decision, and his move had a certain logic behind it. The way Alexander was pitching, it was doubtful he would give up two more hits. By getting into scoring position, the Yankees would need only one single to tie the score. And the Babe had stolen second base off Alexander the day before.[41]

Huggins made no excuses for the outcome and expressed pride in his club, giving special credit to his youngsters and to pitchers Pennock and

Hoyt.[42] Sportswriter James Harrison observed that no seven-game World Series had ever ended "satisfactorily—never a seventh game decided strictly on its merits. Invariably the breaks have decided it."[43]

There was some suspicion that teams had been stretching out the Series in recent years (seven games for the third straight year) to maximize profits.[44] Ruppert commented on the issue. First of all, he claimed that World Series profits had been overestimated, though he provided no numbers. As for rumors of a Series being fixed to go the full seven games, he addressed the matter head on. "Nobody is quicker to investigate rumors of scandal than the owners themselves. We realize we must keep the game clean in order to protect our own property."[45]

Once again a season had taken its toll on Huggins. "The older I grow, the harder it is to manage a ball club. You might think experience would help, and it does. But that's more than offset by the steady grind."[46] He did hire the fiery Art Fletcher as a coach after the season, replacing Fred Merkle.[47] Beginning in 1927, Fletcher would serve as the Yankees' third-base coach; Huggins, who had filled that role since coming to New York, would now do all his managing from the bench. He would lean on his coaches, Fletcher and Charley O'Leary, as his "brain trust" in coming years. They would also be his pinochle partners, providing him with hours of amusement and diversion.

The Yankees' manager was down to 106 pounds at the end of the season and went to Bill Brown's Health Farm in upstate New York, in Garrison.[48] When he returned for his tenth season in New York, Joe Williams noted, "Mr. Huggins seems to have taken on the aspects of a fixture, like the library lions on Fifth Ave. . . . Mr. Huggins and these Yanks seem inevitably merging into one and the same institution."[49] Yet unbeknownst at the time, Huggins had been "on the verge of quitting" before the Yankees' season for the ages, 1927.[50]

29

Winning Pennants Is the
Business of the Yankees

The year 1927 has come to symbolize the era we now remember as the "Roaring Twenties." It was the year of Charles Lindbergh and the *Spirit of St. Louis*; the year of Gene Tunney, Jack Dempsey, and the "Long Count"; the year of Al Capone, America's most notorious bootlegger; the year of Jerome Kern and Oscar Hammerstein's *Showboat*; and the year Al Jolson starred in *The Jazz Singer*, which brought sound to the movies. It was also the year Babe Ruth set a new record for home runs, and the New York Yankees laid claim to being the greatest baseball team ever. A team "greater than any that had gone before, greater than any that followed," wrote Frank Graham.[1]

Graham wrote this in 1943, so the "greater than any that followed" he referred to was a period that included the 1936–39 Yankees, winners of four consecutive World Series. We can argue whether the 1927 New York Yankees were or were not the greatest; certainly, no one was anointing them as such before the season started.[2] Pointing to an aging pitching staff that had finished fourth in the league in ERA in 1926, sportswriter E. G. Brands went so far as to say they were "liable to fall apart and disintegrate this year."[3]

In a poll of the nation's sportswriters taken in the spring of 1927, only half thought the Yankees were strong enough to defend their American League championship. Most of the others picked the Philadelphia Athletics. The Athletics had even greater support in an Associated Press poll, which had them favored by twenty-nine correspondents and the Yankees by just nine.[4] After finishing last in each of the seven seasons following their last pennant in 1914, Connie Mack had slowly led them back: first to respectability, then to pennant contention—they were third in 1926—and now to pennant favorites.

The Athletics featured three young future Hall of Famers: Lefty Grove, Mickey Cochrane, and Al Simmons. Mack had further strengthened his club by adding veteran greats Ty Cobb, Eddie Collins, and Zack Wheat.[5] That such a strong team would finish nineteen games behind suggests how great the 1927 Yankees were.

Mack's signing of Cobb had repercussions in the Bronx. Babe Ruth's three-year contract, signed in 1924 for $52,000 per year, had now expired. Ruth was by far the game's greatest attraction and had long since passed Cobb as its most productive player. Yet Cobb was to be paid between $70,000 and $80,000.[6]

The personal rivalry between the two men was an added incentive for Ruth to demand that he make significantly more money than his old antagonist did. The Babe wrote a letter to Colonel Ruppert asking for a two-year contract at $100,000 per year. If he did not get it, he threatened he would quit baseball. No one took the threat seriously, including Ruppert, and Ruth eventually accepted the Colonel's offer of $70,000 per year for three years.

Ruppert loved going down to Florida every year for spring training. He always was the happiest and most carefree there. He would stay at the Don Cesar Hotel in St. Petersburg Beach, where each morning he would take a long walk on the beach and go for a swim.[7]

On the day Ruppert arrived in Florida in mid-March 1927, he still had two significant holdouts to deal with: Bob Meusel and Herb Pennock.[8] He signed Meusel to a two-year deal that day, but getting an agreement with Pennock proved to be more difficult.[9] A twenty-three-game winner in 1926, he was holding out for $20,000, which would have made him the highest-paid left-handed pitcher in the game's history. "Pennock can hold out for the rest of his life," Ruppert said. "His demands are unreasonable and we are not going to make him another offer."[10]

On March 27, the thirty-three-year-old Pennock signed a three-year contract for an estimated $17,500 per season.[11] He joined Ruth, Brooklyn Robins pitcher Dazzy Vance, and New York Giants outfielder Edd Roush as the only players then currently active to have been signed to three-year contracts.

Miller Huggins had his own opinion about big salaries and, indirectly, long-term contracts. He believed that players should never get the impression that they were indispensable. "Let the players know they must hustle for their jobs," he had written. "Do not let a team get too complacent or too self-satisfied."[12]

A dour man at best, Huggins seemed relatively relaxed and happy in the spring of 1927. He had grown to love his adopted city of St. Petersburg and believed spending the last few winters in the sunshine had done much good for his health. Still, Huggins had been so physically and mentally exhausted at the end of the 1926 season that he had needed that stay at Bill Brown's Health Farm to recover his strength.

Looking ahead, Huggins said he now intended to stay in baseball for the rest of his life, but not necessarily as a manager. As for the upcoming season, he appeared confident he had an even better club than his American League champions of the previous year. "I like my team," Huggins said late in spring training. "In fact I go as far as to say my club is stronger."[13]

He was pleased with the two trades the team had made the past winter, adding catcher Johnny Grabowski and second baseman Ray Morehart from the White Sox and outfielder Cedric Durst and pitcher Joe Giard from the Browns. Grabowski, a three-year veteran, had established himself as one of the best-throwing catchers in the game. He would share the catching duties in 1927 with Benny Bengough and Pat Collins, who had been the team's primary catcher in 1926. None of the three was of the caliber of his former star receiver, Wally Schang, but Huggins was satisfied with what he had, or at least he claimed he was.[14] "I would like to have a great catcher on my club, but I'm not going to worry a great deal because I haven't," he said. "These catchers of mine are not world beaters, but they are good catchers and that is all I ask. The importance of a catcher to a club frequently is overestimated, particularly when the club has a set of smart pitchers, such as ours has."[15]

Morehart, who had been a backup to Eddie Collins with Chicago in 1926, would back up Tony Lazzeri in 1927. The White Sox needed a second baseman to replace Collins, and Lazzeri's emergence in 1926 had made Aaron Ward, a former Huggins favorite whose career had been in decline, expendable. Also expendable was pitcher Sam Jones, who went to the Browns for Giard and Durst. Jones had been a disappointment in

New York since winning twenty-one games in 1923. The following year he won only nine while losing six, and in 1925 he led the league with twenty-one losses.[16]

"Giard was the man I wanted most," Huggins said of the left-handed pitcher he had sent to St. Louis in the December 1924 trade for Urban Shocker. "Both my left-handers are aging," he said, "and you never can tell when they will crack.[17] What I needed was a young southpaw who is coming instead of going. Jones had a bad year last season. I had to shake up the pitching staff, and so I decided to take a chance on Giard." Huggins said he would use Durst as a pinch-hitter and as his left-handed-hitting spare outfielder to complement the right-handed-hitting Ben Paschal.[18] Durst had hit only .234 in his 140 games with the Browns, but he had shown great promise by batting above .340 with Los Angeles of the Pacific Coast League in 1924 and with St. Paul of the American Association in 1925.

Paschal, too, had been a terrific hitter in the Minor Leagues and was hailed by some as the "next Babe Ruth." He had been a solid addition to the Yankees since joining them in 1924, but not good enough to break into an outfield of Ruth, Meusel, and Earle Combs.

Huggins was ahead of his time in believing that psychology played a role in a team's success. "Some people call it luck," he said, "but I call it psychology, which in our business is largely a matter of building and maintaining confidence." He conceded that psychology would go only so far if the team did not "have the players who could hit, run, and field."[19]

The Yankees certainly had the players who could hit, run, and field, but as Bill Corum noted, their pitching was an unknown, with Pennock the only reliable starter. "Shocker has shown signs of slipping," he wrote. "Ruether is an uncertain quantity. Hoyt pitches in streaks. Shawkey is old."[20] Huggins agreed with Corum's assessment but remained optimistic. In an April 3 telegram to the *New York American*, he predicted a hard fight for the pennant. "I believe the deals I made during the winter have strengthened the club behind the bat and have added to the reserve strength of the infield and outfield. I am uncertain only about my pitching, and I would not be surprised if that turned out to be good." He ended on a positive note, writing, "I think New York fans will enjoy the Yanks of 1927."[21]

They would, and so would Ruppert, who preferred runaways by his team both in individual games and pennant races. The Yankees won their first six decisions and were never out of first place all season. A 13–6 win at Philadelphia, on April 21, raised their record to 7-2 and gave them a game-and-a-half lead over Detroit and Washington. After just ten games, Lou Gehrig had nineteen runs batted in, Bob Meusel had fourteen, Tony Lazzeri thirteen, and Babe Ruth, who because he was drawing so many walks—he was walked four times in this game—had just one.

The A's had scored six runs in 4 1/3 innings off starter Waite Hoyt in that April 21 game before Huggins replaced him with right-hander Wilcy Moore, a thirty-year-old rookie. Moore had spent five seasons pitching in the low Minor Leagues before compiling a spectacular 30-4 record to lead the 1926 Greenville (South Carolina) Spinners to the championship of the Class B South Atlantic Association. Moore allowed just one hit in 4 2/3 innings of scoreless relief to gain his first Major League victory. It was the beginning of what would be a sensational year for him. He won nineteen games (19-7) and led the league with a 2.28 earned run average. But it was as a relief pitcher that Moore proved so valuable. He appeared in fifty games, but only twelve were starts. He picked up thirteen of his wins in relief and might have been a twenty-game winner had he not suffered a tough-luck loss at Philadelphia on September 3. He allowed the A's just one run in seven innings, but lost, 1–0, to Lefty Grove, the only time the Yankees were shut out all season.

"I never had his like before," Huggins said. "Moore is the best rescue man I've ever had as long as I've been managing. He is in a class by himself."[22] In August, after Moore had saved another game, Corum wrote, "They call him the big ambulance. Huggins rings the bell and Moore rushes in and administers first aid. He has saved at least ten games this season."[23]

The White Sox had mounted a challenge to the Yankees' domination and trailed by only one game when they came to New York for a four-game series beginning on June 7. The Yankees won the first three games, and while Chicago won the fourth, no other team would come as close again. Ray Schalk, in his first year as manager of the Sox, took the three losses hard. He went so far as to accuse the Yankees of having an unfair advantage: Yankee Stadium. While acknowledging "the Yankees are terrific hitters," he called the Stadium a "trick ball park" that gives them an advantage over other teams. "Consequently the Yankees, particularly Ruth and Gehrig, make comparatively easy home runs which often win games." Schalk went as far as to propose that all parks have uniform measurements.[24]

Huggins had offered his own reason why the Yankees were such heavy hitters. "Just watch these fellows take a toe hold and you have the answer," he said. "Practically every man on the team, except Dugan, holds his bat way down near the handle, and they swing from the hip."[25]

Ruppert had reduced the price of the 22,000 bleacher seats at Yankee Stadium from 75 cents to 50 cents, which resulted in those seats being filled to capacity almost every day. The Yankees led both leagues in attendance, drawing 1,164,015, the most since the Stadium opened five seasons earlier.

On July 4, more than 65,000 were at the Stadium to see the Yankees maul the second-place Senators in both ends of the holiday doubleheader, 12–1 and 21–1. "Those fellows not only beat you, but they eat your heart out," said Senators first baseman Joe Judge after the double loss.[26] George Pipgras and Moore pitched complete games to raise the Yankees' lead over Washington to 11½ games.

Pipgras was a Minor Leaguer when he came to New York in a little-noted 1923 deal with the Red Sox.[27] He had pitched in a combined seventeen games for the Yankees in 1923–24, before becoming a big winner in the Minor Leagues the next two seasons. Huggins brought him back to New York, where he would make twenty-one starts in 1927 and finish with a 10-3 record. "As a baseball man," Ford Frick wrote of Huggins, "his greatest attribute was his patience . . . Once Hug was convinced that a man would make a real ball player he would stay with him for years. Pipgras was developed in that way."[28] "The first time I saw him I knew he was a good pitcher," said Huggins.[29]

Catcher Johnny Grabowski thought Pipgras was the most difficult of the Yankees' pitchers to catch. "He has as much stuff as any pitcher I ever saw, but he is still wild." At the opposite end, he thought Pennock was the easiest to catch. "He has almost perfect control and he throws a light ball." Grabowski said that contrary to popular opinion, Shocker, the spitballer, was easy to catch, much easier than spitballer Red Faber, whom he had caught in Chicago.[30]

Although the Yankees were running away with the pennant, on August 11 they paid the Oakland Oaks $125,000 for infielders Lyn Lary and Jimmie Reese, two of the best players in the Pacific Coast League. While neither man would join the Yankees in 1927, the move outraged the other American League owners, who accused Ruppert of using his checkbook to an unfair advantage.[31] The Yankees' owner was not in the least sympathetic. "If a machine in my business wears out I replace it," the Colonel responded. "I am always looking at improved machines; improved property. I study efficiency in business. Baseball is a sport; it is a hobby, but it is a business. I want the most out of baseball. Not in money alone, but in results. I would rather win a pennant and a World Series than get the money that naturally is made by a winning ball club." Ruppert went on to say, "I want to win the pennant five more years in a row if we can. They can rave about the league going to pieces. It won't do anything of the kind. We are going ahead to get any good ball player we can. Winning pennants is the business of the New York Yankees."[32]

Huggins echoed his boss. "It is our desire to have a pennant winner each year indefinitely. New York fans want championship ball, and the Yankees can be counted on to provide it." Huggins continued, even employing the language of the businessman. "We are prepared to outbid other clubs for young players of quality. What we are after all the time is new material, the best available in the minors and elsewhere, so that it can be developed to fill the places of men who will soon be forced to retire. We have a fine ball team now, but we don't intend to be caught napping."[33]

By July 20, the Yankees had a twelve-game lead on second-place Washington when Huggins, a "chronic pessimist," admitted the Yankees "have a chance to win the pennant again this year."[34] The Colonel, as usual, was at the Stadium on September 13 when the Yankees clinched the pennant, as Pipgras and Hoyt defeated Cleveland by identical 5–3 scores in a doubleheader.

Ruth homered in each game, giving him fifty-two for the season. With fifteen games left, his record home run mark of 59, set in 1921, was in range. On September 30, the next- to-final day of the season, the Babe set a new mark when he smashed number 60 off Washington's Tom Zachary.[35] "Sixty!" Ruth said after the game. "Let's see some son of a bitch try to top that one."[36]

The 1927 Yankees set the American League record for wins (110) and the Major League records for runs and home runs, all since broken. An impressive performance, to be sure, but not one on which Huggins, focused wholly on winning the pennant, placed much value. "I'm not thinking about the records," he had said as far back as July. "I'm only concerned with keeping my team in winning form."[37]

Lou Gehrig had his first great season in 1927. For much of it, he was the home run leader, before Ruth passed him on his way to his record-setting sixty. The Ruth-Gehrig home run race had captivated the fans and was well covered by the nation's newspapers, many of which ran a daily update on where they stood in the race.[38]

In addition to his forty-seven home runs, Gehrig had a .373 batting average, a league-leading fifty-two doubles, and a Major League record 173 runs batted in.[39] He won the League Award, getting seven of the eight first-place votes.[40] The other first-place vote went to Lazzeri, who drove in 102 runs and whose eighteen home runs were third highest in the league.[41] Earle Combs batted .356 and led the American League in hits and triples, while Bob Meusel batted .337 and had 103 runs batted in. Shortstop Mark Koenig (.285), third baseman Joe Dugan (.269), and the catching triumvirate of Collins, Grabowski, and Bengough rounded out the regular starters.

"We never even worried five or six runs behind," Ruth said. "Ruth-Gehrig-Lazzeri-Combs . . . wham, wham, and wham!—no matter who was pitching."[42] The only offensive categories in which New York did not lead the league were doubles and stolen bases. And stolen bases was the only individual offensive category in which a Yankee did not lead—Meusel, with twenty-four, finished second to the Browns' George Sisler, who had twenty-seven. With all the power Huggins had in his everyday lineup, stealing bases did not figure in his offensive scheme.

Aided by the contributions of Pipgras and Moore, the pitching staff that had so worried Huggins in the spring dominated the league. Hoyt (22-7), Shocker (18-6), and Moore (19-7) were 1-2-3 in winning percentage, and Moore (2.28), Hoyt (2.63), and Shocker (2.84) were 1-2-3 in earned run average. The Yankees team ERA of 3.20 was more than a full run lower than the league's seven other teams' combined ERA of 4.27.

The team that Huggins left camp with was the team he kept all season.

His starters remained relatively healthy, making it unnecessary for the Yankees to make trades or call up any players from the Minor Leagues. And when Huggins rested one of his regulars and called on one of his reserves, he expected that substitute to be ready to play. "Huggins instituted a rigid program of behavior for those men who were not in the starting lineup," remembered Waite Hoyt. "If you were an extra for the day, you were expected to pay attention to the game. There was to be no talk about anything but baseball."[43]

As the Yankees drove toward the pennant, Bill Corum looked back on Huggins's ten years as the Yankees' manager. He recalled the criticism Huggins had endured in his early years in New York and how his accomplishments had made that disappear. He dismissed the claims that the Yankees' success was due less to Huggins's leadership than it was to Ruppert's bankroll. Other millionaires in baseball have spent money, Corum wrote, "but they have not been on top five times in seven years as the Yankees have been since 1920."[44]

The National League representative in the 1927 World Series was the Donie Bush–managed Pittsburgh Pirates. Led by the Waner brothers— right fielder Paul and center fielder Lloyd—and third baseman Pie Traynor, the Pirates had held off the defending champion Cardinals to win the pennant by just one and a half games. They had three dependable starting pitchers, twenty-two-game winner Carmen Hill, and nineteen-game winners Ray Kremer and Lee Meadows.

The Yankees were the overwhelming choice to win the Series, yet there were those who thought the Pirates would win. Among them was New York Giants second baseman Rogers Hornsby, who had managed the Cardinals to their 1926 Series win against the Yankees. "The Pirates will outhustle the Yanks, just as all National League teams always do in the classic series with the American League champions," Hornsby said, echoing the older league's customary sense of superiority.[45]

But Huggins had the better team, and he knew it. "The Yankees are ready, as ready as they have been all year for every important test that confronted them," he said. Yet Huggins was not a talkative or a boastful man, far from it. The *New York Times* described him as a little man with tired eyes, who always "looks as though he is being borne down with a great burden."[46] Jacob Ruppert, however, had no hesitation in predicting his team would win the Series. "They will go right on just as if the series games were part of the regular season, and I expect to fly another world's championship pennant from the flagpole next Spring." Ruppert continued to give full credit to Huggins, whom he called one of the smartest men in baseball and one of the finest personally. "He has gone about his work quietly and you hardly ever see him, but you see the results of his planning and of his keen baseball mind."[47]

The experts, excepting Hornsby, were correct in their predictions. The Yankees enhanced their growing reputation as the greatest team ever by sweeping the Series in four games, becoming the first American League team to do so.[48] Hoyt, with relief help from Moore, won the first game, and Pipgras, Pennock, and Moore won the next three with complete games. Ruth hit the only two home runs, and Mark Koenig followed his poor 1926 Series by leading the Yankees in batting with a .500 average. "Pennock will never beat the Pirates," Hornsby had predicted. "That Pittsburgh gang will murder any southpaw."[49] Huggins, aware of Pittsburgh's success against lefthanders—they had batted .334 against them during the season—said that would not prevent him from starting a left-hander in one game of the Series. "I'll start with my right-handers and if they win for me I'll keep on using them," he said. "But if I feel that I need a left-hander I won't hesitate to put him in."[50]

Again Hornsby proved to be a better player than a prognosticator. Pennock had the easiest time of all with the Pirates, allowing just three hits in his 8–1 Game Three victory, a win that raised his World Series record to 5–0. Pennock came close to pitching the first World Series no-hitter that day; the first Pirates' hit was Pie Traynor's single with one out in the eighth inning.

Ban Johnson had recently retired as president of the American League, but still retained the fierce partisanship with which he had challenged the older National League back in 1901. Moments after Pirates pitcher Johnny Miljus threw the wild pitch that allowed Combs to score the run that ended the Series, he sent a congratulatory telegram to Ruppert. "We like to destroy the enemy in that manner," Johnson wrote, reveling in the sweep of Barney Dreyfuss's club. "Four straight victories will have a wholesome effect upon the public mind and strengthen the position of professional baseball."[51]

By winning the Series in four games, the Yankees were obliged to refund $200,000 for tickets that had been purchased in advance for Sunday's scheduled Game Five. "I am tickled to death that our team won," the Colonel said. "But I am happier in what I believe is a great thing for baseball. It will cost us something like $200,000, but there can be no talk now of stringing a series out. We wanted to win in four straight games and we did, because we have a wonderful team."[52]

That both Johnson and Ruppert mentioned the sweep was a good thing for baseball and should not be overlooked. "Even as late as 1927," wrote the *Literary Digest*, "suspicion remained in some quarters that gamblers and greed still played a big role in baseball. So the Yankees' sweep of the Pirates was welcomed by many as proof that, at least in this Series, both teams had played to win." Yet before the Series, there had been a tendency to belittle the New Yorkers, saying they had run away against a very weak American League. Now that they were facing the Pirates, who had won in a league that had several very good clubs, some National League supporters predicted they would be shown in their true colors. "Well, they met the Pirates, and were shown up in their true colors, and those colors proved to be as brilliant as any that have ever been seen on a diamond," wrote the *Literary Digest*. "So hats off to Combs, Koenig, Ruth Gehrig, Meusel, Push'm–Up–Wop [Tony Lazzeri], and all the rest of the celebrated batting order. . . . And hats off to Huggins, the greatest lawyer who ever sat on a bench."[53]

Having piloted his record-breaking team to a World Series sweep, Huggins made his way back to the Florida sunshine for the winter. Even someone like sportswriter Frank Graham, who saw Huggins on a daily basis throughout the season, could not determine where the enigmatic manager found true contentment. "It is doubtful which Huggins enjoys more," Graham wrote, "sitting in the Yankee dugout surrounded and, at times, almost obscured by his ball players, as a pennant fight is waged under his direction, or sitting in a rowboat that bobs lazily so far out on Tampa Bay that the skyline of St. Petersburg is but dimly visible to him as he stares at it dreamily."[54]

Bill Corum believed Ruppert liked the world champions of 1927–28 best, even more than the teams that won three World Series just before the Colonel died. "Ruppert reveled in power and supremacy, and they stood for both—in spades."[55]

Ten years later, in October 1937, Ruppert confirmed that belief. He told Joe Dugan, the third baseman on his 1927 team, that the '27 squad was his favorite. "They were a great bunch, Dugan, really great. They would have beaten even my 1937 team. That's how great they were."[56]

30

Knowing How to Buy and
Knowing How to Build

The Yankees had run away with the pennant in 1927. Yet the consensus in the spring of 1928 was that they were not as strong as they had been in 1927, and the Athletics, their closest competitor, were stronger. However, the experts differed as to whether these degrees of change were enough for the A's to make up the nineteen-game deficit of a year ago. Jacob Ruppert and Miller Huggins thought not. Despite the Yankees' unimpressive play during spring training, both men issued statements declaring they expected the team to win a third straight pennant. "We may not win 110 games this year," said Huggins. "I'm not venturing any guess on that. But I contend that we cannot fall off so badly that we will come to the level of teams which we defeated by 19 games and more. It is not in the cards. . . . Is Gehrig any worse than he was? Of course not. Is Lazzeri? Is Koenig?"[1] Nevertheless, Huggins did not rule out the possibility of complacency. "The toughest opposition which the Yankees will encounter in the coming race will be from the Yankees themselves," he told Bill Slocum. "It is the tendency of a successful ball club to take too much for granted and believe that it can pull itself together at any time."[2]

Opposing batters were having little trouble with the Yankees' pitchers in spring training, but Ruppert, echoing Huggins, assured the fans all was well. "Nothing is the matter with the Yankees' Big Four—Hoyt, Pennock, Moore, and Pipgras," he said. "They are in fine condition but are not being hurried. I believe that Pipgras will be a sensational winner. Beating the Pirates in the World Series last October gave him confidence and prestige, which he still possesses." Ruppert would prove right as Pipgras won twenty-four games to lead the league. He also noted that "Huggins had obtained a promising catcher in [Bill] Dickey."[3]

Nevertheless, spring training had been a time of transition and uncertainty for the pitching staff. Gone were Urban Shocker and Dutch Ruether, seasoned veterans who had combined for thirty-one wins in 1927. Shocker, suffering from a congenital heart condition, was too sick to join the team at training camp, telling the Yankees he was retiring to pursue his business interests. He returned to pitch one final game, appearing in a two-inning mop-up role against Washington on Memorial Day. In early July, with Shocker no longer of any value to the team, Huggins made the emotionally difficult decision to release him. "Although in releasing Shocker Huggins took the only course that was left open to him as manager of the Yankees," wrote Frank Graham, "he was affected to a greater extent by his enforced action than this writer has ever seen him affected by anything."[4]

The Yankees had let Ruether go when they decided his drinking habits were a bad influence on the team's younger players. When no Major League team signed him, he joined the San Francisco Seals of the Pacific Coast League, where he led the league in wins and earned run average. Gone too was Bob Shawkey, who had been a Yankee since 1915, the year Ruppert and Huston bought the club.[5] Wilcy Moore, the rookie sensation of 1927, suffered a sore arm, which only exacerbated the pitching uncertainties Huggins faced. He did have three new pitchers in camp hoping to make the team: veteran Stan Coveleski and two men up from the minors: twenty-eight-year-old Al Shealy and twenty-two-year-old Hank Johnson.[6] Huggins had planned to sign Coveleski in 1927 after the Senators released him in June. But after working out for a while, Coveleski told Huggins he would not be able to pitch that year but would like a trial the following spring. "You can have a trial with me anytime," Huggins replied. "You've been on the square with me and I won't forget it."[7]

Shealy had pitched for Newberry College in South Carolina, which may have been a negative in Huggins's eyes. Despite having played at the University of Cincinnati himself, Huggins believed college players often posed special problems. "College players would be all right if they came to you with the proper attitude on baseball," Huggins said. "They have the anti-minor league complex—don't want to go down for more experience. They have the pride complex. If you take a college pitcher out of the box he gets peeved."[8] Yet as far back as 1920 Huggins had recognized colleges as a breeding ground for especially talented players. "I have high regard for the American university as a developing ground for exceptional ball players," he had said. "One has only to recall that [Eddie] Collins and [George] Sisler came from colleges to understand what I mean."[9]

The Yankees quickly put their travails at spring training behind them by winning 33 of their first 40 games. After sweeping a May 29 double-header from Washington, they had an 8½-game lead over Philadelphia. They were 7 games ahead of their record-setting pace of 1927 and threatening another runaway.[10] Huggins's prediction that the Yankees would not "come to the level of teams which we defeated by 19 games and more" was looking spot on.

In late April, a month past his fiftieth birthday, Huggins reflected on his past in baseball and mentioned a lost opportunity. "If I had to do it all over again I would not be manager of the Yankees or any other ball club. The grand opportunities lie in the business side of baseball—in ownership for example." He said he spoke from the perspective of one who "not only loves baseball but likes financial success and ease in the years past 50." "I saw it and yet my love for playing the game was so great that it kept me from cashing in on that vision. Had I grabbed that Minneapolis [actually St. Paul] chance I would be a millionaire now."[11] He said in recent years several Major League teams had offered him the opportunity to become a manager-owner, but he had turned them down. "Colonel Ruppert and I seem to be definite partners in this Yankee enterprise. It is too late to start building all over again somewhere else."[12]

A doubleheader sweep of the A's on July 1 increased the Yankees lead to 13½ games, 3 games greater than that of the 1927 club at the same time. Pennock, Pipgras, and Hoyt had pitched well, but they were getting no help from the rest of the staff. The biggest disappointment had been Wilcy Moore, who had just one win and two saves, and all had come in the season's first month. "My greatest disappointment has been Moore," Huggins said in early August, after Philadelphia had chopped 7 games off the Yankees' lead. "If he was as good as he was last year we would have won most of the ball games we have lost in the last month."[13]

The need for pitching help forced the Yankees to act. On August 6, they sent $20,000 and a player to be named to St. Paul for veteran Fred Heimach. As part-owner of the Saints, Huggins would profit from the sale. Wanting to avoid any appearance of a conflict of interest, he asked that the Yankees' scouts evaluate Heimach. They confirmed that Heimach would be an asset to the club, and the trade was made.[14] Two weeks later, they acquired another veteran pitcher, claiming Tom Zachary from Washington on waivers. To make room on the roster, they released the thirty-nine-year-old Coveleski. Looking back on the Heimach deal shortly after Huggins's death, sportswriter Bill Slocum praised the manager's ability to balance his duties and responsibilities as a part-owner of the St. Paul team with those as the manager of the Yankees. "Huggins's high sense of propriety would not permit him to recommend a deal in which he might share financially, even with a pennant at stake."[15]

The early threat of a Yankees runaway was short-lived. The team cooled off considerably during the summer, which, combined with a 29-7 streak by Philadelphia, reduced the Yankees' lead over the A's to 3½ games on the morning of August 6. Much of the lead had melted away after a 16-game western trip that began with a July 25 doubleheader in Detroit. They lost 10 of those games, including a 24–6 loss to Cleveland on July 29.[16] The Yankees were generally out-hit, out-pitched, and out-fielded. The fielding woes could be traced in part to the sore arm that had kept second baseman Tony Lazzeri out of the lineup for two weeks.[17] Leo Durocher, a weak-hitting rookie, replaced him, but Huggins considered moving Durocher to shortstop and benching Koenig when Lazzeri returned.

Koenig had been charged with eleven errors on the western swing, with reporters agreeing he could have been charged with several more. Koenig missed Lazzeri, his fellow San Franciscan. They had come up together and formed a close relationship. However, it really did not matter who was at second; Koenig was simply a poor fielder. He had led American League shortstops in errors in each of the previous two seasons and would finish second this season. At spring training in 1927, one reporter called him "one of the most erratic fielders to come up in a long while."[18] "You fellows have been writing so much that the race was all over but the shouting," chided Huggins, "and see what happened? They let down. . . . Anything can happen in a pennant race, and we are not being helped by stuff that makes the team feel that all it has to do is go through the motions."[19]

Huggins's maneuvering of his pitching staff this season drew praise from one unnamed former National League club owner. "I consider Miller

Huggins as one of the greatest managers in the history of baseball," he said in midseason. "You watch him work those pitchers and see what he does at critical times during a game and you will note the mark of a very efficient leader. He has the Yanks playing his type of ball. . . . He eats and sleeps and thinks, just lives baseball."[20]

After twenty-one consecutive road games, the Yankees returned home on August 12. They had won only ten of the games, including the last four. Pennock's three-hit, 8–0 shutout of the Red Sox stretched the winning streak to five. The Yankees were now five games up on Philadelphia, a lead Huggins did not consider safe. "While we have left our slump behind, Connie Mack's club may keep right on winning, waiting for us to slip up here and there."[21]

Pennock's win raised his record to 17-6, but he injured his arm during the game, and it was his final appearance of the season. Losing him was a big setback for Huggins. Unlike some other pitchers he had during his time in New York, Huggins knew he could always depend on Pennock to exercise self-control on and off the field. Pennock was not an overpowering pitcher who could intimidate hitters. His success came primarily from his knowledge of pitching, his ability to locate the ball, and the good fortune of having a great team behind him. Similarly, Frank Graham once asked Hoyt what the secret of pitching success was. Hoyt replied, "Get a job on the Yankees."[22]

The Yankees' lead had been as high as 13½ games on July 1. But from that point on, the A's had continued to gain ground steadily. An embarrassing doubleheader loss to Washington on September 7 dropped the Yankees into a first-place tie with Philadelphia. On September 8 the A's swept two from Boston, while the Yankees were winning a single game, allowing the A's to take over first place by half a game. The next day, a Sunday, the two teams were scheduled to play a doubleheader at Yankee Stadium. What had been a runaway was now a neck-and-neck race, and the fans reacted accordingly.

Three days before the September 9 doubleheader, hordes of people had descended on the Yankees' ticket office. They were looking for the remaining reserved seats. The club had sent thousands of tickets via mail order, and only a few hundred were left for sale on game day. The crowds started forming hours before the office opened, with long lines stretching four abreast. When word came that all the tickets had been sold, there was a rush toward the office, and police from two different precincts had to be called to restore order. On the big day, an estimated crowd of 200,000 was at the Stadium trying to gain admission, and more than 60,000 were still milling around when the first game started. Ticket speculators were getting as much as $20 for a seat and $10 for standing room.[23]

Outside of New York, most of the country's baseball fans were rooting for Mack's team to win the pennant. More accurately, they were rooting for any team except the one from New York to win the pennant. "Things don't look bright for us," Huggins had said a week earlier, "but take my advice and don't bet against us, for we have a habit of playing our best in the pinches. . . . I've got a hunch that, if there is any 'cracking' done, the Athletics will be the ones to do it."[24]

Before the first game of the doubleheader against Philadelphia, Huggins held a meeting with his players, focusing them on the task at hand. "You fellows are standing with your backs against the wall," he said. "You can do one of two things. Either you can quit like curs, or you can go out there on the field and fight like men. You've been whining about bad pitching. I'm not interested in that. You've cried about a lack of base hits. That's no concern of mine. There's just one thing I want to know. Have you got the heart to keep fighting? Have you got the guts to come back for more when you're being licked? That's what I want to know. You've got to show me this afternoon."[25]

It was a speech both challenging and inspiring by the usually taciturn Huggins, not unlike the one he made to rally his club in the spring of 1926. Curiously, two months later, on November 10, Notre Dame football coach Knute Rockne would give his famous "Win One for the Gipper" speech at this same ballpark.

More than 85,000 fans managed to squeeze into the Stadium. Gross receipts were $125,000, with the A's taking home $21,000.[26] Pipgras pitched a 5–0 shutout in the opener, and Bob Meusel's eighth-inning home run with the bases loaded off Eddie Rommel helped Hoyt, in relief of starter Fred Heimach, win the second game, 7–3. Pipgras credited general pitching advice from the departed Bob Shawkey and his start in Game Two of the 1927 World Series for his success this season. "When Hug put me in the World Series game I felt that if he had that much confidence in me

I must have something. So I had confidence in myself. Confidence and control is what I have learned."[27]

Monday was a scheduled off day, and the Yankees would have been within their rights to play one of the Sunday games that day. American League president Ernest Barnard had indicated he would sanction such a move. But Ruppert would not do it, saying it would be breaking faith with the fans. Originally scheduled as a single game, it was rescheduled as a doubleheader to make up for an early-season rainout. By going ahead with the doubleheader, Ruppert lost an estimated $50,000. He had shown again, as he had with his reaction to the games that did not get played in the 1927 Series, that he was a sportsman. Ruppert was a hard-nosed businessman, yet he usually did the honorable thing.

Ed Barrow revealed another facet of Ruppert's largesse. He said that during the 1927 season, the Yankees had issued 100,000 free passes to games at the Stadium. With the average price of a ticket around one dollar, that meant a loss of approximately $100,000 for Ruppert. Moreover, because visiting teams received 25 cents for each paid admission, Ruppert's generosity cost the seven other clubs a combined loss of approximately $25,000.[28]

On Tuesday, September 11, Hank Johnson beat Lefty Grove, 5–3. Grove's loss was his first since early July and ended his fourteen-game winning streak. The Yanks trailed 3–1, but got four runs in the eighth, including Ruth's forty-ninth home run with Lou Gehrig aboard. Philadelphia salvaged the fourth game, 4–3, defeating Hoyt with a two-out ninth-inning home run by Max Bishop.

The next day, some in the press criticized Huggins for not having Gehrig sacrifice after Koenig led off with a single in the sixth inning of a 2–2 game. "If I had asked Gehrig to sacrifice," he said, "the fans would have walked out of the park laughing at me. And they would have been right." As it turned out, Gehrig hit into a double play, and Ruth followed with a single that would have scored Koenig, had he been on second. "But I never have used it [the sacrifice] to any great extent since I got the present slugging array of Yankees together. I have followed the plan of let 'em hit it, and it has been fairly successful for this particular club."[29]

By winning three of four, the Yankees had retaken first place and opened a game-and-a-half lead.[30] They had fifteen games left, all in the West.

The A's, who had played three at Washington and four at Boston before the Yankees' series, also headed West for their final thirteen games. In all, Philadelphia played their final twenty-four games on the road.

The Yankees' first stop was in St. Louis; they arrived on the day of Urban Shocker's funeral, and Ruth, Gehrig, Hoyt, and Earle Combs were among the pallbearers. Shocker had passed away in Denver on September 9, the day of the Yankees-Athletics doubleheader in New York. It is unclear when exactly the Yankees learned that Shocker had died. According to the *New York World*, it was just before they took the field for the opener. However, the *New York Evening Journal* reported they first heard about it following the second game.

Before leaving New York, Huggins assured Ruppert and Barrow that the Yankees would hold onto their lead. "You can go ahead and make all the necessary arrangements for the World Series," he told them.[31] His players appeared just as confident they would be playing more games at Yankee Stadium. They left all their belongings in their lockers.

Philadelphia went 8-5 in the West, while New York won 10 of 15 and clinched the pennant on September 28 at Detroit. It was a subdued celebration in the clubhouse, clouded by the previous day's sprained wrist suffered by Earle Combs in a collision with the outfield wall.[32]

After the Yankees clinched, Joe Vila paid tribute to Huggins. "No manager of a championship team in the history of baseball has overcome so many obstacles as Huggins has encountered during the last three months. . . . Though not a strong man, physically, Huggins has stood the terrific strain with wonderful fortitude. The floundering Yankees owe their new honors to the modest little fellow who has held the reins and worried himself into a state of near collapse."[33]

"Don't congratulate me; congratulate the team," Huggins had said after the clinching.[34] Yet it was under his leadership that the Yankees had now won six of the last eight American League pennants and for the second time had won three in a row. But, as the more astute observers noticed, his strategy in putting his teams together had changed from the 1921–23 winners, built around players acquired from other teams, to the 1926–28 winners, composed mostly of homegrown players. "In winning his first three pennants, Huggins had shown that he knew how to buy," wrote John Kieran. "In winning his last three, he showed that he knew how to build."[35]

Several years later, in looking back at the 1928 season, Al Schacht, the former pitcher and then coach for the Washington Senators, also had praise for Huggins. "My kid brother—why, my aunt for that matter—could have managed the Yankees of 1927. . . . Take the Yankees in 1928, when they were shot through with injuries and handicapped by poor pitching and overconfidence. That's when Miller Huggins proved to me that he was a great manager."[36]

He was helped greatly, of course, by being able to pencil Ruth and Gehrig into his lineup card every day. Both sluggers had sensational years. Ruth led the league in home runs, runs scored, walks, and slugging percentage. Gehrig batted .374 and led the league in runs batted in, doubles, and on-base percentage.[37] "Ruth, Gehrig, and Meusel, hey!" said St. Louis Browns manager Dan Howley. "In my book they're Murder, Malice, and Manslaughter."[38]

The St. Louis Cardinals had won the National League pennant after a close race with the New York Giants, setting up a rematch of the 1926 World Series. Rogers Hornsby, the manager who led St. Louis to victory in 1926, was gone, replaced by Bill McKechnie. Frankie Frisch, who had replaced Hornsby at second base, along with first baseman Jim Bottomley and left fielder Chick Hafey, were the heart of the Cardinals' offense. The Yankees entered the Series hampered by the absence of Pennock and Combs and by injuries to Lazzeri's arm and Ruth's ankle.

Noting all the Yankees' injuries, columnist Joe Williams spoke for many in predicting a Series loss for the New Yorkers. "Broadway doesn't see how Mr. Huggins can win from a team that whipped him two years ago, a team that is essentially unchanged, while he, Mr. Huggins, will be going into the series with a large quantity of his talent on crutches, stretchers, and wheel chairs."[39]

In the opener, Hoyt defeated Bill Sherdel, 4–1, and that was the closest St. Louis came to a victory. The Yankees won the next three games, behind Pipgras, Zachary, and Hoyt again—his sixth Series win—to conclude their second consecutive Series sweep and gain a bit of revenge for their loss in 1926. Huggins handed his starting pitchers the ball and never had to make another move, as they turned in four complete games. Cardinals owner Sam Breadon was so upset over the one-sided result, he fired McKechnie.

Ruth and Gehrig dominated the Series as no teammates ever had done before or since. Gehrig batted .545, with four home runs and nine runs batted in. Cardinals pitchers had walked Ruth eleven times in 1926, but unlike Hornsby, McKechnie wanted his pitchers to challenge the Babe. The result was a .625 batting average, including a three home run onslaught in Game Four. He drew only one walk.

Even the Cardinals' fans recognized they were watching a performance for the ages. John Kieran wrote that after Ruth's third home run, "The left-field bleacherites stood up to greet him when he trotted out to take his position on the field. The Babe made them like him."[40]

"Well, I'll never forget that wild ride back from St. Louis," said Ruppert, who called it and the Yankees' first world championship in 1923 his biggest kicks in baseball. "You couldn't blame the boys for feeling pretty good and wanting to have a lark. Ruth, Gehrig, Durocher, and some of the others went through the train tearing up everybody's pajama shirts. I thought I was pretty smart by locking the door to my stateroom, but when I wouldn't open it, Ruth put his big fist through a panel. They got my shirt, but it was worth it. After winning eight straight World Series games, I didn't mind losing a shirt."[41]

About 3,000 cheering fans were on hand when the Yankees' special train reached Grand Central Terminal. The players had to fight their way through the throng to the Hotel Biltmore, where Governor Al Smith was waiting to add his greeting. Policemen were needed to disentangle Ruth from the crowd, while such "unimportant persons" as owner Jacob Ruppert and Miller Huggins, who guided the Yankees' victory, were swept aside in the crush.

Governor Smith, a candidate for president and about to start on a campaign tour, held his tie and detachable shirt collar in his left hand as he grasped Ruth's hand with his right. "Congratulations on those hits," he said. "If I could count on as many votes as you have kids yelling for you, I'd be sure I'm going to be elected," the governor said.[42]

If not exactly friends, Ruppert and Smith had known each other for a long time. Both had ties to Tammany, and both were Catholics and strongly anti-Prohibition. The Colonel had contributed money to Smith's gubernatorial campaigns, his failed bid for the Democratic presidential nomination in 1924, and now again as the Democratic candidate for president.

Smith's anti-Prohibition stance and Catholicism evoked fierce and wide-spread opposition. Evangelist and former baseball player Billy Sunday's attack on Smith for his opposition to the Eighteenth Amendment was typical. He called Smith's supporters "the damnable whiskey politicians, the bootleggers, crooks, pimps, and businessmen who deal with them." The head of the largest Baptist church in Oklahoma warned his followers, "If you vote for Al Smith, you're voting against Christ and you'll all be damned." The prominent New York City Baptist minister John Roach Straton called Smith "the nominee of the worst forces of hell."[43] Herbert Hoover, the Republican candidate, benefited from the booming economy to defeat Smith easily in the general election, winning forty of the forty-eight states. The New York governor carried six southern states, Massachusetts, and Rhode Island, but failed to win his own state.

"Those eight straight World Series victories in 1927 and 1928 stand as a perpetual monument to Miller Huggins," Ruppert said in 1931.[44] Even Westbrook Pegler, formerly a harsh critic of Huggins's handling of players, had changed his tune. "The minor rowdies of the old band began to pay for their parties in the loss of speed and knack," he wrote. "One by one he [Huggins] eased them out of his force, until finally the greatest cut-up of them all [Babe Ruth] found himself considerably outnumbered by nice young men with respect for authority and an understandable desire to stay up where the wages were good."[45]

Years later, when the Yankees were running away with the 1961 American League race, cries of "Break Up the Yankees" were heard again in the press. The complaint was that Mickey Mantle and Roger Maris should not be on the same team. Frank Graham, a longtime chronicler of the Yankees, recalled that in 1928 there were similar complaints about Gehrig and Ruth. The critics knew Ruth could not be disposed of, but they said Ruppert could get at least $150,000 for Gehrig and, for the good of the game, should sell him. After ignoring these requests for a while, Ruppert finally responded.

"I have no intention of selling Gehrig or any of my players who, in the judgment of Miller Huggins, can help the team win another pennant, if possible, in 1929. I not only have no thought of breaking up the Yankees, but Ed Barrow, Huggins, and myself will exert our best efforts to strengthen them. I do not believe that any of the other club owners are in sympathy with this movement. If any of them is, I advise him to leave the direction of the Yankees to us and to do the best he can to build his own club. Baseball is a sport as well as a business. In every sport the object should be to win on your own merits and not ask the other fellow to weaken himself deliberately to aid your cause."[46]

League president Barnard also believed it would be foolish to ask Ruppert to weaken his club. "I don't imagine Henry Ford would be enthusiastic about reducing the power of his organization in order to make matters easier for his opposition," said Barnard. "Asking Colonel Ruppert to dismantle the Yankees amounts to practically the same thing."[47]

Miller Huggins addressed this topic after the World Series. "Time will take care of the Yankees, as it takes care of everything else. This team, powerful as it is, will crack and break, no matter what any of us does to keep it up. The history of all great teams and all great personal fortunes is the same. They dominate the scene for a while but they don't last. Great teams fall apart and have to be put together again."[48]

Indeed they would have to be put together again. Following their triumph in 1928, the Yankees would return to the World Series only once in the next seven seasons.

Part 8

HUGGINS EXITS

31

The Law of Averages
Catches Up with the Yankees

For the second time in the 1920s, Miller Huggins was attempting to lead the Yankees to a fourth consecutive pennant, something no American League team had ever accomplished.[1] After they swept the 1928 World Series, there had been the usual clamor to "break up the Yankees." Even F. C. Lane, the editor of *Baseball Magazine*, lamented pennant races that featured the Yankees and seven also-rans. "It would be impossible to estimate the damage done to League prosperity by this undesirable state of affairs."[2] Yet Huggins knew how difficult the task would be in 1929. "Who do these people who have raised this cry think the Yankees are that they can go on forever?" he asked.[3]

Born and bred a midwesterner, Huggins now took pride in the nation's biggest city, after having spent more than a decade with the Yankees. "The whole trouble is that we [the Yankees and the Giants] are New York clubs," he said. "If we were located in Kankakee things would be different. . . . 'Beat New York' is the slogan of the land, and when it can't be done, the boys start slinging mud."[4] W. O. McGeehan humorously noted that Colonel Ruppert "did not see why he should pass around players any more than Mr. Rockefeller should pass around oil wells or Mr. Ford automobiles."[5]

"We are bringing in the best men of the minors," Ruppert said when the Yankees bought Lyn Lary and Jimmie Reese from Oakland for $125,000.[6] When he added, "Expense is no consideration," people knew he meant what he said.[7] Ruppert and Huggins realized—as did Barrow—that the Yankees needed a constant infusion of talent if they were to stay on top.

Ruppert understood that continued success, whether in beer or baseball, required constant planning and preparation. "Perhaps neither Reese nor Lary will be able to oust them [Lazzeri and Koenig] from their places in the line-up. But we don't know that. . . . A slide, a broken leg, and the finest ball player may jump into baseball oblivion. That has happened before; it may happen again. We must have replacements."[8]

They also understood that New Yorkers wanted—and expected—the best team for the nation's leading city. "I have to please these people. Yankee fans want a winning ball club," Ruppert explained a decade later. "They won't support a loser."[9] Huggins felt the same way. "A New York club must be a factor in the race year after year. With such keen rivalry and such an exacting public, a manager must keep building all the time. He must never stand pat on what he's got."[10]

Huggins elaborated on the subject early in the 1929 season. "The secret, if secret it is, of keeping a club at the top, then, is being able to select the right men and have them ready at the right time."[11] And there was no one better at finding and securing the right men than Ed Barrow and his scouts.

These Yankees who had won the last three pennants were as talented as the Yankees who had won the first three, but they had a very different personality. Westbrook Pegler was still amazed that the carousing Yankees won those first three, "swinging at the middle ball of every pitch."[12] Pegler still gave Huggins no credit for those early pennants, saying Ruppert and Huston "had clamped a financial half-nelson" on Harry Frazee.

But in recent years Huggins had gotten rid of the "minor rowdies," as Pegler called them, and begun establishing discipline. Ruth's teammates were no longer temperamental stars procured from other teams, but now were soft-spoken ballplayers who never caused trouble—men like Combs, Gehrig, and Lazzeri.

After watching the success of the St. Louis Cardinals and Branch Rickey's growing farm system, the Yankees bought the Chambersburg, Pennsylvania, club of the Blue Ridge League in early 1928.[13] It would not be the last team the Yankees would buy, wrote John Drebinger, because "when Colonel Ruppert goes in for anything, he never plays the game halfway." The *New York Times* reporter was surprised it had taken so long for the Yankees to get going, since Huggins had been "a staunch advocate of the practice for many years."[14]

In 1927 the Yankees' manager had said, "Of course we are trying to buy into the minors! The baseball trend is in that direction. All the majors eventually will own minor league clubs as a matter of self-protection." Huggins explained that the owners of Minor League teams were to blame, since they were pricing their top players for as much as $100,000.[15] Ruppert realized it was a defensive move born from necessity, but took a while to warm to the idea; he would not commit wholeheartedly to the farm system for a few more years.

Huggins had often spoken about "the law of averages." After the 1927 season he noted, "Good as my club is, I can't afford to keep it as it is. . . . This relentless law of averages has broken up every great club in baseball history."[16] Sportswriter Walter Trumbull observed, "The case of Miller Huggins is almost pathetic. He is trying desperately to build up the Yankees. That is a tough job, a little perhaps like trying to add a bit of height to Mount Everest."[17]

Despite Huggins's misgivings, the Yankees went into 1929 with virtually no major roster changes, just as they had in 1924 and 1925.[18] Huggins felt he could get one more pennant out of his core group. "I think we can sneak one in there and then rebuild a bit and maybe win again."[19] Perhaps it was human nature, resistance to change; maybe it was loyalty to the men who had won three straight pennants for him.

The sweep over St. Louis in the 1928 World Series, despite injuries to some key Yankees, probably affected Huggins's thinking. That impressive result, despite injuries to Herb Pennock and Earle Combs, suggested the Yankees were still a juggernaut.[20]

Both men, Ruppert and Huggins—so different in lifestyle and outward appearance—were remarkably similar in some key ways. Both were intensely competitive; losing seemed almost to make them physically ill. "I guess I wasn't born to be a loser," Huggins said late in the 1929 season.[21] Even when the Yankees were winning, Ruppert could not relax—unless the score was very one-sided in their favor. And when they did win, both men fretted about winning again. And again.

While the Colonel said he would spare no expense to buy the best players, stories abound of his tight-fisted negotiations with those already on their roster. Frank Graham noted that it was Ed Barrow who would tell the Colonel "not to yield, or . . . to yield—but only a little."[22] Barrow once told Fred Lieb that had he been sentimental, the Yankees would have won fewer pennants.[23] Barrow sent out the player contracts; he had Ruppert step in when star players held out for more money.

Waite Hoyt had vivid recollections of these negotiations. One year when he met with the Colonel for contract talks, Ruppert commented on photographs of commercial buildings hanging in his office. He took pride in his real estate, his brewery, and his upstate mansion. Yet when Hoyt asked him for a raise, Ruppert allegedly exclaimed, "What do you think I am, a millionaire?"[24]

Joe Dugan was one Yankee who dared to reply to such a comment. When Ruppert explained he could not give raises, the third baseman asked the Colonel if he needed a loan. Ruppert took offense to the question. Dugan later said, "Colonel Ruppert owned half of New York. John Jacob Astor owned the other half."[25]

Going into 1926 and 1927, few newspapermen had picked the Yankees to win the American League pennant. They had been unsure about 1928, but now they swung to the other extreme: the overwhelming majority of them favored New York. The *Sporting News* reported that 78 of 104 writers had done so.[26]

Typical were the comments of respected Chicago sportswriter Irving Vaughn. "This spring nobody is willing to even intimate that the Yanks are disintegrating.[27] Joe Williams was a rare exception, stating the Yankees' "championship structure was crumbling."[28]

Huggins realized he would need a tougher approach with his team this year. The novelty and thrill of winning had worn off, as it had in 1924. He decided to tighten discipline, threaten penalties, and drive his players more than in the past. Williams noted that Huggins used "biting sarcasm"' with some of his players, a tool he had learned in law school.[29] He probably employed it more in 1929 than he had in the previous few years.

Even this club had some "rowdies." When some of his men continued nighttime activities not conducive to performance on the diamond, he lit into his team. "You fellows have won three straight pennants. You are good enough to win another. I'm not going to stand by and see you kick it away."[30]

The Yankees had another tool for discipline this year, at least for one member of the team, Babe Ruth. Just before Opening Day, and three months after his estranged wife had died in a house fire, Ruth married an attractive widow, Claire Hodgson. They had met back in 1923, when she had a small part in a Broadway show. "Claire had many things I did not possess: Culture, background, good looks," he explained.[31] They began seeing each other, and she was not afraid to criticize him. "You drink too much," she told him that year. "Drinking is not good for you." Ruth's reply, somehow preserved for posterity, was "You sound like Miller Huggins."[32]

Waite Hoyt felt that Claire has not gotten enough credit for moderating Ruth's behavior.[33] Ruppert even asked her to travel with the team, which she usually did.[34] Westbrook Pegler wrote of the Babe's new bride, "Mrs. Hodgson now takes rank along with [agent Christy] Walsh and Arthur McGovern, the physical trainer, as one who saved Babe Ruth from improvidence, evil companions, late hours, and deleterious beverages."[35]

Huggins often spoke of "disposition," a vital ingredient for a ballplayer. It was not simply courage, intelligence, or even attitude. It was the ability of a youngster to bide his time on the bench, learn by watching intently, and be ready when the opportunity would arise. "He must work hard, with perhaps nothing in sight; he's got to study players and plays, with only a possible reward in the future; he must be satisfied with his present lot without losing his ambition, and he must be confident in his ability when the chance does come."[36] He added it also meant knocking down the man who stood in his way.

One youngster had that disposition, and plenty of it, and Huggins took to him immediately. The scrappy young infielder probably reminded Huggins of himself, twenty-five years earlier. "He loved me like a father, and I loved him like a son," said Leo Durocher. "I couldn't hit worth a damn. . . . Mr. Huggins kept on telling me I'd stick around for a long time if I kept my cockiness and my scrappiness and that fierce desire to do anything to win. 'Little guys like us can win games,' he would say. 'We can beat 'em,' he would tell me, tapping his head . . . 'up here.'"[37] Durocher said, "Huggins was the only friend I had, the only one who thought I might make good some day."[38] Other Yankees youngsters—including Gehrig, Koenig, and Lazzeri—expressed similar devotion to their little manager.

The mighty Yankees, winners of eight straight World Series games, drew large crowds for spring training. They were the first team to draw 100,000 fans for the exhibition season. Ruppert denied the team made $100,000 in these games. "I wish it were true," he said.[39]

Ruppert was employing an unusual method of evaluating the Yankees' chances in the coming season. Sportswriter Fred Lieb and his wife, Mary, St. Petersburg neighbors of Huggins, dabbled in precognition and the occult. Mary would read Ruppert's palm. When a pennant did not appear to be in the lines, he would cry, "Mary, look again!"[40]

Huggins continued to worry about the Yankees and his own ability to withstand the pressure. He spoke of the "nerve-wracking experience" of the taut 1928 pennant race.[41] He had made an offer to buy the Toledo Mud Hens of the American Association after the 1928 season, an offer that was not publicized in New York and ultimately was not accepted.

He may have been thinking of a fallback option, should his health prevent him from managing. "I don't expect to remain a manager to the end of time, and my health may force me out of the active end any day," he told a Toledo newspaper. "I am not strong and I tire easily. Field or bench directing makes for a hard life."[42]

Huggins gained a measure of relief when Bob Shawkey joined the team as a coach for the pitchers after playing for the International League's Montreal Royals in 1928. He still found respite in his pinochle games with coaches Fletcher and O'Leary. His persona had really not changed much from the solitary, cerebral figure Damon Runyon had described when Huggins arrived in New York a decade earlier. But now he was worn out and continuing to wear down as the 1929 season began.

Transportation was quickly evolving, as automobiles were becoming more affordable for middle-class Americans. With more cars came more accidents. The *Sporting News* wondered if baseball's owners could protect their investment by prohibiting their players from driving, but concluded such a rule would be hard to enforce.[43]

While automobiles were the craze of the times, a war hero aviator was peering into the future and predicting that the cost and time required for coast-to-coast air travel would soon be greatly reduced. Captain Eddie Rickenbacker was presciently envisaging that a World Series between a New York team and one in Los Angeles or San Francisco will give baseball "a playoff it never dreamed of, and both you and I will live to see it."[44]

The Yankees started the season with numbers on the backs of their uniforms, and once again Ruppert did it in a big way, with the biggest numerals that could fit on the players' jerseys. Ruth's "3" was expected to become as famous as Red Grange's "77."[45]

Miller Huggins often said that a manager's toughest job was handling pitchers and that the most difficult aspect of that was deciding when to pull a pitcher.[46] He added that each pitcher handled pressure differently. But this season his mound challenges were far more basic.

Pitching, or the lack thereof, was an ongoing problem for the Yankees in 1929. Herb Pennock did not bounce back from his neuritis; George Pipgras was giving up almost an additional run per game; and the young prospects were either inconsistent or injured.[47] "Every time a Yankee pitcher starts a game," wrote John Drebinger, "three more start right along with him in the bullpen."[48]

There was one bright spot on the Yankees' pitching staff. They had claimed lefty Tom Zachary off waivers from Washington late in the 1928 season.[49] Destined to be remembered as the pitcher who gave up Babe Ruth's sixtieth home run in 1927, he had a 12-0 mark for the 1929 Yankees, still the Major League record for most wins without a defeat in a season.

The left side of the infield was unsettled all season, as Huggins shuffled Durocher, Koenig, Gene Robertson, and Lyn Lary between positions, as well as in and out of the lineup. Lary hit well, but often had mental lapses in the field. In a September game against the Athletics, he held onto the ball too long before throwing it wildly, which allowed the tying run to score. Huggins came storming out of the dugout and pulled the rookie from the game.[50]

The biggest problem was Connie Mack's Athletics, who were emerging as a confident powerhouse. Many Yankees players thought Philadelphia would cool off. They never did. "That business of sitting back and waiting for the A's to crack," wrote Tom Meany, "is like holding a death watch on a wealthy distant and ailing relative."[51]

In late May Huggins told Dan Daniel, "It's going to be harder than we thought."[52] The Yankees had fallen from first place to eight games back by the end of the month. Huggins confided to a Cleveland sportswriter that they would not successfully defend their 1928 title. "Mr. Cobbledick, I don't think the Yankees are going to catch the Athletics. I don't think these Yankees are going to win any more pennants, certainly not this one. They're getting older and they've become glutted with success."[53]

On May 19, the club faced a collapse of a very different sort. A sudden rain squall during a game at Yankee Stadium caused fans sitting in the bleachers to run for cover. Two people, including a student from Hunter College (an all-women's school at the time), were killed, trampled to death in the rush to the exits. Many of the injured were boys who had been sitting in the right-field bleachers, known as "Ruthville," to be close to the Babe.

The district attorney ruled there was no negligence or liability on the part of the Yankees, but the club was tactless in its public response. The Colonel denied charges that the injured were not cared for adequately, and Barrow said no structural or security changes were contemplated. He blamed the accident on an out-of-control crowd, led by rambunctious youths. Only the Babe showed empathy. "I want the name and address of every kid that was hurt," he said.[54]

As the season wore on, Bob Meusel began to fade badly at the plate. The thirty-three-year-old (on July 19) saw his batting average slide more than fifty points below his career average to that point. Because of Huggins's loyalty to a player who had meant so much to the Yankees throughout the decade, he kept Meusel in the starting lineup until September. "We are supposed to be cold and unfeeling in matters of this kind," said Huggins. "His listless way often drew severe criticism, but he has been a great player for this ball club. It isn't an easy thing to do."[55]

A highlight for the team was the emergence of catcher Bill Dickey. He hit .324, the first of ten .300 seasons in the next eleven years. Huggins was not surprised. "I liked him as soon as I saw him throw a ball and swing a bat," he said.[56] Ironically, as the Yankees were faltering, they had strengthened a key position they had not excelled at since Wally Schang was dealt away after the 1925 season.

In the National League, as the Chicago Cubs were streaking to the pennant for the first time since 1910, their manager, Joe McCarthy, was garnering accolades from across the country, and New York was no exception. "His deeds of leadership have fairly electrified the baseball world," wrote Drebinger.[57]

In a mid-July letter he wrote to a young girl in North Carolina, Huggins admitted the Yankees would probably not win the pennant. "That's Okay you know," he wrote, "for the other fellow sometimes must have the reward."[58] By early September, Huggins conceded the pennant to Connie Mack, who had struggled for fifteen years to return the Athletics to the top. "It is probably for the best, too. There is no doubt that the New York fans have become spoiled with championships," he said.[59]

After the 1938 season and the Yankees' third straight championship, cries of "Break up the Yankees" again would sweep the country. Ruppert reminded people that exactly ten years earlier, the same calls were being made. "That [1928] ball club that everyone thought would be unbeatable for years to come was all through. . . . This wonderful ball club that should be broken up fell apart all by itself."[60]

32

No Man Ever Struggled Harder

Ed Barrow looked back at the 1929 season in his autobiography. "Ball teams are like human beings. They are born, live, and die. Time takes care of all things, and in 1929 . . . we began to wear out," he wrote.[1] As the season wore, he and the Colonel could see that Miller Huggins was wearing out, too.

By the time the Philadelphia Athletics had clinched the 1929 pennant, Huggins was an emotional wreck. "He never seemed to enjoy success," Westbrook Pegler wrote. "Even when he was on top of the world in his business he wore a pained, unhappy expression."[2] Huggins's sister made a similar observation. After the Yankees swept the 1928 World Series, Myrtle said he could hardly rest, let alone truly enjoy himself. "His mind was obsessed, as it always was, by baseball. I knew that Miller was beginning to crack, but he wouldn't tear himself away from the game."[3] Huggins suffered from severe headaches during the 1929 season and planned to recover under the care of a doctor during the off-season.[4] He was even considering taking a year off to recuperate. At age fifty-one, he looked like a man in his seventies.

On Labor Day, with the Yankees 13½ games behind the A's, Colonel Ruppert urged his manager to take a leave for the rest of the season. Huggins brushed off the suggestion, saying he wanted to secure second place, which was already fairly secure.[5] He also wanted to continue the rebuilding effort for 1930, which included working with his younger players during September.

The losses his friends and associates had suffered in the Florida real estate collapse weighed on him as well. "He was ultra-conscientious," said Ruppert, who felt "it troubled him to have given advice that was costly to others."[6] Now Huggins worried about the stock market, which had climbed to wild heights. As historian J. C. Furnas wrote, "Wall Street in the latter 1920s was about as implausible a spectacle as Miami in 1925."[7] The only difference was that the investment instruments were securities, not land, and the setting was now national in scale. Both Huggins and Ruppert were warning their players to get out of the stock market.[8]

When a pimple surfaced under Huggins's eye later in the month, coach Art Fletcher urged him to see a doctor. Huggins demurred, maintaining an outward wall of bravado. "Go to a doctor for a red spot on my face? Me—who took the spikes from Frank Chance and Fred Clarke?"[9] Yet the spot on his face had become infected, despite Huggins's efforts to eradicate it with a heat lamp. After one September game, he told Arthur Mann, "I'm so tired, kid. I could sit right here till tomorrow's game."[10]

On September 20, Huggins finally decided to visit a doctor. Fletcher said, "When Miller came in that morning he looked bad. . . . I swear he looked dead already."[11] One of the last Yankees Huggins spoke to in the clubhouse that day was Waite Hoyt, the onetime Schoolboy Wonder who had just turned thirty. Huggins had tried to moderate the behavior of the talented yet hot-headed pitcher over the years, and now was no different. "In baseball especially, you can't do after thirty what you've done before," he told Hoyt. "Every year from now on, if you live soft in the winter, as you have been doing, you'll find it harder to get in condition in the spring. . . . Keep in shape this winter."[12]

As Huggins left the Stadium, he told columnist Ford Frick, "We're licked this year, but next year I'll have another winner."[13] He had not shared his plans in great detail with his coaches, though he probably had a clear idea. He continued to pursue a trade for Boston's Red Ruffing, though many in the press did not understand what Huggins saw in him.[14] "He had a genius for arranging trades, an infinite supply of brains and wisdom," Ruppert later said of his manager. "And he almost always knew exactly what players would do the Yankees the most good."[15]

Though Huggins had minimized his health problems, he knew his condition was no small matter. He confided in Frick, "When I see a doctor this time it will be a tough, tough pull. I'm not going to get well in one or two days. This one is going to be serious."[16]

His doctor had him admitted to Manhattan's St. Vincent's Hospital in Greenwich Village. Huggins was suffering from erysipelas (also known as

St. Anthony's Fire), blood poisoning caused by the *Streptococcus* bacteria. It had spread throughout his body from the boil on his cheek. Influenza had weakened him further, and he soon slipped into unconsciousness.

Ruppert rushed to his manager's bedside and told reporters, "I feel keenly for Huggins. He is a victim of his own courage. . . . No stone will be left unturned to save his life. He is one of the finest men I ever knew."[17] But there were few stones left to turn. Long before the advent of antibiotics, doctors gave him numerous blood transfusions, to no avail.

When he briefly became semiconscious, Huggins asked for his lawyer, to review his will, and his pastor.[18] Near the end, in his delirium he called out for his close friend, Bob Connery, who had rushed in from St. Paul. Around 3:00 PM on the 25th, Jacob Ruppert and Ed Barrow left Huggins's bedside for a late lunch. Shortly thereafter, with his sister and his brother Arthur (Clarence was still in transit from Florida), his pastor, and his friend Connery at his side, Miller Huggins died.[19]

During the Yankees' game at Boston's Fenway Park, the players gathered at home plate, the announcement was made as the flag in center field was slowly lowered halfway down its staff, and there was a moment of silence. The game resumed, and the Yankees rallied for an extra-inning victory, ironically clinching (at least a tie for) second place.[20] All American League games the next day were cancelled. A funeral service was held in New York, with a crowd of 10,000 outside the Church of the Transfiguration.[21] Huggins's body was then taken to Cincinnati for another service and burial at Spring Grove Cemetery.[22]

He left the bulk of his $250,000 estate to his sister. She continued to live in their St. Petersburg home until she took her own life in November 1938.[23]

Frank Graham once wrote of Huggins, "It was his destiny to walk, always, in the shadows of his players."[24] Yet the Yankees' little leader cast a profound shadow on his men, too. Babe Ruth spoke of how much he owed to Huggins after their showdown. Lou Gehrig saw him as a second father, one who expressed confidence in and showed incredible patience with his young first baseman.[25] His two biggest stars needed two very different approaches, and Huggins handled them adroitly. The results were individual and team performances that have stood the test of time.

Accolades rolled in from across the baseball world. No one was better

24. After suspending Babe Ruth and Bob Meusel for the start of the 1922 season, Commissioner Landis allowed them to play in spring training games. Once he had laid down the law, the three have a light-hearted moment in New Orleans, where the Yankees are training. National Baseball Hall of Fame Library, Cooperstown NY.

25. (*opposite*) With Til Huston gone from the Yankees, Jacob Ruppert could finally breathe easier. So could Miller Huggins. Frank Graham wrote, "Save almost in Ruppert's estimation alone, he was just a scrawny little man who happened to be around as the Yankees advanced to a peak." Michael Mumby Collection.

26. (*above*) Managers Miller Huggins and Frank Chance flank Jacob Ruppert prior to the first game at Yankee Stadium. During the off-season, before being named manager of the Red Sox, Chance had lobbied for Huggins's job. "If Huggins resigns and the Yankee owners want me to manage their team I'll gladly accept," he had said. National Baseball Hall of Fame Library, Cooperstown NY.

27. (*opposite*) A pensive Huggins, deep in thought, worried that after three straight pennants, his Yankees were no longer hungry enough. Steve Steinberg Collection.

28. (*above*) Miller Huggins lived with his sister, Myrtle, who was his confidante. They are seen here in front of their new St. Petersburg home, just a short walk from the Yankees' spring training field in late 1924. The strain of the recent pennant race clearly shows on the face of Miller, who looks much older than his forty-six years. *New York Times*/Redux.

29. (*above*) Huggins, Ruppert, and Barrow worked in concert in the 1920s, guiding the Yankees to the top of the baseball world. The three men had a remarkable understanding of organizational success, a perfect alignment of philosophies, and a profound mutual respect. Ruppert had "utter confidence in them," wrote sportswriter Warren Brown. National Baseball Hall of Fame Library, Cooperstown NY.

30. (*opposite top*) Huggins loved spending time in St. Petersburg and was close to Al Lang (*center*), the city's biggest booster, and Walter Ross, a real estate partner of Huggins. The men are heading out for a round of golf, a diversion in which Huggins found some refuge and relaxation. Steve Steinberg Collection.

31. (*opposite bottom*) New York City's newly elected mayor, Jimmy Walker, visits the Yankees during 1926 spring training. "Ruppert was very close to Jimmy Walker. But Jake never asked for a favor," said George Perry, Ruppert's aide. "There was nothing Walker could give Ruppert and there was nothing Ruppert wanted from Jim except his friendship." © Bettmann/CORBIS.

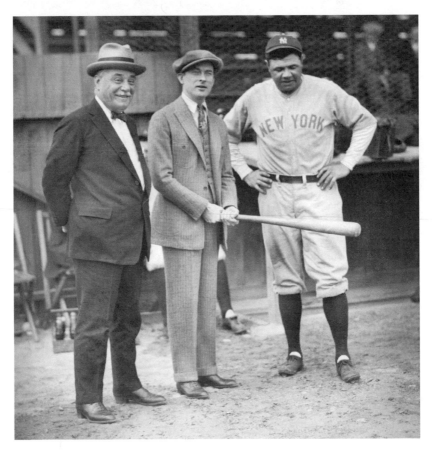

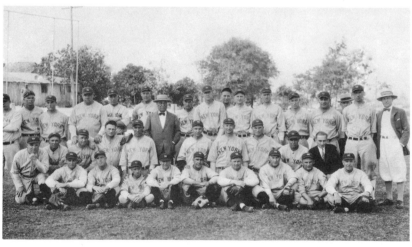

32. (*opposite top*) Babe Ruth and his manager watch the Yankees during 1926 spring training. Once the Colonel had backed his manager to the limit, and Huggins had disciplined the Babe, "to bring the big fellow to his senses," the two men became closer. © Bettmann/CORBIS.

33. (*opposite bottom*) Colonel Ruppert surrounded by his players in a team photo taken at spring training, 1927. Ruppert's longtime adviser, Al Brennan, the Colonel's most intimate friend for more than thirty years, is on the far right with the straw hat. © Bettmann/CORBIS.

34. (*above*) Lou Gehrig rounds third after driving in Earle Combs and Mark Koenig in Game Three of the 1927 World Series. He was out at the plate, trying for an inside-the-park home run. National Baseball Hall of Fame Library, Cooperstown NY.

35. (*above*) Early in 1928, the normally dour Miller Huggins had many reasons to smile, as the Yankees seemed poised for another romp to the pennant. Walter P. Reuther Library, Archives of Labor and Urban Affairs, Wayne State University.

36. (*opposite*) Miller Huggins and his longtime rival, Athletics manager Connie Mack, shake hands before the September 9, 1928, doubleheader at Yankee Stadium. More than 80,000 fans saw the Yankees win both games against their closest rivals. The Rucker Archive.

37. (*above*) The Yankees' owner and his manager both took fierce pride in their city and their ball club. They scoffed at calls to "break up the Yankees" and worried about keeping them on top. Photography Collection, Harry Ransom Center, University of Texas at Austin.

38. (*opposite*) Though Miller Huggins's life revolved around baseball, the pressures of managing took a terrific toll on his already-weak constitution. Keeping on winning pennants, he said, is "altogether different and even tougher" than winning the first one. National Baseball Hall of Fame Library, Cooperstown NY.

39. (*opposite top*) George Perry was the Colonel's longtime public relations man and social secretary. He was often at Ruppert's side, whether on a night out to the theater or a trip to Florida spring training. He played a key role as an intermediary when Joe McCarthy moved from the Cubs to the Yankees. Steve Steinberg Collection.

40. (*opposite bottom*) Myrtle Huggins unveils the monument to her brother, Miller, as Jacob Ruppert and Mayor Jimmy Walker look on. It stood alone in center field for almost a decade, until one was erected for Lou Gehrig in 1941, followed by one for Babe Ruth in 1949. Eventually, Joe DiMaggio and Mickey Mantle joined them. *Cleveland Press* Collection, Cleveland State University Library.

41. (*above*) George Weiss (*left*), director of the Yankees' farm system, and Jacob Ruppert watch Joe DiMaggio play in the Oakland Oaks stadium with West Coast scout Joe Devine. Ruppert had overruled Ed Barrow in starting the Yankees' farm system, a rare intrusion into Barrow's domain and an astute decision that ensured the Yankees' success, especially when he put Weiss in charge. Steve Steinberg Collection.

42. (*opposite top*) (*from left*) Joe McCarthy, Jacob Ruppert, Lou Gehrig, Tony Lazzeri, and a seated Joe DiMaggio celebrate the Yankees' second consecutive World Series victory over the New York Giants. © Bettmann/CORBIS.

43. (*opposite bottom*) Ed Barrow, Joe McCarthy, Mayor Fiorello LaGuardia, and Al Brennan are among those who look on as the memorial plaque to Jacob Ruppert, "Gentleman, American, Sportsman," is unveiled at Yankee Stadium on April 19, 1940. Steve Steinberg Collection.

44. (*above*) Jacob Ruppert poses with close friends Helen Weyant and Fred Wattenberg as the brewery begins production following repeal. Wattenberg was one of the few people who knew of the existence of the "mystery lady." *New York Daily News* via Getty Images.

45. Huggins once said of his boss, "Colonel Ruppert is the most honorable of men and is a stickler for ethics." And Ruppert said of his manager, "He has delivered the goods, always." © Bettmann/CORBIS.

able to observe, extract, and express the crux of a sports personality than Damon Runyon, who captured the essence of Huggins two days after his death.

No man ever struggled harder for the laurels he earned as chief of a crew on the baseball grand circuit. No man was ever more patient under adversity and criticism. And no man ever more thoroughly put to flight his critics and vindicated the confidence his friends had in him. The results are in the records, and baseball judges its people on records.

There it stands—the Huggins score—and it is the measure of managerial greatness. Of baseball genius. A reticent, self-effacing little man, with none of the pomp and truculence attributed to some leaders. Huggins piloted a club, or rather a series of clubs, to all the triumphs that baseball has to offer, including a financial return to the owner beyond his wildest dreams.[26]

A distraught Jacob Ruppert said, "Miller Huggins's death is a deep blow to me. He was a most lovable man, an honest and true friend, a zealous worker. He was a genius in baseball, and I always felt that in him I had a man that would never fail me, and he never did. He was a sick man for a long time but he would not quit despite many urgings, and his own courage and determination to stick it out to the end of the season did much to sap his strength."[27]

When Ruppert looked back at his years as owner of the Yankees in 1931, he said, "From the day Huggins took charge of the team the Yankees were on the upgrade. He brought Ruth to the Yankees. He had the vision and we furnished the money. . . . Getting Huggins was, beyond all question, the most important move toward building the Yankees from almost nothing into a consistent pennant-contending club."[28]

33

Succeeding an Immortal

Miller Huggins's death on September 25 stunned the Yankees' players and created an enormous void in the organization. Jacob Ruppert worked closely with Ed Barrow in the process of selecting a new manager, starting right after the end of the regular season. They were surprised, to say the least, when they were turned down by a number of candidates. Huggins's successor would have to follow a manager who had won six pennants in the past nine seasons. Moreover he would be taking over a team in transition, just as the Athletics were emerging as a potential dynasty.[1]

First, former Pittsburgh manager Donie Bush declined.[2] Then Yankees coach and Huggins's trusted lieutenant, Art Fletcher, who had managed the team for the balance of the 1929 season after Huggins's death, begged off. "Too many headaches and heartaches," he told Frank Graham.[3]

The Yankees then turned to Eddie Collins, now a coach with the Athletics, whom Huggins had recognized as managerial material a few years earlier. When Collins rebuffed New York's initial offer, Ruppert persisted. "Regardless of how you feel about our proposition," Barrow wrote Collins, "Colonel Ruppert would like to see you at his home . . . today."[4] One can only imagine how attractive the offer would have been, but Collins demurred. "Colonel," he told Ruppert at the meeting, "I would feel more comfortable if you did not go further with your offer. I would rather not know what I'm refusing." He agreed with the evaluation of his manager, Connie Mack, that he was not ready for the job. Mack had also told Collins that if he stayed with the A's, "it is our plan to have you succeed me as manager."[5]

Shortly after the World Series, the Yankees hired Bob Shawkey, their longtime pitcher and current coach of the pitchers, to manage the club in 1930.[6] Shawkey, who was hunting in the Canadian wilderness at the time, had not campaigned for the job and may not even have wanted it.[7] Barrow was later quoted as telling Ruppert, "I don't know why I didn't think of him at first."[8] Ruppert also said he was complying with Huggins's wish in trying to explain the logic of the hire.[9] Ruppert was probably trying to put a positive spin on a choice that was disappointing to him.

One name that surfaced in newspaper stories as a possible candidate was former Yankees scout Bob Connery.[10] Neither Tom Meany nor Frank Graham, in their histories of Yankee teams, mentioned that Connery had been offered the managerial position. Yet Connery's close friend, Hartford businessman Mickey Lambert, told a Hartford sportswriter early in 1930 that Connery had been offered the job. Jacob Ruppert had told Connery to fill in his desired salary on a contract. Ruppert also said the Yankees would take the Saints off his hands. Connery turned down the offer, said Lambert, because he wanted to remain the "boss" and because he did not want to have to deal with Babe Ruth or get into arguments with Ed Barrow.[11]

The reality was Barrow and Ruppert did not think of Shawkey because they were not enthusiastic about hiring him. Just a year earlier, Ruppert had explained the challenge of replacing Huggins. If he were to retire, said the Colonel, "It would be well nigh impossible to obtain another manager half as clever as the little fellow."[12] Shawkey later said, "It is hard to be the one who succeeds the immortal."[13]

Shawkey had the added challenge of supervising men who had been his teammates for years.[14] W. O. McGeehan felt it was a great hire, noting Shawkey was "about the most level-headed and even-tempered a player as the National Pastime has produced."[15] But John Drebinger of the *Times* felt that Shawkey's personality "may spell his doom," since he was a "pleasant-spoken, mild-mannered man," whereas managers are supposed to be "severe men and usually are."[16]

Perhaps the bigger stories revolved around two other men who were not hired: Babe Ruth and John McGraw. In the opening chapter of a saga that would play out with increasing friction over the next four years, the Yankees did not offer the managerial job to the Babe. This time it was relatively easy for Ruppert to explain away that option. Even at age thirty-five, Ruth was still at the top of his game, and the Yankees did not want to burden him with the added responsibility of managing. The reality was the Yankees did not—and would not—consider him as a serious candidate. Marshall Smelser, one of Ruth's biographers, wrote, "At no time did Ruppert or Barrow think of Ruth as a manager, not even long enough to have to dismiss the thought."[17]

The most intriguing story revolved around the possibility that John McGraw would become the Yankees' manager. Dan Daniel reported in mid-October that the Yankees would sign him "today" if it were not for his "hold-over contract" with the Giants.[18]

While McGraw had been synonymous with the New York Giants for more than a quarter century, during which time they won ten National League pennants, front-office meddling had made his job more difficult in recent years.[19] When McGraw died in early 1934, Joe Vila—who would follow him to the grave two months later—elaborated on what had almost happened. Had McGraw secured his release from the Giants, "there would be a new contract for $100,000 a year waiting for him in the Yankee Stadium."[20] McGraw instead settled his differences with Giants' owner Charles Stoneham and never mentioned the Yankees' offer.

Would Ruppert have really offered so much money to a fifty-six-year-old skipper who had not won a pennant in the past five seasons? It seems unlikely until one recognizes the club's frustration in finding a suitable candidate. When the *New York Times* reported the persistent McGraw rumors, the Colonel said, "If he is out of a job, I will gladly give him the management of the Yankees. He is a very fine man."[21]

Shawkey guided the Yankees to a third-place finish in 1930, sixteen games behind the powerhouse Athletics and only two games behind New York's 1929 record. He probably did as well as could be expected. After all, it was not that long ago that Miller Huggins had called the Yankees "eight big 'if's' and Lou Gehrig."[22]

Shawkey's biggest contribution would have an impact for far longer than his brief stint as manager; he followed up on Huggins's interest in Red Ruffing and pushed Ed Barrow to trade for the Red Sox pitcher.[23] The Yankees acquired the future Hall of Famer in early May, and in his first of many brilliant seasons with New York, he had a 15-5 record.[24]

After the 1930 World Series, the Yankees signed Joe McCarthy to a two-year contract to replace a surprised and bitter Bob Shawkey. Barrow later wrote, "Easygoing Bob could not drive the Yankees. . . . It hadn't been a very happy year for Bob and he didn't feel that he wanted to go on either."[25] Yet almost a half-century later, the soft-spoken Shawkey still felt a lingering resentment. He told historian Donald Honig that Ruppert and Barrow had assured him he would be re-signed after the Series.[26]

McCarthy had never appeared in a Major League game, though he had come close.[27] When the Yankees acquired Frank Gilhooley from Buffalo of the International League after the 1915 season, Barrow, then the International League president, had recommended that the Yankees also acquire Gilhooley's teammate, Joe McCarthy. They chose not to do so.[28]

Now, fifteen years later, McCarthy was a respected manager, first with Louisville of the American Association and then with the Chicago Cubs. Although McCarthy had led the Cubs to their first World Series in eleven years in 1929 and kept them in or near first place most of the 1930 season, Cubs owner Phil Wrigley had lost faith in him. McCarthy had known it for some time, and he was ready to move on.[29]

The Yankees' hiring of McCarthy revealed Ruppert's business ethics. When Chicago sportswriter Warren Brown learned early in 1930 that McCarthy was on his way out in Chicago, he asked Ruppert confidant George Perry to probe the Colonel's interest in hiring McCarthy. Ruppert practically threw Perry out of his office. "He said Wrigley was a great friend of his," Perry told Brown. "He said Wrigley would never let McCarthy go. He said I was crazy. He ran me out." But, noted Perry, Ruppert did not say no.[30]

Fred Lieb wrote that had McCarthy not been available, the Yankees would have retained Shawkey. But Ruppert and Barrow felt McCarthy was more aggressive and had "more of the spark of leadership."[31] *Baseball Magazine*'s F. C. Lane noted that in Chicago McCarthy had already "won almost universal recognition as being a great manager."[32] The Colonel always wanted to improve his team and win. McCarthy's availability presented the Yankees with a unique opportunity, and they seized it.

As with the firing of Bill Donovan thirteen years earlier, Ruppert found it painful to make the change, even though he knew it was the right move. "I have the highest regard for Shawkey," he told reporters. "He was in a tough spot, and I doubt any manager could have done better." Ruppert got a strong sense of McCarthy from the start. He drove a hard bargain in negotiating his first contract with the Colonel, even though he was unemployed at the time. As with Huggins, Ruppert made it clear McCarthy would be "absolute boss. . . . All we ask is that he give us a winner, bring New York back into the world's series."[33]

At a spring 1931 dinner with sportswriters and the Yankees' team, the two men had an oft-quoted exchange. Ruppert rose and said he could tolerate a second-place finish in McCarthy's first season, but "I warn you, McCardy [as Ruppert pronounced the name], I don't like to finish second." His new manager quickly replied, "Neither do I, Colonel."[34]

At first glance, McCarthy seemed like a very different person than Huggins. Yet a closer look reveals remarkable similarities. Whether Ruppert saw the common traits the men shared from the start is hard to know. But he surely saw them over the next few years. Like Huggins, McCarthy was a serious man who was fixated on winning. Both men were restless perfectionists—never satisfied and always trying to improve. And both had a remarkable ability to spot, develop, and handle young players. In spring training of 1931, after the Yankees had hammered the Minor League Milwaukee Brewers, 19–1, McCarthy told his men, "Against that kind of team, nineteen runs is nothing. We should have scored thirty."[35]

He was even more relentless when the games counted. After the Yankees won the first three games of the 1938 World Series, a reporter asked McCarthy whom he was thinking of starting in Game Five, should the need arise. McCarthy glared and snapped, "What in hell are you talking about?"[36] The Yankees won Game Four to complete the sweep.

In 1937, when Yankees outfielder Roy Johnson said, "What does that guy expect to do—win every game?" McCarthy overheard the remark and told Barrow, "Just get him out of here." Which Barrow soon did.[37] Shortly before he died, Ruppert said that McCarthy did not want what he called "second-division players." He added, "It is a state of mind."[38] McCarthy wanted only players with a winning attitude, players who never accepted losing. In his book on the 1939 Yankees, Richard Tofel described McCarthy as "strict, no nonsense, fundamental, meticulous, unforgiving."[39]

In a 1934 interview with *Baseball Magazine*, entitled "Winning Isn't the Hardest Job," McCarthy almost seemed to be channeling Huggins. He compared a winning ball club to the climber who scaled Mt. Everest and faced the impossible task of staying on top. He also observed that even the best teams grow stale, "as inevitable as the act of [people] growing old." And McCarthy was echoing Ruppert when he compared a baseball team to a machine, with cogs and wheels that had to work together and stay fresh.[40]

Like Huggins, McCarthy was willing and able to sublimate his ego to those of his players. Alan Levy, McCarthy's biographer, wrote that he set rules and expectations—without threats—and "his ego was such that he did not ever need to revel in the fact of him possessing such power."[41] His players simply called him "Joe," just as Huggins's players had called him "Hug."

Both McCarthy and Huggins had to deal with the game's biggest star, Babe Ruth. The Babe resented McCarthy, who chose not to challenge him. He knew Ruth would do his best between the white lines. Which he did.

The Babe was thirty-six years old at the start of the 1931 season, and the twenty-eight-year-old Lou Gehrig seemed poised to become the team's leader. But the colorless Gehrig still was unable to emerge from the shadow of the flamboyant Babe. That was partly because of Ruth's terrific 1931 and 1932 seasons. One Ruth biographer wrote of the aging slugger, "Times changed, presidents retired, aviators fell into the ocean, revolutions swept foreign lands, but Babe Ruth went on forever."[42]

The Yankees won eight more games in 1931 than in 1930 and improved to second place, as the Athletics won their third straight pennant.[43] Ruppert was fully supportive of McCarthy, showing patience and faith in the man he had hired. "He has exceeded my fondest hopes. In spite of all sorts of handicaps, he has made a remarkable showing. Signing him was a ten-strike. But McCarthy must have first-rate players, and I am going to get them for him regardless of cost."[44]

The Minor League talent the Yankees had bought in recent years had simply not justified the high price tags. "I paid $125,000 for [Lyn] Lary and [Jimmie] Reese," Ruppert later said. "It won't happen again."[45] A Los Angeles Times writer noted that the Yankees' struggles over the past three seasons proved that Ruppert would have to "change his idea of buying to that of building."[46] Ruppert apparently agreed.

While neither Barrow nor McCarthy was warm to the idea of buying Minor League teams, Ruppert thought otherwise; he felt the future of the

Yankees required it, something Miller Huggins had spoken of years earlier. Ruppert wielded the owner's ultimate prerogative. In a rare instance of overruling his business manager, the Colonel bought the Newark Bears of the International League after the 1931 season.[47] The Yankees would follow the path established by Branch Rickey and the St. Louis Cardinals, who had acquired a number of Minor League teams.

Dan Daniel provided an inside look at Ruppert's leadership and sensitivity to organizational principles in establishing the Yankees' farm system. He wrote that Ruppert told Barrow, "I now am determined to interfere in a matter of ball club policy, and you know I don't like to do that sort of thing." Barrow realized he could not argue back. "When Ruppert assumed a certain tone of voice, debate was out and compliance came in."[48]

Ruppert needed someone to run the Newark club, and he did not want to burden Barrow with yet another responsibility. He may also have been thinking of the additional Minor League teams the Yankees would buy, as well as the need for a backup to Barrow, who had some health issues at the time. George Weiss, the successful head of the Baltimore Orioles (like Newark, a member of the International League), was the man Ruppert selected.[49] While some accounts credit Barrow with recommending Weiss, most likely Ruppert conducted his own search.[50] Daniel emphasized that Ruppert had hired Weiss without Barrow's involvement.[51]

Weiss would become a passionate proponent of the farm system. Barrow's capable scouts would continue to find promising talent, and Weiss reminded Ruppert and Barrow, "You've got to have a place for them to develop."[52] As with his hires of Miller Huggins and Ed Barrow, Ruppert's selection of McCarthy and Weiss proved to be masterstrokes, crucial for the long-term success of the Yankees. Ruppert had once again hired men whose attention to detail and commitment to winning was paramount. It is not surprising that in *The Yankee Story*, Tom Meany entitled his Weiss chapter, "George Weiss, Perfectionist."

Part 9

THE THIRTIES

34

McCarthy Is My Manager

Jacob Ruppert had a history of hiring exceedingly capable executives for his Yankees and letting them do their jobs. While he signed off on all major decisions and expenditures, he was not a meddler. As Joe McCarthy once said, "Colonel Ruppert was a wonderful man to work for. He never bothered me. He let me run the team."[1]

One area in which Ruppert did take an active role was contract negotiations with Babe Ruth, which became more protracted in the 1930s. Ruppert felt that taking a firm position with the Babe prevented other Yankees from escalating their demands. Ruth did not understand why his 1930 negotiations with the Colonel had been so difficult. "What's $5,000 between us? That's no dough," he said. "I don't see why the Colonel should quibble about $5,000."[2]

As usually happened in an era when ownership had almost total control, the player did most of the compromising; Ruth settled for $80,000 and a two-year deal after demanding $85,000 and a three-year contract. Ruppert did return to the Babe the $5,000 Huggins had fined him back in 1925. "If Huggins had lived, you would not be getting this," the Colonel told him. "But Miller is dead and he won't know."[3]

Some observers felt the Ruth-Ruppert contract disputes were staged to generate publicity for the Yankees. There never seemed to be rancor in the negotiations, though the Babe's wife, Claire, said he hated them.[4] Ruppert did not relish them either. An editorial in *Baseball Magazine* in March 1934 noted, "The genial Colonel has never cared overmuch for the spotlight. . . . He is, first and foremost, a businessman, and showmanship is not his forte."

Salaries were being rolled back across the Major Leagues in the early 1930s, and baseball publications were firmly behind the retrenchment as a necessary reaction to the economic hard times. "Slashing salaries is the new slogan," wrote F. C. Lane in *Baseball Magazine*. "Deflation is the spirit of the times."[5] A *Sporting News* editorial was critical of Ruth's salary demands, noting, "The profligate days are gone and the ballyhoo of the salary struggles . . . leaves everybody cold."[6]

Ruppert and the Babe resumed their contract "dance" in early 1932. The Colonel wanted to roll him back to $70,000. Ruppert had set the stage in December 1931 when he pointed out Ruth was not a one-man team. "I suppose Gehrig didn't help draw all those big crowds last summer?" he asked rhetorically. "Never again will any player get that much [$80,000] a year."[7]

The Babe was now thirty-seven years old, but he was coming off two terrific seasons in which he again led the league in home runs, slugging percentage, and on-base percentage. Westbrook Pegler wrote that Ruth did not seem old because "nothing positive has happened to demonstrate strikingly that he is."[8] Yet Pegler also noted that baseball's reserve clause, which he called "the ingenious 'like it or lump it' clause," allowed the Colonel to offer the Babe only $7,000 if he so chose."[9]

The Babe finally signed a blank contract, into which Ruppert graciously inserted the figure of $75,000.[10] Tom Meany explained that by the time Ruth signed his contracts, there was often very little difference between his number and that of the Colonel. "Ruth had enough native shrewdness to know that it tickled Colonel Ruppert's vanity when he signed sight unseen."[11] Ruppert then would insert a number a little higher than what he said was his top figure.

The Babe had another productive season in 1932.[12] More important, after a second-place finish in 1931, the Yankees surged to the top of the standings in late spring. On July 3 John McGraw, who had stepped down as manager of the Giants a month earlier after thirty years, said they could not be stopped unless they ran into bad breaks.[13] The very next day, such a break occurred when Bill Dickey broke the jaw of Washington outfielder Carl Reynolds in a scuffle at home plate, which resulted in a thirty-day suspension for the Yankees' catcher.

Ruppert took an unusually active role in protesting league president Will Harridge's ruling. "Am astounded at your decision. . . . Its severity is absolutely unwarranted and uncalled for," he wired the league's president.[14] The Colonel's concern can be understood in light of the "irreparable damage" the suspension could inflict on the Yankees and his intense desire to capture his first pennant in four seasons. Yet when Ruppert's appeal was denied, he accepted the decision and was ready to move on, just as he had when he lost his Supreme Court case over Prohibition more than a decade earlier. "As far as I am concerned, it is over," he said of the protest.[15]

The Yankees held on to their lead and returned to the World Series in Joe McCarthy's second season as manager. Their opponent was McCarthy's former team, the Chicago Cubs. When the Yankees swept the Cubs, it marked their third consecutive World Series appearance in which they had won four straight games. Ruppert, on Barrow's recommendation, rewarded McCarthy with a three-year contract, thereby sending a message to Ruth that he would not be needed—or wanted—to manage the club any time soon.

Lou Gehrig continued to be overshadowed by the Babe, and the 1932 World Series was a prime example. Ruth's famous home run in Game 3, the "Called Shot," was quickly gaining mythical status. Yet Gehrig was the real hitting star of the Series, with three home runs and a .529 batting average, compared with the Babe's two home runs and a .333 average. Gehrig's performance was almost lost in the adulation of Ruth.

Once again Ruppert wanted to win the Series quickly and was not concerned about the lost revenue resulting from a sweep. "A world championship means more to me than the money," he said.[16] Despite that philosophy and the heroics of his stars, the Colonel wanted to bring both Ruth's and Gehrig's salaries down again in 1933, "in view of the banking situation."[17] "It may surprise you to learn that we lost money last year," he told reporters in March.[18] Surprise indeed, though the Yankees' financial statement for 1932 did show a very small loss.

The Yankees were not immune from the Depression's impact on baseball: a significant drop in profitability due to a steep decline in revenue, primarily attendance.[19] The economic downturn had an enormous impact on the team's earnings. After generating an average profit of almost $400,000 a year from 1926 to 1929, the Yankees' bottom line averaged only $20,000 from 1930 to 1935.[20]

An editorial in *Baseball Magazine* in May 1933 maintained that while salaries had to be reduced, ticket prices did not "because they were never inflated." By and large, they were not lowered, though many fans "reduced" them by buying bleacher, rather than grandstand, seats.

The Depression had not affected the Yankees' attendance nearly to the extent it hurt most other clubs.[21] They drew more than twice as many fans as any other American League team in 1932 and two-thirds more in 1933. They had a far greater percentage of their ballpark's seating capacity in the 50-cent bleacher seats than other clubs, which allowed plenty of their fans to "trade down" and still attend the games.[22]

On May 30, 1932, the Yankees unveiled a monument in deep center field dedicated to Miller Huggins. Mayor Jimmy Walker and Ruppert led a small group to the monument, which Huggins's sister, Myrtle, unveiled. His visage, on a bronze tablet mounted on a large red granite slab, would grace the Stadium's vast outfield. The Yankees swept a doubleheader from the Red Sox that day, making it an afternoon Huggins would have enjoyed, though he probably would not have wanted the attention the memorial would bring.

The Babe was not concerned about his impending contract talks for 1933. He told the *New York Times*, "The Colonel and I—we always get together when the time comes. I sincerely honor him as a man and always will."[23] Once again they "compromised." Ruth signed for $52,000, a drop of $23,000 from the previous season, while Ruppert moved up his initial offer of $50,000 by $2,000.

The Babe later said that the Colonel's "sob story [of financial difficulties] nearly had me in tears."[24] Ruppert also reduced Gehrig's salary. The payroll of the 1933 Yankees remained far greater than that of any other American League team.[25] However, such a comparison ignores what economist David Surdam calls the "inherent advantage" of big city teams, their larger fan bases. Simply put, the Yankees could spend more dollars on payroll because they had more money coming through the turnstiles. Their payroll was below the league average, as a percentage of revenue.[26]

The Yankees could not repeat in 1933, and neither could Babe Ruth. Age was finally catching up with him, as his batting average plummeted forty points to .301, and he hit only thirty-four home runs—both his lowest tallies as a Yankee, other than his injury-shortened 1925 season. That probably explained why he signed so quickly for $35,000 in 1934. Now, at age thirty-nine, his slide continued as he hit only .288 with twenty-two home runs. Hobbled by injuries, the Babe appeared in only 125 games. "I better get out of this game before I really get killed," he muttered that summer.[27]

Just a few days after Ruth made that comment, on July 24, 1934, one of the Yankees was almost killed on the ball field. Center fielder Earle Combs fractured his skull and suffered other serious injuries when he ran into the concrete outfield wall in St. Louis's Sportsman's Park while chasing a fly ball. He spent weeks in the hospital in critical condition. Even when he eventually recovered, his baseball career was thought to be over. (He did return for one more season.)

At the time of Combs's injury, the Yankees were in second place, just behind the Detroit Tigers; two days later, they pulled into a tie for first. But when the Tigers brought a twelve-game win streak into New York three weeks later, Jacob Ruppert broke a public promise he had made, one that he probably never should have made. It was a rare case of the reticent Colonel saying too much. When he bought the Newark Bears in the fall of 1931, Ruppert had declared that "under no circumstances" would the Yankees weaken the Bears' roster in midseason. "I wouldn't strip Newark of a player if it needed him, even if it meant we had to lose the American League pennant."[28] In early August 1934, the Yankees called up outfielder George Selkirk from Newark, where he was hitting .357.[29] Newark, now managed by Bob Shawkey, did hold on to win the International League pennant that year.

Selkirk hit .313 in forty-six games for the Yankees, but there was no stopping the Tigers. On August 14, two days after Selkirk made his New York debut, the Tigers swept a doubleheader in Yankee Stadium to increase their win streak to fourteen and their lead to six and one-half games.[30] They never surrendered that lead, on their way to their first pennant in twenty-five years. They were managed by catcher Mickey Cochrane, whom they had acquired from the Athletics during the off-season.

Lou Gehrig had one of his greatest seasons in 1934. He won the Triple Crown and finally emerged from Ruth's shadow.[31] On the field, at least, his performance towered over the Babe's. The Colonel rewarded him with a salary increase, though he still made far less than Ruth made in his best years—and even less than the Babe made in 1934.[32] McCarthy designated Gehrig as the Yankees' captain before the 1935 season, the first team captain since Ruth held the post briefly in 1922.[33] The Yankees appeared to be Lou's team for the foreseeable future.

The club's pitching had improved since 1929. In 1931, Red Ruffing was joined in the rotation by a twenty-two-year-old left-hander, Vernon "Lefty" Gomez. Ruppert had spoken excitedly about Gomez a month before Huggins died, when he said his West Coast scout had called him "one of the most remarkable prospects he has seen in many years."[34]

With the economy still mired in the Depression, and the Philadelphia Athletics losing money, Connie Mack continued to sell his stars to generate cash. As early as the Athletics' championship season of 1931, when Ruppert was asked whether he would be interested in any of their players, he declared, "Would I? You bet I would. All Connie Mack has to do is say he is ready to sell, and I'll talk terms with him."[35]

Ruppert most coveted the A's star pitcher, Lefty Grove. But Mack followed his long-standing position of selling talent to weaker clubs.[36] He dealt Grove to the Boston Red Sox and their new owner, Tom Yawkey, for $125,000 in December 1933.[37] Ruppert lamented the sale, saying he would have paid $150,000 for the pitcher and felt Grove would have brought at least two pennants to the Yankees.[38] In the summer of 1934, Ruppert expressed a strong interest in A's slugger Jimmie Foxx, not yet twenty-seven years old, who could have replaced the power of the fading Ruth.[39] But late the following year, Mack again sold his star to the Red Sox for $150,000.[40]

During the 1934 season, some New York sportswriters started referring to McCarthy as "second-place Joe."[41] Still he never came close to facing the harsh criticism and second-guessing in the press that Miller Huggins had faced. Like Huggins, McCarthy had the firm support of Ruppert. The Colonel realized that talk of Ruth's managerial future would intensify as his playing career was coming to an end. So before the start of the season, he had a "heart-to-heart" with McCarthy, reassuring him he would be the club's manager "indefinitely" and that Ruth "never had been seriously considered as leader of the team."[42]

But Ruppert and Barrow had an impending public relations nightmare: how to deal with the Babe. His career as a player was at an end, yet they dared not release a national icon. After the 1933 season, the Colonel had tried to address the issue by offering Ruth the position of manager of the Yankees' top Minor League team, the Newark Bears.[43] It would be an opportunity for him to learn and to show his managerial capabilities.

Ruth rejected the offer out of hand, saying he was a big leaguer and that other superstars—including Ty Cobb, Tris Speaker, and Walter Johnson—became Major League managers without prior experience. To ask him to manage in the Minors, he said, "would be the same, I think, as to ask Colonel Ruppert, one of the foremost brewers in the country, to run a soda fountain."[44]

Ruth's reaction, supported by his wife and his agent, was understandable. But why did the Yankees offer it? And what if he had accepted? Robert Creamer's explanation is most plausible. "Barrow was sure that in time Ruth would get bored with the job or mess it up. In either case, he could be eased out with a minimum of hard feelings, particularly from the public."[45] After the Babe turned the job down, Bob Shawkey was hired as the Newark manager for the 1934 season.[46]

Later that year, Ruth solved the dilemma for the Yankees. Before the 1934 World Series, he asked Ruppert if he was happy with McCarthy, who had one year left on his contract. Ruth said he felt he could do a better job.

"Well, that's too bad, Ruth," replied the Colonel. "I'm sorry, but McCarthy is the manager, and he will continue as manager."[47] The Babe then told three New York sportswriters during the World Series that he would not sign another Yankees' contract unless he was the team's manager. Tom Meany explained that the Babe was "forthright, if not diplomatic."[48] Ed Barrow later wrote that Ruth's statement to the writers was "a great relief. The Babe had made things easier for the Colonel and myself. . . . I don't know what we would have done if the Babe hadn't solved the situation himself."[49]

McCarthy had offered to quit if that would help the situation. But as with Miller Huggins more than a decade earlier, Ruppert stood by his man, even though the Yankees were not champions at the time. "McCarthy, you are not going to quit, and you are my manager," the Colonel told him.[50]

On February 26, 1935, the Yankees released Ruth, who joined the Boston Braves as vice president and assistant manager. Ruppert assumed the role of the magnanimous owner by releasing Ruth without demanding any money from the Braves' owner, Judge Emil Fuchs. "I do not wish

to stand in his way nor to make any profit from his opportunity to better himself."[51]

Ruth's move was a shotgun marriage, and it did not last more than a
few months. The Babe was released by the Braves on June 2 and retired
as an active player. Taylor Spink of the *Sporting News* wrote, "Ruth got
a bum steer from somebody and went to a club which he never should
have joined."[52]

A few weeks earlier, Fuchs was in such difficult financial straits that
he had wanted to introduce dog racing to Braves Field. The proposal
prompted *Baseball Magazine* to editorialize, "His act was, doubtless, the
act of a desperate man who is driven by hard circumstances to grasp at
straws."[53] In his history of the Braves, Harold Kaese described Fuchs as
"almost a farce" who "proceeded inexorably to a tragic conclusion."[54]

Surely Ruppert knew that Fuchs was having financial problems. The
Colonel and Barrow jumped at the opportunity to move Ruth from the
Yankees, even though they knew—or should have known—this was not
an opportunity for him. Taylor Spink wrote that Ruppert, Barrow, and
McCarthy were "in terror lest he remain."[55]

The Colonel later told Daniel that Ruth had made a terrible mistake
by going to the Braves.[56] "Ruth could have remained with the Yankees
forever. Even if I had any idea of letting him go, I could not have fought
public opinion so strongly."[57] Yet would they have kept him? Would he
have wanted to stay? The relationship had already deteriorated beyond
repair. The 1934 season, Leigh Montville wrote, was "one last, fractious
year of a marriage that already was done." And, sadly, "The deal [Ruth's
move from the Yankees to the Braves] had a stench to it from the beginning. The Babe was the only pure heart in the entire proceeding."[58]

Now the man of whom W. O. McGeehan once wrote "did bestride it
[Yankee Stadium] like a Colossus" was gone.[59] Ruppert declared it was
time for the Yankees to move on, which they surely would. "The success of the Yankees is no longer intertwined with, and dependent upon,
the success of Ruth," he said. "There comes a time when a ball player,
brewer, club owner, or artistic genius—especially a club owner—goes
down the hill. Human desire, sentiment cannot stop it."[60]

On July 16, 1935, the Yankees surprised many observers when they
extended McCarthy's contract for two more years, through 1937. Rup-

pert explained, "It is a reward for McCarthy's work. He has the club in first place and always had them in a contending position."[61] However, the Yankees faded down the stretch, while the Detroit Tigers got hot and stayed hot on their way to their second straight pennant.

For the third consecutive season, the Yankees finished in second place; McCarthy took a $7,500 pay cut after failing to deliver a pennant yet again. The team's attendance had dropped almost 23 percent from 1934, and the Tigers outdrew them by almost 400,000. Yet Ruppert continued to believe in his manager; he also desperately wanted to have a championship team once again. "We never have run across anyone else who stressed winning as much as Col. Jake Ruppert," sportswriter Warren Brown wrote.[62] The Colonel was more determined than ever to provide McCarthy with top talent. He continued to purchase Minor League teams; the acquisition of Joplin (Western League) and Oakland (Pacific Coast League) brought the Yankees' farm system to seven clubs. The Colonel's simple directive of three years earlier still applied: "I have told my scouts to go after every prospect."[63]

35

Repeal, Real Estate, and the Third Reich

In September 1930 Texas senator Morris Sheppard, who authored the Prohibition Amendment, declared, "There is as much chance of repealing the Eighteenth Amendment as there is for a hummingbird to fly to the planet Mars with the Washington Monument tied to its tail."[1] Yet forces were stirring at the start of the decade that would empower that little hummingbird. The jobs and tax revenue the liquor industry would generate, combined with the obvious failure of Prohibition to turn the country dry, were too significant to ignore in the current economic climate. Jacob Ruppert was about to reclaim his role as one of the nation's premier brewers.

With New Yorkers, including former governor Al Smith and future mayor Fiorello LaGuardia, leading the battle for Repeal, humorist Will Rogers noted, "There is but one reason that Prohibition won't be repealed. . . . It's because the wrong people want it repealed."[2] As one of LaGuardia's biographers wrote, conservative America "viewed the city, especially New York, as a threat to the staid élan of Protestant small-town America."[3]

In the embers of Al Smith's defeat in the 1928 presidential race were the sparks of a Democratic revival. He had brought together an emerging coalition of Catholic, urban, and working-class voters, as well as the growing anti-Prohibition community. The October 1929 stock market collapse and subsequent Depression helped ignite those sparks. Historian Frederick Lewis Allen wrote that the crash "was destined to be as bewildering and frightening to the rich and the powerful and the customarily sagacious as to the foolish and unwary holder of fifty shares of margin stock."[4]

With massive unemployment and the economy showing no signs of recovering, the governor of New York, Franklin Roosevelt, built on Smith's coalition to capture the presidency in a landslide victory over President Herbert Hoover in 1932. Less than a month after taking office in March 1933, he signed into law a bill legalizing the sale of beer and wine.[5] In the meantime, the states began voting on the Twenty-First Amendment to repeal Prohibition (the Eighteenth Amendment), which would be ratified on December 5, 1933.

During Prohibition, Ruppert "was almost fanatical in his adherence to the law. He would not even have real beer in his home."[6] Even after Roosevelt's election, the Colonel's brewery spokesman said they would not get involved in the battle for Repeal. "We are interested in the brewery business. When the politicians change the law, we will make beer."[7]

As the president of the United States Brewers Association (USBA) again, Jacob Ruppert urged an orderly transition on April 7, the first day beer sales would be legal. He wanted to avoid situations in which celebrating, drunken revelers would provide ammunition to Prohibition forces.[8] For this reason, he asked breweries to begin deliveries in the morning and not at the stroke of midnight. However, a major midwestern brewer, August Busch of St. Louis's Anheuser-Busch, directly contravened Ruppert's guideline and had hundreds of trucks rolling at midnight. It would not be the last time Ruppert and Busch would come into conflict.

The Ruppert Brewery shipped 250,000 cases and 18,000 kegs that first day. Ruppert delivered the first case of his beer to Al Smith at his Fifth Avenue home. The same day, Busch's Clydesdales delivered a case of his beer to Smith at his Empire State Building office.[9]

Ruppert was the beer industry's spokesperson, and he spent more time on brewery matters now. He often repeated his organization's goal. "We don't want people to drink more beer, but more people to drink beer."[10] The Colonel emphasized the key role that the beer industry was playing in the nation's economic recovery. He trumpeted the large tax revenue the industry was generating: almost a half billion dollars in the first two years after Repeal.[11]

As the economy went into a nosedive in the early 1930s, Ruppert donated the use of Yankee Stadium for various charities. In September 1931 the Yankees, Giants, and Dodgers played a round-robin series for the Mayor's

Committee on Unemployment. The Yankees-Giants game drew 60,000 fans and raised almost $60,000 for "families of the idle."[12] The Army-Navy football game was played at the Stadium in December and netted almost $300,000 for charity. Again, Ruppert did not charge rent. As another example of Ruppert's donating Yankee Stadium for charities, the Children's Aid Society used the ballpark for its Sandlot Baseball League games on Saturdays in 1933.[13]

The extent of Ruppert's charitable giving remains unknown. He was a private man and kept the extent of those activities private, too. Shortly after his death, his close aide George Perry wrote, "He was a hard-boiled man to some, but they judged him entirely from externals. The charity he gave never will be known. He never sought publicity that way."[14]

Ruppert was active on a number of fronts in the early 1930s. His Jacob Ruppert Realty Corporation took advantage of depressed real estate prices to acquire prime properties in the city at bargain prices. In the 1929 mayoral race, LaGuardia, then a progressive Republican congressman, based his unsuccessful campaign against Mayor Jimmy Walker on fighting corruption. Among his charges was that Ruppert, a staunch supporter of Walker, had received "Tammany favors in tax matters" and that some of his properties had been grossly undervalued for tax purposes. Ruppert reacted as he sometimes did to criticism, with humor. After denying he had received special treatment, he added, "I could use such favors indeed if they were available."[15] LaGuardia's charges did not stick, and he lost in a landslide.

When Ruppert bought a thirty-six-story building in foreclosure at 44th Street and Fifth Avenue in early 1931, he explained, "I am a firm believer in what is known as the Grand Central Zone. . . . I have evidenced my faith in New York real estate."[16] He had recently bought nearby buildings at Madison Avenue and 39th Street and at Madison and 41st Street.

A year later he purchased another skyscraper, the Commerce Building at 44th Street and Third Avenue, and renamed it the Ruppert Building.[17] The *New York Times* reported that his real estate was then valued at more than $19 million.[18] In the summer of 1933, after the Colonel's Realty Corporation bought yet another building (at 40th and Madison), the *Times* put a value of $35 million on his properties.[19] "The man with money is in a position today," a *Herald Tribune* reporter observed, "to do what Colonel Ruppert has done—grasp opportunities—and there are plenty of them . . . at a marked down price."[20]

Ruppert also invested in an eclectic group of ventures in the 1930s. In 1934 he sponsored Adm. Richard Byrd's second expedition to the South Pole with a large cash infusion. Byrd named his flagship the *Jacob Ruppert* and saluted the Colonel's integrity and sportsmanship when he met the press before heading south.[21]

Distinguished war correspondent Virginia Irwin reported that Ruppert also invested in several money-losing propositions, from a farm raising silkworms to a project of growing edelweiss on top of the Empire State Building. His life, she wrote, was "a blueprint for anybody confronted with the problem of pitching away $40,000,000 in one lifetime."[22] Sportswriter Dan Parker came to a similar conclusion after he reviewed the appraisal of the Colonel's estate. Parker wrote that the Colonel's "bizarre adventures in high finance" resulted in the estate's holding forty-five issues of stock that were now worthless.[23]

Ruppert's hard-nosed approach to controlling his Yankees' salaries certainly contrasts with his free-spending ways in many other ventures or "investments." Does the difference emanate from his personality, that of the benevolent ruler? One who dug in his heels when faced with demands as opposed to when given choices of where to invest? In the former, the recipient (the player) feels he deserves the money; in the latter, the recipient (a start-up, in many cases) is appreciative of the munificence. Also, his tough approach to player payroll mirrored that of virtually every other baseball owner.

While Ruppert probably had been conflicted in the early stages of the Great War, as the United States gradually moved from neutrality in 1914 to joining the Allies in 1917, in the 1930s he opposed his ancestral homeland soon after the Nazis assumed power. On September 20, 1934, he hosted a major charity event in Yankee Stadium. The "Night of Stars" was a gala affair on behalf of German Jewry. The event was headlined by many celebrities, from Irving Berlin and Eddie Cantor to George Jessel and Leopold Stokowski. More than a thousand Jewish groups raised $1,200,000 for the occasion. In announcing the rally in August, five years before the outbreak of World War II, Ruppert framed the issue in no uncertain terms. Calling on "Christian and Jew alike," he declared, "No catastrophe in modern times compares in its tragic effects with the blow that has been struck at the Jewish people in Germany."[24]

The guest of honor at the event was Mayor LaGuardia, who had captured the municipal office in 1933 in his second run. The glitter and allure of the Walker administration had worn thin as the nation slid into the Depression. Scandal and corruption had driven Walker from office late in 1932.[25] LaGuardia quickly emerged as a fierce and outspoken critic of Adolph Hitler.

After President Roosevelt's election, Babe Ruth said that "if real beer comes back," Colonel Ruppert "would be so tickled, he'd never even hear how much I was asking. He'd be a soft touch for me."[26] Of course, if Ruth was serious, he was sadly mistaken. The Colonel was a hard-nosed businessman when negotiating player contracts, regardless of the profits his brewery was generating.

When legalization was approaching, W. O. McGeehan wrote, "When beer comes back . . . the Yankee baseball club, the most expensive of them all, will again become just a toy for Colonel Ruppert."[27] McGeehan was mistaken, as was Billy Fleischmann a decade earlier.[28] Though Ruppert's 1931 feature in the *Saturday Evening Post* was entitled "The Ten Million Dollar Toy," the Yankees were never just a hobby for the Colonel. They provided him with far more than a diversion from his business responsibilities. The challenge of building a winner and the satisfaction of owning a championship team brought meaning and purpose to his life.

In the fall of 1935, after the Yankees had fallen short of the pennant for the third straight season and sixth of the past seven, Joe McCarthy said the Yankees would stand pat and were good enough to win in 1936.[29] The Colonel was never interested in standing pat and wanted to acquire Washington's star second baseman, Buddy Myer, to back up and eventually replace ten-year veteran Tony Lazzeri.[30]

Ruppert was in Los Angeles that fall for the annual USBA convention. The *Los Angeles Times* wrote that the "corpulent, genial, little man" who "talks and does business in big figures" was putting a lot of his 1936 pennant hope in the "lithe figure" of a promising recruit. "If DiMaggio supplies the needed punch at the plate," Ruppert said, "I don't see how we can miss next year."[31]

36

The DiMaggio Years

Occasionally in sport, new champions are sought out and miraculously found to replace the old. DiMaggio was one of those. He would ultimately replace—or come close to replacing—the greatest Yankee in history.

JACK B. MOORE, *Joe DiMaggio*

In 1933, eighteen-year-old Joe DiMaggio batted .340 and hit safely in 61 straight games for the Pacific Coast League's San Francisco Seals. The next season, he batted .341, but played in only 101 games because of a knee injury. Uncertainty as to the extent of the damage to DiMaggio's knee prevented some Major League teams from pursuing him, while economic hard times would not allow others to meet Seals owner Charlie Graham's high asking price.[1]

Yankees Minor League farm director George Weiss and scouts Bill Essick and Joe Devine persuaded Ed Barrow to pursue the young outfielder. "Buy DiMaggio. I think you can get him cheap," Essick told Barrow.[2] A somewhat reluctant Barrow had DiMaggio examined by specialists. When they determined there would be no lasting effects to the knee, Barrow completed the deal on November 21, 1934. The Yankees gave the Seals $25,000 and five nondescript players for DiMaggio.

Eight years earlier, Barrow and Ruppert had taken a similar chance on Tony Lazzeri, another young Pacific Coast League star, whose physical condition (epilepsy in Lazzeri's case) had scared off other teams. They had guessed right then and were hoping DiMaggio would duplicate Lazzeri's success.

As part of the Yankees' agreement with San Francisco, DiMaggio would play for the Seals in 1935 to prove he was not "damaged goods." "And the

Yanks got to keep their money until the kid's knee was proven sound," wrote Richard Ben Cramer, a DiMaggio biographer. His .398 batting average, with 34 homers and 154 runs batted in in 1935, proved that he was not only healthy but also the top prospect in the game. It was "the best deal I ever made," Barrow said years later.[3]

The Colonel got his first look at the man expected to replace Babe Ruth on October 27, 1935, in Oakland. DiMaggio played with a group of Bay area Major Leaguers in a charity game sponsored by the Alameda Elks. He went hitless in two at bats and misplayed his only chance in center field.

When he first met DiMaggio, Ruppert said, prophetically as it turned out, "He seems a difficult man to get acquainted with."[4] Yet Ruppert could not have known that once DiMaggio joined the team, he would never again see a second-place finish. The Yankees had not won a pennant since 1932, but that was about to change. Beginning with his rookie season, 1936, DiMaggio led the Yankees to four consecutive world championships. "He is the best rookie who has broken into the big leagues for years," said his manager, Joe McCarthy.[5]

DiMaggio also was instrumental in changing the culture of the team. "Where Ruth's swagger was emblematic of the Roaring Twenties, the quiet dignity of Gehrig and DiMaggio fit the Depression years," wrote author Neil Sullivan.[6] In 1935, with Ruth gone, Lou Gehrig was poised finally to emerge from the Babe's shadow and become the team's leader. "Gehrig aspires to take Ruth's place," wrote Dan Daniel before the start of spring training.[7] McCarthy had appointed Gehrig team captain in 1935, yet a year later, the twenty-one-year-old DiMaggio had become the Yankees' de facto leader. "Joe became the team's biggest star from the moment he hit the Yankees," remembered Lefty Gomez. "He was as shy as Lou but had an aura about him."[8]

Searching for someone to replace Ruth as the focus of its stories, the New York press had skipped past Gehrig to focus on DiMaggio. "In the forever entwined narrative of the two players' momentarily connected lives," wrote DiMaggio biographer Jack B. Moore, "DiMaggio's domination of Gehrig as the Yankee star adds poignance to Gehrig's sad story, and sharpness to DiMaggio's intense tale of success."[9] Gehrig biographer Jonathan Eig wrote of him, "Between the foul lines, he was terrific, but outside them, he almost never said or did anything interesting enough to satisfy the men who pointed notebooks in his face."[10]

The brawling, free-spirited Yankees of the Huggins-Ruth years would give way to the cold, machinelike efficiency of the McCarthy-DiMaggio Yankees. It was a team of outstanding players: Gehrig, Bill Dickey, Red Rolfe, Joe Gordon, Frank Crosetti, Tommy Henrich, Red Ruffing, and Gomez. Still it was DiMaggio who elevated the Yankees from a very good team to a great one. The success of the DiMaggio-led Yankees brought abundant joy to the Colonel's final years, although that joy did not come without a price.

After making $8,500 as a rookie, an unusually high salary for a first-year player, DiMaggio's salary rose to $15,000 in 1937, a very generous increase. But after his major role in the Yankees' back-to-back World Series wins over Bill Terry's New York Giants, DiMaggio was said to be demanding $40,000 for the 1938 season. The press began speculating about Ruppert and Barrow's counteroffer. "It's $25,000, and I think that is a very fair salary," Ruppert said. "I don't intend to go any higher."[11]

Given the hard economic times, with millions of Americans still unemployed, it was easy to portray DiMaggio as being selfish. After all, Gehrig was coming off a 1937 season in which he batted .351, with 37 home runs and 159 runs batted in, and his reward was a raise of $3,000 to $39,000. This was $1,000 less than DiMaggio wanted.

The Colonel had conducted grueling salary negotiations in the past, with Ruth, Ruffing, and Gomez, among others, but his most difficult were with DiMaggio. "Joe is decidedly the toughest young man I've ever had to deal with," Ruppert said early in the 1938 season. "Ruffing held out longer last year, but he wasn't bullheaded like DiMaggio. This young man left my office on January 21, and I didn't hear from him again until yesterday."[12]

J. G. Taylor Spink, editor of the *Sporting News*, confirmed that Ruppert had his most unpleasant salary negotiations with DiMaggio. According to Spink, though, the newspapers were wrong in saying DiMaggio wanted $40,000 for 1938; he really wanted only $30,000. Ruppert was offering $25,000. At a postseason meeting at Ruppert's office in the brewery, DiMaggio had listened as Ruppert made his case, then got up and left. "Before you go back to San Francisco, give me a ring," Ruppert told him. But DiMaggio left for California without making the call. Spink said Ruppert later told him that had DiMaggio returned to the brewery and restated his reasons, Ruppert would have given him the $30,000. "Joe's returning home without making that call hurt the Colonel's pride," said Spink.[13]

Ruppert voiced his dissatisfaction with DiMaggio while sitting in his private railroad car, en route to the Yankees training camp at St. Petersburg. "DiMaggio is an ungrateful young man, and is very unfair to his teammates, to say the least," he said. "I've offered $25,000 and he won't get a button over that amount. Why, how many men his age earn that much? As far as I'm concerned that's all he's worth to the ball club and if he doesn't sign we'll win the pennant without him."[14]

DiMaggio's demand to meet his price "or else" had infuriated Ruppert. "If he means he will not play baseball this year, then we must accept his decision," the Colonel said. "He will play for $25,000 or not at all."[15] McCarthy sided with Ruppert and Barrow. "The Yankees can get along without DiMaggio. And that $25,000 is final."[16] Now convinced that indeed $25,000 was all he was going to get, DiMaggio wired Barrow that the terms first offered on January 21 were now acceptable and he would be heading from California to New York.[17]

The season had started on April 18, but DiMaggio did not sign his contract until April 25, and then only after a heated conference in Barrow's office. He did not play his first game until April 30. Ruppert had ordered that DiMaggio receive no money from the Yankees until he was in shape to play, a loss of $162 a day. Furthermore, if he wanted to travel with the team he would have to pay his own train fare and hotel and dining bills. "I hope the young man has learned his lesson," said Ruppert.[18]

DiMaggio was the only player who ever incurred Ruppert's real displeasure, wrote columnist Dan Parker shortly after the Colonel's death. He had deeply wounded Ruppert's pride by the utter lack of respect he showed him in the 1938 holdout campaign. Ruppert would have allowed even as great a star as DiMaggio to remain a holdout forever rather than surrender to him after his discourtesy, wrote Parker.[19]

We can only wonder if Ruppert would have indeed sacrificed his team's chances of winning another pennant to satisfy his wounded pride. The Colonel's upper-class breeding set him apart from his employees at the brewery and in baseball. He operated in a world where gentlemen kept their word and treated each other with respect. In his eyes, DiMaggio had violated both those precepts. Yet Ruppert never lost his desire to win. His Yankees had won the last two World Series, and he was anxious to win again in 1938.

The Colonel had always prided himself on being a fan-friendly owner and an innovative businessman. Yet he was slow to accept the two major innovations that surfaced in baseball in the 1930s: night games and radio broadcasts. The Yankees were even slow in holding Ladies Day for their female fans. The custom, introduced in the nineteenth century, did not make its first appearance at Yankee Stadium until April 29, 1938.

When asked about night baseball, after Cincinnati pioneered the concept in 1935, Ruppert had said, "I believe night baseball, given in small doses, has possibilities. I am going to watch the National League's experiment very closely, and if it offers anything of interest to the fans of New York and of value to the club we will go after night baseball in the American League and put it on at the Stadium."[20] Yet there would be no night baseball at Yankee Stadium until 1946, after part-owner and general manager Larry MacPhail, who had brought it to Cincinnati and Brooklyn, succeeded the staunchly opposed Barrow.

By 1938, thirteen of the sixteen Major League teams had all or some of their home games on the radio; most also broadcast re-creations of their road games. The three teams with no radio broadcasts were those in New York, where the Yankees, Giants, and Dodgers had a "gentlemen's agreement" banning them. Late that year, when MacPhail, the new Dodgers' president, declared that he would end the agreement, Ruppert and Giants owner Horace Stoneham felt compelled to go along. Just before Christmas, Ruppert announced that beginning in 1939, the Yankees would broadcast their games on radio. Ruppert's statement followed a similar announcement Stoneham had made two weeks earlier.[21]

Ruppert saw broadcasting games as giving away his product for free. Nevertheless, he described his move as a Christmas gift to fans who were "shut-ins" and could not get to the games. He admitted that during his illness, which dated back to the beginning of the 1938 season, he was able to attend only two games. He said he would have enjoyed listening to the Yankees on the radio rather than getting updates by telephone after each inning.[22] "During my confinement indoors, I found great pleasure in listening to the radio," Ruppert said. "It was fun to me to follow the [World Series] games. And I decided if I could get so much joy out of it, others could too. That's why I have decided to let the Yankees games go on the air."

Ruppert said he did not know whether it would hurt or help attendance, "but I am not considering the financial angle. I don't care whether we make a cent, but I do care that men and women, through illness or accident, who are confined indoors, shall have some happiness brought them by radio."[23]

This was quite a turnaround from earlier in the 1930s, when Ruppert had attacked radio broadcasts of baseball as "ridiculous . . . a menace to the National Game."[24] But much had changed since then, including Ruppert's personal situation and the flamboyant and innovative MacPhail's arrival in Brooklyn. Regardless of whether Ruppert allowed radio for business reasons or for sentimental reasons, he had little choice, considering the Dodgers' action.

Two months earlier, in October 1938, Ruppert had been able to listen to the seventh and deciding game of the Little World Series, which matched his top two farm teams. The Kansas City Blues of the American Association won the game, and the series, over the Newark Bears of the International League.

Ruppert could not lose, no matter who won, unlike the previous year when the 1937 Little World Series matched Newark against the Columbus (Ohio) Red Birds. Columbus was one of the St. Louis Cardinals' two top farm teams; so the series matched Branch Rickey's farm system against that of the Yankees. Ruppert had been in Newark for the first game of the 1937 Little World Series, accompanied by Barrow, McCarthy, Weiss, George Perry, and several Yankees scouts.

Newark had roared through the 1937 International League playoffs, sweeping Syracuse and Baltimore, each in four games.[25] Before the first game against Syracuse, George Weiss had phoned Ruppert. "Four straight in each playoff series suit you all right, Colonel?" Weiss asked. "I always vote for a 'four straight' ticket," Ruppert responded. "And see the same thing in that Little World Series."[26] Newark did win four straight, but only as the result of a spectacular comeback after they had lost the first three games.

As the Yanks prepared to play the Chicago Cubs in the 1938 World Series, following their third consecutive pennant, the old cries of "Break up the Yankees" were again being heard around the American League. Ruppert dismissed them, just as he had in 1932. He pointed out that no one had called for the Philadelphia Athletics to be broken up after their three straight pennants from 1929 to 1931. And when Connie Mack did break them up, Ruppert reminded everyone, it was for money, not out of any sense of charity.

Ruppert suggested that instead of trying to dismantle the Yankees, the other owners spend money to build up their own clubs. "Other clubs must do the same as we are doing, go out and seek players. And you've got to go even deeper than the minor leagues," Ruppert said, reminding everyone they had gotten Gehrig from Columbia, Red Rolfe from Dartmouth, and former Yankee Ben Chapman from a semipro club.[27]

After the Yankees swept the Cubs, the cries to "level the field" grew even louder. And Ruppert continued to defend his approach to winning, eloquently and emphatically, while steadfastly resisting any attempt to break up the Yankees. "When the Detroit Tigers won two pennants in succession [1934 and 1935], nobody called the Tigers a menace to baseball. And nobody cried over the Yankees in the years they didn't win. But when my ball club won in 1936 and again in 1937 and beat the Giants in the World Series there was a great to-do. . . . Winning the world championship is serious business. It's our purpose in baseball. . . . Enterprise and initiative would die if, as has been suggested, all available major-league prospects were pooled and the weaker clubs were allowed first choice of them."[28]

"I have been very fortunate in my choice of men to head the different departments in my baseball organization," Ruppert admitted. "Barrow, my business manager, is recognized as the best there is. Weiss is a genius in minor-league organization and development. And Joe McCarthy, manager of the Yankees, is the best manager in baseball."[29]

Meanwhile, with the repeal of Prohibition, Ruppert's primary business was thriving. By 1936, Ruppert Brewery, with its leading brands, Knickerbocker and Ruppert, was No. 1 in the United States, with sales of over $24 million.[30] And he never missed an opportunity to increase those sales.

One day in October 1937, Ruppert asked Joe Dugan, the onetime Yankees' third baseman, to pay him a visit. Dugan had owned a tavern in upper Manhattan since leaving baseball in 1931.

"You don't sell my beer," Ruppert asked. "Why not?"

Dugan marveled at his former employer. "Imagine a busy man like him knowing I didn't carry his product—and getting disturbed about it! Do you know he keeps intimate tabs on most of his players—not only the current ones, but the old timers?"[31]

"The thing I remember most about the Ruppert Brewery was Colonel Ruppert really ran the place," recalled New York sportscaster Stan Lomax, whose radio show was sponsored by the brewery in the 1930s. "He was in complete charge. He was there every day in the office. He had his finger on every part of the development and sale of that beer. He was a tough guy; he ran the brewery the way he wanted it run."[32]

Still, it was not all business for the Colonel, who had been a longtime patron of the Broadway theater and of Hollywood movies. So in 1937, when the *New York Sun* asked various celebrities to list their top theater performances and favorite movies, he was among those surveyed.[33]

The Colonel, a former congressman, maintained his interest in international affairs. He had recognized the threat of Nazi Germany early on and had never been, even remotely, a part of the pro-Nazi German groups that rose up around America in the 1930s. Pro-German sentiment in the New York area was especially strong in Manhattan's Yorkville section, where Ruppert had his brewery and, to a large extent, his family's roots. He continued to support the cause of German Jewry and was listed as a boxholder for the fifth annual presentation of the "Night of Stars" of the United Palestine Appeal at Madison Square Garden on November 17, 1938. Ruppert was too ill to be there, but two of his players, Lou Gehrig and Lefty Gomez, were among the many sports stars who did attend.

Ruppert's will to win never wavered. He hated losing out in any contest, sporting or otherwise. In December 1938, a month before he died, he read that Walter Briggs, owner of the Tigers, had outbid the Yankees for the Seattle Rainiers' heralded nineteen-year-old pitcher, Fred Hutchinson. He summoned Barrow to his hospital room and demanded to know why the Yankees had been outbid. Barrow assured Ruppert that the Yankees had not been outbid. "Hutchinson is not ready and hasn't enough speed to make him worth that kind of money to us," Barrow explained. "We would have had to send him to Newark. Our scouts did not recommend him at the price." Ruppert, who trusted Barrow, who in turn trusted his scouts, was satisfied; he had not been outbid.[34]

Ruppert's determination not to be outbid came across in a January 1937 interview that appeared in the *Sporting News*. He was reflecting on Judge Landis's decision in December to award teenage sensation Bob Feller to the Cleveland Indians rather than allow all teams to compete for him. "If Feller had been made a free agent, the Yankees would have signed him," he said. "I was determined to cut the purse strings for once, and I told Barrow the sky was the limit." Ruppert confessed he would have gone as high as $100,000, maybe even higher, for Feller, whom he rated in the new super class of players. He added that DiMaggio was also in that class of players he would pay $100,000 to sign. "Say, double that for him— and then some," he added.[35] As demonstrated by his salary battles with DiMaggio and others, he was willing to be very generous in acquiring players, but quite stingy in paying them.

As 1938 ended, and as the nation continued to struggle with recovering from the Depression, Ruppert made this prediction for 1939, with the proviso that peace would prevail. "I see plenty of signs that business, government and labor, after a long period of conflict over new and divergent ideas and demands, are beginning to reconcile their differences in a desire to play ball on a mutually fair and beneficial basis." Ruppert predicted a successful year for business "unless any of the nations plunge into war."[36]

Less than a year later, nations would "plunge into war," but the Colonel would not live to see it.

37

It Took Time for Success
to Become a Tradition

Days after his bitter 1938 salary battle with Joe DiMaggio ended, Jacob Ruppert was diagnosed with phlebitis, the disease that would eventually lead to his death. It was one more piece of bad news in what had been a difficult spring for the Colonel. On March 29 he was in St. Petersburg with the Yankees when he got word that Til Huston had died at age seventy-one. Visibly shaken, he said the death of his former partner had come as a great shock to him. "We had our differences in so far as the conduct of the ball club was concerned, but he was a fine friend, a square shooter, and a grand fighter for the right. That the Colonel sold me his 50 percent interest in the Yankees was due not to any split between us, as we never exchanged a sharp sentence. He felt he did not want to have so much of his capital invested in baseball, and from a business standpoint he was correct."[1] Huston joined Frank Farrell, Bill Devery, Ban Johnson, Harry Frazee, John McGraw, Bill Donovan, and Miller Huggins among those who had played such significant roles in Ruppert's early days in baseball and were now gone.

The Colonel's deteriorating health was starting to take its toll. Scheduled to travel by train to Kansas City for the Blues' 1938 American Association opener, he canceled his reservation. "You've got to go down and take care of the boys yourself," he told Ed Barrow by phone. "The doctor says I have to stay home a few weeks."[2]

Normally a frequent attendee at Yankees home games, he saw only two all season, the home opener and one in August. However, he was among the celebrities at Yankee Stadium on June 22 to see Joe Louis defend his heavyweight title with a one-round knockout of German challenger

Max Schmeling. The fight drew more than 70,000 people, and the gate receipts were in excess of $1 million, providing the Colonel with another lucrative payday.

"I would not object if our new park was used for an occasional big fight, and I would not want too many of those," Ruppert had said before the Stadium opened in 1923. Yet many of the big championship fights since had taken place in the Stadium ring, set up over second base. "The Colonel was very fond of boxing," remembered his longtime confidant, George Perry. "Rarely would he pass up a big fight in New York. And never did he fail to go into the dressing rooms to congratulate the winner and console the loser. He knew a lot about the finer points of boxing."[3]

College football games were another source of revenue for Ruppert. The highlight was the Army–Notre Dame game, played at the Stadium from 1925 to 1947. Boxing and football combined generated almost $150,000 of revenue in 1929 and 1930, a significant addition to the Yankees' bottom line.

Ruppert had attended forty-nine consecutive Yankees World Series games, but his poor health had prevented him from attending the first two games of the 1938 Series in Chicago. He had hoped his doctors would allow him to attend the Series games at Yankee Stadium, but they said no.[4]

Later in October, Ruppert entered Manhattan's Lenox Hill Hospital to undergo a thorough physical examination by his personal physician, Dr. Otto M. Schwerdtfeger. The Colonel had been feeling better, and the visit was a precautionary measure before his annual three-week vacation trip to French Lick. He left the hospital on November 1, with Dr. Schwerdtfeger predicting he "was well on the road to complete recovery."[5]

For the past thirty years, Ruppert had vacationed in French Lick each November, to take the hot springs–fed mineral baths and enjoy walks through the countryside. Wherever he traveled, he enjoyed basking in the reflected glory of owning the Yankees. "I might be the greatest brewer in the world," he once said while at French Lick, "but who would know it way out here in Indiana? But they know all about me because of my connection with the Yankees—and I am only the man who backs the club. I never hit any home runs for the team."[6]

As Ruppert's condition worsened, his phlebitis caused a liver problem that made it difficult for him to digest his food. By late 1938, his weight had dropped from his normal 190 to 100 pounds. He had a heart attack on January 4 and, after some improvement, had a relapse. On January 10, 1939, Father James Kane, of St. Francis de Sales Church on East 96th Street and Madison Avenue, went to the Ruppert home at 1120 Fifth Avenue to administer the last rites of the Catholic Church.[7]

The next day, the *New York Sun* reported Ruppert was near death at his home. His condition became critical, and throughout the night he alternately fell into a coma and regained consciousness. Temporarily emerging from the coma the next morning, he recognized his executive secretary, Al Brennan, who had been his close friend for more than thirty years.

"Hi, Al," he said weakly. "I wish I could get up." Dr. Schwerdtfeger told the press the Colonel was "resting easily and sleeping peacefully." But family and friends knew better. They gathered at his bedside believing his death would occur in "only a matter of hours."[8]

Babe Ruth was one of the last people to see Ruppert. "When all's said and done," the Babe said, "the Colonel was a second father to me." Ruth tried to cheer him, but Ruppert was very weak and could barely speak. "You're going to snap out of it, and you and I are going to the opening game this year together," Ruth said. Then, as he turned to leave, Ruppert summoned him back, held out his hand, and whispered, "Babe." "It was the only time in his life he ever called me Babe to my face. I couldn't help crying when I went out."[9]

While Ruppert's deathbed conversation with Ruth has become part of the lore of both men, it likely did not happen. "Ruth did visit the Colonel," wrote Dan Daniel, a longtime chronicler of Ruppert, "but Jake was too far gone to know what it was about, and he quite definitely did not call him Babe 'for the first time.'"[10]

Jacob Ruppert died on January 13. His doctor attributed his death to phlebitis of his leg.[11] A spokesman for the New York Academy of Medicine said: "The fatalities following phlebitis are comparatively low, even in people of advanced age. In Col. Ruppert's particular case, however, it was not the phlebitis itself that led to his death, but rather the complications that set in following the phlebitis."[12]

Ruppert's funeral was held at St. Patrick's Cathedral, on Fifth Avenue in Manhattan, on January 16, 1939. It was a solemn Requiem Mass, after which he was interred in the family mausoleum in Kensico Cemetery in Westchester County, New York.

His death had a deep emotional impact on Ruth. The Babe, whom Ruppert had made a rich man, and who in turn had enriched the Colonel, recognized Ruppert's contributions to the game. "He brought baseball to the top; picked it up when it was a sort of hit-and-miss thing and made it big business," Ruth said. "He boosted salaries, built the greatest park in the business, and was a fair man to talk and bargain with."[13]

Ruppert's death was mourned in New York's black community as well. William E. Clarke of the *New York Age* wrote that Harlem joined with other sections of New York in grieving over his passing "because of his charitable nature and the many donations he made to young peoples' organizations in Harlem." Clarke believed Ruppert was sympathetic to ending the color line in baseball and that the Yankees would be the first Major League team to place a Negro player on its roster. Ruppert's plan, wrote Clarke, was "to place a colored player on one of his farm teams, possibly the Newark Bears, and if there was no unfavorable reaction, to promote the player to the Yankees after a season or so with the minors."[14]

Ruppert's relations with the city's black community had been mostly positive. Nine years earlier, on July 5, 1930, he had donated the use of Yankee Stadium for a doubleheader between two independent black teams for the benefit of the Brotherhood of Sleeping Car Porters, the nation's first successful black union. The games between the New York Lincoln Giants and the Baltimore Black Sox, the first Negro Leagues clubs to play at the Stadium, drew about 20,000 fans and raised approximately $3,500 for the union.[15] After convincing Ruppert and other Yankees officials to sponsor the fund-raiser, Roy Lancaster, secretary-treasurer of the Brotherhood, declared "the great Yankee Stadium" had been "given to the porters free to aid them in their fight for a higher standard of living. Truly, we have friends in both races."[16]

Beginning in 1936, Negro League games became a regular feature at Yankee Stadium when the Yankees were on the road. A few months after Ruppert died, the Yankees announced the sanction of a Jacob Ruppert Memorial Cup tournament among Negro National League teams, to be played in ten doubleheaders at the Stadium. The Ruppert Trophy would be awarded each year to the championship club. Ed Barrow said the award of this trophy, valued at $500, symbolized a new era of cooperation between the Majors and the Negro National League.[17]

Yet there were, as there always are, differing opinions regarding Ruppert and blacks. An editorial in the *Baltimore Afro-American* took him to task for not doing more to integrate the Major Leagues. The unsigned piece said that while Ruppert was regarded as one of baseball's great owners, he was not a great man in the true sense of that term. "With money, prestige, and almost unlimited power, he could have put on his baseball team one or two colored baseball players and thus revolutionized the whole unsportsmanlike attitude of professional baseball. But he lacked the essential courage. America suffers because a lot of so-called great men, who are looked upon as giants, become chicken hearted when they face color prejudice."[18]

The charge was unfair in that, unlike his contemporary Branch Rickey, Ruppert was not a social visionary. He was, at heart, a consensus-builder who would not choose to find himself on the opposite side of an issue with every other owner.[19] "Let us sit down like sensible men and talk this thing over" had always been one of his favorite expressions.[20]

However, Ruppert, Barrow, or more likely George Weiss can be faulted for actions regarding the seating arrangement for his Minor League team in the American Association. In building his farm system, Ruppert purchased the Kansas City franchise from former Chicago Cubs catcher Johnny Kling in 1937. When Kling took ownership of the franchise in 1933, one of his first acts was to eliminate the segregated seating at Muehlebach Stadium. The policy remained in effect until the Yankees bought the club, whereupon they renamed the park Ruppert Stadium and "the White and Colored signs went right back up."[21] A 1942 article in a black Kansas City newspaper noted that the park was not segregated by race when the Kansas City Monarchs of the Negro Leagues played there. "The truth, pure and simple," it charged, "is that it is the Ruppert Stadium management, not the fans, who bring up and enforce segregation when the Blues play."[22]

Then there was the infamous "Jake Powell affair." Powell had come to the Yankees from Washington in a trade for Ben Chapman on June 14, 1936. The emergence of rookie Joe DiMaggio had made Chapman expendable. So too had his holdouts, his demands to be traded, and his taunting of Jewish spectators at Yankee Stadium with Nazi salutes and anti-Semitic epithets. However, the Yankees may not have fully realized they had traded one bigoted twenty-seven-year-old outfielder for another.

It all began for Powell on July 29, 1938, on radio station WGN in Chicago. During a pregame radio interview with Bob Elson, Powell joked that he kept himself in shape as an offseason policeman in Dayton, Ohio, by "cracking niggers over the head."[23] The remark caused outrage in the black community, especially in Chicago, where they believed the ten-game suspension imposed on Powell by Commissioner Landis was insufficient punishment. The city's leading black newspaper, the *Defender*, wrote: "[Black] fans are wondering why Jake Ruppert, owner of the New York Yankees, who hires Powell, will continue to let him play when Mr. Ruppert enjoys the patronage of thousands of black citizens in his Yankee Stadium and sells his beer all over Harlem to black people, making thousands of dollars from this race."[24]

When black groups threatened to boycott his beer, Ruppert got Powell to visit a Harlem-based newspaper and issue an apology. Ed Barrow attempted to limit the damage with a letter to the *New York Amsterdam News*. "I have personally discussed the Powell matter with several of my colored friends, as well as the two colored servants in my own home," he wrote, "and all of them seem to feel that it was just an unfortunate mistake that cannot happen again."[25]

Nevertheless, the black press was not mollified, and their discontent resurfaced when the Yankees re-signed Powell for the 1939 season. When a black reporter questioned the signing, Barrow was clearly annoyed. "Yes, he is signed up," Barrow said. "But it is not definite that he will be used. That is up to Manager McCarthy." Powell had done all he could to prove he meant no harm, said Barrow.[26]

Barrow's failure to recognize the pain felt in the black community at Powell's re-signing, along with his reliance on his "colored friends" and servants for guidance on the issue, are indications of his insularity, his condescension, and the state of American race relations at the time. But Barrow, like Ruppert, was not a social visionary. His goal was to win championships, and though Powell had not contributed much in 1938, he re-signed him with only that in mind.[27]

On April 19, 1940, a drizzly Friday afternoon, the Yankees defeated the Senators, 5–3, before 15,299 in their home opener. It was the smallest opening day crowd in the eighteen-year history of the Stadium and came on the day the man who was responsible for building it was honored. As a bugler played "Taps," and the Seventh Regiment band played "Just a Song at Twilight," a Ruppert favorite, a plaque was unveiled in center field. Eight years earlier, the Yankees had erected a monument in memory of Ruppert's longtime manager, Miller Huggins. Now the two men whose partnership laid the foundation for baseball's greatest franchise were memorialized in the expanse of outfield of the greatest stadium in baseball. Eventually Ruth and Gehrig, the two players most responsible for the team's success, would join them.

A *Sporting News* editorial of April 18, entitled "A Tribute to Ruppert," noted that his plaque would be next to the monument to Huggins, "who shares with Ruppert the glory that came from these achievements [six pennants and three world championships]. Both lent distinction to the game and their contributions to the sport will long be remembered by the fans of the present generation."[28]

In return, baseball, in general, and the Yankees, in particular, had evolved into the great joy of Ruppert's life. Three years after purchasing the club, he wrote, "I have got a lot of excitement out of this magnate business and no doubt there is much more coming to me before I am through."[29]

Ruppert and Huggins had provided the patience, skill, and commitment to make winning championships the norm for the New York Yankees. Several years after Ruppert's death, John Lardner wrote of the colossus he and Huggins had left behind: "It took time for success to become a tradition."[30]

38

The Mystery Lady

At the time of his death, the estimated worth of Jacob Ruppert's estate ranged between $40 million and $100 million. His 1934 will revealed that he had chosen three women to each receive one-third of the estate.[1] Two were nieces, both of whom lived in Greenwich, Connecticut: Mrs. F. Joseph Holleran and Mrs. J. Basil Maguire. Both were the daughters of Ruppert's youngest sister, Amanda Silleck.[2] The third woman was Helen Weyant, a former Broadway actress who had befriended Ruppert in 1925, when she was twenty-three and he was fifty-seven.[3] Mrs. Holleran had the most direct answer to those who wondered why Miss Weyant, a non-relative, got one-third of the estate. "Miss Weyant is a perfectly charming girl, extremely smart-looking, and very well informed," she said. "She always talks interestingly about any subject that comes up. I met her a number of times at Uncle Jake's place in Garrison, where he entertained his friends. I like her a lot and I know she was my uncle's friend and brought happiness into his life. If he wanted to leave her part of his fortune, I am glad he did. The money was his; why shouldn't it go where he wished; to those who made him happy." Mrs. Holleran added that she was sure Mrs. Maguire felt the same way about Weyant.[4]

It is likely that no one outside of Ruppert's immediate circle had ever heard of Helen Weyant, who lived with her mother on West 55th Street in Manhattan. Her father was the late George Wellington Weyant, a friend of Ruppert's, and her brother Rex had been the Yankees' assistant road secretary for the past three years. Weyant, a native of Winthrop, Massachusetts, had been a chorus girl who had small parts in *Three Cheers* with Will Rogers and in *Sitting Pretty*, among other musical shows, under the name Winthrope Wayne.[5] Her name had never before appeared in the press in this more decorous time. Newspapers described her as a "ward," as "formerly a chorus girl," and, by the *Sporting News*, as "a former show-girl friend."[6]

"I don't know why the Colonel did it, but I feel very honored and a little frightened because this is so tremendous an event," Miss Weyant said. "I had not the slightest idea this was to happen until I attended the reading of the will last Tuesday night at Col. Ruppert's home. The Colonel was a very good friend of the family," she continued. "He knew me as a little girl. I saw him the night before he died. It was after Babe Ruth said goodbye to him. He never had told me he was going to make me a beneficiary in his will. I used to see him quite often, but I never attended a baseball game or a sporting event with him."[7]

"We always got along well together. I think that was because the Colonel liked everything and everybody, and I like everything. He used to talk over his business affairs with me—just sort of thinking out loud, it was without ever calling on me for an answer or advice. . . . I couldn't say just what you could call our relationship outside of friendship," she said.[8]

"Col. Ruppert's interest in Miss Weyant can be explained in a Spanish word, 'sympatico,'—understanding," explained George W. Sutton Jr., who handled public relations for Ruppert. "He was a simple man, and direct, but he had moments of loneliness. Sometimes when he was busy he would stop and ask me about my farm, and talk like that until something turned him back into the business machine. Miss Weyant had a perfect understanding of his simple interests—art, gardening, animals."[9]

A reporter asked the question that had been on many minds. Did he ever propose marriage? "No, he never did," Miss Weyant answered. "He never asked me to dance either. The Colonel didn't care for dancing." She appeared reluctant to define their relationship, but eventually said that it was "like a father and daughter."[10]

Ruppert was far less wealthy than he appeared. A final account filed in Surrogate's Court valued the estate at around only $6 million, providing each of his beneficiaries with trusts of about $2 million. The lower figure was the result of his interests being heavily leveraged with debt.[11]

An attorney for the executors of the Colonel's estate told the Surrogate's Court, "Decedent left an estate in a hopelessly frozen condition. It was burdened with many debts of substantial amounts totaling millions of dollars." A lawyer for one of the beneficiaries described the complex situation. "Various members of the family and the estate are indebted to the Holding Company [which owned the Yankees] and the brewery, which are in turn heavily indebted to Manufacturers Trust Co." The Jacob Ruppert Realty Corporation was in such bad financial condition (past-due mortgages and foreclosure proceedings) that the name of the company was changed to the Forma Corporation.[12]

And while he was the voice and face of his brewery and real estate company, the Colonel owned only 30 percent of each. Family members owned the other 70 percent.[13] A 1957 article in the *St. Louis Post-Dispatch* stated that the estate of George Ruppert held 25.38 percent of the brewery common stock, and J. Ruppert Schalk, a grandson of Jacob Ruppert Sr. and a nephew of the Colonel, owned 11 percent.[14]

Barrow biographer Daniel R. Levitt, who has studied the Yankees' finances, concluded that Ruppert never really had as much money as was credited to him.[15] Ruppert Brewery had lost nearly all its revenue during Prohibition. By the time of Repeal, the Depression was in full swing, and new brewery competition was emerging, both of which prevented a return to pre-Prohibition levels.

The Surrogate's Court proceedings dealt extensively with "the so-called Barrow contract." It turned out that Ed Barrow had indeed paid the Colonel for 10 percent of the Yankees, but the stock was never transferred.[16] In essence, the club's business manager had the right to acquire that stake. So technically Ruppert was correct back in May 1923, when he said he was now the sole owner of the Yankees.[17] This raises an intriguing question: did the Colonel permit Barrow to buy into the Yankees because he needed the money either to buy out Colonel Huston or to meet other obligations?

Then there were the gifts and bad investments the Colonel had made.[18] "No smart business man would go in for some of the Colonel's investments," wrote New York sportswriter Dan Parker, citing his raising of silkworms and other exotic ventures. "Colonel Ruppert made money in baseball," Parker believed, "because he was fortunate enough to hire Ed Barrow to take charge of the New York Yankees." Parker characterized Ruppert in his outside business dealings as a "Midas in reverse," a man who "went for hundreds of sucker plays, and everything he touched turned to dross."[19]

Not everything. The Surrogate's Court concluded the Colonel's stocks and bonds were worth about $1.8 million. But like his other assets, they were pledged as collateral for loans. In the end, they added little value to his estate.[20] Ruppert had no life insurance, and the attorneys spent thousands of hours and dollars unravelling the intricacies of the estate.

Finally, there were the looming state and federal estate taxes due. The trustees decided to challenge the government's valuations, and they put the Yankees up for sale as early as 1940, though no buyer would be found for a number of years. Manufacturers Trust Company, which was owed millions of dollars by the estate, took over as trustee.

So in retrospect, we have to conclude that Jacob Ruppert was not the shrewd businessman he was made out to be. He took on untenable levels of debt in all his companies, including the Yankees. Eventually he even lost his edge in the great brewery his father had started and that he had taken to great heights. In the years before World War I, Ruppert was the leading beer in the country. It dominated the greater New York market and the region's smaller breweries. But after the repeal of Prohibition in 1933, the Ruppert Brewery failed to keep up with changing marketing, tastes, and demographics. These transformations were creating tensions that led to a split in the leadership of the industry in 1936 and, ultimately, to the eclipse of the Ruppert Brewery.

After Repeal, the Colonel had been elected president of the United States Brewers Association, an office he had held for many years before Prohibition. His focus continued to be local distribution and strongly slanted toward selling beer in barrels to restaurants and bars. That beer remained relatively heavy and malty in taste.[21]

Midwestern breweries, led by Anheuser-Busch of St. Louis and Pabst of Milwaukee, were developing national distribution networks with fleets of trucks and offsite bottling plants. They were adding ingredients to reduce costs and create a lighter brew, targeting a younger market, including women, with creative and aggressive marketing campaigns.

The invention of the aluminum can and can liner in the mid-1930s facilitated drinking beer at home and reduced delivery costs by replacing heavier bottles and not requiring backhauls of empty containers. But the key was regulations that allowed the national brewers to ship beer in tanker cars to bottling plants far from their breweries, which the Ruppert-led USBA opposed. With such a distribution network, a brewery a thousand miles from New York could easily invade Ruppert's home base.[22]

In 1936 Anheuser-Busch and Pabst left the USBA and set up a rival organization, leading Ruppert to publicly criticize August "Gussie" Busch.[23] "There may have been personality conflicts between Ruppert and other brewers," wrote Amy Mittelman in *Brewing Battles*. Soon after the death of Ruppert, "a controversial figure in the brewing industry," in Mittelman's words, the organizations merged.[24] In 1957 Busch considered buying the Ruppert Brewery but ultimately declined to do so.[25]

Ruppert's younger brother, George, ran the brewery after Jacob's death, but unlike Barrow with the Yankees, George's stewardship, from 1939 to 1948, was not a success. In *Ambitious Brew*, Maureen Ogle called those ten years, when George stayed with dark, heavy beer, mostly sold in barrels, "years of drift."[26] Yet the trend toward consolidation and new methods of production and distribution began during the Colonel's lifetime, and his brother should not bear all the responsibility for the brewery's decline.

There had been fifteen breweries in Manhattan as late as 1934, but by 1961 only Ruppert's remained. Finally, after ninety-eight years of operation, plagued by declining sales and acrimonious strikes by its workers, the brewery closed at the end of 1965. There were thirty-five "fortress-like red brick buildings" that occupied most of the four blocks from 90th to 94th Streets between Second and Third Avenues. The post–World War II building boom on the East Side continued edging its way north, as "the small bars nestled in the unreconstructed tenements fall one by one." How long before they reach 90th Street, wondered the German-speaking people of Yorkville, who remained fiercely loyal to the brewery?[27] Real estate developer Marvin Kratter, the last in a series of owners of the brewery, eventually levelled the eight-acre property. In 1976 it became the site of the Ruppert and Yorkville Towers, a middle-income housing project.

Knickerbocker Beer continued to be brewed by Rheingold Breweries, which purchased the trademark, formula, and equipment for $12 million. The Knickerbocker brand was discontinued in the 1970s. "This wouldn't have happened if the Colonel had been alive," said one long-time employee.[28]

Jacob Ruppert's name is no longer associated with brewing, but it is and forever will be associated with Yankees baseball. He had stated in his will,

"I have taken a great deal of pride in my connection with the American League Baseball club of New York, Inc. . . . I feel justified in my desire that this enterprise shall be perpetuated." As a reflection of how much Ruppert valued the Yankees above all his other assets, including his brewery and his real estate, he left specific directions that estate taxes should come from those other properties and not the Yankees. Unfortunately, those other companies had so much debt that they could not pay the tax liens.

"The Colonel would want us to carry on, and we've all got to live out our lives," Barrow had said after succeeding Ruppert as the Yankees' president. "The Yankees will be here long after we are gone."[29]

When American League president Will Harridge was asked what would happen to the Yankees with Ruppert gone, Harridge replied, "Nothing. Henry Ford must die some day. Fords will keep running, won't they? Ruppert built up a perfect organization. It could run for years on its present momentum."[30]

Barrow and McCarthy stayed with the Yankees through World War II, at a time the club was administered by the Manufacturers Trust Company, which was actively trying to sell the team.[31] In 1945, as pressure grew on the trust to pay the estate tax, the club and Yankee Stadium were sold to Larry MacPhail, Dan Topping, and Del Webb for close to $3 million.[32]

With a roster of almost all homegrown players, the team won four more pennants in 1939, 1941, 1942, and 1943 and world championships in 1939, 1941, and 1943. George Weiss went on to serve as general manager from 1948 through 1960, during which time the Yankees won ten pennants and seven World Series.

Epilogue

A Legacy of Champions

> You learn eventually that, while there are no villains, there are
> no heroes either. And until you make the final discovery that
> there are only human beings, who are therefore all the more
> fascinating, you are liable to miss something.
>
> PAUL GALLICO, sports editor of the *New York Daily News*,
> in *Farewell to Heroes*

Jacob Ruppert and Miller Huggins joined forces after the 1917 baseball season. Both men were small of stature, yet they were giants of the game. Sharing an unassailable mutual trust and loyalty to each other, their partnership laid the foundation for future Yankees' greatness. From 1918 to 1929, they transformed the Yankees from perennial also-rans into baseball's dominant sports franchise, where it remained for the rest of the twentieth century.

And they did it on baseball's biggest stage. Ruppert and Huggins understood the demands and expectations of managing a team in New York. As early as 1918, during Huggins's first year as the Yankees' manager, Ruppert said, "This is one city where the public demands a winner, but you can't palm off inferior goods on them."[1] Twenty years later, he was saying the same thing. "Second place means about as much as sixth place. Spoiled fans? Nothing of the kind. In New York, we deal in superlatives. People come here to see the best."[2] Huggins spoke of New York's "exacting public," which required the team's manager to keep building. "He can never stand pat on what he's got."[3]

The wealthy, urbane beer baron and the midwestern baseball "lifer," both meticulous planners with an overwhelming need to be the best, built the prototype for a profitable and winning team. The Yankees provided Ruppert with an enormous sense of satisfaction and fulfilled his craving for recognition as the best on a big stage.

The Yankees also provided meaning to Huggins's life. "I don't remember when baseball wasn't the big thing for me. . . . I fell in love. . . . The object of my love, though, was no lady. It was baseball."[4]

Ruppert and Huggins were lifelong bachelors who shared a reputation for being aloof. The Colonel had no close friends among the baseball owners because "there was about him a reserve that made such a relationship difficult."[5] In Huggins's early Yankees years, the press often underestimated and misunderstood him; one writer described him as "strangely complex."[6]

In addition, both men faced personal obstacles. Ruppert and co-owner Til Huston clashed over many matters, especially the continued engagement of Huggins (whom Huston never wanted to hire in the first place), until Ruppert bought him out in 1923. Even that buyout proved taxing; it dragged on for six months. Ruppert also lost his primary source of income, the Ruppert Brewery, when Prohibition became the law of the land early in 1920. At the same time, he was in the midst of an epic struggle with Ban Johnson, the dictatorial president of the American League.

A nervous and unhealthy man, Huggins was forced to withstand the complaints of the press, discontented players, and the ever-present off-field antics of Babe Ruth. Huggins had few friends in the New York press. They were constantly critical of him in his early years and even more so when he failed to win the World Series after acquiring the Babe.

He also had ongoing challenges to his authority from his players, led by Ruth, which culminated in the 1925 showdown. Huggins was constantly "remaking" the Yankees, to improve the team on the field and remove "troublemakers" from the clubhouse. And he faced serious medical problems during his entire tenure, which ended with his death in 1929.

Through it all, Ruppert stood firmly behind his manager. After the Yankees were swept in the 1922 World Series, the Colonel re-signed Huggins and said, "Maybe these people who are firing him and hiring others know more about it than I do. . . . This talk is ridiculous. We are for Huggins, first, last, and all the time."[7] A year later Huggins rewarded him with the Yankees' first world championship.

Jacob Ruppert built an enduring organization by creating a successful business model. Put simply, Ruppert made very shrewd hiring decisions. Of his six most important baseball hires, four were brilliant: managers Huggins and Joe McCarthy, business manager Ed Barrow, and Minor League director George Weiss. He then respected their expertise and did not interfere. His passion for winning was matched by that of his management team.[8] Ruppert identified key elements of success and found them in the makeup of these men: an almost fanatical commitment to winning, great attention to detail, and savvy in evaluating talent. Of equal importance was the Colonel's recognition that they knew more about their jobs than he did. He backed them fully, even when there were calls for their ouster. But he did not abdicate total control; he stayed involved and informed. And occasionally—very occasionally—he stepped in and overruled his men.

Huggins was the man who assembled the team in the late 1910s and 1920s and directed its performance on a day-to-day basis. He knew baseball and the skills necessary to become an accomplished player. After all, he had been a good one himself. He had the elements of success Ruppert was looking for—and more. He had to carry out the vision of winning year after year, with little time for rebuilding. Huggins's ability to evaluate players was legendary: only rarely did someone he gave up on succeed elsewhere. That gift for picking men carried over in the trades he made.[9] And once he saw the potential of a player, he stayed with him for a long time—more than three years in the case of George Pipgras.

Like Ruppert, he developed a clear image of the traits he wanted in a player: the mental toughness, the "disposition," and the focus on "team," qualities he exhibited as a player. Early in his Yankees career, the two men loaded the roster with temperamental stars from other teams. Later on, Huggins asserted more control and allied with Ed Barrow to acquire the types of men the Yankees needed to win.

Ruppert also understood the genius of Huggins that lay beneath his bland exterior, from his uncanny appraisal of talent to his common sense in nurturing the players he believed had that talent. Huggins had the gift of melding the disparate personalities of his players into a winning combination. "I am convinced no other manager could have led the strange collection of temperament that made up the great Yankee baseball team. Huggins had the patience and the understanding to manage the strange and wild mentalities that were on the team," wrote W. O. McGeehan. "He was so inconspicuous that 'he had to die' for his greatness to be fully recognized."[10]

Huggins was the man who persuaded Ruppert to acquire Babe Ruth, though the Colonel did not need too much persuading. With Sunday baseball finally legal in New York, he too understood the potential impact of the Babe—not only on the field but also at the box office.

The Babe, the most colorful player of all time and the best, dominated the game in the 1920s. To showcase him, Ruppert built Yankee Stadium, "the greatest, the most magnificent ball park ever seen," in the words of Frank Graham. "The huge triple-decked grandstand towered, it seemed, almost to the sky."[11] It remains one of the Colonel's greatest achievements.

Unlike Ruppert, who reveled in the adulation of his Yankees, recognition was not important to Huggins. "He played his part on the ball field without giving a thought to the grandstand or the critics," wrote his agent, Christy Walsh. "As for publicity, he loathed it almost as much as he belittled so-called personal popularity."[12] Huggins enjoyed fishing and, in his later years, golf, but he had little personal life. After a ballgame, he began preparing for the next one; after a season, he did the same.

Ruppert, on the other hand, had a full life, with many business and arts interests. Yet he longed for a simpler life, one in which baseball would be his primary focus. "For the last 12 years the Colonel had me plan a summer trip to Europe annually," said George Perry after Ruppert's death. "We would get all the information on ships and sailings, on itineraries, and then he would say that conditions were bad, or that he wanted to stay and see the Yankees win another pennant. He certainly was a slave to his millions and his various enterprises."[13]

It is paradoxical that Ruppert was so successful with the Yankees and his brewery, but so much less successful with his other investments. He created effective business models for the Yankees and for the brewery before Prohibition. He hired brilliantly and understood the chain of command, areas of responsibility, and accountability. After Repeal, changing times and innovations in the industry caught him flat-footed or inflexible to change, or both. Some of his other investments were in schemes so exotic, and so unlikely to succeed, that he seemed to be doing them on a whim, with no expectation of enriching himself. His contribution to the Byrd Expedition, for example, was a venture he knew would provide no monetary return. He simply wanted to be involved with it. And in all his companies, the heavy debt load he took on was simply not sustainable, though the Colonel did not let this affect his lifestyle.

Jack Moore wrote, "In many ways he belonged to the world of New York society that Edith Wharton described so beautifully and devastatingly in her novels. . . . A bon vivant who enjoyed being known throughout his entire lifetime as one of the most eligible bachelors in the city, Ruppert's colonelcy at the age of twenty-two was the result of a two-year stint he enjoyed in the New York National Guard. He relished the title and conducted his affairs with the Yankees as though he were their general."[14]

The Colonel loved nothing more than spending time with his Yankees. Spring training in St. Petersburg was a special time for him, carefree and relaxing. He also loved watching Yankees games from his owner's box in Yankee Stadium, especially when his team was winning by a large margin. Huggins took enormous pride in the success of his players—and his club. "The triumph of the team . . . that's the thrill I get from it now, my appreciation of what winning means to the team," he said.[15]

By the time Huggins died in 1929, the Yankees had established a franchise that was dominant on both the playing field and on the financial statement. Connie Mack, his adversary for a quarter-century, saluted Ruppert when he died. "He came nearer to blending business and sport than any other man I have ever known."[16] Mack had put his finger on a remarkable achievement of the Yankees. They had executed what Henry Fetter, in his economic study on the rise of the Yankees, called "the delicate task of reconciling fandom with business acumen in operating their team."[17]

When Ruppert bought the Yankees, the National League Giants "owned" New York. A few years into his partnership with Huggins— actually, beginning in the early 1920s—the balance of power shifted. At first the shift took place within the confines of the Polo Grounds, where the tenant Yankees began outdrawing their landlords. With the opening of Yankee Stadium, it shifted "across the Harlem River, from Manhattan to the Bronx, never to return."[18] The Yankees had won the battle for baseball supremacy in New York.

"If you became a Yankee, you took on the qualities of breeding which the Yankees exemplified," remembered Waite Hoyt. "You became a Yankee, and that answered a whole lot of questions. For some reason, you were able to perform a little better."[19]

When the Yankees' success led to accusations that they had become too powerful, the Colonel's response always made the same point. "Don't break up my club. Improve the other clubs."[20] Huggins was more of a pessimist and often spoke of the inevitable rise and fall to which all organizations were subject. "We will devote all our time and energy to keeping the Yankees at their present strength," he said after the 1927 season, "but that will not do us any good, for in spite of all we do, the Yankees will tumble. It's the law of averages."[21]

It is both misleading and inaccurate to explain the Yankees' success as simply driven by money. Many sports franchises have had wealthy owners whose expenditures generated little success on the ball field. In one of his final interviews before he died, Ruppert summed up his winning formula. "Money alone does not bring success. You must also have brains, organization, and enterprise. Then you've got something."[22]

In the twelve years they were together, Jacob Ruppert's off-field leadership and Miller Huggins's on-field leadership guided the Yankees to six pennants and three world championships. Yet, while Huggins's managerial contemporaries were elected to baseball's Hall of Fame—Connie Mack and John McGraw in 1937, and Wilbert Robinson in 1945—he did not gain admission until 1964, thirty-five years after his death. Ruppert's three other key employees—Ed Barrow in 1953, Joe McCarthy in 1957, and George Weiss in 1971—were enshrined, but it was not until 2013 that Ruppert joined them and his franchise-building manager in Cooperstown.

NOTES

Prologue

1. Britton was the first female owner of a Major League sports franchise in the United States.
2. Sabermetricians have recognized the 1917 Cardinals as one of the most overachieving teams of all time, comparing their eighty-two wins with their Pythagorean projection of only seventy-one wins. The 1918 team, with many of the same players, won only fifty-one games after Huggins moved on.
3. Joe S. Jackson, Inside Stuff, *Detroit News*, October 26, 1917.
4. George Daley, Comment on Sports, *New York World*, October 29, 1917.
5. Ruppert, "The Ten Million Dollar Toy," 119; Colonel Jacob Ruppert, as told to Daniel, "Behind the Scenes of the Yankees: Robbie Passed Up Stadium Job," *New York World Telegram*, February 18, 1938.
6. Spink's account appeared years later in "Looping the Loops," *Sporting News*, October 21, 1943. Spink was not present at the meeting but probably received firsthand accounts from both Ruppert and Huggins. Ruppert conducted most of his baseball affairs at his brewery rather than at the Yannkees' offices on West Forty-Second Street. Yorkville was the city's German American neighborhood.
7. Ruppert, "The Ten Million Dollar Toy," 119.
8. Bill Slocum, "Miller Huggins, as I Knew Him," *New York American*, September 27, 1929.
9. Damon Runyon, "M. Huggins's Way," *New York American*, June 12, 1918.
10. Miller Huggins, "Serial Story of His Baseball Career: Yankee Berth Gave Huggins Chance to Build Up Real Pennant-Winning Ball Team," *San Francisco Chronicle*, chapter 49, March 10, 1924.
11. Ruppert, "The Ten Million Dollar Toy," 119.
12. Damon Runyon, Between You and Me, *New York American*, September 27, 1929.
13. "Yanks Play for Plattsburg Men," *New York Sun*, September 24, 1917. The Yankees' rookies beat the regulars, 7–5. Ruppert also picked up all the

costs associated with the game. Plattsburgh was often spelled without the
h at that time. The Cardinals' season ended on September 30 and the Yankees' season on October 3.

14. Dan Daniel, High Lights and Shadows in All Spheres of Sport, *New York
Sun*, September 24, 1917.

15. "Huggins Quits Cards to Manage Yanks," *St. Louis Times*, October 26,
1917. This article discussed those August stories.

16. Ban Johnson, *St. Louis Globe-Democrat*, September 15, 1917.

17. W. J. Macbeth, "Johnson's Decision to Go to Trenches Causes Many
Changes in Baseball World," *New York Tribune*, October 17, 1917. See
also *Baltimore Evening Sun*, September 4, 1919, and *New York American*,
January 4, 1921. These accounts suggest that Johnson signed Huggins
illegally while he was still under contract with the Cardinals. At the time,
this story goes, Johnson was thinking of the Cleveland Indians for Huggins, replacing manager Lee Fohl. But the Indians finished the season
strongly and Fohl was retained, while the Yankees faded badly.

18. Spink, *Judge Landis and Twenty-Five Years of Baseball*, 220–21.

19. Bill Corum, Sports, *New York Journal-American*, January 20, 1957, *Sporting News* clip file.

20. Graham, *The New York Yankees*, 31.

21. Jacob Ruppert, *St. Louis Globe-Democrat*, October 26, 1917.

22. William B. Hanna, "One Ambition Realized: Huggins with Yankees
Heart and Soul," *New York Herald*, March 17, 1918.

23. Miller Huggins, "Serial Story of His Baseball Career: Getting New York
Angle Huggins' Biggest Problem at Start of Managership," *San Francisco
Chronicle*, chapter 50, March 11, 1924.

24. Barrow to Huston, October 18, 1917, Steve Steinberg Collection. The letter was addressed to Huston at "Company A, 16th Regiment Engineers
(Railway), American Expeditionary Force in France." Huston almost
certainly received the letter after Huggins was hired.

25. Although the team was known as the Dodgers for most of their years in
Brooklyn, most newspapers called them the Robins during Wilbert Robinson's tenure as manager (1914–31), as a mark of affection for him.

26. Graham, *The New York Yankees*, 32–33. It is hard to believe that Ruppert
would have been so rude to Robinson, even if he had such feelings.

27. Ruppert, "The Ten Million Dollar Toy," 116. Runyon wrote that Ruppert
met with Robinson, who could not assure the Yankees' owner that he was
free to sign with another club. *New York American*, September 27, 1917.

Ruppert could have offered Ebbets compensation to secure Robinson but chose not to do so.

28. The *New York Times* of November 6 reported that Huggins's contract was for $12,500 a year. The *Washington Post* of October 26 reported that it was for $12,000 a year. It is not clear why Huggins did not sign until ten days after the end of the World Series.

29. "Mound City Writers Give High Praise to Huggins as He Goes," *Sporting News*, November 1, 1917.

30. John B. Sheridan, "Close Followers of Baseball Not Surprised over Change," *St. Louis Globe-Democrat*, October 26, 1917.

31. Joe Vila, Setting the Pace, *New York Evening Sun*, October 27, 1917.

32. Editorial, "When the New York Fans Split," *Sporting News*, September 22, 1921. McGraw made the comment when Huggins was hired by the Yankees.

33. *New York Evening Telegram*, October 29, 1917.

1. Everything He Touched Won First Prize

1. Damon Runyon, *New York American*, December 27, 1924.

2. Trachtenberg, "Jake Ruppert Built Dynasties," 19.

3. Ruppert, "Building a Winning Club in New York," 203.

4. Murdock, *Baseball Players and Their Times*, 41.

5. Jay Maeder, "Big Town Biography," quoted in Jimmy Powers's column, *New York Daily News*, March 2, 1939.

6. Smith, *Beer in America*, 151.

7. "Ruppert's Founded in 'Good Old Days,'" *New York Journal-American*, August 4, 1957.

8. *American Brewer* 48 (June 1915): 309.

9. Ruppert descendant K. Jacob Ruppert said the home remained in the family until 1962, when it was donated to the Sisters of St. Ursula as a retreat center.

10. Holland, "The Beer Barons of New York," 404.

11. "The Four Hundred" referred to those who "counted" in New York City society. Social arbiter Ward McAllister claimed in his autobiography, *Society as I Have Found It*, that "the Four Hundred" was derived from the number of people who could be accommodated in Caroline Schermerhorn Astor's ballroom.

12. "Ruppert, Jacob," *The National Cyclopaedia of American Biography*, 29:488.

13. "Mr. Jacob Ruppert, Who Made Fortune as Brewer, Dies at 74," *New York Herald*, May 26, 1915.

14. Edward Rothstein, "A Tipple or Two? It Was Safer than Water," *New York Times*, May 24, 2012.

15. Lagers (beers made with yeast that sinks to the bottom during fermentation) were revolutionary. Because the yeast sank, the beer was clear, not cloudy like ale. For the first time, beer could be served in a clear glass, not an opaque tankard.

16. David Worthington, "How Energy Innovation Made American Beer More Delicious," June 21, 2012. http://www.smartplanet.com/blog /intelligent-energy/how-energy-innovation-made-american-beer -more-delicious/16933.

17. Ice, hauled in from upstate, was initially the lone solution. Blocks were stored in insulated "ice houses" and then floated downriver for distribution. Ice became less desirable over time as greater volumes of beer were brewed, and water became fouled by pollution. Technology breakthroughs, including mechanical refrigeration, were showcased at the United States Centennial in Philadelphia in 1876, where there was a hall dedicated to brewing. John C. de la Vergne founded a refrigeration company in 1880 that brought ammonia-based cooling systems into the mainstream. The system was widely used by 1890, and Jacob Ruppert eventually acquired the business.

18. Smith, *Beer in America*, 153.

19. Two of Ruppert's siblings died young. His brother Frank died of typhoid fever in 1902 at age thirty. His sister Cornelia died in 1896 from a combination of appendicitis and typhoid fever, shortly after her wedding. Cornelia's parents had never forgiven her for her 1895 marriage to Nathan Franko, a divorced Jewish musician, instead of the son of one of the other Bavarian Catholic brewers.

20. "Colonel Jacob Ruppert Dies at His Home," *New York Sun*, January 13, 1939.

21. Trachtenberg, "Jake Ruppert Built Dynasties," 19.

22. "Here's Col. Ruppert," *New York World*, October 5, 1897.

23. Daniel M. Daniel, "Col. Jacob Ruppert, Lonely Bachelor Millionaire. Found Fun in Yanks, after Other Hobbies Palled," *Sporting News*, January 19, 1939.

24. J. G. Taylor Spink, Three and One, *Sporting News*, August 19, 1937.

25. "Col. Ruppert and Babe Ruth Made a Winning Combination," *New York Journal-American*, August 4, 1957.

26. *Time*, September 19, 1932, 28.

27. "Here's Col. Ruppert."

28. *United States Brewers' Association: The Year Book and Proceedings of the Fifty-Second Annual Convention*. New York: United States Brewers' Association, 1912.

29. "Col. Ruppert and Babe Ruth Made a Winning Combination."

30. "Ruppert, Jacob," *The National Cyclopaedia of American Biography*, 29:489.

31. "Seven 'B's' Key to Career of Ruppert," *Chicago Daily News*, January 13, 1939.

32. Frank O'Neill, "Failure behind the Plate Lone Ruppert Regret," *New York Evening Journal*, January 17, 1933.

33. Morris, *Catcher*, 10, 14, and 158.

2. Colonel Makes a Name for Himself

1. Holland, "The Beer Barons of New York," 404.

2. Jacob Ruppert, *Out of the Past* radio program, seventy-first birthday appearance, August 5, 1938.

3. "Colonel" is an honorary title conferred by some American states. Its origin dates back to colonial times.

4. "Ruppert, Jacob" in *Dictionary of American Biography*, vol., 22, suppl. 2, 589–90.

5. "Ruppert Spent Money Fast but Made It Even Faster," *Gloversville (NY) Morning Herald*, January 14, 1939. The monument was built to celebrate the four hundredth anniversary of Columbus's "discovery" of America. It was erected in an area that since 1905 has been called Columbus Circle. http://en.wikipedia.org/wiki/Central_Park.

6. Morton served as vice president of the United States with President Benjamin Harrison from March 4, 1889, to March 4, 1893.

7. Shulman, *Eat the City*, 192.

8. Many German immigrants were educated and affluent. They tended to be Republicans, but began to leave the party around the time of Rutherford B. Hayes's election as president in 1876. The rightward turn of the Republican Party, which was becoming xenophobic, anti-alcohol, and in favor of high tariffs, sent many New York City Germans over to the Democratic Party.

9. Riess, *Touching Base*, 82. Tammany eventually nominated Robert Van Wyck, who won easily and became the first mayor of the city after its consolidation into Greater New York on January 1, 1898.

10. "Colonel Ruppert Off the Ticket," *New York Herald*, October 8, 1897.

11. Isidor Straus and his wife, Rosalie, died when the RMS *Titanic* hit an iceberg on April 14, 1912, and sank the next day.

12. *Brooklyn Daily Eagle*, November 9, 1898.

13. "Ruppert Squarely for Gold Standard," *New York Herald*, December 13, 1899.

14. "O. H. P. Belmont, Too Speedy, Arrested," *New York Herald*, March 26, 1902.

15. "John Gernon Killed Racing Mr. Ruppert," *New York Herald*, June 29, 1912.

16. "Fourteen Members of the Lower House of Congress Are Each Worth a Million or More," *Washington Post*, June 3, 1906.

17. "Bachelors in Congress," *Washington Post*, May 28, 1902.

18. Holland, "The Beer Barons of New York," 405.

19. It was not until 1913 that the Sixteenth Amendment to the Constitution made the income tax a permanent fixture in the United States, giving Congress legal authority to tax income of both individuals and corporations. The revenue obtained from the income tax made Prohibition possible by making up for the lost revenue from the liquor taxes.

20. "Here's Col. Ruppert," *New York World*, October 5, 1897. The *World*, owned by Joseph Pulitzer, was a major voice for the Democratic Party in America and especially in New York.

21. This work schedule was in sharp contrast to young Jacob's long and tedious early days of manual labor in the brewery.

22. "Are Now Qualified Pilots," *New York Times*, June 15, 1896.

23. Standardbred is the official name of American trotting and pacing horses. Characteristics of the breed are similar to those of the thoroughbred, but with modifications due to differences in gait and work. The standardbred is heavier-limbed and more robust than most thoroughbreds, with a longer body and shorter legs.

24. "Horse Breeders Organize," *Washington Post*, November 29, 1906.

25. Ajax was Ruppert's most successful horse. A later horse named Ajax was the famed Australian-bred who dominated Australian racing in the mid- and late 1930s.

26. "Ruppert Not Unknown in World of Sports," *New York Tribune*, January 1915.

27. *New York Tribune*, March 16, 1894, as cited in Riess, *The Sport of Kings and the Kings of Crime*, 162.

28. Riess, *Sport of Kings*, 162–63.

29. In this era, standardbred trotting and pacing race courses were mostly in rural areas with the meets often held as a part of a county fair.

30. Colonel Jacob Ruppert, as told to Daniel, "Behind the Scenes of the Yankees: Ruppert Tells of Early Bid for Giants," *New York World-Telegram*, February 14, 1938.

31. Implicit in Hughes's and his fellow reformers' opposition to racetrack gambling was their well-justified belief that many of the races were fixed. Their opposition was not only to protect the people from the "sin" of gambling but also to protect them from being taken advantage of. The latter motive was behind much of the progressive legislation passed in this era for the protection of the consumer.

32. Riess, *City Games*, 186–87.

33. *Thoroughbred Times* reported that more than 1,500 American horses were sent overseas between 1908 and 1913 and that of them, at least twenty-four were either past, present, or future champions. Racing returned to New York in 1913 after a New York court ruled that oral betting was legal because the Hart-Agnew law only covered bookmakers. On May 30, 1913, thoroughbreds raced at New York's Belmont Park for the first time since 1910.

34. "Ruppert, Jacob" in *Dictionary of American Biography*, volume 22, suppl. 2, 589–90.

35. "Col. Ruppert's Horses Sold," *New York Times*, July 7, 1896.

36. *New York Herald*, October 21, 1895.

37. *New York Times*, June 20, 1897.

38. "Horse Sale's Star Day," *New York Times*, January 31, 1902.

39. "Some Big Figures in the Sporting News," *Boston Daily Globe*, November 1, 1911.

40. "Here's Col. Ruppert," *New York World*, October 5, 1897.

41. A dollar in 1915 was equivalent to more than $22 in 2012.

42. Undated clipping from the *New York Journal-American* morgue housed at the Briscoe Center for American History, University of Texas at Austin.

43. Ruppert's service with the United States Brewers' Association consisted of two stints, one before and one after Prohibition.

44. Shulman, *Eat the City*, 200.

45. Lerner, *Dry Manhattan*, 162.

46. Furnas, *Great Times*, 49–50.

47. *The Year Book and Proceedings of the Fifty-Second Annual Convention of the United States Brewers' Association*, 1912.

48. *Brooklyn Daily Eagle*, January 4, 1912.

49. Banning the manufacture, sale, and transport of alcohol, though not the actual consumption of alcohol, would be the wording used in the Eighteenth Amendment, making Prohibition the law of the land.

50. Taylor, *Inventing Times Square*, 309.

51. *New York Herald*, March 15, 1908.

52. *New York Times*, August 24, 1909.

53. *New York Tribune*, January 20, 1914.

54. Shulman, *Eat the City*, 193–94.

55. Bradley, *Knickerbocker*, 7 and 9. Ruppert sold the brand before Prohibition as well as after Repeal. See, for example, large Ruppert Brewery ads for Knickerbocker beer on the sports pages of the *New York Evening Journal*, February 10 and March 16, 1912.

56. Dan Parker, "The Colonel Always Demanded the Best," *New York Mirror*, January 14, 1939.

3. Ambition and Pluck and Brains

1. John Alexander "Bid" McPhee (1869–1943) played for the Reds from 1882 to 1899 and was elected to the Baseball Hall of Fame by the Veterans' Committee in 2000.

2. Miller Huggins, "Yank Manager Champion Collector Even as Youth," *New York Sun*, May 20, 1924.

3. Procter & Gamble was headquartered in Cincinnati and was probably the source of his name, which at times showed up in box scores spelled "Procter." Huggins was inducted into both the Walnut Hills High School Hall of Fame (1996) and the University of Cincinnati Athletic Hall of Fame (1977).

4. James Thomas Huggins (1846–1913) and Sarah (Reid) Huggins (1848–96) had four children. Miller had two older brothers, Arthur (1875–1963) and Clarence (1876–1955), and a younger sister, Myrtle (1882–1938). James was a phrenologist; at the age of two, his son was "shown" to one of the renowned Fowler brothers, who predicted Miller would make a fortune in an athletic field. *New York World*, October 28, 1917.

5. During his career, Huggins's date of birth was given as March 27, 1880. It was common for players to understate their age, especially when they got

a late start in the Major Leagues. His cemetery record at Spring Grove in Cincinnati lists his birth year as 1880, yet "1878" is etched into his headstone. His official University of Cincinnati record lists 1880. Huggins's official birth record, the 1900 census, and his World War I draft registration all state "1878." These contradictions are not atypical for people born more than a century ago. Only in 2005 was his official baseball birth date corrected to 1878.

6. Damon Runyon, *New York American*, January 1, 1927.

7. Huggins, "Mighty Midget," 18. Years later James Huggins became reconciled to his son's playing baseball and even bragged that the skill he showed was hereditary. Pringle, "A Small Package," 25.

8. Miller Huggins, "Serial Story of His Baseball Career: Writer of Sports Given Credit as Discoverer," *San Francisco Chronicle*, chapter 17, February 1, 1924.

9. The villages of Griffin Corner and Fleischmann incorporated and took the name of Fleischmanns in 1913. A year later, Julius donated two parcels of land to the town for a park. Sive, *Lost Villages*, 53.

10. Evers, *The Catskills*, 545. See also Thorn, "The Last Resort." Charles Fleischmann (1835–97) emigrated from Vienna in 1865.

11. Miller Huggins, "Huggins Wins His Sixth Flag," *New York Sun*, September 29, 1928. Future Major League stars on the team included Doc White and Red Dooin.

12. Miller Huggins file, University of Cincinnati Archives.

13. Huggins, "Mighty Midget," 18. Sportswriter Pat Harmon told this story when Huggins was inducted into the University of Cincinnati Hall of Fame in 1977.

14. Miller Huggins, "How I Got That Way," *New York Evening Post*, October 2, 1926.

15. Miller Huggins, "Serial Story of His Baseball Career: Huggins Reveals How He Was Almost Hired by John J. McGraw to Be a Giant," *San Francisco Chronicle*, chapter 13, January 28, 1924.

16. John McGraw, *New York Herald*, January 17, 1921. Huggins had played for the Shamrocks in 1896; it is possible that he played for them again late in the 1901 season after his St. Paul season had ended.

17. Miller Huggins, "Serial Story of His Baseball Career: Miller Huggins Tells How It Feels to Be Little Man on Diamond," *San Francisco Chronicle*, chapter 14, January 29, 1924. In "Mighty Midget," his sister Myrtle said that he weighed 125 pounds. "He is only an inch or so above five

feet . . . he looks not unlike a jockey grown old," wrote Henry Pringle in "A Small Package," 25.

18. J. Ed Grillo, "Huggins First Man to Fill Biddy McPhee's Shoes," *Cincinnati Commercial Tribune*, March 27, 1904.

19. *New York Sun*, May 20, 1924.

20. George Lennon, "Huggins Alone to Blame If He Fails," *St. Louis Globe-Democrat*, January 5, 1914.

21. *Sporting Life*, November 22, 1902, and June 20, 1903. Clarence worked for the Saints for a number of years.

22. Huggins hit only nine home runs in his Major League career. All were inside-the-park.

23. Miller Huggins, "Huggins, Manager of a Million Dollar Franchise, Played Hookey from Law School to Become Ball Player," *St. Louis Times*, May 17, 1919.

24. John B. Sheridan, Back of the Home Plate, *Sporting News*, April 15, 1920. On June 1, 1910, Huggins had six plate appearances and no at bats (still tied for the all-time record). He walked four times and had two sacrifices.

25. "Huggins Got $1,000 of Purchase Money," *Cincinnati Commercial Tribune*, March 8, 1904.

26. Miller Huggins, "Serial Story of His Baseball Career: Huggins Tells How Ball Players Began to Save Some of Their Money," *San Francisco Chronicle*, chapter 33, February 20, 1924; *Sporting Life*, March 24, 1906, and February 2, 1907. He was still listed as an officer of the Music Hall Amusement Company in Cincinnati City Directories of the early 1920s.

27. John Kieran, Sports of the Times, *New York Times*, September 15, 1927.

28. "Miller Huggins of Cards Is Smallest Player in Majors," *Meriden* (CT) *Daily Journal*, August 7, 1913.

29. "Notes and Gossip of the Game," *Cincinnati Commercial Tribune*, April 16, 1904.

30. *Cincinnati Commercial Tribune*, June 5, 1904.

31. *Cincinnati Enquirer*, April 3, 1904. Huggins would lead the league's second basemen in put-outs (1907), assists (1905 and 1906), and double plays (1906 and 1907).

32. *Cincinnati Commercial Tribune*, June 5, 1904. The colorful and temperamental Donlin hit .351 in 1903 and had a career .333 batting average. Huggins is quoted at length about Keeler in the *St. Louis Times*, May 17, 1919.

33. Ned Hanlon, "Jake [Weimer] and Little Hug Are Shining Examples," *Cincinnati Times-Star*, April 30, 1906.

34. "Field Marshall of the Reds," *Cincinnati Times-Star*, April 14, 1904.

35. Roy Grove, "Huggins Relaxes on Literature between Pennant Games," *St. Louis Times*, September 29, 1922.

36. He had already played in Cuba in the fall of 1902. *Sporting Life*, November 22, 1902.

37. Echevarria, *The Pride of Havana*, 133.

38. *Sporting Life*, January 9, 1909.

39. Egan had a good rookie season but then had a nondescript career. He appeared in fewer than a thousand games with a career batting average of .249. In fairness to Griffith, Huggins had an arm injury and seemed to be on the downside of his career; he had hit only .239 in 1908.

40. *St. Louis Times*, February 10, 1910. The Reds acquired pitcher Fred Beebe and infielder Alan Storke in the deal. Storke died a few weeks after the trade. Besides Huggins, the Cardinals got outfielder Rebel Oakes and pitcher Frank Corridon. Oakes went on to six solid seasons, including two as a player-manager in the Federal League.

41. Clark Griffith, "'I'll Be Cheated When I Trade Hug,' Says Griff," *Cincinnati Times-Star*, February 3, 1910.

42. Herrmann made the remarks at a Cincinnati dinner honoring Huggins after he led the Yankees to their first world championship in 1923. "Early Days of Huggins Recalled," *Cincinnati Enquirer*, September 26, 1929.

43. Miller Huggins, "Serial Story of His Baseball Career: Insists That Trading Spurs a Ball Player On to a Fresh Start," *San Francisco Chronicle*, chapter 35, February 22, 1924.

44. "Regret 'the Rabbit's' Get-Away," *Sporting Life*, July 8, 1911. On July 15 the weekly wrote that "everyone" knew Egan was "a flash in the pan."

45. "May Cost Griff His Job Yet," *Sporting News*, June 29, 1911.

46. *Dayton Daily News*, April 8, 1962. Nelle Hunter, the daughter of a prominent local physician, married Ewing in 1905 in Wapakoneta, where Huggins had played semipro ball in 1898. A few years later, there were vague reports that Huggins would marry. *Sporting Life*, November 10 and December 8, 1906. When Huggins moved to New York in 1918, there were occasional reports that he was dating a Brooklyn girl.

47. Stanley Robison and his brother Frank, Helene Britton's father, had owned the St. Louis team since 1899. They bought the team—then known as the Browns—out of bankruptcy from Chris von der Ahe. They also owned the National League's Cleveland Spiders during that team's entire existence, from 1887 to 1899. Frank Robison had passed away in 1908.

48. The *Federal Express* (later officially known as just the *Federal*) was an overnight passenger train that ran between Washington DC and Boston until 1971.

49. A vivid account of the accident was provided by the *Hartford Courant* on July 9, 2011, around the hundredth anniversary of the accident.

50. The award, an early version of the Most Valuable Player Award, was given only from 1911 to 1914.

51. *Sporting Life*, August 31 and November 2, 1912. Late in the season Huggins expressed unease to the paper over reports that he might take over as manager. The accounts suggested he was trying to undercut Bresnahan, which was not the case, he said. But Huggins may very well have had advance notice of Bresnahan's firing. *Sporting Life*, September 14, 1912.

52. John B. Sheridan, Back of the Home Plate, *Sporting News*, April 15, 1920.

4. No Smarter Man in Baseball

1. *Sporting Life*, August 12, 1911.

2. "National League News in Short Metre," *Sporting Life*, January 3, 1914.

3. Only wins in their final two games prevented the 51-99 Cardinals from losing 100 games. Their most losses since 1913 has been 93 (in 1916 and 1978, the latter a 162-game season).

4. Sid Keener, "Big Change Will Be Made June 15 Unless Huggins Improves," *St. Louis Times*, May 4, 1914. Keener soon grew to admire Huggins's managerial skills.

5. Marion F. Parker, "Huggins' Future," *Sporting Life*, May 16, 1914.

6. "Hug Is Also Canned," *Sporting News*, August 28, 1913. Rumored replacements as manager included Konetchy and even Christy Mathewson.

7. "Huggins Will Quit If Team Doesn't Rally, Friend Says: Little Boss Discouraged," *St. Louis Post-Dispatch*, July 12, 1913.

8. Ed Wray, Wray's Column, *St. Louis Post-Dispatch*, August 7, 1913. At the same time, Huggins made a commitment to St. Louis. He is listed in the city's directory for the first time in 1913, presumably after moving his residence from Cincinnati.

9. The third team was the American League's St. Louis Browns. St. Louis was the nation's fourth largest city in 1910; by 1920 it was ranked sixth in population. The Federal League club, the Terriers, was managed by Chicago Cubs pitching great Mordecai Brown. Steve Evans and Rebel Oakes, Cardinals starting outfielders, joined other Federal League teams, not the Terriers.

10. Schuyler Britton, "Huggins' Future," *Sporting Life*, May 16, 1914.

11. On December 12, 1913, the Cardinals sent Konetchy, pitcher Bob Harmon, and infielder Mike Mowrey to Pittsburgh for pitcher Hank Robinson, outfielders Chief Wilson and Cozy Dolan, and infielders Dots Miller and Art Butler. In this era, managers made all personnel decisions; they often got ownership's approval for major deals.

12. *Sporting Life* had written that if Huggins traded Konetchy and Mowrey, the Cardinals would be "practically, a complete wreck." "The Sayings of St. Louis," *Sporting Life*, November 8, 1913.

13. In his history of the Pirates, Fred Lieb's chapter on the trade is entitled "'Five for Three' Deal Backfires." Pittsburgh's first second-division finish came in 1914. Konetchy hit only .249, and Mowrey missed almost half the season.

14. Miller Huggins, "Serial Story of His Baseball Career: Huggins Defends First Big Trade as One That Helped St. Louis Club," *San Francisco Chronicle*, chapter 39, February 27, 1924.

15. *St. Louis Times*, July 18, 1914. As a rookie, Miller was Honus Wagner's double-play partner on the 1909 world championship Pirates.

16. Based on their pitching styles, Huggins persuaded Perritt to give up the spitball and Doak to take it up. The latter became known as "Spittin' Bill" Doak.

17. The ballpark was known as Robison Field in honor of its two former owners, Helene's father and uncle.

18. Doak tossed a four-hitter, and Huggins scored the game's only run, coming home from second base on a wild pitch that rolled into the overflow crowd behind home plate.

19. W. J. O'Connor, "Hug Wins Recognition as Great Leader by Making Pennant Factor of Tailender," *St. Louis Post-Dispatch*, August 20, 1914.

20. *Baltimore Evening Sun*, August 24, 1914.

21. "McGraw Praises Huggins; Brainy Manager, He Says," *St. Louis Globe-Democrat*, March 7, 1915.

22. "Huggins, Manager of a Million Dollar Franchise, Played Hookey from Law School to Become Ball Player," *St. Louis Times*, May 17, 1919.

23. *Sporting Life*, January 16, 1915.

24. Magee became the player-manager of the Federal League's Brooklyn Tip-Tops. Rebel Oakes, one of the other 1913 Cardinals outfielders, had the same role with the Pittsburgh Rebels.

25. Huggins also tried to bring a player who had jumped to the Federal League from another team back to Organized Baseball. Huggins traveled to Cuba during the off-season, this time to persuade Cuban Armando Marsans (who had jumped from the Reds to the Feds) to join the Cardinals. Huggins was not successful but would manage Marsans (whom he had played against in 1908 exhibition games in Cuba) on the Yankees in 1918.

26. F. C. Lane, "'Pol' Perritt, Pitcher," 29.

27. "Mound City Writers Give Praise to Huggins as He Goes," *Sporting News*, November 1, 1917. Robert Hedges, the owner of the St. Louis Browns, did react to raids on his team by renegotiating contracts, and he prided himself on not losing a single player to the Federal League.

28. Miller Huggins, "Serial Story of His Baseball Career: Woman Owner Wants to Help but Isn't Wised Up on National Game," *San Francisco Chronicle*, chapter 42, March 1, 1924.

29. Bescher and Huggins had been teammates on the 1908–9 Reds. Bescher led the National League in stolen bases four straight seasons, including 1911, when he stole eighty-one. That stood as the National League record for more than a half-century, until Maury Wills broke it in 1962.

30. Huggins signed a three-year contract for $25,000 (total). When he became manager, his annual salary went from $4,000 to $6,000. The Cardinals saved a significant amount of money when they replaced Bresnahan, who had been under contract for $10,000 a year. *Sporting Life*, November 19, 1912, and March 20, 1915.

31. "Kept in the Old League by the Energetic Little Manager, Miller Huggins," *Sporting Life*, December 11, 1915. She did not sell to Ball, and under the terms of the settlement for the end of the Federal League, Ball bought the American League's St. Louis Browns instead. The owner of the Federal League's Chicago Whales, Phil Weeghman, bought the Chicago Cubs, too. They relocated to Weeghman Park, which is now known as Wrigley Field.

32. *Sporting News*, January 19, 1963, as cited in Alexander, *Rogers Hornsby*, 19.

33. George A. Barton, "Uncovering Stars with Famed Scout Connery," *Sporting News*, November 26, 1947. Cardinals scouts Dick Kinsella and Bill Armour had quit in support of Roger Bresnahan when he was fired. *Sporting News*, November 26, 1947.

34. Kelley managed St. Paul and Minneapolis teams for thirty seasons. Connery credited Kelley with helping him secure the scout's position in St. Louis.

35. Ford Frick, "The Life Story of Miller Huggins: Huggins Brought Hornsby to Big League Greatness," *New York Evening Journal*, chapter 4, September 30, 1929.

36. Miller Huggins, "Serial Story of His Baseball Career: Woman Owner Wants to Help," *San Francisco Chronicle*, chapter 48, March 8, 1924. Cubs owner Weeghman was an early bidder for Hornsby, at one point offering $75,000 to the cash-strapped Cardinals.

37. Sid Keener, On the Side Line, *St. Louis Times*, July 3, 1916.

38. It is not known how much Huggins had paid out and whether he was reimbursed, but his generosity has been confirmed by multiple accounts in St. Louis. See "Mound City Writers Give Huggins High Praise as He Goes," *Sporting News*, November 1, 1917, and Sid Keener, On the Side Line, *St. Louis Times*, June 22, 1920.

39. "The Change Huggins Makes," *Sporting News*, November 1, 1917.

40. Unlike many baseball tales, which may actually be myths, this one was described in a number of contemporary papers. See, for example, "Appleton 'Falls for' Ripped Ball Talk and Throws Away Final Game of Series," *New York World*, August 8, 1915. See also Edwin A. Goewey, "The Old Fan Says," *Leslie's Illustrated Weekly*, August 26, 1915, 210. Goewey said that such trickery was "cheating pure and simple" and that the league's president should nullify the game and order it replayed.

41. E-mail from Bill Deane to Steve Steinberg, June 17, 2012. Steinberg had recently come across two of those eight incidents, looking at newspaper accounts of Huggins's Cincinnati years.

42. Harold Lanigan, "Stove League Fuel," *Sporting News*, November 21, 1912.

43. Neither Steve Evans nor Rebel Oakes, prominent leaders of the Fed's recruitment efforts, ever played another Major League game. Lee Magee was purchased by the Yankees in early 1916, one of the new owners' early major cash outlays ($22,500). He did not come close to replicating the success he had in St. Louis and the Federal League.

44. Paul Sallee and Eric Sallee, "Slim Sallee," *Deadball Stars of the National League*, 346. Sallee won almost half of his decisions with the Cardinals, though the team won barely 40 percent of their games and still has the lowest earned run average in team history (1,000 or more innings), 2.67.

45. John McGraw, "McGraw Sizing Up Teams in His Review," *New York Evening World*, June 19, 1916, and Miller Huggins, "How Managers Win," 40.

46. "Huggins May Capture Pennant, but Not in 1915," *St. Louis Post-Dispatch*, June 23, 1915, and "McGraw Praises Huggins; Brainy Manager, He Says," *St. Louis Globe-Democrat*, March 7, 1915.

47. *Chicago Daily News*, April 26, 1919, and *Sporting News*, December 13, 1917.

48. John B. Sheridan, "Miller Huggins, a Lawyer," a 1917 article in the Huggins file at the University of Cincinnati Archives.

49. Billy Murphy, "Mound City Writers Give High Praise to Huggins as He Goes," *Sporting News*, November 1, 1917.

50. H. Perry Lewis, "Huggins Lawyer First, Now an Ardent Student of Baseball," *Philadelphia Public Ledger*, July 25, 1915.

51. Miller Huggins, "Serial Story of His Baseball Career: Huggins Modeled Game on Biddy McPhee's Style," *San Francisco Chronicle*, chapter 21, February 6, 1924.

52. "National League Notes," *Sporting Life*, July 3, 1909. At the height of the Federal League war, Huggins headed a group that included Connery, Kelley, and Cincinnati manager Buck Herzog that offered around $25,000 for the Buffalo club. *Sporting News*, December 17, 1914, and *St. Louis Post-Dispatch*, December 11, 1914. The attempted purchase of the Saints was reported in the *Sporting News*, January 7, 1915. Nothing came of these talks either, but ten years later Huggins and Connery did buy the Saints.

53. As told by Bob Broeg, *Sporting News*, July 29, 1978. Sportswriter Bill Slocum also reported that Huggins wanted to own a Major League club. *New York American*, October 4, 1929.

54. Initially, the ownership group was extremely fragmented and thus unwieldy. Many fans bought one or two shares in the team at $25 each. It was not until December 1919 that one investor, Sam Breadon, emerged to consolidate a large block of stock. Lieb, *The St. Louis Cardinals*, 76.

55. Thomas, *Baseball's First Lady*, 110–11, and an e-mail from Joan Thomas to Steve Steinberg, July 24, 2012. The admission of youngsters, which became known as the "Knothole Gang," was an idea that preceded the arrival of Rickey to the Cardinals.

56. Rickey was also interested in making a move; he did not get along with the Browns' new owner, Phil Ball. Rickey observed the Sabbath and was a tee-

totaler. When Ball met him for the first time, he greeted his manager with, "So you're the Goddamned prohibitionist!" Mann, *Branch Rickey*, 82.

57. The Reds bought Rickey's contact from Dallas of the Texas League in late August 1904. When he refused to play on Sundays for religious reasons, Reds manager Joe Kelley released him in early September before he had played a single game for the Reds. Lowenfish, *Branch Rickey*, 25–28.

58. "Rickey Disagrees with Huggins' Method of Managing Major League Baseball Clubs," *St. Louis Post-Dispatch*, December 21, 1913.

59. Sid Keener, "Why Did Miller Huggins Quit the Cardinals?" *St. Louis Times*, October 29, 1917. The relations between Huggins and Rickey were strained during their season together, and Keener went so far as to call them bitter enemies.

60. Lieb, *The St. Louis Cardinals*, 69.

5. How about the Yankees?

1. Di Salvatore, *A Clever Base-Ballist*, 362.

2. William Lamb, "Andrew Freedman," SABR BioProject, sabr.org/bio project.

3. *Sporting Life*, September 30, 1899, as cited in Lamb, "Andrew Freedman."

4. Frank O'Neill, "Col. Ruppert Reviews Fads," *New York Sun & Globe*," February 2, 1924.

5. Colonel Jacob Ruppert, as told to Daniel, "Behind the Scenes of the Yankees: Ruppert Tells of Early Bid for Giants," *New York World-Telegram*, February 14, 1938, and Official Souvenir Program, Opening Day, Yankee Stadium, April 18, 1923.

6. O'Neill, "Col. Ruppert Reviews Fads."

7. While most reports at the time said Brush paid $150,000 for the Giants, others put the price at $200,000. Moreover, Freedman's choice to sell to Brush rather than Ruppert may have been for reasons other than price.

8. Jacob Ruppert, *Out of the Past* radio program, seventy-first birthday appearance, August 5, 1938.

9. Smelser, *The Life That Ruth Built*, 123.

10. Ruppert, *Out of the Past*.

11. Colonel Jacob Ruppert, as told to Daniel, "Behind the Scenes of the Yankees: Ruppert Tells of Early Struggles," *New York World-Telegram*, February 15, 1938.

12. Graham, *The New York Yankees*, 23. Graham's book was published in 1943, five years after Ruppert's article appeared in the *New York World-Telegram*.

13. Creamer, *Baseball in '41*, 62.

14. Tofel, *A Legend in the Making*, 8.

15. Creamer, *Baseball in '41*, 62.

16. Tofel, *A Legend in the Making*, 8.

17. Appel, *Pinstripe Empire*, 73.

18. *New York Tribune*, December 12, 1922; *New York World-Telegram*, March 29, 1938; *Sporting* News, April 7, 1938; and *New York American*, 1928, undated clipping from the *New York Journal-American* morgue housed at the Briscoe Center for American History, University of Texas at Austin.

19. Taft had bought out Charles Murphy in early 1914 and was now selling the club.

20. Joe Vila, "Wanted the Cubs," *Sporting Life*, January 16, 1915. At the time, Taft was also negotiating with Charles Weeghman, the owner of the Chicago Federal League team, who eventually did buy the Cubs more than a year later.

21. Glenn Stout and Richard Johnson use the phrase "curious ally" in suggesting John McGraw was helping Ban Johnson bring Ruppert and Huston to the Yankees because they both feared the Federal League entering the city. They wanted to shore up the American League team to prevent that from happening. Stout and Johnson, *Yankees Century*, 62.

22. Ruppert, *Out of the Past*.

23. Ruppert, "Behind the Scenes of the Yankees: Ruppert Tells of Early Struggles."

24. Freedman threatened to have a streetcar line run over second base at any prospective site.

25. Sante, *Low Life*, 248.

26. The club was known as the New York Highlanders or New York Americans in its first few years, but some newspapers began using the current name, Yankees, as early as 1904.

27. The Brooklyn National League club was known as the Superbas during the time Ned Hanlon managed the club (1899–1905). The name was a play on Hanlon's Superbas, a popular acrobatic troupe on the vaudeville circuit.

28. New York finished with a 72-62 record in 1903, seventeen games behind the pennant-winning Boston Americans, who then defeated the Pittsburgh Pirates in the first World Series between the National and American Leagues.

29. The Yankees' 103 losses in 1908 remains the club record.

30. On June 1, 1913, the Yankees traded Chase to the White Sox for first baseman Babe Borton and infielder Rollie Zeider. The *New York Globe*'s Mark Roth wrote in disgust: "[Manager Frank] Chance traded Chase for a bunion and an onion."

31. James R. Crowell, "Winning Yankee Team as Wartime Measure," *New York Evening Telegram*, December 17, 1914.

32. *St. Louis Times*, June 11, 1914.

6. The Rocky Road to Ownership

1. Ruppert, "Building a Winning Club in New York," 204.

2. James R. Crowell, "Winning Yankee Team as Wartime Measure," *New York Evening Telegram*, December 17, 1914.

3. Sid Mercer, *New York Globe and Commercial Advertiser*, May 31, 1918.

4. On February 4, 1915, the Yankees purchased first baseman Wally Pipp and outfielder Hugh High from the Detroit Tigers. They also secured the rights to Joe Berger from the Chicago White Sox, Elmer Miller from the St. Louis Cardinals, and Walter Rehg from the Boston Red Sox. Though it was not known at the time, the Yankees' new owners had actually negotiated Pipp's sale to New York a month earlier, at the same time they bought the team.

5. "Chief Devery Sells His Stock in Yankees," *New York Herald*, December 8, 1914.

6. Located in southern Indiana, the town of French Lick had been a vacation spot for the wealthy since the mid-nineteenth century. It was best known for its spa, which contained healing mineral waters.

7. "Yankees Have Not Been Sold—Yet," *New York World*, December 9, 1914.

8. "Ruppert Seeks New Yorks but Has New Rival," *New York Sun*, December 9, 1914.

9. "White Sox Buy Collins," *Baltimore Sun*, December 9, 1914. In the December 16, 1914, issue, *Sporting Life* wrote that "it is believed that the league made up the $50,000 difference between the price demanded and offered for the club." The *New York Sun* wrote that Ruppert would build a $500,000 stadium at Lenox Avenue and 145th Street.

10. "Ruppert Seeks New Yorks, but Has New Rival," *New York Sun*, December 9, 1914.

11. While McGraw was unrivaled in New York, Mack had been even more successful, with six pennants and three world championships to McGraw's five pennants and one world championship.

12. *New York Evening Telegram*, December 9, 1914.

13. "Johnson Remains to Close Sale of Club," *New York Sun*, December 13, 1914.

14. "Wants Five Players and a Live Manager," *New York Sun*, December 19, 1914.

15. Daniel M. Daniel, "Col. Jacob Ruppert, Lonely Bachelor Millionaire, Found Fun in Yanks, After Other Hobbies Palled," *Sporting News*, January 10, 1939.

16. Sid Mercer, "The Colonel," *New York Journal-American*, January 14, 1939.

17. *New York Sun*, December 21, 1914.

18. "Yanks' New Home May Be in Bronx," *Baltimore Evening Sun*, December 12, 1914.

19. "Ruppert and Huston Have Not Lost Hope," *New York World*, December 21, 1914.

20. Sid Mercer, All in a Day's Work, *New York Globe and Commercial Advertiser*, December 28, 1914.

21. "Transfer of Yankee Stock to Be Completed Here," *New York Herald*, December 23, 1914.

22. The tentative agreement reached on the final day of 1914 did not prevent negotiations from continuing into the new year.

23. *Sporting Life*, February 6, 1915.

24. *Reach Official American League Guide, 1915*, 11.

25. Jacob Ruppert, "How I Broke into Baseball," *New York World Magazine*, March 28, 1915.

7. New Owners Get to Work

1. *New York Times*, January 31, 1915.

2. Clifton, *The German-Americans in Politics, 1914–1917*, 53.

3. *New Yorker Herald*, as quoted in "German Editors Here Rail at the President," *New York Sun*, February 13, 1915.

4. The German embassy in America had placed a newspaper advertisement warning people not to sail on the *Lusitania*.

5. The Kaiser had declared the North Sea a war zone in February 1915, but Germany did not start unrestricted submarine (U-boat) warfare until early 1917.

6. Appel, *Pinstripe Empire*, 74.

7. *New Yorker Staats-Zeitung*, quoted in Henderson, *Tammany Hall and the New Immigrants*, 172.

8. Huston to Johnson, telegram, January 11, 1915, Documents from Ruppert Estate, lot 51, Goldin Auctions, July 19, 2014.

9. Haupert and Winter, "Yankees Profits and Promise," 199–200.

10. John Kieran, Sports of the Times, "The Man in the Iron Hat," *New York Times*, March 30, 1938.

11. Lieb, *Baseball as I Have Known It*, 268. In 1946, the New York Knickerbockers basketball team came into existence without any complaints from the New York newspapers.

12. Huston to Ruppert, February 12, 1918, Colonel Til Huston Papers in the Robert Edwards Auctions, May 18, 2013, auction.

13. W. J. Macbeth, "Formal Transfer of the New York Club," *Sporting Life*, February 6, 1915.

14. "Ruppert Finally Buys Yanks," *New York World*, January 1, 1915.

15. Bozeman Bulger, *New York Evening World*, October 20, 1916.

16. Huston did not specify what he meant by "exhibition scheme," but it may have been his plan to stage other events beside baseball in the park they would build.

17. *New York Press*, February 29, 1916.

18. "Transfer of Yankee Stock to Be Completed Here," *New York Herald*, December 23, 1914.

19. P. T. Knox, "'Up to Donovan Now,' Says Captain Huston," *New York Evening Telegram*, January 12, 1915.

20. Like every previous Yankees manager except Stallings, Donovan assumed the role of player-manager. Although he had not pitched in the Major Leagues since 1912, he put himself into nine games in 1915, losing his only three decisions. He would pitch in one game in 1916, which would be the last time a Yankees' manager would play in a league game until Bill Dickey in 1946.

21. "Donovan Will Smile His Way to Success," *New York Sun*, January 3, 1915.

22. Heywood Broun, "Donovan Shies at the Series with Superbas," *New York Tribune*, January 15, 1915.

23. "Yanks Have Grand Chance to Win American Pennant, Says McGraw in Review," *New York Evening World*, July 5, 1916.

24. When Frank Chance managed the Yankees, he had complained about Irwin's scouting skills and asked that he be fired. Steve Steinberg, "Ray Caldwell," SABR BioProject, sabr.org/bioproject.

25. "Says the Yankees Are Not Hopeless," *Baltimore Evening Sun*, January 4, 1915.

26. James Isaminger, *Sporting Life*, January 23, 1915.

27. "Ray Caldwell Hops Back to New Yorks," *New York Sun*, January 7, 1915.

28. Bozeman Bulger, "Yanks Will Pay Caldwell $27,000 to Quit Federals," *St. Louis Post-Dispatch*, January 8, 1915. Despite the headline, Caldwell's salary was likely in the $8,000 to $9,000 range. Steinberg, "Ray Caldwell."

29. Haupert and Winter, "Yankees Profits and Promise," 199.

30. "How the Two Colonels Backed the Yankees," *Literary Digest*, January 13, 1923, 71.

31. Walter Johnson had been baseball's biggest off-season story when he signed to play for the Federal League's Chicago Whales in 1915. Senators president Benjamin Minor then made baseball's best pitcher a new offer, which caused Johnson to renege on his contract with Chicago and re-sign with Washington.

32. The 1915 Tigers won a hundred games, but finished second to the Red Sox.

33. Lyle Spatz, "Wally Pipp," SABR BioProject, sabr.org/bioproject.

34. New York had thirty-one home runs; runner-up Chicago had twenty-five. Roger Peckinpaugh and Lute Boone led the Yankees with five each.

8. Fritz Maisel Follies

1. Sparks, *Frank "Home Run" Baker*, 162.

2. King, "When Did Frank Baker Become 'Home Run' Baker?" 57.

3. Baker had also batted better than .300 in five of his six full seasons, including a .347 mark in 1912.

4. The following week, the Yankees purchased two other Federal League players controlled by Harry Sinclair: pitcher Nick Cullop from the Kansas City Packers, and second baseman Herman "Germany" Schaefer from the Newark Peppers. Cullop was among the league's better pitchers, going 22-11 in 1915, with an earned run average of 2.44. They also purchased Minor League second baseman Joe Gedeon, another player whose contract was controlled by Sinclair.

5. Magee's .323 batting average was second in the league, topped only by Brooklyn teammate Benny Kauff, who batted .342. In 1920 Magee admit-

ted he had been involved in deliberately trying to lose a game as a member of the 1918 Cincinnati Reds, and he was banned from Organized Baseball.

6. In the game of June 28, 1916, Magee had four outfield assists, tying the Major League record.

7. Armando Marsans played twelve seasons (1904–15) in various Cuban and Negro Leagues and eight seasons (1911–18) in the Major Leagues.

8. The other two members of the $100,000 infield were first baseman Stuffy McInnis and shortstop Jack Barry.

9. *Baltimore Evening Sun*, February 22, 1916.

10. Ruppert's closest confidant was Albert Brennan, who had been his personal assistant at the brewery since 1911 and was later his executive secretary and the team's treasurer. However, he was not a "baseball man."

11. "White Sox Want Maisel," *New York Times*, February 17, 1916.

12. Pants Rowland failed to get Maisel or any of the other third basemen he sought. The manager finally found his new third baseman playing shortstop on his own team. Rowland moved Buck Weaver, his shortstop for the past four seasons, to third base in 1916, and Weaver remained there until his career ended following the 1920 season.

13. Maisel would break his collarbone in May and appear in just fifty-three games for the Yankees in 1916.

14. Spatz, "Fritz Maisel for Joe Jackson?"

15. Sam Crane, "Maisel More Valuable Player than Jackson," *New York Evening Journal*, February 19, 1916.

16. Walter St. Denis, "Local Magnates Are Making Good on Promise to Rehabilitate the Yankees," *New York Globe and Commercial Adviser*, February 17, 1916.

17. "Yanks May Close Deal with Red Sox for Tris Speaker," *New York Evening Journal*, April 7, 1916.

18. Speaker's comment is instructive for those fans who think the lack of so-called loyalty to a team is exclusive to modern-day players.

19. Nowadays the press and the teams would also use a Sabermetric value, like Wins Above Replacement (WAR), to compare the two players. WAR purports to measure the number of Wins a player would add to the team above what a bench player or high Minor Leaguer would add. Maisel's WAR value was 3.5 in both 1914 and 1915. Jackson's was 4.6 in 1914 and 2.6 in 1915. Tris Speaker's was 10.0 in 1914 and 7.1 in 1915. For 1916 Speaker's WAR value was 8.6; Jackson's, 7.1; and Maisel's, -0.3. After 1916 Maisel's

career WAR would total 0.6. From 1917 to 1920 Jackson's WAR would total 20.2, and Speaker's would total 27.0 and would be huge in the following few years. The WAR data is from Baseball Reference's most recent update. www.baseball-reference.com.

20. Frederick G. Lieb, "Shift of Star to Yankees Blocked in Indians' Favor, Indications Point to Ban Johnson's Decreeing Transfer of Tris Speaker to Cleveland Club," *New York Press*, April 9, 1916. Even without Speaker, the Red Sox were good enough to win the 1916 pennant and defeat Brooklyn in the World Series.

21. P. T. Knox, "'Help Weaker Clubs' Is Now the Slogan in 'Ban' Johnson's Baseball Organization," *New York Evening Telegram*, April 10, 1916.

22. Sid Mercer, All in a Day's Work, *New York Globe and Commercial Advertiser*, April 10, 1916. The price Cleveland paid for Speaker was actually $55,000.

23. Dan Daniel, *New York Herald*, October 1, 1920.

24. Despite Lieb's claim, Markle's pitching skills by no means vanished. He continued to be very successful in the Minor Leagues, and when the Yankees were desperate for pitching in 1924, they reacquired him from St. Paul of the American Association. He spent a month in New York, going 0-3. Frederick G. Lieb, "Eight Players Are Released by Yanks," *New York Sun*, January 1, 1920.

25. All purchase prices are from the Yankees' player index cards at the National Baseball Hall of Fame and were supplied by Daniel R. Levitt.

26. Sam Murphy, *New York Evening Mail*, June 7, 1920.

9. Anti-German Hysteria

1. "Col. Ruppert a Real Casey," *New York Evening Mail*, March 22, 1916.

2. Smith, *Beer in America*, 153.

3. The multifaceted Fultz was also at various times the head football coach at the University of Missouri, Lafayette College, Brown University, and a baseball coach at the United States Naval Academy, Columbia University, and New York University.

4. "Ruppert Answers Charges of Fultz," *New York Times*, December 7, 1916.

5. Cole, who won only two games in 1915, died of cancer in January 1916.

6. "Charges Are Not Based on Fact, Says Yank Owner," *New York Evening Telegram*, December 7, 1916.

7. The Yankees' major injuries in 1916: mid-May, Fritz Maisel broke his collarbone going for a sinking line drive; early July, Frank Gilhooley broke his ankle; mid-July, Frank Baker broke several ribs going for a foul ball; mid-July, Nick Cullop tore a muscle on his stomach; Ray Caldwell was hit in the knee by a line drive. These and George Mogridge's injured elbow were the major injuries. Many other players had lesser ones.

8. Joe Vila, *New York Evening Sun*, September 25, 1916.

9. Damon Runyon, Th' Mornin's Mornin', *New York American*, February 24, 1917.

10. War was not declared against Austria-Hungary until December 7, 1917.

11. W. J. Macbeth, "In All Fairness," *New York Tribune*, April 1, 1918.

12. "Cobb Presses Speaker for Batting Honors," *New York Evening Journal*, June 8, 1917.

13. After the season, the Yankees included Nunamaker in the multi-player trade with the St. Louis Browns for Del Pratt.

14. Sid Mercer, "Col. Ruppert Ready to Shake Up Yankees," *New York Globe and Commercial Advertiser*, August 27, 1917.

15. "Yanks May Get Walter Johnson in Big Trade," *New York American*, August 27, 1917. Of course the Washington franchise would not be moved for another forty-three years, and then not to Baltimore but to Minnesota. In 1954, the struggling St. Louis Browns would move to Baltimore.

16. W. S. Farnsworth, "Donovan to Remain as Pilot," *New York American*, August 28, 1917.

17. Jacob Ruppert, "The Ten Million Dollar Toy," 116 and 119.

18. Jacob Ruppert, "Building a Winning Club in New York," 203–4.

19. Sam Crane, "Yanks Handicapped in Effort to Make Deal," *New York Evening Journal*, December 31, 1917.

20. Higham, *Stranger in the Land*, 196.

21. Ellis, *Echoes of Distant Thunder*, 170–71. This newspaper deal followed on the heels of the sale of the *New York Evening Mail* to a pro-German newspaperman in 1915.

22. Holland, "The Beer Barons of New York," 405.

23. A. Mitchell Palmer was alien property custodian from October 1917 until March 1919 and President Woodrow Wilson's attorney general from 1919 to 1921. He used the latter office to conduct raids against what he saw as communist and anarchist threats to the country.

24. Christopher Gray, "A Park Ave. Mansion Built with Beer," *New York Times*, July 17, 2005.

25. Ruppert, "The Ten Million Dollar Toy," 18.

10. Impatient City, Unforgiving Press

1. Huggins recognized the importance of money in building a winner in his February 1917 article in *Baseball Magazine*, "How Managers Win."

2. Hochschild, *To End All Wars*, 310 and 331.

3. The amendment passed both houses of Congress on December 18, 1917. It would be ratified on January 16, 1919, when the thirty-sixth of the country's forty-eight states approved it. The separate Volstead Act then provided enforcement details, including the definition of "intoxicating liquors" (any beverage with more than 0.5 percent alcohol) and exclusions to the amendment, such as religious and medical uses of alcohol.

4. For an overview of the ASL, see Daniel Okrent, *Last Call*, 34–42 and 57–65.

5. Asinof, *1919*, 236.

6. Sullivan, *Our Times*, 4:210.

7. *New York Times*, March 22, 1918.

8. *New York Globe and Commercial Advertiser*, as quoted in *Current Opinion*, "New York Scolded for Its Moral and Other Shortcomings," April 1920, 523–24.

9. Frederick G. Lieb, *New York Sun*, March 31, 1918.

10. Right Cross, "Injury Jinx Hands Yanks Severe Jolt," *New York Evening Journal*, July 19, 1916.

11. Myrtle Huggins, "Mighty Midget," 18. Huggins was not starting in the "cellar." The 1917 Yankees had finished in sixth place.

12. Miller Huggins, "Serial Story of His Baseball Career: Getting New York Angle Huggins' Biggest Problem at Start of Managership," *San Francisco Chronicle*, chapter 50, March 11, 1924.

13. Miller Huggins, "Serial Story of His Baseball Career: Duffy Lewis Acquisition Added New Life to Yankees," *San Francisco Chronicle*, chapter 53, March 14, 1924, and *New York Globe and Commercial Advertiser*, February 18, 1918.

14. Sam Crane, "Yanks Must Show 'Pep' to Suit Huggins," *New York Evening Journal*, March 11, 1918. See also Sid Mercer, "Can He 'Color' the Yankees?" *New York Globe and Commercial Advertiser*, January 7, 1918.

15. On January 22, 1918, the Yankees sent pitchers Nick Cullop and Urban Shocker, catcher Les Nunamaker, infielders Joe Gedeon and Fritz Maisel, and $15,000 to St. Louis for Pratt and future Hall of Fame pitcher Eddie Plank. Pratt had an "off" season in 1917, hampered by a broken wrist. The previous four years he had proven to be an iron man, averaging 157 games played a year (including tie games). The forty-two-year-old Plank chose to retire rather than report. Other than Shocker, the players dealt to the Browns contributed little after the trade.

16. Bozeman Bulger, "Ability to See Young Prospects Made Huggins Great Manager," *Atlanta Constitution*, October 1, 1929.

17. Ruppert, "Building a Winning Club in New York," 204.

18. Browns owner Phil Ball had accused Pratt and teammate Johnny Lavan of "laying down" on the team during the 1917 season, a euphemism for not trying and even worse. There was no question about the players' honesty. The men settled their lawsuit out of court. See Steve Steinberg, "Del Pratt," SABR BioProject, Sabr.org/bioproject.

19. Graham, "The Little Miller," 378, and Joe Vila, Setting the Pace, *New York Sun*, December 13, 1928. Originally pitcher Ray Fisher was in the deal, but when he entered the armed forces, Shocker was substituted.

20. Huggins had expressed concern about Caldwell, but decided to give the pitcher, who led the team in wins in 1914, 1915, and 1917, a chance. Monitor, "Huggins Declares He'll Not Trade Ray Caldwell," *New York World*, February 9, 1918. See also Steinberg, "Ray Caldwell," SABR BioProject, Sabr.org/bioproject.

21. "O'Connor Signed to Coach Yanks," *New York Sun*, February 3, 1918. The 1914 Cardinals' pitching staff had a 2.38 earned run average, well below the league average of 2.78. O'Connor also served as a backup catcher for that team.

22. "Yankees Seeking to Pluck the Georgia Peach," *New York Times*, February 16, 1918, and "Huggins Is Determined to Add a Powerful Batter to Roster," *New York Times*, February 18, 1918. Huggins also explored the possibility of acquiring one of the other Detroit outfielders, Harry Heilmann or Bobby Veach.

23. "'Shoeless' Joe Jackson, White Sox Star, Sought by Yankees," *Warren* [PA] *Evening Times*, February 20, 1918.

24. Born Francesco Stephano Pezzolo, Bodie ended up with the last name of a California mining town in which his father had worked. See Baldassaro, *Beyond DiMaggio*, 29–34.

25. The five foot eight, 195-pound Bodie had twice finished third in the American League in home runs. He hit thirty home runs for the San Francisco Seals of the PCL in 1910.

26. Harry Schumacher, "Ping Bodie Brings Powerful Bat and Some Much Needed Color to the Yanks," *New York Globe and Commercial Advertiser*, March 8, 1918, and Schumacher, "Huggins Has Choice of Nine Candidates in Reorganizing Yankee Outfield Works," March 9, 1918. While Bodie was colorful, he had limited baseball skills and thus never attained the rank of a full-fledged star.

27. During 1919 spring training in Florida, W. O. McGeehan of the *New York Tribune* (April 5–6, 1919) described a spaghetti-eating contest between Bodie and an ostrich named Percy. Bodie was declared the winner after downing his eleventh bowl of pasta and Percy collapsed after eating his tenth dish. Many papers and books have accepted this event as real. It apparently never happened. There were no other firsthand accounts of this major event—supposedly promoted by the St. Petersburg Chamber of Commerce—in other New York papers or in the St. Petersburg press. The story was believable because Bodie was such a character. McGeehan was known for his wry sense of humor.

28. Ping Bodie, as quoted in Robert Ripley, *New York Globe and Commercial Advertiser*, June 14, 1918.

29. Sid Mercer, "The Supreme Value of 'Color' in Baseball," 424.

30. Sam Crane, "Yanks Must Show 'Pep' to Suit Huggins," *New York Evening Journal*, March 11, 1918.

31. George Daley, Comment on Sports, *New York World*, April 14, 1919.

32. *New York Times*, February 5, 1918.

33. Sid Mercer, *New York Globe and Commercial Advertiser*, April 15 and 16, 1918. Fred Lieb used that phrase later that season, too. *New York Sun*, June 23, 1918. This was two years before Babe Ruth joined the Yankees.

34. Sam Crane, "Hard-Hitting Yankees Open Season at Home against Senators," *New York Evening Journal*, April 24, 1918.

35. Frederick G. Lieb, "Huggins Adopted Slugging Game When He Came to Yanks," *New York Evening Telegram*, August 19, 1923.

36. Sam Crane, *New York Evening Journal*, July 6, 1918. One of the first rules Huggins announced was a ban on smoking—in the clubhouse and on the field.

37. Miller Huggins, "Huggins, Manager of a Million Dollar Franchise," *St. Louis Times*, May 17, 1919.

38. Hugh Fullerton, "Fullerton Lauds Huggins: Yanks Big Factor in Race," *New York American*, March 11, 1918.

39. Damon Runyon, Th' Mornin's Mornin', *New York Evening Journal*, April 5, 1918.

40. In *Baseball: The Golden Age*, Seymour and Seymour noted that while the auto and the cinema were entertainment alternatives to baseball, they were ultimately beneficial for and contributors to the success of the National Pastime (40–47).

41. Lears, *Rebirth of a Nation*, 339–47.

42. For a discussion of how the war affected the 1918 season, see Steve Steinberg, "World War I and Free Agency," and Charles DeMotte, "How World War I Nearly Brought Down Professional Baseball."

43. The shortened 1918 season had about 20 percent fewer games than 1917, but the drop in attendance was twice as great.

44. Joe Vila, "Joe Vila Draws a Limit on Some Baseball Reformers," *Sporting News*, October 24, 1918.

45. "Ruppert Strongly Opposed to Plan Proposed by Johnson," *New York American*, November 23, 1917, and Frederick G. Lieb, *New York Sun*, November 23, 1917.

46. Jacob Ruppert, *New York American*, May 24, 1918.

47. "Capt. Huston Calls for Baseball to Do More for the Cause," *New York World*, March 24, 1918. Huston felt that at least 25 percent of the World Series proceeds should have been donated, rather than the minuscule amount that was given. He also called the Series a "financial orgy." Huston was an army captain when he enlisted in the Great War. He recruited and then led the Sixteenth Regiment of Engineers in France. General Pershing promoted him to the rank of colonel before the end of the war.

48. Dan Daniel, High Lights and Shadows in All Spheres of Sport, *New York Sun*, July 22, 1918.

49. Huggins had turned forty that spring. The first draft of June 1917 called up men from ages twenty-one through thirty.

50. Stout and Johnson, *Yankee Century*, 73–74, and *Red Sox Century*, 138–39.

51. *New York Evening Journal*, December 17 and 19, 1918.

52. Irving E. Sanborn, *Spalding Official Baseball Guide 1919*, 131.

53. Shawkey would average twenty-nine starts and thirty-nine appearances in his eight full seasons with the Yankees between 1916 and 1924. In 1918, he had two and three, respectively. Shawkey's two 1918 starts came on days off from the navy. After he shut out Washington

and moved the Yankees to within a game of first place, Shawkey was assigned to sea duty.

54. Murdock, *Baseball Players and Their Times*, 30.

55. Craig Wright, "Bender's Comeback Season of 1917," *A Page from Baseball's Past*, August 23, 2013. While he never again appeared in the Major Leagues, he pitched for Richmond of the Virginia League in 1919, where he had a 29-2 record with a 1.06 earned run average.

56. Montville, *The Big Bam*, 69.

57. Sam Crane, *New York Evening Journal*, May 6, 1918. Crane hit three career home runs in the 1880s. Ruth's home run output in 1918 had a strange timeline: he did not hit one after June 30.

58. The following day, May 7, Ruth hit another home run, off Walter Johnson. Johnson led the league with a 1.27 earned run average that year. He gave up only two home runs—both to Ruth.

59. Shocker pitched a twelve-inning complete-game win at the Polo Grounds and, three days later, retired the Yankees in the ninth to preserve another win. He struck out Pratt to end that game. Two days after this 1–0 loss, he again beat New York.

60. Miller Huggins, "Serial Story of His Baseball Career: Duffy Lewis' Acquisition Added New Life to Yankees in 1918," *San Francisco Chronicle*, chapter 53, March 14, 1924.

61. *Sporting News*, August 15, 1918. Rosters also included youngsters not yet ready for big league ball. They included a young pitcher who had played briefly for the Yankees in 1915 and would not win his first game until seven years later, Dazzy Vance. He would go on to a Hall of Fame career with Brooklyn.

62. The complicated dispute is examined in Steinberg's "World War One and Free Agency."

63. Joe Vila, "He Is the Man of the Hour in Gotham," *Sporting News*, June 6, 1918.

64. Joe Vila, "Gotham Knockers Turn on Yankees," *Sporting News*, August 29, 1918.

65. Joe Vila, "Joe Vila in Real Form and Puts Everybody on the Pan," *Sporting News*, August 22, 1918.

66. Grantland Rice, "Hug's New Post Full of Trials," *Cincinnati Post*, October 30, 1917.

67. Istorico, *Greatness in Waiting*, 190, 193.

68. W. S. Farnsworth, "Caldwell, Walters, Love, and Gilhooley to Join Red Sox," *New York American*, December 19, 1918.

11. Nation in Upheaval

1. While the pandemic is known as the "Spanish flu," it did not originate there. A global epidemic is known as a pandemic.
2. Barry, *The Great Influenza*, 239, 302, and 337. Barry wrote that the ships transporting troops became "floating caskets" (306).
3. Barry, *The Great Influenza*, 209–27 and 329.
4. Barry, *The Great Influenza*, 225.
5. Barry, *The Great Influenza*, 331. Katherine and Ira Thomas survived the epidemic. She lived until 1948, and he died ten years later.
6. Barry, *The Great Influenza*, 397. Americans deaths from the influenza epidemic exceeded all American combat deaths of the twentieth century. A most unusual aspect of the disease was that more than half of its victims were between the ages of sixteen and forty, not the very young and the elderly. Another, milder wave of the disease came later in 1919 and continued into early 1920.
7. O'Loughlin was an active American League umpire. Chappell was the "player to be named later" in the February 1916 Joe Jackson trade, coming to the Indians from the White Sox.
8. Major League attendance rose from just over three million in 1918 to six and a half million in 1919. The Yankees' attendance also more than doubled in 1919. The shortened 1919 season rebounded to the attendance of the full 1916 season.
9. Allen, *The Big Change*, 132.
10. Clark, *The World of Damon Runyon*, 48.
11. Ratification by thirty-six of the forty-eight states met the 75 percent requirement. On that day, five states ratified it. The war had added arguments on Prohibition's behalf: keeping the fighting and work forces sober and allowing grain to be directed to the war effort.
12. On January 6, 1920, just days before Prohibition was to go into effect, the Supreme Court ruled that Congress had the power to pass the Volstead Act. The decision stated that whether or not a higher alcohol content was intoxicating was irrelevant. In *Jacob Ruppert vs. Caffey* [Caffey was the U.S. attorney for the Southern District of New York], Justice Louis Brandeis wrote the majority opinion. Brandeis has come under attack for

his decision and the resultant infringement on civil liberties of enforcement. But his latest biographer, Melvin Urofsky, explained the justice's thinking. "In a democracy the people governed, and if occasionally they made the wrong choice, then the country would have to live with it, until a majority chose another path. The people had spoken, whether wisely or not." *Louis Brandeis: A Life*, 621. Ruppert's case was "fast-tracked" through the courts. K. Jacob Ruppert, "In Re John Barleycorn: NYCLA's Role in the Repeal of Prohibition."

13. "Real Beer Goes on Sale Today to Druggists" *New York Tribune*, October 26, 1921.

14. Sunday baseball was legalized in the Midwest in the early twentieth century. The battles took longer in the East, with Pennsylvania not legalizing it until 1933.

15. Sunday, "Keep the Sabbath Undefiled," as quoted in Bevis, *Sunday Baseball*, 178.

16. Editorial, *Baseball Magazine*, May 1921, 554.

17. For analysis of the connection between Prohibition and anti-German war sentiment, see Lerner, *Dry Manhattan*, 30–32, and Furnas, *Great Times*, 274–75.

18. Newsreels became an integral part of the motion-picture experience. As with newspaper coverage after the war, these films made sports coverage, especially baseball, a big part of the cinema.

19. Undated *Variety* articles, http://fultonhistory.com/Fulton.html. Film Clearing House distributed a number of films in 1918 and 1919, including the Jack Dempsey–Jess Willard heavyweight championship fight. Little is known about Ruppert's involvement in the company.

20. "Ruppert Bids for Sunday Baseball," *New York Times*, November 3, 1917.

21. DeMotte, *Bat, Ball, and Bible*, 91.

22. "Browns Beat Yankees in Benefit Game for Engineers," *New York Times*, June 18, 1917.

23. Clark, *The World of Damon Runyon*, 231–32. Boxing had been banned in 1917 and became legal again in early 1920, with passage of the Walker Law.

24. The first Sunday game ever played at the Polo Grounds was a Yankees-Giants exhibition game played for the benefit of the *Titanic* survivors on Sunday, April 21, 1912. "14,083 Fans See Game for Charity," *New York Times*, April 22, 1912.

25. *New York World* and *New York American*, May 5, 1919.

26. Fetter, *Taking on the Yankees*, 71.

27. "Facts Bearing on the Financial Aspects of a New Park for the 'Yankees' Base Ball Club in New York City," Colonel Til Huston Papers in the Robert Edwards Auctions, May 18, 2013 auction. The analysis showed that while the club had an average weekday attendance of 6,495 fans from 1915 to 1920, it averaged 21,115 on Sundays in 1919 and 1920.

28. Thomas, *Walter Johnson*, 157–58.

29. Johnson's biographer and grandson, Henry W. Thomas, calls this game one of his greatest. *Walter Johnson*, 158 and 355.

30. "Yankees and Washington Again Fail to Reach Decision in Long Drawn Game," *New York Times*, May 12, 1919.

31. Davis, *Papa Bear*, 49.

32. Halas, *Halas by Halas*, 48.

12. Season of Transition

1. The ball had traveled more than 500 feet. Meany, *Babe Ruth*, 34–36.

2. Sobol, *Babe Ruth & the American Dream*, 91.

3. Daniel, *The Real Babe Ruth*, 37–38. John McGraw called Ruth's April 4 blast the longest hit he ever saw or expected to see. McGraw, *My Thirty Years in Baseball*, 183–84.

4. "Equals World's Record," *Baltimore Sun*, April 19, 1919, and "Six Homers in a Row," *Baltimore Sun*, April 20, 1919.

5. James J. Corbett, Corbett's Corner, *New York American*, July 24, 1918. Corbett was boxing's world heavyweight champion from 1892 to 1897.

6. The blast cleared the right-field roof and landed in adjacent Manhattan Field, site of an earlier Polo Grounds. Ned Williamson's 1884 mark was set in a small Chicago ballpark. The dimensions of Lakeshore Park were 186 feet in left field, 300 feet in center field, and 190 feet in right field. Ruth hit one more to finish 1919 with an almost incomprehensible twenty-nine home runs. He also led the league in runs batted in (not an official statistic until the following year) and two more recent offensive measures, on-base percentage and slugging percentage.

7. Hoyt later said of this game, "I had my first lesson in the cost of playing with the world's greatest ball player." Hoyt, *Babe Ruth as I Knew Him*, 7. Hoyt had signed with the New York Giants at the age of fifteen.

8. *New York Times*, March 16, 1919, as quoted in Sparks, *Frank "Home Run" Baker*, 203.

9. Their Murderers' Row was very effective in 1919: Baker had ten home runs, Pipp, Peckinpaugh, and Lewis each hit seven, Bodie hit six, and Pratt had four. The Red Sox got only four home runs from players other than Ruth and finished far behind the Yankees with thirty-three.

10. John B. Sheridan, the *Sporting News* columnist, was from St. Louis, where he had organized and managed that top sandlot team, the Wabadas.

11. Sammy Vick, the right fielder, hit .248 in his only season as a regular. Duffy Lewis was the third regular outfielder. Another Yankee right fielder, George Halas, appeared in only twelve games.

12. There are no "Caught Stealing" records for 1919. But in 1920 Bodie stole six bases and was caught stealing fourteen times.

13. Hyatt Daab, Timely News and Views in the World of Sport, *New York Evening Telegram*, October 26, 1920.

14. Owens reversed his ninth-inning call after consulting with umpire Bill Dinneen and ruled that Washington's Patsy Gharrity had successfully stolen home.

15. *St. Louis Star*, July 17, 1917. On May 15, 1912, Ty Cobb had a notorious incident when he climbed into the stands and attacked a fan who had been berating him. The fan turned out to have been severely disabled.

16. Okkonen, *The Ty Cobb Scrapbook*, 137.

17. Shirley Povich, July 19, 1961, column, in Povich, *All Those Mornings at the Post*, 210.

18. Today 1919 is recognized as Cobb's eleventh title. At the time, he was considered to have won the 1910 batting race. Only years later did a correction of Cobb's hits total give the 1910 title to Cleveland's Napoleon Lajoie.

19. Damon Runyon, "Ruth Greatest Showman in All Sports," Babe Ruth Scrapbooks, National Baseball Hall of Fame Library and Archives.

20. Stump, *Cobb*, 288–89.

21. "Yanks Buy Babe Ruth for $125,000," *New York Times*, January 6, 1920.

22. *Detroit Free Press*, August 24, 1919; *Detroit News*, August 25, 1919; *Detroit Journal*, August 25, 1919.

23. New York sent Caldwell, pitcher Slim Love, catcher Roxy Walters, outfielder Frank Gilhooley, and $15,000 to Boston for pitchers Shore and Dutch Leonard and outfielder Lewis. Love would win only six more games, Walters would not hit above .201 the next four seasons, and Gilhooley would play only one more year.

24. "Lewis, Leonard, and Shore Come to the Yankees in Big Trade," *New York Herald*, December 19, 1918.

25. "Still a Clever Trader," *Sporting News*, December 26, 1918.

26. "Leonard Balks at Coming to Yankees," *New York Sun*, December 20, 1918. The Yankees sold Leonard to Detroit for $12,000, and the Red Sox returned $10,000 of the $25,000 they had received in the trade. John Sheridan wrote that a mere $1,000 separated Leonard and the Yankees in the contract dispute and that his loss probably cost the Yankees the 1919 pennant. Back of the Home Plate, January 1, 1920.

27. Lewis had remarkable success with Salt Lake City in the Pacific Coast League afterward. From 1921 to 1924 (the last three seasons as a player-manager), he played regularly and hit .403, .362, 358, and .392.

28. Frederick G. Lieb, "Yankees Fail to Get a Hit Off Ray Caldwell," *New York Sun*, September 11, 1919.

29. Lewis, *The Cleveland Indians*, 104–5. The contract required Caldwell to get drunk and then gradually prepare for his next start.

30. Sam Crane, *New York Evening Journal*, September 11, 1919.

31. John B. Sheridan, Back of the Home Plate, *Sporting News*, July 24, 1919. Sheridan felt that Huggins was sticking with Baker, Bodie, Lewis, and Pratt too long.

32. E-mails from Black Sox historian Gene Carney to Steve Steinberg, March 23 and 24, 2008. Carney discovered that Huggins had offered Jackson a five-year deal at $20,000 a year after the 1919 World Series, a year before the Black Sox "fix" was exposed. Huggins's offer was stricken from Jackson's 1924 trial record (his lawsuit for back pay against the White Sox), Carney suggested, so Huggins would not be charged with tampering.

33. W. S. Farnsworth, "Huggins' Mistakes Costly," *New York American*, August 12, 1919.

34. J. V. Fitz Gerald, "Robinson to Lead Yanks Is Latest Rumor," *Washington Post*, September 4, 1919.

35. *Chicago Daily News*, October 14, 1919. In "The Ten Million Dollar Toy," Ruppert said Huggins never had a formal contract after that first two-year deal. They had an understanding that Huggins would give him a two-year notice if he was going to leave.

36. "Robbie Decides He'll Stay with Ebbets," *Sporting News*, October 2, 1919.

37. Editorial, "No Glittering Knight Is Robbie," *Sporting News*, October 2, 1919. The editorial felt that Robinson did not command much more stature than Huggins did.

38. Hugh Fullerton, *Atlanta Constitution*, June 17, 1919, and Dan Daniel, "Hammer Throwers Are Out for Miller Huggins," *New York Sun*, August 1, 1919.

39. Damon Runyon, undated clipping from the *New York Journal-American* morgue housed at the Briscoe Center for American History, University of Texas at Austin.

40. Daniel, "Hammer Throwers Are Out for Miller Huggins."

41. Shortstop, "Huggins Fails to Snare Popularity," *New York Sun*, June 15, 1919.

42. Daniel, "Hammer Throwers Are Out for Miller Huggins."

43. Myrtle Huggins, "Mighty Midget," 31.

44. Eig, *Luckiest Man*, 42.

45. Sid Mercer, "Split-Up of World's Series 'Windfall' Does Not Suit Members of Huggins' Team," *New York Globe and Commercial Advertiser*, March 8, 1920. The Yankees had $13,000 to distribute. Pitchers Bob McGraw and Allan Russell, traded to the Red Sox midseason, were given full shares. Trainer Doc Woods, groundskeeper Phil Schenck, and two front-office men, Mark Roth and Charlie McManus, were given partial shares. The third-place money was not distributed until early 1920 because of a dispute discussed in the next chapter.

46. John Kieran, Sports of the Times, *New York Times*, June 17, 1929.

47. John B. Sheridan, Back of the Home Plate, *Sporting News*, April 15, 1920.

48. Jacob Ruppert, "President will Give Huggins Free Reign in Buying Players," *New York American*, January 5, 1919.

49. Miller Huggins, "Watch the Yankees Next Season," *New York Evening Telegram*, February 4, 1918.

13. Battle Leads to a War

1. Russell would win seventy games in an eleven-year career (1915–25), including the 1924–25 pennant-winning Washington Senators. McGraw would not win a game with Boston, and he resurfaced on the 1920 Yankees, where he also was winless.

2. Mays's earned run average of 2.47 in Boston was well below the league's 1919 average of 3.22.

3. Meany, *The Yankee Story*, 29–30.

4. When New York Justice Robert F. Wagner granted the Yankees a temporary injunction in the Mays case (see further), he included Hooper's testimony. Black Sox Scandal papers, Chicago History Museum. For some

reason, papers relating to the Wagner injunction rulings are in the Black Sox Scandal papers.

5. Seymour and Seymour, *Baseball: The Golden Age*, 264. In late May in Philadelphia, an angry Mays had thrown a ball at a fan in the stands and hit him in the head.

6. F. C. Lane, "A Startling Baseball Tragedy," 523.

7. On September 16, 1915, Cobb responded by throwing his bat at Mays. After order was restored, Mays hit the Tigers' star in the wrist. Years later, when Mays threw at him, Cobb bunted and went to first base with his spikes up and bloodied the leg of Mays, who was covering first on the play. Sowell, *The Pitch That Killed*, 15.

8. Tris Speaker, *Sporting News*, May 30, 1918. The men were teammates on the 1915 Red Sox. Mays led American League pitchers in Hit Batsmen in 1917 and was second in both 1918 and 1919.

9. F. C. Lane, "Carl Mays' Cynical Definition of Pitching Efficiency," 391.

10. Hal Lebovitz, "Carl Mays Interview," February 1961, Mays bio file, *Sporting News*.

11. Murdock, *Baseball between the Wars*, 34–36. Hoyt and Mays were roommates on the 1919 Red Sox, and Hoyt confirmed that Mays spoke of knocking men down. The Red Sox had just acquired Hoyt, which may have made Mays expendable.

12. J. G. Taylor Spink, *Judge Landis and Twenty-Five Years of Baseball*, 50.

13. Til Huston testimony, Mays injunction hearing, Chicago Black Sox Scandal papers, Chicago History Museum.

14. When Frazee bought the Red Sox, Sid Mercer wrote, "The suddenness of the transfer has rather shocked Ban Johnson." All in a Day's Work, *New York Globe and Commercial Advertiser*, November 3, 1916.

15. Murdock, *Ban Johnson*, 159.

16. "Huston Threatens to Wage War on Johnson Unless Suspension of Mays Is Lifted," *Washington Post*, August 2, 1919.

17. John Kieran, Sports of the Times, "The Man in the Iron Hat," *New York Times*, March 30, 1938.

18. "Mays' Suspension Starts A. L. War," *New York Times*, August 1, 1919.

19. Colonel Jacob Ruppert, as told to Daniel, "Behind the Scenes of the Yankees: Ruppert Almost Broke Up AL," *New York World-Telegram*, February 16, 1938. Ruppert's recollection of details, including the chronology of events, years after they occurred, was sometimes hazy and even contradictory.

20. In early 1916 Johnson lent $100,000 to James Dunn to facilitate his purchase of the Indians; Dunn had paid back half of the loan. This was not confirmed until the upcoming court hearings before Justice Wagner. While some contemporary accounts said the Yankees blamed Johnson for not letting them have a chance to land either Speaker or Joe Jackson, the reality as discussed earlier suggested that the Yankees may indeed have had an opportunity to acquire them.

21. Murdock, *Ban Johnson*, 169.

22. Til Huston, "Yanks Fire First Shot; Big Baseball War Is On," *New York American*, August 5, 1919.

23. Sid Mercer, "The Colonel," *New York Journal-American*, January 15, 1939.

24. William H. Wright, "Mays Case," *New York World*, August 6, 1919.

25. Wagner later was a four-term U.S. senator and was active in passing New Deal legislation. His son, Robert Jr., was New York City mayor from 1954 to 1965.

26. When the National Commission awarded Philadelphia Athletics pitcher Scott Perry to the National League's Boston Braves, Mack's American League team secured a court injunction to retain Perry. See Macht, *Connie Mack: The Turbulent and Triumphant Years, 1915–1931*, 138–58.

27. Mays had an earned run average of 1.65 for the Yankees in 120 innings. Combined with his Red Sox performance, his ERA of 2.10 was the league's fourth best.

28. See, for example, "The Principle in the Mays Case," *Sporting News*, August 7, 1919. The editorial did wonder why Johnson had not suspended Mays earlier. An editorial a week later stated, "When they [the Yankees' owners] recover from their madness, they'll regret what they did."

29. Scribbled by Scribes, *Sporting News*, October 2, 1919.

30. Sheridan, Back of the Home Plate, *Sporting News*, January 1, 1920.

31. "Yanks' Owners Are Sustained by Court," *New York Times*, October 16, 1919. Murdock wrote that Wagner's ruling was incorrect and unjust. Mays had violated the rules, he wrote. The pitcher should have been disciplined, and it was not ethical for any club to negotiate for him. Johnson appealed the Wagner ruling and lost. *Ban Johnson*, 168–72.

32. Huston testimony, Mays injunction hearing, Chicago Black Sox Scandal papers, Chicago History Museum. Huston also noted the case of pitcher Dutch Leonard, who refused to pitch for the Yankees after the Red Sox had traded him in December 1918.

33. Sid Mercer, All in a Day's Work, "Johnson Offers Another Affront," *New York Globe and Commercial Advertiser*, November 6, 1919.

34. Murdock, *Ban Johnson*, 172.

35. The Loyal Five were the owners of the Cleveland, Detroit, Philadelphia, St. Louis, and Washington clubs.

36. Macht, *Connie Mack*, 209–10.

37. "Ban Johnson Crushes Opposing Faction at American League Meeting and Grasps Reins," *New York Times*, December 11, 1919. Ruppert's resolution to strip Johnson of his power lost by a 5–3 vote.

38. January 31, 1920, lawsuit. Murdock, *Ban Johnson*, 176. In his January 1, 1920, column, Back of the Home Plate, in the *Sporting News*, John B. Sheridan made a strong defense of Johnson and all he had done for baseball. Sheridan criticized the Yankees' owners for "trying to smear Johnson with a technical, legal decision."

39. "As Old Saying Is: Truth Prevails," *Sporting News*, January 15, 1920.

40. Black Sox Scandal papers, Chicago History Museum.

41. "Baseball Again Suffers from Picayune Politics," *New York Sun*, January 19, 1919. The third member of the commission was National League president John Heydler.

42. Spink, *Judge Landis and Twenty-Five Years of Baseball*, 41–44. The complex dueling claims for Sisler revolved around the Pirates' purchasing Sisler's contract from a Minor League club. The commission ruled that Sisler was a minor when he signed with that club and that he never reported to it anyway. "Barney was an implacable enemy [of Herrmann], and cried for vengeance," wrote Spink.

43. Cook, *August "Garry" Herrmann*, 244–45.

44. "Called Man of the Hour," *Sporting News*, January 15, 1920.

45. Seymour and Seymour, *Baseball: The Golden Age*, 271. Back in August 1919, when Ruppert offered to settle matters at an owners' meeting—without Ban Johnson present—Ball declined, replying, "Your business sagacity and acumen in the Mays matter does not appeal to us. Your sportsmanship smells to heaven." To which Ruppert replied, "Refusal not unacceptable in view of your gratuitous insult in reply to polite invitation." Sowell, *The Pitch That Killed*, 53.

46. Monitor, "Johnson Disgusted, May Quit Baseball," *New York World*, February 12, 1920. Should Ruppert and the other board member, Washington's Clark Griffith, split on an issue, a Chicago federal judge would

break the tie. ("Name withheld but known" was the way John Sheridan referred to the judge.) At those same meetings, Judge Landis was named as one of the five finalists for the job of chairman of the National Commission. New York state senator and future New York City mayor Jimmy Walker was one of the other finalists.

47. Damon Runyon, Th' Mornin's Mornin', "Ban's Mexican Stand-Off," *New York American*, February 12, 1920.

48. Monitor, "Johnson Disgusted, May Quit Baseball."

49. Joe Vila, "Biggest Victory Won in Taking Game out of Lawyers' Hands," and editorial, "Bitter Is This Pill," *Sporting News*, February 19, 1920.

50. Murdock, *Ban Johnson*, 177.

51. John B. Sheridan, Back of the Home Plate, *Sporting News*, April 15, 1920.

52. Frank Graham, Graham's Corner, "The Little Miller," *New York Journal-American*, February 5, 1964, and Graham, "The Little Miller," 378.

53. Westbrook Pegler, "Wanted to Fire Him, but the Little Runt Won Three Flags," *United News*, September 19, 1923.

54. Joe Vila, Setting the Pace, *New York Sun*, September 26, 1929.

14. Home Is No Longer a Home

1. Murdock, *Ban Johnson*, 175.

2. "Ban Johnson Denies Charge," *Los Angeles Times*, December 28, 1919, and "Insurrecto Attacks Prove Boomerangs," *Sporting News*, January 8, 1920.

3. "Ball Makes Public a Johnson Letter," *New York Times*, February 8, 1920.

4. Michael T. Lynch's *Harry Frazee, Ban Johnson, and the Feud That Nearly Destroyed the American League* does an excellent job of covering this specific episode as well as the larger conflict.

5. "Ball Makes Public a Johnson Letter."

6. The diary of Chicago White Sox secretary Harry Grabiner was discovered in a wall at Comiskey Park in 1963. In return for Stoneham's evicting the Yankees, Grabiner wrote, Johnson promised Stoneham veto power over the selection of the Yankees' new owners. Bill Veeck, *The Hustler's Handbook*, 289. A February 8, 1920, *New York Times* article confirms that in 1919 Stoneham gave the Yankees notice to vacate the Polo Grounds.

7. "Col. Ruppert Dies at 71; Brewer, Owner of the Yankees," *New York World-Telegram*, January 13, 1939.

8. Jacob Ruppert, as told to Dan Daniel, "Behind the Scenes of the Yankees: Ruppert Almost Broke Up the AL," *New York World-Telegram*, February 16, 1938. See also "Colonel Ruppert Dies at 71," *New York World-Telegram*, January 13, 1939.

9. "Yanks Lose Home at Polo Grounds," *New York Times*, May 15, 1920.

10. *Baltimore Evening Sun*, February 29, 1916.

11. "Yanks Must Find Own Ball Field," *New York Sun*, May 15, 1920. Hempstead was the son-in-law of former Giants owner John Brush.

12. "Hunt for Home Is Spared to Yanks," *New York Times*, May 22, 1920.

13. Mrs. John McGraw, *The Real McGraw*, 277–78, and Frank Graham, *The New York Yankees*, 75.

14. Sid Mercer, *New York Evening Journal*, May 18, 1920. Mercer noted it was the Yankees who did not want overlapping home games, not the Giants. Were the National League to schedule such conflicting dates in New York, the American League would have retaliated in other cities where their team was more popular, such as in Chicago.

15. For the scheduling policy under the National Agreement, see Sid Mercer, *New York Evening Journal*, May 18, 1920, and *New York Times*, May 22, 1920. Actual Sunday game dates may have been slightly different than the original schedules, because of rainouts.

16. The Dodgers had significantly more Sunday home dates than either the Giants or the Yankees (around nineteen vs. twelve to thirteen) in the early 1920s.

17. McGraw, *The Real McGraw*, 277.

18. Frederick G. Lieb, *New York Evening Telegram*, May 15, 1920. When Stoneham bought the Giants, McGraw acquired a small stake in the team.

19. The fact that the Yankees were close to or in first place during these games also helped bring out the crowds. They played a single game on June 22 and a five-game series included two doubleheaders at the end of the month.

20. "Red Sox Take First; Yanks Take Second," *New York Times*, June 28, 1919.

21. "Ruth Knocks Out His 26th Home Run," *New York Times*, September 9, 1919.

22. The Yankees hosted the league-leading Cleveland Indians on May 15 and 16. The May 16 game drew more than 38,000 fans, and newspapers reported that the crowd broke the Polo Grounds record of 38,281, set at

Game One of the 1911 World Series, and that of a similar crowd at the "Merkle game" of October 1908.

23. "Stoneham Discusses Move," *New York Times*, May 15, 1920.
24. Jacob Ruppert, as told to Daniel, "Behind the Scenes of the Yankees: Ruppert Buys Out Huston." A day earlier, in the same series of articles, Ruppert told an amazing story. He said that at one point he had agreed to buy the Washington Senators (who were struggling financially), with Frazee and Comiskey and move them to Brooklyn. He had an agreement with the Brooklyn Dodgers for this team to buy a half interest in Ebbets Field, where the team would play its games. Just how owners of one team would be able to own a second one was not clear. ("Syndicate ball" had been outlawed.) Ruppert said that Johnson "killed" this deal.
25. Jacob Ruppert, *Out of the Past* radio program, seventy-first birthday appearance, August 5, 1938.
26. "Yanks Lose Home at Polo Grounds," *New York Times*, May 15, 1920.
27. "Ban and Garry Show Class in Persuading Stoneham to Relent," *Sporting News*, May 27, 1920. See also "Hunt for Home Is Spared for Yanks."
28. This was only three months after the Yankees' owners had led the battle against Johnson. They had secured virtually everything they wanted—except the removal of Johnson. Did Johnson make a deal with his foes, agreeing to support them in their ballpark negotiations in exchange for their allowing him to remain as league president?

15. Buying the Babe

1. "Ban on 2.75 Beers in Wartime Upheld by Supreme Court," *New York Times*, January 6, 1920. The Volstead Act had defined beverages of 0.5 percent or more as intoxicating. In *Jacob Ruppert vs. Caffey* 251 US 264 (1920), the court dismissed the action brought by Ruppert for an injunction restraining the federal government from stopping the sale of 2.75 percent beer.
2. Ruppert's attorneys argued that the 2.75 percent alcoholic beverages manufactured during World War I did not come under the heading of "intoxicating beverages" because in order to get drunk, one would have to drink more beer with that amount of alcohol in it than the human system could consume. Noon, *Yuengling*, 112.
3. Although called the Yankees as early as 1904 and almost universally since 1913, some newspapers occasionally called each city's team "Americans" or "Nationals" in reference to its league.

4. "Ruth Bought by New York Americans for $125,000, Highest Price in Baseball's Annals," *New York Times*, January 6, 1920.

5. Frederick G. Lieb, "Ruth Brings Joy to Yankee Fandom," *New York Sun*, January 6, 1920.

6. "Babe Ruth Accepts Terms of Yankees," *New York Times*, January 7, 1920.

7. "The High Cost of Home Runs," *New York Times*, January 7, 1920.

8. Joe Vila, "Ruppert Belittles Suggestion Yanks Should Aid Weak Clubs," *Sporting News*, November 10, 1932.

9. Seth Livingstone, "Fenway at 100: 'The Blessing of the Bambino,'" *USA TODAY*, February 28, 2012.

10. Ruth had eleven home runs (tied with Tilly Walker of the Athletics) in 1918 and twenty-nine home runs in 1919.

11. Livingstone, "Fenway at 100."

12. Ruth's $10,000 salary was already one of the highest in the game. According to Michael Haupert, who has researched baseball contracts of Hall of Famers, Walter Johnson was making $12,000 in 1920, Eddie Collins was making $15,000, and Ty Cobb was making $20,000. www.baseball-reference.com.

13. "Ruth Thought Only of Making Homers," *New York Sun*, January 7, 1920.

14. Harvey Frommer, http://bleacherreport.com, April 9, 2012.

15. Daniel, *The Real Babe Ruth*, 40–41.

16. Appel, *Pinstripe Empire*, 96.

17. Livingstone, "Fenway at 100."

18. Ruppert, "The Ten Million Dollar Toy," 18.

19. Considine, *The Babe Ruth Story*, 81.

20. Ed Fitz Gerald, "The Round-Up," *Washington Post*, January 8, 1920.

21. Ruppert, "The Ten Million Dollar Toy," 18.

22. Appel, *Pinstripe Empire*, 96.

23. Based on his financial obligations and actual actions going forward, it seems unlikely Frazee ever meant to use this money to get new players.

24. Linn, *The Great Rivalry*, 84.

25. "Babe Ruth Accepts Terms of Yankees," *New York Times*, January 7, 1920. In 1918, Ruth had walked out on his team, jumping to a shipbuilding team. In 1919, he had almost come to blows with manager Ed Barrow.

26. Barrow, *My Fifty Years in Baseball*, 108.

27. Barrow's rant aside, Russell did well in Boston in 1919. He appeared in 21 games, with a 10-4 record and a 2.52 earned run average. Frederick G.

Lieb, "Inside of Baseball's Most Famous Deals," *Sporting News*, November 11, 1943.

28. Richard Sandomir, "Setting Record Straight on Ruth," *New York Times*, July 24, 2003.

29. Levitt, Armour, and Levitt, "History versus Harry Frazee," 32.

30. Babe Ruth, "Babe Ruth Tells in His Own Book of Baseball," *New York World*, January 8, 1929.

31. W. R. Hoefer, "The Reign of the Wallop," 375.

32. "Home Run King Wallops Ball out of Park," *St. Louis Globe-Democrat*, May 24, 1920. Ruth said that he was one of only three "free swingers" in the teens; the others were Chicago's Joe Jackson and Detroit's Sam Crawford. Daniel, *The Real Babe Ruth*, 105.

33. Pitchers had been increasingly tampering with the ball, which affected its flight and made it harder to hit. All trick pitches were banned at once, except for the spitball, which was given a one-year reprieve, and it too would become illegal starting in 1921. Seventeen Major League pitchers were allowed to continue throwing the pitch for the rest of their careers.

34. Rule 14, Section 4, and Rule 30, Section 2. *Reach Official American League Baseball Guide*, 396, 401. See Steve Steinberg's "The Spitball and the End of the Deadball Era."

35. In *The Pitch That Killed*, Mike Sowell notes that the rule to keep clean, white balls in play was instituted at the start of the 1920 season. But owners grumbled about the increased cost, and during the season, umpires were directed to back off on replacing balls so often. After Ray Chapman was killed in August by a pitch he may not have seen, fresh balls became a staple in the game.

36. Until 1901 in the National League and 1903 in the American League, a foul ball was not charged as a first or second strike.

37. Tom Shibe of the A. J. Reach Company declared that the ball "has not been changed one iota and no effort has been made to turn out a livelier ball." *New York Evening Telegram*, June 5, 1920. In 1949, George Reach, then in his eighties, said that his company at times did adjust the ball's liveliness. But back in 1921, he had insisted there were no changes, and his reputation for integrity, wrote *Baseball Magazine*, was that of a man whose word could not be questioned. F. C. Lane, "Has the 'Lively' Ball Revolutionized the Game?" September 1921, 438. Historian Bill Curran noted that if the owners had wanted to produce a livelier ball, they had no reason to keep that a secret. *Big Sticks*, 65–85.

38. The most widely publicized tests were done by Columbia University chemistry professor Harold Fales, comparing the balls of 1914, 1923, and 1925. "Magnates Approve the 'Rabbit Ball;' Tests Show No Alteration," *New York Times*, July 16, 1925.

39. Wagenheim, *Babe Ruth*, 62.

16. The Risks of Ruth

1. Stout and Johnson, *Red Sox Century*, 146–47.

2. Levitt, Armour, and Levitt, "History versus Harry Frazee."

3. Smelser, *The Life That Ruth Built*, 312. Barrow was silent on the subject in his autobiography.

4. Creamer, *Babe*, 289.

5. Smith, *Babe Ruth's America*, 92–93. The infection sidelined Ruth for a week. Some accounts said it was a mosquito bite.

6. *New York Evening Telegram*, October 11, 1921. The abscess was drained repeatedly.

7. Smith, *Babe Ruth's America*, 148, and Ken Sobol, *Babe Ruth & the American Dream*, 184.

8. Ed Sullivan, undated article, Babe Ruth Scrapbook, National Baseball Hall of Fame and Archives.

9. Smelser, *The Life That Ruth Built*, 145.

10. Creamer, *Babe*, 142.

11. Douglas, *Terrible Honesty*, 65–66.

12. Smith, *Babe Ruth's America*, 148, and Ken Sobol, *Babe Ruth & the American Dream*, 110. The Packard was considered one of the finest luxury cars in the 1920s.

13. *New York World*, March 21, 1920, and Considine, *The Babe Ruth Story*, 85 and 86.

14. Sid Mercer, *New York Globe and Commercial Advertiser*, January 7, 1920.

15. The fine was not nearly as significant as the amount of money—more than $40,000—Ruth stood to make for his barnstorming. World Series participants had been banned from playing exhibition games after the Series ended. The rule emanated from the 1910 world champion Athletics being embarrassed by Cuban teams on a trip that the former saw as a "joy ride." The rule would be changed in 1922.

16. During the 1922 season, Ruth was ejected from games by three of baseball's most respected umpires: George Hildebrand, Bill Dinneen, and Tom Connolly. Ban Johnson followed all three ejections with suspensions.

17. Daniel, *The Real Babe Ruth*, 112.

18. Hoyt, *Babe Ruth as I Knew Him*, 5.

19. Lieb, *Baseball as I Have Known It*, 159. The woman was reportedly the wife of a Louisiana legislator.

20. Creamer, *Babe*, 238.

21. Daniel, *Babe Ruth: Idol of the American Boy*, 19–20. Ruth actually did follow one of his commandments: "Remember that it is important to be able to 'take it.' Gameness is vital in baseball, and in your lifework."

22. Gallen, *The Baseball Chronicles*, 29.

23. Creamer, *Babe*, 330.

24. Lieb, *Baseball as I Have Known It*, 158.

25. Colonel Til Huston papers in the Robert Edwards Auctions, May 18, 2013 auction, Lot 1284. When the detective mentioned that Ruth went hitless against Walter Johnson (a May 2 shutout), a chorus girl told him, "I'll bet they are all drunk again. We know Ruth and a lot of the players."

26. Williams, *The Joe Williams Baseball Reader*, 77.

27. Smelser, *The Life That Ruth Built*, 134, 239. The Yankees insured Ruth for $150,000 at first and later doubled the amount.

17. Ruth Roars into the Twenties

1. Daniel R. Levitt's review of the Yankee records has noted a few things. Because Ruth's 1920 bonus was paid in February 1921, some sources have reported his 1921 salary as $30,000. The Babe was also paid a bonus of $50 for each home run he hit in 1921. E-mail from Dan Levitt to Steve Steinberg, June 18, 2006.

2. Sid Mercer, "The Problem of Handling Ruth," *New York Globe and Commercial Advertiser*, January 6, 1920.

3. "He is an inveterate cigar smoker," one sportswriter observed. "Except at meals, on the ball fields and when asleep, he invariably has a long weed tilted at a rakish angle in his mouth." James P. Sinnott, "Babe Ruth Is No Bloomer," *New York Evening Mail*, March 24, 1920.

4. Reisler, *Babe Ruth*, 24.

5. *New York American*, February 17, 1920.

6. On February 11, 1920, Oh Boy won first prize in all three categories in which he was entered. Ruppert's St. Bernard bitch, Bulgari, won second in the overall category and first in the two categories in which only bitches competed. One year earlier, Oh Boy and Ruppert's other St. Bernards had won five trophies at the Westminster show.

7. Sid Mercer, "The Colonel," *New York Journal-American*, January 17, 1939.

8. *Variety*, January 16, 1920.

9. Bodie had left spring training in Jacksonville to return to New York on personal business. "He will never be seen in a Yankee uniform as long as I am connected with the club," vowed Huggins. Sam Crane, "Miller Huggins 'Fires' Ping Bodie," *New York Evening Journal*, March 26, 1920. Sid Mercer wrote in the March 26 *New York Globe* that Bodie would soon be traded to the Red Sox. He was not. Despite Huggins's outburst, Bodie was with the Yankees until he broke an ankle in a September 8 exhibition game in Pittsburgh.

10. W. S. Farnsworth, "Outfield Job for Meusel," *New York American*, January 23, 1920.

11. Baker, who was at the opener, was still undecided about whether he would play in 1920. En route from Los Angeles to New York, after signing Ruth, Huggins was instructed by a Ruppert telegram to stop off in Trappe, Maryland, and try to convince Baker to play with the Yankees in 1920. At the opener, Baker promised Huggins he would make his decision within a week, which he did, deciding, as he had in a salary dispute in 1915, to sit out the year.

12. "Ruppert Library Sold," *New York Times*, April 15, 1920. Ruppert never stated publicly why he sold these collections, but it was likely done to replace the rental income he was losing from the saloons that rented street-level shops in his buildings.

13. Arthur Robinson, "Concerning Babe Ruth," *New York American*, July 18, 1920.

14. "Supreme Court Ends Hope of the 'Wets,'" *Washington Post*, June 8, 1920.

15. "Dry Laws Upheld In Unanimous View of Supreme Court," *New York Times*, June 7, 1920.

16. "Liquor Dead as Slavery, Counsel for 'Drys' Says," *Washington Post*, June 8, 1920.

17. Asinof, *1919*, 261.

18. Okrent, *Last Call*, 346.

19. Lerner, *Dry Manhattan*, 84.

20. Asinof, *1919*, 262.

21. Turesky, "A World Almost Apart: Baseball and American Life in the Twenties," 10.

22. Hyatt Daab, Timely Views and News in the World of Sport, *New York Evening Telegram*, May 28, 1920.

23. Frederick G. Lieb, "Huggins Thinks Outlook Bright," *New York Evening Telegram*, May 14, 1920. During the 1920 season, the Yankees won games by scores of 11–0, 11–3 (twice), 14–0, 17–0, 20–5, 19–3, 10–0, and 13–3.

24. Damon Runyon, *New York American*, May 24, 1920.

25. The top three hitters in the American League on July 24 were Tris Speaker (.418); Joe Jackson (.399); and George Sisler (.397). Ruth would end the season in fourth place in batting behind Sisler, the leader, Speaker, and Jackson.

26. Daniel, *The Real Babe Ruth*, 152.

27. Alexander, *Ty Cobb*, 158–59.

28. Arthur Robinson, "Yankees Intimate Rivals Are Trying to 'Shoo-In' Cleveland," *New York American*, August 11, 1920.

29. Hyatt Daab, Timely Views and News in the World of Sport, *New York Evening Telegram*, August 10, 1920.

30. The Browns' Shocker always asked to start two games of any four-game series vs. New York. It was "revenge" for him, against the team that shipped him away. However, he had started only once for the Browns in the recently completed five-game series. And while Ehmke did appear twice for the Tigers in their four-game series against the Yankees, one was a start and one was a one-inning relief appearance.

31. Murdock, *Baseball Players between the Wars*, 7.

32. Sowell, *The Pitch That Killed*, 174.

33. *Baseball Magazine*, as quoted in Sowell, *The Pitch That Killed*, 16–17.

34. Harry Schumacher, "Fans Fear Incident May Ruin Carl Mays," *New York Globe and Commercial Advertiser*, August 18, 1920.

35. In his first five seasons in the league, 1915–19, Mays hit forty-nine batters. During that same period, Walter Johnson, the league's best pitcher, and one who never has been accused of throwing at batters, hit fifty-seven.

36. "No Ball Strike, Say Managers," *New York Evening Telegram*, August 18, 1920.

37. William B. Hanna, "Chapman Dead; Mays Is Exonerated of Blame," *New York Sun and Herald*, August 18, 1920.

38. "Ray Chapman's Body Sent to Cleveland," *Boston Globe*, August 18, 1920. The Yankees were one of only a few teams that wore a black armband in memory of Chapman for the remainder of the 1920 season.

39. "Yankee Owners Score Johnson," *New York Evening Telegram*, August 21, 1920.

40. Reisler, *Babe Ruth*, 198.

41. Warburton, "The 1921 AL Race.

42. Harry Schumacher, "Huggins's Judgment Suicidal to Yankees," *New York Globe and Commercial Advertiser*, September 17, 1920. Schumacher had an equally harsh subtitle for his article: "Choice of Quinn to Pitch Critical Game Was a Terrible Blow to Yankees' Pennant Hopes."

43. Harry Schumacher, "Yankees Are Bringing Shattered Hopes Home," *New York Globe and Commercial Advertiser*, September 22, 1920.

44. Huggins was very fond of Fewster, perhaps identifying with the slightly built youngster. In 1918, Huggins had called him as good a prospect as he had ever seen. But after Fewster suffered a near-fatal beaning by Brooklyn's Jeff Pfeffer in a March 25, 1920, exhibition game, Huggins reinserted Pratt at second base, where he played the whole season.

45. James P. Sinnott, "Yankee Dissensions Due to Benching of Pratt," *New York Evening Mail*, April 19, 1920.

46. "Ruth Means Pennant Winner for New York," *New York Evening Telegram*, February 23, 1920.

47. On September 26, when news of the 1919 scandal became public, White Sox owner Charles Comiskey suspended the seven involved players who were still active. At the time, the White Sox were only a half-game behind Cleveland, and while they won three of their final five, the Indians won six of eight to win the pennant by two games.

48. Sam Murphy, *New York Evening Mail*, September 21, 1920.

49. For Barry Bonds to have matched Ruth's hitting 15 percent of his league's home runs in 2001, the season he hit a record-breaking 73, he would have had to hit 443 home runs.

50. Ruth's .847 slugging percentage in 1920 remained the Major League's best until 2001, when Barry Bonds of the San Francisco Giants compiled a .863 slugging percentage.

51. The sixty-one home runs hit by Yankees other than Babe Ruth was itself greater than any other American League club. Second to New York's 115 were the St. Louis Browns, with 50. Second to Ruth's 54 was George Sisler of the Browns, with 19. Conversely, the Yankees were one of the slowest teams in baseball; only the Philadelphia Athletics, with 50, had fewer stolen bases than the 64 they had.

52. F. C. Lane, "Secret of My Heavy Hitting," 420.

53. Haupert and Winter, "Yankees Profits and Promise," 201.

54. Sid Mercer, "Babe Ruth Will Pay for Himself in One Year," *New York Evening Journal*, May 14, 1920.

55. Turesky, "A World Almost Apart: Baseball and American Life in the Twenties," 64.

56. Neither the Giants nor the Yankees allowed fans on the field at the Polo Grounds, although doing so would have meant more revenue for them. That practice had been instituted by John T. Brush during his years as owner of the Giants.

57. Sam Murphy, "Babe Ruth Greatest Player Ever; Cobb or Old Stars Not His Equal," *New York Evening Mail*, June 2, 1920.

18. Squabbling Owners and Scandal

1. Pitcher Eddie Cicotte and outfielder Joe Jackson confessed before a Chicago grand jury in late September. Johnson had rallied his "Loyal Five" owners in support of his obstructionism.

2. Grantland Rice, "The Sportlight," *New York Tribune*, October 2, 1920.

3. Hyatt Daab, Timely News and Views in the World of Sport, *New York Evening Telegram*, September 27, 1920.

4. Sid Mercer, Sid Mercer's Close-Ups, *New York Evening Journal*, October 18, 1920.

5. Helyar, *Lords of the Realm*, 542.

6. Harry Schumacher, "Only Lasker Plan Will Prevent Baseball War," *New York Globe and Commercial Advertiser*, October 21, 1920. For some reason, Lasker felt that Ruppert was the weakest link in the pro-Landis forces. He thought that Ruppert was "money mad" and might waver if there was a baseball war. Perhaps Ruppert's efforts to reach a compromise and avoid that war concerned Lasker. Seymour and Seymour, *The Golden Age of Baseball*, 317.

7. Whether the scandal would have been prevented is questionable. For the previous two decades, there had been many "clues" of corruption, almost all of which had been ignored by the National Commission.

8. Harry Schumacher, "Seems Determined to Keep League at War," *New York Globe and Commercial Advertiser*, December 20, 1920.

9. "Ruppert Halts Building Plan in Agreement with Giants," *New York American*, October 21, 1920.

10. A rival league, the Federal League, had brought an antitrust suit in Landis's court in 1915. He delayed ruling until the league had disintegrated a year later.

11. Turesky, "A World Almost Apart: Baseball and American Life in the Twenties," 96. In the trial of the International Workers of the World (IWW), for their antiwar and subversive activities, Landis handed down a number of twenty-year sentences. They were considered so harsh that President Calvin Coolidge commuted all of them in 1923, an action that elicited outrage from Landis.

12. Frederick G. Lieb, "Baseball Peace Again Is Near," *New York Evening Telegram*, November 11, 1920.

13. Hyatt Daab, Timely News and Views in the World of Sport, *New York Evening Telegram*, October 21, 1920. Johnson even threatened to revoke the charters of the three rebellious franchises and reclaim their players, including, of course, Babe Ruth.

14. Runyon, editorial, *New York American*, November 11, 1920. St. Louis Browns business manager Bob Quinn told some of the other owners, "If my two boys wanted to fight over anything so silly, I would spank them both." David Pietrusza, *Judge and Jury*, 167.

15. The eleven clubs had said that they would place a twelfth team in Detroit, which must have been a persuasive tool in getting Detroit Tigers owner Frank Navin to be amenable to a settlement.

16. Rosenberg, "Here Comes the Judge!" 118.

17. White, *Creating the National Pastime*, 106.

18. Dos Passos, *Mid-Century*, 156.

19. Spatz and Steinberg, *1921*, 13.

20. Voigt, "The Chicago Black Sox and the Myth of Baseball's Single Sin." Landis also banned a handful of other players whom he found easy to discredit.

21. Frank Graham, "'Must Divorce Baseball and Gambling,' Says Judge Landis," *New York Sun*, November 29, 1920.

22. Harold Seymour and Dorothy Seymour, *Baseball: The Golden Age*, 278, 281.

23. Hugh Fullerton, "Baseball on Trial," 184.

24. Damon Runyon, "Postscript on Sports Writing," as quoted in Clark, *The World of Damon Runyon*, 101.

25. Clark, *The World of Damon Runyon*, 102.

26. "Yankee Owners Give Praise to Comiskey," *New York Times*, September 29, 1920.

27. "White Sox Indicted," *Los Angeles Times*, September 29, 1920.

28. John B. Sheridan, Back of the Home Plate, *Sporting News*, November 4, 1920. When the Black Sox scandal became public, Christy Mathewson (Chase's manager in Cincinnati, who had presented persuasive evidence against Chase in 1918) told Fullerton, "Damn them [the owners]. They have it coming to them. I caught two crooks [Chase and Heinie Zimmerman], and they whitewashed them." *Sporting News*, October 17, 1935.

29. William L. Chenery, "Foul Ball!" *New York Times*, October 3, 1920.

19. Huggins Stays

1. Coincidentally, Jersey City was managed by Bill Donovan, Ruppert's manager in 1915–17, whom he had replaced with Miller Huggins.

2. Dempsey won the title on July 4, 1919, when he knocked champion Jess Willard down seven times in the first round, on the way to a third-round TKO when Willard could not answer the bell for Round Four.

3. Turesky, "A World Almost Apart: Baseball and American Life in the Twenties," 54.

4. Allen, *Only Yesterday*, 69 and 179.

5. Parrish, *Anxious Decades*, 159.

6. Hugh Fullerton, *New York Evening Mail*, August 15, 1921.

7. Joe Vila, "Yanks Must Test the Feeling of Fans in Foreign Fields," *Sporting News*, September 2, 1920.

8. Sid Mercer, "The Jury Is Still Out," *New York Evening Journal*, October 22, 1920.

9. Damon Runyon, *New York American*, October 29, 1920.

10. John B. Sheridan, Back of the Home Plate, *Sporting News*, April 15, 1920.

11. Sam Murphy, *New York Evening Mail*, September 21, 1920.

12. "Many a Man Picked to Lead the Yanks," *New York American*, October 16, 1920.

13. Tom Rice, *Brooklyn Daily Eagle*, October 27, 1920.

14. Jacob Ruppert, as told to Daniel, "Behind the Scenes of the Yankees: Robbie Passed Up Stadium Job," *New York World-Telegram*, February 18, 1938.

15. Charles Ebbets, *New York Globe and Commercial Advertiser*, October 15, 1920.

16. "Huggins Surprised at Report; Not Worried," *New York Evening Telegram*, October 12, 1920.
17. "Robbie Will Sign for 3 Years, Ebbets Confers with Huggins," *New York American*, October 13, 1920. Robinson, it was generally agreed, had the ability to get his team to overachieve.
18. Robinson had been making an annual salary of $9,000, and Huggins was making $12,000. Robinson was reported to have been offered either $15,000 or $18,000 by the Yankees. He signed with Brooklyn for $15,000, plus a $5,000 bonus for winning the pennant.
19. George Perry served for fourteen years as Ruppert's personal secretary and the primary contact between the Colonel and the press.
20. George Perry, "Behind the Scenes with Ruppert's Inside Man," *Sporting News*, March 2, 1939.
21. Edward T. Murphy, "Huggins Discusses Yankees," *New York Sun*, October 30, 1920. Harding ran against, and defeated, another Ohioan, Governor James Cox.
22. Jacob Ruppert, "Huggins Will Lead Yankees," *New York Evening Telegram*, October 28, 1920.
23. Sam Murphy, *New York Evening Mail*, October 23, 1920.
24. Joe Vila, "Gotham Fans Given Batch of Real Dope," *Sporting News*, November 4, 1920.
25. Scribbled by Scribes, *Sporting News*, January 22, 1920.
26. Barrow, *My Fifty Years in Baseball*, 110.
27. Graham, *The New York Yankees*, 53.
28. Barrow, *My Fifty Years in Baseball*, 126.
29. Krichell, a former Major League catcher, would take over the Yankees' scouting in the mid-1920s and remain in that position for more than three decades. During that time Krichell signed many future Yankees stars, including Lou Gehrig, Tony Lazzeri, Charlie Keller, Red Rolfe, Phil Rizzuto, Vic Raschi, and Whitey Ford.
30. Meany, *Yankee Story*, 59.

20. One of the Fiercest Pennant Battles

1. Frederick G. Lieb, "Huggins Thinks Outlook Bright," *New York Evening Telegram*, May 14, 1920.
2. Washington led the league with 160 stolen bases, and Philadelphia was last, with 50. The Yankees were one of four American League teams

whose 1920 stolen base success rate was below 50 percent. The league average was just .517.

3. "Huggins to Make Changes," *New York Times*, October 30, 1920.

4. *New York Evening Mail*, April 9, 1921.

5. Hoyt had missed a good part of the 1920 season due to a double hernia, the result of an immature "prank."

6. Roth's final season in the big leagues was 1921. He was injured for a good part of the season, played in only forty-three games, and had just one stolen base. The Yankees had expected much more from someone who had stolen 160 bases over the past five seasons, including a career-high 51 with the 1917 Indians.

7. *New York Evening Telegram*, January 3, 1921.

8. Walter Trumbull, The Listening Post, *New York Herald*, March 21, 1921.

9. The scheme for such a commission provided for either a one-man or three-man board, which would be granted absolute power in the regulation of professional sports in New York State.

10. Hyatt Daab, "Experts Oppose Placing All Sports under Single Commission Rule," *New York Evening Telegram*, January 20, 1921.

11. Bill Slocum, "Miller Huggins, as I Knew Him," *New York American*, October 3, 1929.

12. Spatz and Steinberg, *1921*, 85.

13. *Sporting News*, January 13, 1921.

14. Frederick G. Lieb, "Yankees to Be a Slugging Nine," *New York Evening Telegram*, March 3, 1921.

15. Ralph Davis, *Pittsburgh Press*, quoted in *Cleveland Press*, August 31, 1921.

16. "Yankees Stronger, Faster, and More Versatile than in 1920, Says Huggins," *New York Globe and Commercial Advertiser*, April 13, 1921.

17. William B. Hanna, *New York Herald*, March 3, 1921.

18. Harry Schumacher, "Miller Huggins Confronted by Big Task in Managing the Yankees in 1921 Campaign," *New York Globe and Commercial Advertiser*, October 30, 1920.

19. Dan Daniel, *New York Evening Telegram*, September 24, 1920.

20. Sid Mercer, "Punctured Pitching Staff Flops Yanks," *New York Evening Journal*, April 27, 1921.

21. On May 2, Huggins had signaled Mays to walk Boston's Tim Hendryx, with two outs and first base open in the ninth inning of a 1–1 game. Mays chose to pitch to Hendryx, who then singled to drive in the winning run.

New York Herald, May 4, 1921, quoting the *Boston Daily Globe*, May 3, 1921.

22. Hugh Fullerton, On the Screen of Sport, New York *Evening Mail*, April 27, 1921. Fullerton does not give a specific date for this incident, but it appears to be the Yankees' 8–4 win over the Red Sox on April 20.

23. "Huggins Says He'll Use Mays in Games with Cleveland," *New York Evening Telegram*, May 13, 1921.

24. George Daley, George Daley's Sport Talk, *New York World*, July 11, 1921.

25. W. J. Macbeth, "In All Fairness," *New York Tribune*, July 25, 1921.

26. Babe Ruth, "Yankees Will Annex Pennant," *New York American*, July 28, 1921.

27. Hugh Fullerton, On the Screen of Sport, *New York Evening Mail*, July 16, 23, and 25, 1921.

28. Graham, *New York Yankees*, 63.

29. *Sporting News*, August 18, 1921.

30. "Wolves Howl All in Vain," *Sporting News*, September 29, 1921.

31. Damon Runyon, "Yankees Win Pennant as 30,000 Fans Go Wild," *New York American*, October 2, 1921.

32. Damon Runyon, "Huggins," *New York American*, October 3, 1921.

33. This would be the first World Series broadcast on the radio, albeit to a limited number of outlets. More fans would follow the games via a medium that had become popular in many of the nation's biggest cities. Several New York City newspapers had set up "boards" outside their offices that would allow thousands of those without radios to follow the play-by-play action and see lifelike players hit the ball and run the bases.

34. The Old Sport's Musings, *Philadelphia Inquirer*, October 10, 1921.

35. Ruth also led the American League with 145 walks and a still Major League record of 457 total bases. His slugging percentage remains the second highest in American League history, topped only by his 1920 mark.

36. Hynd, *The Giants of the Polo Grounds*, 220.

37. Sid Mercer, "Whole City Busy with 'Dope,'" *New York Evening Journal*, October 3, 1921. One can almost sense Mercer looking down his nose at the newer, unsophisticated Yankees fans, "the element that loves the spectacular."

38. Sam Crane, "Crane Picks Giants to Defeat Yankees for World's Title," *New York Evening Journal*, October 3, 1921.

39. William B. Hanna, "Giants Appear the More Resourceful; Yanks Have Strong, Concentrated Attack," *New York Herald*, October 2, 1921.

40. "Hug May Capture Pennant, but Not in 1915—Says McGraw," *St. Louis Post-Dispatch*, June 23, 1915.

41. "Yankees Only Playing Their Usual Game, Says Huggins," *New York Tribune*, October 7, 1921.

42. *New York Tribune*, October 7, 1921.

43. Sid Mercer, "Series Tie Hard Blow to Yanks," *New York Evening Journal*, October 12, 1921.

44. Mays had suffered several late-inning collapses during the season, including a memorable one in Game Four of the World Series. The consensus in this September game was that Huggins had stayed with him too long. However, Mays did distinguish himself in the Series by allowing no walks in the twenty-six innings he pitched.

45. Frederick G. Lieb, *New York Evening Telegram*, December 12, 1922.

46. Joe Vila, "Ruppert and Barrow Ignore Campaign against Huggins," *Sporting News*, November 3, 1921.

47. With the trade of Del Pratt after the 1920 season and Peckinpaugh after the 1921 season, Huggins had gotten rid of the two players who conceivably threatened his job.

48. Going to Boston, along with Peckinpaugh, were pitchers Jack Quinn, Rip Collins, Bill Piercy, and $150,000.

49. Bill Piercy, who was 5-4 for the Yankees in 1921, pitched four more seasons in the big leagues, going 22-38. Rip Collins had won fourteen games as a rookie in 1920 and eleven in 1921. He would pitch in the American League for another nine years, twice winning fourteen games. Quinn, who was thirty-eight, had an 8-7 record in 1921, which led Huggins to believe his career was over. But Quinn would pitch in the big leagues for another twelve years and win 122 more games.

50. *Sporting News*, January 12, 1922.

51. Spatz, *Yankees Coming, Yankees Going*, 42. Peckinpaugh never would play for Boston. Exactly three weeks after this trade, the Red Sox sent him to Washington as part of a three-team deal that also included the Athletics.

52. Hugh Fullerton, On the Screen of Sport, *New York Evening Mail*, April 13, 1922.

53. Frederick G. Lieb, "Ruppert Defends Miller Huggins," *New York Evening Telegram*, November 4, 1921.

21. *Struggles and Troubles*

1. Frederick G. Lieb, *New York Evening Telegram*, November 29, 1921. Some newspapers reported that Huggins was merely recuperating from tonsillitis.

2. "Miller Huggins on a Sick Bed," *Los Angeles Times*, October 25, 1921.

3. Will Wedge, *New York Sun*, May 29, 1924. Waite Hoyt said that Huggins could not keep his legs still and had either "traveling palsy" or neuritis. Murdock, *Baseball between the Wars*, 35–36.

4. Pringle, "A Small Package," 25.

5. The reports varied widely, from Huggins managing the St. Louis Cardinals (Henry Farrell, *Pittsburgh Chronicle*, October 25, 1921) or managing a Minor League team (Hugh Fullerton, *New York Evening Mail*, October 31, 1921) to buying a team (Sid Mercer, *New York Evening Journal*, October 18, 1921) or practicing law in Cincinnati (*St. Louis Times*, April 7, 1922).

6. Harold C. Burr, "Old Yank-Giant Rivalry Forgotten as Last Flag Flies for Lost Leader," *Brooklyn Daily Eagle*, September 26, 1929.

7. Graham, "The Little Miller," 378. One of the casualties was former New York mayor John Purroy Mitchel, who fell to his death during a military training flight in the summer of 1918. One of Huggins's pitchers on the 1917 Cardinals, Marvin Goodwin, was killed in an Army Reserve flight in 1925.

8. *St. Louis Times*, September 29, 1922.

9. Joe Williams, By Joe Williams, *New York Evening Telegram*, September 29, 1927. Flowers became the world middleweight champion in 1926 and lost his title to Mickey Walker in a controversial decision at the end of that year.

10. Graham, *The New York Yankees*, 74. After that article appeared, Huggins forbade his players to go to the Little Club, a popular night spot. But the city had many others. One wonders if the move from Shreveport to New Orleans was Huggins's choice, or whether it was the Colonels' (and Barrow's) desire to generate larger crowds and thus more revenue from the larger city. The availability of Heinemann Park, home of the Minor League New Orleans Pelicans, was also a factor.

11. Asinof, *1919*, 274.

12. Landis had often imposed harsh penalties from the bench on violators of the Volstead Act. Yet his biographer relates the story of a 1922 gathering at which Landis made a toast to the Eighteenth Amendment, before lead-

ing the partygoers in drinking alcohol. Pietrusza, *Judge and Jury*, 314. The consumption of alcohol, as opposed to its production, sale, or transport, was not a violation of the Volstead Act. Still, such an action on the part of the commissioner was incongruous at best.

13. Joe Vila, "What Difference, Really, If Huggins Is to Be Actual Boss?" *Sporting News*, January 5, 1922.

14. Hugh Fullerton, On the Screen of Sport, *New York Evening Mail*, April 13, 1922.

15. "Mays Threatens to Quit after $200 Fine," *New York American*, April 6–7, 1922. It marked a first public indication of a serious rift between the pitcher and his manager, who would have "no love lost" for each other. *New York Evening Telegram*, April 6, 1922.

16. Editorial, "The Crisis with the Yankees," *Sporting News*, April 13, 1922. See also the editorial of March 23, 1922, "Dissipating a Myth."

17. The terms of the National Agreement barred the owners from contesting the decisions of the commissioner. Anyway, as Sid Mercer noted, there was no way the Colonels would "repudiate" Landis after leading the battle that installed him. "Huggins Will Manage Cardinals, Is Rumor," *New York Evening Journal*, October 18, 1921.

18. Honig, *Baseball America*, 139.

19. "Huggins Releases Six Yank Players; Landis Praises Players," *New York Times*, March 25, 1922. Landis had ruled that Ruth and Meusel could play in spring training games.

20. Robert Smith, *Babe Ruth's America*, 123.

21. Ruth hit only .315 in 1922, his lowest batting average as a Yankee—except for 1925—until 1933, when he was thirty-eight years old. His power numbers were still quite impressive: thirty-five home runs in only 110 games. He finished third in the home run race, behind the Browns' Ken Williams, who had thirty-nine, and Philadelphia's Tilly Walker, who had thirty-seven. Ruth also had a league-best slugging percentage of .672.

22. Ruth threw dirt at umpire George Hildebrand and called umpire Bill Dinneen "one of the vilest names known," in Johnson's words. Both were respected umpires. Two months later, Ruth was "tossed" by future Hall of Fame umpire Tom Connolly for using what Johnson called "vulgar and vicious language."

23. Joe Vila, "Ruth's Case Proves a Hero's Day Is Short in New York," *Sporting News*, June 1, 1922.

24. Joe Vila, "Woes of New York Fans Do Not Bring Tears from Rest of World," *Sporting News*, July 27, 1922.

25. Hugh Fullerton, On the Screen of Sport, *New York Evening Mail*, no date, Babe Ruth scrapbook, National Baseball Hall of Fame and Archives. Fullerton felt that Ruth should be disciplined.

26. James K. McGuinness, Sporting Spotlight, *New York Evening Telegram*, July 5, 1922.

27. Whether Hoyt punched or merely pushed Huggins differed from one account to another. The Yankees' pitcher was upset when Huggins ordered him to walk a batter in the final inning. After the walk, the Red Sox scored three times for a 5–2 win. At six feet and 180 pounds, Hoyt was much larger than Huggins.

28. Hugh Fullerton, On the Screen of Sport, *New York Evening Mail*, June 1, 1922.

29. Frederick G. Lieb, "Eleven Years in the Game, Yet the 'School Boy,'" *Sporting News*, March 3, 1927.

30. "Huggins May Move Meusel," *New York Globe and Commercial Advertiser*, March 29, 1923. Meusel hit .319 in 1922 (tied with catcher Wally Schang), second best on the team to Wally Pipp's .329. Huggins's respect for Meusel's playing grew over the years.

31. Joe Vila, "Landis Has Goods on Some of the Gambling Yankee Men," *Sporting News*, July 6, 1922.

32. Shocker brought a 17-8 record against New York into the game. A couple of days later, he checked into a hospital with a thigh injury and missed almost a month of the season. He would lose six of his next eight decisions against the Yankees in 1922.

33. Graham, *The New York Yankees*, 81–82.

34. Sid Keener, "Huggins May Quit Baseball after Operation to Take Up Law Practice at Cincinnati," *St. Louis Times*, April 7, 1922. See also Hugh Fullerton, "Operation upon Huggins Seen as End of B. B. Days," *Chicago Daily Tribune*, October 11, 1922.

35. Arthur Mann, "Miller Huggins, Unhappy Warrior, Overcame Ridicule, Hatred, Prima Donnas to Lead Earlier Yanks to Top," *Sporting News*, November 2, 1939.

36. "Use Black Jack, Yank Boss Tells Pilot Huggins," undated newspaper article, Bill Loughman private collection.

37. Barrow, *My Fifty Years in Baseball*, 138. Barrow wrote that both Yankees owners tended to go into the clubhouse after games to discuss with their manager what had transpired.

38. Barrow, *My Fifty Years in Baseball*, 137.

39. Creamer, *Babe*, 262–63.

40. Harry Schumacher, "Commissioner Landis Warns Ball Players in Serious Talk in Boston," *New York Globe and Commercial Advertiser*, June 27, 1922. See also "Yankees Win, 6–4; Judge Landis Tells Players What's What," *Boston Globe*, June 27, 1922. Landis said the punishment would be a five-year suspension.

41. Wagenheim, *Babe Ruth*, 137. A half-century after the incident occurred, Yankees center fielder Whitey Witt told Wagenheim the story. While he placed the conversation in 1925, it probably occurred in 1922, based on other accounts.

42. Alexander, *Our Game*, 145.

43. Joe Vila, "New York Sure It Is Already Settled," *Sporting News*, April 27, 1922.

44. James O'Leary, "Scott Completes String of 900 Successive Games," *Boston Sunday Globe*, June 25, 1922. Following the 1921 season, when Scott's streak had reached 832, statistician Al Munro Elias, writing in the 1922 *Baseball Bat Bag*, said that during the 1920 season, Scott had broken George Pinckney's record of 577 consecutive games played.

45. Boston got some real talent in the July 23 deal, though O'Doul would have great hitting seasons after he left Boston.

46. Spatz, *Yankees Coming, Yankees Going*, 43.

47. Lane, "The All-American Baseball Club of 1922," 309.

48. *Reach Official American League Baseball Guide, 1923*, 14.

49. John B. Sheridan, Back of the Home Plate, *Sporting News*, August 3, 1922.

50. Scribbled by Scribes, *Sporting News*, August 10, 1922.

51. Irving Vaughn, "Red Sox-Yankees Trades Arouse Fans of Nation," *Chicago Daily Tribune*, July 26, 1922.

52. Steinberg, "The Curse of the Hurlers."

53. Sid Mercer, "Huggins Will Be Firm with Temperamental Stars Next Season," *New York Evening Journal*, October 21, 1922.

54. Haupert, "Babe Ruth: Better than the Dow Jones," 13. From 1922 to 1926, Ruth's contract prohibited him from drinking or staying out past 1 AM. He obviously did not comply with these clauses, though the amount of money he was fined for these violations is not known.

55. Meany, *The Yankee Story*, 75. The Yankees beat the White Sox, 7–5. Two days earlier, Ruth's tenth-inning home run also beat the White Sox. Robert Creamer says that it was Huggins's scout and friend, Bob Connery, not Roth, with whom he was talking. *Babe*, 279–80.

56. Sid Keener, "Huggins, Manager of a Million Dollar Franchise, Played Hookey from Law School to Become Ball Player," *St. Louis Times*, May 17, 1919.

57. Colonel Til Huston papers in the Robert Edwards Auctions, May 18, 2013, auction, Lot 1284.

58. Sid Keener, *St. Louis Times*, October 10, 1922.

59. James Enright, "Roaring '20s—Great Time for Waite Hoyt," *Sporting News*, August 7, 1965.

60. Damon Runyon, Between You and Me, *New York American*, September 17, 1929. Runyon said he did not know Huggins before he came to the Yankees. So he is probably referring to the late (and not the early) teens.

61. On August 1 in Chicago, the Yankees were losing 5–1 in the top of the fifth inning, which had to be completed for the game to become official. Huggins stalled long enough for the game to be called on account of rain.

62. Frank Graham, "The Little Miller," *New York Journal-American*, December 13, 1964, and Al DeMaree, "Miller Huggins Kidded Again about Height," *Boston Globe*, September 4, 1925. The game in question took place on August 13, 1922, in Washington, when Witt and Huggins were ejected in the first inning.

63. Shocker did beat the Yankee four times in 1922; he insisted on starting twice in four-game series against them. New York had beaten him by the score of 2–1 in the opening game of the September series, and he failed to protect a 2–1 lead in the final game, which New York won, 3–2.

64. Harry Schumacher, *New York Globe and Commercial Advertiser*, October 2, 1922.

65. After posting an 11-4 mark and a league-best 2.63 earned run average, Douglas was banned by the commissioner when he wrote a compromising letter while recovering from a drunken binge. He suggested he would go fishing and hurt his Giants' (and manager John McGraw's, with whom he had constantly fought) pennant chances in exchange for "some inducement."

66. Hugh Fullerton, "Fullerton Picks the Yankees to Overwhelm McGraw's Men," *Chicago Daily Tribune*, October 1, 1922, and "Hugh Fullerton Picks Yanks to Smother Giants," *Chicago Daily Tribune*, October 2, 1922.

67. John Kieran, "Huggins Makes No Secret of Today's Pitching Selection," *New York Tribune*, October 4, 1922.

68. After giving up three first-inning runs, Bob Shawkey was brilliant for the next nine. The controversial decision to call the game—when there still seemed to be sufficient daylight—was made by umpire George Hildebrand. He feared that if the Giants scored in a time-consuming top of the eleventh inning, he might have to call the game with darkness falling in the bottom of the inning. The score would then revert to the 3–3 tie that was the score after ten full innings, which would surely trigger an outcry from the Giants.

69. Huston wanted all the money (over $120,000) to go to the Veterans of Foreign Wars for a home for indigent soldiers. Ruppert wanted to spread the money among different New York City charities. In the end, $50,000 went to the VFW, and the rest went to other groups. *New York Tribune*, October 13 and December 16, 1922.

70. Frederick G. Lieb, "41 Years Ago They Played Tie Contest and Lost Four," *Sporting News*, October 19, 1963. Bush probably used a word far more pejorative than "oaf."

71. Damon Runyon, *New York American*, October 9, 1922.

72. F. C. Lane, "The Manager Who Lost," 303.

73. Graham, *The New York Yankees*, 87.

74. Lieb, "41 Years Ago They Played Tie Contest and Lost Four."

75. Lieb, "Huggins Again to Lead the Yankees," *New York Evening Telegram*, October 12, 1922.

76. Frank Graham, *New York Sun*, October 9, 1922.

77. Joe Vila, Setting the Pace, *New York Sun*, October 9, 1922. Vila noted that Ruth was particularly weak on change-of-pace pitches and low balls.

78. Grantland Rice, "Giants Win Title; Take 4th Straight from Yanks, 5–3," *New York Tribune*, October 9, 1922.

79. Sid Keener, *St. Louis Times*, October 10, 1922.

80. Sid Mercer, Sid Mercer's Close-Ups, *New York Evening Journal*, October 10, 1922.

81. Mann, "Miller Huggins, Unhappy Warrior."

82. Editorial, "Huggins and His Job," *Sporting News*, October 26, 1922.

83. Frank O'Neill, "Changes Threaten the Yankees," *New York Sun*, October 10, 1922.

84. Ford Frick, "Huggins Born 49 Years Ago, Starred with Cardinals," *New York Evening Journal*, September 25, 1929.

1. Harry Schumacher, "Ruppert Intends to Perpetuate Yankees' Policy; Huston Not Forced Out," *New York Globe and Commercial Advertiser*, December 13, 1922.

2. Ruppert agreed to pay $500,000 in cash and $75,000 a year for ten years. In a December 11, 1922, letter to his attorney, Huston wrote, "Perfect safety in securing the deferred payments is the prime essence of the trade to me. Anything else will defeat the negotiations." Colonel Til Huston papers in the Robert Edwards Auctions, May 18, 2013, auction, Lot 1284.

3. Barrow, *My Fifty Years in Baseball*, 123. Ruppert's obituary in the *New York Sun* said, "Temperamentally neither man was gaited to be a partner. They were both individuals of strong wills and opinions." January 13, 1939.

4. Huston papers in the Robert Edwards Auctions.

5. Levitt, *Ed Barrow*, 203.

6. Sid Mercer, "Colonel Huston Steps Out; Was a Credit to Baseball," *New York Evening Journal*, December 13, 1922.

7. Col. Jacob Ruppert, as told to Daniel, "Behind the Scenes of the Yankees: Ruppert Buys Out Huston," *New York World-Telegram*, February 17, 1938.

8. "Huggins May Stay as Yanks' Manager," *New York Times*, October 10, 1922, and "Huggins Will Manage Yankees Next Season," *New York Tribune*, October 10, 1922.

9. Joe Vila, "Ruppert Scores Biggest Win of Whole Year for Yankees," *Sporting News*, May 31, 1923. The dynamics of how Ruppert was able to get his way with his fifty-fifty partner so often must have been fascinating.

10. Frederick G. Lieb, "Col. Ruppert Soon to Become Sole Boss of the Yankee Club," *New York Evening Telegram*, December 13, 1922.

11. W. A. Phelon, "The Grand Panorama of Winter Baseball," 405.

12. Editorial, "And Mr. Huston Retires," *Sporting News*, December 28, 1922. See also the *Sporting News* editorial of January 11, 1923, "Colonel Huston Is In Again."

13. Frederick G. Lieb, *New York Evening Telegram*, December 12, 1922.

14. John B. Sheridan, Back of the Home Plate, *Sporting News*, December 25, 1919.

15. Mercer, "Colonel Huston Steps Out; Was a Credit to Baseball."

16. Joe Vila, "Under Ruppert Huggins Is to Be One Real Manager," *Sporting News*, December 28, 1922.

17. Mercer, "Colonel Huston Steps Out; Was a Credit to Baseball."

18. Sid Mercer, "Huston Will Continue as Part Owner of Yankee Team," *New York Evening Journal*, January 5, 1923.

19. W. J. Macbeth, "Col. Huston Will Retain His Interest," *New York Tribune*, January 5, 1923.

20. Francis C. Richter, Casual Comment, *Sporting News*, January 18, 1923.

21. "Col. Ruppert Said He and Col. Huston 'Agreed to Agree,'" *New York World*, January 6, 1923.

22. W. J. Macbeth, "Yankee Deal for Eddie Collins Said to Be Almost Completed," *New York Tribune*, January 11, 1923.

23. Warren W. Brown, "Huggins Earns Cheers of Yank Fans," *New York Evening Mail*, September 4, 1922.

24. Monitor, "Would Groom Second Baseman to Succeed Huggins as Manager," *New York World*, January 14, 1923. George Daley wrote under the pseudonym of "Monitor."

25. F. C. Lane, "What Has Blocked One of Baseball's Biggest Deals," 435.

26. Monitor, "Would Groom Second Baseman to Succeed Huggins as Manager."

27. Huston was paid a total of $1,175,000: $450,000 down and the balance in nine annual payments, the first for $85,000 and the rest for $80,000. Executed Purchase and Sale Agreement, Huston papers in the Robert Edwards Auctions.

28. "Ruppert Completes Deal for Yankees," *New York Times*, May 22, 1923. Ruppert's brother, George, took over as the club's vice president. Huston remained a director of the team, apparently did not attend any board meetings, and withdrew as a director in the summer of 1924 when Ruppert paid off the note early. *Sporting News*, August 21, 1924.

29. Levitt, *Ed Barrow*, 203–4. Barrow borrowed the $300,000 from his former business associate, stadium concessionaire Harry Stevens.

30. Meany, *The Yankee Story*, 55.

31. Before the buyout, Barrow had informed Ruppert that he was thinking of pursuing the American League presidency, as Ban Johnson was thinking of retiring. Levitt, *Ed Barrow*, 203.

32. "Huston Sells to Ruppert," *New York Sun*, May 22, 1923.

33. Huston papers in the Robert Edwards Auctions. Although these hand-written letters were drafts that may not have been sent, they reveal how Huston had come to feel.

34. Huston papers in the Robert Edwards Auctions.

35. Editorial, "Victory for Law and Order," *Sporting News*, May 31, 1923, and Francis C. Richter, Casual Comment, *Sporting News*, January 4, 1923.

36. Graham, *The New York Yankees*, 93.

37. "Ruppert Completes Deal for Yankees," *New York Times*, May 22, 1923. The "one really good player" was probably Roger Peckinpaugh.

38. Francis C. Richter, Casual Comment, *Sporting News*, June 7, 1923. The Yankees outdrew the Giants at the Polo Grounds by more than 500,000 fans (32%) in 1920–21.

39. W. B. Hanna, "Ruppert Buys Huston Shares in Yankees," *New York Tribune*, May 22, 1923.

40. Graham, *The New York Yankees*, 92. In his autobiography, Barrow says he "made" Ruppert send the telegram. Barrow, *My Fifty Years in Baseball*, 139.

41. Ford Frick, "Life Story of Miller Huggins," part 5, *New York Evening Journal*, October 1, 1929.

42. Frederick G. Lieb, "Huggins Will Stay with Yankees Indefinitely," *New York Evening Telegram*, December 26, 1924. This quote appeared in more than one publication. Sometimes it was said to cover 1919 to 1923. See Graham, *The New York Yankees*, 35, and Barrow, *My Fifty Years in Baseball*, 140.

23. Happiest Day of My Life

1. Bronx County Historical Society. http://www.bronxhistoricalsociety .org.

2. Commissioner Landis traveled from his Manhattan hotel to the Yankees' opening game by subway.

3. Neil Sullivan, *The Diamond in the Bronx*, 43 and 46.

4. Jay Maeder, "Big Town Biography," *New York Daily News*, March 2, 1999.

5. John Kieran, "The Man in the Iron Hat," *New York Times*, March 30, 1938.

6. To erect this extraordinary structure, it took two million board feet and 600,000 lineal feet of lumber, 2,500 tons of structural steel, 1,000 tons of

reinforcing steel, 500 tons of iron, and four miles of piping. Then 45,000 cubic yards of earth was needed to fill and level the ground, and then more than 100,000 square feet of sod was trucked in from Long Island to create the playing surface.

7. "Size of Stadium Impresses Crowd," *New York Times*, April 19, 1923.

8. Robinson and Jennison, *Yankee Stadium*, 13.

9. Frederick G. Lieb, *New York Evening Telegram*, November 24, 1922.

10. Yankee Stadium's big fights were not restricted solely to the heavy-weights. On July 23, more than 60,000 people saw local favorite Benny Leonard defend his world lightweight title with a unanimous fifteen-round decision over Philadelphia's Lew Tendler.

11. Levitt, *Ed Barrow*, 198. The Yankees' financial records at the Hall of Fame Library and Archives have an entry for December 1922 that the Yankees received the loan at 7 percent interest from the league. Principal was due in the amount of $40,000 per year for ten years.

12. Schenck had been the groundskeeper at Hilltop Park, the Yankees' original ballpark, but lost his job in 1913 when the Yankees became tenants of the Giants at the Polo Grounds. When they moved to Yankee Stadium, the popular groundskeeper was rehired. During the interim, Schenck worked as the groundskeeper for Fordham University's ball fields on the Rose Hill campus in the Bronx.

13. The previous record was 43,620 set at Boston's Braves Field in the fifth game of the 1916 World Series between Brooklyn and the Boston Red Sox. The Red Sox used Braves Field, rather than the smaller-capacity Fenway Park, in both the 1915 and 1916 World Series. Lowry, *Green Cathedrals*, 31.

14. As early as 1917, cartoonist and columnist Robert Ripley wrote that Harry Stevens had concessions at five ballparks and four of the nation's biggest race tracks, including Belmont Park. "He serves different items at different places," Ripley wrote. "At Belmont, it's champagne and lobster; at the six-day bike races, it's hot dogs." Credit for the success of the business belonged to his son, Frank, Stevens told Ripley. Robert Ripley, "Catering to Sport Fans," *New York Globe and Commercial Advertiser*, June 16, 1917.

15. Entering the 1923 season, Shawkey was also the all-time Yankees' leader in wins with 120.

16. Ruth, playing right field, also committed the first error in the new stadium when he dropped a fly ball. Ruth was in his third Yankee opener; he

played center field in the first one (1920), left field in the second (1921), and was on suspension for the 1922 opener.

17. Spatz, *New York Yankee Openers*, 93.

18. W. B. Hanna, "Ruppert Buys Huston's Share of Yankees," *New York Tribune*, May 22, 1923.

19. Joe Vila, "Yankees in West and Giants in East Make It Monotonous," *Sporting News*, May 24, 1923.

20. Lane, "The Shadow of New York on the Baseball Diamond," 398.

21. Joe Vila, "If Ruppert Has Doubts He Is the Only One of Such Mind," *Sporting News*, July 12, 1923.

22. If Ruppert had one disappointment in this championship season, it was in home attendance. Due in large part to a runaway pennant race, the Yankees drew only 1,007,066. That was less than in any of the three preceding years at the Polo Grounds, but still considerably more than the 820,780 the Giants drew at the Polo Grounds in 1923.

23. Vila, "If Ruppert Has Doubts He Is the Only One of Such Mind."

24. Ruth's .393 batting average was the highest of his career, but was good for only second place behind Detroit's Harry Heilmann, who batted .403.

25. Ruth's 170 walks and .545 on-base percentage remain American League single-season records.

26. In 1922, the American League created the League Award to honor "the baseball player who is of the greatest all-around service to his club." The voters included one writer from each American League city, and Ruth got all eight votes. A player could win the award only once. The National League began making a League Award in 1924, but allowed for repeat winners. The American League dropped the award after 1928, and the National League dropped it after 1929.

27. Far from being a one-dimensional team, the Yankees also led the American League in fielding percentage.

28. "Huggins Is Signed Again as Manager," *New York Times*, October 8, 1923.

29. The Yankees had not had a proven left-hander in their starting rotation since George Mogridge (1916–20).

30. "Yanks Get Pennock from the Red Sox," *New York Times*, January 31, 1923.

31. *New York World*, January 31, 1923.

32. Sid Mercer, "Huggins Figures Mays Can Win 25 Games," *New York Evening Journal*, April 17, 1923.

33. "Ruth Offers to Work on Slab for Yankees," *Cleveland Plain Dealer*, July 20, 1923.

34. "Extends Huggins's Term as Manager," *New York Herald*, October 8, 1923.

35. "Huggins Is Signed Again as Manager," *New York Times*, October 8, 1923.

36. Ford Frick, *New York Evening Journal*, October 9, 1923. Evidently Frick felt confident that his readers were familiar with Napoleon, Ulysses S. Grant, and former British prime ministers William Gladstone and Benjamin Disraeli.

37. Christy Walsh, "Adios to Ghosts!" *Cleveland News*, September 21, 1937.

38. Lieb, *The Baseball Story*, 229.

39. "Old Sport," *Philadelphia Inquirer*, August 20, 1923.

40. As they had in 1921 and 1922, the teams would alternate being the home team in every other game through the first six games. A seventh game, if necessary, would be decided by a coin toss, which the Yankees won. McGraw would not let the Giants use the visitors' clubhouse at Yankee Stadium. He had them dress for their Yankee Stadium games in their own clubhouse at the Polo Grounds.

41. During the season, the Yankees had been more successful on the road (52-24) than at home (46-30).

42. One game of the 1922 Series ended in a tie.

43. Creamer, *Stengel*, 168.

44. Frederick G. Lieb, "Col. Ruppert Ridicules Idea of 'Weakening Yankees'; We're Out to Win, Let Others Build to Our Strength," *Sporting News*, October 6, 1938.

45. Huggins, "Serial Story of His Baseball Career: Miller Huggins Tells How He Figured on McGraw Making a Mistake," *San Francisco Chronicle*, chapter 12, January 27, 1924.

46. Appel, *Pinstripe Empire*, 139.

47. Damon Runyon, "Deserved Tribute to Colonel Ruppert," *Reach Official American League Guide, 1924*, 243.

48. Gallagher, *The Yankee Encyclopedia*, 406.

49. Robert F. Kelley, "Yanks Finally Come to End of Their Long Trail," *New York Evening Post*, October 16, 1923. The lyric includes the phrase, "There's a long, long night of waiting, Until my dreams all come true," which likely resonated with the Colonel.

50. Harry Cross, "It's All in the Game," *New York Evening Post*, October 16, 1923.

1. Huggins, "The Danger of Too Much Success," 543.

2. Dan Daniel, "Yankees Scorched by Hot Talk on Training by Chief Huggins," *New York Telegram and Evening Mail*, March 25, 1924.

3. Huggins, "The Danger of Too Much Success," 543.

4. Daniel, "Yankees Scorched by Hot Talk on Training by Chief Huggins."

5. "Yanks to Abandon New Orleans Camp," *New York Times*, January 31, 1924, and "Yanks Will Train at St. Petersburg," *New York Times*, July 8, 1924.

6. Editorial, "Records and Loss of Sleep," *Sporting News*, March 20, 1924.

7. Scott broke George Pinkney's nineteenth-century mark of 577 later in the 1920 season.

8. Graham, *Lou Gehrig*, 92–93.

9. "Gehrig Leaves Yanks to Play under Option in Hartford," *New York Times*, April 15, 1924.

10. Unidentified newspaper clipping in the Miller Huggins scrapbook, National Baseball Hall of Fame Library and Archives.

11. "Yank Chief Finds Rookies Enigma While Training," *New York Telegram and Evening Mail*, March 12, 1924.

12. Joe Vila, Setting the Pace, *New York Sun*, July 13, 1923. The new owners were led by former Browns business manager Bob Quinn.

13. "Outfielder Combs Bought by Yanks," *New York Times*, January 8, 1924. This report said there was opposition to the deal within the club, possibly from Barrow or Huggins, but Ruppert had insisted on making it.

14. Ruppert to Earle Combs, February 7, 1924, Combs family papers, SABR Research Library.

15. Baxter, In the Press Box, *Washington Post*, February 28, 1924. Ruppert said the team's regulars had averaged $12,500 in salary and World Series shares. The latter was almost half the total. http://www.baseball-almanac.com/ws/wsshares.shtml.

16. Will Wedge, "Why Ruppert Likes Flags," *New York Sun*, April 7, 1924.

17. Frank O'Neill, "Ruppert of the Yankees Once upon a Time Almost Bought Giants," *Sporting News*, February 21, 1924.

18. Joe Vila, "Big Disappointment for Ruppert if Yanks Fail to Come Through," *Sporting News*, April 10, 1924.

19. Sid Mercer, "Ruppert, Mere Fan Few Years Ago, Now Owns the Richest Club," *New York Evening Telegram*, December 30, 1922.

20. W. O. McGeehan, "Ruppert Lives to Learn Baseball Men Have Class," *Sporting News*, December 27, 1923.

21. Damon Runyon, Runyon Says, *New York American*, December 27, 1924.

22. Sid Mercer, "The Colonel: Victory Always His Aim," *New York Journal-American*, January 20, 1939.

23. Frederick G. Lieb, "Ruppert Praises Work of Huggins," *New York Evening Telegram*, September 21, 1923.

24. Motor vehicle fatalities in the United States, which had totaled less than 100 in 1902 and 1,000 in 1908, exceeded 18,000 in 1924 and would rise to more than 30,000 by 1930. Carter et al., *Historical Statistics of the United States*, vol. 4.

25. The *New York Daily Mirror*, begun in June 1924, was the competing tabloid of the Hearst chain.

26. Perrett, *America in the Twenties*, 78. In Congress Ruppert had served on the Immigration Committee, where he opposed literacy tests for new immigrants.

27. The law included the National Origins Act, whose quota limited annual immigration from a country to 2 percent of the U.S. population from that country, based on the 1890 census, just before large numbers of immigrants came to America from those regions.

28. Higham, *Strangers in the Land*, 159 and 324. See also Miller, *New World Coming*, 93 and 147. British and Irish immigration dropped about 20 percent after the restrictive law was passed, but that from Italy and Eastern Europe dropped 90 percent.

29. Lieb, "Baseball—The Nation's Melting Pot."

30. Lieb, *Baseball as I Have Known It*, 132. It is unclear whether the Bush-Huggins flare-up at the end of the 1922 World Series was the source of the conflict or a symptom of a bigger problem.

31. McGarigle, *Baseball's Great Tragedy*, 198. The book is almost a collaborative effort; McGarigle quotes heavily from Mays throughout.

32. Murdock, *Baseball between the Wars*, 36.

33. Frederick G. Lieb, *New York Telegram and Evening Mail*, July 12, 1924.

34. Frederick G. Lieb, *New York Telegram and Evening Mail*, August 12, 1924. Lieb reported that Herrmann paid the Yankees $25,000 for Mays.

35. "Editorial Comment," *Baseball Magazine*, February 1924, 386.

36. Arthur Robinson, *New York American*, February 7, 1924. With Ruppert's consolidation of ownership and Barrow's buying into ownership, the latter had no reason to leave New York.

37. Graham, "The Little Miller," 378. Ruel is listed as five foot nine and 150 pounds, taller and heavier than Huggins.

38. Thomas, *Walter Johnson*, 187.

39. The previous four seasons, Johnson had a 57-52 record and did not lead the league in any major statistical category other than strikeouts in 1921 and 1923.

40. Judge, *Damn Senators*, 75.

41. Frederick G. Lieb, "Huggins Will Stay with the Yankees Indefinitely," *New York Telegram and Evening Mail*, December 26, 1924.

42. "Yanks Again Lose to Senators, 5–1," *New York Times*, August 30, 1924.

43. "Notes of the Nationals," *Washington Post*, September 15, 1924.

44. Marberry led the league in Games, Games Finished, and Saves (the latter computed retroactively), the first of three straight seasons he did so. His fifteen Saves that year were the most to that point, a mark Marberry would tie in 1925 and surpass in 1926.

45. "Twirlers Worry Huggins," *New York Telegram and Evening Mail*, July 3, 1924.

46. F. C. Lane, "The Man Who Led the Yankees to Their First Pennant," 596.

47. Markle was a bust in 1924, too. He lost his three starts and had an 8.87 earned run average.

48. After posting a 19-6 record with a 3.13 earned run average in 1923, Pennock fashioned a 21-9 mark with a 2.83 ERA in 1924.

49. Miller Huggins file, National Baseball Hall of Fame Library and Archives.

50. Damon Runyon, Runyon Says, *New York American*, September 20, 1924.

51. Joe Vila, "It Begins to Look Like Dodgers against Senators to Joe Vila," *Sporting News*, September 11, 1924.

52. Babe Ruth went only 2-for-10 in the series.

53. Judge, *Damn Senators*, 104. The Tigers were in first place themselves as late as August 12.

54. Gallico, *The Golden People*, 200.

55. Alexander, *Ty Cobb*, 172.

56. Editorial, *Sporting News*, July 31, 1924. The Yankees also played exhibition games that season in New Jersey, Louisville, Utica, Syracuse, and Buffalo, all to generate extra revenue for Ruppert and the club.

57. Washington's pennant left St. Louis as the only "pennant-less" Major League city; St. Louis had two teams, the Browns and the Cardinals.

58. The Yankees again drew more than 1 million fans in 1924 (and did so for the fifth straight season). They also widened the gap with the Giants

slightly (from 1923). Their 1920 mark of 1,289,422, the Babe's first season in New York, remained their top turnout until they surpassed 1.3 million fans in 1946.

59. The May 1923 buyout called for nine quarterly payments to Huston. Trust Agreement in the Robert Edwards Auctions, May 18, 2013, auction.

60. Frederick G. Lieb, "Huggins Will Stay with Yanks Indefinitely; No Longer Has Any Thought of Retiring," *New York Telegram and Evening Mail*," December 26, 1924.

61. Ford Frick, "Frick's Comments," *New York Evening Journal*, June 19, 1924.

62. Miller Huggins, "Serial Story of His Baseball Career: Babe Ruth Is One of Few Ballplayers Who Never Want an Alibi," *San Francisco Chronicle*, chapter 24, February 9, 1924.

63. Miller Huggins, "Serial Story of His Baseball Career: Ruth Is Most Remarkable Figure Baseball Has Ever Known, Declares Huggins," chapter 23, February 8, 1924.

64. Lieb, "Huggins Will Stay with Yanks Indefinitely."

65. Ford Frick, "Huggins Ready to Break Up Team for New Talent," *New York Evening Journal*, October 28, 1924.

66. Arthur Mann, "Miller Huggins, Unhappy Warrior, Overcame Ridicule, Hatred, Prima Donnas to Lead Earlier Yanks to Top," *Sporting News*, November 2, 1939. While Huggins and Mann did not mention a player by name, Aaron Ward was a promising young Yankee who was a starter at twenty-three, benched at twenty-nine, traded by the Yankees at thirty, and out of the Major Leagues a year later.

67. Lieb, "Huggins Will Stay with Yanks Indefinitely."

68. Frank Graham, Graham's Corner, *New York Journal-American*, July 1962.

69. Holtzman, *No Cheering in the Press Box*, 10.

25. New Homes for Single Men

1. "Connery in New York to Form Alliance with Yanks," *St. Paul Press*, January 20, 1925.

2. "Owner of Saints Denies New York Baseball Stories," *St. Paul Dispatch*, January 20, 1925. See also the *St. Paul Daily Light*, January 1, 1925.

3. Steinberg, "The St. Paul–New York Underground Railroad," 38.

4. Levitt, *Ed Barrow*, 277.

5. Two documents confirm Huggins's investment: a 1925 stock certificate reflecting his ownership of fifty shares in the team, and a letter from Huggins to Connery confirming the former's investment. Steinberg, "The St.

Paul–New York Underground Railroad," 41–43. St. Louis banker Leo Daly was a third investor.

6. In the past, Huggins had thought of buying and running a Minor League club and no longer managing in the Major Leagues. In St. Paul, he was simply a passive investor.

7. "Two More Scouts Join Yank Staff," *New York Times*, December 16, 1925. Bob Gilks and Ed Holly were two other Yankees scouts.

8. Colonel Til Huston papers in the Robert Edwards Auctions, May 18, 2013, auction. There is no evidence Huggins opposed the farm system in the early 1920s. Until the Cardinals won the 1926 National League pennant, there was no evidence that Rickey's radical approach would pay off.

9. Levitt, *Ed Barrow*, 214.

10. Daniel M. Daniel, "From Peanuts to Pennants: The Story of Edward G. Barrow," chapter 10, February 1938.

11. Fountain, *Under the March Sun*, 22. See chapter 2, "St. Petersburg's Mr. Baseball."

12. McCarthy, *Baseball in Florida*, 147.

13. Fountain, *Under the March Sun*, 30.

14. Joe Williams, Joe Williams Says, *New York Evening Telegram*, March 9, 1927.

15. Huggins first appeared in the Manhattan and Bronx Directory in 1925, at 364 St. Nicholas Avenue, near West 128th Street.

16. Huggins and his sister were listed in Cincinnati directories through 1924, which is also the first year they appeared in the St. Petersburg one.

17. W. O. McGeehan, Down the Line, *New York Herald Tribune*," March 11, 1925. Florida's west coast, where many Major League clubs held their spring training, was often called the Ivory Belt. The state's east coast was known as the Gold Coast.

18. The ballpark was renamed Miller Huggins Field in a March 1931 ceremony, and in 1963 was renamed Huggins-Stengel Field, after another successful Yankees' manager, Casey Stengel. The Huggins home was at 1416 Second Street North.

19. Kelley had moved across the river and was now the owner and manager of the Minneapolis Millers of the American Association.

20. Warren Brown, So They Tell Me, *Chicago Herald and Examiner*, September 27, 1929.

21. Bill Corum, Sports, *New York Evening Journal*, March 9, 1927. Huggins mentioned Yale and Princeton as two of the "great universities" his son could have attended. *New York Evening Journal*, December 23, 1939.

22. Dan Daniel, "Late Chief's Policies to Govern New Yank Pilot," *New York Evening Telegram*, September 27, 1929. Daniel revealed these comments only after Huggins's death.

23. Arthur Mann, "Miller Huggins, Unhappy Warrior, Overcame Ridicule, Hatred, Prima Donnas to Lead Earlier Yanks to Top," *Sporting News*, November 2, 1939. Mann was born in 1901 and married in 1923.

24. E-mail from K. Jacob Ruppert to Steve Steinberg, April 15, 2013. Ruppert sold the family home to developer Sam Minskoff and moved from 1115 Fifth Avenue to 1120 Fifth Avenue.

25. Betty Kirk, "Jacob Ruppert, 'Born Bachelor,' Sees Day Coming with Marriage Extinct," *New York Evening Telegram*, June 13, 1928.

26. The property is now St. Basil Academy, a children's refuge of the Greek Orthodox Church, which acquired it in 1944. http://saintbasilacademy.org/about_us/estate_history.

27. Sportswriter Tom Meany wrote that the only baseball item in the mansion was an ashtray with a batter as an ornament. He said that the estate never had a visitor from the Yankees, not even Ed Barrow or Miller Huggins. "Old Estate No Reminder of Ruppert Dynasty," *PM*, March 28, 1943. The Saint Basil Academy web site, however, says Ruppert had numerous Yankees as guests.

28. Frommer, *Five O'Clock Lightning*, 58–59.

29. Damon Runyon, Runyon Says, *New York American*, December 27, 1924.

30. Lieb, *Baseball as I Have Known It*, 228.

31. Betty Kirk, "Jacob Ruppert, 'Born Bachelor.'"

32. Lieb, *Baseball as I Have Known It*, 228.

33. Shulman, *Eat the City*, 217.

34. *Bachelor*, May 1937, 51.

35. Louis E. Bisch, M.D., "What Is a Bachelor?" *Bachelor*, April 1937, 9. It is not known if Ruppert cooperated with the magazine or agreed to appear in it.

36. Hiram Jefferson Herbert, "Why a Bachelor?" *Bachelor*, May 1937, 9.

37. Kirk, "Jacob Ruppert, 'Born Bachelor.'"

38. Holland, "The Beer Barons of New York," 405.

39. Kirk, "Jacob Ruppert, 'Born Bachelor.'"

40. She appeared in five plays between 1922 and 1929. Her brother, Rex, would become the Yankees' assistant traveling secretary in 1936.

1. After winning three straight pennants from 1906 to 1908 and falling to second place in 1909, the Cubs won the 1910 pennant by 13 games.
2. Frederick G. Lieb, "Mental Disintegration Huggins' Fear," *New York Evening Telegram*, April 8, 1925.
3. "Harris and Huggins Enter Early Claims for Pennant Honors," *Sporting News*, April 9, 1925.
4. Editorial, "The Mystery of the Yanks," *Sporting News*, June 25, 1925.
5. W. O. McGechan, Down the Line, *New York Herald Tribune*, March 11, 1925.
6. Milt Gaston and Joe Giard were promising prospects. Gaston spent ten more years in the Majors as a journeyman pitcher. The Yankees reacquired Giard before the 1927 season, his last in the Majors, when they sent Sam Jones to the Browns. Giard recorded no decisions for the '27 Yankees.
7. Lieb, "Mental Disintegration Huggins's Fear." Shocker had a number of run-ins with Browns owner Phil Ball. The irascible Ball was more than willing to trade his ace.
8. Dan Daniel, Daniel's Dope, *New York World-Telegram*, July 7, 1941. The *New York Evening World* of September 13, 1924, said the Yankees had indeed offered Bush and Gehrig to the Browns for Shocker. The December 12, 1924, *New York Times*, just days before the trade, wrote that the Browns wanted Gehrig. Evidently, however, the Browns wanted more pitching instead.
9. "Gehrig Ready to Quit, Changes Mind after Session with Huggins," chapter 18 of Gehrig's life story, *New York American*, September 17, 1927.
10. "Hug Class of Bunch as Pilot, Says Gehrig," chapter 26 of Gehrig's life story, *New York American*, September 28, 1927.
11. Bozeman Bulger, *Newspaper Alliance*, September 28, 1929.
12. Frank Graham, "Players Make the Manager," *New York Sun*, August 14, 1926.
13. Creamer, *Babe*, 289.
14. "Yank Chief Finds Rookies Enigma While Training," *New York Telegram and Evening Mail*, March 12, 1924.
15. Barrow, *My Fifty Years in Baseball*, 190.
16. Norman Baxter, In the Press Box, *Washington Post*, April 28, 1925.

17. Miller Huggins, *New York World*, May 5, 1925.
18. Lieb, *The Baseball Story*, 240.
19. The Yankees also sent three players to the Saints: catcher Fred Hofmann, pitcher Oscar Roettger, and infielder Ernie Johnson.
20. W. O. McGeehan, Down the Line, *New York Herald Tribune*, October 4, 1925.
21. Gehrig had only twenty-three at bats the first six weeks of the season.
22. Pipp has been immortalized in one of baseball's enduring myths, as well as in the English language. To be "pipped" or "wallypipped" has entered our slang, referring to someone who took a day off and was replaced permanently.
23. "Pickups and Putouts," *New York Times*, August 10, 1925.
24. Joe Vila, "Youngsters Instill New Spirit into Wavering Ranks of Yanks," *Sporting News*, June 18, 1925.
25. Frederick G. Lieb, Cutting the Plate, *New York Evening Post*, July 26, 1927.
26. John B. Foster, "Yankee Management Gambled One Year Too Long," *St. Louis Post-Dispatch*, June 15, 1925.
27. Davis J. Walsh, "Yankees' Stars to Move On," *New York Evening Journal*, July 28, 1925.
28. Joe Vila, "Yanks beyond Control of 'Hug,' According to Gotham Gossips," *Sporting News*, June 25, 1925. Stallings had managed the Yankees in 1909–10.
29. Joe Vila, "Ruth May Pay Heavy Penalty for Getting Back Too Quickly," *Sporting News*, July 2, 1925.
30. Joe Vila, "Feeling Grows Yanks Conspire to Ride Miller Huggins Out," *Sporting News*, July 23, 1925.
31. Scribbled by Scribes, *Sporting News*, August 6, 1925.
32. "Yanks Play Browns in 2 Games Today," *New York Times*, June 26, 1925.
33. W. O. McGeehan, "The Invalid Yanks," *New York Herald Tribune*, June 21, 1925. In one of the first issues of the *New Yorker*, Morris Markey wrote about the quality of colorful writing on the sports pages, topped by the "sardonic humor" of McGeehan. "The Current Press," 15.
34. Smelser, *The Life That Ruth Built*, 316. See also Wagenheim, *Babe Ruth*, 142, and Considine, *The Babe Ruth Story*, 140.
35. Graham, *The New York Yankees*, 32, and Murdock, *Baseball Players and Their Times*, 32.

36. Ford Frick, *New York Evening Journal*, October 1, 1929, and Arthur Mann, "Miller Huggins, Unhappy Warrior, Overcame Ridicule, Hatred, Prima Donnas to Lead Earlier Yanks to Top," *Sporting News*, November 2, 1939.

37. Joe Williams, By Joe Williams, *New York Evening Telegram*, September 24, 1929.

38. Mrs. Babe Ruth, *The Babe and I*, 87.

39. Fowler, *Skyline*, 107.

40. Smelser wrote that this happened in late June in Boston, 316; Wagenheim placed it in Cleveland in late August, 142. In both series, Ruth hit home runs.

41. Five thousand dollars was an incredible sum at the time, around the annual salary of the average ballplayer. For Ruth, the fine amounted to almost 10 percent of his $52,000 annual salary.

42. Huggins was reported to have kept a chart of four years of insubordination by the Babe. *New York American*, September 1, 1925. The recently surfaced Huston papers reveal that the Yankees had an investigator following Ruth even during the successful 1923 season. He reported on alcohol-fueled parties attended by Ruth and other Yankees with Broadway chorus girls. Colonel Til Huston papers in the Robert Edwards Auctions, May 18, 2013, auction. (The story of a detective spending time undercover with the team took place during the disastrous 1922 campaign.)

43. Babe Ruth Transaction Card, National Baseball Hall of Fame Library and Archives.

44. "Ruth Fined $5,000; Costly Star Banned for Acts Off Field," *New York Times*, August 30, 1925.

45. Damon Runyon, Runyon Says, *New York American*, September 2, 1925.

46. Heywood Broun, It Seems to Me, *Boston Daily Globe*, September 2, 1925.

47. Miller Huggins, "Serial Story of His Baseball Group: Babe Ruth Is One of Few Ballplayers Who Never Want an Alibi," chapter 24, February 9, 1924.

48. "Yankee Owner Will Uphold Action of Manager Huggins," *Washington Post*, August 31, 1925.

49. F. C. Lane, "A Fallen Idol," 558.

50. Ruth, "I Have Been a Babe and a Boob."

51. "Ruth Sees Ruppert; Waves Olive Branch," *New York Times*, September 2, 1925.

52. Damon Runyon, Runyon Says, *New York American*, September 3, 1925.

53. Lipsky, *How We Play the Game*, 106.

54. Ed Wray, "Huggins Is Wearing His Spurs, Although It Is Only December," *Sporting News*, December 10, 1925.

55. Ruth, "I Have Been a Babe and a Boob."

56. In his Yankees' team history, Graham says the conversation took place in 1928, not 1925. In his team history, Tom Meany places it in 1925.

57. Frank Graham, "Prefers Old Type of Player," *New York Sun*, June 22, 1926.

58. Barrow, *My Fifty Years in Baseball*, 142.

59. John Kieran, Sports of the Times, *New York Times*, October 23, 1928.

60. Hugh Bradley, "The Barrow Story: Built an Empire but Always Considered Himself a Player," December 1953, *New York Journal-American* morgue files, Harry Ransom Humanities Research Center, University of Texas at Austin.

27. Boom to Bust, Bust to Boom

1. "A Funny Game, Says Huggins," *New York Sun*, August 31, 1926.

2. "Frederick G. Lieb, "Rebuilding of His Own Team," *New York Evening Telegram*, February 20, 1926.

3. Allen, *Only Yesterday*, 241–42.

4. Frank Graham, Graham's Corner, *New York Journal-American*, March 27, 1943.

5. Arthur Mann, "Miller Huggins, Unhappy Warrior, Overcame Ridicule, Hatred, Prima Donnas to Lead Earlier Yanks to Top," *Sporting News*, November 2, 1939. Other accounts say that Huggins sold his stock portfolio of his own volition later in the 1920s, when he felt uncomfortable with the inflated market. See Smith, *Babe Ruth's America*, 176–77.

6. Lieb, "Rebuilding of His Own Team."

7. Moore, *Anything Goes*, 326.

8. *Brooklyn Daily Eagle*, February 18, 1926, and *New York Evening Telegram*, February 20, 1926. Pegler later wrote that his March 1926 column attacking Huggins "so aroused him [Huggins] that he renounced Florida real estate." But Huggins sold his holdings almost a month before the infamous article appeared.

9. "Miller Huggins Dies," *New York Herald Tribune*, September 26, 1929.

10. Bill Slocum, "Miller Huggins, as I Knew Him," *New York American*, October 1, 1929.

11. "Baseball Magnate Buys Island Land," *St. Petersburg Evening Independent*, September 25, 1925. The corporation had paid-in capital of $500,000. *New York Sun*, October 30. 1925.
12. "Colonel Ruppert Authorizes Interview Which Expresses His Faith in the West Coast," *St. Petersburg Evening Independent*, March 10, 1926.
13. Moore, *Anything Goes*, 158.
14. Smith, *Babe Ruth's America*, 176.
15. Koenig had appeared in twenty-eight games for the Yankees in 1925, when he hit only .209, after hitting .308 that year in St. Paul.
16. Will Wedge, "Business Instinct in Baseball," *New York Sun*, April 17, 1926.
17. Ford Frick, "Huggins Dims Hopes of Annexing Pennant This Year," *New York Evening Journal*, March 2, 1926.
18. Ed Wray, *St. Louis Post-Dispatch*, April 4, 1926.
19. "Baseball," *New York Times*, March 8, 1926.
20. Graham, *Lou Gehrig*, 111. Pipp batted only .230 as a part-time player in 1925.
21. The Pacific Coast League had a very long season. The thin, high desert air obviously aided his long-ball hitting.
22. Appel, *Pinstripe Empire*, 146.
23. When Lazzeri had a seizure, it usually occurred in the morning.
24. Robinson, *Iron Horse*, 107. They are fewer reports of Huggins spending time with Koenig on fielding, though he turned out to be a much more erratic fielder than Lazzeri. His nervous temperament may have played a role in his committing so many errors.
25. Meany, *The Yankee Story*, 80–81.
26. "Miller Huggins, Yanks' Manager, Dies," *New York Herald Tribune*, September 26, 1929.
27. Frank Graham, Graham's Corner, *New York Journal-American*, March 27, 1943.
28. "Many Praise Huggins as Clean Sportsman," *New York Times*, September 26, 1929.
29. Mosedale, *The Greatest of All*, 61. Koenig added, "Barrow could make you feel like a midget, but Huggins made you feel like a giant."
30. *New York Evening Telegram*, April 16, 1926.
31. Manning Vaughn, "Putting 'em on the Pan," unknown newspaper, May 23, 1927. Vaughn wrote for Milwaukee newspapers.
32. Joe Williams, *The Joe Williams Baseball Reader*, 70.

33. Montville, *The Big Bam*, 111.

34. Stout, *Yankees Century*, 117.

35. Frick, "Huggins Dims Hopes of Annexing Pennant This Year."

36. *New York American*, early February 1926, Babe Ruth scrapbook, National Baseball Library and Archives.

37. Westbrook Pegler, "Yankees Pretty Fair Ball Players, but Not Ball Team," *Chicago Daily Tribune*, March 14, 1926.

38. Westbrook Pegler, "Yanks Social Leaders While Robins and Braves Just Toil," *Chicago Daily Tribune*, March 6, 1926.

39. "Huggins Defends Yankees," *New York Sun*, March 19, 1926.

40. W. O. McGeehan, Down the Line, *New York Herald Tribune*, March 21, 1926.

41. "Yanks Prove That Pitchers Are Not Their Only Asset," *New York Evening Telegram*, March 30, 1926, and "Robbie Pities Pitchers Who Face Murderers' Row," *New York Evening Telegram*, April 5, 1926.

42. "Jacob Ruppert, 'Only a Fan,' Makes Some Critical Deductions," *Sporting News*, April 1, 1926, and "Ruppert Smiles as Canary Once More Gobbles Cat," *New York Evening Telegram*, March 26, 1926.

43. *New York Evening Telegram*, April 8, 1926.

28. Huggins Silences His Critics, for Good

1. Clark, *The World of Damon Runyon*, 240. New York City historian Oliver Allen has noted that Walker's first term did have accomplishments: the first citywide sanitation system, the first hospital department, a new dock for ocean liners, and many new highways. Allen, *The Tiger*, 237.

2. Fowler, *Skyline*, 58. One story reflects the city and the times, as well as Walker: One afternoon a rumor was afloat that Walker had been shot. When reporters tracked him down, he said, "Gentlemen, at this time of day I am not even half shot." Abels, *In the Time of Silent Cal*, 96.

3. Spink, Three and One, *Sporting News*, March 2, 1939.

4. Morris, *Incredible New York*, 340.

5. Sullivan, *Our Times*, 4:210.

6. James M. Gould, "Who Will Win the Big League Pennants in 1926?" 531.

7. Frederick G. Lieb, "Lieb Selects Yankees and Pirates as Pennant Winners," *New York Evening Telegram*, April 12, 1926. Many of the predictions came out before the long win streak. Some early prognosticators might have revised their calls just before the season started.

8. Billy Evans, How They Look to Billy Evans, *Sporting News*, April 8, 1926.

9. "Ruth Gets Homer; Yanks Win, 3–1," *New York Times*, April 24, 1926.

10. Ruffing would have a 39-96 record with Boston from 1925 to 1930.

11. Frederick G. Lieb, *New York Evening Post*, December 10, 1927. Huggins spoke to Red Sox president Bob Quinn about possible trades for Ruffing.

12. James R. Harrison, "Huggins Talks of Flag Outlook," *New York Times*, May 12, 1926.

13. Graham, *The New York Yankees*, 117.

14. W. O. McGeehan, Down the Line, *New York Herald Tribune*, April 10, 1926.

15. Joe Vila, "Yankees Hold Own on First Road Test," *Sporting News*, June 24, 1926.

16. "A Rich Mixture of Beer, Baseball, Bachelorhood," *News-Week*, August 7, 1937, 21.

17. Harrison, "Huggins Talks of Flag Outlook."

18. *New York Times*, August 12 and August 13, 1926.

19. "Huggins Pulling for Giants," *New York Sun*, July 28, 1926.

20. Editorial, "They Have Earned Praise," *Sporting News*, June 17, 1926.

21. Frederick G. Lieb, "Yankees Travelling on a New Wave of Prosperity," *New York Evening Journal*, May 17, 1926.

22. Arthur Robinson, "Profiles: The Babe," *New Yorker*, July 31, 1926.

23. Charyn, *Gangsters and Gold Diggers*, 17.

24. Tullius, *I'd Rather Be a Yankee*, 44.

25. Joe Vila, Setting the Pace, *New York Sun*, July 3, 1925.

26. W. B. Hanna, "Lively Ball Not Only Cause of Accidents," *New York Herald Tribune*, June 21, 1925.

27. "Baseball Men Are Certain Lively Sphere Is Menace," *New York Evening Telegram*, August 1, 1929.

28. "Channel Exploit Thrills the City," *New York Times*, August 7, 1926.

29. "Gertrude of Arc," *New York Times*, August 11, 1926. See also Stout, *Young Woman and the Sea*, 284–85.

30. The Yankees sent pitcher Garland Braxton and outfielder Nick Cullop to Washington after the season to complete the trade. This was not the pitcher Nick Cullop, whom the Yankees had acquired from the Federal League ten years earlier.

31. "New York Yankees, Still in Batting Slump, Drop Another to Cleveland," *New York Times*, September 18, 1926.

32. James R. Harrison, "Yanks Lose Fourth to Indians, 3–1," *New York Times*, September 19, 1926. When New York pitcher Urban Shocker

walked Speaker intentionally, the Indians' leader started mocking and taunting him. Huggins did not take kindly to the insults.

33. Ruether had pitched well in the second game of the series, losing 2–1.

34. After their early-season sixteen-game win streak, the Yankees won only 55 percent of their games. After August 1, they played the last two months of the season five games below .500.

35. Editorial, "Hail New York," *Sporting News*, September 26, 1929.

36. John Kieran, Sports of the Times, *New York Times*, September 26, 1929.

37. Westbrook Pegler, "Yankees Victory Gives Experts Sock on Chin," *Chicago Daily Tribune*, September 28, 1926.

38. Smelser, *The Life That Ruth Built*, 194–95 and 317. Smelser gave full credence to Carl Mays's criticism of Huggins.

39. Frank Getty, "Miller Huggins, Manager of League-Leading Yankees, Explaining What Is Needed to Make a Successful Pilot," *United News*, August 16, 1926.

40. The Cards surprised most prognosticators and edged Cincinnati by two games. Arm trouble prevented Carl Mays from pitching after September 14, which hurt his Reds down the stretch.

41. Smelser, *The Life That Ruth Built*, 341, and Montville, *The Big Bam*, 236.

42. "Boss Huggins Has No Alibis," *Los Angeles Times*, October 11, 1926.

43. James R. Harrison, "Alexander Again the Hero," *New York Times*, October 11, 1926.

44. The players shared in the revenue of only the first four games. So any "plot" to stretch out a Series would not benefit them.

45. "Five-Game Series Costly to Clubs, Says Ruppert," *Washington Post*, November 3, 1926.

46. F. C. Lane, "Huggins and Harmony," 535.

47. Fletcher, most recently the manager of the Philadelphia Phillies, had been a fiery infielder for John McGraw's Giants for more than a decade.

48. "Miller Huggins Taking on Weight," *New York American*, October 22, 1926. Brown's retreat was featured in a 1939 article in the U.S. Chamber of Commerce's monthly magazine. "Bill Brown's business is making business men do things they don't want to do. Hated, but healthful things." Angell, "Bill Brown Rebuilds Executives," 31.

49. Joe Williams, By Joe Williams, *New York Evening Telegram*, April 9, 1927.

50. Bill Slocum, "Miller Huggins, as I Knew Him," *New York American*, October 4, 1929.

1. Graham, *The New York Yankees*, 127.
2. While he may have changed his mind later, in 1928 Ed Barrow thought the 1919 Chicago White Sox had been a better team than the 1927 Yankees.
3. E. G. Brands, *Collyer's Eye*, April 9, 1927.
4. Mosedale, *The Greatest of All*, 183.
5. Mack had also attempted to sign Tris Speaker, as had Miller Huggins and Ed Barrow of the Yankees, but Speaker chose to sign with the Washington Senators. Alexander, *Ty Cobb*, 195.
6. Alexander, *Ty Cobb*, 195. Cobb's pay was a combination of salary, bonuses, and a portion of exhibition-game gate receipts.
7. Bill Corum, Corum Says, *Chicago Sunday Herald and Examiner*, January 15, 1939.
8. Throughout Ed Barrow's tenure as business manager, Ruppert handled the contract negotiations with the stars, and Barrow handled those with the lesser players. Levitt, *Ed Barrow*, 230.
9. Some estimates at the time had Meusel signing for $17,500 per season, but Michael Haupert's research of transaction cards at the Hall of Fame Library and Archives places the amount at $13,000 per season.
10. "Herb Pennock Last Holdout in Yank Rank," *Evening Leader* (Corning NY), March 27, 1927.
11. Pennock was independently wealthy from his parents' sale of their road and farm equipment business late in the nineteenth century, and he never hesitated to stretch out contract negotiations.
12. Miller Huggins, *New York Telegram and Evening Mail*, December 26, 1924.
13. Will Wedge, "Huggins Likes Yanks' Chances," *New York Sun*, March 31, 1927.
14. Huggins had traded Schang after his .240 season in 1925, but Schang would prove his manager wrong by outhitting his replacements with the Yankees for each of the next three seasons.
15. Joe Vila, Setting the Pace, *New York Sun*, January 4, 1928.
16. Jones lasted another nine seasons in the American League after leaving New York. Pitching for mostly second division teams in St. Louis, Washington, and Chicago, he won ninety-four games and lost ninety-three.
17. One of the "aging" left-handers Huggins was referring to was his ace, Herb Pennock. The other was Dutch Ruether, whose four wins by mid-

May helped the Yankees to their fast start in 1927. Both men were thirty-three years old.

18. James R. Harrison, "Yanks Trade Jones for Giard-Durst," *New York Times*, February 9, 1927. Giard and Durst were of little help to New York.

19. Austen Lake, *Boston Evening Transcript*, April 30, 1927.

20. Bill Corum, "Ruppert's Rifles Are Powerful," *New York Evening Journal*, April 2, 1927. Shocker and Shawkey were both thirty-six.

21. "Yankees Retain Punch of 1926, Huggins Wires to *New York American*," *New York American*, April 3, 1927.

22. Will Wedge, "Huggins Praises Wilcy Moore," *New York Sun*, June 23, 1927.

23. Bill Corum, "Dr. Wilcy Moore, Specialist," *New York American*, August 14, 1927.

24. Joe Vila, Setting the Pace, *New York Sun*, June 10, 1927.

25. Pat Robinson, "Huggins Banks on Slugging to Put Yanks on Top in Race," *New York Evening Telegram*, March 25, 1927.

26. Graham, *Lou Gehrig*, 118.

27. On January 3, 1923, the Yankees had sent catcher Al DeVormer and cash to the Boston Red Sox for Minor League pitcher George Pipgras and Minor League outfielder Harvey Hendrick.

28. Ford Frick, *New York Evening Journal*, September 26, 1929.

29. "Huggins Says Yanks Have Pitchers Also," *New York Times*, August 7, 1927.

30. Frank Graham, "Grabowski Fortified Yanks," *New York Sun*, June 2, 1927. Shocker bluffed using the spitball a lot more than he threw it.

31. Lyn Lary would not play for the Yankees until 1929, and Jimmie Reese would not do so until 1930.

32. Frank O'Neill, "Loud Wails in Wake of Yank Deal," *New York Evening Journal*, January 6, 1928.

33. Miller Huggins, *Sporting News*, August 4, 1927.

34. *New York Sun*, July 20, 1927.

35. Ruth played in the season finale the next day, but went 0-for-3, with a walk.

36. Appel, *Pinstripe Empire*, 156.

37. Frank Graham, *New York Sun*, July 22, 1927.

38. On August 21, Ruth and Gehrig each had thirty-nine home runs. From that point on, Gehrig hit only eight, while Ruth hit twenty-one.

39. Babe Ruth had held the record with 171 runs batted in in 1921. Until recently, Gehrig had been credited with 175 runs batted in, but an investigation by Herman Krabbenhoft of the Society for American Baseball Research discovered RBI errors in four games that resulted in a net loss of two runs batted in.

40. The American League would drop the award after the 1928 season, and the National League would do so after the 1929 season. Both leagues would institute the Most Valuable Player Award in 1931, which remains in existence today.

41. Because a player could win the award only once, Babe Ruth, the 1922 winner, was ineligible.

42. Appel, *Pinstripe Empire*, 153.

43. Fleming, *Murderers' Row*, 11.

44. Bill Corum, "Huggins, Pilot of Few If Any Mistakes, Has Genius for Picking Men," *New York American*, September 11, 1927.

45. "Hornsby Predicts Pirate Victory," *New York Times*, October 2, 1927.

46. "Yankees Are Ready, Their Leader Says," *New York Times*, October 2, 1927.

47. "Ruppert Forecasts Triumph for Yankees," *New York Times*, October 2, 1927.

48. The only National League team that had won the Series in four games was the 1914 Boston Braves in their stunning upset of the Philadelphia Athletics.

49. "Hornsby Predicts Pirate Victory."

50. Rud Rennie, "Huggins Ready to Put Southpaw in Box Despite Pirates' Record," *New York Herald Tribune*, October 4, 1927.

51. "We Like to Destroy the Enemy, Ban Johnson Wires Ruppert," *New York Times*, October 9, 1927.

52. "Ruppert Happy, Though Smile Cost $200,000 in Receipts," *New York Times*, October 9, 1927.

53. "How the Yanks' Four Straight Gave Baseball a Good Name," *Literary Digest*, 64. Lazzeri's stardom did not prevent the press from continuing to use disparaging ethnic terminology in referring to him.

54. Frank Graham, "Huggins Can Go Fishing Now," *New York Sun*, October 12, 1927.

55. Bill Corum, "The Four-Straight Man," *New York Journal-American*, January 15, 1939.

56. Williams, *The Joe Williams Baseball Reader*, 68.

1. Frank O'Neill, "Huggins Is Undaunted by Slump," *New York Evening Journal*, April 6, 1928.

2. Bill Slocum, *New York American*, March 28, 1928.

3. Joe Vila, Setting the Pace, *New York Sun*, April 3, 1928. The Yankees had purchased Dickey's contract from Jackson (Mississippi) of the Cotton States League at the Minor League meetings in Dallas in December 1927.

4. Frank Graham, "Yankees Release Shocker," *New York Sun*, July 6, 1928.

5. Shawkey spent the 1928 season, his final one as a full-time active player, splitting eighteen decisions with Montreal of the International League.

6. Johnson had pitched in a combined twenty-five games for the Yankees in 1925–26, but spent the entire 1927 season with Milwaukee of the American Association, where he went 18-10.

7. Frank Graham, "Signs Covey, Awaits Shocker," *New York Sun*, April 10, 1928.

8. Dan Daniel, Daniel's Dope, *New York Evening Telegram*, May 7, 1928.

9. Miller Huggins, *New York Evening Telegram*, December 22, 1920.

10. As May turned to June, Babe Ruth already had nineteen home runs, three more than he had at that time during his record-setting season the previous year.

11. In late 1914, Huggins, Cardinals scout Bob Connery, and St. Paul manager Mike Kelley had tried to buy the Saints, but nothing came of it. *Sporting News*, January 7, 1915. Ten years later Huggins and Connery did buy the Saints.

12. Dan Daniel, "Life Dream of Huggins, 49 Today, Has Been to Own Club," *New York Evening Telegram*, April 28, 1928. Huggins was still using 1879 as his birth year.

13. Rud Rennie, "Huggins Blames Yankee Slump on Poor Pitching, Weak Infield," *New York Herald Tribune*, August 5, 1928.

14. Steinberg, "The St. Paul–New York Underground Railroad," 38–43.

15. Bill Slocum, "Miller Huggins, as I Knew Him," *New York American*, October 4, 1929.

16. The twenty-four runs remain the most runs the Yankees have allowed in a single game.

17. Lazzeri played second on July 30 and then not again until August 15. He played just 110 games in the field in 1928.

18. Pat Robinson, "Yankee Success May Hinge on Keystone Combination," *New York Evening Telegram*, March 21, 1927.

19. Unsourced clipping in Miller Huggins's file, dated July 26, 1928, Baseball Hall of Fame Library and Archives.

20. Dan Daniel, Daniel's Dope, *New York Evening Telegram*, July 20, 1928. The owner was likely Garry Herrmann, who knew Huggins well and had sold his shares in the Cincinnati Reds a year earlier.

21. Dan Daniel, "Huggins Convinced Slump of Champions Is at an End," *New York Evening Telegram*, August 13, 1928.

22. Steinberg, "Pitchers in Pinstripes: Unheralded Stars of the 1920s," 484.

23. "Police Quell Fans' Riot at Yank Offices," *New York American*, September 7, 1928.

24. Miller Huggins, *Washington Post*, September 1, 1928.

25. Frank O'Neill, "Drama, Thrills Galore on Stadium Green," *New York Evening Journal*, September 10, 1928.

26. The league's other owners were quick to forget their complaints about New York's dominance when games against the Yankees, home and away, helped greatly to fill their coffers.

27. Rud Rennie, "'Farmer Boy Makes Good in Big City' Applies to Rise of Pipgras," *New York Herald Tribune*, July 8, 1928.

28. Joe Vila, Setting the Pace, *New York Sun*, February 28, 1928.

29. Bill Slocum, "Let the Hitters Hit; That's Hug's Theory," *New York American*, September 16, 1928.

30. The Yankees, who finished just 2½ games ahead of the second-place Athletics, had remarkable success against them, winning 16 of the 22 games the teams played.

31. "Dan Daniel, "Huggins Insists His Team Will Return with Pennant," *New York Evening Telegram*, September 14, 1928.

32. The injury limited Combs to just one plate appearance in the World Series, as Huggins platooned right-handed-hitting Ben Paschal and left-handed-hitting Cedric Durst in center field.

33. Joe Vila, Setting the Pace, *New York Sun*, September 29, 1928.

34. Will Wedge, "Huggins Wins His Sixth Flag," *New York Sun*, September 29, 1928.

35. John Kieran, Sports of the Times, *New York Times*, September 26, 1929.

36. Joe Vila, Setting the Pace, *New York Sun*, February 4, 1932.

37. Until recently, Gehrig and Ruth had been recognized as co-leaders in runs batted in with 142 each. A thorough review of their runs batted in total

by Herman Krabbenhoft of the Society for American Baseball Research revealed that Gehrig should be credited with 147 runs batted in and Ruth with 146.

38. Joe Vila, Setting the Pace, *New York Sun*, December 21, 1928.

39. Joe Williams, *New York Evening Telegram*, October 2, 1928.

40. John Kieran, Sports of the Times, *New York Times*, October 11, 1928.

41. Frederick G. Lieb, "Col. Ruppert Ridicules Idea of 'Weakening Yankees'; We're Out to Win, Let Others Build to Our Strength," *Sporting News*, October 6, 1938.

42. "Ruppert and Huggins Lost in Rush as Cheering Fans Crowd about The Babe," *Evening Leader* (Corning NY), October 11, 1928.

43. Parrish, *Anxious Decades*, 214.

44. Ruppert, "The Ten Million Dollar Toy," 18.

45. Westbrook Pegler, "Nobody's Business," *Washington Post*, October 14, 1928.

46. Frank Graham, *New York Journal-American*, September 11, 1961.

47. Joe Williams, *New York Evening Telegram*, July 11, 1928.

48. Joe Vila, Setting the Pace, *New York Sun*, December 26, 1928.

31. The Law of Averages

1. The New York Giants had won four straight National League pennants from 1921 to 1924. Hughie Jennings's Detroit Tigers (1907–9) and Huggins's Yankees (1921–23 and 1926–28) had won three straight in the American League.

2. Lane, "The Yankee Peril," 339.

3. Graham, *Lou Gehrig*, 126.

4. Joseph Gordon, "Yankee Pilot Waxes Furious at Accusation," *New York American*, December 16, 1927.

5. Mosedale, *The Greatest of All*, 167.

6. The Yankees purchased the men in the summer of 1927 and agreed to leave them with Oakland for the 1928 season. Most of the money was for Lary; Ed Barrow later called it a terrible deal.

7. Dan Daniel, Daniel's Dope, *New York Evening Telegram*, August 30, 1929. Among the other highly regarded and expensive prospects who joined the Yankees in 1928 and 1929 were Sam Byrd, Dusty Cooke, Gordon Rhodes, and Roy Sherid. For a variety of reasons, none came close to meeting expectations. But one youngster did emerge as a star, catcher Bill Dickey.

8. Frank O'Neill, "Loud Wails in Wake of Yank Deal," *New York Evening Journal*, January 6, 1928.

9. Rennie, "Stop Squawking," 11.

10. Bozeman Bulger, "Development of Hornsby Outstanding Huggins Achievement," *Atlanta Constitution*, September 29, 1929. Hornsby began developing into one of the game's greatest hitters under Huggins's tutelage.

11. "Miller Huggins Answers the Question, 'How Do You Do It?'" *Los Angeles Times*, April 24, 1929.

12. Westbrook Pegler, "Nobody's Business," *Chicago Daily Tribune*, October 14, 1928.

13. They renamed the team the Young Yanks and appointed Tommy Clarke, a former catcher and Cincinnati teammate of Huggins back in 1909, as manager.

14. John Drebinger, "Yankees Purchase Minor League Club," *New York Times*, January 11, 1929. See also Joe Vila, "Ruppert Makes First Real Move in Baseball Agricultural Field," *Sporting News*, January 17, 1929.

15. Gordon, "Yankee Pilot Waxes Furious at Accusation."

16. Frederick G. Lieb, "The Hot Stove League," *New York Evening Post*, December 10, 1927.

17. Walter Trumbull, The Listening Post, *New York Evening Post*, December 13, 1927.

18. The Yankees released third baseman Joe Dugan after the 1928 season; he had appeared in only ninety-four games in 1928. He was replaced by Gene Robertson, whom the Yankees would sell during the 1929 season.

19. Dan Daniel, "Miller Huggins Is Near Death," *New York Evening Telegram*, September 23, 1929.

20. Pennock did not pitch, and Combs had but one plate appearance in the Series.

21. *Cincinnati Post*, September 23, 1929.

22. Graham, *The New York Yankees*, 139.

23. Frederick G. Lieb, "Yankees' Pennants at Half-Staff for Barrow," *Sporting News*, December 23, 1953.

24. Pat Harmon, *Cincinnati Post*, August 27, 1984, as quoted in Cook, *Waite Hoyt*, 61.

25. Cook, *Waite Hoyt*, 61.

26. Dick Farrington, "Major League Writers Pick Yankees and Cubs to Win Pennants," *Sporting News*, April 11, 1929. Seventeen picked the Athletics.

27. Irving Vaughn, "Babe and Yanks to Be More Powerful than Last Season," *Chicago Daily Tribune*, March 19, 1929.

28. Joe Williams, By Joe Williams, *New York Evening Telegram*, April 27, 1929.

29. Joe Williams, By Joe Williams, *New York Evening Telegram*, September 8, 1928 dateline.

30. Joe Williams, By Joe Williams, *New York Evening Telegram*, April 27, 1929.

31. Considine, *The Babe Ruth Story*, 176.

32. Montville, *The Big Bam*, 179.

33. Hoyt, *Babe Ruth as I Knew Him*, 34.

34. Mrs. Babe Ruth, *The Babe and I*, 95–96, and Smelser, *The Life That Ruth Built*, 399.

35. Westbrook Pegler, "Babe Reticent about It," *Chicago Daily Tribune*, April 17, 1929.

36. John Kieran, "Disposition an Important Asset to Big Leaguers," *New York Herald Tribune*, May 27, 1923.

37. Durocher, *Nice Guys Finish Last*, 46.

38. "All Yankees Are Grief-Stricken," *New York Herald Tribune*, September 26, 1929.

39. Joe Williams, By Joe Williams, *New York Evening Telegram*, April 8, 1929.

40. Lieb, *Baseball as I Have Known It*, 227–28.

41. Miller Huggins, "Is a World Series a Toss-Up?" 533.

42. Dick Meade, "Random Shots," *Toledo News-Bee*, September 25, 1929.

43. Editorial, "Players and Automobiles," *Sporting News*, April 18, 1929.

44. Joe Williams, By Joe Williams, *New York Evening Telegram*, August 26, 1929. Rickenbacker, a Medal of Honor winner, lived until 1973, a decade after both the San Francisco Giants and Los Angeles Dodgers had faced the New York Yankees in the World Series.

45. John Drebinger, "40,000 See Yanks Beat Red Sox, 7–3," *New York Times*, April 19, 1929. The Yankees had numbers that corresponded with where they hit in the batting order: Ruth hit third, Gehrig, who hit fourth, was "4," etc. Grange was the nation's most famous football player. He turned professional in 1925 after graduating from the University of Illinois, where he wore Number 77. Former Yankees' right fielder (in 1919) and current Chicago Bears owner George Halas signed him to a professional contract.

46. Huggins, "The Toughest Problem," 537.

47. Pennock had been suffered from this inflammation of the nerves in the shoulder of his pitching arm since the summer of 1928. See "65,000 See Yanks and Indians Divide," *New York Times*, August 20, 1928. Miller Huggins suffered from neuritis of his leg for years. Graham, *The New York Yankees*, 156.

48. John Drebinger, "Ruth Slams Homer as Yanks Win, 8–3," *New York Times*, May 6, 1929.

49. Zachary had a 3-3 record with New York late in the 1928 season, the wins helping the Yankees secure the pennant. He had won two games for the Senators in the 1924 World Series.

50. Joe Vila, "Huggins Prepares to Renovate Yanks," *Sporting News*, September 12, 1929. See also James Isaminger's article in the same issue.

51. Tom Meany, "Yankee Spirit Is at Fever Pitch as Crucial Western Trip Begins," *New York Evening Telegram*, July 5, 1929.

52. Dan Daniel, "Will to Win Resurgent on His Club, Says Huggins," *New York Evening Telegram*, May 22, 1929. .

53. Meany, *The Yankee Story*, 70. Gordon Cobbledick was a *Cleveland Plain Dealer* sportswriter.

54. "Clears Ball Club in Stadium Deaths," *New York Times*, May 21, 1929.

55. Bill Slocum, "Miller Huggins, as I Knew Him," *New York American*, September 27, 1929.

56. George Moriarty, "Calling Them," 506.

57. John Drebinger, "Joe McCarthy—Specialist in Managing," *New York Times*, September 13, 1929.

58. Letter from Miller Huggins to Dorothy Fitz, July 15, 1929, Doug Lowry Collection.

59. W. O. McGeehan, Down the Line, *New York Herald Tribune*, September 8, 1929.

60. Rennie, "Stop Squawking," 60.

32. No Man Ever Struggled Harder

1. Barrow, *My Fifty Years in Baseball*, 152.

2. Westbrook Pegler, "Mr. Huggins, Persistent Person," *Washington Post*, September 25, 1929.

3. Myrtle Huggins, "Mighty Midget," 36.

4. "Young, Up-and-at-'em Club Is Plan of Miller," *New York Evening Telegram*, September 21, 1929, and "Huggins of Yankees Is Critically Ill," *New York Times*, September 23, 1929.

5. After dropping a doubleheader to the A's on Labor Day, the Yankees were still 6½ games up on Cleveland, who had won a doubleheader that day. Huggins probably did not want to leave on such a "losing note."

6. Ruppert, "The Ten Million Dollar Toy," 119.

7. Furnas, *Great Times*, 521–22.

8. Eig, *Luckiest Man*, 85, and Cook, *Waite Hoyt*, 112. Huggins had already largely gotten out of the stock market. The extent of Ruppert's exposure to the market is not known.

9. Babe Ruth, *Babe Ruth*, 176. Frank Chance and Fred Clarke were early twentieth-century player-managers of the Chicago Cubs and Pittsburgh Pirates, respectively. Both were tough and aggressive players, as was Huggins.

10. Arthur Mann, "Miller Huggins, Unhappy Warrior, Overcame Ridicule, Hatred, Prima Donnas to Lead Earlier Yanks to Top," *Sporting News*, November 2, 1939.

11. Tullius, *I'd Rather Be a Yankee*, 100.

12. Graham, *The New York Yankees*, 158.

13. Ford C. Frick, "Huggins, a Constant Planner, Saw Yanks 1930 Winners," *New York Evening Journal*, October 2, 1929.

14. "Why Ruffing? His pitching percentage is lower than the rating of the Red Sox, though at first glance that might seem impossible," wrote John Kieran. Sports of the Times, *New York Times*, August 18, 1929. Ruffing finished the season with a 9-22 record. His record his first five seasons was 39-93.

15. Ruppert, "The Ten Million Dollar Toy," 119. Bob Shawkey said that Huggins had offered the Red Sox $50,000 for Ruffing. *New York Evening Telegram*, May 7, 1930.

16. Frick, "Huggins, a Constant Planner, Saw Yanks 1930 Winners."

17. "Huggins Weaker; High Fever Holds," *New York Times*, September 25, 1929.

18. Rev. J. E. Price of the Washington Heights Methodist Episcopal Church was "a life-long friend." "Miller Huggins Dies; Many Pay Tribute," *New York Times*, September 26, 1929.

19. One newspaper described his passing as follows: "His death was caused by pyaemia, the process of pus-forming organisms in the blood, with infection of the face, and edema, the filling of the lungs with water, as contributory causes." "Yankee Idol Goes Home," *Los Angeles Times*, September 26, 1929.

20. Yankees' coach Art Fletcher had taken over as acting manager for the balance of the season.

21. The church, on East 29th Street, was also known as the "Little Church around the Corner."

22. Huggins, the son of a devout Methodist, died in a Catholic hospital, his New York funeral was held in an Episcopal church, and his Cincinnati funeral was in a Presbyterian church.

23. *New York Sun*, November 2, 1938. Fred Lieb, who was her neighbor in St. Petersburg, mistakenly placed her suicide in the summer of 1942. Lieb, *Baseball as I Have Known It*, 230. Huggins also left $10,000 to each of his brothers. One of them, Clarence, moved into the house after Myrtle's death and lived there until he died in 1955.

24. Frank Graham, "The Little Miller," *New York Journal-American*, December 13, 1964.

25. "Many Praise Huggins as Clean Sportsman," *New York Times*, September 26, 1929.

26. Damon Runyon, Between You and Me! *New York American*, September 27, 1929.

27. "Many Praise Huggins as Clean Sportsman."

28. Ruppert, "The Ten Million Dollar Toy," 119.

33. Succeeding an Immortal

1. The team needed to rebuild an aging pitching staff and address weaknesses on the left side of the infield and the decline of Bob Meusel in the outfield.

2. On the day Barrow called to offer him the job, Bush was in Chicago, signing to manage the White Sox.

3. Graham, *The New York Yankees*, 162. After managing the Philadelphia Phillies from 1923 to 1926, "I promised my wife and myself I would never go through that again. And I never will." Barrow, *My Fifty Years in Baseball*, 153.

4. Ed Barrow to Eddie Collins, October 5, 1929, Steve Steinberg Collection.

5. Collins, "Out at Second," 84. Mack did not retire until 1950, when he was 87. Collins was hired as the vice president and general manager of the Boston Red Sox in 1933.

6. Shawkey was hired for $15,000. Surdam notes that Huggins was making "over $39,000" in 1929, far more than the $25,000 that was reported in the press. *Wins, Losses, and Empty Seats*, 87. On the same day they hired Shawkey, the Yankees sold Bob Meusel to the Cincinnati Reds.

7. "Yankee Telegram to Shawkey Cost the New Manager $31," *New York Times*, October 24, 1929. Indian guides delivered the telegram by sleigh in Quebec's Laurentian Mountains.

8. Levitt, *Ed Barrow*, 247.

9. John Drebinger, "Shawkey Named Yankees' Manager," *New York Times*, October 18, 1929.

10. On October 18, 1929, Bill Corum predicted that Connery would be the new Yankees manager. Sports with Bill Corum, *New York American*.

11. Calling 'em Right with Albert Keane, *Hartford Courant*, May 5, 1930.

12. Joe Vila, "Huggins Banked on Young Box Men to Carry Yanks Through," *Sporting News*, July 14, 1928.

13. Levy, *Joe McCarthy*, 147.

14. When Waite Hoyt crossed Shawkey early in the 1930 season, he traded Hoyt, along with Mark Koenig, to the Tigers. Hoyt went on to win seventy more games.

15. W. O. McGeehan, Down the Line, *New York Herald Tribune*, October 19, 1929.

16. John Drebinger, "Players of the Game," *New York Times*, October 25, 1929.

17. Smelser, *The Life That Ruth Built*, 427.

18. Dan Daniel, "Fletcher Probable Choice to Succeed Huggins," *New York Evening Telegram*, October 16, 1929.

19. The Giants' ownership had forced the trading of Rogers Hornsby and Burleigh Grimes after the 1927 season, their first with the Giants. In 1928, the club fell just two games short of the pennant. Hornsby hit .387 for the Cubs, and Grimes won twenty-five games for the Pirates that year.

20. Joe Vila, Setting the Pace, *New York Sun*, February 26, 1934.

21. "Yanks Pick Pilot; Name Not Revealed," *New York Times*, October 15, 1929.

22. "Huggins Sees Dire Fate for Club," *Washington Post*, October 28, 1928. Among other "question marks," Ruth was turning thirty-four, Lazzeri had missed a quarter of the 1928 season due to injury, Combs suffered a serious wrist injury at the end of that season, and Dickey had played only ten Major League games. There was also concern about Pennock's ongoing neuritis.

23. "Why Ruffing? After five innings he's done," complained Barrow to Shawkey, who replied, "He won't be done when I tell him a few things." Barrow's curt reply: "Okay, it's your funeral." Unsourced clip-

ping in Bob Shawkey's file, National Baseball Hall of Fame Library and Archives.

24. The Yankees sent utility outfielder Cedric Durst and $50,000 to the Red Sox for Ruffing, who was twenty-five years old when the Yankees acquired him.

25. Barrow, *My Fifty Years in Baseball*, 154. Frank Graham wrote of the players taking advantage of Shawkey. *The New York Yankees*, 166.

26. Honig, *The Man in the Dugout*, 178. Shawkey said he went to the Yankees' offices one day that fall and saw McCarthy coming out of Barrow's office. "I knew what had happened," he said.

27. McCarthy was the first man without Major League playing experience to manage the Yankees. The Yankees' chief scout, Paul Krichell, had been a Buffalo teammate of McCarthy in 1914.

28. Levy, *Joe McCarthy*, 13. Gilhooley hit .322 for Buffalo that season; McCarthy hit .266.

29. Wrigley never forgave McCarthy for the Cubs' blowing an 8–0 lead in Game 4 of the 1929 World Series. Wrigley made one of the great personnel blunders in baseball history when he replaced McCarthy with Rogers Hornsby, who would be fired by the Cubs less than two years later. Ehrgott, *Mr. Wrigley's Ball Club*, 206–7 and 250–53.

30. Brown, *The Chicago Cubs*, 119.

31. Fred Lieb, Cutting the Plate, *New York Evening Post*, October 11, 1930.

32. F. C. Lane, "Why Big League Managers Fail," 341.

33. "McCarthy Signs for 2 Years as Yankees Manager," *Chicago Daily Tribune*, October 15, 1930.

34. Graham, *The New York Yankees*, 176–77.

35. Robinson, *Iron Horse*, 143.

36. Alexander, *Breaking the Slump*, 165, quoting the *Chicago Daily Tribune*, October 10, 1938.

37. Alexander, *Breaking the Slump*, 135.

38. Rennie, "Stop Squawking," 61.

39. Tofel, *A Legend in the Making*, 17.

40. Joseph McCarthy, "Winning Isn't the Hardest Job," 339.

41. Levy, *Joe McCarthy*, 146.

42. Sobol, *Babe Ruth & the American Dream*, 222.

43. The 1931 Yankees won ninety-four games, the same number as the 1922 pennant winners and three more games than the 1926 Yankees.

44. Joe Vila, Setting the Pace, *New York Sun*, September 2, 1931.

45. "Ruppert, Yankees' Sole Owner for 10 Years, Glories in Team," *New York Herald Tribune*, June 2, 1933.

46. J. P. Gallagher, "Indifferent Success of Yankees Proves Wealthy Magnates Can't Buy Pennants," *Los Angeles Times*, June 20, 1930.

47. Unlike the Chambersburg team the Yankees had bought in 1929, Newark was at the highest level of the Minor Leagues.

48. Dan Daniel, "Over the Fence," *Sporting News*, January 18, 1961. See also Daniel, "Old-Fashioned Weiss," *Sporting News*, October 22, 1947.

49. Weiss had bought the New Haven club of the Eastern League back in 1919, when he was only twenty-three years old. When Jack Dunn, the owner of the Orioles, passed away late in 1928, Weiss sold the New Haven club and left for Baltimore and the higher-level International League.

50. In *My Fifty Years in Baseball* (180, 189), Barrow wrote that he had recommended Weiss. Frank Graham supported Barrow's account in *The New York Yankees*, 189. However, Tom Meany said Ruppert made the selection and that Barrow had recommended Bob Connery. *The Yankee Story*, 149. And Dan Daniel went into detail in a number of *Sporting News* articles that Ruppert drove the selection process.

51. Daniel, "Over the Fence."

52. Graham, *The New York Yankees*, 191.

34. McCarthy Is My Manager

1. Honig, *The Man in the Dugout*, 86.

2. William E. Brandt, "Ruth Rejects $85,000 for 1930," *New York Times*, March 8, 1930. The Ruth salary numbers are based on contemporary newspaper accounts and quotes from the parties involved.

3. Creamer, *Babe*, 350. Ruth's previous contract, from 1927 to 1929, paid him $70,000 a year.

4. Mrs. Babe Ruth, *The Babe and I*, 83.

5. Lane, "Slashing Baseball Salaries," 401 and 402.

6. Editorial, "Ruth and $50,000," *Sporting News*, January 26, 1933.

7. "Ruppert to Slash Ruth's $80,000 Salary," *New York Times*, December 5, 1931.

8. Westbrook Pegler, "Someone Ought to Tell Babe How Much $70,000 Really Is," *Chicago Daily Tribune*, March 16, 1932.

9. Westbrook Pegler, "Ruth Is Tonic for Panic in Red Sox Camp," *Chicago Daily Tribune*, May 29, 1932.

10. Smelser, *The Life That Ruth Built*, 441. Ruth also was to receive 25 percent of exhibition game profits.

11. Meany, *Babe Ruth*, 144.

12. For the seventh straight season, he hit more than 40 home runs (41). His .341 batting average and league-leading on-base percentage and second-best slugging percentage were also impressive.

13. John McGraw, "Yankees Almost Cinch," *Los Angeles Times*, July 3, 1932.

14. "Dickey of Yankees Draws $1,000 Fine," *New York Times*, July 10, 1932.

15. "Dickey Ruling Upheld by Directors," *Washington Post*, July 12, 1932. Harridge later called it his toughest decision. Mark Armour, "Will Harridge," SABR BioProject, sabr.org/bioproject.

16. Joe Vila, Setting the Pace, *New York Sun*, September 9, 1932.

17. "Ruth Unrelenting on $25,000 Slash," *New York Times*, March 6, 1933.

18. "Ruth and Ruppert Clash on Salary," *New York Times*, March 14, 1933. The Yankees' financial documents show a loss of $4,730 in 1932. Haupert and Winter, "Pay Ball."

19. Surdam, *Wins, Losses, and Empty Seats*, 86 and 91. In the early 1930s, most teams did not bring salaries down enough to offset the declining revenue.

20. Haupert and Winter, "Pay Ball." The Yankees lost money in three of those six years and made less than $100,000 in two of the other three seasons.

21. "Ruth Unrelenting on $25,000 Slash." While the Yankee's attendance rose 5.5 percent in 1932, that of the other American League teams dropped 26.9 percent. Still the Yankees' attendance had fallen 17.7 percent since 1930.

22. Walter Schmidt, "Baseball's Forgotten Man, the Bleacherite," *New York Times*, May 21, 1933. Yankee Stadium had 22,000 (31 percent) bleacher seats. The Giants, by comparison, started the 1932 season with only 5,400 bleacher seats at the Polo Grounds; they added 4,300 more during the season.

23. "Stage Now Set for Annual Drama Featuring Ruth and Col. Ruppert," *New York Times*, January 4, 1933.

24. Wagenheim, *Babe Ruth*, 216.

25. The Yankees' payroll of almost $295,000 was more than $100,000 greater than any other American League club. And only one National League club had a team payroll even close to that of the Yankees, the Cubs at $266,000 (Levitt, *Ed Barrow*, table 14). Gehrig finished second (to Jimmie Foxx) in the MVP voting that year; Ruth was in sixth place.

26. Surdam, *Wins, Losses, and Empty Seats*, 86 and 91. Surdam looks at 1929, 1933, and 1939. He includes coaches' and managers' salaries in tables 8 and 17, pages 322 and 331.

27. James M. Kahn, "Yanks Will Go On without Ruth," *New York Sun*, July 19, 1934.

28. "Mamaux Renamed Newark Manager," *New York Times*, December 4, 1931.

29. The Yankees sent outfielder Cleo Carlyle (whose rights they controlled) from Hollywood of the Pacific Coast League to Newark when they took Selkirk.

30. The games drew one of the largest crowds in Yankee Stadium history, almost 80,000 fans. Another 20,000 clashed with police outside the Stadium when they were turned away.

31. Gehrig finished only fifth in the voting for the league's MVP award, won by Mickey Cochrane.

32. Gehrig reportedly signed for $30,000 (Eig, *Luckiest Man*, 194) or $31,000 (Robinson, *Iron Horse*, 212).

33. After one of the Babe's suspensions during the 1922 season, Ban Johnson had stripped Ruth of his captaincy.

34. Dan Daniel, Daniel's Dope, *New York Evening Telegram*, August 29, 1929. That scout, Bill Essick, would prove right: Gomez won eighty-seven games during his first four full seasons with New York.

35. Joe Vila, Setting the Pace, *New York Sun*, September 2, 1931.

36. E-mail from Norman Macht, Connie Mack biographer, September 21, 2013.

37. Mack sold Grove, pitcher Rube Walberg, and infielder Max Bishop to Boston for the cash and two players. Harry Frazee had sold the Red Sox to Yawkey earlier that year for $1,200,000.

38. "Ruppert Says He Would Have Paid $150,000 for Grove," *New York Herald Tribune*, February 7, 1934.

39. "Ruth to Be with Yankees in '35, Says Ruppert, Who Covets Foxx," *New York Herald Tribune*, August 18, 1934.

40. Three other players were involved in the deal. One who came to the A's was a former Yankee pitcher, Gordon "Dusty" Rhodes, who was a Yankee prospect in 1929, but never developed as expected due to arm problems.

41. Meany, *Babe Ruth*, 157.

42. Joe Vila, "M'Carthy Heats Up over Yank Outlook," *Sporting News*, April 19, 1934.
43. Creamer, *Babe*, 374, and Levitt, *Ed Barrow*, 292. Some accounts place this offer after the 1934 season, not before. See Graham, *The New York Yankees*, 201, and Considine, *The Babe Ruth Story*, 205.
44. Montville, *The Big Bam*, 324–25.
45. Creamer, *Babe*, 374.
46. John Drebinger, "Shawkey Named Newark Manager for 1934," *New York Times*, December 30, 1933.
47. Creamer, *Babe*, 377.
48. Meany, *Babe Ruth*, 154. Meany, Joe Williams, and Dan Daniel were the three writers with whom Ruth spoke. Williams broke the story.
49. Barrow, *My Fifty Years in Baseball*, 169–70.
50. Barrow, *My Fifty Years in Baseball*, 171.
51. Graham, *The New York Yankees*, 204.
52. J. G. Taylor Spink, Three and One: Looking Them Over, *Sporting News*, June 13, 1935.
53. Editorial, *Baseball Magazine*, March 1935, 434. The magazine's publication lead time meant it went to press before Ruth had joined the Braves.
54. Kaese, *The Boston Braves*, 101–2.
55. J. G. Taylor Spink, Three and One: Looking Them Over, *Sporting News*, March 7, 1935.
56. Dan Daniel, "Colonel Ruppert's Death," *New York Evening Telegram*, January 14, 1939.
57. Appel, *Pinstripe Empire*, 183.
58. Montville, *The Big Bam*, 325 and 337.
59. W. O. McGeehan, Down the Line, *New York Herald Tribune*, September 22, 1933.
60. Dan Daniel, "Ruppert Sees Boom Year and Pennant for Yanks," *New York Evening Telegram*, undated article in Jacob Ruppert file, National Baseball Hall of Fame Library and Archives.
61. Max Kase, "McCarthy's New Pact Signing Is Tonic to Yankee Ball Club," *New York Evening Journal*, July 17, 1935. After the Yankees won on July 16, they had stretched their lead over the Tigers to two and one-half games.
62. Warren Brown, "All in a Week," *Chicago Herald and Examiner*, January 15, 1939.

63. Dan Daniel, "Game Coming Back Bigger than Ever," *Sporting News*, January 19, 1933.

35. Repeal, Real Estate, and Third Reich

1. Okrent, *Last Call*, 330.
2. Lerner, *Dry Manhattan*, 279.
3. Kessner, *Fiorello H. LaGuardia*, 115.
4. Allen, *Only Yesterday*, 282.
5. The Cullen-Harrison Act legalized the manufacture and sale of beer and wine not exceeding 3.2 percent alcoholic content.
6. "Ruppert Dies at His Home," *New York Sun*, January 13, 1939.
7. "Wine and Beer Men Assailed by Doubt," *New York Times*, November 11, 1932.
8. "Friday Morning Beer," *Washington Post*, April 6, 1933. See also "Beer Floods Nation at Midnight," *New York Herald Tribune*, April 7, 1933.
9. "Six Big Horses Bring Smith a Case of Beer," *New York Times*, April 8, 1933. The Anheuser-Busch case was put on an airplane in St. Louis at midnight.
10. "Ruppert Sees Nickel Beer If Tax Is Halved," *New York Herald Tribune*, October 9, 1934. In its annual report, the USBA noted that per capita beer consumption rose to 9.9 gallons in 1934, still far below the record year of 1914, when 21 gallons were consumed per person. It would continue to rise, reaching 18.6 gallons in 1945 and 22.6 gallons in 1990. http://eh.net/?s=annual+Beer+consumption+per+capita.
11. "Legal Beer Marks Its 2nd Year Today," *New York Times*, April 7, 1935. The tax revenue consisted of $360 million of federal taxes, $80 million in state taxes, and $40 million in local taxes.
12. The Yankees won the series, beating both of the other New York teams. The games grossed more than $200,000. *New York Times*, August 28, September 10, and September 25, 1931.
13. "Sandlot Baseball Again at Stadium," *New York Times*, June 11, 1933, and "Boys' Team Gets Sandlot Trophy," *New York Times*, October 11, 1933.
14. J. G. Taylor Spink, Three and One: Looking Them Over, *Sporting News*, March 2, 1939.
15. "LaGuardia Names 5 in New Tax Attack," *New York Times*, October 3, 1929.
16. "Col. Ruppert Buys Fifth Ave. Building," *New York Times*, February 1, 1931. The "Grand Central Zone" is the area around Grand Central Ter-

minal [railroad station], at 42nd Street and Park Avenue in Midtown Manhattan.

17. *New York Herald Tribune*, January 6, 1932, and February 29, 1932.

18. *New York Times*, June 16, 1932.

19. "Col. Ruppert Buys Another Skyscraper," *New York Herald Tribune*, July 18, 1933.

20. "Observations Here and There in Real Estate," *New York Herald Tribune*, February 18, 1931.

21. "Byrd Names Ship for Chief Backer," *New York Times*, September 22, 1933. Most reports estimated the Colonel's contribution at $250,000.

22. Virginia Irwin, "Tossed Away Millions of Dollars," *St. Louis Post-Dispatch*, February 13, 1946, George Weiss Scrapbooks, National Baseball Hall of Fame Library and Archives. Irwin was one of the first American reporters to cover the fall of Berlin, when she slipped into the German capital in advance of American troops in 1945. Sorel, *The Women Who Wrote the War*, 212–13 and 365–69.

23. Parker, "The $40,000,000 Touch."

24. "Plan Open Air Festival for Aid of Jews," *New York Herald Tribune*, August 10, 1934, and "Baseball Magnate Aids Jewish Cause," *New York Times*, August 9, 1934. Jessel served as the master of ceremonies.

25. Governor Roosevelt had appointed former judge Samuel Seabury to investigate the magistrate courts and police department. Seabury's hearings exposed the corruption of the Walker administration. The mayor resigned on September 1, 1932, and joined his mistress, actress Betty Compton, in Europe.

26. "Ruth Pins His Hope of Big Salary on Beer," *New York Times*, December 23, 1932.

27. W. O. McGeehan, Down the Line, *New York Herald Tribune*, March 18, 1933.

28. Fleischmann, Ruppert's aide, had predicted that the Colonel would lose interest in the Yankees and sell them once he won the World Series.

29. "Joe McCarthy Thinks Yankees Will Win in 1936," *Chicago Daily Tribune*, December 8, 1935.

30. "Ruppert Anxious to Get Infielder," *New York Times*, October 23, 1935. Myer remained with the Senators, where he ended his career in 1941.

31. Jack Singer, "'Yankee Hopes Depend on DiMaggio,' Ruppert," *Los Angeles Times*, October 22, 1935.

1. The Seals originally had considered asking $75,000 for DiMaggio, but lowered the price after his knee injury.
2. Neyer and Epstein, *Baseball Dynasties*, 135.
3. Cramer, *Joe DiMaggio*, 69.
4. Cramer, *Joe DiMaggio*, 73.
5. F. C. Lane, "The Greatest Rookie of the Decade," 441.
6. Sullivan, *The Diamond in the Bronx*, 71.
7. Daniel M. Daniel, "Gehrig, Compromising on Pay, Signs Up for Reported $30,000," *Sporting News*, February 21, 1935.
8. Robinson, *Iron Horse*, 216.
9. Moore, *Joe DiMaggio*, 27.
10. Eig, *Luckiest Man*, 204.
11. Cramer, *Joe DiMaggio*, 115.
12. "Joe Toughest of Them All, Says Col. Ruppert," *New York Sun*, April 21, 1938.
13. J. G. Taylor Spink, Three and One, *Sporting News*, January 19, 1939.
14. Cramer, *Joe DiMaggio*, 116.
15. Jay Maeder, "Big Town Biography," *New York Daily News*, March 2, 1999.
16. The *Sporting News* reported DiMaggio eventually signed for $27,500.
17. Cramer, *Joe DiMaggio*, 117.
18. Cramer, *Joe DiMaggio*, 118.
19. Dan Parker, "The Colonel Always Demanded the Best," *New York Mirror*, January 14, 1939.
20. Dan Daniel, "Ruppert Sees Boom Year and Pennant for Yanks," *New York World-Telegram*, undated clip from the Jacob Ruppert file, National Baseball Library and Archives.
21. The Yankees and Giants shared radio station WABC in 1939 and 1940, carrying only home games. The teams used the same announcers, who shifted from the Polo Grounds to Yankee Stadium, depending on which team was playing at home. If one was on the road while the other had an off day, they would do a re-creation of the game being played. November 5, 2013, e-mail from Chuck Hildebrandt, chairman of SABR's Baseball and the Media Research Committee.
22. "Ruppert Sees Action as Gift to Shut-In Fans," *New York Sun*, December 22, 1938.

23. Rud Rennie, "Yankees Agree to Broadcast All Home Games," *New York Herald Tribune*, December 23, 1938.

24. *Sporting News*, November 10, 1932.

25. Minor League experts Bill Weiss and Marshall Wright rated the 1937 Newark Bears the third best Minor League team ever and the 1938 Bears the sixteenth best. MiLB.com. Among the future Yankees stars who were on one or both of those clubs were Spud Chandler, Ernie Bonham, Joe Gordon, Tommy Henrich, Charlie Keller, Johnny Lindell, and Marius Russo.

26. Mayer, *The 1937 Newark Bears*, 259.

27. Frederick G. Lieb, "Col. Ruppert Ridicules Idea of 'Weakening Yankees'; We're Out to Win, Let Others Build to Our Strength," *Sporting News*, October 6, 1938.

28. Rennie, "Stop Squawking," 11–12. Ruppert would prove to be very wrong here. Just such a system, the amateur draft, went into effect in 1965 and has allowed weaker teams to become more competitive.

29. Rennie, "Stop Squawking," 61.

30. J. G. Taylor Spink, Three and One, *Sporting News*, January 19, 1939.

31. Williams, *The Joe Williams Baseball Reader*, 68.

32. Anderson, *From Beer to Eternity*, 22.

33. Ruppert listed his top five theater performances as Edwin Booth in *Hamlet*, Robson and Crane in *The Henrietta*, Kyrie Bellew in *Raffles*, Nat Goodwin in *When We Were 21*, and Wilson Lackaye in *Trilby*. His top five movies were *Mutiny on the Bounty*, *Birth of a Nation*, *Snow White and the Seven Dwarfs*, *It Happened One Night*, and *Little Caesar*.

34. J. G. Taylor Spink, Three and One, *Sporting News*, January 19, 1939. Hutchinson won only three games for the Tigers in both 1939 and 1940 before coming back from World War II with five excellent seasons from 1946 to 1950.

35. "Game Will Surpass '27–'28 Peak This Year—Ruppert," *Sporting News*, January 7, 1937.

36. Dan M. Daniel, "Ruppert Sees New Trade and Labor Accord," *New York Herald Tribune*, December 31, 1938.

37. It Took Time for Success

1. John Kieran, Sports of the Times, "The Man in the Iron Hat," *New York Times*, March 30, 1938.

2. "Ruppert Saw Only Two Ball Games during '38," *New York Herald Tribune*, January 14, 1939.

3. J. G. Taylor Spink, Three and One, *Sporting News*, March 2, 1939.

4. Arthur E. Patterson, "Ruppert Barred from Stadium and Peep at Yankees by Illness," *New York Herald Tribune*, October 8, 1938.

5. "Ruppert Leaves Hospital," *New York Herald Tribune*, November 2, 1938.

6. Sid Mercer, "The Colonel," *New York Journal-American*, January 16, 1939.

7. "Col. Jacob Ruppert Dies at 71; Brewer, Owner of the Yankees," *New York Herald Tribune*, January 14, 1939.

8. *New York Sun*, January 11, 1939.

9. Howard Whitman, "Ruppert Makes Up with Babe—Dies with Smile," *New York Daily News*, January 14, 1939.

10. Daniel M. Daniel, "Those Yankees Carry On," 479.

11. The Department of Medicine at the NYU Langone Medical Center defines phlebitis as the term for the swelling of a vein, most often in one's leg. Thrombophlebitis is the term for inflammation of a vein caused by a blood clot. The term is often shortened to phlebitis. When the clot is embedded into a deep vein, thrombophlebitis can become much more serious. The condition, appropriately named deep vein thrombosis, can cause blood clots in the lungs (pulmonary embolism), heart attack, and stroke.

12. *New York Journal-American*, January 13, 1939.

13. *New York Evening Post*, January 14, 1939.

14. William E. Clarke, "Sports of the Age," *New York Age*, January 21, 1939.

15. Lawrence D. Hogan, "The Negro Leagues Discovered an Oasis at Yankee Stadium," *New York Times*, February 12, 2011.

16. Bruns, *Negro Leagues Baseball*, 39.

17. *New York Age*, June 2, 1939.

18. "Great Jake Ruppert," *Baltimore Afro-American*, January 28, 1939.

19. Branch Rickey's decision to sign Jackie Robinson for the Brooklyn Dodgers, which came seven years after Ruppert's death, was opposed by all fifteen of the other owners.

20. *New York Evening Telegram*, December 18, 1926.

21. Bogen, *Johnny Kling*, 203.

22. *Kansas City Call*, May 22, 1942.

23. Despite his claim, Jake Powell was not a police officer in Dayton or anywhere else.

24. *Chicago Defender*, August 6, 1938.

25. "Jake Powell Case Seethes," *New York Amsterdam News*, August 13, 1938.

26. Harry B. Webber, "Yankee Boss Touchy about Jake Powell," *Afro American*, February 11, 1939.

27. Powell was the fifth outfielder on the Yankees' powerhouse of 1938 and 1939. He batted .256 in forty-five games in 1938 and would bat just .244 in thirty-one games in 1939.

28. "A Tribute to Ruppert," *Sporting News*, April 18, 1940.

29. Ruppert, "Building a Winning Club in New York," 254.

30. John Lardner, "The Peerage, Self-Elevated," *Newsweek*, September 29, 1941, 48.

38. The Mystery Lady

1. The primary source of the estate matters in this chapter is the Jacob Ruppert Estate File Number 1939–0202 of the New York County Surrogate's Court. Ruppert created two trusts for each woman, one for his baseball assets and the other for the rest of his estate. The trustees, Ruppert's brother George, his brother-in-law, H. Garrison Silleck Jr., and his attorney, Byron Clark, would run the businesses (Ed Barrow was a fourth trustee for the Yankees), with the income going to the women. He also left $150,000 to Lenox Hill Hospital, as well as sixty-five paintings and sculptures to New York's Metropolitan Museum of Art.

2. Amanda Ruppert Silleck died in 1952. Garrison was her husband.

3. In addition to willing her one-third of his estate, Ruppert also left Miss Weyant $300,000 in cash.

4. "Three Ruppert Legatees Share Friendship Too," *New York Herald Tribune*, January 22, 1939.

5. Weyant's full name was Helen Winthrope Wayne Weyant. She is listed in the Internet Broadway Database (ibdb.com) as having appeared in five shows between 1922 and 1928.

6. Frommer, *Five O'Clock Lightning*, 200.

7. "Legacy Frightens Colonel's Friend," *New York Journal-American*, January 20, 1939.

8. "Ruppert Gift Stuns Actress," *New York World-Telegram*, January 21, 1939. Helen Weyant outlived Ruppert by forty-six years. She died in Westchester County, New York, in July 1985. She never married. Her estate of about $6 million—similar in value to that of Jacob Ruppert—consisted of the Ruppert trusts and the Weyant family fortune. She left the money to eight charities, including the Salvation Army and the ASPCA.

9. "New Owners of Yanks Recover Enough to Talk," *Chicago Daily Tribune*, January 22, 1939.

10. "Miss Weyant Tells of Ruppert Friendship," *New York Journal-American*, January 21, 1939.

11. The Colonel may not have paid out dividends from the Yankees or the brewery, but the family borrowed heavily from both.

12. This was done to protect the Ruppert name and the ability of the brewery and baseball club to finance their operations.

13. In explaining why he had not left any of his estate to his brother, George, the Colonel noted in a supporting document to his will that George had inherited a stake in the brewery from their father upon his death in 1915.

14. "Busch Gives Up Efforts to Buy Ruppert Firm," *St. Louis Post-Dispatch*, July 18, 1957.

15. Levitt, *Ed Barrow*, 319, and April 20, 2012, e-mail from Levitt.

16. At first the executors denied Barrow's claim, and he commenced legal action against the estate in the New York Supreme Court. Eventually, the contract was found in the Colonel's personal safe, and the matter was resolved.

17. Actually George Ruppert owned about 3 percent of the Yankees' stock.

18. See chapter 35, "Real Estate, Repeal, and the Third Reich," and Virginia Irwin, "Tossed Away Millions of Dollars," *St. Louis Post-Dispatch*, February 13, 1946.

19. Parker, "The $40,000,000 Touch."

20. The executors sold the Colonel's Garrison estate for $75,000 and his yacht, *Yankee*, for $50,000. His Florida property was deemed "of comparatively small value."

21. Before Prohibition, brewers had close relationships with saloons and even owned them. After Prohibition, they were forbidden to do so because of the bad reputation attached to saloons.

22. "Brewers' Civil War," *Business Week*, July 2, 1938, and "Brewers Split on Promotion Plan," *Business Week*, October 31, 1936.

23. "Busch Chided by Ruppert," *New York Times*, February 10, 1936, and "Brewing Unity Set Back," *New York Times*, July 17, 1936. The new trade group was called Brewing Industry, Inc.

24. Mittelman, *Brewing Battles*, 109, 122.

25. "Talks Called Off on Ruppert Deal," *New York Times*, July 18, 1957. Busch had bought the St. Louis Cardinals four years earlier.

26. Ogle, *Ambitious Brew*, 230.

27. A. J. Glass, "The Fight to Save Ruppert Brewery," *New York Herald Tribune*, February 20, 1961.

28. "Ruppert Brewery Closed Here," *New York Times*, January 1, 1966.

29. Harold C. Burr, "Ed Barrow to Guide Baseball Destinies of Ruppert's Empire," *New York Evening Post*, January 14, 1939.

30. Bob Considine, On the Line, *New York Mirror*, January 17, 1939.

31. That bank contested the tax valuation of the estate and thus secured a delay in the payment of the estate taxes. This avoided having to liquidate the ball club at a "fire sale" price.

32. Armour and Levitt, "The Yankees Ownership," 2.

Epilogue

1. Ruppert, "Building a Winning Club in New York," 253.

2. Dan Daniel, "Colonel Ruppert Blasts Yank Break-Up Idea," *Sporting News*, January 13, 1938.

3. Bozeman Bulger, "Development of Hornsby Outstanding Huggins Achievement," *New York Evening World*, September 29, 1929.

4. Miller Huggins, "How I Got That Way," *New York Evening Post*, October 2, 1926.

5. Graham, *The New York Yankees*, 248.

6. Harold Schumacher, "Miller Huggins, a Very Superstitious Manager," *New York Globe and Commercial Advertiser*," October 3, 1922.

7. John Kieran, "Huggins Will Manage Yanks Next Season, Says Club Owner," *New York Herald Tribune*, October 10, 1922.

8. The two hires that were not successful—managers Bill Donovan and Bob Shawkey—were made under some duress. In both cases, Ruppert had set his sights higher, but the men he wanted were not available.

9. Huggins's talents in these areas were already recognized when he was the Cardinals' manager.

10. W. O. McGeehan, Down the Line, *New York Herald Tribune*, September 27, 1929.

11. Graham, *The New York Yankees*, 91.

12. Christy Walsh, *South Bend [Indiana] News-Times*, September 1929, exact date not known.

13. J. G. Taylor Spink, Three and One: Looking Them Over, *Sporting News*, March 2, 1939.

14. Moore, *Joe DiMaggio*, 37.

15. Huggins, "How I Got That Way."

16. "Athletes, Sportsmen, Leaders Saddened by Death of Ruppert," *New York Herald Tribune*, January 14, 1939.
17. Fetter, *Taking on the Yankees*, 31.
18. Fetter, *Taking on the Yankees*, 18.
19. Murdock, *Baseball between the Wars*, 43.
20. Rennie, "Stop Squawking," 11.
21. Frank Graham, "The Little Miller," 364.
22. Rennie, "Stop Squawking," 61.

BIBLIOGRAPHY

Abels, Jules. *In the Time of Silent Cal.* New York: G. P. Putnam's Sons, 1969.

Alexander, Charles C. *Breaking the Slump: Baseball in the Depression Era.* New York: Columbia University Press, 2002.

————. *John McGraw.* New York: Viking, 1988.

————. *Our Game.* New York: Henry Holt, 1992.

————. *Rogers Hornsby.* New York: Henry Holt, 1995.

————. *Spoke: A Biography of Tris Speaker.* Dallas: Southern Methodist University Press, 2007.

————. *Ty Cobb.* London: Oxford University Press, 1984.

Allen, Frederick Lewis. *The Big Change: America Transforms Itself, 1900–1950.* New York: Harper and Row, 1986.

————. *Only Yesterday: An Informal History of the 1920s.* New York: Perennial Classics, 2000.

————. *Since Yesterday: The 1930s in America.* New York: Perennial Library, 1940.

Allen, Lee. *100 Years of Baseball.* New York: Bartholomew House. 1950.

————. *The Cincinnati Reds: An Informal History* New York: G. P. Putnam's Sons. 1948.

————. *Cooperstown Corner: Columns from the Sporting News, 1962–1969.* Cleveland: Society for American Baseball Research, 1990.

————. *Hot Stove League.* Mattituck NY: Amereon House, 1955.

Allen, Oliver E. *New York, New York: A History of the World's Most Exhilarating & Challenging City.* New York: Atheneum, 1990.

————. *The Tiger: The Rise and Fall of Tammany Hall.* Boston: Addison-Wesley, 1993.

Anderson, Will. *From Beer to Eternity.* Lexington MA: Stephen Greene Press, 1987.

Angell, Orson, "Bill Brown Rebuilds Executives." *Nation's Business*, June 1939, 31–32.

Appel, Marty. *Pinstripe Empire: The New York Yankees from before the Babe to after the Boss.* New York: Bloomsbury, 2012.

Armour, Mark. *"Will Harridge."* SABR BioProject, sabr.org/bioproject.

Armour, Mark, and Daniel R. Levitt, "The Yankees' Ownership." In *Bridging Two Dynasties: The 1947 New York Yankees*, ed. Lyle Spatz, 1–4. Lincoln: University of Nebraska Press and the Society for American Baseball Research, 2013.

Asinof, Eliot. *1919: America's Loss of Innocence*. New York: Donald I. Fine, 1990.

Bak, Richard. *Cobb Would Have Caught It: The Golden Age of Baseball in Detroit*. Detroit: Wayne State University Press, 1991.

————. *Lou Gehrig: An American Classic*. Dallas: Taylor, 1995.

————. *Peach: Ty Cobb in His Time and Ours*. Ann Arbor: Sports Media Group, 2005.

Baldassaro, Lawrence. *Beyond DiMaggio: Italian Americans in Baseball*. Lincoln: University of Nebraska Press, 2011.

Baron, Stanley. *Brewed in America: A History of Beer and Ale in the United States*. Boston: Little, Brown, 1962.

Barr, Andrew. *Drink: A Social History of America*. New York: Carroll & Graff, 1999.

Barrow, Edward G., with James M. Kahn. *My Fifty Years in Baseball*. New York: Coward-McCann, 1951.

Barry, John M. *The Great Influenza: The Epic Story of the Deadliest Plague in History*. London: Penguin Books, 2004.

"Baseball and Beer." *News-Week*, January 23, 1939, 30.

"Beer Bust." *Business Week*, April 4, 1936, 14.

"Beer's Honeymoon." *Business Week*, April 19, 1933, 10–11.

Bevis, Charlie. *Sunday Baseball: The Major Leagues' Struggle to Play Baseball on the Lord's Day, 1876–1934*. Jefferson NC: McFarland, 2003.

Black Sox Scandal Papers. Chicago History Museum.

Bloodgood, Clifford. "Tramping the Ivory Trail with Paul Krichell." *Baseball Magazine*, June 1938, 295 (3).

Bogen, Gil. *Johnny Kling: A Baseball Biography*. Jefferson NC: McFarland, 2006.

Bradley, Elizabeth L. *Knickerbocker: The Myth behind New York*. New Brunswick NJ: Rivergate Books, 2009.

"Brewers' Civil War." *Business Week*, July 2, 1938, 20.

"Brewers Split on Promotion Plan." *Business Week*, October 31, 1936, 31–32.

"Brewery Disunion." *Business Week*, July 25, 1935, 30.

Britt, Albert, ed. "The Jinx Braver." *Outing*, March 1918, 420–22.

Brown, Warren. *The Chicago Cubs*. Carbondale: Southern Illinois University Press, 2001. Originally published in New York by G. P. Putnam's Sons, 1946.

Browning, Reed. *Baseball's Greatest Season: 1924*. Amherst: University of Massachusetts Press, 2003.

Bruns, Roger A. *Negro Leagues Baseball*. Santa Barbara: ABC-CLIO, 2012.

Brunsvold, Sara K. *The Life of Lou Gehrig: Told by a Fan*. Skokie IL: Acta Sports, 2006.

Bryson, Bill. *One Summer: America, 1927*. New York: Doubleday, 2013.

Buchanan, Andy, and John Buchanan. *Wise Guide Yankee Stadium: The Fan Navigator to Yankee Stadium*. Chicago: Wise Guides, 2007.

Burns, Ric, and James Sanders. *New York: An Illustrated History*. New York: Alfred A. Knopf, 1999.

Carmichael, John P. *My Greatest Day in Baseball*. Lincoln: Bison Books, 1996. Originally copublished in New York by Grosset and Dunlap and by A. S. Barnes, 1945.

Carter, Susan B., Scott S. Gartner, Michael R. Haines, Alan L. Olmstead, Richard Sutch, and Gavin Wright, eds. *Historical Statistics of the United States: Earliest Times to the Present*. Vol. 4. New York: Cambridge University Press, 2006.

Chamlee, Roy Zebulon. "The Sabbath Crusade, 1810–1920." PhD diss., George Washington University, 1968.

Charyn, Jerome. *Gangsters and Gold Diggers*. New York: Four Walls Eight Windows, 2003.

———. *Joe DiMaggio: The Long Vigil*. New Haven: Yale University Press, 2011.

Clark, Tom. *The World of Damon Runyon*. New York: Harper & Row, 1978.

Clavin, Tom. *The DiMaggios: Three Brothers, Their Passion for Baseball, Their Pursuit of the American Dream*. New York: HarperCollins, 2013.

Clifton, James Child. *The German-Americans in Politics, 1914–1917*. Madison: University of Wisconsin Press, 1939.

Cobb, William R., ed. *Babe Ruth: Playing the Game, My Early Years in Baseball*. New York: Dover Publication, 2011.

Cochran, Thomas C. *The Pabst Brewing Company*. London: Oxford University Press, 1948.

Collins, Eddie, with Boyden Sparkes. "Out at Second." *Saturday Evening Post*, June 23, 1934, 18 (5).

Colver, J. Newton. "Are the Yanks the Strongest Club in Baseball History?" *Baseball Magazine*, November 1927, 557 (3).

———. "Are the Yanks the Strongest Club in Baseball History? Part II," *Baseball Magazine*, December 1927, 309 (4).

Considine, Bob. *The Babe Ruth Story*. New York: E. P. Dutton, 1948.

Cook, William A. *August "Garry" Herrmann: A Biography*. Jefferson NC: McFarland, 2008.

———. *Waite Hoyt: A Biography of the Yankees' Schoolboy Wonder*. Jefferson NC: McFarland, 2004.

Cooper, Brian E. *Red Faber: A Biography of the Hall of Fame Spitball Pitcher*. Jefferson NC: McFarland, 2007.

Corzine, Nathan M. "American Game, American Mirror: Baseball, Beer, the Media, and American Culture, 1933–1954." MA thesis, University of Missouri, Columbia, 2004.

Cottrell, Robert A. *Blackball, the Black Sox, and the Babe*. Jefferson NC: McFarland, 2002.

Cramer, Richard Ben. *Joe DiMaggio: The Hero's Life*. New York: Simon & Schuster, 2000.

Creamer, Robert W. *Babe: The Legend Comes to Life*. New York: Penguin, 1974. Originally published in New York by Simon & Schuster, 1974.

———. *Baseball in '41: A Celebration of Baseball's Best Season Ever in the Year America Went to War*. New York: Viking, 1991.

———. Stengel: His Life and Times. Lincoln: University of Nebraska Press, 1996.

Crosby, Alfred W. *America's Forgotten Pandemic: The Influenza of 1918*. Cambridge: Cambridge University Press, 2003.

Curran, William. *Big Sticks: The Batting Revolution of the Twenties*. New York: William Morrow, 1990.

Daniel, Daniel M. "1935 a Big Year for the Yankees." *Baseball Magazine*, March 1935, 437 (4).

Daniel, Dan, with anecdotes by H. G. Salsinger. *The Real Babe Ruth*. St. Louis: Sporting News, 1948.

Daniel, Dan. *Babe Ruth: The Idol of the American Boy*. Racine WI: Whitman, 1930.

Daniel, Daniel M. "The Hero of the World's Series." *Baseball Magazine*, December 1932, 291 (3).

———. "Night Baseball Nothing New." *Baseball Magazine*, February 1935, 389 (3).

————. "Those Yankees Carry On." *Baseball Magazine*, March 1939, 435 (4).

Davis, Jeff. *Papa Bear: The Life and Legacy of George Halas*. New York: McGraw-Hill, 2006.

DeMotte, Charles. *Bat, Ball & Bible: Baseball and Sunday Observance in New York*. Dulles VA: Potomac Books, 2012.

————. "How World War I Nearly Brought Down Professional Baseball." In *The Cooperstown Symposium on Baseball and American Culture, 2009–2010*, ed. William M. Simons, 214–24. Jefferson NC: McFarland, 2011.

Derr, Mark. *A Dog's History of America: How Our Best Friend Explored, Conquered, and Settled a Continent*. New York: North Point Press, 2004.

Dewey, Donald, and Nicholas Acocella. *The Biographical History of Baseball*. New York: Carroll & Graff, 1995.

Di Salvatore, Bryan. *A Clever Base-Ballist: The Life and Times of John Montgomery Ward*. Baltimore: Johns Hopkins University Press, 1999.

Dos Passos, John. *Mid-Century*. Boston: Houghton Mifflin, 1961.

Douglas, Ann. *Terrible Honesty: Mongrel Manhattan in the 1920s*. New York: Farrar, Straus and Giroux, 1995.

Drebinger, John. "How Long Can the Yanks Stay on Top?" *Baseball Magazine*, December 1937, 291 (3).

Durocher, Leo. *Nice Guys Finish Last*. New York: Simon & Schuster, 1975.

Echevarria, Roberto. *The Pride of Havana: A History of Cuban Baseball*. New York: Oxford University Press, 1999.

Ehrgott, Robert. *Mr. Wrigley's Ball Club: Chicago and the Cubs during the Jazz Age*. Lincoln: University of Nebraska Press, 2013.

Eig, Jonathan. *Luckiest Man: The Life and Death of Lou Gehrig*. New York: Simon & Schuster, 2005.

Elias, Al Munro. "Miller Huggins." *Baseball Magazine*, March 1918, 433–34.

Ellis, Edward Robb. *Echoes of Distant Thunder: Life in the United States, 1914–1918*. New York: Kodansha International, 1996. Originally published in New York by Coward, McCann & Geoghegan, 1975.

Evers, Alf. *The Catskills: From Wilderness to Woodstock*. Garden City NY: Doubleday, 1972.

Fetter, Henry D. *Taking on the Yankees: Winning and Losing in the Business of Baseball*. New York: W. W. Norton, 2003.

Fleitz, David. *More Ghosts in the Gallery*. Jefferson NC: McFarland, 2007.

————. *Shoeless: The Life and Times of Joe Jackson*. Jefferson NC: McFarland, 2001.

Fountain, Charles. *Sportswriter: The Life and Times of Grantland Rice*. Bridge-water CT: Replica Books, 2000.

————. *Under the March Sun: The Story of Spring Training*. New York: Oxford University Press, 2009.

Fowler, Gene. *Skyline: A Reporter's Reminiscence of the '20s*. New York: Viking, 1961.

Frazee, Harry. "The Reasons Which Led Me to Sell 'Babe' Ruth. *Baseball Magazine*, April 1920, 626 (2).

Frommer, Harvey. *Five O'Clock Lightning: Babe Ruth, Lou Gehrig, and the Greatest Baseball Team in History: The 1927 New York Yankees*. Hoboken NJ: John Wiley & Sons, 2008.

————. *A Yankee Century*. New York: Berkley, 2002.

Fullerton, Hugh. "Baseball on Trial," *New Republic*, October 20, 1920, 183–84.

————. "Can Babe Ruth Come Back?" *Liberty*, May 1, 1926.

————. "Peckinpaugh's Greatest Thrill: A Baseball Classic for 1921." *Liberty*, May 4, 1929, 67–68.

Furnas, J. C. *Great Times: An Informal Social History of the United States, 1914–1929*. New York: G. P. Putnam's Sons, 1974.

————. *Stormy Weather, Crosslights on the Nineteen Thirties: An Informal Social History of the United States, 1929–1941*. New York: G. P. Putnam's Sons, 1977.

Gallagher, Mark. *The Yankee Encyclopedia*. Champaign IL: Sagamore, 1996.

Gallen, David. *The Baseball Chronicles*. New York: Carroll & Graf, 1991.

Gallico, Paul W. *Farewell to Sport*. Evanston IL: Holtzman Press, 1938.

————. *The Golden People*. New York: Doubleday, 1965.

Gettelson, Leonard. "Miller Huggins' Last Flag." *Baseball Magazine*, December 1929, 315 (4).

————. "The Yankees Great Winning Streak." *Baseball Magazine*, August 1926, 393 (2).

Godin, Roger A. *The 1922 St. Louis Browns: Best of the American League's Worst*. Jefferson NC: McFarland, 1991.

Goewey, Edwin A. "The Old Fan Says." *Leslie's Illustrated Weekly*, August 26, 1915, 210.

Goldberg, David J. *Discontented America: The United States in the 1920s*. Baltimore: Johns Hopkins University Press, 1999.

Goldstein, Ed. "The Yankee-California Collection." *Baseball Research Journal* 19 (1990): 54–56.

Gomez, Vernona, with Lawrence Goldstone. *Lefty: An American Odyssey*. New York: Ballantine Books, 2012.

Gorman, Robert, and David Weeks. *Death at the Ballpark: A Comprehensive Study of Game-Related Fatalities, 1862–2007*. Jefferson NC: McFarland, 2009.

Gould, James M. "Who Will Win the Big League Pennants in 1926?" *Baseball Magazine*, May 1926, 531–33.

Graff, Henry F. "Jacob Ruppert." *Dictionary of American Biography, Supplement Two*. New York: Charles Scribner's Sons, 1958, 589–90.

Graham, Frank. *Baseball Extra*. New York: A. S. Barnes, 1954.

———. "The Little Miller." *Baseball Magazine*, January 1930, 363 (4).

———. *Lou Gehrig: A Quiet Hero*. New York: Putnam, 1942.

———. *McGraw of the Giants: An Informal Biography*. New York: Putnam & Sons, 1944.

———. *The New York Yankees*. New York: G. P. Putnam's Sons, 1948.

Graham, Frank, Jr. *A Farewell to Heroes*. New York: Viking, 1981.

Gribetz, Louis J., and Joseph Kaye. *Jimmy Walker: The Story of a Personality*. New York: Dial Press, 1932.

Griffith, Clark. "Why the Spit Ball Should Be Abolished." *Baseball Magazine*, July 1917.

Halas, George Stanley. *Halas by Halas: The Autobiography of George Halas*. New York: McGraw-Hill, 1979.

Halberstam, David. *Sports on New York Radio: A Play-by-Play History*. Chicago: Masters, 1999.

Hanrahan, Tom. "Which Batter Had the Greatest Eye?" *By the Numbers*, Statistical Analysis Committee, Society for American Baseball Research, May 2009, 6–10.

Harper, William A. *How You Played the Game: The Life of Grantland Rice*. Columbia: University of Missouri Press, 1999.

Harries, Meirion, and Suzie Harries. *The Last Days of Innocence: America at War, 1917–1918*. New York: Random House, 1997.

Harris, Stanley. *Playing the Game: From Mine Boy to Manager*. New York: Frederick A. Stokes, 1925.

Harrison, Mitchell C., comp. *New York State's Prominent and Progressive Men. An Encyclopaedia of Contemporaneous Biography, Volume II*. New York: New York Tribune, 1900, 295–98.

Hartzell, Scott Taylor. *St. Petersburg: An Oral History*. Sarasota: Pineapple Press, 1996.

Haupert, Michael. "Babe Ruth: Better than the Dow Jones." *Outside the Lines*, Business of Baseball Research Committee, Society for American Baseball Research (Spring 2008): 1 (7).

————. "The Odd Fellows and the Colonels: Innovation and Survival in Segregated Baseball." *Black Ball*, Spring 2008, 79–92.

Haupert, Michael J., and Kenneth Winter. "Pay Ball: Estimating the Profitability of the New York Yankees, 1915–1937." *Essays in Economic and Business History* 21 (Spring 2003): 89–102.

————. "Yankees Profits and Promise: The Purchase of Babe Ruth and the Building of Yankee Stadium." In *The Cooperstown Symposium on Baseball and American Culture*, ed. William M. Simons, 197–214. Jefferson NC: McFarland, 2003.

Helyar, John. *Lords of the Realm: The Real History of Baseball*. New York: Villard Books, 1994.

Henderson, Thomas H. *Tammany Hall and the New Immigrants: The Progressive Years*. New York: Arno Press, 1976.

Hernon, Peter, and Terry Ganey. *Under the Influence: The Unauthorized Story of the Anheuser-Busch Dynasty*. New York: Simon & Schuster, 1991.

Higham, John. *Stranger in the Land: Patterns of American Nativism, 1860–1925*. New York: Atheneum, 1970. Originally published in New Brunswick by Rutgers University Press, 1955.

Hochschild, Adam. *To End All Wars: A Story of Loyalty and Rebellion, 1914–1918*. Boston: Houghton Mifflin Harcourt, 2011.

Hoefer, W. R. "Curbing the Yankees." *Baseball Magazine*, January 1939, 365 (3).

————. "The Reign of the Wallop." *Baseball Magazine*, July 1923, 365 (3).

Holland, Gerald. "The Beer Barons of New York." *American Mercury*, August 1931, 401–7.

Holtzman, Jerome, ed. *No Cheering in the Press Box*. New York: Holt, Rinehart & Winston, 1974.

Honig, Donald. *Baseball America: The Heroes of the Game and the Times of Their Glory*. New York: Macmillan, 1985.

————. *Baseball When the Grass Was Real*. Lincoln: University of Nebraska Press, 1993.

————. *The Man in the Dugout*. Lincoln: University of Nebraska Press, 1977.

Hotaling, Ed. *The Great Black Jockeys: The Life and Times of the Men Who Dominated America's First National Sport*. Rocklin CA: Forum, 1999.

"How the Two 'Colonels' Backed the 'Yankees.'" *Literary Digest*, January 13, 1923, 69–71.

"How the Yanks' Four Straight Gave Baseball a Good Name," *Literary Digest*, October 22, 1927, 64–67.

Hoyt, Waite. *Babe Ruth as I Knew Him*. New York: Dell, 1948.

Huggins, Miller. "The Danger of Too Much Success." *Baseball Magazine*, November 1924, 543 (2).

————. "The Difficulty of Doping Out a Pennant Race." *Baseball Magazine*, July 1925, 351.

————. "How Managers Win: The Secret of a Baseball Leader's Success." *Baseball Magazine*, February 1917, 39–40.

————. "Is a World Series a Toss-Up?" *Baseball Magazine*, November 1929, 533 (2).

————. "The Leading Points of a Winning Ball Club." *Baseball Magazine*, September 1919, 259 (7).

————. "The Toughest Problem." *Baseball Magazine*, May 1929, 537 (3).

————. "The Yankees' Big Lead and Their Prospects." *Baseball Magazine*, November 1923, 533 (3).

Huggins, Myrtle, as told to John B. Kennedy. "Mighty Midget." *Collier's*, May 24, 1930, 18 (3).

Huhn, Rick. *Eddie Collins: A Baseball Biography*. Jefferson NC: McFarland, 2008.

————. *The Sizzler: George Sisler, Baseball's Forgotten Great*. Columbia: University of Missouri Press, 2004.

Huntington, C. P. "The Real Reason for the Yankees' Great Slump." *Baseball Magazine*, October 1925, 498 (2).

Hynd, Noel. *The Giants of the Polo Grounds*. New York: Doubleday, 1988.

Irons, Craig Lynn. "Babe Ruth and the New York City Press, 1919–1932." Manuscript in SABR Research Library, 1996.

Istorico, Ray. *Greatness in Waiting: An Illustrated History of the Early New York Yankees, 1903–1919*. Jefferson NC: McFarland, 2008.

Jenkinson, Bill. *The Year Babe Ruth Hit 104 Home Runs*. New York: Carroll and Graf, 2007.

Johnson, Walter. "What I Pitch to Babe Ruth and Why." *Baseball Magazine*, September 1920, 478 (4).

Johnston, Alva. "Beer and Baseball." *New Yorker*, September 24, 1932.

Jones, David, ed. *Deadball Stars of the American League*. Washington DC: Potomac Books, 2006.

Judge, Mark Gauvreau. *Damn Senators: My Grandfather and the Story of Washington's Only World Series Championship*. San Francisco: Encounter Books, 2003.

Kaese, Harold. *The Boston Braves: 1871–1953*. Boston: Northeastern University Press, 2004. Originally published in New York by G. P. Putnam's Sons, 1948.

Kammer, David John. "Take Me Out to the Ballgame: American Cultural Values as Reflected in the Architectural Evolution and Criticism of the Modern Baseball Stadium." PhD diss., University of New Mexico, 1982.

Kanfer, Stefan. *A Summer World*. New York: Farrar, Strauss and Giroux, 1989.

Kavanagh, Jack, and Norman L. Macht. *Uncle Robbie*. Cleveland: Society for American Baseball Research, 2000.

Kelley, Brent E. *They Too Wore Pinstripes: Interviews with 20 Glory-Days New York Yankees*. Jefferson NC: McFarland, 1998.

Kennedy, David M. *Over Here: The First World War and American Society*. New York: Oxford University Press, 1980, 2004.

Kessner, Thomas. *Fiorello H. LaGuardia and the Making of Modern New York*. New York: McGraw-Hill, 1989.

King, Steven A. "When Did Frank Baker Become 'Home Run' Baker?" *Baseball Research Journal* 42, no. 2 (2013): 57–60.

Knoedelseder, William. *Bitter Brew: The Rise and Fall of Anheuser-Busch and America's King of Beers*. New York: Harper Business, 2012.

Kofoed, J. C. "The New School of Big League Managers." *Baseball Magazine*, September 1917, 487 (4).

Lackey, Mike. *Spitballing: The Baseball Days of Long Bob Ewing*. Wilmington OH: Orange Frazer Press, 2013.

Lamb, Chris. "L'Affaire Jake Powell: The Minority Press Goes to Bat against Segregated Baseball." *Journalism & Mass Communication Quarterly*, 1999.

Lamb, William. "Andrew Freedman." SABR BioProject, sabr.org/bioproject.

———. "Bill Devery." SABR BioProject, sabr.org/bioproject.

———. "Frank Farrell." SABR BioProject, sabr.org/bioproject.

Landis, Lincoln. *From Pilgrimage to Promise: Civil War Heritage and the Landis Boys of Logansport, Indiana*. Westminster MD: Heritage Books, 2006.

Lane, F. C. "The All-American Baseball Club of 1922." *Baseball Magazine*, December 1922, 307 (6).

Lane, F. C. "Back of the Stars That Shine." *Baseball Magazine*, November 1928, 545 (4).

American League (*continued*)
   salaries in, 441n25; Scott Perry in,
   113; in St. Louis, 356n9, 358n31;
   stolen bases in, 167, 397n2; strikeout record in, 415n39; on Sunday baseball, 272; team names
   in, 386n3; trading in, 71, 72, 80;
   umpire in, 97, 375n7; Yankee pennants in, 273, 277, 281, 307, 323,
   432n1; and Yankee Stadium, 199,
   410n11. *See also* Major Leagues
American Mercury, 18
America's Loss of Innocence (Asinof), 86
Anheuser-Busch brewery, 313, 336,
   337, 444n9. *See also* breweries
Anti-Saloon League (asl), 85–86, 144
Appel, Marty, xv, 49, 131
Appleton, Ed, 41
Arion Society, 21, 22
Armour, Bill, 358n33
Armour, Mark, 132
Army-Navy football game, 314
Army–Notre Dame football game,
   327
Asinof, Eliot, 86, 145
aspca, 449n8
Association of Trotting Horse Breed-
   ers, 22
Astor, Caroline Schermerhorn, 347n11
Astor, John Jacob, 22, 284
Astor, William Waldorf, 198
Astor family, 14, 185–86
Atlanta ga, 235
Atlantic Yacht Club, 22
Austin, Jimmy, 182
Austria-Hungary, 369n10
automobiles, 90, 136–37, 214, 243,
   286, 373n40, 389n12, 414n24

Bachelor magazine, 225, 418n35
Bailey, J. W., 22
Baker, Frank "Home Run": 1916
   season, 76, 77; 1919 season, 103,
   378n9; 1920 season, 142, 391n11;
   injuries of, 77, 183, 369n7; with
   New York Yankees, 69–73, 114,
   168, 171, 379n31; as star player, 89;
   Ty Cobb's run-in with, 104
Baker, Newton, 91
Baker, Ottalee, 142
Ball, Phil, 40, 116, 118, 358n31,
   360n56, 371n18, 383n45, 419n7
Baltimore Afro-American, 330
Baltimore baseball teams, 51, 69, 322.
   See also Baltimore Orioles
Baltimore Black Sox, 329
Baltimore md, 48, 79, 145, 369n15
Baltimore Orioles, 31, 47, 52, 66, 102,
   300, 440n49. *See also* Baltimore
   baseball teams
Baltimore Sun, 56, 58
Bancroft, Dave, 175
Baptist churches, 86, 276
Barnard, Ernest, 272, 277
Barnes, Jesse, 175
barnstorming tours, 137, 180, 389n15.
   See also Major Leagues, exhibition
   games in
Barrow, Ed: on 1917 season, 5; on
   1927 team, 427n2; on 1929 season, 290; and Babe Ruth, 102, 128,
   131–33, 136, 252, 308–10, 387n25,
   387n27; in Baseball Hall of Fame,
   344; biography of, xv–xvi, 335;
   and black community, 329–31; as
   business manager, xii, 162–63, 196,
   323, 335, 341, 427n8; on buyout,

Tullius, John. *I'd Rather Be a Yankee*. New York: Macmillan, 1986.

Turesky, David S. "A World Apart: Baseball and American Life in the Twenties." BA honors thesis, Amherst College, 1972.

United States Brewers' Association: The Year Book and Proceedings of the Fifty-Second Annual Convention. New York: United States Brewers' Association, 1912.

Urofsky, Melvin I. *Louis Brandeis: A Life*. New York: Schocken Books, 2009.

Vancil, Mark, and Alfred Santasiere III. *Yankee Stadium: The Official Retrospective*. New York: Pocket Books, 2008.

Veeck, Bill, with Ed Linn. *The Hustler's Handbook*. New York: Simon & Schuster, 1989. Originally published in New York by G. P. Putnam's Sons, 1965.

Vickers, Raymond. *Panic in Paradise: Florida's Banking Crash of 1926*. Tuscaloosa: University of Alabama Press, 1994.

Vincent, David. *Home Run: The Definitive History of Baseball's Ultimate Weapon*. Washington DC: Potomac Books, 2007.

Vitty, Cort. "Yankee Catchers during the Miller Huggins Era." *Baseball Research Journal* 42, no. 1 (2013): 106–10.

Voigt, David Q. "The Chicago Black Sox and the Myth of Baseball's Single Sin." In *America through Baseball*, 65–76. Chicago: Nelson-Hall, 1976.

Wagenheim, Kal. *Babe Ruth: His Life and Legend*. New York: Henry Holt, 1974.

Walker, Stanley. *City Editor*. Baltimore: Johns Hopkins University Press, 1999. Originally published in New York by Frederick A. Stokes, 1934.

Walsh, Christy. "Adios to Ghosts." *Cleveland News*, September 21, 1937.

Warburton, Paul. "The 1921 AL Race." *National Pastime* 18 (1998): 103–6.

Wheeler, Lonnie, and John Baskin. *The Cincinnati Game*. Wilmington OH: Orange Fraser Press, 1998.

"When 'Babe' Ruth Was Beaten by John McGraw." *Literary Digest*, December 2, 1922, 57–61.

White, G. Edward. *Creating the National Pastime: Baseball Transforms Itself, 1903–1953*. Princeton: Princeton University Press, 1996.

Wiggins, Robert Peyton. *The Federal League of Base Ball Clubs*. Jefferson NC: McFarland, 2009.

Willey, Ken. *Baseball's Golden Half-Century, 1910–1959*. City of Industry CA: Glenleaf, 2007.

Williams, Joe. *The Joe Williams Baseball Reader*. Chapel Hill: Algonquin Books, 1989.

———. *Yankees Century*. Boston: Houghton Mifflin Harcourt, 2002.

Stump, Al. *Cobb: A Biography*. Chapel Hill: Algonquin Books, 1994.

Sullivan, Dean A. *Middle Innings: A Documentary History of Baseball, 1900–1948*. Lincoln: Bison Books, 2001.

Sullivan, George, and John Powers. *Yankees: An Illustrated History*. Englewood Cliffs NJ: Prentice-Hall, 1982.

Sullivan, Mark. *Our Times: The United States 1900–1925. Vol. 4: The War Begins, 1909–1914*. New York: Charles Scribner's Sons, 1932.

———. *Our Times: The United States 1900–1925. Vol. 5: Over Here, 1914–1918*. New York: Charles Scribner's Sons, 1933.

———. *Our Times: The United States 1900–1925. Vol. 6: The Twenties*. New York: Charles Scribner's Sons, 1935.

Sullivan, Neil J. *The Diamond in the Bronx: Yankee Stadium and the Politics of New York*. New York: Oxford University Press, 2001.

Surdam, David George. *Wins, Losses, and Empty Seats: How Baseball Outlasted the Great Depression*. Lincoln: University of Nebraska Press, 2011.

Swanson, Harry. *Ruthless Baseball*. Bloomington IN: Author House, 2004.

Tan, Cecilia. *The 50 Greatest Yankee Games*. Hoboken NJ: John Wiley, 2005.

"Taps for Huggins: A Great Little Bear-Tamer." *Literary Digest*, October 12, 1929, 39 (3).

Taylor, William R., ed. *Inventing Times Square: Commerce and Culture at the Crossroads of the World*. New York: Russell Sage Foundation, 1991.

Thomas, Henry W. *Walter Johnson: Baseball's Big Train*. Washington DC: Phenom Press, 1995.

Thomas, Joan M. *Baseball's First Lady: Helene Hathaway Robison Britton and the St. Louis Cardinals*. St. Louis: Reedy Press, 2010.

Thorn, John. "The Last Resort." *Voices: The Journal of New York Folklore* 36 (Spring/Summer 2010).

———. "Shoeless Joe, the Bambino, the Big Bankroll, and the Jazz Age." *NINE: A Journal of Baseball History & Culture* 21, no. 1 (Fall 2012): 118–27.

Tofel, Richard. *A Legend in the Making: The New York Yankees in 1939*. Chicago: Ivan R. Dee, 2003.

Trachtenberg, Leo. "Jake Ruppert Built Dynasties." *Yankees Magazine*, June 20, 1985, 19 (3).

———. "Miller Huggins. *Yankees Magazine*, July 21, 1983, 18–19.

———. "The Travails of Miller Huggins." *Baseball History*, Summer 1987, 48–60.

———. *The Ty Cobb S...*

...rent, Daniel. I...

...ner, 201...

Palmer, Ste...

August 19...

Parker, Dan. "T...

Parrish, Michael ...

1920–1941. New...

Perrett, Geoffrey. *Am...*

Schuster, 1982.

Phelon, W. A. "Glimpses...

Little Player." *Baseball ...*

———. "The Grand Panora...

February 1923, 405–6.

———. "The Passing Show." *Ba...*

Pietrusza, David. *Judge and Jury: 7...*

tain Landis. South Bend IN: Diamo...

Povich, Lynn, Maury Povich, and Davi...

the Post. New York: Public Affairs, 20...

Povich, Shirley. *The Washington Senators*. N...

1954.

Pringle, Henry F. "A Small Package." *New Yor...*

Reisler, Jim. *Babe Ruth: Launching the Legend*. Ne...

———, ed. *Guys, Dolls, and Curveballs*. New York...

Rennie, Rud. "The Decline of a Once Great Team."...

October 1934, 491 (2).

———. "Stop Squawking!" *Collier's*, March 4, 1939, 11 (...

Ribowsky, Mark. *The Complete History of the Home Run*. Ne...

2003.

"A Rich Mixture of Beer, Baseball, Bachelorhood." *News-Week*,...

1937, 21.

Riess, Steven A. "The Baseball Magnates and Urban Politics in the...

sive Era: 1885–1920." *Journal of Sports History* 1, no. 1 (1974): 41–6...

———. *City Games: The Evolution of American Urban Society and the R...*

Sports. Urbana: University of Illinois Press, 1991.

———. *The Sport of Kings and the Kings of Crime: Horse Racing, Politics, a...*

Organized Crime in New York, 1865–1913. Syracuse: Syracuse University...

Press, 2011.

Robinson, Arthur. "M...

Robinson, Ray. *Iron Horse*... nial, 1990.

———. "Profiles: The...

Robinson, Ray, and Christop...
Drama, Glamour, and Glory.

Ruel, Harold "Muddy." "A Playe... ?ine, February 1929, 399–400.

Ruppert, Jacob. "Building a Winning...

———. "The Ten Million Dollar Toy."... 1931, 18 (4).

Col. Jacob Ruppert. "*Baseball Maga*...

Ruppert, K. Jacob. "In Re John Barleycorn: ... Prohibition," Part I, *New York County Lawy*...

"Ruppert's Surprise." *News-Week*, January 30, 19...

Ruth, Babe, with Joe Winkworth. "I Have Been a B... October 12, 1925, 15.

Ruth, Mrs. Babe, with Bill Slocum. *The Babe and I.* Ne... 1959.

Sanborn, Irving E. "Consider the Pitchers: They Shine No... They Spit." *Baseball Magazine*, September 1920, 475 (4).

———. *Spalding Official Baseball Guide 1919.*

Sante, Luc. *Low Life: Lures and Snores of Old New York.* New Yo... Strauss and Giroux, 1991.

Seymour, Harold, and Dorothy Z. Seymour. *Baseball: The Golden A*... York: Oxford University Press, 1971.

Shawkey, Bob. "The Veteran of the Yankees' Hurling Staff." *Baseball Ma*... ?ine, July 1926, 349–50.

Shulman, Robin. *Eat the City: A Tale of Fishers, Foragers, Butchers, Farmers, and Brewers Who Built New York.* New York: Crown, 2012.

Sive, Robinson. *Lost Villages: Historic Driving Tours in the Catskills.* Delhi NY: Delaware County Historical Association 1998.

Moore, Lucy. *Anything Goes: A Biography of the Roaring Twenties.* New York: Overlook Press, 2010.

Moriarty, George. "Calling Them." *Baseball Magazine*, October 1929, 506.

Morris, Lloyd. *Incredible New York.* New York: Random House, 1951.

Morris, Peter. *Catcher: How the Man behind the Plate Became an American Folk Hero.* Chicago: Ivan R. Dee, 2009.

———. *A Game of Inches: The Stories behind the Innovations That Shaped Baseball.* Vol. 1, *The Game on the Field.* Chicago: Ivan R. Dee, 2006.

———. *A Game of Inches: The Stories behind the Innovations That Shaped Baseball.* Vol. 2, *The Game behind the Scenes.* Chicago: Ivan R. Dee, 2006.

Mosedale, John. *The Greatest of All: The 1927 New York Yankees.* New York: Dial Press, 1983 Originally published in New York by Dial Press, 1974.

Murdock, Eugene C. *Ban Johnson: Czar of Baseball.* Westport CT: Greenwood Press, 1982.

———. *Baseball between the Wars: Memories of the Game by the Men who Played It.* Westport CT: Meckler, 1992.

———. *Baseball Players and Their Times: Oral Histories of the Game.* Westport CT: Meckler, 1991.

Nadel, Stanley. *Little Germany: Ethnicity, Religion, and Class in New York City, 1945–80.* Urbana: University of Illinois Press, 1990.

Nathanson, Mitchell. *A People's History of Baseball.* Urbana: University of Illinois Press, 2012.

The National Cyclopaedia of American Biography. Vol. 29. New York: James White, 1941.

"New York Scolded for Its Moral and Other Shortcomings." *Current Opinion*, April 1920, 523–24.

Neyer, Rob, and Eddie Epstein. *Baseball Dynasties: The Greatest Teams of All Time.* New York: W. W. Norton, 2000.

Noon, Nark A. *Yuengling: A History of America's Oldest Brewery.* Jefferson NC: McFarland, 1997.

O'Connor, Richard. *Heywood Broun: A Biography.* New York: G. P. Putnam's Sons, 1975.

Official Souvenir Program, Opening Day, Yankee Stadium, April 18, 1923.

Ogle, Maureen. *Ambitious Brew: The Story of American Beer.* Orlando: Harcourt, 2006.

Okkonen, Marc. *Baseball Uniforms of the 20th Century.* New York: Sterling, 1991.

Mann, Arthur, *Branch Rickey: American in Action*. Boston: Houghton Mifflin, 1957.

Markey, Morris, "The Current Press." *New Yorker*, October 24, 1925, 15–16.

Mason, Ward. "The Star of the 1916 Recruits: Rogers Hornsby." *Baseball Magazine*, October 1916, 45–48.

Mayer, Ronald A. *The 1937 Newark Bears: A Baseball Legend*. East Hanover NJ: Vintage Press, 1980.

Mays, Carl. "My Attitude toward the Unfortunate Chapman Affair." *Baseball Magazine*, November 1920, 573 (4).

———. "What I Have Learned from Four World Series." *Baseball Magazine*, November 1922, 544 (3).

McCarthy, Joseph. "Winning Isn't the Hardest Job." *Baseball Magazine*, July 1934, 339 (3).

McCarthy, Kevin M. *Baseball in Florida*. Sarasota: Pineapple Press, 1996.

McDermott, J. R. "Miller Huggins, the Midget Manager." *Baseball Magazine*, October 1913, 59–67.

McGarigle, Bob. *Baseball's Great Tragedy: The Story of Carl Mays, Submarine Pitcher*. Jericho NY: Exposition Press, 1972.

McGovern, Arthur A. "'If I Can Come Back, Anybody Can,' Says Babe Ruth." *Collier's*, March 26, 1927, 15 (3).

McGraw, John. *My Thirty Years in Baseball*. Lincoln: Bison Books, 1995. Originally published in New York by Boni and Liveright, 1923.

McGraw, Mrs. John, with Arthur Mann. *The Real McGraw*. New York: David McKay, 1953.

Meany, Tom. *Babe Ruth: The Big Moments of the Big Fellow*. New York: A. S. Barnes, 1947.

———. *The Yankee Story*. New York: Dutton, 1960.

Mercer, Sid, "The Supreme Value of 'Color' in Baseball." *Baseball Magazine*, August 1920, 423 (5).

Miller, Nathan. *New World Coming: The 1920s and the Making of Modern America*. Cambridge MA: Da Capo Press, 2003.

Mittelman, Amy. *Brewing Battles: A History of American Beer*. New York: Algora, 2007.

Montville, Leigh. *The Big Bam: The Life and Times of Babe Ruth*. New York: Broadway Books, 2006.

Moore, Jack B. *Joe DiMaggio: A Bio-Bibliography*. Westport CT: Greenwood Press, 1986.

Levitt, Daniel R., Mark L. Armour, and Matthew Levitt. "History versus Harry Frazee: Re-revising the Story." *Baseball Research Journal* 37 (2008): 26–41.

Levy, Alan H. *Joe McCarthy: Architect of the Yankee Dynasty*. Jefferson NC: McFarland, 2005.

Lewis, Franklin A. *The Cleveland Indians*. New York: Putnam, 1949.

Lieb, Frederick G. *Baseball as I Have Known It*. Lincoln: Bison Books, 1996. Originally published in New York by Coward, McCann, and Geoghegan, 1977.

———. *The Baseball Story*. New York: Putnam, 1950.

———. "Baseball—The Nation's Melting Pot." *Baseball Magazine*, August 1923, 393 (4).

———. *The Boston Red Sox*. New York: Putnam, 1947.

———. *The Detroit Tigers*. New York: Putnam, 1946.

———. "The Manager's Part in Winning a Championship." *Baseball Magazine*, November 1921, 535 (3).

———. *The Pittsburgh Pirates*. Carbondale: Southern Illinois University Press, 2003. Originally published in New York by G. P. Putnam's Sons, 1948.

———. *The St. Louis Cardinals*. New York: G. P. Putnam's Sons, 1945.

Light, Jonathan Fraser. *The Cultural Encyclopedia of Baseball*. Jefferson NC: McFarland, 1997.

Linn, Ed. *The Great Rivalry: The Yankees and the Red Sox, 1901–1990*. New York: Ticknor & Fields, 1991.

Lipsky, Richard. *How We Play the Game: Why Sports Dominate American Life*. Boston: Beacon Press, 1981.

Lipsyte, Robert, and Peter Levine. *Idols of the Game: A Sporting History of the American Century*. Atlanta: Turner, 1995.

Lowenfish, Lee. *Branch Rickey: The Ferocious Gentleman*. Lincoln: University of Nebraska Press, 2007.

Lowry, Philip J. *Green Cathedrals: The Ultimate Celebration of Major League and Negro League Ballparks*. New York: Walker, 2006.

Lynch, Michael T. *Harry Frazee, Ban Johnson, and the Feud That Nearly Destroyed the American League*. Jefferson NC: McFarland, 2008.

Macht, Norman L. *Connie Mack and the Early Years of Baseball*. Lincoln: University of Nebraska Press, 2007.

———. *Connie Mack: The Turbulent and Triumphant Years, 1915–1931*. Lincoln: University of Nebraska Press, 2012.

Lane, F. C. "A Rival for Babe Ruth." *Baseball Magazine*, July 1922, 361 (2).

Lane, F. C. "Secret of My Heavy Hitting: An Interview with the King of Sluggers, Babe Ruth." *Baseball Magazine*, August 1920, 419 (7).

Lane, F. C. "The Shadow of New York on the Baseball Diamond." *Baseball Magazine*, August 1923, 397 (3).

Lane, F. C. "Should the Spitball Be Abolished?" *Baseball Magazine*, June 1919, 67 (5).

Lane, F. C. "Slashing Baseball Salaries." *Baseball Magazine*, February 1932, 401 (3).

Lane, F. C. "A Startling Baseball Tragedy." *Baseball Magazine*, October 1920, 523 (4).

Lane, F. C. "Those Mid-Summer Trades." *Baseball Magazine*, October 1922, 504 (5).

Lane, F. C. "What Has Blocked One of Baseball's Biggest Deals." *Baseball Magazine*, March 1923, 435 (4).

Lane, F. C. "Why Big League Managers Fail." *Baseball Magazine*, January 1932, 341 (3).

Lane, F. C. "Will the Major Leagues Adopt Night Baseball?" *Baseball Magazine*, October 1935, 487 (5).

Lane, F. C. "The Yankee Peril." *Baseball Magazine*, January 1929, 339 (3).

Lane, F. C. "The Yankees' New Home, Baseball's Largest and Costliest Stadium." *Baseball Magazine*, May 1923, 552 (6).

Lane, F. C. "The Yankees' Pitching Ace." *Baseball Magazine*, February 1923, 395 (2).

Lardner, John. "The Peerage, Self-Elected." *Newsweek*, September 29, 1941, 48.

Lears, Jackson. *Rebirth of a Nation: The Making of Modern America, 1877–1920*. New York: Harper Perennial, 2009.

Leavengood, Ted. *Clark Griffith: The Old Fox of Washington Baseball*. Jefferson NC: McFarland, 2011.

Leighton, Isabel, *The Aspirin Age, 1919–1941*. New York: Touchstone, 1976.

Lerner, Michael A. *Dry Manhattan: Prohibition in New York City*. Cambridge: Harvard University Press, 2007.

Levitt, Daniel R. *The Battle That Forged Modern Baseball: The Federal League Challenge and Its Legacy*. Lanham MD: Ivan R. Dee, 2012.

———. *Ed Barrow: The Bulldog Who Built the Yankees' First Dynasty*. Lincoln: University of Nebraska Press, 2008.

———. Yankees Financial Records. National Baseball Library and Archives, Cooperstown NY.

Lane, F. C. "Baseball Problems of the Winter Meetings." *Baseball Magazine*, December 1933, 291 (4).

Lane, F. C. "Baseball's Big Question Mark: Will Babe Ruth Come Back?" *Baseball Magazine*, April 1923, 483 (3).

Lane, F. C. "Baseball's Dictator." *Baseball Magazine*, January 1921, 413 (6).

Lane, F. C. "Baseball's Master Builder." *Baseball Magazine*, October 1936, 485 (2).

Lane, F. C. "The Battle of the Hold-Outs." *Baseball Magazine*, April 1932, 483 (4).

Lane, F. C. "The Biggest Managerial Job in Baseball." *Baseball Magazine*, May 1931, 551 (2).

Lane, F. C. "Can Babe Ruth Repeat?" *Baseball Magazine*, May 1921, 555–57.

Lane, F. C. "Carl Mays' Cynical Definition of Pitching Efficiency," *Baseball Magazine*, August 1928, 391–92.

Lane, F. C. "A Fallen Idol." *Baseball Magazine*, November 1925, 558 (2).

Lane, F. C. "The Greatest Rookie of the Decade." *Baseball Magazine*, September 1936, 441 (3).

Lane, F. C. "Has the 'Lively' Ball Revolutionized the Game?" *Baseball Magazine*, September 1921, 435 (7).

Lane, F. C. "The Home-Run Epidemic." *Baseball Magazine*, July 1921, 339 (4).

Lane, F. C. "How Babe Ruth Wins for the New York Yankees." *Baseball Magazine*, June 1921, 291–93.

Lane, F. C. "Huggins and Harmony." *Baseball Magazine*, November 1926, 535 (2).

Lane, F. C. "Huggins vs. McGraw." *Baseball Magazine*, December 1923, 291 (5).

Lane, F. C. "If I Were Only Young Once More!" *Baseball Magazine*, November 1924, 531 (3).

Lane, F. C. "In the Glare of the Spotlight." *Baseball Magazine*, June 1932, 299 (3).

Lane, F. C. "The Man Who Led the Yankees to Their First Pennant." *Baseball Magazine*, December 1921, 595–96.

Lane, F. C. "The Manager Who Lost." *Baseball Magazine*, December 1922, 303–4.

Lane, F. C. "'Pol' Perrit, Pitcher." *Baseball Magazine*, June 1915, 29 (7).

Lane, F. C. "Preparing for a World's Series." *Baseball Magazine*, October 1937, 489 (4).

Boston Red Sox (*continued*)
380n45, 382n32, 391n9, 400n51,
400nn47–49, 404n45, 425n11,
428n27, 436n15, 439n24
Boston Terrier dogs, 25. *See also* dogs
Bottomley, Jim, 274
boxing: and Babe Ruth, 137; film of,
376n18; governance of, 169; of
James Corbett, 377n5; legalization
of, 100, 246; popularity of, 158,
396n2; reporter's comment about,
178, 401n9; at Yankee Stadium,
199, 326–27, 410n10
Boyle's Thirty Acres, 158
Bradley, Elizabeth, 28
Brandeis, Louis, 375n12
Brands, E. G., 254
Braves Field, 310, 410n13
Braxton, Garland, 425n30
Breadon, Sam, 274, 360n54
Brennan, Al, 225, 328, 367n10
Bresnahan, Roger, 36, 37, 356n51,
358n30, 358n33
breweries: competition of, 313, 336–
37; in New York, 14–15, 28, 336–
37, 348n17; role in economic
recovery, 313–14, 444n5, 444n10;
and saloons, 336, 450n21; and Sunday baseball, 99; World War I
effect on, 61, 81, 98, 375nn11–12;
Yankee players at, 182. *See also*
alcohol; Anheuser-Busch brew-
ery; Jacob Ruppert Brewery; Pabst
brewery; Prohibition
Brewers Board of Trade, 28
Brewing Battles (Mittelman), 337
Brewing Industry, Inc., 450n23
Bridgeport CT, 36

Briggs, Walter, 324
Brisbane, Arthur, 81, 106
Britton, Helene: as Cardinals' owner,
1, 36, 345n1; father of, 355n47;
refusal of Federal League players,
42; salaries paid by, 40, 41; sale of
Cardinals, 43, 358n31; support of
Miller Huggins, 38
Britton, Schuyler, 38, 42
Bronx, 19, 28, 58, 91, 198, 410n12
Brooklyn (Dodgers): Jeff Pfeffer
with, 393n44; Miller Huggins's
trick on, 41
Brooklyn NY, 14, 103, 386n24
Brooklyn Daily Eagle, 27
Brooklyn Dodgers: 1926 season,
244; charity games of, 313–14,
444n12; Dazzy Vance with,
374n61; game schedules of, 121,
385n16; home field of, 386n24;
Jackie Robinson with, 448n19;
night baseball of, 321; ownership
of, 99, 192; radio broadcasts of,
321, 322; Wilbert Robinson with,
5–6, 79, 107, 160, 161, 346n25,
397n18; in World Series (1916),
368n20, 410n13; in World Series
(1920), 158, 160
Brooklyn Robins, 100, 255, 346n25
Brooklyn Superbas, 52, 65, 66, 362n27
Brooklyn Tip-Tops, 40, 70, 357n24,
366n5
Brotherhood of Sleeping Car Porters, 329
Broun, Heywood, 233
Brown, Bill, 253, 256, 426n48
Brown, Mordecai, 356n9
Brown, Warren, 297, 311

Brush, John T., 48, 361n7, 385n11, 394n56
Bryan, William Jennings, 20, 61
Buffalo Bisons, 43, 67, 297, 360n52, 439n27, 439n28
Bulgari (dog), 117, 390n6
Bulger, Bozeman, 64, 228
Burns, George, 200
Busch, August, 313, 337
Bush, Donie, 262, 294, 437n2
Bush, Joe: 1923 season, 202–3; acquisition of, 176; and Miller Huggins, 215, 230, 414n30; to St. Louis Browns, 227–28, 419n8; in World Series (1922), 186, 187, 406n70; in World Series (1923), 205
Bushwick section (Brooklyn), 14
Butler, Art, 357n11
Byrd, Richard, 315, 343, 445n21
Byrd, Sam, 432n7

Caffey, Jacob Ruppert vs., 375n12, 386nn1–2
Caldwell, Ray: 1917 season, 79; antics of, 93; with Boston Red Sox, 105, 106, 378n23, 379n29; with Cleveland Indians, 106; injury of, 369n7; with New York Yankees, 66, 67, 88, 371n20; rumor about, 56
California, 214, 286, 371n24, 434n44. *See also* Los Angeles CA; Oakland CA; Pacific Coast League; San Francisco CA; Vernon CA
"Called Shot" by Ruth, 305
Cantor, Eddie, 315
Capone, Al, 254
Carlyle, Cleo, 442n29
Carnegie, Andrew, 14

Carney, Gene, 379n32
Carpentier, Georges, 158
Carrigan, Bill, 160
cars. *See* automobiles
catcher(s): in 1927 season, 256, 259; in 1928 season, 266; in 1929 season, 288; Jacob Ruppert as, 17; Muddy Ruel as, 103, 167, 168; Wally Schang as, 168; Yankees' problems with, 78
Catholic Club, 22
Catholic religion, 14, 15, 26, 139, 275–76, 312, 328, 437n22
Catholic University of America, 79
Central Opera House (NYC), 14
Central Park, 21
Chalmers Award, 36, 356n50
Chambersburg (PA) baseball team, 282, 433n13, 440n47
Champion Young Stormer (dog), 24
Chance, Frank, 6, 53, 200, 227, 291, 363n30, 366n24, 436n9
Chandler, Spud, 447n25
Chapman, Ben, 323, 330
Chapman, Ray, 147–48, 150, 388n35, 392n38
Chappell, Larry, 97, 375n7
charity: in black community, 329; to Byrd expedition, 315, 343, 445n21; game for in Oakland, 318; of Helen Weyant, 449n8; from World Series, 187, 190, 406n69; at Yankee Stadium, 313–16, 444n12
Charyn, Jerome, 249
Chase, Hal, 52–53, 156, 363n30, 396n28
Chesbro, Jack, 52, 69
Chicago Bears, 101, 434n45

Chicago Cubs: 1910 season, 227, 419n1; 1929 season, 288; Frank Chance with, 53, 436n9; Joe McCarthy with, 288, 297, 439n29; Johnny Kling with, 330; management of, 356n9; Miller Huggins's injury against, 33; ownership of, 48, 50, 152, 358n31, 359n36, 362n19; pitchers with, 250; president of, 141; Rogers Hornsby with, 438n19; salaries of, 441n25; in World Series (1918), 94; in World Series (1932), 305; in World Series (1938), 323

Chicago Defender, 331

Chicago IL: American League meetings in, 57–58, 116–17; batting record in, 377n6; black community in, 331; exhibition game en route to, 218; Federal League team in, 57; game schedules in, 121, 385n14; Republican National Convention in, 144; World Series (1938) in, 327

Chicago Whales, 59, 358n31

Chicago White Sox: 1919 team, 427n2; 1920 season, 147–50; 1921 season, 172; 1922 season, 186, 197, 405n55, 405n61; 1923 season, 203; 1927 season, 258; Babe Ruth against, 143; Clark Griffith with, 52; Eddie Collins with, 55, 70, 194; and Frank Baker acquisition, 69; and Fritz Maisel trade, 71; Hal Chase to, 53, 363n30; Jack Quinn with, 94; Joe Jackson with, 71–72, 88, 106, 375n7, 379n32, 388n32; Johnny Grabowski with, 259; management of, 160, 437n2; ownership of, 94, 114, 152, 154, 395n13; Ping

Bodie against, 104; secretary of, 384n6; suspensions of, 156, 393n47; in World Series (1917), 4; in World Series (1919), 106; world tour of (1914), 66; and Yankee player acquisitions, 88, 193, 256, 363n4. *See also* Black Sox scandal

Children's Aid Society, 314

Chill, Ollie, 180

Church of the Transfiguration, 292, 437n21

Cicotte, Eddie, 394n1

Cincinnati Enquirer, 30, 33

Cincinnati OH: Ban Johnson and Til Huston from, 112; leagues' agreement in, 51; Miller Huggins in, 32–33, 161, 211, 223, 239, 292, 353n5, 355n42, 356n8, 401n5, 417n16, 437n22; Procter and Gamble in, 352n3

Cincinnati Reds: 1926 season, 426n40; Armando Marsans with, 358n25; Bob Meusel to, 437n6; Branch Rickey with, 361n57; Carl Mays to, 215, 216; Hal Chase with, 396n28; leadership of, 30, 34, 35, 55, 56, 115, 431n20; Lee Magee with, 367n5; Miller Huggins's love of, 29; Miller Huggins with, xv, 31–34, 223, 354n31, 355nn39–40, 358n29, 359n41, 433n13; night baseball of, 321

cinema: in 1927, 254; and Babe Ruth, 136, 137, 249; and baseball, 90, 99, 214, 373n40, 376n18; Jacob Ruppert as fan of, 324, 447n33

Claridge Hotel (NYC), 49

Clark, Byron, 449n1

Clark, Tom, 97–98

Eagle's Rest, 25, 224, 226, 418n26. *See also* Garrison NY

earned run average (ERA): of 1914 Cardinals, 371n21; in 1926 season, 254; in 1927 season, 261; of Allen Russell, 387n27; of Carl Mays, 380n2, 382n27; of Chief Bender, 374n55; of Cliff Markle, 415n47; of Herb Pennock, 415n48; of Phil Douglas, 405n65; of Slim Sallee, 359n44; of Walter Johnson, 374n58

Eastern European immigrants, 26, 215, 414n28

Eastern League, 212, 440n49

Ebbets, Charles, 6, 79, 99, 160, 161, 347n27

Ebbets Field, 100, 386n24

Echevarria, Robert, 34

Ed Barrow (Levitt), xv–xvi

edelweiss, 315

Ederle, Gertrude, 249–50

Egan, Dick, 35, 355n39

Ehmke, Howard, 147, 200, 392n30

Ehret, George, 14–15, 81

Ehret, George, Jr., 81

Eig, Jonathan, 108, 318–19

Eighteenth Amendment. *See* Prohibition

Elberfeld, Kid, 52, 53

Elias, Al Munro, 404n44

Elkus, Gleason, and Proskauer, 62–63

Elson, Bob, 331

embargo, munitions, 61

Emerson, Ralph Waldo, 198

Empire State Building, 313, 315

English Channel, 249–50

English Jockey Club, 22

Essick, Bill, 222, 317, 442n34

Evans, Billy, 247

Evans, Steve, 42, 356n9, 359n43

Evers, Johnny, 33

Ewing, Bob, 36, 355n46

exhibition games. *See* barnstorming tours; Major Leagues, exhibition games in

Faber, Red, 259

Fales, Harold, 389n38

Fallon, William, 156

farm system: black player in, 329; Til Huston on, 222, 417n8; of Yankees, 282–83, 299–300, 307, 311, 317, 322, 330, 433n13, 440n47. *See also* Minor Leagues; specific teams

Farnsworth, W. S., 79

Farrell, Duke, 66, 88

Farrell, Frank, 49, 51–53, 55–59, 67, 326

Federal Express train, 36, 356nn48–49

Federal League: antitrust lawsuit of, 153–54, 395n10; Buffalo Bisons in, 360n52; in Chicago, 362n20, 366n31; disputes of, 123; end of, 42, 72; John McGraw's attitude toward, 50, 362n21; Lee Magee in, 40, 70, 357n24, 359n43; Organized Baseball players to, 39–40, 70, 357n24, 358n25, 358n27, 359n43; Ray Caldwell in, 67; Rebel Oakes in, 355n40, 359n43; settlement regarding Polo Grounds, 120; team in St. Louis, 38–41, 356n9, 358n31; wooing of Jacob Ruppert, 57, 58; wooing of Roger Peckinpaugh, 59; Yankee players from, 70, 366n4, 425n30

Feller, Bob, 325

Felsch, Happy, 74

Fenway Park, 110–11, 129, 131, 132, 292, 410n13

Fewster, Chick, 149, 183, 393n44

Film Clearing House, 99, 376n18

Firpo, Luis Angel, 199

Fisher, Ray, 66, 371n19

fishing, 220, 223, 240, 342

Fitz Gerald, Ed, 131

"five-for-three" trade, 38, 357n11

Flagler, Henry, 239

Fleischmann, Billy, 49, 56–57, 65, 213–14, 316, 445n28

Fleischmann, Charles, 30

Fleischmann, Herrmann, 56

Fleischmann, Julius, 30, 31, 43, 56, 353n9

Fleischmann, Max, 30, 43

Fleischmanns NY, 30, 353n9

Fleischmann's Mountain Tourists, 30

Fletcher, Art, 253, 286, 291, 294, 426n47, 437n20

Florida: Clarence Huggins in, 292; Jacob Ruppert in, 255, 450n20; Miller Huggins in, 35, 220, 223, 239–40, 245, 264; Myrtle Huggins in, 223, 292; real estate boom and bust in, 239–40, 248, 290, 422n8; spring training in, 223, 417n17. *See also specific cities*

Florida East Coast Railway, 239

Florida Keys, 137

Flower, Roswell P., 18, 22

Flowers, Tiger, 178, 401n9

flu. *See* influenza

Fohl, Lee, 346n17

football, 101, 158, 271, 314, 327, 368n3, 434n45

Ford, Russ, 66

Ford, Whitey, 397n29

Fordham University, 410n12

Forma Corporation, 335. *See also* Jacob Ruppert Realty Corporation

Foster, John, 230

foul-strike rule, 133, 388n36

Fountain, Charles, 222

Fountain Square, 32

"Four Hundred," 14, 347n11

Fowler, Gene, 232, 246

Fowler brothers, 352n4

Foxx, Jimmie, 308, 441n25

France, 5, 63, 79, 80, 85, 91, 118, 144, 207, 373n47

Franko, Nahan, 348n19

Frazee, Elsie, 129

Frazee, Harry: and Ban Johnson, 92, 94, 111–12, 114, 127, 153; finances of, 184; and Jacob Ruppert, 326; release of Ed Barrow, 163; on risks of Babe Ruth, 135, 137, 143; sale of Babe Ruth, 93, 115, 129–33, 140, 387n23; and sale of Red Sox, 212, 381n14, 442n37; trade of Carl Mays, 110–12, 114; and Washington Senators, 386n24; Yankee players from, 105, 202, 212, 282; at Yankee Stadium, 200

Frazee, Max, 132

Freedman, Andrew, 47–48, 51, 361n7, 362n24

Free Silver, 20

French Lick IN, 55–57, 76, 327, 363n6

Frick, Ford, 204, 219, 232, 241, 243, 259, 291, 412n36

Frisch, Frankie, 203, 274

Fuchs, Judge Emil, 309–10

Kieran, John, 63, 108, 112, 235, 251, 275, 436n14
Kilroe, Edwin Patrick, 142
Kinsella, Dick, 358n33
Kling, Johnny, 330
Knickerbocker (Bradley), 28
Knickerbocker brand, 28, 63, 323–24, 337, 352n55
Knickerbocker Greys, 16
Knothole Gang, 43, 360n55
Knox, P. T., 73
Koenig, Mark: 1926 season, 241–43, 252, 423n15, 423n24; 1927 season, 261, 263, 264; 1928 season, 269, 272; 1929 season, 282, 287; acquisition of, 229; on Miller Huggins, 242, 285, 423n29; trade of, 438n14
Konetchy, Ed, 37, 38, 356n6, 357nn11–13
Krabbenhoft, Herman, 429n39, 432n37
Kremer, Ray, 262
Krichell, Paul, 163, 222, 397n29, 439n27

labor unions. *See* organized labor
Lackaye, Wilson, 447n33
Ladies Day, 321
LaGuardia, Fiorello, 144–45, 312, 314, 316
Lajoie, Napoleon, 67, 378n18
Lakeshore Park, 377n6
Lamb, William, 47
Lambert, Mickey, 295
Lambs Club, 22
Lancaster, Roy, 329
Landis, Kenesaw Mountain: and baseball governance, 94, 116, 153–55, 169, 384n46, 394n6, 395n10; on Black Sox scandal, 155, 395n20; on Babe Ruth, 180, 183; on Bob Feller, 325; disciplining of players, 137, 180, 182–83, 331, 402n17, 402n19, 404n40; on IWW sentences, 154, 395n11; on managers as owners, 222; on Prohibition, 179, 401n12; on trade rules, 183–84; at World Series (1923), 205, 207; at Yankee Stadium, 200
Lane, F. C.: on Babe Ruth, 233; on Carl Mays, 110, 111; on Joe Dugan trade, 183; on Joe McCarthy, 297; on lively ball, 388n37; on Miller Huggins, 187, 194; on New York baseball teams, 201; on salaries, 304; on Yankees' dominance, 281
Lang, Al, 222–23
Lanigan, Harold, 41
Lannin, Joseph, 65, 72, 73
Larchmont Yacht Club, 22
Lardner, John, 332
Lary, Lyn, 259–60, 281–82, 287, 299, 428n31, 432n6
Lasker, Albert, 152, 394n6
Laurentian Mountains, 438n7
Lavan, Johnny, 371n18
Lazzeri, Tony: 1926 season, 241–42; 1927 season, 256, 258, 261, 264; 1928 season, 269, 274, 430n17, 438n22; 1929 season, 282; demeanor of, 282, 423n24; injuries and illness of, 242, 274, 317, 423n23, 438n22; on Miller Huggins, 285; press on, 264, 429n53; replacement of, 316; signing of, 397n29; in World Series (1926), 252

kees, 69, 70, 75; rumors about, 55, 56, 364n11; and Scott Perry, 113, 382n26; and Yankee management, 294, 437n5. *See also* Philadelphia Athletics

Macon GA, 76

MacPhail, Larry, 321, 322, 338

Macy's department stores, 19

Madison Square Garden, 24, 25, 141, 324

Magee, Lee, 39–40, 42, 70, 77, 78, 357n24, 366n5, 367n6

Maguire, Mrs. J. Basil, 333

Maisel, Fritz, 58, 69, 71–72, 77, 367n19, 367nn12–13, 369n7, 371n15

Major Leagues: American League as part of, 51; attendance (1918–19), 375n8; Babe Ruth's batting records in, 128, 129, 393n50; Bill Donovan in, 365n20; charity game in Oakland, 318; draft in, 323, 447n28; exhibition games in, 3–4, 34, 137, 179, 180, 218, 223, 244, 286, 346n13, 358n25, 389n15, 391n9, 393n44, 415n56, 427n6, 441n10; female ownership in, 345n1; in Florida, 223, 417n17; George Halas in, 101; during Great Depression, 305–6; home runs in, 103, 261; integration of, 329–31; Joe McCarthy in, 297; Kenesaw Landis's ruling on, 153–54; management in, 53, 309, 439n27; Miller Huggins in, 32, 268, 353n5, 354n22, 360n53; New York teams in, 201; outfield assists record in, 367n6; pennantless teams in (1924), 415n57; power structure of, 94, 110, 113, 115, 152–

57, 169, 180, 395n14, 402n17; public attitude toward, 263; radio broadcasts in, 321; rule changes in 1920, 133–34; salaries in, 303–4, 387n12; spitballs in, 388n33; transformation of play in, 127; walks record in, 399n35; win record in, 287; Yankee records in, 151, 260–61. *See also* American League; National League; Organized Baseball

Manhattan, 14, 19, 52, 119, 129–30, 327, 333, 337. *See also* New York City

Manhattan Club, 22

Manhattan Field, 103, 143, 377n6

Mann, Arthur, 188, 220, 224, 232, 291, 416n66

Man O'War (horse), 158

Mansfield (OH) Haymakers, 29, 31

Mantle, Mickey, xv, 276

Manufacturers Trust Co., 335, 336, 338

Marberry, Firpo, 217, 415n44

Maris, Roger, 276

Markey, Morris, 420n33

Markle, Cliff, 74–75, 217, 368n24, 415n47

Marlin TX, 50

Marquard, Rube, 70

Marsans, Armando, 34, 70, 358n25, 367n7

Mathewson, Christy, 39, 56, 70, 107, 356n6, 396n28

Mayor's Committee on Unemployment, 313–14

Mays, Carl: 1919 season, 113, 382n27; 1921 season, 176; 1923 season, 202, 203; acquisition of, xiii; with Boston

McQuade, Francis X., 122
McQuillan, Hugh, 184, 249
Meadows, Lee, 262
Meany, Tom: on Babe Ruth, 309, 443n48; on Eagle's Rest, 418n27; on George Weiss, 300, 440n50; on Philadelphia Athletics, 287; on rebuilding team, 422n56; on salaries, 304; on Yankee management, 295; on Yankees' transformation, 163, 195
Mencken, H. L., 145, 179
Méndez, José, 34
Mercer, Sid: on American League owners, 55; on attitudes toward money, 57; on Babe Ruth, 137, 151, 184–85; on baseball governance, 152–53, 402n17; on Carl Mays trade, 114; on Jacob Ruppert, 141, 214; on Miller Huggins, 159, 175; on New York baseball teams, 174, 399n37; on Ping Bodie, 391n9; on pitching staff, 171; on player acquisitions, 73; on players' performance, 78, 89; on Polo Grounds controversy, 121, 385n14; on Red Sox ownership, 381n14; on Til Huston, 192
Merkle, Fred, 253
"Merkle game," 386n22
Methodist religion, 29, 86, 437n22
Metropolitan Museum of Art (NY), 449n1
Meusel, Bob: 1922 season, 403n30; 1923 season, 203; 1927 season, 258, 261, 264; 1928 season, 271, 274; 1929 season, 288; aging of, 437n1; and Ben Paschal, 257; car accident of, 214;

to Cincinnati Reds, 437n6; contract with Yankees, 255, 427n9; injury of, 218, 248; and Miller Huggins, 181, 231–32, 235, 248; punishment of, 180, 186, 402n19; talent of, 142; trade rumors about, 182, 193, 194, 231; in World Series (1923), 205, 206; in World Series (1926), 252
Miami Daily News, 239
Miami FL, 141, 240
Middletown CT, 137
Midwest, 86, 376n14
Milan, Clyde, 79
Milk Fund, 199
Miller, Elmer, 183, 363n4
Miller, Jack "Dots," 38, 357n11, 357n15
Miller Huggins Field, 223, 417n18
Millrocks (baseball team), 17
Milwaukee Brewers, 298
Milwaukee WI, 336, 430n6
Minneapolis Millers, 359n34, 417n19
Minnesota, 223, 369n15
Minor, Benjamin, 366n31
Minor Leagues: Bob Connery in, 40; Cliff Markle in, 368n24; Ed Barrow with, 162; effect of World War I on, 94; George Pipgras in, 259; George Sisler in, 383n42; Mark Koenig in, 242; and Miller Huggins, 31, 33, 220–22, 401n5, 416n5, 417n6; Milwaukee Brewers in, 298; in New Orleans, 401n10; segregation in, 329, 330; Wilcy Moore in, 258; Yankee players from, 213, 222, 257, 266, 299–300, 307, 323, 366n4, 428n27, 430n3, 447n25; Yankees' ownership in, 282–83, 307, 309, 311, 317, 440n47. *See also* farm system

Minskoff, Sam, 418n24

Mitchel, John Purroy, 68, 401n7

Mitchell, Johnny, 183

Mittelman, Amy, 337

Mogridge, George, 75, 77, 79, 148, 168, 171, 216, 369n7, 411n29

Monitor (George Daley pseud.), 117

Montreal Royals, 286, 430n5

Montville, Leigh, 93, 231, 310

Moore, Jack B., 318, 343

Moore, Wilcy, 258, 259, 261, 263, 266–68

Morehart, Ray, 256

Morgan, J. P., 22

Morris, Lloyd, 246

Morris, Peter, 17

Morton, Levi P., 18–19, 349n6

Most Valuable Player award, 356n50, 429n40, 441n25, 442n31. *See also* Chalmers Award

Mountain Athletic Club, 30, 353n11

movies. *See* cinema

Mowrey, Mike, 357nn11–13

Muehlebach Stadium, 330

Municipal Council (NY), 15

"Murderers' Row," 89, 103–4, 372n33, 378n9

Murdock, Eugene, 92, 111, 112, 114, 117, 382n31

Murphy, Charles, 48, 362n19

Murphy, Jack, 148, 151, 160

Murphy, Sam, 75, 162

Murray, George, 202

Murray brewery, 14

Museum of American Folk Art, 132

MVP. *See* Most Valuable Player award

Myer, Buddy, 316

Napoleon, 204, 251, 412n36

Nashville TN, 141

National Commission: Ban Johnson against, 152; and Black Sox scandal, 394n7; chairmanship of, 384n46; on contested Athletics player, 113, 382n26; end of, 94, 115–16; John Heydler with, 383n41; and Polo Grounds controversy, 120; on shortened 1918 season, 91; withholding of third-place money, 114, 116, 380n45

National German-American Alliance, 61, 62, 81

National League: 1921 pennant race, 173; 1926 pennant race, 250; 1928 pennant race, 274; 1929 pennant race, 288; American League players from, 51, 52; Andrew Freedman's effect on, 47; awards in, 411n24, 429n40; Baltimore Orioles in, 31; Ban Johnson's revenge on, 2, 4; and baseball governance, 115, 152, 154, 169; batters in, 206; Brooklyn Dodgers in, 5, 107; Brooklyn Superbas in, 362n27; Cincinnati Reds in, 30; Cleveland Spiders in, 355n47; disputes with American League, 123; Federal League players in, 40, 42; first interleague World Series of, 362n28; foul-strike rule in, 388n36; Frank Chance in, 53; game schedules in, 385n14; hidden ball trick in, 41; Joe Kelley in, 66; Miller Huggins in, 33, 90; and National Commission, 383n41; Ned Hanlon in,

New York Daily Mirror, 414n25

New York Daily News, 12, 214, 218

New Yorker, 249, 420n33

New Yorker Herold, 62

New Yorker Staats-Zeitung, 28, 62

New York Evening Journal, 72, 80, 273, 352n55

New York Evening Mail, 74, 162, 171, 369n21

New York Evening Post, 207

New York Evening Sun, 51, 77, 159

New York Evening Telegram, 73, 160–61, 388n37

New York Evening World, 64, 419n8

New York Giants: 1921 season, 173; 1923 season, 201, 411n22; 1924 season, 218; 1928 season, 274, 438n19; Art Fletcher with, 426n47; Babe Ruth against, 102; on baseball governance, 153; charity games of, 313–14, 376n24, 444n12; in Cuba, 50; dominance of, 66, 86, 174, 184, 201, 213, 218, 343–44, 415n58, 432n1; Edd Roush with, 255; Federal League players with, 40; Frank Baker's home runs against, 70; Harry Sparrow with, 144; Jacob Ruppert at games of, 59–60; Joe DiMaggio against, 319; John McGraw's contract with, 296; on lively ball, 249; ownership and management of, 6, 47–51, 192–93, 200, 296, 304, 361n7, 384n6, 385n11, 394n56, 438n19; Phil Douglas with, 405n65; at Polo Grounds, 58, 64, 118–23, 151, 197, 385n14, 394n56, 409n38, 410n12; radio broadcasts of, 321, 446n21;

Roger Bresnahan with, 36; Slim Sallee to, 42; at St. Louis Cardinals (1914), 39; Sunday games of, 100, 120–21, 192, 385nn15–16; and trade deadlines, 184; in World Series (1917), 4; in World Series (1921), 173–75, 177–78, 197, 412n40; in World Series (1922), 186–88, 191, 197, 406n68, 412n40; in World Series (1923), 203–6; world tour of (1914), 66; Yankees' effect on, 50, 54, 59. *See also* McGraw, John

New York Globe, 66, 72, 86, 88, 363n30

New York Herald, 24, 55, 105

New York Herald-Tribune, 49, 314–15

New York Highlanders, 52, 64, 362n26. *See also* New York Yankees

New York Institute for the Blind, 52

New York Journal-American, 13

New York Knickerbockers, 63, 365n11

New York Lincoln Giants, 329

New York National Guard, 18, 343

New York Nautical College, 22

New York Press, 73, 74

New York State: Al Smith votes in, 276; boxing in, 199, 246, 326–27; governorship of, 312–13; horse racing in, 23; Prohibition in, 145; sports commission in, 169, 398n9; Sunday baseball in, 98, 100, 120, 246

New York Sun, xvi, 107, 115–16, 324, 328, 363n9, 407n3

New York Supreme Court, 113, 114, 450n16. *See also* courts of law

New York Times: on 1924 pennant race, 217; on 1926 season, 250; on

61, 80–81; as law, 98, 99, 144–45, 305, 375nn11–12; New York Yankees' flouting of, 141, 179, 182, 401n12; repeal of, 312–13, 323–24, 335, 336, 444n5, 444n11. *See also* alcohol; breweries

prostitution, 27–28

Protestant religion, 14, 26, 99, 312

Providence Grays, 65

Pulitzer, Joseph, 350n20

Quebec, 438n7

Quinn, Bob, 395n14, 413n12, 425n11

Quinn, Jack, 66, 94, 101, 102, 149, 168, 393n42, 400nn48–49

rabbit ball, 247. *See also* baseballs

radio broadcasts, 172, 321, 322, 324, 331, 399n33, 446n21. *See also* press

Raschi, Vic, 397n29

Reach, George, 388n37

Reach Official American League Guide, 59, 90

real estate business: of Miller Huggins, 33, 194, 223, 239–40, 251, 290, 422n8; of Ruppert, 13, 58, 239, 240, 248, 284, 314–15, 335, 337, 338, 391n12, 423n11

Reed, Matilda, 223

Reese, Jimmie, 259–60, 281–82, 299, 428n31, 432n6

Rehg, Walter, 363n4

Rennie, Rud, 49

Republican National Convention, 144

Republicans, 98, 169, 349n8

reserve clause, 304

Reserve Engineers Regiment, 99–100

Reynolds, Carl, 304

Rheingold Breweries, 337

Rhinebeck-on-the-Hudson, 13, 22, 24, 25

Rhodes, Gordon "Dusty," 432n7, 442n40

Rice, Grantland, 95, 98, 101, 152, 175, 188

Rice, Tom, 160

Richmond (va) baseball team (Colts), 374n55

Rickard, Tex, 190

Rickenbacker, Eddie, 286, 434n44

Rickey, Branch: on "addition by subtraction," 53; and Miller Huggins, 44, 361n59; Minor League teams of, 282, 300, 322, 417n8; as social visionary, 330, 448n19; with St. Louis Cardinals, 1, 3, 4, 6, 44, 222, 282, 300, 360n56

Ringling, John, 190

Ripley, Robert, 410n14

Rizzuto, Phil, 397n29

"Roaring Twenties," 254, 318

Robertson, Gene, 287, 433n18

Robinson, Hank, 357n11

Robinson, Jackie, 448n19

Robinson, Mary, 161

Robinson, Wilbert: in Baseball Hall of Fame, 344; management style of, 90, 397n17; as manager candidate, 5–6, 79, 107, 117, 160–62, 379n37, 397n18; as part of Giants purchase, 48; and team ownership, 192; on Yankees' batting, 244

Robison, Frank De Haas, 39, 47–48, 355n47, 357n17

Robison, Stanley, 36, 39, 47–48, 355n47, 357n17

Index   509

building ballpark, 122; as businessman, 25, 28, 60, 70, 213, 260, 297,
300, 303–4, 313–16, 320–25, 329–
31, 334–37, 341–43, 351n43, 367n10,
413n15, 445n28, 447n28; buyout of
Til Huston, 188, 190–93, 195–97,
218, 335, 407n2, 407n9, 408nn27–
28, 416n59; and Carl Mays, 112–14,
116, 148, 381n19, 383n45; challenge of Prohibition, 98; charity of,
187, 314–16, 329, 406n69, 444n12,
445n21; childhood of, 15–17; collections of, 25, 28, 142–43, 391n12,
449n1; as Colonel, 214, 343, 349n3;
contract negotiations of, 107, 255,
297–98, 307, 427n8, 427n11; death
of, 326, 328–29, 407n3; description
of, 11–12, 20–21, 49, 63–64, 214,
272, 314, 315, 320–21, 334; desire
to win, 176, 184, 201, 213–14, 220,
227, 231, 247–48, 257–58, 260, 276–
77, 281, 283, 286, 289, 297–98, 300,
305, 311, 316, 321, 323–25, 331; on
disability clause, 77; on fan injuries and deaths, 288; farm teams of,
282–83, 300, 307, 440n50; Florida
real estate of, 239–40; on German
Jewry, 315–16; on Gertrude Ederle,
249–50; and horses, 23–24, 27; illness of, 23, 321–22, 324, 326–28,
448n11; investigation of players,
182–83; and Joe DiMaggio, 318–21;
and Joe McCarthy, 297–99, 303–
11; legacy of, xiii, 337–40, 344; on
manager candidates, 294–97, 341,
451n8; and Miller Huggins, xvi,
1–7, 11–16, 79–81, 130, 159–63,
173, 176, 177, 182, 187, 188, 191–92,

194, 196, 197, 202–4, 207, 213, 218,
220–22, 230, 231, 240, 262–63, 268,
276, 290–93, 306, 340–41, 345n6,
379n35, 409n40; monument to, xv,
331–32; and moral reform, 26–
28; personal life of, 20–22, 224–
25, 324, 342–43, 350n21, 418n24,
447n33; personal secretary of,
397n19; on player acquisitions, 69,
72, 87, 89, 93, 168–69, 213, 221–22,
234, 260, 283–84, 299–300, 308,
311, 317, 324–25, 413n13; political life of, 19–21, 28, 246, 275–76,
314, 324; during Prohibition, 312,
313; purchase of Yankees, 47–60,
62–65, 267, 361n12, 362n21, 363n9;
on sale of Red Sox, 212; and spring
training, 222, 255; on Sunday baseball, 99–101, 272; on ticket sales,
142, 259, 264; and Til Huston, 80,
108, 179, 185, 188, 195–96, 340,
407n3, 409n33; traffic violations of,
20; on Washington Senators purchase, 386n24; wealth of, 12–15, 20,
21, 57, 85, 95, 109, 118–19, 141–43,
151, 169, 218, 260, 262, 272, 281,
284, 305, 314–16, 331, 333–36, 338,
391n12, 415n56, 449n1, 450n11; and
Wilbert Robinson, 5, 346nn25–26;
on World Series (1922), 187, 188;
on World Series (1923), 205–7, 275,
412n49; on World Series (1926),
253; on World Series (1927), 262–
63; on World Series (1928), 206,
275; on World War I, 62, 78, 91–
92, 95; on Yankees' batting, 244;
and Yankee Stadium, 198–200,
247–48, 260, 343

risks of, 131, 132, 135–39, 222, 387n25, 390n25; salary of, 129, 139, 140, 255, 303–7, 316, 319, 387n12, 390n1, 421n41, 440nn2–3, 441n10; skill of, 102–5, 377n6, 388n32; smoking of, 140, 390n3; transformation of baseball, 146; uniform of, 287, 434n45; and Wally Pipp, 182; in World Series (1921), 174, 399n35; in World Series (1922), 186–88, 406n77; in World Series (1923), 205–6; and Yankees' dominance, 276; Yankees' release of, 132; at Yankee Stadium, 200, 259

Ruth, Claire, 232, 285, 303

"Ruthville," 288

Ryan, Rosy, 205, 206

Sabbatarians, 98

Salamanca NY, 67

Sallee, "Slim," 38–39, 42, 359n44

saloons, 85–86, 144, 336, 450n21

Salt Lake City team (Bees), 241–42

Salvation Army, 449n8

San Diego Union, 148

Sandlot Baseball League, 314

San Francisco CA, 88, 269, 286, 317–20

San Francisco Giants, 393n50, 434n44

San Francisco Seals, 267, 317–18, 372n25, 446n1

Sante, Luc, 51

Saturday Evening Post, xvi, 81, 316

saves, 415n44

Schacht, Al, 274

Schaefer, Herman "Germany," 366n4

Schalk, J. Ruppert, 335

Schalk, Ray, 258–59

Schang, Wally, 167–68, 202, 230, 235, 256, 288, 403n30, 427n14

Schenck, Phil, 199, 380n45, 410n12

Schmeling, Max, 326–27

Schumacher, Harry, 149, 393n42

Schwerdtfeger, Otto M., 327, 328

Scott, Everett, 176, 183, 202, 211–12, 229, 235, 404n44, 413n7

Seabury, Samuel, 445n25

Seattle Rainiers, 324

Selkirk, George, 307, 442n29

Seventh Regiment Band, 200, 332

Seymour, Dorothy, 110, 151, 155, 373n40

Seymour, Harold, 110, 151, 155, 373n40

Shamrocks (Cincinnati), 31, 353n16

Shawkey, Bob: 1916 season, 77; 1917 season, 79; 1919 season, 102–3; 1923 season, 200, 202, 410n15; 1927 season, 257, 428n20; acquisition of, 75; career of, 267, 430n5; as manager, xii, 294–97, 307, 309, 437n6, 438n14, 439nn25–26, 451n8; and Miller Huggins, 168, 232; in navy, 92, 373n53; personality of, 295, 297; pitching advice from, 271–72, 286; on Red Ruffing, 436n15; in World Series (1922), 406n68; in World Series (1923), 205

Shealy, Al, 267

Sheepshead Bay racetrack, 24

Sheppard, Morris, 312

Sherdel, Bill, 274

Sherid, Roy, 432n7

Sheridan, John: on Ban Johnson, 114, 117, 383n38; on baseball governance, 383n46; on Black Sox scandal,

Sheridan, John (*continued*)
156; on Dutch Leonard trade,
379n26; on Miller Huggins, 6, 32,
36, 106, 108–9, 160, 379n31; on
New York baseball teams, 184;
sandlot team of, 378n10; on Til
Huston, 192, 383n38
Shibe, Tom, 388n37
Shibe Park, 141–42
Shocker, Urban: 1926 season, 247,
425n32; 1927 season, 257, 261,
428n20; funeral of, 273; illness
of, 267; pitching style of, 259,
428n30; with St. Louis Browns,
93, 374n59, 419n7; trade of, 87–
88, 227–28, 371n15, 371n19, 419n8;
against Yankees, 147, 180, 182, 186,
392n30, 403n32, 405n63
Shore, Ernie, 105–6, 139, 378n23
Showboat, 254
Shreveport LA, 138, 170, 178, 401n10
Shulman, Robin, 26, 28
silkworms, 315, 335
Silleck, Amanda Ruppert, 15, 333, 449n2
Silleck, H. Garrison, Jr., 449nn1–2
Simmons, Al, 255
Simms, Edward F., 191
Sinclair, Harry, 57, 70, 366n4
Sinnott, James P., 150
Sir Barton (horse), 158
Sisler, George, 116, 261, 268, 383n42,
392n25, 393n51
Sisters of St. Ursula, 347n9
Sitting Pretty, 333
Skinner, Camp, 202
Slocum, Bill, 3, 240, 266, 269, 360n53
Smelser, Marshall, 231–32, 235, 251,
296, 421n40, 426n38

Smith, Al, 100, 200, 275–76, 312, 313
Smith, Robert, 240–41
Smith, William, 56
Society as I Have Found It (McAllister), 347n11
Society for American Baseball
Research, 429n39, 432n37
Somers, Charles, 73
Sousa, John Philip, 200
South Atlantic Association, 258
Southern League, 43
South Pole, 315, 343
Sowell, Mike, 388n35
Spalding Guide, 92
Spanish-American War, 50
Sparrow, Harry, 65–66, 144, 162
Speaker, Tris: 1920 season, 392n25;
with Boston Red Sox, 131, 133;
with Cleveland Indians, 72–73,
106, 112–13, 170, 183, 250, 368n22,
425n32; hit by pitch, 111, 381n8;
insurance of, 141; on Joe Dugan
trade, 183; as manager, 309; on
Ray Chapman's death, 148; WAR
value of, 367n19; with Washington
Senators, 427n5; Yankees' attempt
to acquire, 72–73, 367n18, 382n20
Spink, Taylor, 2, 3, 16, 111, 179, 310,
319–20, 345n6, 383n42
Spirit of St. Louis, 254
spitball, 259, 357n16, 388n33, 428n30.
See also pitcher(s)
Sporting Life, 35, 36, 59, 356n51,
357n12, 363n9
Sporting News: on 1926 season, 251; on
1929 pennant race, 284; on automobiles, 286; on Babe Ruth, 310;
on Ban Johnson, 115, 117, 383n38;

on baseball governance, 116; on
Black Sox scandal, 156; on Cardinals' 1917 season, 2; on Carl
Mays, 111, 113, 382n28; on exhibition games, 218; on George Weiss,
440n50; on Helen Weyant, 334;
John Sheridan with, 378n10; on
Miller Huggins, 6, 32, 36, 37, 41,
94, 106, 107, 159–60, 162, 170, 173,
188, 212, 248–49, 379n37; on Monument Park honorees, xvi, 332; on
New York baseball teams, 184, 197;
on player acquisitions, 105, 128,
325; on player quality during war,
94; on Ruppert family business,
15–16; on salaries, 304, 319–20; on
St. Paul Saints ownership, 360n52;
on Til Huston, 192; on Yankees'
intent to win, 176; on Yankees
ownership, 179, 191, 196
sports: governance of, 169, 246,
398n9; lack of security in, 138;
media coverage of, 99, 376n18,
420n33; popularity of, 158–60,
249–50
Sports Museum of New England, 129
Sports View column, 72
Spring Grove Cemetery, 292, 353n5
stadium(s): intent to build, 51, 56, 58,
64–65, 179, 362n24, 363n9; and
Sunday baseball, 100; ticket prices
at, 142; Yankees' lack of, 114–15,
153. *See also individual stadiums*
Stallings, George, 52–53, 65, 66, 77,
90, 160, 231, 365n20
St. Basil's Academy, 418n26
St. Bernard dogs, 12, 24–25, 117, 141,
390n6. *See also* dogs

St. Denis, Walter, 72
St. Domingo (horse), 22
Steinbrenner, George, xi
Stengel, Casey, 205, 417n18
Stevens, Frank, 199–200, 410n14
Stevens, Harry M., 199–200, 408n29,
410n14
St. Francis de Sales Church, 328
St. Louis Browns: 1916 season, 77;
1917 season, 371n18; 1920 season,
393n51; 1922 season, 180, 181, 183,
186, 402n21; Babe Ruth against,
133, 182; Bob Quinn with, 395n14;
Branch Rickey with, 1, 44, 360n56;
Carl Mays against, 113; Dan Howley with, 274; and Federal League,
358n27; George Sisler with, 116,
383n42; Lee Magee with, 70;
Muddy Ruel with, 103; ownership
of, 116, 118, 355n47, 358n31, 419n7;
pitching against Yankees, 146–47,
392n30; relocation of, 369n15; stolen bases by, 261; in Sunday game,
99–100; on trade rules, 183–84;
Yankees' trades with, 72, 87, 93,
227–28, 256, 257, 369n13, 371n15,
374n59, 419n6, 419n8
St. Louis Cardinals: 1913 season, 37,
356n3; 1914 season, 371n21; 1927
season, 262; 1928 season, 273–
75, 283; Armando Marsans with,
358n25; Branch Rickey with, 1, 3,
4, 6; farm system of, 282, 300, 322,
417n8; finances of, 40–41, 359n36,
359n38; Grover Cleveland Alexander with, 250; Lee Magee with, 70,
359n43; Miller Huggins with, xv,
1–4, 35–44, 87, 89, 95, 104, 175,

Walsh, Ed, 186

Walters, Roxy, 378n23

Waner, Lloyd, 262

Waner, Paul, 262

Wanninger, Pee Wee, 230

Wapakoneta OH, 355n46

Warburg, Felix, 14

Ward, Aaron: 1925 season, 230; 1927 season, 256; injury of, 142; position of, 171; promise of, 416n66; trade rumors about, 182, 193, 194, 231; in World Series (1923), 205

Washington DC, 20, 79, 356n48, 427n16

Washington Heights, 52

Washington Heights Methodist Episcopal Church, 436n18

Washington Post, 20, 107, 213, 347n28

Washington Senators: 1920 season, 167, 397n2; 1921 season, 171; 1922 season, 405n62; 1924 season, 216–18, 415n57; 1925 season, 229; 1926 season, 247; 1927 season, 258–60; 1928 season, 267, 268, 270, 273; 1932 season, 304; 1940 season, 331–32; Allen Russell with, 380n1; Al Schacht with, 274; and baseball governance, 383n46; Buddy Myer with, 316; in first Yankees' Sunday game, 100–101; Jacob Ruppert's attempt to purchase, 386n24; Miller Huggins's outburst against, 104; move of, 79, 369n15; Roger Peckinpaugh with, 400n51; Stan Coveleski with, 267; stolen bases by, 378n14; Tom Zachary with, 287, 435n49; trades with, 79, 106, 168, 250, 269, 330, 425n30; Tris Speaker

with, 427n5; against Yankees, 67, 68, 89, 167, 373n53

Washington Times, 81, 369n21

Wattenberg, Fred, 225

Watterson, Henry, 27

Wawa PA, 136

Wayne, Winthrop. *See* Weyant, Helen "Winnie"

Weaver, Buck, 74, 367n12

Webb, Del, 338

Wedge, Will, 178

Weeghman, Charlie, 57, 359n36, 362n20

Weeghman Park, 358n31

Weiss, Bill, 447n25

Weiss, George: in Baseball Hall of Fame, 344; and Joe DiMaggio, 317; at Little World Series, 322; as manager, 338; with Minor League, 323, 341; with Newark Bears, 300, 440nn49–50; and segregation, 330

Westchester County NY, xiii, 328

Western League, 31, 75, 311

Westminster Kennel Club Dog Show, 25, 117, 141, 390n6

West Point (military academy), 15–16, 18, 224

West Side Park, 158

Weyant, George Wellington, 333

Weyant, Helen "Winnie," xiii, 225–26, 333–34, 418n40, 449n3, 449n5, 449n8

Weyant, Rex, 333, 418n40

WGN radio, 331

Wheat, Zack, 255

Wheeler, Wayne B., 144

White, Doc, 353n11

White, G. Edward, 154

White Construction Company, 198–99

Whitney, Harry Payne, 207

Wilhelm II, Kaiser, 14

Willard, Jess, 199, 376n18, 396n2

Willebrandt, Mabel, 145

Williams, Joe, 139, 178, 222–23, 232, 274, 284, 443n48

Williams, Ken, 402n21

Williamsburg section (Brooklyn), 14

Williamson, Ned, 103, 377n6

Wills, Maury, 358n29

Wilson, Chief, 357n11

Wilson, Woodrow, 61–62, 98, 369n23

Windsor, Ontario, 158

Wins Above Replacement (war), 367n19

Winter, Kenneth, 63

Winthrop MA, 333

Witt, Whitey, 186, 200, 217, 235, 404n41, 405n62

Wolcott Hotel, 57, 59, 64

Wolverton, Harry, 53

women: and alcohol consumption, 85–86, 179, 336; attitudes toward, 223–26, 334, 355n46; Babe Ruth with, 136–39, 390n19, 390n25; in Jacob Ruppert's will, 333, 449n1

Woods, Doc, 143, 380n45

Woollcott, Alexander, 225

World Series: with Babe Ruth, 132; and barnstorming tours, 180, 389n15; California teams in, 286, 434n44; Chicago Cubs in, 6; compensation for Yankees players, 67; Jacob Ruppert at, 327; as Jacob Ruppert's goal, 214, 298, 445n28; managers in, 31; Miller Hug-gins's failure to win, 340; National League in, 429n48; New York teams in, 205, 217, 286; players' checks for, 213; proceeds from, 108, 187, 190, 253, 380n45, 413n15, 426n44; on radio, 172, 322, 399n33; throwing of 1919, 152; Wally Schang in, 168; won by Athletics, 364n11; won by Red Sox, 133; won by Yankees, xv, 254, 318, 332, 338, 344; Yankee participation after 1928, 277

World Series (1903), 362n28

World Series (1911), 50, 70, 386n22

World Series (1915), 410n13

World Series (1916), 92, 410n13

World Series (1917), 4, 91

World Series (1918), 91, 373n47

World Series (1919), 106, 152, 379n32

World Series (1920), 158, 160

World Series (1921), 136, 173–78, 197, 201, 400n44

World Series (1922), 186–88, 190–91, 201, 203, 206, 230, 340, 406n68, 412n42, 414n30

World Series (1923), 201, 203–7, 211, 275, 412n40

World Series (1924), 218, 435n49

World Series (1926), 252–53, 262, 263, 274, 275, 426n44

World Series (1927), 262–64, 266, 271–72, 276

World Series (1928), 206, 273–76, 283, 431n32, 433n20

World Series (1929), 297, 439n29

World Series (1932), 305

World Series (1934), 309

World Series (1936), 319